Database Systems

INTERNATIONAL COMPUTER SCIENCE SERIES

Consulting Editor **A D McGettrick** University of Strathclyde

SELECTED TITLES IN THE SERIES

Software Development with Z *J Wordsworth*

Program Verification *N Francez*

Performance Modelling of Communication Networks *P Harrison and N Patel*

Concurrent Systems: An Integrated Approach to Operating Systems, Database, and Distributed Systems *J Bacon*

Introduction to Parallel Processing *B Codenotti and M Leoncini*

Concurrent Programming *A Burns and G Davies*

Comparative Programming Languages (2nd edn) *L Wilson and R Clark*

Functional Programming *R Plasmeijer and M van Eekelen*

Object-Oriented Database Systems: Concepts and Architectures *E Bertino and L D Martino*

Programming in Ada (4th edn) *J Barnes*

Software Design *D Budgen*

Ada from the Beginning (2nd edn) *J Skansholm*

Programming Language Essentials *H E Bal and D Grune*

Human–Computer Interaction *J Preece et al.*

Distributed Systems: Concepts and Design (2nd edn) *G Coulouris, J Dollimore and T Kindberg*

Fortran 90 Programming *T M R Ellis, I Philips and T Lahey*

Parallel Processing: The Transputer and its Applications *E Hull, D Crookes and P Sweeney*

Foundations of Computing: System Development with Set Theory and Logic *T Scheurer*

Database Systems
A Practical Approach to Design, Implementation and Management

Thomas M. Connolly

Carolyn E. Begg

Anne D. Strachan

University of Paisley

ADDISON-WESLEY
Harlow, England • Reading, Massachusetts • Menlo Park, California
New York • Don Mills, Ontario • Amsterdam • Bonn • Sydney • Singapore
Tokyo • Madrid • San Juan • Milan • Mexico City • Seoul • Taipei

Addison Wesley Longman Limited
Edinburgh Gate
Harlow, Essex
CM20 2JE
England

The programs in this book have been included for their instructional value. They have been tested with care but are not guaranteed for any particular purpose. The publisher does not offer any warranties or representations, nor does it accept any liabilities with respect to the programs.

Many of the designations used by manufacturers and sellers to distinguish their products are claimed as trademarks. Addison-Wesley has made every attempt to supply trademark information about manufacturers and their products mentioned in this book. A list of the trademark designations and their owners appears on page xxxi.

Cover designed by op den Brouw, Design & Illustration, Reading
and printed by The Riverside Printing Co. (Reading) Ltd.
Typeset by Colset Ptd Ltd, Singapore
Printed and bound in Great Britain by Biddles Ltd, Guildford and King's Lynn.

First printed 1995
Reprinted 1996 (twice), 1997 (twice)

ISBN 0-201-42277-8

British Library Cataloguing-in-Publication Data
A catalogue record for this book is available from the British Library.

Library of Congress Cataloging-in-Publication Data
Connolly, Thomas M.
    Database systems : a practical approach to design, implementation, and management / Thomas M. Connolly. Carolyn E. Begg, Anne D. Strachan.
        p.   cm. — (International computer science series)
    Includes bibliographical references and index.
    ISBN 0-201-42277-8
    1. Database design.   2. Database management.   I. Begg, Carolyn E.
II. Strachan, Anne D.   III. Title.   IV. Series.
QA76.9.D26C66   1996
005.74—dc20   95-26031
                                                              CIP

Publisher's acknowledgements
The publisher wishes to thank the following for permission to reproduce the material. Figure 4.6 material from: Earl, M.J. (1989). *Management Strategies for Information Technology,* Hemel Hempstead: Prentice-Hall International (UK) Ltd; Loring, P. and De Garis, C. (1992). 'The changing face of Data Administration' in Clarke, R. and Cameron, J. (eds) *Managing Information Technology's Organisational Impact II,* A (3), J.F.I.P.: Amsterdam: Elsevier Science.

To Sheena, for her patience and understanding during the last three years.

To Kathryn, for the constant pleasure she has given us since her birth.

To my Mother, who died during the writing of this book – sleep peacefully, Mum.

Thomas M. Connolly

To my Mother and Father and, in particular, to Alan, for his support and understanding.

Carolyn Begg

To Paul, for his encouragement and support.

Anne Strachan

Preface

Background

The history of database research over the past 30 years is one of exceptional productivity that has led to the database system becoming arguably the most important development in the field of software engineering. The database is now the underlying framework of the information system, and has fundamentally changed the way many organizations operate. In particular, the developments in this technology over the last few years have produced systems that are more powerful and more intuitive to use. This has resulted in database systems becoming increasingly available to a wider variety of users. Unfortunately, the apparent simplicity of these systems has led to these users creating databases and applications without the necessary knowledge to produce an effective and efficient system. And so the 'software crisis' or, as it is sometimes referred to, the 'software depression' continues.

The original stimulus for this book came from the authors' work in industry, providing consultancy on database design for new software systems or, as often as not, resolving inadequacies with existing systems. Added to this, the authors' move to academia brought similar problems from different users – students. The objective of this book, therefore, is to provide a textbook that introduces the theory behind databases as clearly as possible and, in particular, provides a methodology for database design that can be used by both technical and non-technical readers.

The methodology presented in this book for relational Database Management Systems (DBMSs) – the predominant system for business applications at present – has been tried and tested over the years in both industrial and academic environments. It consists of two main phases: logical database design and physical database design. The first phase starts with the production of a conceptual data model that is independent of all physical considerations. This model is then refined into a logical data model by removing constructs that cannot be represented in relational systems. In the second phase, the logical data model is translated into a physical design for the target DBMS. The physical design phase considers the storage structures and access methods required for efficient access to the database on secondary storage.

The methodology in each phase is presented as a series of steps. For the inexperienced designer, it is expected that the steps will be followed in the order described, and guidelines are provided throughout to help with this process. For the experienced designer, the methodology can be less prescriptive, acting more as a checklist. To help the reader understand these important issues, the book has two chapters providing comprehensive worked examples, based on an integrated case study, *DreamHome*. In addition, a second case study, *Wellmeadows Hospital*, is provided to allow readers to try out the methodology for themselves.

The book also examines in some depth:

- the latest standard in SQL, SQL-92, including embedded SQL;
- the concepts and problems with the emerging distributed database system and object database system;
- the new Object Database Management Group standard for object database systems.

Intended Audience

This book is intended to be used as a textbook for a one- or two-semester course in database management or database design in an introductory undergraduate course, in a graduate or advanced undergraduate course. Such courses are usually required in an information systems, business IT, or computer science curriculum.

The book is also intended as a reference book for IT professionals, such as systems analysts or designers, application programmers, systems programmers, database practitioners and for independent self-teachers. Owing to the widespread use of database systems nowadays, these professionals could come from any type of company that requires a database.

It would be helpful for students to have a good background in the file organization and data structures concepts covered in Appendix A before covering the material in Chapter 9 on physical database design. This background ideally will have been obtained from a prior course. If this is not possible, then the material in Appendix A can be presented near the beginning of the database course, immediately following Chapter 1.

An understanding of a high-level programming language, such as 'C', would be advantageous for Sections 12.5 and 12.6 on embedded and dynamic SQL.

Distinguishing Features

(1) An easy-to-use, step-by-step methodology for logical database design, based on the widely-accepted Entity–Relationship model, with normal-

ization used as a validation technique. There is an accompanying chapter showing the methodology in use and a separate chapter showing how database design fits into the overall systems development lifecycle.

(2)   An easy-to-use, step-by-step methodology for physical database design, covering the mapping of the logical design to a physical implementation, selecting file organizations and indexes appropriate for the applications, and when to introduce controlled redundancy. There is an accompanying chapter showing the methodology in use.

(3)   A clear and easy-to-understand presentation, with definitions clearly highlighted, chapter objectives clearly stated and chapters summarized. Numerous examples and diagrams provided throughout each chapter to illustrate the concepts. There is a realistic case study integrated throughout the book and a second case study that can be used as a student project.

(4)   Extensive treatment of the latest formal and *de facto* standards: SQL (Structured Query Language), QBE (Query-By-Example) and the ODMG (Object Database Management Group) standard for object databases.

(5)   Two tutorial-style chapters on the new SQL (SQL–92) standard, covering both interactive and embedded SQL.

(6)   A tutorial-style chapter on QBE.

(7)   Comprehensive coverage of the relational data model.

(8)   Comprehensive coverage of the concepts and issues relating to the increasingly important area of distributed database management systems.

(9)   Comprehensive introduction to the concepts and issues relating to the increasingly important area of object-oriented database systems, including a review of the ODMG standard and a preview of the next SQL standard, SQL3.

(10) Introduction to DBMS system implementation concepts, including concurrency and recovery control, and security and integrity.

(11) An overview of legacy systems and a detailed comparison of the three traditional data models.

Pedagogy

Before starting to write any material for this book, one of the objectives was to produce a textbook that would be easy for the readers, whatever their background and experience, to follow and understand. From the authors' experience of using textbooks, which clearly was quite considerable before undertaking a project of this size, and also from listening to colleagues, clients and students, there were a number of design features that readers liked and disliked. With these comments in mind, the following style and structure was adopted:

- A set of objectives, clearly identified at the start of each chapter.
- Each important concept that is introduced is clearly defined and highlighted. The style used is that such concepts are boxed.
- Diagrams are liberally used throughout to help support and clarify concepts.
- A very practical orientation. To this end, each chapter contains many worked examples to help illustrate the concepts covered.
- A summary at the end covering the main concepts introduced.
- A set of review questions, the answers to which can be found in the text.
- A set of exercises that can be used by teachers or individuals to demonstrate and test the individual's understanding of the chapter.

Instructor's Manual

A comprehensive supplement containing numerous instructional resources is available for this textbook, upon request from Addison-Wesley. The accompanying manual includes:

- *Course structures*   This includes suggestions for the material to be covered in a variety of courses.
- *Teaching suggestions*   These include lecture suggestions, teaching hints and student project ideas that make use of the chapter content.
- *Solutions*   Sample answers are provided for all review questions and exercises.
- *Examination questions*   Examination problems (similar to the questions and exercises from the text) with solutions.
- *Transparency masters*   A set of masters for overhead transparencies of enlarged illustrations and tables from the text help the instructor to associate lectures and class discussion to material in the text. There is also a set of transparencies containing lecture notes for the main chapters in this book.

Organization of this Book

Part 1   Background

Part 1 of the book serves to introduce the field of database systems and database design, introducing the relational model, which is the main focus of attention.

Chapter 1 introduces the field of database management, examining the problems with the precursor to the database system, the file-based system, and the advantages offered by the database approach. It provides a description of *DreamHome*, a case study that is used extensively throughout the book. It also provides a second case study, the *Wellmeadows Hospital*, which can be used as a student project.

Chapter 2 examines the database environment, discussing the advantages offered by the three-level ANSI-SPARC architecture, introducing the most popular data models, and outlining the functions that should be provided by a multi-user DBMS. The chapter also looks at the underlying software architecture for DBMSs, which could be omitted for a first course in database management.

Chapter 3 introduces the concepts behind the relational model, the most popular data model at present, and the one most chosen for standard business applications. After introducing the terminology and showing the relationship with mathematical relations, the relational integrity rules, entity integrity and referential integrity, are discussed.

A short overview of relational algebra and relational calculus is presented with examples to illustrate all the operations. This could be omitted for a first course in database management. However, relational algebra is needed to understand fragmentation in Chapter 16 on distributed databases. In addition, the comparative aspects of the procedural algebra and the non-procedural calculus act as a useful precursor for the study of SQL in Chapters 11 and 12, although not essential. The chapter concludes with an overview on views, which is expanded upon in Chapter 12.

Chapter 4 completes the introduction to the first part of the book. This chapter presents an overview of the main phases of the information systems lifecycle, and discusses how these relate to the development of database applications. In particular, it emphasizes the importance of database design and shows how the process can be decomposed into two stages: logical database design and physical database design. It also shows how the design of the application (the functional approach) affects database design (the data approach). The chapter also examines the applicability of Computer-Aided Software Engineering (CASE) tools to the database lifecycle.

A crucial stage in the database application lifecycle is the selection of an appropriate DBMS. This chapter discusses the process of DBMS selection and provides some guidelines and recommendations. The chapter concludes with a discussion of the Data Administrator (DA) and the Database Administrator (DBA), the main personnel responsible for the planning, design and administration of a database.

Part 2 Methodology

Part 2 of the book presents a methodology for both logical and physical database design for relational systems.

Chapter 5 covers the concepts of Chen's Entity–Relationship (ER) model, and the Enhanced Entity-Relationship (EER) model, which allows more advanced data modelling using subclasses and superclasses. The EER model is a popular high-level conceptual data model and is a fundamental technique of the logical database design methodology presented herein. A worked example taken from the *DreamHome* case study is used to demonstrate how to create an EER model.

Chapter 6 examines the concepts behind normalization, which is another important technique used in the logical database design methodology. Using a series of worked examples drawn from the integrated case study, it demonstrates how to transition a design from one normal form to another and shows the advantages of having a logical database design that conforms to each of the normal forms up to, and including, Boyce–Codd normal form.

Chapter 7 presents a step-by-step methodology for logical database design for the relational model. It shows how to decompose the design into more manageable areas based on individual user views, and then provides guidelines for identifying entities, attributes, relationships and keys. It shows how to create a data model for each user view, validate it, and then map it to a data model suitable for implementation in a relational system. To complete the logical design methodology, the chapter shows how to merge the resulting data models together into a global data model that represents the part of the enterprise being modelled.

Chapter 8 provides a realistic worked example of the logical database design methodology taken from the *DreamHome* case study. It illustrates the creation and validation of local data models for two user views, and illustrates how to merge the resulting views together.

Chapter 9 presents a step-by-step methodology for physical database design and implementation for relational systems. It shows how to take the global data model developed during logical database design and how, using a variety of techniques, to design and implement it in a relational system. The methodology addresses the performance of the resulting implementation by providing guidelines for choosing file organizations and storage structures, and by considering denormalization – the introduction of controlled redundancy.

Chapter 10 provides a realistic worked example of the physical database design methodology taken from the *DreamHome* case study. It illustrates the implementation of part of the global logical data model derived in Chapter 8 using the PC database management system, Paradox for Windows.

Part 3   Database Languages

Part 3 of the book looks at the two main languages of relational systems: SQL and QBE.

Chapter 11 introduces the new 1992 SQL standard, SQL-92. The chapter is presented as a worked tutorial, giving a series of worked examples that demonstrate the main concepts of SQL. In particular, it concentrates on the data manipulation statements: SELECT, INSERT, UPDATE and DELETE. It also covers the SQL-92 data types and shows basic forms of the data definition statements.

Chapter 12 covers the more advanced features of the SQL-92 standard. Again, the chapter is presented as a worked tutorial. This chapter looks at views, the Integrity Enhancement Feature (IEF) and the more advanced features of the data definition statements, including the access control statements GRANT and REVOKE. There are two sections that examine embedded and dynamic SQL, with sample programs in 'C'. For an introductory course in databases, these two sections could be omitted.

Chapter 13 is another practical chapter that looks at the interactive query language, Query-by-Example (QBE), which has acquired the reputation of being one of the easiest ways for non-technical computer users to access information in a database. QBE is demonstrated using Paradox for Windows 5.1.

Part 4   Selected Database Issues

Part 4 of the book examines four specific topics that the authors consider necessary for a modern course in database management.

Chapter 14 is divided into two main areas: database integrity and security. Security is considered not just in the context of DBMS security but also in the context of the security of the DBMS environment. Thus, the chapter examines both computer-based and non-computer-based solutions, concluding with a presentation of risk analysis.

Chapter 15 concentrates on three of the functions that a Database Management System (DBMS) should provide, namely transaction management, concurrency control and recovery control. These functions are intended to ensure that the database is reliable and remains in a consistent state, when multiple users are accessing the database and in the presence of failures of both hardware and software components.

Distributed database management system (DDBMS) technology is one of the current major developments in the database systems area. The previous chapters of this book concentrate on centralized database systems: that is, systems with a single logical database located at one site under the control of a single DBMS. **Chapter 16** discusses the concepts and problems of distributed database management systems, where users can not only access the database at their own site but also access data stored at remote sites. There are claims that in the next ten years centralized database systems will be an 'antique curiosity' as most organizations move towards distributed database systems.

The preceding chapters of this book concentrate on the relational model and relational systems. The justification for this is that such systems are currently the predominant DBMS for traditional business database applications. However, relational systems are not without their failings, and the object database, or object-oriented database, is a major development in the database systems area that attempts to overcome these failings. **Chapter 17** examines this development in some detail. After presenting the main concepts of object orientation, the chapter examines two approaches that are being investigated: extending the relational model or producing a new data model based on object concepts. The chapter examines two new emerging but contrasting standards: the next SQL standard, called SQL3, and the new *de facto* object database standard from the Object Database Management Group (ODMG). The chapter also examines how the methodology presented in Part 2 of the book may be extended for object databases.

Appendices

Appendix A provides some background information on file organization and storage structures that is necessary for an understanding of the physical database design methodology presented in Chapter 9.

Appendix B introduces the basics of the network data model.

Appendix C introduces the basics of the hierarchical data model, concentrating in particular on the concepts of the hierarchical product IMS (Information Management System).

Appendix D compares and contrasts the features of the three traditional data models.

Appendix E summarizes the steps in the methodology presented in Chapter 7 and 9 for logical and physical database design.

The logical organization of the book and the suggested paths through it are illustrated in Figure P.1.

Corrections and Suggestions

As a textbook of this size is so vulnerable to errors, disagreements, omissions and confusion, your input is solicited for future reprints and editions. Comments, corrections and constructive suggestions should be sent to Addison-Wesley, or by electronic mail to:

conn-ci0@paisley.ac.uk

Acknowledgements

This book is the outcome of many years of work by the authors in industry, research and academia. It is therefore difficult to name all the people who have directly or indirectly helped us in our efforts; an idea here and there may have appeared insignificant at the time but may have had a significant causal effect. For those people we are about to omit, we apologize now. However, special thanks and apologies must first go to our families, who over the years have been neglected, even ignored, during our deepest concentrations. Next, we should like to thank Dr Simon Plumtree and Nicky Jaeger, our editors, for their help, encouragement and professionalism throughout the years. We should also like to thank the reviewers of the book, who contributed their comments, suggestions and advice. In particular, we would like to mention: William H. Gwinn, Instructor, Texas Tech University; Adrian Larner, De Montfort University, Leicester; Professor Andrew McGettrick, University of Strathclyde; Dennis McLeod, Professor of Computer Science, University of Southern California; Josephine DeGuzman Mendoza, Associate Professor, California State University; Jeff Naughton, Professor A.B. Schwarzkopf,

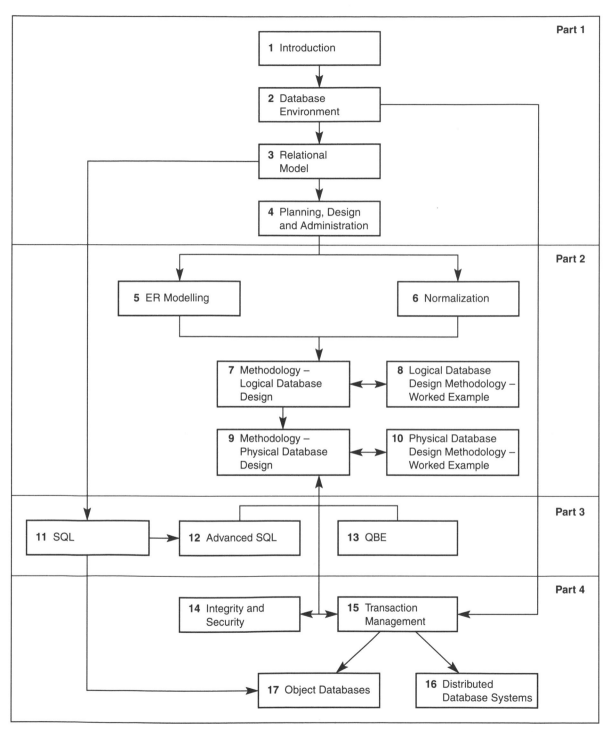

Figure P.1 Logical organization and suggested paths through it.

University of Oklahoma; Junping Sun, Assistant Professor, Nova Southeastern University; Donovan Young, Associate Professor, Georgia Tech; Dr. Barry Eaglestone, Lecturer in Computer Science, University of Bradford. Many others are still anonymous to us – we thank you for the time you must have spent on the manuscript. We should like to express our gratitude to John Wade of IBM for reading and commenting on the IMS material. Special thanks must go to our excellent production editor, Martin Tytler, for his patience and assistance throughout the production process, and to our proofreader, Lionel Browne, for the outstanding work in spotting and resolving all the inconsistencies and irregularities in the typeset manuscript. We should also like to thank Malcolm Bronte-Stewart for the *DreamHome* concept, Moira O'Donnell for ensuring the accuracy of the *Wellmeadows Hospital* case study, and Thomas's secretary Lyndonne MacLeod, for managing his administrative duties during the years.

Thomas M. Connolly
Carolyn Begg
Anne Strachan
Glasgow, September 1995

Brief Contents

Appendices

Contents

Appendices

Part One

Background

1 Introduction to Databases

Chapter Objectives

In this chapter you will learn:

- Some common uses of database systems.
- The characteristics of file-based systems.
- The problems with the file-based approach.
- The meaning of the term database.
- The meaning of the term Database Management System (DBMS).
- The typical functions of a DBMS.
- The major components of the DBMS environment.
- The personnel involved in the DBMS environment.
- The history of the development of database systems.
- The advantages and disadvantages of database systems.

The history of database system research is one of exceptional productivity and startling economic impact. Barely 20 years old as a basic science research field, database research has fueled an information services industry estimated at $10 billion per year in the U.S. alone. Achievements in database research underpin fundamental advances in communications systems, transportation and logistics, financial management, knowledge-based systems, accessibility to scientific literature, and a host of other civilian and defense applications. They also serve as the foundation for considerable progress in the basic science fields ranging from computing to biology.   (Silberschatz *et al.*, 1991)

This quotation is from a recent workshop on database systems, and it provides substantial motivation for the study of the subject of this book: **the database system**.[†] The database system is arguably the most important development in the field of software engineering. The database is now the underlying framework of the information system, and has fundamentally changed the way many organizations operate. Database technology has been an exciting area to work in and, since its emergence, has been the catalyst for many significant developments in software engineering. The workshop emphasized that the developments in database systems were not over, as some people thought. In fact (to paraphrase an old saying), it may be that we are only *at the end of the beginning* of the development. The applications that will have to be handled in the future are so much more complex that we will have to rethink many of the algorithms, such as the file storage and access algorithms, currently being used. The development of these original algorithms has had significant ramifications in software engineering and, without doubt, the development of new algorithms will have similar effects.

Throughout this book, we illustrate concepts using a case study based on a fictitious estate agency called *DreamHome*. We provide a detailed introduction to this case study in Section 1.7. At the end of this introductory chapter, we present a second case study that is intended to provide an additional realistic project for the reader. There will be exercises based on these two case studies at the end of many chapters.

1.1   Introduction

The database is now such an integral part of our day-to-day life that often we are not aware we are using one. To start our discussion of databases, in this section we examine some applications of database systems. For the purposes of this discussion, we can consider a database to be a collection of related data and the Database Management System (DBMS) to be the software that manages and controls access to the database. We provide accurate definitions in Section 1.3.

[†] Some authors make a distinction between database system and database management system, the database system being the application software. In this book we make no distinction.

When you purchase goods from your local **supermarket**, it is likely that a database will be accessed. The checkout assistant will run a bar code reader over each of your purchases. This will be linked to a database application program, which uses the bar code to find out the price of the item from a products database. The program then reduces the number of such items in stock and rings the price up on the till. If the reorder level falls below a threshold, the system may automatically place an order to obtain more stocks of that item. If a customer telephones the supermarket, an assistant can check whether an item is in stock by running an application program that determines availability from the database.

When you purchase goods using your **credit card**, the assistant normally checks that you have sufficient credit left to make the purchase. This check may be carried out by telephone or it may be done automatically by a card reader linked to a computer system. In either case, there is a database somewhere that contains information about the purchases you have made using your credit card. To check your credit, there is an application program that uses your credit card number to check that the price of the goods you wish to buy together with the sum of the purchases you have already made this month is within your credit limit. When the purchase is confirmed, the details of the purchase are added to this database. The application program will also access the database to check that the credit card is not on the list of stolen or lost cards before authorizing the purchase. There will be other application programs to send out monthly statements to each card holder and to credit accounts when payment is received.

When you make enquiries about a holiday, the **travel agent** may access several databases containing holiday and flight details. When you book your holiday, the database system has to make all the necessary booking arrangements. In this case, the system has to ensure that two different agents do not book the same holiday or overbook the seats on the flight. For example, if there is only one seat left on the flight from London to New York and two agents try to reserve the last seat at the same time, the system has to recognize this situation, allow one booking to proceed and inform the other agent that there are now no seats available. The travel agent may have another, usually separate, database system for invoicing.

Whenever you visit your local **library**, there is probably a database containing details of the books in the library, details of the users, reservations and so on. There will be a computerized index, which allows users to find a book based on its title, or its authors or its subject area. The database system will handle reservations to allow a user to reserve a book and to be informed by post when the book is available. The system will also send out reminders to borrowers who have failed to return books on the due date. Typically, the system will have a bar code reader, similar to that used by the supermarket described earlier, which is used to keep track of books coming in and going out of the library.

Whenever you wish to take out **insurance**, for example personal insurance, building or contents insurance for your house, or car insurance, your broker may access several databases containing figures for various insurance organizations. After personal details, such as name, address, age and whether you drink or smoke, have been supplied, they are used by the database system to determine the cost of the insurance. The broker can search several databases to find the organization that gives you the best deal.

If you are at **university**, there will be a database system containing information about yourself, the course you are enrolled in, details about your grant, the modules you have taken in previous years or are taking this year and details of all your past examination results. There may also be a database containing details relating to the next year's admissions and a database containing details of the staff who work at the university, giving personal details and salary-related details for the payroll office.

1.2 Traditional File-Based Systems

It is almost a tradition that comprehensive database books introduce the database system with a review of its predecessor, the file-based system. We will not depart from this tradition. Although the file-based approach is largely obsolete, there are very good reasons for studying it:

- Understanding the problems inherent in file-based systems may prevent us from repeating these problems in database systems. In other words, we should learn from our earlier mistakes. Actually, using the word 'mistakes' is derogatory and does not give any cognizance to the work that served a useful purpose for many years. However, we have learned from this work that there are better ways to handle data.

- If you wish to convert a file-based system to a database system, understanding how the file system works will be extremely useful, if not essential.

1.2.1 File-Based Approach

File-based system	A collection of application programs that perform services for the end users such as the production of reports. Each program defines and manages its own data.

File-based systems were an early attempt to computerize the manual filing system that we are all familiar with. For example, in an organization a manual file is set up to hold all external and internal correspondence relating to a project, product, task, client or employee. Typically, there are many such files, and for safety they are labelled and stored in one or more cabinets. For security, the cabinets may have locks or may be located in secure areas of the building. In our own home, we probably have some sort of filing system, which contains receipts, guarantees, invoices, bank statements and such like. When we need to look something up, we go to the filing system and search through the system starting from the first entry until we find what we want. Alternatively, we may have an indexing system that helps us locate what we want more quickly. For example, we may have divisions in the filing system or separate folders for different types of items that are in some way *logically related*.

The manual filing system works well while the number of items to be stored is small. It even works quite adequately when there are large numbers of items and we have only to store and retrieve them. However, the manual filing system breaks down when we have to cross-reference or process the information in the files. For example, a typical estate agent's office might have a separate file for each property for sale or rent, each potential buyer and renter and each member of staff. Consider the effort that would be required to answer the following questions:

- What three-bedroom properties do you have for sale with a garden and garage?
- What flats do you have for rent within three miles of the city centre?
- What is the average house price?
- What is the average rent for a two-bedroom flat?
- What is the total annual salary bill for staff?
- What was last year's monthly turnover derived from property sales?
- How does last month's turnover compare with the projected figure for this month?
- What is the expected monthly turnover for the next financial year?

Increasingly nowadays, clients, senior managers and staff want more and more information. In some areas, there is a legal requirement to produce detailed monthly, quarterly and annual reports. Clearly, the manual system is totally inadequate for this type of work. The file-based system was developed in response to the needs of industry for more efficient data access. However, rather than establish a centralized store for the organization's operational data, a decentralized approach was taken, where each department, with the assistance of **Data Processing (DP)** staff, stored and controlled its own data. To understand what this means, let us again consider the estate agency example.

The Sales Department are responsible for the selling and renting of properties. For example, whenever a client approaches the Sales Department with a view to marketing his or her property for rent, a form is completed, similar to that shown in Figure 1.1(a). This gives details of the property such as address and number of rooms together with the owner's details. The Sales Department also handle enquiries from potential renters, and a form similar to the one shown in Figure 1.1(b) is completed for each one. With the assistance of the DP Department, the Sales Department create an information system to handle the renting of property. The system consists of three files containing property, owner and renter details, as illustrated in Figure 1.2. For simplicity, we omit details relating to members of staff, branch offices and business owners.

The Contracts Department are responsible for handling the lease agreements associated with properties for rent. Whenever a client agrees to rent a

(b)

DreamHome
Renter Details

Renter Number: *CR74*

First Name *Mike*   Last Name *Ritchie*

Address *18 Tain Street*
Gourock
PA1G 1YQ   Tel No. *01475 392178*

Property Requirement Details

Preferred
Property Type *House*   Maximum
Monthly Rent *750*

General Comments *Currently living at home with parents*
Getting married in August

Seen By *Ann Beech*   Date *24-Mar-95*

Branch No *B3*   Branch City *Glasgow*

(a)

DreamHome
Property for Rent Details

Property Number : *PG21*

Address *18 Dale Rd*   Allocated to Branch:

Area *Hyndland*   *163 Main Street,*
Partick, Glasgow

City *Glasgow*

Postcode *G12*   Branch No *B3*

Type *House*   Rent *600*   Staff Responsible

No of Rooms *5*   *Ann Beech*

Owner's Details

Name *Carol Farrel*   Business Name

Address *6 Achray St,*
Glasgow
G32 9DX   Address

Tel No. *0141-357-7419*   Tel No.

Owner No. *CO87*   Owner No.

Contact Name

Business Type

Figure 1.1 Sales Department forms: (a) Property for Rent Details form; (b) Renter Details form.

PROPERTY_FOR_RENT

Pno	Street	Area	City	Pcode	Type	Rooms	Rent	Ono
PA14	16 Holhead	Dee	Aberdeen	AB7 5SU	House	6	650	CO46
PL94	6 Argyll St	Kilburn	London	NW2	Flat	4	400	CO87
PG4	6 Lawrence St	Partick	Glasgow	G11 9QX	Flat	3	350	CO40
PG36	2 Manor Rd		Glasgow	G32 4QX	Flat	3	375	CO93
PG21	18 Dale Rd	Hyndland	Glasgow	G12	House	5	600	CO87
PG16	5 Novar Dr	Hyndland	Glasgow	G12 9AX	Flat	4	450	CO93

OWNER

Ono	FName	LName	Address	Tel_No
CO46	Joe	Keogh	2 Fergus Dr, Banchory, Aberdeen AB2 7SX	01224-861212
CO87	Carol	Farrel	6 Achray St, Glasgow G32 9DX	0141-357-7419
CO40	Tina	Murphy	63 Well St, Shawlands, Glasgow G42	0141-943-1728
CO93	Tony	Shaw	12 Park Pl, Hillhead, Glasgow G4 0QR	0141-225-7025

RENTER

Rno	FName	LName	Address	Tel_No	Pref_Type	Max_Rent
CR76	John	Kay	56 High St, Putney, London SW1 4EH	0171-774-5632	Flat	425
CR56	Aline	Stewart	64 Fern Dr, Pollock, Glasgow G42 0BL	0141-848-1825	Flat	350
CR74	Mike	Ritchie	18 Tain St, Gourock PA1G 1YQ	01475-392178	House	750
CR62	Mary	Tregear	5 Tarbot Rd, Kildary, Aberdeen AB9 3ST	01224-196720	Flat	600

property, a form is filled in by one of the Sales staff giving the renter and property details, as shown in Figure 1.3. This form is passed to the Contracts Department, who allocate a lease number and complete the payment and rental period details. Again, with the assistance of the DP Department, the Contracts Department create an information system to handle lease agreements. The system consists of three files storing lease, property and renter details, containing similar data to that held by the Sales Department, as illustrated in Figure 1.4.

The situation is illustrated diagrammatically in Figure 1.5. It shows each department accessing their own files through application programs written specially for them. Each set of departmental application programs handles data entry, file maintenance and the generation of a fixed set of specific reports. What is more important, the physical structure and storage of the data files and records are defined in the application code.

We can find similar examples in other departments. For example, the Payroll Department store details relating to each employee's salary, namely:

Staff_Salary(Staff Number, First Name, Last Name, Address, Sex, Date of Birth, Salary, National Insurance Number, Branch Number)

Figure 1.2 The Property_for_Rent, Owner and Renter files used by Sales.

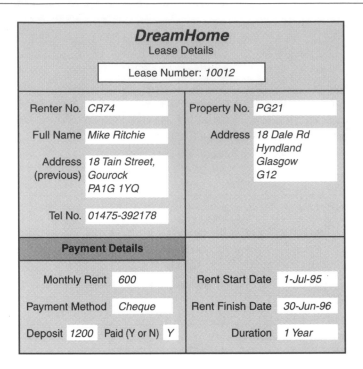

Figure 1.3 Lease Details form.

LEASE

Lno	Pno	Rno	Rent	Payment	Deposit	Paid	Start	Finish	Duration
10024	PA14	CR62	650	Visa	1300	Y	1-Jun-95	31-May-96	12
10075	PL94	CR76	400	Cash	800	N	1-Aug-95	31-Jan-96	6
10012	PG21	CR74	600	Cheque	1200	Y	1-Jul-95	30-Jun-96	12

PROPERTY_FOR_RENT

Pno	Street	Area	City	Pcode	Rent
PA14	16 Holhead	Dee	Aberdeen	AB7 5SU	650
PL94	6 Argyll St	Kilburn	London	NW2	400
PG21	18 Dale Rd	Hyndland	Glasgow	G12	600

RENTER

Figure 1.4
The Lease,
Property_for_Rent
and Renter files used
by contracts.

Rno	FName	LName	Address	Tel_No
CR76	John	Kay	56 High St, Putney, London SW1 4EH	0171-774-5632
CR74	Mike	Ritchie	18 Tain St, Gourock PA1G 1YQ	01475-392178
CR62	Mary	Tregear	5 Tarbot Rd, Kildary, Aberdeen AB9 3ST	01224-196720

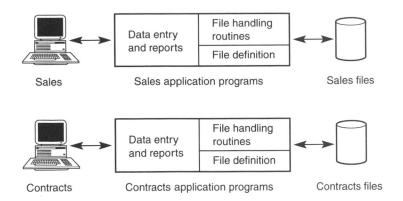

Sales Files

>   **Property_for_Rent**(Property Number, Street, Area, City, Post Code, Property Type,
>   Number of Rooms, Monthly Rent, Owner Number)
>
>   **Owner**(Owner Number, First Name, Last Name, Address, Telephone Number)
>
>   **Renter**(Renter Number, First Name, Last Name, Address, Telephone Number,
>   Preferred Type, Maximum Rent)

Contracts Files

>   **Lease**(Lease Number, Property Number, Renter Number, Monthly Rent,
>   Payment Method, Deposit, Paid, Rent Start Date, Rent Finish Date, Duration)
>
>   **Property_for_Rent**(Property Number, Street, Area, City, Post Code, Monthly Rent)
>
>   **Renter**(Renter Number, First Name, Last Name, Address, Telephone Number)

Figure 1.5
File-based
processing.

The Personnel Department also store staff details, namely:

>   **Staff**(Staff Number, First Name, Last Name, Address, Telephone Number,
>   Position, Sex, Date of Birth, Salary, National Insurance Number,
>   Branch Number)

It can be seen quite clearly that there is a significant amount of duplication of data in these departments, and this is generally true of file-based systems. Before we discuss the limitations of this approach, it may be useful to understand the terminology used in file-based systems. A file is simply a collection of **records**, which contain logically related **data**. For example, the Property_ for_Rent file in Figure 1.2 contains six records, one for each property. Each record contains a logically connected set of one or more **fields**, where each field represents some characteristic of the real-world object that is being modelled. In Figure 1.2, the fields of the Property_for_Rent file represent characteristics of properties, such as address, property type and number of rooms.

1.2.2   Limitations of the File-Based Approach

This brief description of traditional file-based systems should be sufficient to allow us to discuss the limitations of this approach. We list five problems in Table 1.1.

Table 1.1 Limitations of file-based systems.

Separation and isolation of data

Duplication of data

Data dependence

Incompatibility of files

Fixed queries/proliferation of application programs

Separation and isolation of data

When data is isolated in separate files, it is more difficult to access data that should be available. For example, if we want to produce a list of all houses, say, that match the requirements of potential renters, we need to create a temporary file of those renters who have 'house' as the preferred type, and then search the Property_for_Rent file for those properties whose property type is house and whose rent is less than the renter's maximum rent. With file systems, such processing is difficult. The application programmer must synchronize the processing of two files to ensure the correct data is extracted. This difficulty is compounded if we require data from more than two files.

Duplication of data

Due to the decentralized approach taken by each department, the file-based approach encouraged, if not necessitated, the uncontrolled duplication of data. For example, in Figure 1.5 we can clearly see that there is duplication of both property and renter details in the Sales and Contracts Departments. Uncontrolled duplication of data is undesirable for several reasons.

(a)   Duplication is wasteful. It costs time and money to enter the data more than once. Furthermore, it takes up additional storage space, again with associated costs. Often, the duplication of data can be avoided by sharing data files.

(b)   Perhaps more important, duplication can lead to loss of data integrity; in other words, the data is no longer consistent. For example, consider the duplication of data between the Payroll and Personnel Departments listed above. If an employee moves house and the change of address is communicated only to Personnel and not to Payroll, the person's payslip will be sent to the wrong address. A more serious problem occurs if an employee is promoted to a more senior position with an associated increase in salary. Again, the change is notified to Personnel but the change does not filter through to Payroll. Now, the employee is receiving the wrong salary. When this error is detected, it will take time and effort to resolve it. Both these examples illustrate inconsistencies that may result from the duplication of data. As there is no automatic way for Personnel to update the data in the Payroll files, it is not difficult to foresee such inconsistencies arising. Even if Payroll is notified of the changes, it is possible that the data will be entered incorrectly.

Data dependence

As we have already mentioned, the physical structure and storage of the data files and records are defined in the application code. This means that changes to an existing structure are difficult. For example, increasing the size of the Property_for_Rent address field from 40 to 41 characters sounds like a simple change, but it requires the creation of a one-off program (that is, a program that is run only once and can then be discarded) that converts the Property_for_Rent file to the new format. This program has to:

- Open the original Property_for_Rent file for reading.
- Open a temporary file with the new structure.
- Read a record from the original file, convert the data to conform to the new structure and write it to the temporary file. Repeat for all records in the original file.
- Delete the original Property_for_Rent file.
- Rename the temporary file as Property_for_Rent.

In addition, all programs that access the Property_for_Rent file must be modified to conform to the new file structure. There might be many such programs that access the Property_for_Rent file. Thus, the programmer needs to identify all the affected programs, modify them and then retest them. Note that a program does not even have to use the address field to be affected; it has only to use the Property_for_Rent file. Clearly, this could be very time-consuming and subject to error. This characteristic of file-based systems is known as **program–data dependence.**

Incompatible file formats

As the structure of files is embedded in the application programs, the structure is dependent on the application programming language. For example, the structure of a file generated by a COBOL program may be different from the structure of a file generated by a C program. The direct incompatibility of such files makes them difficult to process jointly.

For example, suppose that the Contracts Department want to find the names and addresses of all owners whose property is currently under lease. Unfortunately, Contracts do not hold the details of property owners; this is held only by the Sales Department. However, Contracts have the Property Number, which can be used to find the corresponding Property Number in the Sales Department's Property_for_Rent file. This file holds the Owner Number, which can be used to find the owner details in the Owner file. The Contracts Department program in COBOL and the Sales Department program in C. Therefore, to match Property Numbers in the two Property_for_Rent files requires the application programmer to write software to convert the files to some common format to facilitate processing. This again can be time-consuming and costly.

Fixed queries/proliferation of application programs

From the end users' point of view, file-based systems proved to be a great improvement over manual systems. Consequently, the requirement for new or modified queries grew. However, file-based systems are very dependent upon the application programmer. Any queries or reports that are required have to be written by the application programmer. As a result, two things happened. In some organizations, the type of query or report that could be produced was fixed. There was no facility for asking unplanned (that is, spur-of-the-moment or ad-hoc) queries either about the data itself or about which types of data were available.

In others, there was a proliferation of files and application programs. Eventually, this reached a point where the work could not be handled by the DP Department's current resources. This put tremendous pressure on the DP staff, resulting in programs that were inadequate or inefficient in meeting the demands of the users, documentation that was limited and maintenance that was difficult. Often, functionality was omitted; there was no provision for security or integrity; recovery in the event of failure of hardware or software was limited or non-existent; access to the files was restricted to one user at a time – there was no provision for shared access by staff in the same department.

In either case, the outcome was not acceptable. Another solution was required.

1.3   Database Approach

All the above limitations of the file-based approach can be attributed to two factors:

(1)   The definition of the data is embedded in the application programs, rather than being stored separately and independently.

(2)   There is no control over the access and manipulation of data beyond that imposed by the application programs.

To become more effective, a new approach was required. What emerged were the **database** and the **Database Management System (DBMS)**.

1.3.1   The Database

> **Database**   A shared collection of logically related data (and a description of this data), designed to meet the information needs of an organization.

Let us examine this definition in detail to understand this concept fully. The database is a single, large repository of data, which is defined once and used simultaneously by many departments and users. Instead of disconnected files with redundant data, all data is integrated with a minimum amount of dupli-

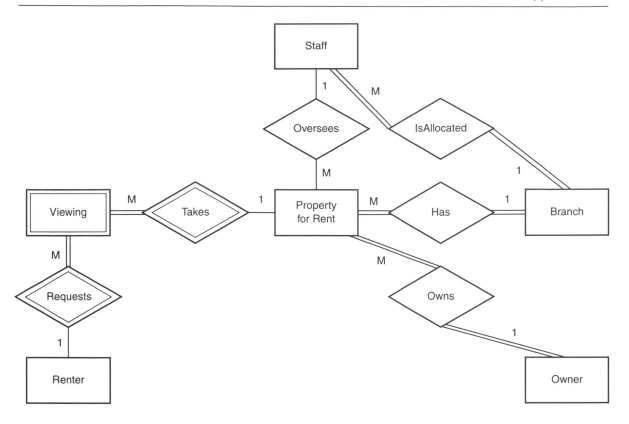

Figure 1.6
Example entity–
relationship diagram.

cation. The database is no longer owned by one department but is now a shared corporate resource. The database holds not only the organization's operational data but, in addition, it holds a description of this data. For this reason, a database is also defined as *a self-describing collection of integrated records*. The description of the data is known as the **system catalog** (or **data dictionary** or **metadata** – the 'data about data'). It is the self-describing nature of a database that provides **program–data independence**.

The approach taken with database systems, whereby we separate the definition of data from the application programs, is very similar to the approach taken in modern software development, whereby we provide an' internal definition of an object and a separate external definition. The users of an object see only the external definition and are unaware of how the object is defined and how it functions. One advantage of this approach, known as **data abstraction**, is that we can change the internal definition of an object without affecting the users of the object, provided the external definition remains the same. In the same way, the database approach separates the structure of the data from the application programs and stores it in the database. If new data structures are added or existing structures are modified then the application programs are unaffected, provided they do not directly depend upon what has been modified. For example, if we add a new field to a record or create a new file, existing applications are unaffected. However, if we remove a field from a file that an application program uses, then that application program is affected by this change and must be modified accordingly.

The final term in the definition of a database that we should explain is 'logically related'. When we analyse the information needs of an organization, we attempt to identify entities, attributes and relationships. An **entity** is a distinct object (a person, place or thing, concept or event) in the organization that is to be represented in the database. An **attribute** is a property that describes some aspect of the object that we wish to record, and a **relationship** is an association between several entities. For example, Figure 1.6 shows an Entity–Relationship (ER) diagram for part of *DreamHome*. It consists of:

- six entities (the rectangles): Branch, Staff, Property_for_Rent, Owner, Renter and Viewing;
- six relationships (the diamonds): IsAllocated, Has, Oversees, Owns, Requests and Takes.

The database represent the entities, the attributes and the logical relationships between the entities. In other words, the database holds data that is logically related. We will discuss the entity–relationship model in detail in Chapter 5.

1.3.2 The Database Management System (DBMS)

DBMS	A software system that enables users to define, create and maintain the database and which provides controlled access to this database.

The DBMS is the software that interacts with the users' application programs and the database. Typically, a DBMS provides the following facilities:

- It allows users to define the database, usually through a **Data Definition Language** (DDL). The DDL allows users to specify the data types and structures, and the constraints on the data to be stored in the database.
- It allows users to insert, update, delete and retrieve data from the database, usually through a **Data Manipulation Language** (DML). Having a central repository for all data and data descriptions allows the DML to provide a general enquiry facility to this data, called a **query language**. The provision of a query language alleviates the problems with file-based systems where the user has to work with a fixed set of queries or there is a proliferation of programs, giving major software management problems.

    There are two types of DML, **procedural** and **non-procedural**, which we can distinguish according to the retrieval operations. The main difference between them is that procedural languages manipulate the database record by record, while non-procedural languages operate on sets of records. Consequently, procedural languages specify *how* the output of a DML statement is to be obtained, while non-procedural DMLs describe only *what* data is to be obtained. The most common type of non-procedural language is the Structured Query Language (SQL – pronounced 'S-Q-L' or sometimes 'See-Quel'), which is now both the standard and the *de facto* language for relational database systems. To emphasize the importance of SQL, we devote two chapters, Chapters 11 and 12, to a comprehensive study of this language.

- It provides controlled access to the database. For example, it may provide:

  - a security system, which prevents unauthorized users from accessing the database;
  - an integrity system, which maintains the consistency of stored data;
  - a concurrency control system, which allows shared access of the database;
  - a recovery control system, which restores the database to a previous consistent state following a hardware or software failure;
  - a user-accessible catalog, which contains descriptions of the data in the database.

The database approach is illustrated diagrammatically in Figure 1.7, based on the file approach of Figure 1.5. It shows the Sales and Contracts Departments using their application programs to access the database through the DBMS. Each set of departmental application programs handles data entry, data maintenance and the generation of reports. However, compared with the file-based approach, the physical structure and storage of the data are now managed by the DBMS.

With this functionality, the DBMS is an extremely useful tool. However, from the end users' point of view, who are not interested in how complex or easy a task is, it could be argued that the DBMS has made things more complex because they now see more data than they actually need or want. For example, the details that the Contracts Department want to see for a rental property, as shown in Figure 1.5, have changed in the database approach, shown in Figure 1.7. Now the database also holds the property type, the number of rooms and the owner details. In recognition of this problem, a DBMS provides another facility known as a **view mechanism**, which allows each user to have his or her own view of the database. The DDL allows views to be defined, where a view is a subset of the database. For example, we could set up a view that allows the Contracts Department to see only the data that they want to see for rental properties.

As well as reducing complexity by letting users see the data in the way that they want to see it, views have several other benefits:

- Views provide a level of security. Views can be set up to exclude data that some users should not see. For example, we could create a view that allows a branch manager and the Payroll Department to see all staff data, including salary details. However, we could create a second view that other staff would use, which excludes salary details.

- Views provide a mechanism to customize the appearance of the database. For example, the Contracts Department may wish to call the Monthly Rent field by the simpler name, Rent.

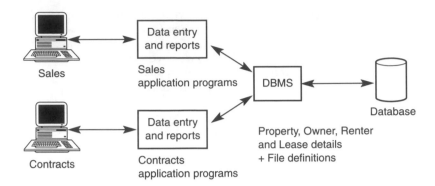

Figure 1.7
Database processing.

Property_for_Rent(Property Number, Street, Area, City, Post Code, Property Type, Number of Rooms, Monthly Rent, Owner Number)

Owner(Owner Number, First Name, Last Name, Address, Telephone Number)

Renter(Renter Number, First Name, Last Name, Address, Telephone Number), Preferred Type, Maximum Rent)

Lease(Lease Number, Property Number, Renter Number, Payment Method, Deposit, Paid, Rent Start Date, Rent Finish Date)

- A view can present a consistent, unchanging picture of the structure of the database, even if the underlying database is changed (for example, fields added or removed, relationships changed, files split, restructured or renamed). If fields are added or removed from a file, and these fields are not required by the view, the view is not affected by this change. Thus, a view helps provide the program–data independence we mentioned earlier.

The above discussion is general. The actual level of functionality offered by a DBMS differs from product to product. For example, a DBMS for a personal computer may not support concurrent shared access, and it may only provide limited security, integrity and recovery control. However, modern large multi-user DBMS products offer all the above functions and much more. Modern systems are extremely complex pieces of software consisting of millions of lines of code, with documentation comprising many volumes. This is a result of having to provide software that handles requirements of a more general nature. Furthermore, the application of database systems nowadays requires a system that provides almost 100% reliability, even in the presence of hardware or software failures. The DBMS is continually evolving and has to be expanded to cope with new user requirements. For example, some applications now require the storage of graphic images, video, sound, and so on. To reach this market, the DBMS must change. It is likely that new functionality will always be required, so that the functionality of the DBMS will never become static. We will discuss the basic functions provided by a DBMS in detail in later chapters.

1.3.3   Components of the DBMS Environment

We can identify five major components in the DBMS environment: hardware, software, data, procedures and people, as illustrated in Figure 1.8.

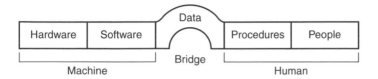

Figure 1.8   DBMS environment.

Hardware

The DBMS and the applications require hardware to run. The hardware can range from a single personal computer to a single mainframe to a network of computers. The particular hardware depends on the organization's requirements and the DBMS used. Some DBMSs run only on particular hardware or operating systems, while others run on a wide variety of hardware and operating systems. A DBMS requires a minimum amount of main memory and disk space to run, but this minimum configuration may not necessarily give acceptable performance. A simplified hardware configuration for the estate agents is illustrated in Figure 1.9. It consists of a network of mini-computers, with a central computer located in London running the **backend** of the DBMS: that is, the part of the DBMS that manages and controls access to the database, and several computers at various locations running the **front-end** of the DBMS: that is, the part of the DBMS that interfaces with the user. This is called a **client–server** architecture: the backend is the server and the frontends are the clients. We will discuss this type of architecture further in the next chapter.

Software

The software component comprises the DBMS software itself together with the operating system, including network software if the DBMS is being used over a network, and the application programs. Typically, application programs are written in a third-generation programming language, such as C, COBOL, Fortran, Ada or Pascal, or using a fourth-generation language, such as SQL, embedded in a third-generation language. The target DBMS may have its own fourth-generation tools that allow rapid development of applications through the provision of non-procedural query languages, reports generators, forms generators, graphics generators and application generators. The use of fourth-generation tools can improve productivity significantly and produce programs that are easier to maintain. We will discuss fourth-generation tools in Section 2.2.3.

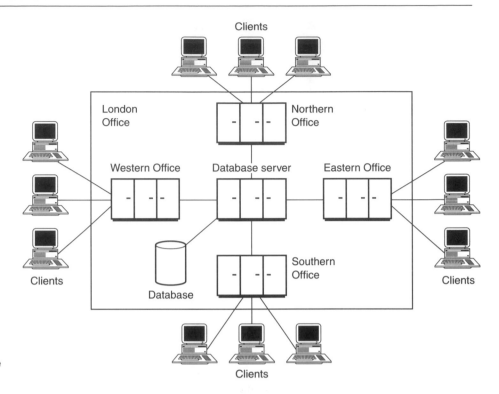

Figure 1.9
DreamHome hardware configuration.

Data

Perhaps the most important component of the DBMS environment, certainly from the end users' point of view, is the data. From Figure 1.8, we observe that the data acts as a bridge between the machine components and the human components. The database contains both the operational data and the metadata, the 'data about data'. The structure of the database is called the **schema**. In Figure 1.7, the schema consists of four files, or **tables**, namely: Property_for_Rent, Owner, Renter and Lease. The Property_for_Rent table has nine fields, or **attributes**, namely: Property Number, Street, Area, City, Post Code, Property Type, Number of Rooms, Monthly Rent and Owner Number. The Owner Number attribute models the relationship between Property_for_Rent and Owner: that is, an owner *Owns* a property for rent, as depicted in the entity–relationship diagram of Figure 1.6. For example, in Figure 1.2 we observe that Owner CO46, Joe Keogh, owns property PA14.

The system catalog contains data such as:

- names, types and sizes of data items;
- names of relationships;
- integrity constraints on the data;
- names of authorized users who have access to the data;
- what indexes and what storage structures are being used, such as hashing, inverted files or B^+-Trees.

We will discuss the system catalog in more detail in the next chapter.

Procedures

Procedures refer to the instructions and rules that govern the design and use of the database. The users of the system and the staff that manage the database require documented procedures on how to use or run the system. These may consist of instructions on how to:

- Log on to the DBMS.
- Use a particular DBMS facility or application program.
- Start and stop the DBMS.
- Make backup copies of the database.
- Handle hardware or software failures. This may include procedures on how to identify the failed component, how to fix the failed component (for example, telephone the appropriate hardware engineer) and, following the repair of the fault, how to recover the database.
- Change the structure of a table, reorganize the database across multiple disks, improve performance or archive data to secondary storage.

People

The final component is the people involved with the system. We discuss this component in Section 1.4.

1.3.4 Database Design – The Paradigm Shift

Until now, we have taken it for granted that there is a structure to the data in the database. For example, we have identified four tables in Figure 1.7, Property_for_Rent, Renter, Owner and Lease. But how did we get this structure? The answer is quite simple: the structure of the database is determined during **database design**. However, carrying out database design can be extremely complex. To produce a system that will satisfy the organization's information needs requires a different approach to that of file-based systems, where the work was driven by the application needs of individual departments. For the database approach to succeed, the organization now has to think of the data first and the application second. This change in approach is sometimes referred to as a *paradigm shift*. For the system to be acceptable to the end users, the database design activity is crucial. A poorly designed database will generate errors that may lead to bad decisions being made, which may have serious repercussions for the organization. On the other hand, a well designed database produces a system that provides the correct information for the decision making process to succeed.

The objective of this book is to help effect this paradigm shift. We devote several chapters to the presentation of a complete methodology for database design. We present it as a series of simple-to-follow steps, with guidelines provided throughout. For example, in the entity–relationship diagram of Figure 1.6, we have identified six entities and six relationships. We will provide guidelines to help identify the entities, attributes and relationships that have to be represented in the database.

Unfortunately, database design methodologies are not very popular; most organizations and individual designers rely very little on methodologies for conducting the design of databases, and this is commonly considered a major cause of failure in the development of information systems. Due to the lack of structured approaches to database design, the time or resources required for a database project are typically underestimated, the databases developed are inadequate or inefficient in meeting the demands of applications, documentation is limited and maintenance is difficult.

1.4 Roles in the Database Environment

In this section, we examine the fifth component of the DBMS environment: the **people**. We can identify four distinct types of people: data and database administrators, database designers, application programmers and end users.

1.4.1 Data and Database Administrators

The database and the DBMS are corporate resources that must be managed like any other resource. Data and database administration are the roles generally associated with the management and control of a DBMS and its data. The **Data Administrator (DA)** is responsible for the management of the data resource including database planning, development and maintenance of standards, policies and procedures and logical database design. The DA consults with and advises senior managers, ensuring that the direction of database development will ultimately support corporate objectives.

The **Database Administrator (DBA)** is responsible for the physical realization of the database system, including physical database design and implementation, security and integrity control, maintenance of the operational system and ensuring satisfactory performance for the applications and users. The role of the DBA is more technically oriented than the role of the DA, requiring detailed knowledge of the target DBMS and the system environment. In some organizations there is no distinction between these two roles. In others, the importance of the corporate resources is reflected in the allocation of teams of staff dedicated to each of these roles. We will discuss data and database administration in more detail in Chapter 4.

1.4.2 Database Designers

In large database design projects, we can distinguish between two types of designers: logical database designers and physical database designers. The **logical database designer** is concerned with identifying the data (that is, the entities and attributes), the relationships between the data and the constraints on the data that is to be stored in the database. The logical database designer must have a thorough and complete understanding of the organization's data and of the **business rules**. Business rules describe the main characteristics of the data *as viewed by the organization*. Examples of business rules are:

- A member of staff cannot handle the sale or rent of more than ten properties at the same time.
- A member of staff cannot handle the sale or rent of their own property.
- A solicitor cannot act for both the buyer and seller of a property.

To be effective, the logical database designer must involve all prospective database users in the development of the data model, and the involvement should begin as early in the process as possible. Logical database design is independent of implementation details such as the target DBMS, application programs, programming languages or any other physical considerations.

The **physical database designer** takes the logical data model and decides how it is to be physically realized. This involves:

- mapping the logical data model into a set of tables and integrity constraints;
- selecting specific storage structures and access methods for the data to achieve good performance for the database activities;
- designing any security measures required on the data.

Many parts of physical database design are highly dependent on the target DBMS, and there may be more than one way of implementing a mechanism. Consequently, the physical database designer must be fully aware of the functionality of the target DBMS and must understand the advantages and disadvantages of each alternative for a particular implementation. The physical database designer must be capable of selecting a suitable storage strategy that takes account of usage. Whereas logical database design is concerned with the *what*, physical database design is concerned with the *how*. It requires different skills, which are often found in different people. We present a methodology for logical database design in Chapter 7 and one for physical database design in Chapter 9.

1.4.3 Application Programmers

Once the database has been implemented, the application programs that provide the required functionality for the end users must be implemented. This is the responsibility of the **application programmers**. Typically, the application programmers work from a specification produced by systems analysts. Each program contains statements that request the DBMS to perform some operation on the database. This includes retrieving data, inserting, updating and deleting data. The programs may be written in a third-generation programming language or a fourth-generation language, as discussed in the previous section.

1.4.4 End-Users

The end-users are the 'clients' for the database – the database has been designed and implemented, and is being maintained to serve their information needs. End-users can be classified according to the way they use the system:

- **Naïve users** are typically unaware of the DBMS. They access the database through specially written application programs, which attempt to make the operations as simple as possible. They invoke database operations by entering simple commands or choosing options from a menu. This means that they do not need to know anything about the database or the DBMS. For example, the checkout assistant at the local supermarket uses a bar code reader to find out the price of the item. However, there is an application program present that reads the bar code, looks up the price of the item in the database, reduces the database field containing the number of such items in stock and rings up the price on the till.

- **Sophisticated users**. At the other end of the spectrum, the sophisticated end-user is familiar with the structure of the database and the facilities offered by the DBMS. Sophisticated end-users may use a high-level query language such as SQL to perform the required operations. Some sophisticated end-users may even write application programs for their own use.

1.5 The History of Database Systems

We have already seen that the predecessor to the database system was the file-based system. However, there was never a time when the database approach began and the file-based system ceased. In fact, the file-based system is still in existence today in specific areas. It has been suggested that the database system has its roots in the 1960s Apollo moon-landing project, which was initiated in response to President J.F. Kennedy's objective of landing a man on the moon by the end of the decade. At that time, there was no system available that would be able to handle and manage the vast amounts of information that the project would require.

As a result, North American Aviation (now Rockwell International), the prime contractor for the project, developed software known as **GUAM (Generalized Update Access Method)**. GUAM was based on the concept that smaller components come together as parts of larger components, and so on, until the final product is assembled. This structure, which conforms to an upside-down tree, is also known as a **hierarchical structure**. In the mid-1960s, IBM joined NAA to develop GUAM into what is now known as **IMS (Information Management System)**. The reason why IBM restricted IMS to the management of hierarchies of records was to allow the use of serial storage devices, most notably magnetic tape, which was a market requirement at that time. This restriction was subsequently dropped. Although one of the earliest commercial database systems, IMS is still the main hierarchical database used by most large mainframe installations.

In the mid-1960s, another significant development was the emergence of **IDS (Integrated Data Store)** from General Electric. This work was headed by one of the early pioneers of database systems, Charles Bachmann. This development led to a new type of database system known as the **network** database system, which had a profound effect on the information systems of that generation. The network database was developed partly to address the need to represent more complex data relationships than could be modelled with hierarchical structures, and partly to impose a database standard. To help establish such standards, the Conference on DAta SYstems Languages (**CODASYL**), comprising representatives of the US Government and the world of business and commerce, formed a List Processing Task Force in 1965, subsequently renamed the **Data Base Task Group (DBTG)** in 1967. The terms of reference for the DBTG were to define standard specifications for an environment that would allow database creation and data manipulation. A draft report was issued in 1969 and the first definitive report in 1971. The DBTG proposal identified three components:

- the network **schema** – the logical organization of the entire database as seen by the DBA – which includes a definition of the database name, the type of each record and the components of each record type;
- the **subschema** – the part of the database as seen by the user or application program;
- a data management language to define the data characteristics and the data structure, and to manipulate the data.

For standardization, the DBTG specified three distinct languages:

- a schema **Data Definition Language (DDL)**, which enables the DBA to define the schema;
- a subschema **DDL**, which allows the application programs to define the parts of the database they require;
- a **Data Manipulation Language (DML)**, to manipulate the data.

Although the report was not formally adopted by the American National Standards Institute (ANSI), a number of systems were subsequently developed following the DBTG proposal. These systems are now known as CODASYL or DBTG systems. The hierarchical and CODASYL approaches represented the **first generation** of DBMSs. However, these two models have some fundamental disadvantages:

- Complex programs have to be written to answer even simple queries based on navigational record-oriented access.
- There is minimal data independence.
- There is no widely accepted theoretical foundation.

In 1970, E. F. Codd of the IBM Research Laboratory produced his highly influential paper on the relational data model. This paper was very timely and addressed the disadvantages of the former approaches. Many experimental relational systems were implemented thereafter, with the first commercial products appearing in the late 1970s and early 1980s. Of particular note is the System R project at IBM's San Jose Research Laboratory in California, which was developed during the late 1970s (Astrahan *et al.*, 1976). This project was designed to prove the practicality of the relational model by providing an implementation of its data structures and operations, and led to two major developments:

- the development of a structured query language called SQL, which has since become the standard language for relational systems;
- the production of various commercial relational database management system products during the 1980s; for example, DB2 and SQL/DS from IBM and ORACLE from ORACLE Corporation.

Now there are several hundred relational DBMSs for both mainframe and microcomputer environments, though many are stretching the definition of the relational model. Other examples of multi-user relational systems are INGRES from Relational Technology Inc. (now Computer Associates: The ASK Group), Informix from Informix Software Inc. and Sybase from Sybase Inc. Examples of microcomputer-based relational DBMSs are Paradox and dBaseIV from Borland, Access from Microsoft, FoxPro and R:base from Microrim. Relational DBMSs are referred to as **second-generation** DBMSs. We discuss the relational data model in Chapter 3.

However, the relational model is not without its failings, and in particular its limited modelling capabilities. There has been much research since then attempting to address this problem. In 1976, Chen presented the entity–relationship model, which is now a widely accepted technique for database design and the basis for the methodology presented in Chapter 7 of this book. In 1979, Codd himself attempted to address some of the failings in his original work with an extended version of the relational model called RM/T (1979) and recently RM/V2 (1990). The attempts to provide a data model that represents the real world more closely have been loosely classified as **semantic data modelling**.

In response to the increasing complexity of database applications, two 'new' data models have emerged: the **Object-Oriented Data Model** (OODM) and the **Extended Relational Data Model** (ERDM). However, unlike previous models, the actual composition of these models is not clear. This evolution represents **third-generation** DBMSs, which we will discuss in detail in Chapter 17.

1.6 Advantages and Disadvantages of Database Systems

The database management system has promising potential advantages. Unfortunately, there are also disadvantages. In this section, we examine these advantages and disadvantages.

Table 1.2 Advantages of database systems.

Control of data redundancy

Data consistency

More information from the same amount of data

Sharing of data

Improved data integrity

Improved security

Enforcement of standards

Economy of scale

Balanced conflicting requirements

Improved data accessibility and responsiveness

Increased productivity

Improved maintenance through data independence

Increased concurrency

Improved backup and recovery services

Advantages

The advantages of database systems are listed in Table 1.2.

Control of data redundancy

As we discussed in Section 1.2, the traditional file-based systems waste space by storing the same information in more than one file. For example, in Figure 1.5, we stored similar data for properties for rent and renters in both the Sales and Contracts Departments. In contrast, the database approach attempts to eliminate the redundancy by integrating the files so that several copies of the same data are not stored. However, the database approach does not eliminate redundancy entirely, but controls the amount of redundancy inherent in the database. Sometimes, it is necessary to duplicate key data items to model relationships. At other times, it is desirable to duplicate some data items to improve performance. The reasons for controlled duplication will become clearer as you read the next few chapters.

Data consistency

By eliminating or controlling redundancy, we are reducing the risk of inconsistencies occurring. If a data item is stored only once in the database, any update to its value has to be performed only once and the new value is immediately available to all users. If a data item is stored more than once and the system is aware of this, the system can ensure that all copies of the item are kept consistent. Unfortunately, many of today's DBMSs do not automatically ensure this type of consistency.

More information from the same amount of data
With the integration of the operational data, it may be possible for the organization to derive additional information from the same data. For example, in the file-based system illustrated in Figure 1.5, the Contracts Department do not know who owns a leased property. However, the Sales Department have no knowledge of lease details. When we integrate these files together, the Contracts Department has access to owner details and the Sales Department has access to lease details. We may now be able to derive more information from the same amount of data.

Sharing of data
Typically, files are owned by the people or departments that use them. On the other hand, the database belongs to the entire organization and can be shared by all authorized users. In this way, more users share more of the data. Furthermore, new applications can use the existing data in the database and then require only additional data that is not currently stored, rather than having to define all data requirements again. The new applications can also rely on the functions provided by the DBMS, such as data definition and manipulation, rather than having to provide these functions themselves.

Improved data integrity
Database integrity refers to the validity and consistency of stored data. Integrity is usually expressed in terms of **constraints**, which are consistency rules that the database is not permitted to violate. Constraints may apply to data items within a single record or they may apply to relationships between records. For example, an integrity constraint could state that an employee's salary cannot be greater than £40,000 or that the branch number contained in the employee's record, representing the branch that the employee works at, corresponds to an existing branch office. Again, integration allows the DBA to define, and the DBMS to enforce, integrity constraints.

Improved security
Database security is the protection of the database from unauthorized users. Without suitable security measures, integration makes the data more vulnerable than file-based systems. However, integration allows the DBA to define, and the DBMS to enforce, database security. This may take the form of user names and passwords to identify people authorized to use the database. The access that an authorized user is allowed on the data may be restricted by the operation type (retrieval, insert, update, delete). For example, the DBA has access to all the data in the database; a branch manager may have access to all data that relates to his or her branch office; and a sales assistant may have access to all data relating to properties but no access to sensitive data, such as salary details.

Enforcement of standards
Again, integration allows the DBA to define and enforce the necessary standards. These may include departmental, organizational, country or international standards for such things as data formats to facilitate exchange of data between systems, naming conventions, documentation standards, update procedures and access rules.

Economy of scale
Combining all of an organization's operational data into one database with the applications that are required can result in cost savings. In this case, the budget that would normally be allocated to each department for the development and maintenance of their file-based systems can be combined, possibly resulting in a lower total cost, leading to an economy of scale. The combined budget can be used to buy a system configuration that is more suited to the organization's needs. This may consist of one large, powerful computer or a network of smaller computers.

Balanced conflicting requirements
Each user or department has needs that may be in conflict with the needs of other users. Since the database is under the control of the DBA, the DBA can make decisions about the design and operational use of the database that provide the best use of resources for the organization as a whole. These decisions will provide optimal performance for important applications, possibly at the expense of less critical ones.

Improved data accessibility and responsiveness
Again, as a result of integration, data that crosses departmental boundaries is directly accessible to the end-user. This provides a system with potentially much more functionality, which for example, can be used to provide better services to the end-user or the organization's clients. Many DBMSs provide query languages or report writers that allow users to ask ad-hoc questions and obtain the required information almost immediately at their terminals, without requiring a programmer to write some software to extract this information from the database. For example, a branch manager could list all flats with a monthly rent greater than £400 by entering the following SQL command at a terminal:

```
SELECT *
FROM Property_for_Rent
WHERE type = 'Flat' AND rent > 400;
```

Increased productivity
As mentioned previously, the DBMS provides many of the standard functions that the programmer would normally have to write in a file-based application. At a basic level, the DBMS provides all the low-level file-handling routines that are typical in application programs. The provision of these functions allows the programmer to concentrate more on the specific functionality required by the users without having to worry about low-level implementation details. Many DBMSs also provide a fourth-generation environment consisting of tools to simplify the development of database applications. This results in increased programmer productivity and reduced development time (with associated cost savings).

Improved maintenance through data independence
In file-based systems, the descriptions of the data and the logic for accessing the data are built into each application program, making the programs dependent on the data. A change to the structure of the data, for example making

an address 41 characters instead of 40 characters, or a change to the way the data is stored on disk, can require substantial alterations to the programs that are affected by the change. In contrast, a DBMS separates the data descriptions from the applications, thus making applications immune to changes in the data descriptions. This is known as **data independence** and is discussed further in Section 2.1.5. The provision of data independence simplifies database application maintenance.

Increased concurrency

In some file-based systems, if two or more users are allowed to access the same file simultaneously, it is possible that the accesses will interfere with each other, resulting in loss of information or even loss of integrity. Many DBMSs manage concurrent database access and ensure such problems cannot occur. We will discuss concurrency control in Chapter 15.

Improved backup and recovery services

Many file-based systems place the responsibility on the user to provide measures to protect the data from failures to the computer system or application program. This may involve taking a nightly backup of the data. In the event of a failure during the next day, the backup is restored and the work that has taken place since this backup is lost and has to be reentered. In contrast, modern DBMSs provide facilities to minimize the amount of processing that can be lost following a failure. We will discuss recovery control in Chapter 15.

Disadvantages

The disadvantages of the database approach are summarized in Table 1.3.

Table 1.3 Disadvantages of database systems.

Complexity
Size
Cost of DBMS
Additional hardware costs
Cost of conversion
Performance
Higher impact of a failure

Complexity

The provision of the functionality we expect of a good DBMS makes the DBMS an extremely complex piece of software. Database designers and developers, the data and database administrators and end-users must understand this functionality to take full advantage of it. Failure to understand the system can lead to bad design decisions, which can be disastrous for an organization.

Size
The complexity and breadth of functionality makes the DBMS an extremely large piece of software, occupying many megabytes of disk space and requiring substantial amounts of memory to run efficiently.

Cost of DBMS
The cost of DBMSs varies significantly, depending on the environment and functionality provided. For example, a single-user DBMS for a personal computer may only cost £500. However, a large mainframe multi-user DBMS servicing hundreds of users can be extremely expensive, perhaps £100,000 to £500,000. There is also the recurrent annual maintenance cost, which is typically a percentage of the list price.

Additional hardware costs
The disk storage requirements for the DBMS and the database may necessitate the purchase of additional storage space. Furthermore, to achieve the required performance, it may be necessary to purchase a larger machine, perhaps even a machine dedicated to running the DBMS. The procurement of additional hardware results in further expenditure.

Cost of conversion
In some situations, the cost of the DBMS and extra hardware may be insignificant compared with the cost of converting existing applications to run on the new DBMS and hardware. This cost also includes the cost of training staff to use these new systems, and possibly the employment of specialist staff to help with the conversion and running of the system. This cost is one of the main reasons why some organizations feel tied to their current systems and cannot switch to database technology.

Performance
Typically, a file-based system is written for a specific application, such as invoicing. As a result, performance is generally very good. However, the DBMS is written to be more general, to cater for many applications rather than just one. The effect is that some applications may not run as fast any more.

Higher impact of a failure
The centralization of resources increases the vulnerability of the system. Since all users and applications rely on the availability of the DBMS, the failure of any component can bring operations to a halt.

1.7 The *DreamHome* Case Study

This case study describes a company called *DreamHome*, which specializes in the management of properties for rent on behalf of the owners. The company offers a complete service to owners who wish to rent out their furnished property.

The service provided by *DreamHome* includes advertising the property in the local or national press (when necessary), interviewing prospective renters, organizing visits to the property by prospective renters and negotiating the lease agreement. Once rented, *DreamHome* assumes responsibility for the property, which involves regular property inspections by *DreamHome* staff.

Listed below is a description of the data recorded, maintained and accessed at each branch office to support the day-to-day operation and management of the *DreamHome* company.

Branch offices

DreamHome has several branch offices located throughout the United Kingdom. Each branch office is identified by a unique branch number and has an address (street, area, city, postcode), telephone number and fax number. Each branch office has members of staff.

Staff

Each *DreamHome* branch office has a manager responsible for overseeing the operations of the office. The *DreamHome* company closely follows the performance of its managers, and notes the date that each manager assumed his or her position at their current branch office. Each manager is allocated an annual car allowance and a monthly bonus payment based upon his or her performance in the property for rent market.

Each *DreamHome* branch office has members of staff with the job title of Supervisor (sometimes called Senior Administrator). Supervisors are responsible for the day-to-day activities of a dedicated group of staff (minimum of five and a maximum of ten members of staff) responsible for the management of property for rent. The administrative work of each group of staff is supported by a secretary.

Each member of staff is given a staff number, unique across all branch offices. Information held on each member of staff includes the name (first and last name), address, telephone number, sex, date of birth, national insurance number (NIN), job title (position), salary and the date the member of staff joined the *DreamHome* company. Additional information held on staff with the job title of Secretary is their typing speed.

It is company policy to record the details of the next-of-kin of members of staff and this includes the next-of-kin's full name, relationship to the member of staff, address and telephone number. Only the details of a single next-of-kin are held for each member of staff.

An example of the *DreamHome* form used to record the details of a member of staff called John White based at the London branch office is shown in Figure 1.10.

Property for rent

Each *DreamHome* branch office has properties for rent that are identified by a property number, which is unique across all branch offices. The details of property for rent include the full address (street, area, city, postcode), type

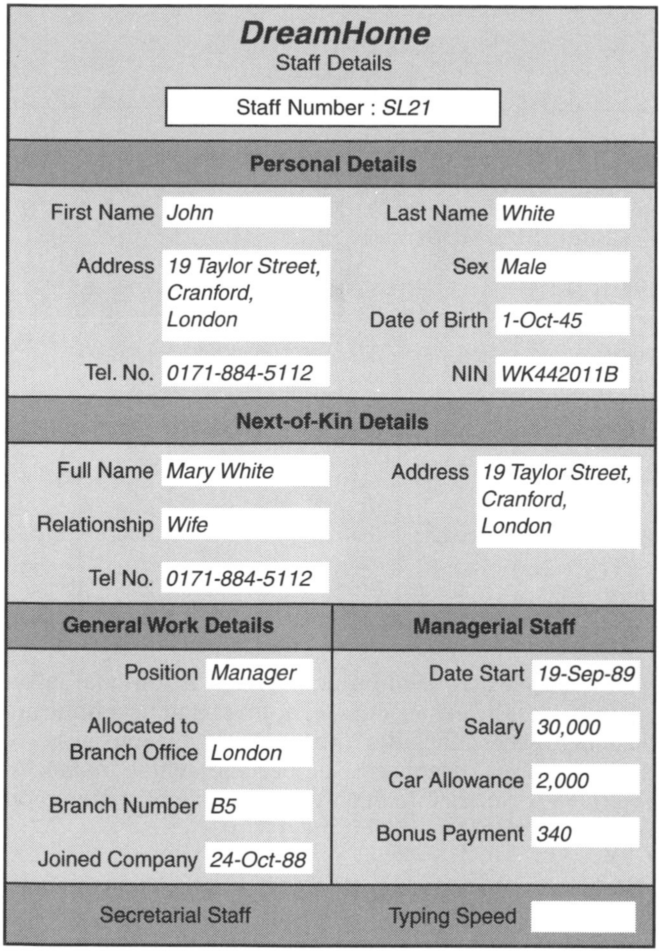
DreamHome
Staff Details

Staff Number : *SL21*

Personal Details

First Name	*John*	Last Name	*White*
Address	*19 Taylor Street, Cranford, London*	Sex	*Male*
		Date of Birth	*1-Oct-45*
Tel. No.	*0171-884-5112*	NIN	*WK442011B*

Next-of-Kin Details

Full Name	*Mary White*	Address	*19 Taylor Street, Cranford, London*
Relationship	*Wife*		
Tel No.	*0171-884-5112*		

General Work Details		**Managerial Staff**	
Position	*Manager*	Date Start	*19-Sep-89*
Allocated to Branch Office	*London*	Salary	*30,000*
Branch Number	*B5*	Car Allowance	*2,000*
Joined Company	*24-Oct-88*	Bonus Payment	*340*
Secretarial Staff		Typing Speed	

Figure 1.10 *DreamHome* Staff Details form.

of property, number of rooms and monthly rent. The monthly rent for a property is reviewed annually. Most of the properties rented out by *DreamHome* are flats. Each property for rent is assigned to a specific member of staff who is responsible for the management of that property. A member of staff may only manage a maximum of 20 properties for rent, at any one time.

When a property is withdrawn from the *DreamHome* company and is no longer available for rent, it is company policy to retain the information associated with this property for a minimum of three years.

An example of a *DreamHome* report listing the details of properties for rent available at the Glasgow branch office is shown in Figure 1.11.

Property owners

The *DreamHome* company manages property for private or business owners. Each private owner and business owner is uniquely identified by an owner

DreamHome Property for Rent							
Page 1						Date 12-May-96	

Branch Number B3   Telephone Number 0141-339-2178

Branch Office Address 163 Main Street, Partick, Glasgow G11 9QX   Fax Number 0141-339-4439

Property Number	Street	Area	City	Postcode	Type	No of Rooms	Monthly Rent
PG4	6 Lawrence St	Partick	Glasgow	G11 9QX	Flat	3	350
PG36	2 Manor Road		Glasgow	G32 4QX	Flat	3	375
PG21	18 Dale Road	Hyndland	Glasgow	G12	House	5	600
PG16	5 Novar Drive	Hyndland	Glasgow	G12 9AX	Flat	4	450

Figure 1.11
DreamHome report listing properties for rent.

number, which is unique across all branch offices. Additional information on private owners includes the owner's name, address and telephone number. The details of business owners includes the name of the business, the type of business, business address, telephone number and contact name. An example of the *DreamHome* form used to record the details of a single property for rent and the owner was shown in Figure 1.1(a).

Clients/renters

When a client first contacts a *DreamHome* branch office, his or her details are recorded. This includes the client's name (first and last name), address, telephone number, preferred type of accommodation and the maximum rent the client is prepared to pay. As a prospective renter, each client is given a unique number called the renter number, which is unique across all branch offices. It is *DreamHome*'s company policy to interview all prospective clients wishing to rent property from the company. The information recorded about each interview is the date of the interview, the member of staff who conducted the interview and any general comments about the prospective renter. An example of the *DreamHome* form used to record the details of a prospective renter called Mike Ritchie was shown in Figure 1.1(b).

Property viewings

In most cases, a prospective renter will request to view one or more properties before renting. The details of each viewing are recorded and include the date of the viewing and any comments by the prospective renter regarding the suitability or otherwise of the property.

Property advertising

In the case of properties that prove difficult to rent out, the *DreamHome* company will advertise these properties in local and national newspapers. For each advert, the company notes the date the property is advertised and the cost. Only appropriate newspapers are used to advertise *DreamHome*'s properties and the details of each newspaper used by the company include the newspaper name, address, telephone number, fax number and contact name.

Lease agreements

The *DreamHome* company is responsible for drawing up the terms of the lease (rental) agreement between a client and a property. The lease agreement details the lease number, the monthly rent, the method of payment, the rental deposit, whether the deposit is paid, the date the rent starts and finishes, the duration of the lease and the member of staff who arranged the lease. The minimum and maximum duration for a single lease period are three months and 1 year, respectively. The lease number is unique across all branch offices. *DreamHome*'s clients can rent out one or more properties, at any one time.

When a lease agreement expires between a client and a property, it is *DreamHome*'s company policy to retain this information for a minimum of three years. An example of the *DreamHome* form used to record the details of a lease agreement between a renter called Mike Ritchie and a property located in Glasgow was shown in Figure 1.3.

Property inspections

As part of the service to property owners, the *DreamHome* company is responsible for undertaking regular inspections of property to ensure that the property is being correctly maintained. Each property is inspected at least once over a six month period. However, *DreamHome* staff are only required to inspect property that is currently being rented or is available for rent. For each inspection, the company notes the date of the inspection and any comments regarding the state of the property given by the member of staff undertaking the inspection. An example of a property inspection report is given in Figure 1.12.

Branch office operations

At each *DreamHome* branch office the following operations are undertaken to ensure that the appropriate information is available to the staff to ensure that the office is efficiently and effectively managed and to support the services provided to owners and renters of property. Each operation is associated with a specific business function within the *DreamHome* company. These functions are the responsibility of members of staff with particular job titles (positions). The main user or group of users of each operation is given in brackets at the end of the description of each operation.

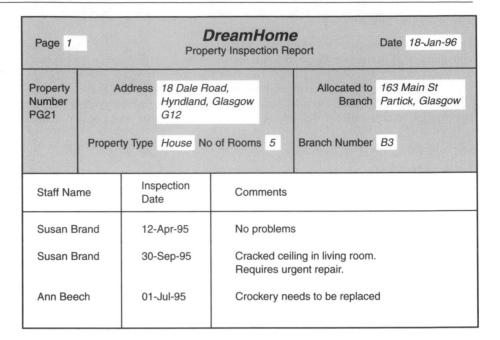

Figure 1.12
DreamHome Property
Inspection Report.

(a) Create and maintain records recording the details of members of staff and their next-of-kin at each branch office (Manager).

(b) Produce a report listing the details of staff at each branch office (Manager).

(c) Produce a list of staff supervised by a named Supervisor (Manager and Supervisor).

(d) Produce a list of Supervisors at each branch office (Manager and Supervisor).

(e) Create and maintain records recording the details of property for rent (and their owners) available at each branch office (Supervisor).

(f) Produce a report listing the details of property for rent at each branch office (all staff).

(g) Produce a list of properties for rent managed by a specific member of staff (Supervisor).

(h) Create and maintain records describing the details of prospective renters at each branch office (Supervisor).

(i) Produce a list of prospective renters registered at each branch office (all staff).

(j) Search for properties for rent that satisfy a prospective renter's requirements (all staff).

(k) Create and maintain records holding the details of viewings by prospective renters to properties for rent (all staff).

(l)   Produce a report listing the comments of prospective renters concerning a specific property for rent (all staff).

(m)   Create and maintain records detailing the adverts placed in newspapers for properties for rent (all staff).

(n)   Produce a list of all adverts for a specific property (Supervisor).

(o)   Produce a list of all adverts placed in a specific newspaper (Supervisor).

(p)   Create and maintain records describing the details of lease agreements between a renter and a property (Manager and Supervisor).

(q)   List the details of the lease agreement for a specific property (Manager and Supervisor).

(r)   Create and maintain records describing the details of inspections of properties for rent (all staff).

(s)   Produce a list of all inspections of a specific property (Supervisor).

1.8   Student Project – The *Wellmeadows Hospital* Case Study

This case study describes a small hospital called *Wellmeadows*, which is located in Edinburgh. The *Wellmeadows Hospital* specializes in the provision of health care for elderly people. Listed below is a description of the data recorded, maintained and accessed by the hospital staff to support the management and day-to-day operations of the *Wellmeadows Hospital*.

Wards

The *Wellmeadows Hospital* has 17 wards with a total of 240 beds available for short- and long-stay patients, and an out-patient clinic. Each ward is uniquely identified by a number (for example, ward 11) and also a ward name (for example, Orthopaedic), location (for example, E Block), total number of beds and telephone extension number (for example, Extn. 7711).

Staff

The *Wellmeadows Hospital* has a Medical Director, who has overall responsibility for the management of the hospital. The Medical Director maintains control over the use of the hospital resources (including staff, beds and supplies) in the provision of cost-effective treatment for all patients.

The *Wellmeadows Hospital* has a Personnel Officer who is responsible for ensuring that the appropriate number and type of staff are allocated to each ward and the out-patient clinic.

The information stored on each member of staff includes a staff number, name (first and last) full address, telephone number, date of birth, sex, national insurance number (NIN), position held, current salary, salary scale, qualifications (which includes date of qualification, type, name of institution) and work experience details (which includes the start and finish dates, position, name of organization).

The type of employment contract for each member of staff is also recorded including the number of hours worked per week, whether the member of staff is on a permanent or temporary contract and the type of salary payment (weekly/monthly).

An example of a *Wellmeadows Hospital* form used to record the details of a member of staff called Moira Samuel working in ward 11 is shown in Figure 1.13.

Wellmeadows Hospital
Staff Form

Staff Number: *S011*

Personal Details

First Name	*Moira*	Last Name	*Samuel*
Address	*49 School Road Broxburn*	Sex	*Female*
		Date of Birth	*30-May-61*
Tel. No.	*01506-45633*	NIN	*WB123423D*

Position	*Charge Nurse*	Allocated to ward	*11*
Current Salary	*18,760*		
		Hours/Week	*37.5*
Salary Scale	*1C scale*		
Paid Weekly or Monthly (Enter W or M)	*M*	Permanent or Temporary (Enter P or T)	*P*

Qualification(s)		**Work Experience**	
Type	*BSc Nursing Studies*	Position	*Staff Nurse*
Date	*12-Jul-87*	Start Date	*23-Jan-90*
Institution	*Edinburgh Unit*	Finish Date	*1-May-93*
		Organization	*Western Hospital*

Note: Please enter additional qualifications/work experience overleaf

Figure 1.13
Wellmeadows Hospital member of staff form.

Each ward and the out-patient clinic has a member of staff with the position of Charge Nurse. The Charge Nurse is responsible for overseeing the day-to-day operation of the ward/clinic. The Charge Nurse is allocated a budget to run the ward and must ensure that all resources (staff, beds and supplies) are used effectively in the care of patients. The Medical Director works closely with the Charge Nurses to ensure the efficient running of the hospital.

A Charge Nurse is responsible for setting up a weekly staff rota, and must ensure that the ward/clinic has the correct number and type of staff on duty at any time during the day or night. In a given week, each member of staff is assigned to work an early, late or night shift.

As well as the Charge Nurse, each ward is allocated senior and junior nurses, doctors and auxiliaries. Specialist staff (for example, consultants, physiotherapists) are allocated to several wards or the clinic.

An example of a *Wellmeadows Hospital* report listing the details of the staff allocated to ward 11 is shown in Figure 1.14.

Page	1	**Wellmeadows Hospital** Ward Staff Allocation	Week beginning	9-Jan-96

Ward Number	Ward 11	Charge Nurse	Moira Samuel
Ward Name	Orthopaedic	Staff Number	S011
Location	Block E	Tel Extn	7711

Staff No.	Name	Address	Tel No	Position	Shift
S098	Carol Cummings	15 High Street Edinburgh	0131-334-5677	Staff Nurse	Late
S123	Morgan Russell	23A George Street Broxburn	01506-67676	Nurse	Late
S167	Robin Plevin	7 Glen Terrace Edinburgh	0131-339-6123	Staff Nurse	Early
S234	Amy O' Donnell	234 Princes Street Edinburgh	0131-334-9099	Nurse	Night
S344	Laurence Burns	1 Apple Drive Edinburgh	0131-344-9100	Consultant	Early

Figure 1.14
Wellmeadows Hospital report listing ward staff.

Patients

When a patient is first referred to the hospital they are allocated a unique patient number. At this time, additional details of the patient are also recorded including the name (first and last name), address, telephone number, date of birth, sex, marital status, date registered with the hospital and the details of the patient's next-of-kin.

Patient's next-of-kin

The details of a patient's next-of-kin are also recorded and include the next-of-kin's full name, relationship to the patient, address and telephone number.

Local doctors

Patients are normally referred to the hospital for treatment by their local doctor. The details of local doctors are held including their full name, clinic number, address and telephone number. The clinic number is unique throughout the United Kingdom.

An example of a *Wellmeadows Hospital* patient registration form used to record the details of a patient called Anne Phelps is shown in Figure 1.15.

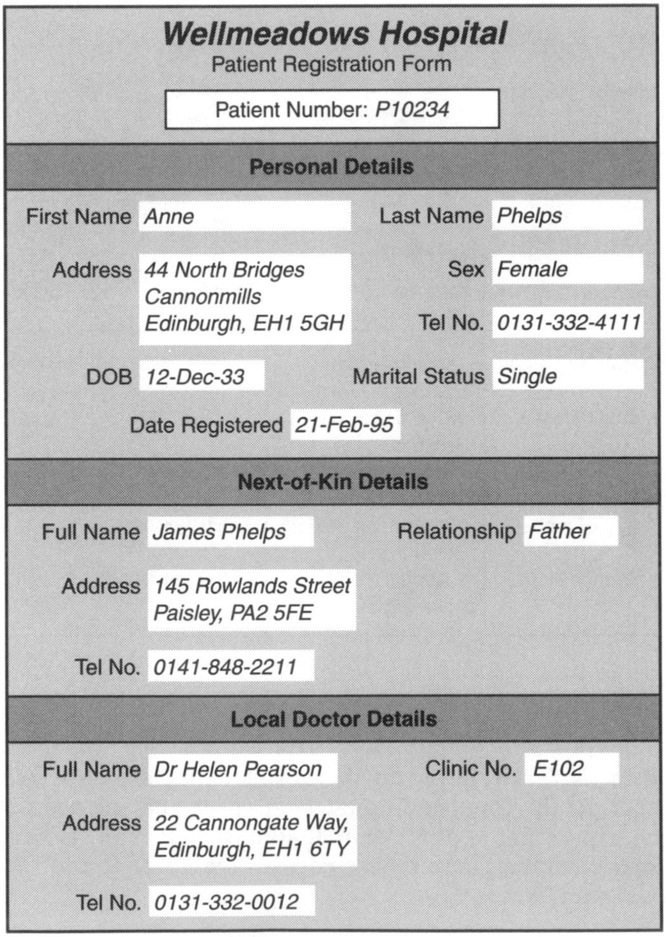

Figure 1.15
Wellmeadows Hospital
Patient Registration
Form.

Wellmeadows Hospital
Patient Registration Form

Patient Number: *P10234*

Personal Details

First Name *Anne*	Last Name *Phelps*
Address *44 North Bridges Cannonmills Edinburgh, EH1 5GH*	Sex *Female*
	Tel No. *0131-332-4111*
DOB *12-Dec-33*	Marital Status *Single*
Date Registered *21-Feb-95*	

Next-of-Kin Details

Full Name *James Phelps*	Relationship *Father*
Address *145 Rowlands Street Paisley, PA2 5FE*	
Tel No. *0141-848-2211*	

Local Doctor Details

Full Name *Dr Helen Pearson*	Clinic No. *E102*
Address *22 Cannongate Way, Edinburgh, EH1 6TY*	
Tel No. *0131-332-0012*	

Patient appointment

When a patient is referred by his or her doctor to attend the *Wellmeadows Hospital*, the patient is given an appointment for an examination by a hospital consultant.

Each appointment is given a unique appointment number. The details of each patient's appointment are recorded, and include the name and staff number of the consultant undertaking the examination, the date and time of the appointment and the examination room (for example, Room E252).

As a result of the examination, the patient is either recommended to attend the out-patient clinic or is placed on a waiting list until a bed can be found in an appropriate ward.

Out-patients

The details of out-patients are stored and include the patient number, name (first and last name), address, telephone number, date of birth, sex and the date and time of the appointment at the out-patient clinic.

In-patients

The Charge Nurse and other senior medical staff are responsible for the allocation of beds to patients on the waiting list.

The details of patients currently placed in a ward and those on the waiting list for a place on a ward are recorded. This includes the patient number, name (first and last name), address, telephone number, date of birth, sex, marital status, the details of the patient's next-of-kin, the date placed on the waiting list, the ward required, expected duration of stay (in days), date placed in the ward, date expected to leave the ward and the actual date the patient left the ward, when known.

When a patient enters the ward they are allocated a bed with a unique bed number. An example of a *Wellmeadows Hospital* report listing the details of patients allocated to ward 11 is shown in Figure 1.16.

Patient medication

When a patient is prescribed medication, the details are recorded. This includes the patient's name and number, drug number and name, units per day, method of administration (for example, oral, intravenous (IV)), start and finish date. The medication (pharmaceutical supplies) given to each patient is monitored.

An example of a *Wellmeadows Hospital* report used to record the details of medication given to a patient called Robert MacDonald is shown in Figure 1.17.

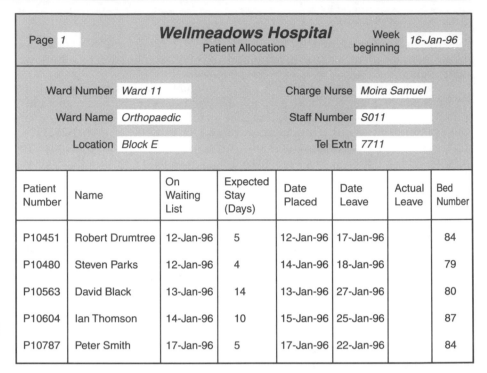

Figure 1.16
Wellmeadows Hospital report listing ward patients.

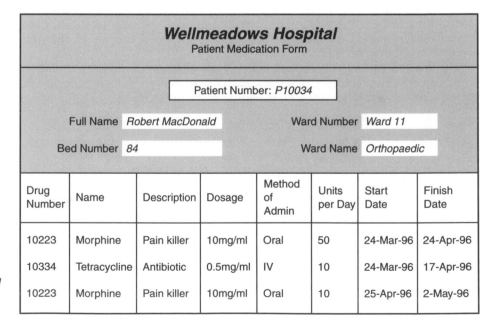

Figure 1.17
Wellmeadows Hospital patient's medication report.

Surgical and non-surgical supplies

The *Wellmeadows Hospital* maintains a central stock of surgical (for example, syringes, sterile dressings) and non-surgical (for example, plastic bags, aprons) supplies. The details of surgical and non-surgical supplies include the item number and name, item description, quantity in stock, reorder level and cost per unit. The item number uniquely identifies each type of surgical or non-surgical supply. The supplies used by each ward are monitored.

Pharmaceutical supplies

The hospital also maintains a stock of pharmaceutical supplies (for example, antibiotics, pain killers). The details of pharmaceutical supplies include drug number and name, description, dosage, method of administration, quantity in stock, reorder level, cost per unit. The drug number uniquely identifies each type of pharmaceutical supply. The pharmaceutical supplies used by each ward are monitored.

Ward requisitions

When required, the Charge Nurse may obtain surgical, non-surgical and pharmaceutical supplies from the central stock of supplies held by the hospital. This is achieved by ordering supplies for the ward using a requisition form. The information detailed on a requisition form includes a unique requisition number, the name of the member of staff placing the requisition and the number and name of the ward. Also included is the item or drug number, name, description, dosage and method of administration (for drugs only), cost per unit, quantity required and date ordered. When the requisitioned supplies are delivered to the ward, the form must be signed and dated by the Charge Nurse who initiated the order.

An example of a *Wellmeadows Hospital* requisition form used to order supplies of morphine for ward 11 is shown in Figure 1.18.

Suppliers

The details of the suppliers of the surgical, non-surgical and pharmaceutical items are stored. This information includes the supplier's name and number, address, telephone and fax number. The supplier number is unique for each supplier.

Operations

The following operations are undertaken to ensure that the appropriate information is available to enable the staff to manage and oversee the day-to-day running of the *Wellmeadows Hospital*. Each operation is associated with a specific function within the hospital. These functions are the responsibility of members of staff with particular job titles (positions). The main user or group

Wellmeadows Hospital
Central Store
Requisition Form

Requisition Number: *034567712*

Ward Number *Ward 11*   Requisitioned By *Moira Samuel*

Ward Name *Orthopaedic*   Requisition Date *15-Feb-96*

Item/Drug Number	Name	Description	Dosage (Drugs Only)	Method of Admin	Cost per Unit	Quantity
10223	Morphine	Pain killer	10mg/ml	Oral	27.75	50

Received By: _____   Date Received: _____

Figure 1.18
Wellmeadows Hospital ward requisition form.

of users of each operation is given in brackets at the end of the description of each operation.

(a) Create and maintain records recording the details of members of staff (Personnel Officer).

(b) Search for staff who have particular qualifications or previous work experience (Personnel Officer).

(c) Produce a report listing the details of staff allocated to each ward (Personnel Officer and Charge Nurse).

(d) Create and maintain records recording the details of patients referred to the hospital (all staff).

(e) Create and maintain records recording the details of patients referred to the out-patient clinic (Charge Nurse).

(f) Produce a report listing the details of patients referred to the out-patient clinic (Charge Nurse and Medical Director).

(g) Create and maintain records recording the details of patients referred to a particular ward (Charge Nurse).

(h) Produce a report listing the details of patients currently located in a particular ward (Charge Nurse and Medical Director).

(i) Produce a report listing the details of patients currently on the waiting list for a particular ward (Charge Nurse and Medical Director).

(j) Create and maintain records recording the details of medication given to a particular patient (Charge Nurse).

(k)   Produce a report listing the details of medication for a particular patient (Charge Nurse).

(l)   Create and maintain records recording the details of suppliers for the hospital (Medical Director).

(m)   Create and maintain records detailing requisitions for supplies for particular wards (Charge Nurse).

(n)   Produce a report listing the details of supplies provided to specific wards (Charge Nurse and Medical Director).

Chapter Summary

- The database system is now the underlying framework of the information system and has fundamentally changed the way many organizations operate. The database system remains a very active research area and many significant problems have still to be satisfactorily resolved.

- The predecessor to database systems was the **file-based system**, which is a collection of application programs that perform services for the end users, usually the production of reports. Each program defines and manages its own data. Although the file-based system was a great improvement on the manual filing system, it still had significant problems, mainly the amount of data redundancy present and program–data dependence.

- The database approach emerged to resolve the problems with the file approach. A **database** is a shared collection of logically related data (and a description of this data), designed to meet the information needs of an organization. A **DBMS** is a software system that enables users to define, create and maintain the database, and also provides controlled access to this database.

- The database includes both the data and the definition of the data. All access to the database is through the DBMS. The DBMS provides a **Data Definition Language (DDL)**, which allows users to define the database, and a **Data Manipulation Language (DML)**, which allows users to insert, update, delete and retrieve data from the database.

- The DBMS provides controlled access to the database. It provides security, integrity, concurrency and recovery control, and a user-accessible catalogue. It also provides a view mechanism to simplify the data that users have to deal with.

- The DBMS environment consists of hardware (the computer), software (the DBMS, operating system and applications programs), data, procedures and people. The people include data and database administrators, database designers, application programmers and end users.

- The roots of the DBMS lie in file-based systems. The hierarchical and CODASYL systems represent the first generation of DBMSs. The **hierarchical model** is typified by IMS (Information Management System) and the **network** or **CODASYL model** by IDS (Integrated Data Store), both developed in the mid-1960s. The **relational model**, first proposed by E. F. Codd in 1970, represents the second generation of DBMSs. It has had a fundamental effect on the DBMS community and there are now over 100 relational DBMSs. The third generation of DBMSs are represented by the **extended relational** DBMS and the **object-oriented** DBMS.

■ Some advantages of the database approach include control of data redundancy, data consistency, sharing of data and improved security and integrity. Some disadvantages include complexity, cost, reduced performance and higher impact of a failure.

REVIEW QUESTIONS

1.1 List four examples of database systems other than those listed in Section 1.1.

1.2 Discuss each of the following terms:

(a) data

(b) database

(c) database management system

(d) data independence

(e) security

(f) integrity

(g) views.

1.3 Describe the approach taken to the handling of data in the early file-based systems. Discuss the disadvantages of this approach.

1.4 Describe the main characteristics of the database approach, and contrast it with the file-based approach.

1.5 Describe the five components of the DBMS environment and discuss how they relate to each other.

1.6 Discuss the roles of the following personnel in the database environment:

(a) data administrator

(b) database administrator

(c) logical database designer

(d) physical database designer

(e) application programmer

(f) end-users.

1.7 Discuss the advantages and disadvantages of database processing.

EXERCISES

1.8 Interview some users of database systems. Which DBMS facilities do they find most useful and why? Which DBMS facilities do they find least useful and why? What do these users perceive to be the advantages and disadvantages of the DBMS?

1.9 Write a small program that allows entry and display of renter details including a renter number, name, address, telephone number, preferred number of rooms and maximum rent. The details should be stored in a file. Enter a few records and display the details. Now repeat this process but rather than writing a special program, use any DBMS that you have access to. What can you conclude from these two approaches?

1.10 Study the *DreamHome* case study presented in Section 1.7. In what ways would a DBMS help this organization? What data can you identify that needs to be represented in the database? What relationships exist between the data? What queries do you think are required?

1.11 Study the *Wellmeadows Hospital* case study presented in Section 1.8. In what ways would a DBMS help this organization? What data can you identify that needs to be represented in the database? What relationships exist between the data?

2 Database Environment

Chapter Objectives

In this chapter you will learn:

- The purpose and origin of the three-level database architecture.
- The contents of the external, conceptual and internal levels.
- The purpose of the external/conceptual and the conceptual/internal mappings.
- The meaning of logical and physical data independence.
- The distinction between a Data Definition Language (DDL) and a Data Manipulation Language (DML).
- A classification of data models.
- The purpose and importance of conceptual modelling.
- The typical functions and services a DBMS should provide.
- The components of a DBMS.
- The meaning of client–server architecture and the advantages of this type of architecture for a DBMS.
- The function and importance of the data dictionary.

A major aim of a database system is to provide users with an abstract view of data, by hiding certain details of how data is stored and manipulated. Therefore, the starting point for the design of a database must be an abstract and general description of the information requirements of the organization that is to be represented in the database. In this chapter, and throughout this book, we use the term organization loosely, to mean the whole organization or part of the organization. For example, in the *DreamHome* case study we may be interested in modelling:

- the 'real world' **entities** Staff, Property, Owners and Renters;
- **attributes** describing properties or qualities of each entity (for example, Staff have a Name, Address and Salary);
- **relationships** between these entities (for example, Staff *Manages* Property).

Furthermore, since a database is a shared resource, each user may require a different view of the data held in the database. To satisfy these needs, the architecture of most commercial DBMSs available today is based to some extent on the so-called ANSI-SPARC architecture.

In this chapter, we discuss various architectural and functional characteristics of database systems, including the ANSI-SPARC architecture and its associated benefits, the functions that we would expect a database system to provide, and the architecture for a database system. The examples in this chapter are drawn from the *DreamHome* case study introduced in Section 1.7.

Much of the material in this chapter provides important background information on databases. However, the reader that is new to the area of database systems may find some of this material difficult to appreciate on a first reading. Do not be too worried about this, but be prepared to revisit parts of this chapter at a later date when you have read subsequent chapters of the book.

2.1 The Three-Level ANSI-SPARC Architecture

An early proposal for a standard terminology and general architecture for database systems was produced in 1971 by the DBTG (Data Base Task Group) appointed by the Conference on Data Systems and Languages (CODASYL, 1971). The DBTG recognized the need for a two-level approach with a system view called the **schema** and user views called **subschemas**. A similar terminology and architecture were produced in 1975 by the American National Standards Institute (ANSI) Standards Planning and Requirements Committee (SPARC), ANSI/X3/SPARC (ANSI, 1975). ANSI-SPARC recognized the need for a three-level approach with a data dictionary. These proposals reflected those published by the IBM user organizations Guide and Share some years previously, and concentrated on the need for an implementation-independent layer to isolate programs from underlying representational issues (Guide/Share, 1970). Although the ANSI-SPARC model did not become a standard, it still provides a basis for understanding some of the DBMS functionalities.

For our purposes, the fundamental point of these and later reports is the identification of three levels of abstraction: that is, three distinct levels at which data items can be described. The levels form a **three-level architecture** comprising an **external**, a **conceptual** and an **internal** level, as depicted in Figure 2.1. The objective of the three-level architecture is to separate each user's view of the database from the way it is physically represented. There are several reasons why this separation is desirable:

- Each user should be able to access the same data, but have a different customized view of the data. Each user should be able to change the way he or she views the data, and this change should not affect other users.

- Users should not have to deal directly with physical database storage details, such as indexing or hashing (see Appendix A – File Organization and Storage Structures). In other words, a user's interaction with the database should be independent of storage considerations.

- The Database Administrator (DBA) should be able to change the database storage structures without affecting the users' views.

- The internal structure of the database should be unaffected by changes to the physical aspects of storage, such as the changeover to a new storage device.

- The DBA should be able to change the conceptual or global structure of the database without affecting all users.

The way users perceive the data is called the **external level**. The way the DBMS and the operating system perceive the data is the **internal level**. The internal level is where the data is actually stored using the data structures and file organizations described in Appendix A. The **conceptual level** provides both the **mapping** and the desired **independence** between the external and internal levels.

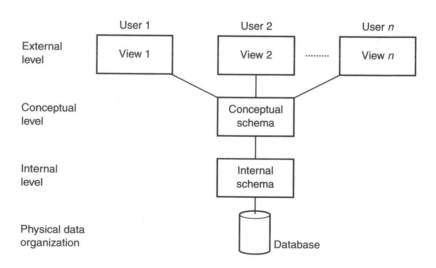

Figure 2.1 The ANSI-SPARC three-level architecture.

2.1.1 External Level

External level	The user's view of the database. This level describes that part of the database that is relevant to a particular user.

The external level consists of a number of different external views of the database. Each user has a view of the 'real world' represented in a form that is familiar for that user. The external view includes only those entities, attributes and relationships in the 'real world' that the user is interested in. Other entities, attributes or relationships that are not of interest may be represented in the database, but the user will be unaware of them.

In addition, different views may have different representations of the same data. For example, one user may view dates in the form (day, month, year), while another may view dates as (year, month, day). Some views might include derived or calculated data, data not actually stored in the database as such, but created when needed. For example, in the *DreamHome* case study, we may wish to view the age of a member of staff. However, it is unlikely that ages would be stored, as this data would have to be updated on a daily basis. Instead, the member of staff's date of birth would be stored and age would be calculated by the DBMS when it is referenced. Views may even include data combined or derived from several entities. We will discuss views in more detail in Sections 3.5 and 12.1.

2.1.2 Conceptual Level

Conceptual level	The community view of the database. This level describes *what* data is stored in the database and the relationships among the data.

The middle level in the three-level architecture is the conceptual level. This level contains the logical structure of the entire database as seen by the DBA. It is a complete view of the data requirements of the organization that is independent of any storage considerations. The conceptual level represents:

- all entities, their attributes and their relationships;
- the constraints on the data;
- semantic information about the data;
- security and integrity information.

The conceptual level supports each external view, in that any data available to a user must be contained in, or derivable from, the conceptual level. However, this level must not contain any storage-dependent details. For instance, the description of an entity should contain only data types of attributes (for example, integer, real, character) and their length (such as the maximum number of digits or characters), but not any storage considerations, such as the number of bytes occupied.

2.1.3 Internal Level

Internal level	The physical representation of the database on the computer. This level describes *how* the data is stored in the database.

The internal level covers the physical implementation of the database to achieve optimal run-time performance and storage space utilization. It covers the data structures and file organizations used to store data on storage devices. It interfaces with the operating system access methods (file management techniques for storing and retrieving data records) to place the data on the storage devices, build the indexes, retrieve the data, and so on. The internal level is concerned with such things as:

- storage space allocation for data and indexes;
- record descriptions for storage (with stored sizes for data items);
- record placement;
- data compression and data encryption techniques.

Below the internal level there is a **physical level** that may be managed by the operating system under the direction of the DBMS. However, the functions of the DBMS and the operating system at the physical level are not clear cut and vary from system to system. Some DBMSs take advantage of many of the operating system access methods, while others use only the most basic ones and create their own file organizations. The physical level below the DBMS consists of items only the operating system knows, such as exactly how the sequencing is implemented and whether the fields of internal records are stored as contiguous bytes on the disk.

2.1.4 Schemas, Mappings and Instances

The overall description of the database is called the **database schema**. There are three different types of schema in the database and these are defined according to the levels of abstraction of the three-level architecture illustrated in Figure 2.1. At the highest level, we have multiple **external schemas** (also called **subschemas**), which correspond to different views of the data. At the conceptual level, we have the **conceptual schema**, while at the lowest level of abstraction we have the **internal schema**.

The conceptual schema describes all the data items and relationships between data items, together with integrity constraints. There is only one conceptual schema per database. At the lowest level, the internal schema is a complete description of the internal model. It contains the definitions of stored records, the methods of representation, the data fields and the indexes and hashing schemes used, if any. Again, there is only one internal schema.

The DBMS is responsible for mapping between these three types of schema. It must also check the schemas for consistency; in other words, the DBMS must check that each external schema is derivable from the conceptual schema, and it must use the information in the conceptual schema to map between each external schema and the internal schema. The conceptual schema is related to the internal schema through a **conceptual/internal mapping**. This enables the DBMS to find the actual record or combination of records in physical storage that constitute a **logical record** in the conceptual schema, together with any constraints to be enforced on the operations for that logical record. It also allows any differences in entity names, attribute names, attribute order, data types, and so on, to be resolved. Finally, each external schema is related to the conceptual schema by the **external/conceptual mapping**. This enables the DBMS to map names in the user's view onto the relevant part of the conceptual schema.

An example of the different levels is shown in Figure 2.2. Two different external views of staff details exist: one consisting of a staff number, Sno, a first and last name, an age and a salary; a second consisting of a staff number, Staff_No, a last name and the number of the branch the member of staff works at, Bno. These external views are merged into one conceptual view. In this merging process, the major difference is that the age field has been changed into a date of birth field, DOB. The DBMS maintains the external/conceptual mapping; for example, it maps the Sno field of the first external view to the field Staff_No of the conceptual record. The conceptual level is then mapped to the internal level, which contains a physical description of the structure for the conceptual record. At this level, we see a definition of the structure in a high-level language. The structure contains a pointer, *next*, which allows the list of staff records to be physically linked together to form

Figure 2.2
Differences between the three levels.

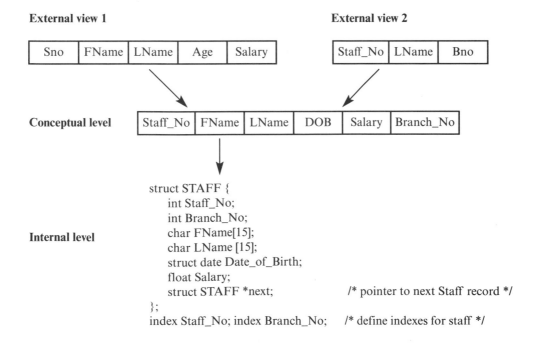

a chain. Note that the order of fields at the internal level is different from that of the conceptual level. Again, the DBMS maintains the conceptual/internal mapping.

It is important to distinguish between the description of the database and the database itself. The description of the database is the **database schema**. The schema is specified during the database design process and is not expected to change frequently. However, the actual data in the database may change frequently; for example, it changes every time we insert details of a new member of staff or a new property. The data in the database at any particular point in time is called a **database instance**. Therefore, many database instances can correspond to the same database schema.

The schema is sometimes called the **intension** of the database, while an instance is called an **extension** (or **state**) of the database.

2.1.5 Data Independence

A major objective for the three-level architecture is to provide **data independence**, which means that upper levels are unaffected by changes to lower levels. There are two kinds of data independence: **logical** and **physical**.

Logical data independence	Logical data independence refers to the immunity of external schemas to changes in the conceptual schema.

Changes to the conceptual schema, such as the addition or removal of new entities, attributes or relationships, should be possible without having to change existing external schema or having to rewrite application programs. Clearly, the users for whom the changes have been made need to be aware of them, but what is important is that other users should not be.

Physical data independence	Physical data independence refers to the immunity of the conceptual schema to changes in the internal schema.

Changes to the internal schema, such as using different file organizations or storage structures, using different storage devices, modifying indexes or hashing algorithms, should be possible without having to change the conceptual or external schemas. From the user's point of view, the only effect that may be noticed is a change in performance. In fact, a deterioration in performance is the most common reason for internal schema changes. Figure 2.3 illustrates where each type of data independence occurs in relation to the three-level architecture.

The two-stage mapping in the ANSI-SPARC architecture may be less efficient, but provides greater data independence. However, for more efficient mapping, the ANSI-SPARC model allows the direct mapping of external schemas on to the internal schemas, thus by-passing the conceptual schema. This, of course, reduces data independence, so that every time the internal

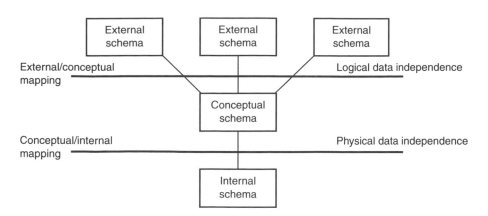

Figure 2.3 Data independence and the ANSI-SPARC three-level architecture.

schema changes, the external schema and any dependent application programs may also have to change.

2.2   Database Languages

A data sublanguage consists of two parts: a **Data Definition Language** (DDL) and a **Data Manipulation Language** (DML). The DDL is used to specify the database schema and the DML is used to both read and update the database. These languages are called **data sublanguages** because they do not include constructs for all computing needs, such as those provided by the high-level programming languages. Many database systems have a facility for **embedding** the sublanguage in a high-level programming language such as COBOL, Fortran, Pascal, Ada, C. In this case, the high-level language is sometimes referred to as the **host language**. To compile the embedded file, first the commands in the data sublanguage are removed from the host-language program and replaced by function calls. The pre-processed file is then compiled, placed in an object module, linked with a library containing the replaced functions provided with the DBMS and executed when required. Most data sublanguages also provide non-embedded, or **interactive**, commands that can be input directly from a terminal.

2.2.1   The Data Definition Language (DDL)

> **DDL**   A descriptive language that allows the DBA or user to describe and name the entities required for the application and the relationships that may exist between the different entities.

The database schema is specified by a set of definitions expressed by means of a special language called a Data Definition Language (DDL). The DDL is used to define a schema or to modify an existing one. It cannot be used to manipulate data.

The result of the compilation of the DDL statements is a set of tables stored in special files collectively called the **data dictionary**. The data dictionary integrates the **metadata**: that is, data that describes objects in the database, and makes it easier for them to be accessed or manipulated. The meta-data contain definitions of records, data items and other objects that are of interest to users or are required by the DBMS. The DBMS normally consults the data dictionary before the actual data is accessed in the database. The terms **catalog** and **directory** are also used to describe the data dictionary. Data dictionaries are discussed further in Section 2.7.

At a theoretical level, we could identify different DDLs for each schema in the three-level architecture, namely a DDL for the external schemas, a DDL for the conceptual schema and a DDL for the internal schema. However, in practice, there is one comprehensive DDL that allows specification of at least the external and conceptual schemas.

2.2.2   The Data Manipulation Language (DML)

DML   A language that provides a set of operations that support the basic data manipulation operations on the data held in the database.

Data manipulation operations usually include the following:

- the insertion of new data into the database,
- the modification of data stored in the database,
- the retrieval of data contained in the database,
- the deletion of data from the database.

Therefore, one of the main functions of the DBMS is to support a data manipulation language in which the user can construct statements that will cause such data manipulation to occur. Data manipulation applies to the external and conceptual levels as well as to the internal level. However, at the internal level we must define rather complex low-level procedures that allow efficient data access. In contrast, at higher levels emphasis is placed on ease of use, and effort is directed at providing efficient user interaction with the system.

DMLs are distinguished by their underlying retrieval constructs. We can distinguish between two types of DML: **procedural** and **non-procedural**. The prime difference between these two data manipulation languages is that in procedural languages the database statements treat records individually, while in non-procedural languages the statements operate on sets of records. Consequently, procedural languages specify *how* the output of a DML statement must be obtained, while non-procedural DMLs describe only *what* output is to be obtained.

Procedural DMLs

Procedural DML	A language that allows the user to tell the system exactly *how* to manipulate the data.

With a procedural DML, the user, or more normally the programmer, specifies what data is needed and how to obtain it. This means that the user must express all the data access operations that are to be used by calling appropriate procedures to obtain the information required. Typically, such a procedural DML retrieves a record, processes it and, based on the results obtained by this processing, retrieves another record that would be processed similarly, and so on. This process of retrievals continues until the data requested from the retrieval has been gathered. Network and hierarchical DMLs are normally procedural (see Section 2.3).

Non-procedural DMLs

Non-procedural DML	A language that allows the user to state *what* data is needed rather than *how* it is to be retrieved.

Non-procedural DMLs allow the required data to be specified in a single retrieval or update statement. With non-procedural DMLs, the user specifies what data is required without specifying how it is to be obtained. The DBMS translates a DML statement into a procedure (or set of procedures) that manipulates the required sets of records. This frees the user from having to know how data structures are internally implemented and what algorithms are required to retrieve and possibly transform the data, thus providing users with a considerable degree of data independence. Relational database systems usually include some form of non-procedural language for data manipulation, typically SQL (Structured Query Language) or QBE (Query-by-Example). Non-procedural DMLs are normally easier to learn and use than procedural DMLs as less work is done by the user and more by the DBMS. We will examine SQL in detail in Chapters 11 and 12, and QBE in Chapter 13.

　　　　The part of a non-procedural DML that involves data retrieval is called a **query language**. A query language can be defined as a high-level special-purpose language used to satisfy diverse requests for the retrieval of data held in the database. The term 'query' is therefore reserved to denote a retrieval statement expressed in a query language. The terms query language and data manipulation language are commonly used interchangeably, although this is technically incorrect.

2.2.3 4GL

4GL stands for **Fourth-Generation Language**. There is no consensus about what constitutes a 4GL; it is essentially a shorthand programming language.

An operation that requires hundreds of lines in a third-generation language (3GL), such as COBOL, typically requires only 10–20 lines in a 4GL.

Compared with a 3GL, which is procedural, a 4GL is non-procedural; the user defines *what* is to be done, not how. A 4GL is expected to rely largely on much higher-level components known as fourth-generation tools. The user is not expected to define the steps a program needs to perform a task, but instead defines parameters for the tools that use them to generate an application program. It is claimed that 4GLs can improve productivity by a factor of ten, at the cost of limiting the types of problems that can be tackled. 4GLs encompass:

- presentation languages, such as query languages and report generators;
- speciality languages, such as spreadsheets and database languages;
- application generators that define, insert, update and retrieve data from the database to build applications;
- very high-level languages that are used to generate application code.

SQL and QBE, mentioned above, are examples of 4GLs. We now briefly discuss some of the other types of 4GLs.

Forms generators

A forms generator is an interactive facility for rapidly creating data input and display layouts for screen forms. The forms generator allows the user to define what the screen is to look like, what information is to be displayed and where on the screen it is to be displayed. It may also allow the definition of colours for screen elements and other characteristics, such as bold, underline, blinking, reverse video, and so on. The better forms generators allow the creation of derived attributes, perhaps using arithmetic operators or aggregates, and the specification of validation checks for data input.

Report generators

A report generator is a facility for creating reports from data stored in the database. It is similar to a query language in that it allows the user to ask questions of the database and retrieve information from it for a report. However, in the case of a report generator, we have much greater control over what the output looks like. We can let the report generator automatically determine how the output should look or we can create our own customized output reports using special report-generator command instructions.

There are two main types of report generator: language oriented and visually oriented. In the first case, we enter a command in a sublanguage to define what data is to be included in the report and how the report is to be laid out. In the second case, we use a facility similar to a forms generator to define the same information.

Graphics generators

A graphics generator is a facility to retrieve data from the database and display the data as a graph showing trends and relationships in the data. Typically, it allows the user to create bar charts, pie charts, line charts, scatter charts, and so on.

Application generators

An application generator is a facility for producing a program that interfaces with the database. The use of an application generator can reduce the time it takes to design an entire software application. Application generators typically consist of pre-written modules that comprise fundamental functions that most programs use. These modules, usually written in a high-level language, constitute a 'library' of functions to choose from. The user specifies *what* the program is supposed to do; the application generator determines *how* to perform the tasks.

2.3   Data Models and Conceptual Modelling

We mentioned earlier that a schema is written using a data definition language. In fact, it is written in the data definition language of a particular DBMS. Unfortunately, this type of language is too low-level to describe the data requirements of an organization in a way that is readily understandable by a variety of users. What we require is a higher-level description of the schema: that is, a **data model**.

Data model	An integrated collection of concepts for describing data, relationships between data and constraints on the data in an organization.

A model is a representation of 'real world' objects and events and their associations. It is an abstraction that concentrates on the essential, inherent aspects of an organization and ignores the accidental properties. A data model represents the organization itself. It should provide the basic concepts and notations that will allow database designers and end users to unambiguously and accurately communicate their understanding of the organizational data. A data model can be thought of as comprising three components:

(1)   a structural part, consisting of a set of rules according to which databases can be constructed;

(2)   a manipulative part, defining the types of operations that are allowed on the data (this includes the operations that are used for updating or retrieving data from the database and for changing the structure of the database);

(3)   possibly a set of integrity rules, which ensures that the data is accurate.

The purpose of a data model is to represent data and to make the data understandable. If it does this, then it can be easily used to design a database. To reflect the ANSI-SPARC architecture introduced in Section 2.1, we can identify three related data models:

(1)   an external data model, to represent each user's view of the organization, sometimes called the **Universe of Discourse** (UoD);

(2)   a conceptual data model, to represent the logical (or community) view that is DBMS independent;

(3)   an internal data model, to represent the conceptual schema in such a way that it can be understood by the DBMS.

There have been many data models proposed in the literature. They fall into three broad categories: **object-based** data models; **record-based** data models; and **physical** data models. The first two are used to describe data at the conceptual and external levels, the latter is used to describe data at the internal level.

2.3.1   Object-Based Data Models

Object-based data models use concepts such as entities, attributes and relationships. An **entity** is a distinct object (a person, place or thing, concept or event) in the organization that is to be represented in the database. An **attribute** is a property that describes some aspect of the object that we wish to record and a **relationship** is an association between entities. Some of the more common types of object-based data models are:

- entity–relationship
- semantic
- functional
- object-oriented.

The entity–relationship model has emerged as one of the main techniques for conceptual database design, and forms the basis for the database design methodology used in this book. The object-oriented data model extends the definition of an entity to include not only the attributes that describe the **state** of the object but also the actions that are associated with the object, that is, its **behaviour**. The object is said to **encapsulate** both state and behaviour. We will look at the Entity–Relationship model in depth in Chapter 5 and the object-oriented model in Chapter 17.

2.3.2   Record-Based Data Models

In a record-based model, the database consists of a number of fixed-format records of possibly differing types. Each record type defines a fixed number of fields, each typically of a fixed length. There are three principal types of record-based logical data model: the **relational data model**; the **network data model**; and the **hierarchical data model**. The hierarchical and network data models were developed almost a decade before the relational data model, and so their links to traditional file processing concepts are more evident.

Relational data model

The relational data model is based on the concept of mathematical relations. In the relational model, data and relationships are represented as tables, each of which has a number of columns with a unique name. Figure 2.4 is a sample instance of a relational schema for part of the *DreamHome* case study, showing branch and staff details. For example, it shows that employee John White of 19 Taylor St in London is a manager with a salary of £30,000, who works at branch (Bno) B5, which from the first table is at 22 Deer Rd in Sidcup, London. It is important to note that there is a relationship between Staff and Branch: a member of staff *works* at a branch office. However, there is no explicit link between these two tables; it is only by knowing that the attribute Bno in the Staff relation is the same as the Bno of the Branch relation that we can establish that a relationship exists.

Note that the relational data model requires only that the database be perceived by the user as tables. However, this perception applies only to the logical structure of the database, that is, the external and conceptual levels of the ANSI-SPARC architecture. It does not apply to the physical structure of the database, which can be implemented using a variety of storage structures. We will discuss the relational data model in Chapter 3.

BRANCH

Bno	Street	Area	City	Pcode	Tel_No	Fax_No
B5	22 Deer Rd	Sidcup	London	SW1 4EH	0171-886-1212	0171-886-1214
B7	16 Argyll St	Dyce	Aberdeen	AB2 3SU	01224-67125	01224-67111
B3	163 Main St	Partick	Glasgow	G11 9QX	0141-339-2178	0141-339-4439
B4	32 Manse Rd	Leigh	Bristol	BS99 1NZ	0117-916-1170	0117-776-1114
B2	56 Clover Dr		London	NW10 6EU	0181-963-1030	0181-453-7992

Figure 2.4 A sample instance of a relational schema.

STAFF

Sno	FName	LName	Address	Tel_No	Position	Sex	DOB	Salary	NIN	Bno
SL21	John	White	19 Taylor St, Cranford, London	0171-884-5112	Manager	M	1-Oct-45	30000	WK442011B	B5
SG37	Ann	Beech	81 George St, Glasgow PA1 2JR	0141-848-3345	Snr Asst	F	10-Nov-60	12000	WL432514C	B3
SG14	David	Ford	63 Ashby St, Partick, Glasgow G11	0141-339-2177	Deputy	M	24-Mar-58	18000	WL220658D	B3
SA9	Mary	Howe	2 Elm Pl, Aberdeen AB2 3SU		Assistant	F	19-Feb-70	9000	WM532187D	B7
SG5	Susan	Brand	5 Gt Western Rd, Glasgow G12	0141-334-2001	Manager	F	3-Jun-40	24000	WK588932E	B3
SL41	Julie	Lee	28 Malvern St, Kilburn NW2	0181-554-3541	Assistant	F	13-Jun-65	9000	WA290573K	B5

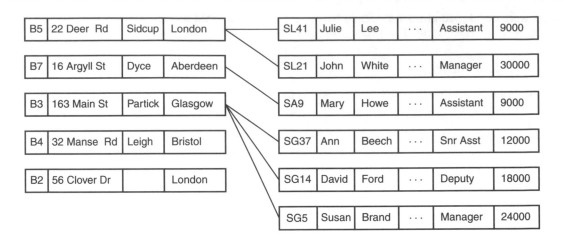

Figure 2.5 A sample instance of a network schema.

Network data model

In the network model, data is represented as collections of **records** and relationships are represented by **sets**. Compared with the relational model, relationships are explicitly modelled by the set, which become pointers in the implementation. The records are organized as generalized graph structures with records appearing as **nodes** and sets as **edges** in the graph. Figure 2.5 illustrates an instance of a network schema for the same data set presented in Figure 2.4. The most popular network database system is Computer Associates' IDMS/R. We will discuss the network data model in more detail in Appendix B.

Hierarchical data model

The hierarchical model is a restricted type of network model. Again, data is represented as collections of **records** and relationships are represented by **sets**. However, the hierarchical model allows a node to have only one parent. A hierarchical model can be represented as a tree graph, with records appearing as nodes, also called **segments**, and sets as edges. Figure 2.6 illustrates an instance of a hierarchical schema for the same data set presented in Figure 2.4. The principal hierarchical database system is IBM's IMS, although IMS also provides non-hierarchical features. We will discuss the hierarchical data model in Appendix C.

Record-based (logical) data models are used to specify the overall structure of the database and a higher-level description of the implementation. Their main drawback lies in the fact that they do not provide adequate facilities for explicitly specifying constraints on the data, whereas the object-based data models lack the means of logical structure specification, but provide more semantic substance by allowing the user to specify constraints on the data.

The majority of modern commercial systems are based on the relational

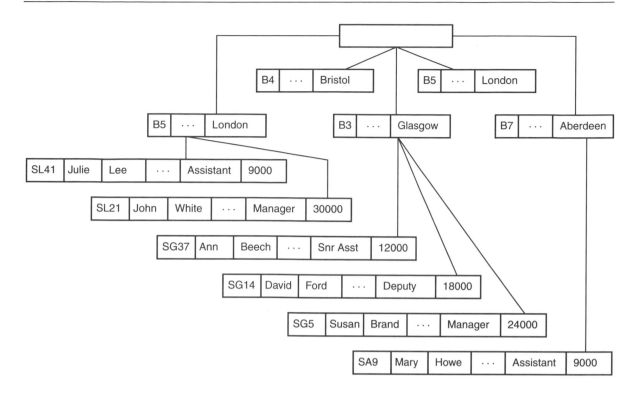

Figure 2.6 A sample instance of a hierarchical schema.

paradigm, whereas the early database systems were based on either the network or hierarchical data models. The latter two models still require the user to have knowledge of the physical database being accessed, whereas the former provides a substantial amount of data independence. Hence, while relational systems adopt a declarative approach to database processing (that is, they specify *what* data is to be retrieved), network and hierarchical systems adopt a navigational approach (that is, they specify *how* the data is to be retrieved).

2.3.3 Physical Data Models

Physical data models describe how data is stored in the computer, representing information such as record structures, record orderings and access paths. There are not as many physical data models as logical data models, the most common ones being the *unifying model* and the *frame memory*.

2.3.4 Conceptual Modelling

From an examination of the three-level architecture, we can see that the conceptual schema is the 'heart' of the database. It supports all the external views and is, in turn, supported by the internal schema. However, the internal schema is merely the physical implementation of the conceptual schema. The conceptual schema should be a complete and accurate representation of the data requirements of the enterprise[†]. If this is not the case, some information about the enterprise will be missing or incorrectly represented and we will have difficulty fully implementing one or more of the external views.

Conceptual modelling or conceptual database design is the process of constructing a model of the information use in an enterprise that is independent of implementation details, such as the target DBMS, application programs, programming languages or any other physical considerations. This model is called a **conceptual data model**. Conceptual models are also referred to as logical models in the literature. However, in this book we make a distinction between conceptual and logical data models. Whereas the conceptual model is independent of all implementation details, the logical model assumes knowledge of the underlying data model of the target DBMS. In Chapter 7, we present a methodology for database design that produces a logical model based on the relational data model. We discuss database design in more detail in Section 4.3.

2.4 Functions of a DBMS

In this section, we look at the types of functions and services we would expect to be provided by a database management system. Codd lists eight services that should be provided by any full-scale DBMS (Codd, 1982).

(1) *Data storage, retrieval and update*

> A DBMS must furnish users with the ability to store, retrieve and update data in the database.

This is the fundamental function of a DBMS. From the discussion in Section 2.1, clearly in providing this functionality the DBMS should hide the internal physical implementation details (such as file organization and storage structures) from the user.

(2) *A user-accessible catalog*

> A DBMS must furnish a catalog in which descriptions of data items are stored and which is accessible to users.

[†] When we are discussing the organization with respect to database design we normally refer to the business or organization as the *enterprise*.

A key feature of the ANSI-SPARC architecture is the recognition of an integrated **data dictionary** to hold data about the schemas, users, applications, and so on. The dictionary is expected to be accessible to users as well as to the DBMS. A data dictionary or **catalog** is a repository of information describing the data in the database; it is, the 'data about the data' or **meta-data**. The amount of information and the way the information is used vary with the DBMS. Typically, the data dictionary stores:

- names, types and sizes of data items;
- names of relationships;
- integrity constraints on the data;
- names of authorized users who have access to the data;
- external, conceptual and internal schemas and the mappings between the schemas, as described in Section 2.1.4;
- usage statistics, such as the frequencies of transactions and counts on the number of accesses made to objects in the database.

Some benefits of a data dictionary are as follows:

- Information about data can be collected and stored centrally. This helps to maintain control over the data as a resource.
- The meaning of data can be defined, which will help other users understand the purpose of the data.
- Communication is simplified, since exact meanings are stored. The data dictionary may also identify the user or users who own or access the data.
- Redundancy and inconsistencies can be identified more easily since the data is centralized.
- Changes to the database can be recorded.
- The impact of a change can be determined before it is implemented, since the data dictionary records each data item, all its relationships and all its users.
- Security can be enforced.
- Integrity can be ensured.
- Audit information can be provided.

Some authors make a distinction between data dictionary and data directory, where a data directory holds information relating to where data is stored and how it is stored. We use the more general term **data dictionary** in this book to refer to all repository information. We discuss the data dictionary in more detail in Section 2.7.

(3) *Transaction support*

> A DBMS must furnish a mechanism which will ensure that either all the updates corresponding to a given transaction are made or that none of them are made.

A transaction is a series of actions, carried out by a single user or application program, which accesses or changes the contents of the database. For example, some simple transactions for the *DreamHome* case study might be to add a new member of staff to the database, to update the salary of a particular member of staff, or to delete a property from the register. A more complicated example might be to delete a member of staff from the database *and* to reassign the properties that he or she handled to another member of staff. In this case, there is more than one change to be made to the database. If the transaction fails during execution, perhaps because of a computer crash, the database will be in an **inconsistent** state. Some changes will have been made and others not. Consequently, the changes that have been made will have to be undone to return the database to a consistent state again. We will discuss transaction support in Chapter 15.

(4) *Concurrency control services*

> A DBMS must furnish a mechanism to ensure that the database is updated correctly when multiple users are updating the database concurrently.

One major objective in using a DBMS is to enable many users to access shared data concurrently. Concurrent access is relatively easy if all users are only reading data, as there is no way that they can interfere with one another. However, when two or more users are accessing the database simultaneously and at least one of them is updating data, there may be interference that can result in inconsistencies. For example, consider two transactions T_1 and T_2, which are executing concurrently as illustrated in Figure 2.7.

Time	T_1	T_2	bal_x
t_1		read(bal_x)	100
t_2	read(bal_x)	$bal_x = bal_x + 100$	100
t_3	$bal_x = bal_x - 10$	write(bal_x)	200
t_4	write(bal_x)		90
t_5			90

Figure 2.7 The lost update problem.

T_1 is withdrawing £10 from an account (with balance bal_x) and T_2 is depositing £100 into the same account. If these transactions were executed

serially, one after the other with no interleaving of operations, the final balance would be £190 regardless of which was performed first. Transactions T_1 and T_2 start at nearly the same time and both read the balance as £100. T_2 increases bal_x by £100 to £200 and stores the update in the database. Meanwhile, transaction T_1 decrements its copy of bal_x by £10 to £90 and stores this value in the database, overwriting the previous update and thereby 'losing' £100.

The DBMS must ensure that, when multiple users are accessing the database, interference cannot occur. We will discuss this issue fully in Chapter 15.

(5) *Recovery services*

> A DBMS must furnish a mechanism for recovering the database in the event that the database is damaged in any way.

When discussing transaction support, we mentioned that if the transaction fails the database has to be returned to a consistent state. This may be a result of a system crash, media failure, a hardware or software error causing the DBMS to stop, or it may be the result of the user detecting an error during the transaction and aborting the transaction before it completes. In all these cases, the DBMS must provide a mechanism to recover the database to a consistent state. Again, we will discuss recovery control in Chapter 15.

(6) *Authorization services*

> A DBMS must furnish a mechanism to ensure that only authorized users can access the database.

It is not difficult to imagine instances where we would want to protect some of the data stored in the database from being seen by all users. For example, we may want only branch managers to see salary-related information for staff and prevent all other users from seeing this data. Additionally, we may want to protect the database from unauthorized access. The term **security** refers to the protection of the database against unauthorized access, either intentional or accidental. We expect the DBMS to provide mechanisms to ensure the data is secure. We will discuss security in Chapter 14.

(7) *Support for data communication*

> A DBMS must be capable of integrating with communication software.

Most users access the database from terminals. Sometimes, these terminals are connected directly to the computer hosting the DBMS. In other cases, the terminals are at remote locations and communicate with the computer hosting the DBMS over a network. In either case, the DBMS receives requests as **communications messages** and responds in a similar way. All such transmissions are handled by the Data Communication Manager (DCM). Although the DCM is not part of the DBMS, it is necessary for the DBMS to be capable of being integrated with a variety of DCMs, if the system is to be commercially viable. Even DBMSs for personal computers should be capable of being run on a local area network so that one centralized database can be established for users to share, rather than having a series of disparate databases, one for each user. This does not imply that the database has to be distributed across the network; rather that users should be able to access a centralized database from remote locations.

(8) *Integrity services*

> A DBMS must furnish a means to ensure that both the data in the database and changes to the data follow certain rules.

Database integrity refers to the correctness and consistency of stored data. It can be considered as another type of database protection. While it is related to security, it has wider implications; integrity is concerned with the quality of data itself. Integrity is usually expressed in terms of constraints, which are consistency rules that the database is not permitted to violate. For example, we may want to specify a constraint that no member of staff can handle more than 10 properties at the one time. Here, we would want the DBMS to check when we assign a property to a member of staff that this limit would not be exceeded and to prevent the assignment from occurring if the limit has been reached. We will discuss integrity control in Chapter 14.

In addition to these eight services, we could also reasonably expect the following two services to be provided by a DBMS:

(9) *Services to promote data independence*

> A DBMS must include facilities to support the independence of programs from the actual structure of the database.

We discussed the concept of data independence in Section 2.1.5. Data independence is normally achieved through a view or subschema mechanism. Physical data independence is easier to achieve; there are usually several types of changes that can be made to the physical characteristics of the database without affecting the views. However, complete logical data independence is more difficult to achieve. The addition of a new entity, attribute or relationship can usually be accommodated, but not their removal. In some systems, any type of change to an existing component in the logical structure is prohibited.

(10) *Utility services*

> A DBMS should provide a set of utility services.

Utility programs help the DBA to administer the database effectively. Some utilities work at the external level, and consequently could have been produced by the DBA. Other utilities work at the internal level and can be provided only by the DBMS vendor. Examples of utilities of the latter kind are:

- import/export facilities, to load/unload the database from/to flat files;
- monitoring facilities, to monitor database usage and operation;
- statistical analysis programs, to examine performance or usage statistics;
- index reorganization facilities, to reorganize indexes and their overflows;
- garbage collection and reallocation, to remove deleted records physically from the storage devices, to consolidate the space released and to reallocate it where it is needed.

2.5   Components of a DBMS

DBMSs are highly complex and sophisticated pieces of software that aim to provide the services discussed in the previous section. It is not possible to generalize the component structure of a DBMS as they vary greatly from system to system. However, it is useful when trying to understand database systems to try to view the components and the relationships between them. In this section, we present a possible architecture for a DBMS.

A DBMS is partitioned into several software components (modules), each of which is assigned a specific operation. As stated previously, some of the functions of the DBMS are supported by the underlying operating system. However, the operating system provides only basic services and the DBMS must be built on top of it. Thus, the design of a DBMS must take into account the interface between the DBMS and the operating system.

The major software components in a DBMS environment are depicted in Figure 2.8. This diagram shows how the DBMS interfaces with other software components, such as user queries and access methods (file management techniques for storing and retrieving data records). For a detailed coverage of access methods and their performance, see Teorey and Fry (1982) and Weiderhold (1983).

Figure 2.8 shows the following components:

- *Query processor* This is a major DBMS component that transforms queries into a series of low-level instructions directed to the Database Manager.

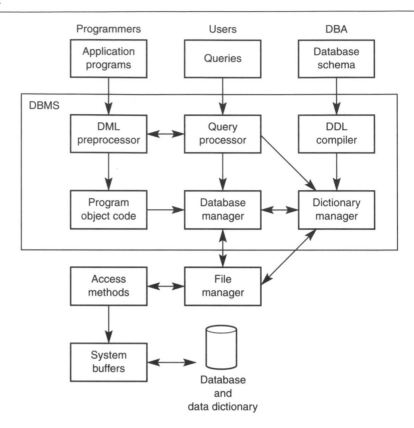

Figure 2.8 Major components of a DBMS.

- *Database manager (DM)* The DM interfaces with user-submitted application programs and queries. The DM accepts queries and examines the external and conceptual schemas to determine what conceptual records are required to satisfy the request. The DM then places a call to the File Manager to perform the request. The components of the DM are shown in Figure 2.9.

- *File manager* The file manager manipulates the underlying storage files and manages the allocation of storage space on the disk. It establishes and maintains the list of structures and indexes defined in the internal schema. If hashed files are used it calls on the hashing functions to generate record addresses. However, the file manager does not directly manage the physical input and output of data. Rather it passes the requests on to the appropriate access methods, which either read data from or write data into the system buffer.

- *DML preprocessor* This module converts DML statements embedded in an application program into standard function calls in the host language. The DML preprocessor must interact with the query processor to generate the appropriate code.

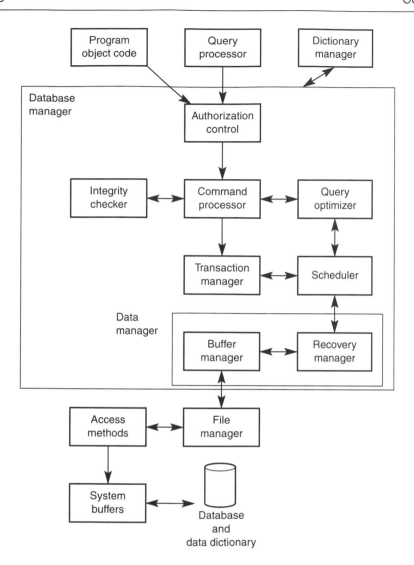

Figure 2.9
Components of a
database manager.

- *DDL compiler*   The DDL compiler converts DDL statements into a set of tables containing metadata. These tables are then stored in the data dictionary while control information is stored in data file headers.
- *Dictionary manager*   The dictionary manager manages access to and maintains the data dictionary. The data dictionary is accessed by most DBMS components.

The major software components for the database manager are as follows:

- *Authorization control* This module checks that the user has the necessary authorization to carry out the required operation.

- *Command processor* Once the system has checked that the user has authority to carry out the operation, control is passed to the command processor.

- *Integrity checker* For an operation that changes the database, the integrity checker checks that the requested operation satisfies all necessary integrity constraints (such as key constraints).

- *Query optimizer* This module determines an optimal strategy for the query execution.

- *Transaction manager* This module performs the required processing of operations it receives from transactions.

- *Scheduler* This module is responsible for ensuring that concurrent operations on the database proceed without conflicting with one another. It controls the relative order in which transaction operations are executed.

- *Recovery manager* This module ensures that the database remains in a consistent state in the presence of failures. It is responsible for transaction commit and abort.

- *Buffer manager* This module is responsible for the transfer of data between main memory and secondary storage, such as disk and tape. The recovery manager and the buffer manager are sometimes referred to collectively as the *data manager*.

We will discuss the last four modules in more detail in Chapter 15. In addition to the above modules, several other data structures are required as part of the physical level implementation. These structures include data and index files and the data dictionary. An attempt has been made to standardize database management systems, and a reference model has been proposed by the Database Architecture Framework Task Group (DAFTG, 1986). The purpose of this reference model is to define a conceptual framework aiming to divide standardization attempts into manageable pieces and to show at a very broad level how these pieces could be interrelated.

2.6 Multi-User DBMS Architectures

In this section, we look at the common architectures that are used to implement multi-user database management systems, namely teleprocessing, file-server and client–server.

2.6.1 Teleprocessing

The traditional architecture for multi-user systems was teleprocessing, where there is one computer with a single CPU and a number of terminals, as

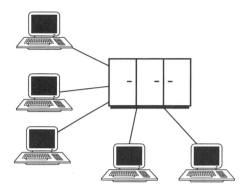

Figure 2.10
Teleprocessing
topology.

illustrated in Figure 2.10. All processing is performed within the boundaries
of the same physical computer. User terminals are typically 'dumb' ones,
incapable of functioning on their own. They are cabled to the central computer. The terminals send messages via the communications control subsystem
of the operating system to the user's application program, which in turn, uses
the services of the DBMS. In the same way, messages are routed back to the
user's terminal. Unfortunately, this architecture placed a tremendous burden
on the central computer, which not only had to run the application programs
and the DBMS, but also had to carry out a significant amount of work on
behalf of the terminals (such as formatting data for display on the screen).

In recent years, there have been significant advances in the development
of high-performance personal computers and networks. There is now an identifiable trend in industry towards **downsizing**, that is, replacing expensive
mainframe computers with more cost-effective networks of personal computers that achieve the same, or even better, results. This trend has given
rise to the next two architectures that we discuss, namely file-server and
client-server.

2.6.2   File-Server

In a file-server environment, the processing is distributed about the network,
typically a Local Area Network (LAN). The file-server holds the files required
by the applications and the DBMS. However, the applications and the DBMS
run on each workstation, requesting files from the file-server when necessary,
as illustrated in Figure 2.11. In this way, the file-server simply acts as a shared
hard disk drive. The DBMS on each workstation sends requests to the file-
server for all data the DBMS requires that is stored on disk. This approach
can generate a significant amount of network traffic, which can lead to performance problems. For example, consider a user request that requires the name
of staff who work in the branch at 163 Main St. We can express this request
in SQL (see Chapter 11) as:

> SELECT fname, lname
> FROM branch b, staff s
> WHERE b.bno = s.sno AND b.street = '163 Main St';

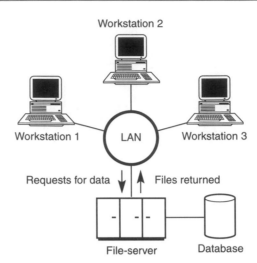

Figure 2.11
File-server
architecture.

As the file-server has no knowledge of SQL, the DBMS has to request the files corresponding to the Branch and Staff relations from the file-server, rather than just the staff names that satisfy the query.

The file-server architecture, therefore, has three main disadvantages:

(1)   There is a large amount of network traffic.

(2)   A full copy of the DBMS is required on each workstation.

(3)   Concurrency, recovery and integrity control are more complex because of multiple DBMSs accessing shared files.

2.6.3   Client–Server

To overcome the disadvantages of the first two approaches, the client–server architecture was developed. Client–server refers to the way in which software components interact to form a system. As the name suggests, there is a **client** process, which requires some resource, and a **server**, which provides the resource. There is no requirement that the client and server must reside on the same machine. In practice, it is quite common to place a server at one site in a local area network and the clients at the other sites. Figure 2.12 illustrates the client–server architecture and Figure 2.13 shows some possible combinations of the client–server topology.

In the database context, the client manages the user interface, acting as a sophisticated workstation on which to run database applications. The client takes the user's request, checks the syntax and generates database requests in SQL or another database language. It then transmits the message to the server, waits for a response and formats the response for the end user. The server accepts and processes the database requests, then transmits the results back to the client. The processing involves checking authorization, ensuring integrity, maintaining the data dictionary and performing query and

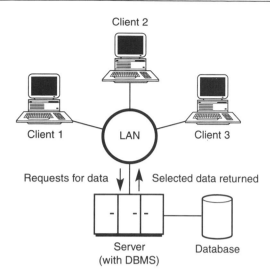

Figure 2.12
Client–server
architecture.

update processing. In addition, it also provides concurrency and recovery control. The operations of client and server are summarized in Table 2.1.

There are many advantages to this type of architecture. For example:

- It enables wider access to existing databases.

- Increased performance – if the clients and server reside on different computers then different CPUs can be processing applications in parallel. It should also be easier to tune the server machine if its only task is to perform database processing.

- Hardware costs may be reduced – it is only the server that requires storage and processing power sufficient to store and manage the database.

- Communication costs are reduced – applications carry out part of the operations on the client and send only requests for database access across the network, resulting in less data being sent across the network.

- Increased consistency – the server can handle integrity checks, so that constraints need be defined and validated only in the one place, rather than having each application program perform its own checking.

- It maps onto open-systems architecture quite naturally.

Some database vendors have used this architecture to indicate distributed database capability: that is, a collection of multiple, logically interrelated databases, distributed over a computer network. However, although the client–server architecture can be used to provide distributed DBMSs, it is not of itself a distributed DBMS. We will discuss distributed databases in more detail in Chapter 16.

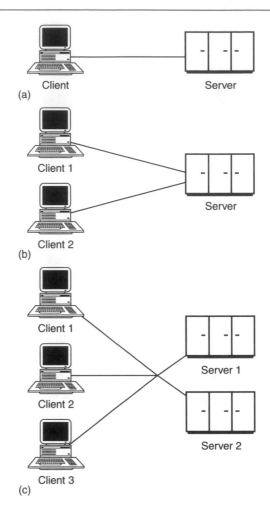

Figure 2.13
Alternative client–server topologies: (a) single client, single server; (b) multiple clients, single server; (c) multiple clients, multiple servers.

Table 2.1 Summary of client–server functions.

Client	Server
Manages the user interface	Accepts and processes database requests from clients
Accepts and checks syntax of user input	Checks authorization
Processes application	Ensures integrity constraints not violated
Generates database requests and transmits to server	Performs query/update processing and transmits response to client
Passes response back to user	Maintains data dictionary
	Provides concurrent database access
	Provides recovery control

2.7 Data Dictionaries

In Section 2.4, we stated that a DBMS should have a user-accessible catalogue or data dictionary. To conclude this chapter on the database environment, we examine data dictionaries in some further detail.

Data dictionary	A repository of information describing the data in the database: that is, the metadata or the 'data about the data'.

The DBMS data dictionary is one of the fundamental components of the system. Many of the software components that we described in Section 2.5 rely on the data dictionary for information. For example, the Authorization Control module uses the data dictionary to check whether a user has the necessary authorization to carry out the requested operation. To perform this check, the data dictionary has to store:

- the names of users authorized to use the DBMS;
- the names of the data items in the database;
- the data items that each user can access and the type of access allowed: for example, insert, update, delete or read access.

As another example, the integrity checker module uses the data dictionary to check that the requested operation satisfies all necessary integrity constraints. To perform this check, the data dictionary has to store:

- the names of the data items in the database,
- the types and sizes of the data items,
- the constraints on each data item.

A data dictionary system can be either active or passive. An **active** system is always consistent with the database structure, because it is maintained automatically by the system. On the other hand, a **passive** system may not be consistent with the database, as changes are initiated by the users. If the data dictionary is part of the DBMS, we refer to it as an **integrated** data dictionary. A **standalone** data dictionary has its own specialized DBMS. A standalone data dictionary may be preferable in the initial stages of design as this delays the commitment to a particular target DBMS for the organization for as long as possible. However, the disadvantage is that once the DBMS has been selected and the database implemented it is more difficult to keep the standalone data dictionary consistent with the database. This problem could be minimized if it was possible to transfer the design data dictionary into the DBMS dictionary. Until recently, this was not an option; however, the development of standards for data dictionaries may now make this more realistic. We discuss these standards briefly in the following section.

2.7.1 Information Resource Dictionary System (IRDS)

In many systems, the data dictionary is an internal component of the DBMS that stores only information directly relating to the database. However, the data held by the DBMS is usually only part of the total information requirements of an organization. Typically, there will be additional information held in other tools, such as CASE tools, documentation tools, and configuration and project management tools. Each of these tools will have its own internal data dictionary that is accessible from other external tools. Unfortunately, as a result there has been no general way to share these different sets of information across different groups of users or applications.

Recently, there has been an attempt to standardize the interface to data dictionaries to make them more accessible and shareable. This has led to the development of the Information Resource Dictionary System (IRDS). An IRDS is a software tool that can be used to control and document an organization's information resources. It provides a definition for the tables that comprise the data dictionary and the operations that can be used to access these tables. The operations provide a consistent method for accessing the data dictionary and a way to transfer data definitions from one dictionary to another. For example, information stored in an IRDS-compliant DB2 data dictionary could be moved to an IRDS-compliant INGRES data dictionary or accessed by an INGRES application using IRDS services.

One of the main strengths of IRDS is the extensibility of the data dictionary. Thus, if a user wishes to store definitions for a new type of information in a tool, for example project management reports in a DBMS, the IRDS for the DBMS can be extended to include this information. IRDS has been adopted as a standard by the International Standards Organization (ISO, 1990; 1993).

The IRDS standards define a set of rules on how information is stored and accessed in the data dictionary. The IRDS has three objectives:

- extensibility of data,
- integrity of data,
- controlled access to data.

The IRDS is based on a services interface, which consists of a set of functions that can be called to access the data dictionary. The services interface can be invoked from the following types of user interfaces:

- panel,
- command language,
- export/import files,
- application programs.

The panel interface consists of a set of panels or screens, each of which provides access to a prescribed set of services. This interface may be similar to QBE (Query-by-Example) and allows the user to browse and change the dictionary data. The Command Language Interface (CLI) consists of a set of

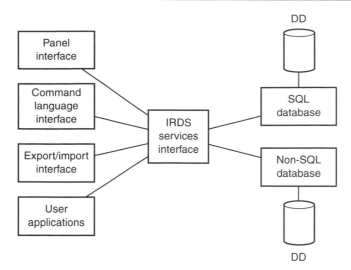

Figure 2.14 IRDS services interface.

commands or statements that allows the user to perform operations on the dictionary data. The CLI can be invoked interactively from a terminal or embedded in a high-level programming language. The export/import interface generates a file that can be moved between IRDS-compliant systems. The standards define a common format for the interchange of information. The standards do not require that the underlying database for the data dictionary conform to one particular data model, so that the IRDS services interface may connect heterogeneous database systems, as shown in Figure 2.14.

Chapter Summary

- The ANSI-SPARC database architecture uses **three levels** of abstraction: **external**, **conceptual** and **internal**. The external level consists of the users' views of the database. The **conceptual level** is the community view of the database. It specifies the information content of the entire database, independent of storage considerations. The **internal level** is the computer's view of the database. It specifies how data is represented, how records are sequenced, what indexes and pointers exist, and what hashing scheme, if any, is used.

- The **external/conceptual mapping** transforms requests and results between the external and conceptual levels. The **conceptual/internal mapping** transforms requests and results between the conceptual and internal levels.

- A **database schema** is a description of the database structure. Data independence makes each level immune to changes to lower levels. **Logical data independence** refers to the immunity of external schemas to changes in the conceptual schema. **Physical data independence** refers to the immunity of the conceptual schema to changes in the internal schema.

- A data sublanguage consists of two parts: a **Data Definition Language (DDL)** and a **Data Manipulation Language (DML)**. The DDL is used to specify the database schema and the DML is used to both read and update the database.

- A **data model** is a collection of concepts that can be used to describe a set of data, the operations to manipulate the data and a set of integrity rules for the data. They fall into three broad categories, **object-based** data models, **record-based** data models and **physical** data models. The first two are used to describe data at the conceptual and external levels; the latter is used to describe data at the internal level.

- Object-based data models include the entity–relationship, semantic, functional and object-oriented models. Record-based data models include the relational, network and hierarchical models.

- Conceptual modelling is the process of constructing a detailed architecture for a database that is independent of implementation details, such as the target DBMS, application programs or programming languages or any other physical considerations. The design of the conceptual schema is critical to the overall success of the system. It is worth spending the time and energy necessary to produce the best possible conceptual design.

- Client–server architecture refers to the way in which software components interact. There is a **client** process, which requires some resource, and a **server**, which provides the resource. Typically, the client handles the user interface and the server handles the database functionality.

- The **data dictionary** is one of the fundamental components of a DBMS. It contains 'data about the data' or **metadata**. The dictionary should be accessible to users. The Information Resource Dictionary System is a new ISO standard that defines a set of access methods for a data dictionary. This allows dictionaries to be shared and transferred from one system to another.

REVIEW QUESTIONS

2.1 Discuss the concept of data independence and explain its importance in a database environment.

2.2 To address the issue of data independence, the ANSI-SPARC three-level architecture was proposed. Compare and contrast the three levels of this model.

2.3 What is a data model? Discuss the main types of data models.

2.4 Discuss the function and importance of conceptual modelling.

2.5 Describe the types of facilities you would expect to be provided in a multi-user DBMS.

2.6 Of the facilities described in your answer to question 2.5, which ones do you think would *not* be needed in a standalone PC database management system? Provide justification for your answer.

2.7 Describe the main components in a DBMS and suggest which components are responsible for each facility identified in Question 2.5.

2.8 What is meant by the term 'client–server architecture' and what are the advantages of this approach? Compare the client–server architecture with two other architectures.

2.9 Discuss the function and importance of the data dictionary.

EXERCISES

2.10 Analyse the DBMSs that you are currently using. Determine each system's compliance with the functions that we would expect to be provided by a DBMS. What types of languages does each system provide? What type of architecture does each DBMS use? Check the accessibility and extensibility of the data dictionary. Is it possible to export the data dictionary to another system?

2.11 Write a program that stores names and telephone numbers in a database. Write another program that stores names and addresses in a database. Modify the programs to use external, conceptual and internal schemas. What are the advantages and disadvantages of this modification?

2.12 Write a program that stores names and dates of birth in a database. Extend the program so that it stores the format of the data in the database; in other words, create a data dictionary. Provide an interface that makes this data dictionary accessible to external users.

2.13 How would you modify this program to conform to a client–server architecture? What would be the advantages and disadvantages of this modification?

3 The Relational Model

Chapter Objectives

In this chapter you will learn:

- The origins of the relational model.
- The terminology of the relational model.
- How tables are used to represent data.
- The connection between mathematical relations and relational model relations.
- Properties of database relations.
- How to identify candidate, primary and foreign keys.
- The meaning of entity integrity and referential integrity.
- The categories of relational Data Manipulation Languages (DMLs).
- How to form queries in relational algebra.
- How relational calculus queries are expressed.
- The purpose and advantages of views in relational systems.
- Criteria for the evaluation of relational database management systems.

The Relational Database Management System (RDBMS) has become the dominant data-processing software in use today. This software represents the second generation of DBMS and is based on the relational data model introduced by E. F. Codd (1970). In the relational model, all data is logically structured within relations (tables). Each relation has a name and is made up of named **attributes** (columns) of data. Each **tuple** (row) contains one value per attribute. A great strength of the relational model is this simple logical structure. Yet, behind this simple structure is a sound theoretical foundation that is lacking in the first generation of DBMSs: that is, the network and hierarchical DBMSs.

We devote a significant amount of this book to the RDBMS, in recognition of the importance of these systems. In this chapter, we discuss the basic principles of the relational data model. In Chapters 7, 8, 9 and 10, we present a complete methodology for relational database design. We also devote two Chapters, 11 and 12, to the formal and *de facto* standard language for RDBMSs, Structured Query Language (SQL). The examples in this chapter are drawn from the *DreamHome* case study introduced in Section 1.7.

3.1 Brief History of the Relational Model

The relational model was first proposed by E. F. Codd, in the seminal paper 'A relational model of data for large shared data banks' (Codd, 1970). This paper is now generally accepted as a landmark in database systems, although it should be noted that a set-oriented model had already been proposed (Childs, 1968). The relational model's objectives were specified as follows:

- To allow a high degree of data independence. Application programs must not be affected by modifications to the internal data representation, particularly by the changes of file organizations, record orderings and access paths.

- To provide substantial grounds for dealing with data semantics, consistency and redundancy problems. In particular, Codd's paper introduces the concept of **normalized** relations, that is, relations that have no repeating groups. (The process of normalization will be discussed in Chapter 6.)

- To enable the expansion of set-oriented data manipulation languages.

Although interest in the relational model came from several directions, the most significant research may be attributed to three projects with rather different perspectives. The first of these, at IBM's San Jose Research Laboratory in California, was the prototype relational database management system, System R, which was developed during the late 1970s (Astrahan *et al.*, 1976). This project was designed to prove the practicality of the relational model by providing an implementation of its data structures and operations. It also proved to be an excellent source of information about implementation concerns such as concurrency control, query optimization, transaction management, data security and integrity, recovery techniques, human factors and user interfaces, and led to the publication of many research papers and to the development of other prototypes. In particular, the System R project led to two major developments:

- the development of a structured query language called SQL (pronounced 'S-Q-L' or sometimes 'See-Quel'), which has since become the formal International Standards Organization (ISO) and the *de facto* standard relational language;

- the production of various commercial relational DBMS products during the 1980s: for example, DB2 and SQL/DS from IBM and ORACLE from ORACLE Corporation.

The second project to have been significant in the development of the relational model was the INGRES (INteractive GRaphics REtrieval System) project at the University of California at Berkeley, which was active at about the same time as the System R project. The INGRES project involved the development of a prototype RDBMS, with the research concentrating on the same overall objectives as the System R project. The research led to an academic version of INGRES, which contributed to the general appreciation of relational concepts. This project spawned the commercial products INGRES from Relational Technology Inc. (now Computer Associates: The ASK Group) and the Intelligent Database Machine from Britton Lee Inc.

The third project was the Peterlee Relational Test Vehicle at the IBM UK Scientific Centre in Peterlee (Todd, 1976). This project had a more theoretical orientation than the System R and INGRES projects and was significant, principally for research into such issues as query optimization and evaluation, and functional extension.

Commercial systems based on the relational model started to appear in the late 1970s and early 1980s. Now there are several hundred relational DBMSs for both mainframe and microcomputer environments, even though many do not strictly adhere to the definition of the relational model. Examples of microcomputer-based relational DBMSs are Paradox and dBaseIV from Borland, Access from Microsoft, FoxPro and R:base from Microrim.

Due to the popularity of the relational model, many non-relational systems now provide a relational user interface, irrespective of the underlying model. Computer Associates' IDMS, formerly the example of the network model, has become IDMS/R and IDMS/SQL, supporting a relational view of data. Other mainframe DBMSs that support some relational features are Computer Corporation of America's Model 204 and Software AG's ADABAS.

Some extensions to the relational model have also been proposed to capture more closely the meaning of data (for example, Codd, 1979), to support object-oriented concepts (for example, Stonebraker and Rowe, 1986) and to support deductive capabilities (for example, Gardarin and Valduriez, 1989). We discuss some of these extensions in Chapter 17 on Object Databases.

3.2   Terminology

The relational model is based on the mathematical concept of a **relation**, which is physically represented as a **table**. Codd, a trained mathematician, used terminology taken from mathematics, principally set theory and predicate logic. In this section, we explain the terminology and structural concepts of the relational model.

3.2.1   Relational Data Structure

Relation   A relation is a table with columns and rows.

A relational DBMS requires only that the database be perceived by the user as tables. Note, however, that this perception applies only to the logical structure of the database: that is, the external and conceptual levels of the ANSI-SPARC architecture discussed in Section 2.1. It does not apply to the physical structure of the database, which can be implemented using a variety of storage structures (see Appendix A).

Attribute   An attribute is a named column of a relation.

In the relational model, relations are used to hold information about the objects to be represented in the database. A relation is represented as a two-dimensional table in which the rows of the table correspond to individual records and the table columns correspond to attributes. Attributes can appear in any order and the relation will still be the same relation, and therefore convey the same meaning.

For example, the information on branch offices is represented by the Branch relation, having columns for attributes Bno (the branch number), Street, Area, City, Pcode, Tel_No and Fax_No. Similarly, the information on staff is represented by the Staff relation, having columns for attributes Sno (the staff number), FName, LName, Address, Tel_No, Position, Sex, DOB (date of birth), Salary, NIN (national insurance number) and Bno (the number of the branch the staff member works at). Figure 3.1 shows instances of the Branch and Staff relations. As you can see from this example, a column contains values of a single attribute; for example, the Bno columns contain only numbers of existing branch offices.

Domain   A domain is the set of allowable values for one or more attributes.

Domains are an extremely powerful feature of the relational model. Every attribute in a relational database is defined on a domain. Domains may be distinct for each attribute, or two or more attributes may have the same

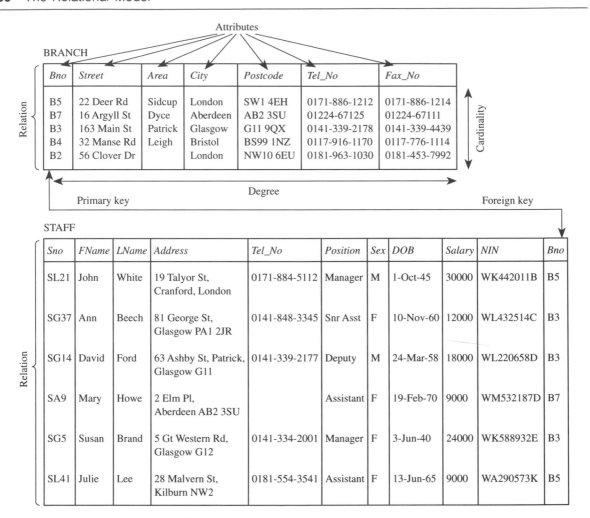

Figure 3.1 Instances of the Branch and Staff relations.

domain. Figure 3.2 shows the domains for some of the attributes of the Branch and Staff relations. Although there are seven attributes in the Branch relation, there are only six domains represented, as the two attributes Tel_No and Fax_No take their values from the same domain. Note that, at any given time, typically there will be values in a domain that do not currently appear as a value in the corresponding attribute.

The domain concept is important because it allows the user to define in a central place the meaning and source of values that attributes can hold. As a result, more information is available to the system when it undertakes the execution of a relational operation, and operations that are semantically incorrect can be avoided. For example, it is not sensible to compare a street name with a telephone number, even though the domain definitions for both of these attributes are character strings. On the other hand, the monthly rental

Attribute	Domain Name	Meaning	Domain Definition
Bno	BRANCH_NUMBERS	The set of all possible branch numbers	character: size 3, range B01–B99
Street	STREET_NAMES	The set of all street names in Britain	character: size 25
Area	AREA_NAMES	The set of all area names in Britain	character: size 20
City	CITY_NAMES	The set of all city names in Britain	character: size 15
Pcode	POST_CODES	The set of all post codes in Britain	character: size 8
Tel_No	TELFAX_NUMBERS	The set of all telephone and fax numbers in Britain	character: size 13
Fax_No	TELFAX_NUMBERS	The set of all telephone and fax numbers in Britain	character: size 13
Sex	SEX	The sex of a person	character: size 1, value M or F
DOB	DATES_OF_BIRTH	Possible values of staff birth dates	date, range from 1-Jan-20, format dd-mmm-yy
Salary	SALARIES	Possible values of staff salaries	monetary: 7 digits, range 6000.00–40000.00

on a property and the number of months a property has been leased have different domains (the first a monetary value, the second an integer value), but it is still a legal operation to multiply two values from these domains. As these two examples illustrate, a complete implementation of domains is not straightforward and, as a result, many RDBMSs do not support them fully.

Figure 3.2 Domains for some attributes of the Branch and Staff relations.

> **Tuple**   A tuple is a row of a relation.

The elements of a relation are the rows or tuples in the table. In the Branch relation, each row contains seven values, one for each attribute. Tuples can appear in any order and the relation will still be the same relation, and therefore convey the same meaning.

The structure of a relation, together with a specification of the domains and any other restrictions on possible values, is sometimes called its **intension**, which is usually fixed unless the meaning of a relation is changed to include additional attributes. The tuples are called the **extension** (or **state**) of a relation, which changes over time.

> **Degree**   The degree of a relation is the number of attributes it contains.

The Branch relation in Figure 3.1 has seven attributes or degree seven. This means that each row of the table is a seven-tuple, containing seven values. A relation with only one attribute would have degree one and be called a **unary** relation or one-tuple. A relation with two attributes is called **binary,** one with three attributes is called **ternary**, and after that the term **n-ary** is usually used. The degree of a relation is part of the intension of the relation.

> **Cardinality** The cardinality of a relation is the number of tuples it contains.

By contrast, the number of tuples is called the **cardinality** of the relation and this changes as tuples are added or deleted. The cardinality is a property of the extension of the relation and is the particular instance of the relation at any given moment. Finally, we have the definition:

> **Relational database** A collection of normalized relations.

Alternative terminology

The terminology for the relational model can be quite confusing. We have introduced two sets of terms. In fact, there is a third set of terms that is sometimes used. A relation may be referred to as a **file**, the tuples as **records** and the attributes as **fields**. This terminology stems from the fact that physically the RDBMS may store each relation in a file. Table 3.1 summarizes the different terms for the relational model.

Table 3.1 Alternative terminology for relational model terms.

Formal terms	Alternative 1	Alternative 2
Relation	Table	File
Tuple	Row	Record
Attribute	Column	Field

3.2.2 Mathematical Relations

To understand the true meaning of the term **relation,** we have to review some concepts from mathematics. Suppose that we have two sets, D_1 and D_2, where $D_1 = \{2, 4\}$ and $D_2 = \{1, 3, 5\}$. The **Cartesian product** of these two sets, written $D_1 \times D_2$, is the set of all ordered pairs such that the first element is a member of D_1 and the second element is a member of D_2. An alternative way of expressing this is to find all combinations of elements with the first from D_1 and the second from D_2. In our case, we have:

$$D_1 \times D_2 = \{(2, 1), (2, 3), (2, 5), (4, 1), (4, 3), (4, 5)\}$$

Any subset of this Cartesian product is a relation. For example, we could produce a relation R such that:

$$R = \{(2, 1), (4, 1)\}$$

We may specify which ordered pairs will be in the relation by giving some condition for their selection. For example, if we observe that R includes all those ordered pairs in which the second element is 1, then we could write R as:

$$R = \{(x, y) \mid x \in D_1, y \in D_2, \text{ and } y = 1\}$$

Using these same sets, we could form another relation, S, in which the first element is always twice the second. Thus, we could write S as:

$$S = \{(x, y) \mid x \in D_1, y \in D_2, \text{ and } x = 2y\}$$

or, in this instance,

$$S = \{(2, 1)\}$$

since there is only one ordered pair in the Cartesian product that satisfies this condition. We can easily extend the notion of a relation to three sets. Let D_1, D_2 and D_3 be three sets. The Cartesian product $D_1 \times D_2 \times D_3$ of these three sets is the set of all ordered triples such that the first element is from D_1, the second element is from D_2 and the third element is from D_3. Any subset of this Cartesian product is a relation. For example, suppose we have:

$$D_1 = \{1, 3\} \qquad D_2 = \{2, 4\} \qquad D_3 = \{5, 6\}$$
$$D_1 \times D_2 \times D_3 = \{(1,2,5),(1,2,6),(1,4,5),(1,4,6),(3,2,5),(3,2,6),$$
$$(3,4,5),(3,4,6)\}$$

Any subset of these ordered triples is a relation. We can extend the three sets and define a general relation on n domains. Let $D_1, D_2, \ldots, D_n$ be n sets. Their Cartesian product is defined as:

$$D_1 \times D_2 \times \ldots \times D_n = \{(d_1, d_2, \ldots, d_n) \mid d_1 \in D_1, d_2 \in D_2, \ldots, d_n \in D_n\}$$

and is usually written as:

$$\underset{i=1}{\overset{n}{X}} D_i$$

Any set of n-tuples from this Cartesian product is a relation on the n sets. Note that in defining these relations we had to specify the sets, or **domains**, from which we chose values.

3.2.3   Database Relations

Applying these concepts to databases, we have:

Relation schema	A relation name followed by a set of attribute and domain name pairs.

Let $A_1, A_2, \ldots, A_n$ be attributes with domains $D_1, D_2, \ldots, D_n$. Then the set $\{A_1:D_1, A_2:D_2, \ldots, A_n:D_n\}$ is a relation schema. A relation R defined by a relation schema S is a set of mappings from the attribute names to their corresponding domains. Thus, relation R is a set of n-tuples:

$$(A_1:d_1, A_2:d_2, \ldots, A_n:d_n) \text{ such that } d_1 \in D_1, d_2 \in D_2, \ldots, d_n \in D_n$$

Each element in the n-tuple consists of an attribute and a value for that attribute. Normally, when we write out a relation as a table, we list the attribute names as column headings and write out the tuples as rows having the form $(d_1, d_2, \ldots, d_n)$, where each value is taken from the appropriate domain. In this way, we can think of a relation in the relational model as any subset of the Cartesian product of the domains of the attributes. A table is simply a physical representation of such a relation.

In our example, the Branch relation shown in Figure 3.1 has attributes Bno, Street, Area, City, Pcode, Tel_No and Fax_No, each with its corresponding domain. The Branch relation is any subset of the Cartesian product of the domains, or any set of seven-tuples in which the first element is from the domain BRANCH_NUMBER, the second is from the domain STREET_NAME, and so on. One of the seven-tuples is:

$$\{(\text{B5, 22 Deer Rd, Sidcup, London, SW1 4EH, 0171–886–1212,}$$
$$\text{0171–886–1214})\}$$

or more correctly:

$$\{(\textbf{Bno: } \text{B5, } \textbf{Street: } \text{22 Deer Rd, } \textbf{Area: } \text{Sidcup, } \textbf{City: } \text{London,}$$
$$\textbf{Pcode: } \text{SW1 4EH, } \textbf{Tel\_No: } \text{0171–886–1212, } \textbf{Fax\_No: } \text{0171–886–1214})\}$$

The Branch table is a convenient way of writing out all the seven-tuples that form the relation at a specific moment in time, which explains why table rows in the relational model are called tuples.

3.2.4 Properties of Relations

A relation has the following characteristics:

- The relation name has a name that is distinct from all other relations.
- Each cell of the relation contains exactly one atomic (single) value.
- Each attribute has a distinct name.
- The values of an attribute are all from the same domain.
- The order of attributes has no significance.
- Each tuple is distinct; there are no duplicate tuples.
- The order of tuples has no significance, theoretically. (However, in practice, the order may affect the efficiency of accessing tuples.)

To illustrate what these restrictions mean, consider again the Branch relation shown in Figure 3.1. Since each cell should contain only one value, it is illegal to store two telephone numbers for a single branch office in a single cell. In other words, relations do not contain repeating groups. A relation that satisfies this property is said to be **normalized** or in **first normal form**. (Normal forms are discussed in Chapter 6 on Normalization.)

The column names listed at the tops of columns correspond to the attributes of the relation. The values in the Bno attribute are all from the domain of BRANCH_NUMBERS; we should not allow a postcode value to appear in this column.

Provided an attribute name is moved along with the attribute values, we can interchange columns. The table would represent the same relation if we were to put the Fax_No attribute before the Pcode attribute, although for readability, it makes more sense to keep the address elements together.

There can be no duplicate tuples in a relation. For example, the row (B5, 22 Deer Rd, Sidcup, London, SW1 4EH, 0171–886–1212, 0171–886–1214) appears only once. The rows can be interchanged at will, so the records of branch B5 and B4 can be switched, and the relation will still be the same relation.

Most of the properties specified for relations result from the properties of mathematical relations:

- Since a relation is a set, the order of elements does not count. Therefore, in a relation the order of tuples is immaterial.

- In a set, no elements are repeated. Similarly, in a relation, there are no duplicate tuples.

- When we derived the Cartesian product of sets with simple, single-valued elements such as integers, each element in each tuple was single-valued. Similarly, each cell of a relation contains exactly one value. However, a mathematical relation need not be normalized. Codd chose to disallow repeating groups to simplify the relational data model.

- In a relation, the possible values for a given position are determined by the set or domain on which the position is defined. In a table, the values in each column must come from the same attribute domain.

However, in a mathematical relation, the order of elements in a tuple is important. For example, the ordered pair (1,2) is quite different from the ordered pair (2,1). This is not the case for relations in the relational model, which specifically require that the order of attributes be immaterial. The reason is that the column headings tell us to which attribute the value belongs. This means that the order of column headings in the intension is immaterial, but once the structure of the relation is chosen, the order of elements within the tuples of the extension must match the order of attribute names.

3.2.5   Relational Keys

We need to be able to identify uniquely each tuple in a relation by the values of its attributes. In this section, we explain the terminology used for relational keys.

> **Superkey** An attribute or a set of attributes that uniquely identifies a tuple within a relation.

Since a superkey may contain additional attributes that are not necessary for unique identification, we are interested in identifying superkeys that contain only the attributes necessary for unique identification.

> **Candidate key** A superkey such that no proper subset is a superkey within the relation.

A candidate key, K, for a relation R has two properties therefore:

- **Uniqueness** In each tuple of R, the values of K uniquely identify that tuple.
- **Irreducibility** No proper subset of K has the uniqueness property.

There may be several candidate keys for a relation. When a key consists of more than one attribute, we call it a **composite key**. Consider the Branch relation shown in Figure 3.1. Given a value of City, we would expect to be able to determine several branch offices (for example, London has two branch offices). This attribute cannot be selected as a candidate key. On the other hand, since *DreamHome* allocate each branch office a unique branch number, then given a branch number value, Bno, we can determine at most one tuple, so that Bno is a candidate key. Similarly, Tel_No and Fax_No are also candidate keys for this relation.

Now consider a relation Viewing, which contains information relating to properties viewed by potential renters. The relation comprises a renter number (Rno), a property number (Pno), a date of viewing (Date) and optionally a comment. Given a renter number, Rno, there may be several corresponding viewings for different properties. Similarly, given a property number, Pno, there may be several renters who view this property. Therefore, Rno by itself or Pno by itself cannot be selected as a candidate key. However, the combination of Rno and Pno identifies at most one tuple. If we need to cater for the possibility that a renter may view a property more than once, then we could add Date to the composite key. However, we assume that this is not necessary.

Note that an instance of a relation cannot be used to prove that an attribute or combination of attributes is a candidate key. The fact that there are no duplicates for the values that appear at a particular moment in time does not guarantee that duplicates are not possible. However, the presence of duplicates in an instance can be used to show that some attribute combination is not a candidate key. Identifying a candidate key requires that we know the real-world meaning of the attribute(s) involved so that we can decide whether duplicates are possible. Only by using this semantic information can we be certain that an attribute combination is a candidate key. For example, from the data presented in Figure 3.1, we may think that a suitable candidate key for the Staff relation would be LName, the employee's surname. However, although there is only a single value of White, if a new member of staff with the surname White joins the company, this would invalidate the choice of LName as a candidate key.

> **Primary key**   The candidate key that is selected to identify tuples uniquely within the relation.

Since a relation has no duplicate tuples, it is always possible to uniquely identify each row. This means that a relation always has a primary key. In the worst case, the entire set of attributes could serve as the primary key, but usually some smaller subset is sufficient to distinguish the tuples. The candidate keys that are not selected to be the primary key are called **alternate keys**. For the Branch relation, if we choose Bno as the primary key, Tel_No and Fax_No would then be alternate keys. For the Viewing relation, there is only one candidate key, comprising Rno and Pno, so these attributes would automatically form the primary key.

> **Foreign key**   An attribute or set of attributes within one relation that matches the candidate key of some (possibly the same) relation.

When an attribute appears in more than one relation, its appearance usually represents a relationship between tuples of the two relations. For example, the inclusion of Bno in both the Branch and Staff relations is quite deliberate and links branch to the details of staff working at each branch. In the Branch relation, Bno is the primary key. However, in the Staff relation the Bno attribute exists to allow us to match staff to the branch office they work in. In the Staff relation, Bno is a foreign key. We say that the attribute Bno in the Staff relation **targets** the primary key attribute Bno in the **home relation**, Branch. These common attributes play an important role in performing data manipulation, as we will see in later sections.

3.2.6 Representing Relational Database Schemas

A relational database consists of any number of relations. The relation schemas for the rental part of the *DreamHome* case study is:

Branch	(<u>Bno</u>, Street, Area, City, Pcode, Tel_No, Fax_No)
Staff	(<u>Sno</u>, FName, LName, Address, Tel_No, Position, Sex, DOB, Salary, NIN, Bno)
Property_for_Rent	(<u>Pno</u>, Street, Area, City, Pcode, Type, Rooms, Rent, Ono, Sno, Bno)
Renter	(<u>Rno</u>, FName, LName, Address, Tel_No, Pref_Type, Max_Rent)
Owner	(<u>Ono</u>, FName, LName, Address, Tel_No)
Viewing	(<u>Rno</u>, <u>Pno</u>, Date, Comment)

Figure 3.3 Instance of the *DreamHome* rental database.

BRANCH

Bno	Street	Area	City	Pcode	Tel_No	Fax_No
B5	22 Deer Rd	Sidcup	London	SW1 4EH	0171–886–1212	0171–886–1214
B7	16 Argyll St	Dyce	Aberdeen	AB2 3SU	01224–67125	01224–67111
B3	163 Main St	Partick	Glasgow	G11 9QX	0141–339–2178	0141–339–4439
B4	32 Manse Rd	Leigh	Bristol	BS99 1NZ	0117–916–1170	0117–776–1114
B2	56 Clover Dr		London	NW10 6EU	0181–963–1030	0181–453–7992

STAFF

Sno	FName	LName	Address	Tel_No	Position	Sex	DOB	Salary	NIN	Bno
SL21	John	White	19 Taylor St, Cranford, London	0171–884–5112	Manager	M	1-Oct–45	30000	WK442011B	B5
SG37	Ann	Beech	81 George St, Glasgow PA1 2JR	0141–848–3345	Snr Asst	F	10–Nov–60	12000	WL432514C	B3
SG14	David	Ford	63 Ashby St, Partick, Glasgow G11	0141–339–2177	Deputy	M	24–Mar–58	18000	WL220658D	B3
SA9	Mary	Howe	2 Elm Pl, Aberdeen AB2 3SU		Assistant	F	19–Feb–70	9000	WM532187D	B7
SG5	Susan	Brand	5 Gt Western Rd, Glasgow G12	0141–334–2001	Manager	F	3–Jun–40	24000	WK588932E	B3
SL41	Julie	Lee	28 Malvern St, Kilburn NW2	0181–554–3541	Assistant	F	13–Jun–65	9000	WA290573K	B5

PROPERTY_FOR_RENT

Pno	Street	Area	City	Pcode	Type	Rooms	Rent	Ono	Sno	Bno
PA14	16 Holhead	Dee	Aberdeen	AB7 5SU	House	6	650	CO46	SA9	B7
PL94	6 Argyll St	Kilburn	London	NW2	Flat	4	400	CO87	SL41	B5
PG4	6 Lawrence St	Partick	Glasgow	G11 9QX	Flat	3	350	CO40	SG14	B3
PG36	2 Manor Rd		Glasgow	G32 4QX	Flat	3	375	CO93	SG37	B3
PG21	18 Dale Rd	Hyndland	Glasgow	G12	House	5	600	CO87	SG37	B3
PG16	5 Novar Dr	Hyndland	Glasgow	G12 9AX	Flat	4	450	CO93	SG14	B3

RENTER

Rno	FName	LName	Address	Tel_No	Pref_Type	Max_Rent
CR76	John	Kay	56 High St, Putney, London SW1 4EH	0171–774–5632	Flat	425
CR56	Aline	Stewart	64 Fern Dr, Pollock, Glasgow G42 0BL	0141–848–1825	Flat	350
CR74	Mike	Ritchie	18 Tain St, Gourock PA1G 1YQ	01475–392178	House	750
CR62	Mary	Tregear	5 Tarbot Rd, Kildary, Aberdeen AB9 3ST	01224–196720	Flat	600

OWNER

Ono	FName	LName	Address	Tel_No
CO46	Joe	Keogh	2 Fergus Dr, Banchory, Aberdeen AB2 7SX	01224–861212
CO87	Carol	Farrel	6 Achray St, Glasgow G32 9DX	0141–357–7419
CO40	Tina	Murphy	63 Well St, Shawlands, Glasgow G42	0141–943–1728
CO93	Tony	Shaw	12 Park Pl, Hillhead, Glasgow G4 0QR	0141–225–7025

VIEWING

Rno	Pno	Date	Comment
CR56	PA14	24–May–95	too small
CR76	PG4	20–Apr–95	too remote
CR56	PG4	26–May–95	
CR62	PA14	14–May–95	no dining room
CR56	PG36	28–Apr–95	

Figure 3.3 continued

The common convention for representing a relation schema is to give the name of the relation, followed by the attribute names in parentheses. Normally, the primary key is underlined.

The conceptual model or schema is the set of all these schemas for the database. Figure 3.3 shows an instance of this database.

3.3 Relational Integrity

In the previous section, we discussed the structural part of the relational data model. As stated in Section 2.3, a data model has two other parts: a manipulative part, defining the types of operations that are allowed on the data, and a set of integrity rules, which ensure that the data is accurate. In this section, we discuss the relational integrity rules and in the following section, we discuss the relational manipulation operations.

Since every attribute has an associated domain, there are constraints (called **domain constraints**) in the form of restrictions on the set of values allowed for the attributes of relations. In addition, there are two important **integrity rules**, which are constraints or restrictions that apply to all instances of the database. The two principal rules for the relational model are known as **entity integrity** and **referential integrity**. Before we define these terms, it is necessary to understand the concept of nulls.

3.3.1 Nulls

> **Null** Represents a value for an attribute that is currently unknown or is not applicable for this tuple.

A null can be taken to mean the logical value 'unknown'. It can mean that a value is not applicable to a particular tuple, or it could merely mean that no value has yet been supplied. Nulls are a way to deal with incomplete or exceptional data. However, a null is not the same as a zero numeric value or a text string filled with spaces; zeros and spaces are values, but a null represents the absence of a value. Therefore, nulls should be treated differently from other values. Some authors use the term 'null value'. In fact, a null is not a value but represents the absence of a value and so the term 'null value' is deprecated.

For example, in the Viewing relation shown in Figure 3.3, the Comment attribute may be undefined until the potential renter has visited the property and returned his or her comment to the agency. Without nulls, it becomes necessary to introduce false data to represent this state or to add additional attributes that may not be meaningful to the user. In our example, we may try to represent a null comment with the value '−1'. Alternatively, we may add a new attribute 'Has Comment Been Supplied?' to the Viewing relation, which contains a Y (Yes), if a comment has been supplied and N (No), otherwise. Both these approaches can be confusing to the user.

Nulls can cause implementational problems. The difficulty arises because the relational model is based on first-order predicate calculus, which is a two-valued or Boolean logic – the only values allowed are true or false. Allowing nulls means that we have to work with a higher-valued logic, such as three- or four-valued logic (Codd, 1986, 1987, 1990). It should be noted that not all relational systems support nulls.

The incorporation of nulls in the relational model is a contentious issue. Codd (1990) now regards nulls as an integral part of the model. Others consider this approach to be misguided, believing that the missing information problem is not fully understood, that no fully satisfactory solution has been found and, consequently, that the incorporation of nulls in the relational model is premature (see for example, Date, 1995).

We are now in a position to define the two relational integrity rules.

3.3.2 Entity Integrity

The first integrity rule applies to the primary keys of base relations. For the present, we define a base relation as a relation that corresponds to an entity in the conceptual schema (see Section 2.1). We will provide a more precise definition in Section 3.5.

> **Entity integrity** In a base relation, no attribute of a primary key can be null.

By definition, a primary key is a minimal identifier that is used to identify tuples uniquely. This means that no subset of the primary key is sufficient to provide unique identification of tuples. If we allow a null for any part of a primary key, we are implying that not all of the attributes are needed to distinguish between tuples, which contradicts the definition of the primary key. For example, as Bno is the primary key of the Branch relation, we should not be able to insert a tuple into the Branch relation with a null for the Bno attribute.

If we were to examine this rule in detail, we would find some anomalies. First, why does the rule apply only to primary keys and not alternate keys as well? Secondly, why is the rule restricted to base relations? For example, using the data of the Staff relation shown in Figure 3.3, consider the query 'List all staff telephone numbers'. This will produce a unary relation consisting of the attribute Tel_No. By definition, this attribute must be a primary key, but it contains a null (corresponding to staff number SA9). Since this relation is not a base relation, the model allows the primary key to be null. There have been several attempts to redefine this rule (see, for example, Codd, 1988; Date, 1990).

3.3.3 Referential Integrity

The second integrity rule applies to foreign keys.

Referential integrity	If a foreign key exists in a relation, either the foreign key value must match a candidate key value of some tuple in its home relation or the foreign key value must be wholly null.

For example, Bno in the Staff relation is a foreign key targeting the Bno attribute in the home relation, Branch. It should not be possible to create a staff record with branch number B25, for example, unless there is already a record for branch number B25 in the Branch relation. However, we should be able to create a new staff record with a null branch number. This allows for the situation where a new member of staff has joined the company but has not yet been assigned to a particular branch office.

3.3.4 Enterprise Constraints

Enterprise constraints	Additional rules specified by the users or database administrators of a database.

It is also possible for users to specify additional constraints that the data must satisfy. For example, if an upper limit of 20 members of staff has been placed upon a branch office, then the user must be able to specify it and expect the DBMS to enforce it, such that a new member of staff cannot be added to the Staff relation if the number of staff currently assigned to a particular branch is 20. Unfortunately, the level of support for relational integrity varies from system to system. We discuss the implementation of relational integrity in Chapters 9, 10, 12 and 14.

3.4   Relational Languages

The third part of a data model is the manipulative part. There are a variety of languages used by relational DBMSs for manipulating relations. Some of them are **procedural**, meaning that the user tells the system exactly how to manipulate the data. Others are **non-procedural**, which means that the user states *what* data is needed rather than *how* it is to be retrieved.

In this section, we concentrate on relational algebra and relational calculus, as defined by Codd (1971) as the basis for relational languages. Informally, we may describe the relational algebra as a (high-level) procedural language: it can be used to tell the DBMS how to build a relation from one or more relations in the database. Again, informally, we may describe relational calculus as a non-procedural language: it can be used to formulate the definition of a relation in terms of one or more database relations. However, formally the relational algebra and relational calculus are equivalent to one another. For every expression in the algebra, there is an equivalent expression in the calculus (and vice versa).

Relational calculus is used to measure the selective power of relational languages. A language that can be used to produce any relation that can be derived using relational calculus is said to be **relationally complete**. Most relational query languages are relationally complete but have more expressive power than relational algebra or relational calculus because of additional operations such as calculated, summary and ordering functions.

Both the algebra and the calculus are formal, non-user-friendly languages. They have been used as the basis for other, higher-level Data Manipulation Languages (DML) for relational databases. They are of interest because they illustrate the basic operations required of any DML and because they serve as the standard of comparison for other relational languages. We discuss other types of languages in Section 3.4.3.

3.4.1   Relational Algebra

Relational algebra is a theoretical language with operations that work on one or more relations to define another relation without changing the original relations. Thus, both the operands and the results are relations, and so the output from one operation can become the input to another operation. This allows us to nest expressions in relational algebra, just as we can nest arithmetic operations. This property is called **closure**: relations are closed under the algebra, just as numbers are closed under arithmetic operations.

Relational algebra is a relation-at-a-time (or set) language in which all tuples, possibly from several relations, are manipulated in one statement without looping. There are several variations of syntax of relational algebra commands and we will use a common symbolic notation for the commands and

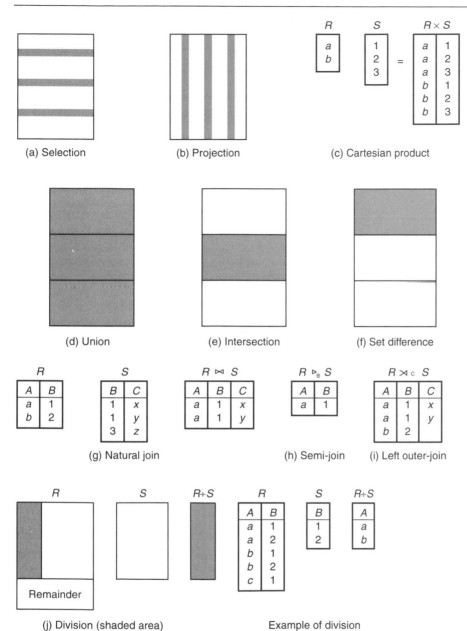

Figure 3.4 Illustration showing the function of the relational algebra operations.

present it informally. The interested reader is referred to Ullman (1988) for a more formal treatment.

There are many variations of the operations that are included in relational algebra. Codd (1972a) originally proposed eight operations, but several others have been developed. The five fundamental operations in relational algebra, *Selection*, *Projection*, *Cartesian product*, *Union* and *Set difference*, allow us to perform most of the data retrieval operations that we are interested in. In addition, there are also the *Join, Intersection* and *Division* operations, which can be expressed in terms of the five basic operations. The function of the operations is illustrated diagrammatically in Figure 3.4.

The selection and projection operations are **unary** operations, since they operate on one relation. The other operators work on pairs of relations and are therefore called **binary** operations. In the following definitions, let R and S be two relations defined over the attributes $A = (a_1, a_2, \ldots, a_N)$ and $B = (b_1, b_2, \ldots, b_M)$ respectively. We use the *DreamHome* rental database example shown in Figure 3.3 to illustrate these operations.

Selection (or Restriction)

$\sigma_{\text{predicate}}(R)$	The selection operator works on a single relation R and defines a relation that contains only those tuples (rows) of R that satisfy the specified condition (*predicate*).

Example 3.1

List all staff with a salary greater than £10,000.

$$\sigma_{\text{salary} > 10000}(\text{STAFF})$$

Here, the input relation is Staff and the predicate is salary > 10000. The selection defines a relation containing only those Staff tuples with a salary greater than £10,000. The result of this operation is shown in Figure 3.5. More complex predicates can be generated using the logical operators **AND**, **OR** and **NOT**.

Sno	FName	LName	Address	Tel_No	Position	Sex	DOB	Salary	NIN	Bno
SL21	John	White	19 Taylor St, Cranford, London	0171–884–5112	Manager	M	1-Oct–45	30000	WK442011B	B5
SG37	Ann	Beech	81 George St, Glasgow PA1 2JR	0141–848–3345	Snr Asst	F	10–Nov–60	12000	WL432514C	B3
SG14	David	Ford	63 Ashby St, Partick, Glasgow G11	0141–339–2177	Deputy	M	24–Mar–58	18000	WL220658D	B3
SG5	Susan	Brand	5 Gt Western Rd, Glasgow G12	0141–334–2001	Manager	F	3–Jun–40	24000	WK588932E	B3

Figure 3.5 Selecting Salary > £10,000 from Staff relation.

Projection

$\Pi_{col1, \, ..., \, coln}(R)$	The projection operator works on a single relation R and defines a relation that contains a vertical subset of R, extracting the values of specified attributes and eliminating duplicates.

Example 3.2 _____

Produce a list of salaries for all staff, showing only the Sno, FName, LName and Salary details.

$$\Pi_{sno,fname,lname,salary}(\text{STAFF})$$

In this example, the operation defines a relation that contains only the designated Staff attributes *Sno*, *FName*, *LName* and *Salary*, in the specified order. The result of this operation is shown in Figure 3.6.

Sno	FName	LName	Salary
SL21	John	White	30000
SG37	Ann	Beech	12000
SG14	David	Ford	18000
SA9	Mary	Howe	9000
SG5	Susan	Brand	24000
SL41	Julie	Lee	9000

Figure 3.6 Projecting Staff relation over *Sno*, *FName*, *LName* and *Salary* attributes.

Cartesian product

$R \times S$	The Cartesian product operator defines a relation that is the concatenation of every tuple of relation R with every tuple of relation S.

The selection and projection operations allow us to extract information from only one relation. There are obviously cases where we would like to combine information from several relations. The Cartesian product operator multiplies two relations to define another relation consisting of all possible pairs of tuples from the two relations. Therefore, if one relation has I tuples and N attributes and the other has J tuples and M attributes, the Cartesian product relation will contain $(I*J)$ tuples, with $(N + M)$ attributes. It is possible that the two relations may have attributes with the same name. In this case, the attribute names are prefixed with the relation name to maintain the uniqueness of attribute names within a relation.

Example 3.3 _____

List the names and comments of all renters who have viewed a property.

The names of renters are held in the Renter relation and the details of viewings are held in the Viewing relation. To obtain the list of renters and the comments of properties they have viewed, we need to combine these two relations:

$$(\Pi_{\text{rno,fname,lname}}(\text{RENTER})) \times (\Pi_{\text{rno,pno,comment}}(\text{VIEWING}))$$

This result of this operation is shown in Figure 3.7.

Renter.Rno	FName	LName	Viewing.Rno	Pno	Comment
CR76	John	Kay	CR56	PA14	too small
CR76	John	Kay	CR76	PG4	too remote
CR76	John	Kay	CR56	PG4	
CR76	John	Kay	CR62	PA14	no dining room
CR76	John	Kay	CR56	PG36	
CR56	Aline	Stewart	CR56	PA14	too small
CR56	Aline	Stewart	CR76	PG4	too remote
CR56	Aline	Stewart	CR56	PG4	
CR56	Aline	Stewart	CR62	PA14	no dining room
CR56	Aline	Stewart	CR56	PG36	
CR74	Mike	Ritchie	CR56	PA14	too small
CR74	Mike	Ritchie	CR76	PG4	too remote
CR74	Mike	Ritchie	CR56	PG4	
CR74	Mike	Ritchie	CR62	PA14	no dining room
CR74	Mike	Ritchie	CR56	PG36	
CR62	Mary	Tregear	CR56	PA14	too small
CR62	Mary	Tregear	CR76	PG4	too remote
CR62	Mary	Tregear	CR56	PG4	
CR62	Mary	Tregear	CR62	PA14	no dining room
CR62	Mary	Tregear	CR56	PG36	

Figure 3.7 Cartesian product of reduced Renter and Viewing relations.

In its present form, this relation contains more information than we require. For example, the first tuple of this relation contains different Rno values. To obtain the required list, we need to carry out a selection operation on this relation to extract those tuples where Renter.Rno = Viewing.Rno. The complete operation is thus:

$$\sigma_{\text{renter.rno = viewing.rno}}\left(\left(\Pi_{\text{rno,fname,lname}}(\text{RENTER})\right) \times \left(\Pi_{\text{rno,pno,comment}}(\text{VIEWING})\right)\right)$$

The result of this operation is shown in Figure 3.8. The combination of Cartesian product and selection can be reduced to a single operator, *join*, as we will see shortly.

Renter.Rno	FName	LName	Viewing.Rno	Pno	Comment
CR76	John	Kay	CR76	PG4	too remote
CR56	Aline	Stewart	CR56	PA14	too small
CR56	Aline	Stewart	CR56	PG4	
CR56	Aline	Stewart	CR56	PG36	
CR62	Mary	Tregear	CR62	PA14	no dining room

Figure 3.8 Restricted Cartesian product of reduced Renter and Viewing relations.

Union

> $R \cup S$ The union of two relations R and S with I and J tuples, respectively, is obtained by concatenating them into one relation with a maximum of $(I + J)$ tuples, duplicate tuples being eliminated. R and S must be union-compatible.

Union is possible only if the schema of the two relations match, that is, if they have the same number of attributes with matching domains; in other words, the relations must be **union-compatible**. Note that, in some cases, the projection operator may be used to make two relations union-compatible.

Example 3.4

Construct a list of all areas where there is either a branch or a property.

$$\Pi_{area}(BRANCH) \cup \Pi_{area}(PROPERTY\_FOR\_RENT)$$

To produce union-compatible relations, we first use the projection operator, to project the Branch and Property_for_Rent relations over the attribute Area. We then use the union operator to combine these new relations. The result of this operation is shown in Figure 3.9.

Area
Sidcup
Dyce
Partick
Leigh
Dee
Kilburn
Hyndland

Figure 3.9 Union of two relations.

Set difference

> $R - S$ The difference operator defines a relation consisting of the tuples that are in relation R, but not in S. R and S must be union-compatible.

Example 3.5

City
Bristol

Figure 3.10 Set Difference of two relations.

Construct a list of all cities where there is a branch office but no properties.

$$\Pi_{\text{city}}(\text{BRANCH}) - \Pi_{\text{city}}(\text{PROPERTY\_FOR\_RENT})$$

In a similar way to the previous example, we produce union-compatible relations by projecting the Branch and Property_for_Rent relations over the attribute City. We then use the set difference operator to combine these new relations. The result of this operation is shown in Figure 3.10.

The Join operators

Usually, we want only combinations of the Cartesian product that satisfy certain conditions and so we would normally use a join operator instead of the Cartesian product operator. The join operation is one of the essential operations in relational algebra. It allows us to combine two or more relations to form a new relation. Join is a derivative of Cartesian product; it is equivalent to performing a selection, using the join predicate as the selection formula, over the Cartesian product of the two operand relations. The join is one of the most difficult operations to implement efficiently in a relational DBMS and one of the reasons why relational systems have intrinsic performance problems.

There are various forms of join operator, each with subtle differences, some more useful than others:

- theta-join
- equi-join (a particular type of theta-join)
- natural join
- outer join
- semi-join.

Theta-join (θ-join)

> $R \bowtie_F S$ The theta-join operator defines a relation that contains tuples satisfying the predicate F from the Cartesian product of R and S. The predicate F is of the form $R.a_i \; \theta \; S.b_i$ where θ may be one of the comparison operators ($<$, $<=$, $>$, $>=$, $=$, $\sim=$).

We can rewrite the theta-join in terms of the basic selection and Cartesian product operations:

$$R \bowtie_F S = \sigma_F(R \times S)$$

As with Cartesian product, the degree of a theta-join is the sum of the degrees of the operand relations R and S. In the case where the predicate

F contains only equality ($=$), the term **equi-join** is used instead. Let us look again at the query posed in Example 3.3.

Example 3.6

List the names and comments of all renters who have viewed a property.

In Example 3.3, we used the Cartesian product and selection operations to obtain this list. However, the same result is obtained using the equi-join operator:

$$\text{RENTER} \bowtie_{\text{renter.rno = viewing.rno}} \text{VIEWING}$$

The result of this operation is shown in Figure 3.11.

Rno	FName	LName	Address	Tel_No	Pref_Type	Max_Rent	Rno	Pno	Date	Comment
CR76	John	Kay	56 High St, Putney, London SW1 4EH	0171–774–5632	Flat	425	CR76	PG4	20–Apr–95	too remote
CR56	Aline	Stewart	64 Fern Dr, Pollock, Glasgow G42 0BL	0141–848–1825	Flat	350	CR56	PA14	24–May–95	too small
CR56	Aline	Stewart	64 Fern Dr, Pollock, Glasgow G42 0BL	0141–848–1825	Flat	350	CR56	PG4	26–May–95	
CR56	Aline	Stewart	64 Fern Dr, Pollock, Glasgow G42 0BL	0141–848–1825	Flat	350	CR56	PG36	28–Apr–95	
CR62	Mary	Tregear	5 Tarbot Rd, Kildary, Aberdeen AB9 3ST	01224–196720	Flat	600	CR62	PA14	14–May–95	no dining room

Figure 3.11 Equi-join of Renter and Viewing relations.

Natural join

> $R \bowtie S$ The natural-join is an equi-join of the two relations R and S over all common attributes x. One occurrence of each common attribute is eliminated from the result.

The degree of a natural join is the sum of the degrees of the relations R and S less the number of attributes in x. For example, the natural join of Renter and Viewing (RENTER $\bowtie$ VIEWING) returns the same relation as shown in Figure 3.11 with one of the columns entitled Rno omitted.

Outer join
Often in joining two relations, a tuple in one relation does not have a matching tuple in the other relation; in other words, there is no matching value in the

join columns. The user may want a row from one of the relations to appear in the result even when there is no matching value in the other relation. This may be accomplished using the outer-join.

> $R \righttie S$ The outer join is a join in which tuples from R that do not have matching values in the common columns of S are also included in the result relation.

Missing values in the second relation are set to null. The outer join is becoming more widely available in relational systems and is now a specified operator in the new SQL standard (see Section 11.3.7). The advantage of an outer join is that information is preserved; that is, the outer join preserves tuples that would have been lost by other types of join.

Example 3.7

Produce a status report on property viewings.

In this case, we want to produce a relation consisting of the properties that have been viewed with comments and those that have not been viewed. This can be achieved using the following outer join:

$$\Pi_{\text{pno,street,city}}(\text{PROPERTY\_FOR\_RENT}) \righttie \text{VIEWING}$$

The resulting relation is shown in Figure 3.12. Note that property PL94 has had no viewings, but this tuple is still contained in the result with nulls for the attributes from the Viewing relation.

Figure 3.12 Outer-join of Property_for_ Rent and Viewing relations.

Pno	Street	City	Rno	Date	Comment
PA14	16 Holhead	Aberdeen	CR56	24–May–95	too small
PA14	16 Holhead	Aberdeen	CR62	14–May–95	no dining room
PL94	6 Argyll St	London	**null**	**null**	**null**
PG4	6 Lawrence St	Glasgow	CR76	20–Apr–95	too remote
PG4	6 Lawrence St	Glasgow	CR56	26–May–95	
PG36	2 Manor Rd	Glasgow	CR56	28–Apr–95	

Strictly speaking, Example 3.7 is a **left (natural) outer-join** as it keeps every tuple in the left-hand relation in the result. Similarly, there is a **right outer join** that keeps every tuple in the right-hand relation in the result. There is also a **full outer join** that keeps all tuples in both relations, padding tuples with nulls when no matching tuples are found.

Semi-join

> $R \triangleright_F S$ The semi-join operator defines a relation that contains the tuples of R that participate in the join of R with S.

The advantage of a semi-join is that it decreases the number of tuples that need to be handled to form the join. It is particularly useful for computing joins in distributed systems (see Sections 16.4.2 and 16.5.3). We can rewrite the semi-join using the projection and join operations:

$$R \triangleright_F S = \Pi_A (R \bowtie_F S) \quad A \text{ is the set of all attributes for } R.$$

This is actually a semi-theta-join; there are variants for semi-equi-join and semi-natural join.

Example 3.8

List complete details of all staff who work at the branch in Partick.

If we are interested in seeing only the attributes of the Staff relation, we can use the following semi-join operation, producing the relation shown in Figure 3.13.

$$\text{STAFF} \triangleright_{\text{staff.bno = branch.bno and branch.area = 'Partick'}} \text{BRANCH}$$

Sno	FName	LName	Address	Tel_No	Position	Sex	DOB	Salary	NIN	Bno
SG37	Ann	Beech	81 George St, Glasgow PA1 2JR	0141-848-3345	Snr Asst	F	10-Nov-60	12000	WL432514C	B3
SG14	David	Ford	63 Ashby St, Partick, Glasgow G11	0141-339-2177	Deputy	M	24-Mar-58	18000	WL220658D	B3
SG5	Susan	Brand	5 Gt Western Rd, Glasgow G12	0141-334-2001	Manager	F	3-Jun-40	24000	WK588932E	B3

Figure 3.13 Semi-join of Staff and Branch relations.

Intersection

> $R \cap S$ The intersection consists of the set of all tuples that are in both R and S. R and S must be union-compatible.

We can express the intersection operator in terms of the set difference operation:

$$R \cap S = R - (R - S)$$

Division

The division operator is useful for a particular type of query that occurs quite frequently in database applications. Assume relation R is defined over the attribute set A and relation S is defined over the attribute set B such that $B \subseteq A$ (B is a subset of A). Let $C = A - B$, that is, C is the set of attributes of R that are not attributes of S. We have the following definition of the division operator:

$R \div S$ The division consists of the set of tuples from R defined over the attributes C that match the combination of **every** tuple in S.

We can express the division operator in terms of the basic operations:

$$T_1 = \Pi_C(R)$$
$$T_2 = \Pi_C((S \times T_1) - R)$$
$$T = T_1 - T_2$$

Example 3.9

Identify all renters who have viewed all properties with three rooms.

We can use the selection operator to find all properties with three rooms followed by the projection operator to produce a relation containing only these property numbers. We can then use the following division operator to obtain the new relation shown in Figure 3.14.

$$(\Pi_{\text{rno, pno}}(\text{VIEWING})) \div (\Pi_{\text{pno}}(\sigma_{\text{rooms}=3}(\text{PROPERTY\_FOR\_RENT})))$$

$\Pi_{\text{rno,pno}}(\text{VIEWING})$

Rno	Pno
CR56	PA14
CR76	PG4
CR56	PG4
CR62	PA14
CR56	PG36

$\Pi_{\text{pno}}(\sigma_{\text{rooms}=3}(\text{PROPERTY\_FOR\_RENT}))$

Pno
PG4
PG36

RESULT

Rno
CR56

Figure 3.14 Result of division operation on Viewing and Property_for_Rent relations.

3.4.2 Relational Calculus

A certain order is always explicitly specified in a relational algebra expression, and a strategy for evaluating the query is implied. In relational calculus, there is no description of how to evaluate a query; a relational calculus query specifies *what* is to be retrieved rather than *how* to retrieve it.

The relational calculus is not related to differential and integral calculus in mathematics, but takes its name from a branch of symbolic logic called the **predicate calculus**. When applied to databases, it is found in two forms: **tuple-oriented** relational calculus, as originally proposed by Codd (1972a), and **domain-oriented** relational calculus, as proposed by Lacroix and Pirotte (1977). We will not give a formal definition of relational calculus, but we will provide an overview of it. The interested reader is again referred to Ullman (1988).

In first-order logic or predicate calculus, a **predicate** is a truth-valued function with arguments. When we substitute values for the arguments, the function yields an expression, called a **proposition**, that can be either true or false. For example, the sentences 'John White is a member of staff' and 'John White earns more than Ann Beech' are both propositions, since we can determine whether they are true or false. In the first case, we have a function 'is a member of staff' with one argument (John White); in the second case, we have a function 'earns more than' with two arguments (John White and Ann Beech). On the other hand, 'Look at that!' is not a predicate.

If a predicate contains a variable, as in 'x is a member of staff', there must be an associated **range** for x. When we substitute some values of the range for x, the proposition may be true; for other values, it may be false. For example, if the range is the set of all people and we replace x by John White, the proposition, 'John White is a member of staff', is true. If we replace x by the name of a person who is not a member of staff, the proposition is false.

If P is a predicate, then we can write the set of all x such that P is true for x as:

$$\{x \mid P(x)\}$$

We may connect predicates by the logical connectives AND ($\wedge$), OR ($\vee$), and NOT ($\sim$) to form **compound predicates**.

Tuple-oriented relational calculus

In tuple-oriented relational calculus we are interested in finding tuples for which a predicate is true. The calculus is based on the use of **tuple variables**. A tuple variable is a variable that 'ranges over' a named relation: that is, a variable whose only permitted values are tuples of the relation. (The word *range* here does not correspond to the mathematical use of range, but corresponds to a mathematical domain.)

For example, to specify the range of a tuple variable T as the Staff relation, we write:

RANGE OF T IS STAFF

To express the query 'Find the set of all tuples T such that $P(T)$ is true', we can write:

$$\{T \mid P(T)\}$$

P is called a **formula** (or **well-formed formula**, or **wff** in mathematical logic). For example, to express the query 'Find the Sno, FName, LName, Address, Tel_No, Position, Sex, DOB, Salary, NIN and Bno of all staff earning more than £10,000', we can write:

RANGE OF T IS STAFF

$\{T \mid T.Salary > 10000\}$

T.Salary means the value of the Salary attribute for the tuple T. To find a particular attribute, such as Salary, we would write:

RANGE OF T IS STAFF

$\{T.Salary \mid T.Salary > 10000\}$

There are two **quantifiers** used with formulae to tell how many instances the predicate applies to. The **existential quantifier** $\exists$ ('there exists') is used in formulae that must be true for at least one instance, such as:

RANGE OF B IS BRANCH

$\exists B(B.Bno = T.Bno \land B.City = \text{'London'})$

This means 'There exists a Branch tuple that has the same Bno as the Bno of the current Staff tuple, T, and is located in London'. The **universal quantifier** $\forall$ ('for all') is used in statements about every instance, such as:

$\forall T(T.City \sim = \text{'London'})$

This means 'For all Staff tuples, the address is not in London'. Using the equivalence rules for logical operations, we can rewrite this as:

$\sim \exists T(T.City = \text{'London'})$

which means 'There are no staff with an address in London'.

Tuple variables are called **free variables** unless they are qualified by a $\forall$ or $\exists$, in which case they are called **bound variables**. As with the English alphabet, in which some sequences of characters do not form a correctly structured sentence, so in calculus not every sequence of formulae is acceptable. The formulae should be those sequences that are unambiguous and make sense. A (well-formed) formula in predicate calculus is defined by the following rules:

- If P is an n-ary formula (a predicate with n arguments) and $t_1, t_2, \ldots, t_n$ are either constants or variables, then $P(t_1, t_2, \ldots, t_n)$ is a formula.
- If t_1 and t_2 are either constants or variables from the same domain and θ is one of the comparison operators ($<, <=, >, >=, =, \sim=$) then $t_1 \; \theta \; t_2$ is a formula.
- If F_1 and F_2 are formulae, so are their conjunction, $F_1 \land F_2$; their disjunction, $F_1 \lor F_2$; and the negation, $\sim F_1$. Also, if F is a formula with free variable X, then $\exists X(F)$ and $\forall X(F)$ are both formulae.

Example 3.10 _____

List the staff who manage properties in Glasgow.

> RANGE OF S IS STAFF
>
> RANGE OF P IS PROPERTY_FOR_RENT
>
> $\{S \mid \exists P(P.sno = S.sno \land P.city = \text{'Glasgow'})\}$

The Sno attribute in the Property_for_Rent relation holds the staff number of the member of staff who manages the property. We could reformulate the query as 'For each member of staff whose details we want to list, there exists a tuple in the relation Property_for_Rent for that member of staff with the value of the attribute City in that tuple being Glasgow.'

Note that in this formulation of the query, there is no indication of a strategy for executing the query – the DBMS is free to decide the operations and their execution order to fulfil the request. On the other hand, the equivalent relational algebra formulation would be 'Select tuples from Property_for_Rent such that the City is Glasgow and perform their join with the Staff relation'.

Before we complete this section, we should mention that it is possible for a calculus expression to generate an infinite set. We have avoided this problem by using range variables that are defined by a separate RANGE statement. However, some authors do not use this statement but instead define the range explicitly within the formula. In this case, it is possible to define an infinite set; for example:

$$\{S \mid \sim (S \in \text{Staff})\}$$

would mean the set of tuples that are not in the Staff relation. Such an expression is said to be **unsafe**. To avoid this, we have to add a restriction that all values that appear in the result must be values in the domain of the formula. In this example, the domain of the formula is the set of all values appearing in the Staff relation. The interested reader is referred to Ullman (1988).

Domain-oriented relational calculus

In domain-oriented relational calculus, we use variables that take their values from domains instead of tuples of relations. If $P(d_1, d_2, \ldots, d_n)$ stands for a predicate with variables $d_1, d_2, \ldots, d_n$, then:

$$\{d_1, d_2, \ldots, d_n \mid P(d_1, d_2, \ldots, d_n)\}$$

means the set of all domain variables $d_1, d_2, \ldots, d_n$ for which the predicate $P(d_1, d_2, \ldots, d_n)$ is true. In the domain-oriented relational calculus, we often want to test for a **membership condition**, to determine whether values belong to a relation. The expression $R(x, y)$ evaluates to true *if and only if* there is a tuple in relation R with values x, y for its two attributes.

Example 3.11

Find the surnames of all managers who have salaries above £10,000.

{LName | ∃ Position, ∃ Salary
  (STAFF(LName, Position, Salary) AND Position = 'Manager'
  AND Salary > 10000)}

This query is **safe**. When the domain relational calculus is restricted to safe expressions, it is equivalent to the tuple relational calculus restricted to safe expressions, which in turn is equivalent to relational algebra. This means that for every relational algebra expression there is an equivalent expression in the relational calculus, and for every tuple or domain relational calculus expression there is an equivalent relational algebra expression.

3.4.3   Other Languages

Although relational calculus is hard to understand and use, it was recognized that its non-procedural property is exceedingly desirable, and this resulted in a search for other easy to use non-procedural techniques. This led to another two categories of relational languages: transform-oriented and graphical.

Transform-oriented languages are a class of non-procedural languages that use relations to transform input data into required outputs. These languages provide easy-to-use structures for expressing what is desired in terms of what is known. SQUARE (Boyce *et al.*, 1975), SEQUEL (Chamberlin *et al.*, 1976) and SEQUEL's offspring, SQL, are all transform-oriented languages.

Graphical languages provide the user with a picture or illustration of the structure of the relation. The user fills in an example of what is wanted and the system returns the required data in that format. QBE (Query-by-Example) is an example of a graphical language (Zloof, 1977). We will demonstrate the capabilities of QBE in Chapter 13.

Another category is **fourth-generation languages** (4GLs), which allow a complete customized application to be created using a limited set of commands in a user-friendly, often menu-driven environment (see Section 2.2). Some systems accept a form of *natural language*, a restricted version of natural English, sometimes called a **fifth-generation language** (5GL), although this development is still in its infancy.

3.5   Views

In the three-level architecture presented in Chapter 2, we described an external view as the structure of the database as it appears to a particular user. In the relational model, the word 'view' has a slightly different meaning. Rather than it being the entire external model of a user, a view is a **virtual relation** or, in other words, a relation that does not actually exist. A view can be constructed by performing operations such as the relational algebra selection, projection, join or other calculations on the values of existing base relations. Thus, an external model can consist of both base (conceptual-level) relations and views derived from the base relations. In this section, we discuss virtual relations or **views** in relational systems.

3.5.1 Terminology

The relations we have been dealing with so far in this chapter are known as base relations:

Base relation	A named relation, corresponding to an entity in the conceptual schema, whose tuples are physically stored in the database.

We can define views in terms of base relations:

View	A view is the dynamic result of one or more relational operations operating on the base relations to produce another relation. A view is a **virtual relation** that does not actually exist in the database but is produced upon request by a particular user, at the time of request.

A view is a relation that appears to the user to exist, can be manipulated as if it were a base relation, but does not exist in storage in the sense that the base relations do (although its definition is stored in the system catalog). The contents of a view are defined as a query on one or more base relations. Any operations on the view are automatically translated into operations on the relations from which it is derived. Views are **dynamic**, meaning that changes made to the base relations that affect the view are immediately reflected in the view. When users make permitted changes to the view, those changes are made to the underlying relations. In this section we describe the purpose of views and briefly examine restrictions that apply to updates made through views. However, we defer treatment of how views are defined and processed until Section 12.1.

3.5.2 Purpose of Views

The view mechanism is desirable for several reasons:

- It provides a powerful and flexible security mechanism by hiding parts of the database from certain users. The user is not aware of the existence of any attributes or tuples that are missing from the view.

- It permits users to access data in a way that is customized to their needs, so that the same data can be seen by different users in different ways, at the same time.

- It can simplify complex operations on the base relations. For example, if a view is defined as a join of two relations, the user may now perform the more simple unary operations of selection and projection on the view, which will be translated by the DBMS into equivalent operations on the join.

A view should be designed to support the external model that the user finds familiar. For example:

- A user might need Branch records that contain the names of managers as well as the other attributes already in Branch. This view is created by joining the Branch and Staff relations and then projecting on the attributes of interest.
- Another user might need to see Staff records without the Salary attribute. For this user, a projection is performed to create a view that does not have the Salary attribute.
- Attributes may be renamed, so that the user accustomed to calling the Bno of branches by the full name Branch Number may see that column heading. The order of columns may be changed, so that Bno may appear as the last column instead of the first column in a view.
- A member of staff may see property records only for those properties that they manage. Here, a selection operation is performed so that only a horizontal subset of the Property_for_Rent relation is seen.

Although all of these examples demonstrate that a view provides logical data independence (see Section 2.1.5), views allow more significant logical data independence when the conceptual level is reorganized. If a new attribute is added to a relation, existing users can be unaware of its existence if their views are defined to exclude it. If an existing relation is rearranged or split up, a view may be defined so that users can continue to see their original views. In the case of splitting up a relation, the original relation can be recreated by defining a view from the join of the new relations, provided that the split is done in such a way that the original can be reconstructed. We can ensure that this is possible by placing the primary key in both of the new relations. Thus, if we originally had a Renter relation of the form:

Renter (<u>Rno</u>, FName, LName, Address, Tel_No, Pref_Type, Max_Rent)

we could reorganize it into two new relations:

Renter_Details (<u>Rno</u>, FName, LName, Address, Tel_No)
Renter_Reqts (<u>Rno</u>, Pref_Type, Max_Rent)

Users and applications could still access the data using the old relation structure, which would be recreated by defining a view called Renter as the natural join of Renter_Details and Renter_Reqts, with Rno as the join attribute.

3.5.3 Updating Views

All updates to a base relation should be immediately reflected in all views that reference that base relation. Similarly, if a view is updated, then the underlying base relation should reflect the change. However, there are restrictions on the types of modifications that can be made through views. We summarize below the conditions under which most systems determine whether an update is allowed through a view:

- Updates are allowed through a view defined using a simple query involving a single base relation and containing either the primary key or a candidate key of the base relation.

- Updates are not allowed through views involving multiple base relations.

- Updates are not allowed through views involving aggregation or grouping operations.

Classes of views have been defined, which are **theoretically not updatable**, **theoretically updatable** and **partially updatable**. Views are discussed in more detail in Section 12.1.

3.6 When is a DBMS Relational?

As we mentioned in Section 3.1, there are now several hundred relational DBMSs for both mainframe and microcomputer environments. Unfortunately, some do not strictly follow the definition of the relational model. In particular, some traditional vendors of DBMS products based upon network and hierarchic data models have implemented a few relational features to claim they are in some way relational. Concerned that the full power and implications of the relational approach were being distorted, Codd (1985a, 1985b) specified 12 rules (13 with Rule 0, the foundational rule) for a relational DBMS. These rules form a yardstick against which the 'real' relational DBMS products can be identified.

Over the years, Codd's rules have caused a great deal of controversy. Some argue that these rules are nothing more than an academic exercise. Some claim that their products already satisfy most, if not all, rules. This discussion generated an increasing awareness within the user and vendor communities of the essential properties for a true relational DBMS.

To emphasize the implications of the rules, we have reorganized the rules into the following five functional areas:

(1)   foundational rules
(2)   structural rules
(3)   integrity rules
(4)   data manipulation rules
(5)   data independence rules.

Foundational rules (Rule 0 and Rule 12)

Rules 0 and 12 provide a litmus test to assess whether a system is a relational DBMS. If these rules are not complied with, the product should not be considered relational.

Rule 0 – Foundational rule

> For any system that is advertised as, or claimed to be, a relational database management system, that system must be able to manage databases entirely through its relational capabilities.

This rule means that the DBMS should not have to resort to any non-relational operations to achieve any of its data management capabilities such as data definition and data manipulation.

Rule 12 – Nonsubversion rule

> If a relational system has a low-level (single-record-at-a-time) language, that low level cannot be used to subvert or bypass the integrity rules and constraints expressed in the higher-level relational language (multiple-records-at-a-time).

This rule requires that all database access be controlled by the DBMS so that the integrity of the database cannot be compromised without the knowledge of the user or the Database Administrator (DBA). However, this does not prohibit the use of a language with a record-at-a-time interface.

Structural rules (Rule 1 and Rule 6)

The fundamental structural concept of the relational model is the table. Codd states that an RDBMS must support several structural features, including tables, domains, primary and foreign keys. There should be a primary key for each relation in the database.

Rule 1 – Information representation

> All information in a relational database is represented explicitly at the logical level and in exactly one way – by values in tables.

This rule requires that all information, even the metadata held in the system catalog, must be stored as relations, and managed by the same operational functions as would be used to maintain data. The reference to 'logical level' means that physical constructs, such as indexes, are not represented and need not be explicitly referenced in a retrieval operation, even if they exist.

Rule 6 – View updating

> All views that are theoretically updatable are also updatable by the system.

This rule deals explicitly with view tables. In Section 12.1.5, we discuss the conditions for view updatability. This rule states that if a view is theoretically updatable, then the DBMS should be able to perform the update. No system truly supports this feature, because conditions have not been found yet to identify all theoretically updatable views.

Integrity rules (Rule 3 and Rule 10)

Codd specifies two data integrity rules. The support of data integrity is an important criterion when assessing the suitability of a product. The more integrity constraints that can be maintained by the DBMS product, rather than in each application program, the better the guarantee of data quality.

Rule 3 – Systematic treatment of null values

> Null values (distinct from the empty character string or a string of blank characters and distinct from zero or any other number) are supported for representing missing information and inapplicable information in a systematic way, independent of data type.

Rule 10 – Integrity independence

> Integrity constraints specific to a particular relational database must be definable in the relational data sublanguage[†] and storable in the catalog, not in the application programs.

Codd makes a specific point that integrity constraints must be stored in the system catalogue, rather than encapsulated in application programs or user interfaces. Storing the constraints in the system catalog has the advantage of centralized control and enforcement.

Data manipulation rules (Rule 2, Rule 4, Rule 5 and Rule 7)

There are 18 manipulation features that an ideal relational DBMS should support. These features define the completeness of the query language (where, in this sense, 'query' includes insert, update and delete operations). The data manipulation rules guide the application of the 18 manipulation features. Adherence to these rules insulates the user and application programs from

---

[†] A sublanguage is one that does not attempt to include constructs for all computing needs. Relational algebra and relational calculus are database sublanguages.

the physical and logical mechanisms that implement the data management capabilities.

Rule 2 – Guaranteed access

> Each and every datum (atomic value) in a relational database is guaranteed to be logically accessible by resorting to a combination of table name, primary key value and column name.

Rule 4 – Dynamic on-line catalogue based on the relational model

> The database description is represented at the logical level in the same way as ordinary data, so that authorized users can apply the same relational language to its interrogation as they apply to the regular data.

This rule specifies that there is only one language for manipulating metadata as well as data, and moreover, that there is only one logical structure (relations) used to store system information.

Rule 5 – Comprehensive data sublanguage

> A relational system may support several languages and various modes of terminal use (for example, the *fill-in-the-blanks* mode). However, there must be at least one language whose statements can express all of the following items: (1) data definition; (2) view definition; (3) data manipulation (interactive and by program); (4) integrity constraints; (5) authorization (6) transaction boundaries (begin, commit, and rollback).

Note that the new ISO standard for SQL provides all these functions, so any language complying with this standard will automatically satisfy this rule (see Chapters 11 and 12).

Rule 7 – High-level insert, update, delete

> The capability of handling a base relation or a derived relation (that is, a view) as a single operand applies not only to the retrieval of data but also to the insertion, update, and deletion of data.

Data independence rules (Rule 8, Rule 9 and Rule 11)

Codd defines three rules to specify the independence of data from the applications that use the data. Adherence to these rules ensures that both users and developers are protected from having to change the applications following low-level reorganizations of the database.

Rule 8 – Physical data independence

> Application programs and terminal activities remain logically unimpaired whenever any changes are made in either storage representations or access methods.

Rule 9 – Logical data independence

> Application programs and terminal activities remain logically unimpaired when information-preserving changes of any kind that theoretically permit unimpairment are made to the base tables.

Rule 11 – Distribution independence

> The data manipulation sublanguage of a relational DBMS must enable application programs and inquiries to remain logically the same whether and whenever data are physically centralized or distributed.

Distribution independence means that an application program that accesses the DBMS on a single computer should also work without modification, even if the data is moved about from computer to computer, in a network environment. In other words, the end-user should be given the illusion that the data is centralized on a single machine, and the responsibility of locating the data from (possibly) multiple sites and recomposing it should always reside with the system. Note that this rule does not say that to be fully relational the DBMS must support a distributed database, but it does say that the query language would remain the same if and when this capability is introduced and the data is distributed. Distributed databases will be discussed in Chapter 16.

Chapter Summary

- A mathematical **relation** is a subset of the Cartesian product of two or more sets. In database terms, a relation is any subset of the Cartesian product of the domains of the attributes. A relation is normally written as a set of n-tuples, in which each element is chosen from the appropriate domain.

- Relations are physically represented as **tables**, with the rows corresponding to individual tuples and the columns to attributes.

- The structure of the relation, with domain specifications and other constraints, is part of the **intension** of the database, while the relation with all its tuples written out represents an instance or **extension** of the database.

- Properties of database relations are: each cell contains exactly one atomic value, attribute names are distinct, attribute values come from the same domain, attribute order is immaterial, tuple order is immaterial and there are no duplicate tuples.

- The **degree** of a relation is the number of attributes, while the **cardinality** is the number of tuples. A **unary** relation has one attribute, a **binary** relation has two, a **ternary** relation has three and an **n-ary** relation has n attributes.

- A **superkey** is a set of attributes that identifies tuples of the relation uniquely, while a **candidate key** is a minimal superkey. A **primary key** is the candidate key chosen for use in identification of tuples. A relation must always have a primary key. A **foreign key** is an attribute or set of attributes within one relation that is the candidate key of another relation.

- A **null** represents a value for an attribute that is unknown at the present time or is not defined for this tuple.

- **Entity integrity** is a constraint that states that in a base relation no attribute of a primary key can be null. Referential integrity states that foreign key values must match a candidate key value of some tuple in the home relation or be wholly null.

- Relational data manipulation languages are sometimes classified as **procedural** or **non-procedural, transform-oriented, graphical, fourth generation** or **fifth generation**. Relational algebra is a formal procedural language. Its operations include selection, projection, Cartesian product, union, intersection, set difference, division and several types of joins. **Relational calculus** is a formal non-procedural language that uses predicates. Relational algebra is logically equivalent to a safe subset of relational calculus (and vice versa).

- A **view** in the relational model is a **virtual relation**. The view provides security and allows the designer to customize a user's model. Views are created dynamically for users. Not all views are updatable.

REVIEW QUESTIONS

3.1 Discuss each of the following concepts in the context of the relational data model:
(a) relation
(b) attribute
(c) tuple
(d) intension and extension
(e) degree and cardinality.

3.2 Discuss the differences between the candidate keys and the primary key of a relation. Explain what is meant by a foreign key. How do foreign keys of relations relate to candidate keys?

3.3 Define the two principal integrity rules for the relational model. Discuss why it is desirable to enforce these rules.

3.4 Define the five basic relational algebra operations. Define the remaining three relational algebra operations in terms of the five basic operations.

3.5 What is a view? Discuss the difference between a view and a base relation. Explain what happens when a user accesses a database through a view.

EXERCISES

The following tables form part of a database held in a relational DBMS:

Hotel   (Hotel_No, Name, Address)
Room   (Room_No, Hotel_No, Type, Price)
Booking   (Hotel_No, Guest_No, Date_From, Date_To, Room_No)
Guest   (Guest_No, Name, Address)

where Hotel contains hotel details and Hotel_No is the primary key

Room contains room details for each hotel and Hotel_No/Room_No forms the primary key

Booking contains details of the bookings and the primary key comprises Hotel_No, Guest_No and Date_From

and Guest contains guest details and Guest_No is the primary key.

3.6 Generate the relational algebra for the following queries:
(a) List all hotels.
(b) List all single rooms with a price below £20 per night.
(c) List the names and addresses of all guests.
(d) List the price and type of all rooms at the Grosvenor Hotel.
(e) List all guests currently staying at the Grosvenor Hotel.
(f) List the details of all rooms at the Grosvenor Hotel, including the name of the guest staying in the room, if the room is occupied.
(g) List the guest details (Guest_No, Name and Address) of all guests staying at the Grosvenor Hotel.

3.7 Using relational algebra, create a view of all rooms in the Grosvenor Hotel, excluding price details. What would be the advantages of this view?

3.8 Produce the equivalent tuple and domain relational calculus statements for the above queries.

3.9 Explain how the entity and referential integrity rules apply to these relations.

3.10 Analyse the RDBMSs that you are currently using. Determine the support the system provides for primary keys, alternate keys, foreign keys, relational integrity and views. What types of relational languages does the system provide? For each of the languages provided, what are the equivalent operations for the eight relational algebra operations?

4 Database Planning, Design and Administration

Chapter Objectives

In this chapter you will learn:

- The main phases that form the lifecycle of an information system.
- The relationship between the information system lifecycle and the development of a database application system.
- The main stages of the database application lifecycle.
- The main phases of database design: logical and physical database design.
- The benefits of CASE support during the database application lifecycle.
- The types of criteria to use in evaluating a DBMS.
- How to evaluate and select a DBMS.
- The distinction between data administration and database administration.
- The roles and functions of data and database administration.
- The organizational position of data and database administration.

Software has now surpassed hardware as the key to the success of many computer-based systems. Unfortunately, the track record at developing software systems is not particularly impressive. The last few decades have seen the proliferation of software applications, ranging from small, relatively simple applications consisting of a few lines of code, to large, complex applications consisting of millions of lines of code. Many of these applications required constant maintenance. This involved correcting faults that had been detected, implementing new user requirements and modifying the software to run on new or upgraded platforms. The effort spent on maintenance began to absorb resources at an alarming rate. As a result, many major software projects were late, over budget, unreliable, difficult to maintain and performed poorly. This led to what has become known as the 'software crisis'. Although this term was first used in the late 1960s, more than 30 years later, the crisis is still with us. As a result, some authors now refer to the software crisis as the 'software depression'.

As an indication of this crisis, the US Army found that of several Federal projects:

- 47% were delivered, but not used.
- 29% were paid for, but not delivered.
- 19% were abandoned or reworked.
- 3% were used after changes were made.
- **Only 2%** were used as delivered.

There are several major reasons for the failure of software projects:

- lack of a complete requirements specification;
- lack of an appropriate development methodology;
- poor decomposition of design into manageable components.

In this chapter, we present an overview of the main phases of the information systems lifecycle, and discuss how this relates to the development of database applications. We then discuss the activities that should be undertaken at each stage of the database application lifecycle to produce a successful system. Many of these activities will be expanded upon in later chapters. We conclude with a discussion of the main personnel responsible for the planning, design and administration of a database.

4.1 Overview of the Information Systems Lifecycle

Information system	The resources that enable the collection, management, control and dissemination of information throughout an organization.

Since the 1970s, database systems have been gradually replacing file-based systems as part of an organization's Information System (IS) infrastructure. At the same time, there has been a growing recognition that information is an important corporate resource that should be treated with respect, like all other organizational resources. This resulted in many organizations setting up whole departments or functional areas responsible for the management of corporate information and the corporate database. The roles of the Data Administrator (DA) and Database Administrator (DBA) have also been identified, and given the responsibility for overseeing and controlling the activities associated with the corporate data and database application lifecycle, respectively.

A computer-based information system includes the following components:

- database,
- database software,
- application software,
- computer hardware including storage media,
- personnel using and developing the system.

The database is a fundamental component of an information system, and its development and usage should be viewed from the perspective of the wider requirements of the organization. Therefore, the lifecycle of an organizational information system is inherently linked to the lifecycle of the database system that supports it. Typically, the stages in the lifecycle of an information system include: planning, requirements collection and analysis, design (including database design), prototyping, implementation, testing, conversion and operational maintenance. In this chapter, we review each of the stages of the IS lifecycle from the perspective of developing a database application system. However, it is important to recognize that the development of a database should also be viewed from the broader perspective of developing a component part of the larger organization IS. The information systems lifecycle is also known as the **Software Development Lifecycle (SDLC)**. Throughout this book, we use only the term 'information system lifecycle'.

4.2   The Database Application Lifecycle

As previously described, a database system is a fundamental component of the larger organization information system. Therefore, the database application lifecycle is inherently associated with the information system lifecycle. The stages of the database application lifecycle are shown in Figure 4.1. It is important to recognize that the stages of the database application lifecycle are not strictly sequential, but involve some amount of repetition of stages, sometimes known as **feedback loops**. For example, problems encountered dur-

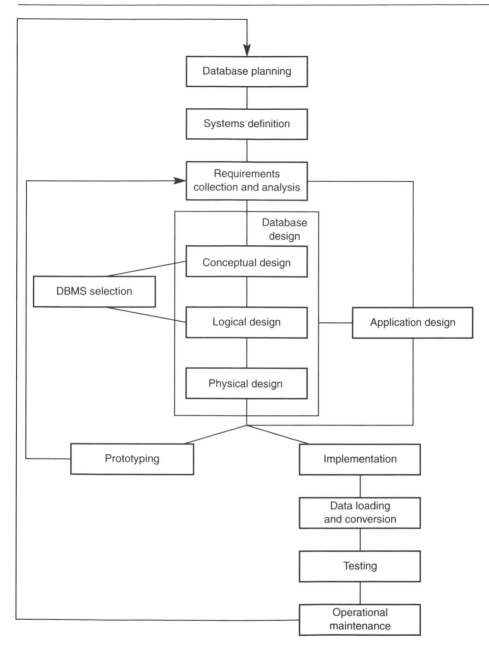

Figure 4.1 The database application lifecycle.

ing database design may necessitate additional requirements collection and analysis. As there are feedback loops between most stages, we show only some of the more obvious ones.

The main activities associated with each stage are listed below.

- *Database planning* This involves planning how the stages of the lifecycle can be realized most efficiently and effectively.

- *System definition* This involves specifying the scope and boundaries of the database application, its users and application areas.

- *Requirements collection and analysis* This involves the collection and analysis of the requirements of users and application areas.

- *Database design* This includes the conceptual, logical and physical design of the database itself.

- *DBMS selection (optional)* This involves selecting a suitable DBMS for the information system.

- *Application design* This involves designing the application programs that use and process the database.

- *Prototyping (optional)* This involves building a working model of the database application system, which allows the designers or users to test the system.

- *Implementation* This involves creating the conceptual, external and internal database definitions and the application programs.

- *Data conversion and loading* This stage is required when replacing an old system with a new system. The data is loaded directly from the old system to the new system or, if appropriate, the old database file(s) are converted to the format required by the new DBMS and then loaded. Any application programs from the old system are also be converted for use by the new system, if possible.

- *Testing* The database application system is tested and validated against the requirements specified by the users.

- *Operational maintenance* The database application system is fully implemented. The system is continuously monitored and maintained. When required, new requirements are incorporated into the database application system through the preceding stages of the lifecycle.

The design, implementation and loading or data conversion phases are part of the design and implementation phases of the larger information systems lifecycle listed in Section 4.1. In the following sections, we review the activities associated with each stage of the database application lifecycle in more detail. For small database applications, with a small number of users, the lifecycle need not be very complex. However, when designing a medium to large database application with tens to thousands of users, using hundreds of queries and application programs, the lifecycle can become extremely complex. Throughout this chapter, we concentrate on activities associated with the development of medium to large database applications.

4.2.1 Database Planning

Database planning	The management activities that allow the stages of the database application to be realized as efficiently and effectively as possible.

As with all software planning, database planning has three main components: the work to be done; the resources with which to do it; and the money to pay for it all. Database planning must be integrated with the organization's overall planning strategy as one of its main purposes is to support the business activities and strategies. As database activities lie within the Information Technology (IT)/Information System (IS) area, any development strategies are influenced by the broader IT/IS development strategies. Clear distinctions are now made in large organizations between IT and IS and, when planning for information systems (that is, deciding what to do with IT), several methodologies are advocated, each of which complements the others in resolving the three main issues involved in formulating IS strategy. These three issues are:

- identification of business plans and goals with subsequent determination of information systems needs;
- evaluation of current information systems to determine existing strengths and weaknesses;
- appraisal of IT opportunities that might yield competitive advantage.

The methodologies used to resolve these issues are outside the scope of this book; however, the interested reader is referred to Earl (1989) for a fuller discussion.

To support database planning, a **corporate data model** can be developed that shows the main entities and relationships of the organization and identifies the functional areas of the organization. Typically, the corporate data model is represented as a simplified Entity–Relationship (ER) diagram (see Chapter 5). The model does not necessarily have to be fully normalized, but it indicates, for example, where data sharing is necessary between different functional areas. Typically, the functional areas for development are assigned priorities in line with corporate strategy and help to define the scope of the database for system development. The data administrator can then develop plans to achieve these development goals. The corporate data model for *DreamHome* is shown in Figure 4.2. For simplicity, only three functional areas are identified: Buying, Rentals and Advertising.

Database planning should also include the development of standards that govern how data will be collected, how the format should be specified, what necessary documentation will be needed, and how design and implementation should proceed. Standards can be very time-consuming to develop and maintain, requiring resources to set them up initially, and to continue maintaining them. However, a well-designed set of standards provides a basis for training staff and measuring quality control, and can ensure that work conforms to a pattern, irrespective of staff skills and experience. For example, specific rules may govern how data items can be named in the data dictionary which, in turn, may prevent both redundancy and inconsistency. Any legal or company requirements concerning the data should be documented, such as the stipulation that some types of data must be treated confidentially.

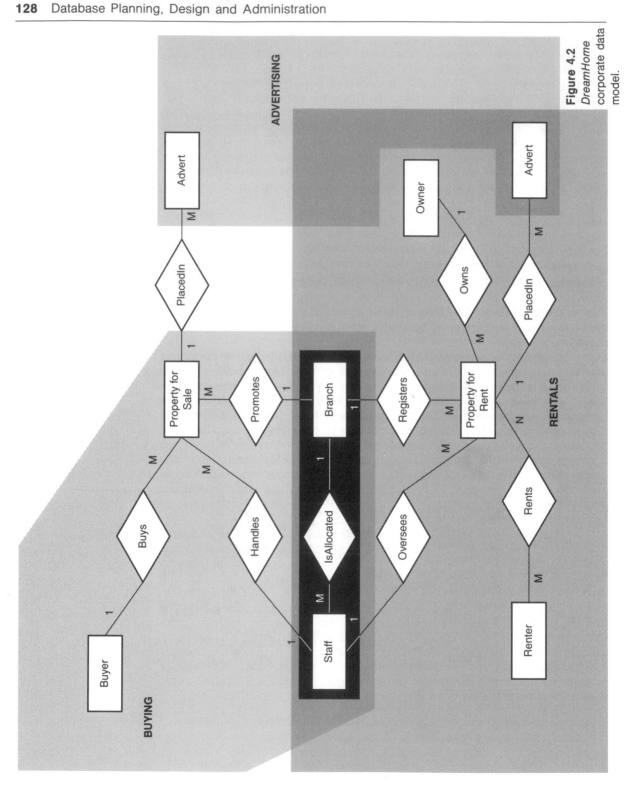

Figure 4.2
DreamHome corporate data model.

4.2.2 System Definition

System definition	The scope and boundaries of the database application including its major application areas and user groups.

Before attempting to design a database application system, it is essential that we first identify the boundaries of the system that we are investigating and how it interfaces with other parts of the organizational information system. It is important that we include within our system boundaries not only the current users and application areas, but also future users and applications.

4.2.3 Requirements Collection and Analysis

Requirement	A feature to be included in the new system.

Database design is based on information about the organization that is to be served by the database. This information may be gathered in the following ways:

- interviewing individuals within the enterprise, particularly those who are regarded as experts within a specific area of interest;
- observing the enterprise in operation;
- examining documents, in particular those used to record or display information;
- using questionnaires to gather information from a wide number of users;
- using experience from the design of similar systems.

The information gathered should include the main application areas and user groups; the documentation used or generated by these application areas or user groups; the details of the transactions required by each application area or user group; and a prioritized list of requirements of each application area or user group.

This activity results in a users' requirements specification of the enterprise, possibly as a set of documents describing the enterprise's operations from different viewpoints. The activity is a preliminary stage to logical database design, during which the users' requirement specification is analysed to identify the necessary details. The amount of data gathered depends on the nature of the problem and the policies of the enterprise. Too much study too soon leads to *paralysis by analysis*. Too little thought can result in an unnecessary waste of both time and money by working on the wrong solution to the wrong problem. A comprehensive discussion of analysis techniques is outside the scope of this book; however, the interested reader is referred to Senn (1989).

The information collected at this stage may be poorly structured and include some informal requests, which must be converted into a more structured statement of requirements. This is achieved using **requirements**

specification techniques, which include, for example: Structured Analysis and Design (SAD) techniques, Data Flow Diagrams (DFD) and Hierarchical Input Process Output (HIPO) charts supported by documentation. As we will see shortly, CASE tools may provide automated assistance to ensure that the requirements are complete and consistent.

Identifying the required functionality for a database system is a critical activity, as systems with inadequate or incomplete functionality will annoy the users, which may lead to their rejection or to underutilization of the system (Bailey, 1989). However, excessive functionality can also be problematic as it can over complicate a system making it difficult to implement, maintain, use or learn.

4.2.4 Database Design

Database design	The design of the database model that will support the organization's operations and objectives.

The major aims of database design are:

- to represent the data and the relationships between data required by all major application areas and user groups;
- to provide a data model that supports any transactions required on the data;
- to specify a design that will achieve the stated performance requirements for the system such as response time.

Unfortunately, these aims are not always easy to achieve, and sometimes require compromises to be made, particularly to achieve acceptable system performance. The two main approaches to the design of a database system are referred to as the 'top-down' and 'bottom-up' approaches. The **bottom-up** approach begins at the fundamental level of attributes, which are grouped into entities and relationships. As the process continues we identify and add new relationships between entities. The process of normalization, which we discuss in Chapter 6, also represents a bottom-up approach to design. Normalization involves the identification of the required attributes and their subsequent decomposition into normalized tables based on functional dependencies between them.

The bottom-up approach is appropriate for the design of simple databases with a relatively small number of attributes. However, this approach becomes difficult when applied to the design of more complex databases with a larger number of attributes, where it is difficult to establish all the functional dependencies between the attributes. As the logical data model for complex databases may contain hundreds to thousands of attributes, it is essential to establish an approach that will simplify the design procedure. Also in the initial stages of establishing the data requirements for a complex database, it may be difficult to establish all the attributes to be included in the logical data model.

A more appropriate strategy for the design of complex databases is to use the **top-down** approach. This approach starts with the development of data models that contain a few high-level entities and then applies successive top-down refinements to identify lower-level entities, attributes and relationships. The top-down approach is illustrated by using the concepts of the Entity–Relationship (ER) model. This approach begins with the identification of entities and relationships between the entities, which are of interest to the organization. For example, we may identify entities Client, Property and Owner, and relationships for Client *Rents* Property and Owner *Owns* Property. Building a high-level data model using the concepts of the ER model will be described in Chapter 5.

There are other approaches to database design such the inside-out approach and the mixed strategy approach. The **inside-out** approach is related to the bottom-up approach but differs by first featuring a set of major concepts and spreading out to consider other concepts associated with those first identified. The **mixed strategy** approach uses both the top-down and bottom-up approach for various parts of the model and then, finally, combines all parts together.

We discuss database design further in Section 4.3. Throughout the remainder of this chapter, and in subsequent chapters, when we are discussing the organization with respect to database design we normally refer to the organization as the *enterprise*.

4.2.5 DBMS Selection

DBMS selection	The selection of an appropriate DBMS to support the information system.

If no DBMS exists, an appropriate part of the lifecycle in which to make a selection is between the conceptual and logical database design (see Section 4.3). However, selection could be done at any time prior to logical design provided sufficient information is available regarding system requirements such as performance, ease of restructuring, security and integrity constraints. Any additional DBMSs would also be selected now after the target application's requirements have been investigated. The selection process is covered in more detail in Section 4.6.

4.2.6 Application Design

Application design	The design of software programs that will use and process the database.

From Figure 4.1, observe that database and application design are parallel activities of the database application lifecycle. In most cases, it is not possible to complete the application design until the design of the database itself has taken place. On the other hand, the database exists to support the applications, and so there will be information fed from application design into database design.

In the application design phase, we must ensure that all of the functionality stated in the users' requirements specification is present in the application design for the database system. This involves designing the application programs that will use and process the data in the database. This activity includes **transaction design** – the design of the database access requirements, which we discuss in Section 4.4.

In addition to designing how the required functionality is to be achieved, we have to design an appropriate user interface to the database applications. This interface should present the required information to the users in a user-friendly way. The importance of user interface design is sometimes ignored or left until late in the design stages. However, it should be realized that the interface may be one of the most important components of the system. If it is easy to learn, simple to use, straightforward and forgiving, the users will be inclined to make good use of what information is presented. On the other hand, if the interface has none of these characteristics, the system will undoubtedly cause problems. In Section 4.4, we present some general guidelines that will result in a friendly, efficient interface.

4.2.7   Prototyping

At various points throughout the design process, we have the option to either fully implement the database application or build a prototype. The benefits of using the prototype approach, and when it is appropriate to use such an approach, are described in this section.

Prototyping   Building a working model of a database application system.

A prototype is a working model that does not normally have all of the required features or provide all of the functionality of the final system. The purpose of developing a prototype database application is to allow users to use the system to identify the features of the system that work well, or are inadequate, and if possible to suggest improvements or even new features to the database application. This process allows those involved in designing and implementing the database application to check that their interpretation of the users' requirements of the systems is compatible with the users' expectations of the system. Prototypes also have the major advantage of being relatively inexpensive and quick to build.

Testing and reviewing the users' reactions to the prototype is an iterative process. The benefit of using a prototype approach is that it can greatly clarify the users' requirements for both the users and developers of the system, and can also be used to test the feasibility of a particular system design. The stages involved in the prototype development method are shown in Figure 4.3 (Senn, 1989).

Prototyping is a very effective development method under particular circumstances. For example, prototyping is useful when clarification of users'

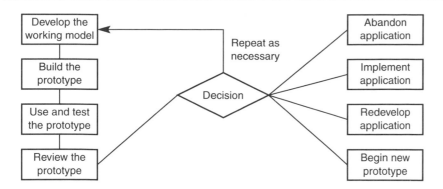

Figure 4.3
Prototype
development
method.

requirements is required before fully implementing a database application system that is associated with high cost, high risk or new technology.

4.2.8   Implementation

Implementation	The physical realization of the database and application designs.

On completion of the design stages (which may or may not have involved prototyping), we are now in a position to implement the database and the applications. The database implementation is achieved using the Data Definition Language (DDL) of the selected DBMS. The DDL statements are compiled and used to create the database schemas and empty database files. Any specified user views are also defined at this stage.

The application programs are implemented using the preferred third- or fourth-generation language. Parts of these applications are the database transactions, which are implemented using the Data Manipulation Language (DML) of the target DBMS, possibly embedded within a host programming language such as C, COBOL, Fortran, Ada or Pascal. We also implement the other components of the application design including, for example, menu screens, data entry forms and reports. Again, the target DBMS may have its own fourth-generation tools that allow rapid development of applications through the provision of non-procedural query languages, reports generators, forms generators, graphics generators and application generators.

Security and integrity controls for the application are also implemented. Some of these controls are implemented using the DDL, but others may need to be defined outside the DDL, for example, using the supplied DBMS utilities or written into the application programs, although, as we will see in later chapters, this is not desirable.

4.2.9 Data Conversion and Loading

Data conversion and loading	Transferring any existing data into the new database and converting any existing applications to run on the new database.

This stage is required only when a new database system is replacing an old system. Nowadays, it is common for a database system to have a utility that loads existing files into the new database. The utility usually requires the specifications of the source file and the target database, and then automatically converts the data to the required format of the new database files. Note that, where applicable, application programs from the old system can also be converted for use by the new system. Whenever conversion and loading are required, the process should be properly planned to ensure a smooth transition to full operation.

4.2.10 Testing

Testing	The process of executing the application programs with the intent of finding errors.

Before going live, the newly developed database application system should be thoroughly tested. This is achieved using carefully planned test strategies and realistic data so that the entire testing process is methodically and rigorously carried out. Note that in our definition of testing we have not used the commonly held view that testing is the process of demonstrating that faults are not present. In fact, testing cannot show the absence of faults; it can show only that software faults are present. If testing is conducted successfully, it will uncover errors with the application programs and possibly the database structure. As a secondary benefit, testing demonstrates that the database and the application programs *appear* to be working according to their specification and that performance requirements appear to have been satisfied. In addition, metrics collected from the testing stage will provide a measure of software reliability and software quality.

As with database design, the users of the new system should be involved in the testing process. The ideal situation for system testing is to have a test database on a separate hardware system, but often this is not available. If real data is to be used, it is essential to have backups taken in case of error. After testing is completed, the application system is ready to be 'signed off' and handed over to the users.

Testing strategies

There are various testing strategies available to assess the completeness and correctness of a database system. The main testing strategies include:

- top-down testing
- bottom-up testing
- thread testing
- stress testing.

Each of these testing strategies has its own particular advantages and limitations. When testing larger systems, a selection of these strategies is normally used. Different techniques may be used for different parts of the system and at different stages of the testing process (Sommerville, 1992).

It is sensible to adopt an incremental approach when testing a system. That is, rather than combine and test all modules as a whole, the system should be built and tested in increments. The process should continue until all modules have been integrated into the total system. In this way, when a defect is detected the problem can often be localized to the most recently added module and its interfaces.

Top-down testing starts at the subsystem level with modules represented by stubs, which are simple components that have the same interface as the module but no functional code. Each function is represented by a stub. Finally, the program components are replaced by the actual code and this is tested. The advantage of this strategy is that design errors may be detected early in the testing phase, avoiding extensive redesign or re-implementation. Also, a limited working system is available at an early stage of the development and can demonstrate the feasibility of the system. One disadvantage of this strategy is that program stubs must be produced to simulate lower levels of the system. Also, test output may be difficult to observe from higher levels of a system that do not normally produce an output unless artificially forced to do so.

Bottom-up testing works in the opposite direction to that of top-down testing. It starts testing the modules at the lower levels of the hierarchy and then works up, until the final module is tested. The advantages and disadvantages of bottom-up testing are the reverse of those described for top-down testing.

Thread testing is a strategy that is associated with real-time systems, which are usually made up of a number of cooperating processes and may be interrupt driven. These systems are difficult to test because of the time-dependent interactions between processes in the system. Thread testing is a strategy that follows individual processes. The processing of each external event 'threads' its way through the system processes. This strategy involves identifying and executing each possible processing 'thread'. It is impossible to completely thread test a system because of the vast number of possible input and output combinations.

Some systems are designed to handle maximum or minimum loads. **Stress tests** are designed to ensure that the system can handle its intended loads. This often involves planning a series of tests where the load is continually increased until the system fails. This strategy has two main advantages: it tests the behaviour of the system, and stresses the system to allow any defect to appear that would not normally be identified.

4.2.11 Operational Maintenance

Operational maintenance	The process of monitoring and maintaining the system following installation.

In the previous stages, the database application system has been fully implemented and tested. The system now moves into a maintenance stage that involves the following activities:

- Monitoring the performance of the system. If the performance falls below an acceptable level, this may require tuning or reorganization of the database.
- Maintaining and upgrading the database application system (when required). New requirements are incorporated into the database application system via the preceding stages of the lifecycle.

Once the database system is fully operational, close monitoring takes place to ensure that performance levels remain within acceptable levels. A DBMS normally provides various utilities to aid database administration including utilities to load data into a database, and to monitor the system. The utilities that allow system monitoring give information on, for example, database usage, locking efficiency (including number of deadlocks that have occurred, and so on) and query statement execution. Database administration can use this information to tune the system to give better performance, for example, by creating additional indexes to speed up queries, by altering storage structures or by combining or splitting tables.

The monitoring process continues throughout the life of an application and in time may lead to reorganization of the database to satisfy the changing requirements. These changes in turn provide information on the likely evolution of the system and the future resources that may be needed. This, together with knowledge of proposed new applications, enables database administration to engage in capacity planning and to notify or alert senior staff to adjust plans accordingly. If the DBMS lacks certain utilities, the DBA staff would either develop them as required, or, if specially developed tools were commercially available from other sources, purchase them.

When a new application system is brought online, the users should operate it in conjunction with the old system for a period of time. This is to safeguard current operations in case of unanticipated problems with the new system. Periodic checks on data consistency between the two systems need to be made, and only when both systems appear to be producing the same results consistently, should the old system be dropped. If the changeover is too hasty, the end result could be disastrous. Despite the foregoing assumption that the old system may be dropped, there may be situations where both systems are maintained. This is often the case if a system has to be kept running whether or not the computer system is functioning, health care systems being one example.

4.3 Overview of Database Design

In Section 4.2.4, we outlined the objectives of database design and the approaches that can be taken to produce this design. In this section, we discuss the process of database design in more detail. This process, known as **data modelling**, is one of the two major components of system development, the other being **process modelling**. Data models have two main purposes:

- to assist in the understanding of the meaning (semantics) of the data;
- to facilitate communication about the information requirements.

Understanding the meaning of the data

Building a data model requires answering questions about entities, relationships and attributes. In doing so, the designers discover the semantics of the enterprise's data, which exist whether or not they happen to be recorded in a formal data model. Entities, relationships and attributes are fundamental to all enterprises. However, their meaning may remain poorly understood until they have been correctly documented. A data model makes it easier to understand the meaning of the data. Thus, we model data to ensure that we understand:

- each user's perspective of the data;
- the nature of the data itself, independent of its physical representations;
- the use of data across applications.

Communicating information requirements

Data models can be used to convey the designer's understanding of the information requirements of the enterprise. Provided both parties are familiar with the notation used in the model, it will support communication between the users and designers. Increasingly, enterprises are standardizing the way that they model data by selecting a particular approach to data modelling and using it throughout their database development projects. The most popular high-level data model used in database design, and the one we use in this book, is based on the concepts of the Entity–Relationship (ER) model. We will describe entity–relationship modelling in detail in the next chapter.

In this book, we consider database design to be composed of two major phases: logical database design and physical database design.

In the remainder of this section, we provide an overview of the activities associated with these phases. A detailed description of the phases will be provided in Chapters 7 and 9.

4.3.1 Logical Database Design

Logical database design	The process of constructing a model of the information use in an enterprise based on one model of data, but independent of a particular DBMS and other physical aspects.

The approach we take in this book is to divide logical database design into three main activities:

- The production of a **conceptual data model** for each user view or functional area of the enterprise.
- The production of a **logical data model** for each user view. Each logical data model, derived from the corresponding conceptual model, is validated to ensure that it is properly normalized and that it supports the necessary transactions.
- The production of a **global logical data model**, formed by merging the logical models.

We now briefly explain the objectives of these activities.

Conceptual data model

Conceptual data model	A model of the information use in an enterprise, without regard to its physical aspects.

The creation of the conceptual data model is the first activity of logical database design. The conceptual data model represents the required data and the relationships between that data to be held in the database. This data model is independent of implementation details such as the target DBMS software, application programs, programming languages, hardware platform or any other physical considerations.

Logical data model

Logical data model	A model of the information use in an enterprise based on the model of data underlying the target DBMS.

Whereas the conceptual data models are independent of all physical considerations, the logical models are derived knowing the underlying data model of the target DBMS. In other words, we know that the DBMS is, for example, relational, network, hierarchic or object-oriented. However, we ignore any other aspects of the chosen DBMS and, in particular, any physical details, such as storage structures or indexes.

Throughout the process of developing a logical data model, we continually test and validate the model against the users' requirements. We use **normalization** to test the correctness of a logical data model. This ensures that the relations ultimately derived from the data model do not display data redundancy, which can cause update anomalies when implemented. Chapter 6 will illustrate the problems associated with data redundancy and will detail the process of normalization.

Once the logical data models have been produced for each view, we merge these models together to form one global logical data model. (We discuss the approaches to merging user views shortly.) The global logical data model is a source of information for the physical design process, providing the physical database designer with a vehicle for making trade-offs that are very important to efficient database design. The global model also serves an important role during operational maintenance. Properly maintained and kept up to date, the global model allows future changes to application programs or data to be accurately and efficiently represented by the database. It also reduces or eliminates the need to recreate the global model every time an application is modified or a new one is started.

Logical database design is an iterative process, which has a starting point and an almost endless procession of refinements. It should be viewed as a learning process. As the designers come to understand the workings of the enterprise and the meanings of its data, and express that understanding in the chosen model, the information gained may well necessitate changes to earlier parts of the design. Consequently, any methodology used for logical database design should not be prescriptive, but should act as a framework to help the designers carry out the activity effectively.

Logical database design is critical to the overall success of the system. If the design is not a true representation of the enterprise, it will be difficult, if not impossible, to define all the required user views (external schemas) or to maintain database integrity. It may even prove difficult to define the physical implementation or to maintain acceptable system performance. On the other hand, the ability to adjust to change is one hallmark of good logical design. Therefore, it is worthwhile spending the time and energy necessary to produce the best possible logical design.

We should attempt to produce an *optimal* logical data model that meets the following criteria (Fleming and Von Halle, 1989):

- *Structural validity*   Consistency with the way the enterprise defines and organizes information.

- *Simplicity*   Ease of understanding by information systems professionals and users including non-technical professionals.

- *Expressability*   Ability to distinguish between different types of data, relationship types and constraints.

- *Nonredundancy*   Exclusion of extraneous information; in particular, the representation of any one piece of information exactly once.

- *Shareability*   Not specific to any particular application or technology; thereby usable by many.

- *Extensibility* Ability to evolve to support new requirements with minimal affect on existing users.
- *Integrity* Consistency with the way the enterprise uses and manages information.
- *Diagrammatic representation* Ability to represent a model using easily understood diagrammatic notation.

However, sometimes these criteria are not compatible. For example, in attempting to achieve greater *Expressability* in a data model, we may lose *Simplicity*.

Merging user views

There are two major approaches to designing the global data model, which is a representation of multiple user views of the organization, namely the **centralized** approach and the **view integration** approach.

Centralized approach	Merge separate user requirements lists that represent distinct user views into a single set of user requirements. Then build the global logical data model.

The first approach is referred to as the **centralized** (or one-shot) approach, and involves collating the users' requirements for different application areas or user groups into a single list of requirements. The essential characteristic of this approach is that the lists of requirements are collated *before* building the logical data model. This approach is workable provided the database system being described is not overly large nor complex.

View integration approach	Merge separate logical data models that represent distinct user views into one global logical data model.

The second approach is referred to as the **view integration** approach, and involves the merging of separate data models based on distinct user views into one **global logical data model**. This approach is perhaps easier to manage as the work is first divided into more manageable parts. The difficulty arises when we try to merge the data models, which may have been produced by different designers, and may use different terminology for the same item and even the same terminology for different items.

In Chapter 7, we will present a methodology for database design that uses the view integration approach. The methodology will provide a practical step-by-step guide on how to perform the view integration approach. Chapter 8 will demonstrate view integration in action by providing a comprehensive worked example.

4.3.2 Physical Database Design

Physical database design	The process of producing a description of the implementation of the database on secondary storage; it describes the storage structures and access methods used to effectively access data.

Physical database design is the second main phase of the database design process, during which the designer decides how the database is to be implemented. The previous stage of the database application lifecycle involved the identification of the logical structure for the database (that is, entities, relationships and attributes). The development of this structure was DBMS-independent, although constrained to a particular data model such as the relational, network or hierarchic. However, in developing the physical database design, we must first know the target database system. Therefore, physical design is tailored to a specific DBMS system. There is feedback between physical and conceptual/logical design, because decisions are taken during physical design for improving performance that may affect the structure of the conceptual schema.

In general, the main aim of physical database design is to describe how we intend to physically implement the logical database design. For the relational model, this involves:

- deriving a set of relational tables and the constraints on these tables from the information presented in the global logical data model;
- identifying the specific storage structures and access methods for the data to achieve an optimum performance for the database system;
- designing and describing the security protection for the system.

Ideally, logical database design for larger systems should be separated from physical design for three main reasons:

- It deals with a different subject matter – the *what*, not the *how*.
- It is performed at a different time – the *what* must be understood before the *how* can be determined.
- It requires different skills, which are often found in different people.

In Chapter 2, we discussed the three-level ANSI-SPARC architecture for a database system, consisting of external, conceptual and internal schemas. Figure 4.4 illustrates the correspondence between this architecture and logical and physical database design. In Chapter 9, we will describe in detail the physical database design phase of the methodology presented in this book, and we provide a comprehensive worked example in Chapter 10.

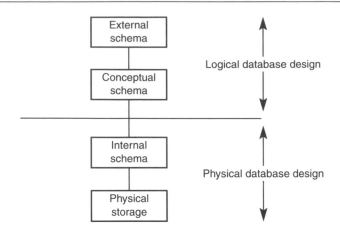

Figure 4.4 Data modelling and the ANSI-SPARC architecture.

4.4 Application Design

In Section 4.2.6, we outlined the objectives of application design. In this section, we briefly examine two aspects of application design, namely transaction design and user interface design.

4.4.1 Transaction Design

Database transaction	An operation that requires access to a database and is a representation of a 'real world' event.

Transactions are representations of events that occur in the part of the 'real world' that a database represents. These transactions have to be applied to the database to ensure that data held by the database remains current with the 'real world' situation and to support the information needs of the users.

The purpose of transaction design is to define and document the high-level characteristics of the transactions required on the database system. This activity should be carried out early in the design process to ensure that the logical data model is capable of supporting all the required transactions. It is important that the characteristics of each transaction are documented such as the information required by the transaction, its importance to the users and the expected rate of usage.

There are several techniques available for specifying the high-level characteristics of transactions, such as identifying the following details:

- data to be used by the transaction,
- the functional characteristic of the transaction,
- the output of the transaction.

There are three main types of transactions: retrieval transactions, update transactions and mixed transactions.

- **Retrieval transactions** are used to retrieve data for display on the screen or in the production of a report. For example, the requirement to search for and display on screen the details of a property for rent for a given property number, is an example of a retrieval transaction.

- **Update transactions** are used to insert new records, delete old records or modify existing records in the database. For example, the requirement to insert the details of a new property for rent into the database is an example of an update transaction.

- **Mixed transactions** are used for more complex applications that require the retrieval and updating of data. For example, the requirement to search for and display on screen the details of a property for rent (given the property number) and then update the value of the monthly rent is an example of a mixed transaction.

The design of a database transaction is based on the information given in the users' requirements specification. There are many techniques for requirements specification that include a notation for specifying the transactions required by the users. These transactions can be complex operations that, when analysed, are actually composed of many operations, each of which constitutes a single transaction.

4.4.2 User Interface Design Guidelines

Before implementing a form or report, it is essential that we first design the layout. Listed below are useful guidelines to follow when designing forms or reports (Shneiderman, 1992):

- meaningful title,
- comprehensible instructions,
- logical grouping and sequencing of fields,
- visually appealing layout of the form,
- familiar field labels,
- consistent terminology and abbreviations,
- consistent use of colour,
- visible space and boundaries for data-entry fields,
- convenient cursor movement,
- error correction for individual characters and entire fields,
- error messages for unacceptable values,
- optional fields marked clearly,
- explanatory messages for fields,
- completion signal.

A short explanation for each of these guidelines is given below.

Meaningful title

The information conveyed by the title should clearly and unambiguously identify the purpose of the form.

Comprehensible instructions

Familiar terminology should be used to convey instructions to the user. The instructions should be brief; however, when more information is required help screens should be made available. Instructions should be written in a consistent grammatical style using a standard format.

Logical grouping and sequencing of fields

Fields that are related should be positioned together on the form. The sequencing of fields should be logical and consistent.

Visually appealing layout of the form

The form should present an attractive interface to the user. The form should appear balanced with fields or groups of fields evenly positioned throughout the form. There should not be areas of the form that have too few or too many fields. Fields or groups of fields should be separated by a regular amount of space. Where appropriate, fields should be vertically or horizontally aligned. In cases where a form on screen has a hardcopy equivalent, the appearance of both should be consistent.

Familiar field labels

Field labels should be familiar. For example, if Sex was replaced by Gender it is possible that some users would be confused.

Consistent terminology and abbreviations

An agreed list of familiar terms and abbreviations should be used consistently.

Consistent use of colour

Colour should be used to improve the appearance of a form and to highlight important fields or important messages. To achieve this, colour should be used in a consistent and meaningful way. For example, fields with a white background may indicate data-entry fields and those with a blue background may indicate display-only fields.

Visible space and boundaries for data-entry fields

A user should be visually aware of the total amount of space available for each field. This allows a user to consider the appropriate format for the data before entering the values into a field.

Convenient cursor movement

A user should easily identify the operation required to move a cursor throughout the form. Simple mechanisms such as using the Tab key, arrows or the mouse pointer should be used.

Error correction for individual characters and entire fields
A user should easily identify the operation required to make alterations to field values. Simple mechanisms should be available such as using the Backspace key or by overtyping.

Error messages for unacceptable values
If a user attempts to enter incorrect data into a field, an error message should be displayed. The message should inform the user of the error and indicate permissible values.

Optional fields marked clearly
Optional fields should be clearly identified for the user. This can be achieved using an appropriate field label or by displaying the field using a colour that indicates the type of the field. Optional fields should be placed after required fields.

Explanatory messages for fields
When a user places a cursor on a field, information about the field should appear in a regular position on the screen such as a window status bar.

Completion signal
It should be clear to a user when the process of filling in fields on a form is complete. However, the option to complete the process should not be automatic as the user may wish to review the data entered.

4.5   CASE Support

Part of this planning process may also involve the selection of suitable Computer-Aided Software Engineering (CASE) tools. In its widest sense, CASE can be applied to any tool that supports software engineering. Appropriate productivity tools are needed by data administration to permit the database development activities to be carried out as efficiently and effectively as possible. These tools may include a data dictionary to store information about the application's data, and design tools to support data analysis. The tools permit development of the corporate data model and the logical data model (see Section 4.2.4), and support the prototyping of applications.

CASE tools may be divided into two categories: upper-CASE and lower-CASE, as illustrated in Figure 4.5. **Upper-CASE** tools are intended to support the initial stages of the database application lifecycle, from planning through to logical and physical database design. **Lower-CASE** tools support the later stages of the lifecycle, from implementation through testing to operational maintenance.

As CASE is a workstation technology, the environment must accommodate high-quality networking, electronic mail and other communications capabilities. Although the operating system preference for most engineering workstations is UNIX, many systems can now run on high-end personal computers under DOS and Microsoft Windows.

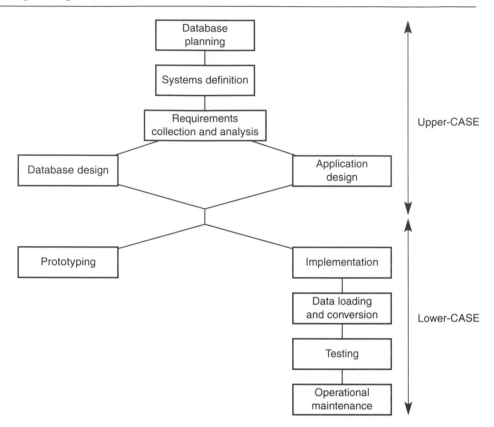

Figure 4.5
Application of
CASE tools.

Benefits of CASE

The use of appropriate CASE tools should improve the system development productivity. We use the term 'productivity' to relate both to the efficiency of the development process and to the effectiveness of the developed system. **Efficiency** refers to the cost, in terms of time and money, of realizing the information system. CASE tools aim to support and automate the development tasks and thus improve efficiency. **Effectiveness** refers to the extent to which the system satisfies the information needs of its users. In the pursuit of greater productivity, raising the effectiveness of the development process may be even more important than increasing its efficiency. For example, it would not be sensible to develop an information system extremely efficiently when the product is not what the users want. In this way, effectiveness is related to the quality of the final product. Since computers are better than humans at certain tasks, for example consistency checking, CASE tools can be used to increase the effectiveness of some tasks in the development process.

CASE tools provide the following benefits that improve productivity:

- *Standards* CASE tools help to enforce standards on a project or across the organization. They encourage the production of standard test components that can be reused, thus simplifying maintenance and increasing productivity.

- *Integration*   CASE tools store all the information generated in a repository, or data dictionary, as discussed in Section 2.7. Thus, it should be possible to store the data gathered during all the stages of the information system lifecycle. The data then can be linked together to ensure that all parts of the system are integrated. In this way, information systems no longer have to consist of independent, unconnected components.

- *Support for standard methods*   Structured techniques make significant use of diagrams, which are difficult to draw and maintain manually. CASE tools simplify this process, resulting in documentation that is correct and more current.

- *Consistency*   Since all the information in the data dictionary is inter-related, CASE tools can check its consistency.

- *Automation*   Some CASE tools can automatically transform parts of a design specification into executable code. This reduces the work required to produce the implemented system, and may eliminate errors that arise during the coding process.

For further information on CASE systems see Fisher (1988), QED (1989), McClure (1989), Gane (1990) and Batini *et al.* (1992).

4.6   DBMS Selection

A crucial stage in the database application lifecycle is the selection of an appropriate DBMS. Generally, unless there are very exceptional circumstances, it is *not* recommended that any organization takes steps to design and implement their own DBMS, as the process is extremely complex, time-consuming and expensive. Although DBMS selection may be infrequent, as business needs expand or existing systems are replaced, it becomes necessary at times to evaluate new DBMS products. The aim is to select a system that permits expansion and enables speedier, easier application development balanced against costs that include the cost of the DBMS product, additional hardware costs, changeover costs (both in time and money) and training costs.

Ideally, before engaging in a selection process, the detailed requirements have been obtained and are fully documented. A thorough analysis of user needs is usually undertaken as part of the study to determine whether the database approach is justified, and no evaluation of DBMSs should begin until a complete detailed specification of requirements is available. However, despite these assertions, it has been found that some organizations make a selection based upon cost or the characteristics of the vendor alone, and the database administration staff have to work around the failings of the DBMS to stand a chance of producing a successful system. Dunnachie (1984) mentions that requirements should have been obtained, but 'more than likely they have not [been]', and warns against minimizing the additional time necessary to determine them. Despite this warning, it is likely that some organizations will continue to purchase DBMS products without prior determination of requirements.

A simple approach to selection is to check off DBMS features against requirements although, in practice, it is more complicated than this. If an organization is selecting a DBMS for the first time, there is an opportunity to ensure that this move is well planned by considering all current and future requirements. Usually, this is not the case, and there may be various situations within an organization that have to be dealt with. These include people favouring one particular system, groups of users attempting to make their requirements top priority whether or not they are in the long-term interests of the organization, and any need to link the new software to existing software or match it to existing hardware.

4.6.1 Choosing the Best System

The process of selecting a DBMS is summarized in Table 4.1, although the size and resources of an organization influence how fully this is undertaken.

Table 4.1 Summary of selection process.

Full requirement specification available as initial input
Define terms of reference of study
Identify possible products
Shortlist two or three products
Evaluate products
Recommend selection and produce report

It has been known for the selection process to take up to nine months, and it has been suggested that the order of two to five years should be allowed for both requirements collection and DBMS appraisal (Frost, 1984). Clearly, many organizations could not afford such a length of time. The final selection of a product will be based on the results of the evaluation process coupled with cost and the vendor's characteristics. A final report of the process with recommendations should be prepared for the selection committee.

Full requirements specification available

Requirements specification for the application or applications should have been undertaken prior to DBMS appraisal.

Define terms of reference of study

Prior to any software evaluation, terms of reference for the study should be established stating the objectives and scope, which will indicate the tasks that need to be undertaken. The document should include information to produce a preliminary list of products for consideration, what criteria will be used to evaluate them and all constraints and timescales amongst other detail. The selection process needs to be well-planned, with projected meetings and presentations identified so that advance notice can be given to everyone involved in the selection process.

Although a group of staff representing different skills may form the selection committee, this is often not an ideal way to proceed. A less time-consuming way is for two or three people to lead the process and report back informally using meetings or presentations. In practice, the number of people involved and the structure of the selection process will vary between organizations.

Identify possible products

The information contained in the terms of reference is used to draw up a preliminary list of products for consideration. The terms of reference may also contain possible sources of information about products. Decisions to list a product include whether it is available on particular hardware, how compatible it is with other software, and the cost and nature of the user base. DBMS vendors now make their software available across a range of hardware platforms. Another factor in deciding to list a product may be how soon a new upgrade is received for a particular hardware platform after the first release.

User support is also a deciding factor and some idea of this may be obtained by talking to the vendor. In addition, the vendor may also be willing to supply a list of current users who can be contacted. Talking to existing users of a particular product can produce useful information, not only on how good the support is, but also on how the product supports particular applications, and whether or not certain hardware platforms are more problematic than others.

Shortlist two or three products

A shortlist of two or three products should be produced from the preliminary list, usually by an analysis of features of each system. Different authors propose various features that could be assessed as either groups (for example, data definition features) or individually (for example, data types provided). The features or criteria should be specified in the terms of reference document. Table 4.2 gives some possible features that might be considered. Other factors that should be taken into account include:

- the budget available;
- likely costs, which will include licence fees and maintenance;
- hardware and additional software requirements;
- estimated data volumes allowing for growth over a particular time period;
- estimated transaction rates, which will have been determined in the requirements analysis;

Table 4.2 Some grouped selection criteria.

Data definition	Physical definition
Primary key enforcement	File structures available
Foreign key specification	File structure maintenance
Data types available	Ease of reorganization
Domain specification	Indexing
Ease of restructuring	Variable length fields/records
Integrity controls	Data compression
View mechanism	Encryption routines
Data dictionary	Memory requirements
Data independence	Storage requirements
Type of data model used	

Accessibility	Transaction handling
Query language: SQL-compliant	Backup and recovery routines
Other system interfacing	Checkpointing facility
Interfacing to 3GLs	Logging facility
Multi-user	Granularity of concurrency
Security	Deadlock resolution strategy
– Access controls	
– Authorization mechanism	

Utilities	Development
Performance measuring	4GL tools
Tuning	CASE tools
Load/unload facilities	Windows capabilities

Other features	
Upgradibility	Operating system required
Vendor stability	Cost
User base	Interoperability with other DBMSs
Training and user support	Distributed facilities
Documentation	Portability
	Hardware required
	Network support
	Object-oriented capabilities
	Online help
	Standards used

Table 4.3 Analysis of criteria/features.

DBMS: Sample product

Vendor: Sample vendor

Criteria/Features	Comment	Rating	Weighting	Score
File structures available	Choice of 4	8	0.15	1.2
File structure maintenance	NOT self-regulating	6	0.2	1.2
Ease of reorganization		4	0.25	1.0
Indexing		6	0.15	0.9
Variable length fields/records		6	0.15	0.9
Data compression	Specify with file structure	7	0.05	0.35
Encryption routines	None	0	0.05	0
		5.3	1.0	5.55
Physical definition group		5.55	0.25	1.5

- performance requirements, which may have been stipulated by some users;
- existing expertise within the organization.

If features are checked off simply with an indication of how good or bad each is, it may be difficult to see which systems are worth further investigation. A more useful approach is to weight each feature with respect to its importance to the organization, and to obtain an overall weighted value that can be compared for each product. Groups of features could also be weighted, especially if some are not considered as important as others. This again produces a weighted value that can be compared for each product. Table 4.3 illustrates this type of analysis. The drawback with this type of analysis is that no idea of performance is obtained. This is covered by the next step.

Evaluate products

The shortlisted products are now evaluated more thoroughly, with vendors being given the opportunity to make presentations and give demonstrations. Potential users could also be involved in these meetings to give additional feedback. Each vendor should be fully briefed on what is required including the level of detail, and how much time they have for their presentation, to avoid them giving a sales-oriented presentation. Demonstrations are more useful if the vendors are willing to develop part of a required system specification to show the capabilities of the software. To enable an equal comparison to be made, the same specification should be given to all vendors. However, this will cost more in time and money, and vendors may have resource problems to do this quickly. Nevertheless, if this is done, a better comparison can be achieved.

Benchmarking can also be used in evaluation. Some tests have been developed and used in research and in the commercial world, but to undertake a complicated benchmark can be very time-consuming, and simple ones do not indicate very much. Vendors should be able to supply performance figures, and visiting or talking to other users should yield more information. If they are unwilling to do this, they may have something to hide, or else may simply be protecting their base.

Recommend selection and produce report

The final stage for the evaluation team to complete is to document the evaluation process. Details of the criteria applied and how each system measured up to them should be included, along with a recommendation for a particular product. This report should be considered by the selection committee, possibly in conjunction with a verbal presentation by the evaluation team. A verbal presentation is less time-consuming, and also offers the opportunity for the selection committee to question the evaluation team.

4.7   Data and Database Administration

Current trends increasingly acknowledge the importance of data, and consequently information, to an organization, with the need to manage it properly. This information arises from data collected, generated and used solely within an organization (the corporate data resource), and it may also be derived from externally generated data, such as financial or stock market data. Data is now recognized as a resource to be maintained properly.

Due to the rapid pace of technological developments, the changing nature of working environments requires up-to-date, reliable information, and therefore proper management of corporate data in order to respond appropriately and quickly. This response may be in terms of increased efficiency, better customer support, developing new businesses or finding niche markets. As we mentioned at the start of this chapter, the roles of the Data Administrator (DA) and Database Administrator (DBA) are responsible for overseeing and controlling the activities associated with the corporate data and database application lifecycle, respectively. In this final section of the chapter, we discuss the roles and functions of these positions.

To put the discussion into perspective, in Table 4.4 we list the stages of the database lifecycle and indicate the contribution made by each role. From this table, we can see that the DA role is more heavily involved in the initial stages of the lifecycle, from planning through to logical database design. In contrast, the DBA role becomes more involved in the subsequent stages, from physical database design to implementation and testing.

Table 4.4 Functions of the DA and DBA during the database application lifecycle.

Stage	Major role	Minor role
Database planning	DA	DBA
System definition	DA	DBA
Requirements collection and analysis	DA	DBA
Conceptual database design	DA	DBA
DBMS selection	DBA	DA
Logical database design	DA	DBA
Physical database design	DBA	DA
Implementation	DBA	DA
Testing	DBA	DA
Data conversion and loading	DBA	DA
Operational maintenance	DBA	DA

4.7.1 Data Administration Role

Data administration	The management of the data resource, including database planning, development and maintenance of standards, policies and procedures, and conceptual and logical database design.

In principle, the data administration role has responsibility for the corporate data resource, which includes non-computerized data, but in practice is often concerned solely with managing the shared data of the key users or key application areas. The number of staff assigned to this role varies depending on the size of the organization. A large, well-funded organization is likely to have several specialist staff under the control of a manager, the Data Administrator (DA). The DA has the primary responsibility of consulting with and advising senior managers, and ensuring that the direction of database development will ultimately support corporate objectives.

The position of data administration is usually within the Information Systems (IS) or Information Technology (IT) areas of an organization. The area of IS focuses on application needs, addressing issues of *what* should be done with the technology to enable an organization to develop competitively. On the other hand, IT focuses on supporting IS strategies and therefore IT strategy is concerned with *how* to implement and deliver business and management information systems (Earl, 1989).

Organizational structures vary, and in some situations data administration is a distinct role, in others it may be combined with database administration. However, as we will see shortly, data administration and database administration are distinct roles having specific responsibilities that complement each other (GUIDE, 1978; Brathwaite, 1985). Where the data administration function is present it usually co-exists with the database administration function, and if there is only one function present, it is usually database administration (Strachan, 1994). Some recent organizational structures are shown in Figure 4.6. Two of the structures show the DA reporting to the IT Director or Chief Information Officer (CIO), while the third variation has both data administration and database administration roles one level lower.

In current strategic IS/IT thinking, there is now greater emphasis on the importance of the DA. All organizations are assumed to use IT and are developing as information-based enterprises. Consequently, there is an urgent requirement to merge IS/IT and business strategy to create a more flexible organization that can cope with rapid change, provide a more creative and innovative environment and permit the redesign of business processes as necessary. This change in emphasis means that DAs increasingly need to understand the business as well as IT, and therefore have a crucial role in helping to develop IS strategy and ensuring that it is aligned to corporate strategy. This change in thinking reflects the dramatic changes that have occurred, from the initial use of computers to control aspects of the business more efficiently, through making the business more effective, to enabling change and innovation.

4.7.2 Data Administration Functions

The functions of data administration are as follows:

- selecting appropriate productivity tools;
- assisting in the development of a strategic IS plan by undertaking feasibility studies and planning for database development;
- developing a corporate data model, or enterprise model, which shows functional areas and is a good starting point for database development;
- determining the organization's data requirements;
- setting data collection standards and establishing data formats;
- estimating volumes of data and likely growth;
- determining patterns and frequencies of data usage;
- determining data access requirements and safeguards for both legal and company requirements;
- undertaking conceptual and logical database design;
- liaising with database administration staff and application developers to ensure applications meet all stated requirements;
- user education for data standards and legal responsibilities;
- keeping up to date with developments;
- ensuring documentation is complete, including the enterprise model, standards, policies, procedures, use of the data dictionary and controls on end users;
- managing the data dictionary;
- user liaison to determine new requirements and to resolve difficulties over data access or performance.

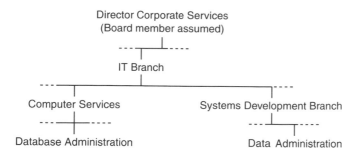

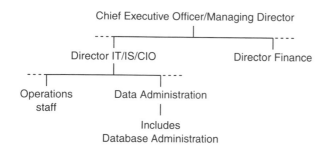

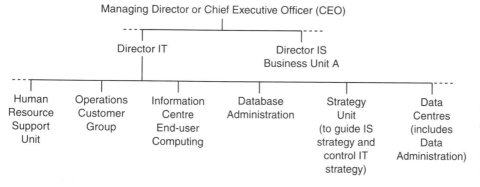

Figure 4.6 Some organizational positions of data/database administration.

4.7.3 Database Administration Role

Database administration	The management of the physical realization of a database system, including physical database design, implementation including setting security and integrity controls, monitoring system performance and reorganizing the database as necessary.

The database administration role is more technically oriented than the data administration role, requiring knowledge of specific DBMSs and the operating system environment. Although the primary responsibilities are centred on developing and maintaining systems using the DBMS software to its fullest extent, database administration staff also assist data administration staff in other areas, as we indicated in Table 4.4.

The number of staff employed in this role also varies between organizations. If several staff are employed, the Database Administrator (DBA) leads the group, and would be expected to have a recognized position in the organization's hierarchy. If only one person is in the role, he or she is unlikely to have a high status.

If there is no defined data administration role, there may be a managerially oriented DBA who would also assume responsibility for some of data administrations functions: for example, engaging in planning for database development; undertaking logical database design; managing the data dictionary; determining both access requirements and legal requirements; and generally liaising with users. However, if only a technically oriented database administration role exists, these types of functions may be undertaken either wholly or partly by systems analysts/designers and application developers. The position of database administration in an organization is similar to that of data administration (see Figure 4.6).

4.7.4 Database Administration Functions

The functions of database administration are as follows:

- evaluating DBMSs and recommending the most suitable one;
- carrying out physical database design;
- implementing/modifying a physical database design and initially having responsibility for loading the database;
- defining security and integrity constraints;
- liaising with application developers;
- developing test strategies;
- training users;
- having responsibility for signing off the implemented database application;
- monitoring system performance and tuning the database as appropriate;
- performing backups routinely;
- ensuring recovery mechanisms and procedures are in place;
- ensuring documentation is complete including in-house produced material;
- keeping up to date with software and hardware developments and costs, and installing updates as necessary.

4.7.5   Comparison of Data and Database Administration Roles

We have looked at the roles and associated functions of data administration and database administration. In this final section, we briefly contrast these roles. Table 4.5 summarizes the *main* task differences of the two roles. Perhaps the most obvious difference lies in the nature of the work carried out. The DA role tends to be much more managerial, whereas the DBA tends to be a more technical role. We end this chapter by summarizing the types of skills required by the two roles in Table 4.6.

Table 4.5   DA and DBA – main task differences.

Data administration	Database administration
Involved in strategic IS planning	Evaluates new DBMSs
Determines long-term goals	Executes plans to achieve goals
Enforces standards, policies and procedures	Enforces standards, policies and procedures
Determines data requirements	Implements data requirements
Develops corporate data model	Implements global logical data model
Coordinates system development	Monitors and controls database
Managerial orientation	Technical orientation
DBMS independent	DBMS dependent

Table 4.6   Desirable skills.

Managerial	Technical
Business understanding	DP background
Ability to coordinate people and plans	Knowledge of structured methodologies
Analytical skills	– Data flow diagrams
Negotiation skills	– Structure charts
Arbitration skills	– Software development
Written and oral communication skills	Database design and modelling
Ability to lead and motivate	Data dictionary management
Ability to withstand pressure and stress due to the management of change	

Chapter Summary

- The database is a fundamental component of an information system, and its development and usage should be viewed from the perspective of the wider requirements of the organization. Therefore, the lifecycle of an organizational information system is inherently linked to the lifecycle of the database system that supports it.

- The stages of the database application lifecycle include: database planning, system definition, requirements collection and analysis, database design, DBMS selection, application design, prototyping, implementation, conversion and data loading, testing and operational maintenance.

- Database design is divided into three phases: conceptual, logical and physical database design. **Conceptual design** constructs a model of the information use in an enterprise that is free of physical considerations. **Logical design** is similar to conceptual design, but assumes knowledge of the underlying data model of the target DBMS. **Physical design** produces a description of the implementation of the database on secondary storage. Physical design is tied to the target DBMS.

- Selecting a DBMS requires planning, and sufficient time must be allocated to the evaluation process.

- **Data administration** is oriented towards IS planning, and involves setting standards and determining associated policies and procedures. Development of the corporate data model and logical database design are also responsibilities.

- **Database administration** is oriented towards defining, monitoring and maintaining database systems. Physical database design and implementation are included in the responsibilities, as are the specification of backup and recovery procedures.

- Data administration is predominantly involved in functions associated with the initial stages of the database application lifecycle prior to any implementation being carried out.

- Database administration is mainly involved in functions associated with the later stages of the database application lifecycle. These are concerned with physical design, system implementation, testing and maintenance.

REVIEW QUESTIONS

4.1 Discuss the relationship between the information system lifecycle and the database application lifecycle.

4.2 Describe the purpose of each of the phases of the database application lifecycle.

4.3   Identify some of the techniques available to help document the users' requirements specification.

4.4   Describe the main aims of the conceptual and logical database design phases.

4.5   Explain why it is necessary to select the target DBMS before beginning the physical database design phase. Describe the main aims of the physical database design phase.

4.6   Describe the prototype approach and identify the potential advantages of using this approach.

4.7   Outline the procedure for selecting a DBMS.

4.8   Define the roles of data administration and database administration.

4.9   Explain the functions of data administration and database administration, and make a comparison between them.

4.10   Explain how the roles of data administration and database administration differ from and/or complement each other during the different phases of the database application lifecycle.

4.11   Describe the ideal skills that are required by data administrators and database administrators.

EXERCISES

4.12   This exercise is intended only to give a feel for DBMS evaluation and selection: consequently it is not expected that detailed requirements will be obtained, nor necessarily a full set of selection criteria. The time spent should therefore be within reasonable limits, unless, of course, you wish to spend several months or more on the exercise.

(a)   Determine the user and business requirements for a personnel system, and then choose a set of criteria that you consider important in the selection of an appropriate DBMS.

(b)   List possible DBMS products that should be considered and produce a shortlist of two by eliminating the others. Document and present your reasons.

(c)   Evaluate the two remaining DBMS products with respect to your requirements and select the one most suitable.

4.13   Investigate your organization with regard to the management of the data resource. In particular determine whether:

(a) A corporate data model exists and how it influences development of systems.

(b) Someone has overall responsibility for the data resource, and what functions they do in fact carry out.

(c) All necessary data is available on demand to senior management.

If some (or all) points are not satisfied, determine how lack of any apparent data management is detrimental to the organization.

4.14 Investigate your organization to determine whether a recognized database administration role exists. Find out how it is organized; its scope of operation; its responsibilities and the functions undertaken.

Part Two

Methodology

5 Entity–Relationship Modelling

Chapter Objectives

In this chapter you will learn:

- The use of high-level conceptual data models to support database design.
- The basic concepts associated with the Entity–Relationship (ER) model, a high-level conceptual data model.
- A diagrammatic technique for displaying an ER model.
- How to identify problems called connection traps, which may occur when creating an ER model.
- The limitations of the basic ER modelling concepts and the requirements to model more complex applications using enhanced data modelling concepts.
- The main concept associated with the Enhanced Entity–Relationship (EER) model called specialization/generalization.
- A diagrammatic technique for displaying specialization/generalization in an EER model.
- The use of Computer Aided Software Engineering (CASE) tools to support database design, including ER modelling.

The Entity–Relationship (ER) model is a high-level conceptual data model developed by Chen (1976) to facilitate database design. A conceptual data model is a set of concepts that describe the structure of a database and the associated retrieval and update transactions on the database. The main purpose for developing a high-level data model is to support a user's perception of data, and to conceal the more technical aspects associated with database design. Furthermore, a conceptual data model is independent of the particular DBMS and hardware platform that is used to implement the database.

In this chapter, we begin by describing the basic concepts of the entity–relationship model, and illustrate how these concepts may be represented pictorially as an ER diagram. We next identify potential problems associated with the development of an ER model called connection traps (Howe, 1989).

We also recognize the inherent problems associated with representing complex applications using the concepts of the ER model (Schmidt and Swenson, 1975). In response to the limitations of the basic ER model, additional 'semantic' concepts were added to the original ER model resulting in development of the Enhanced Entity–Relationship (EER) model. In this chapter, we describe the main concept associated with the EER model called specialization/generalization.

We demonstrate the process of building an EER data model based on the Manager's view of the *DreamHome* case study (see Section 1.7). The EER model shown in Figure 5.1 is an example of one of the possible end products of this process. This figure is presented at the start of this chapter to show the reader an example of the type of model that we can build using EER modelling. At this stage, the reader should not be concerned about fully understanding this model, as the concepts shown in Figure 5.1 are discussed in detail throughout this chapter.

We conclude this chapter with a brief look at an example of a Computer Aided Software Engineering (CASE) tool called Software through Pictures (StP), which provides support for database design, including ER modelling.

5.1 The Concepts of the Entity–Relationship Model

The basic concepts of the entity–relationship model include **entity types, relationship types** and **attributes**. These basic concepts are demonstrated using examples from the *DreamHome* case study.

5.1.1 Entity Types

Entity type	An object or concept that is identified by the enterprise as having an independent existence.

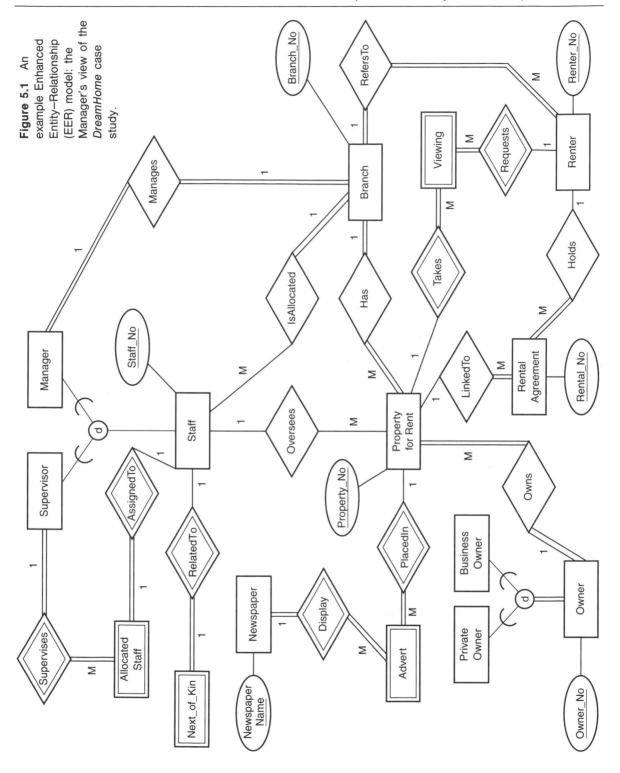

Figure 5.1 An example Enhanced Entity–Relationship (EER) model: the Manager's view of the *DreamHome* case study.

The basic concept of the ER model is an entity type, which represents a set of 'objects' in the 'real world' with the same properties. An entity type has an independent existence and can be an object with a physical (or 'real') existence or an object with a conceptual (or 'abstract') existence, as listed in Figure 5.2.

Physical existence	
Staff	Part
Property	Supplier
Customer	Product
Conceptual existence	
Viewing	Sale
Inspection	Work experience

Figure 5.2 Examples of entities with a physical or conceptual existence.

Note that we are only able to give a working definition of an entity type as no strict formal definition exists. This means that different designers may identify different entities.

Entity   An object or concept that is uniquely identifiable.

Each uniquely identifiable object of an entity type is referred to simply as an entity. Other authors may refer to our definition of an entity as an **entity occurrence** or **entity instance**. Throughout this chapter, we only use the terms 'entity type' or 'entity'. However, note that we use the more general term 'entity' where the meaning is obvious.

We identify each entity type by a name and a list of properties. A database normally contains many different entity types. Examples of entity types are shown in Figure 5.1, such as Staff, Branch and Next_of_Kin. Although an entity type has a distinct set of attributes, each entity has its own values for each attribute. We can classify entities as being strong or weak entity types.

Weak entity type   An entity type that is existence-dependent on some other entity type.

Strong entity type   An entity type that is *not* existence-dependent on some other entity type.

A weak entity type is dependent on the existence of another entity. For example, dependents of members of staff are weak entities because they cannot exist in the model if the corresponding member of staff does not exist. An example of a weak entity is the Next_of_Kin entity, shown in Figure 5.1. An entity is referred to as being a strong entity, if its existence does not depend upon the existence of another entity. Examples of strong entities include the Staff and Branch entities, shown in Figure 5.1. Weak entities are sometimes referred to as **child**, **dependent** or **subordinate** entities and strong entities as **parent**, **owner** or **dominant** entities.

Diagrammatic representation of an entity

Each strong entity type is shown as a rectangle, labelled with the name of the entity. For a weak entity type, the rectangle has double lines. Figure 5.3 demonstrates the diagrammatic representation of strong (Staff and Branch) and weak (Next_of_Kin) entity types.

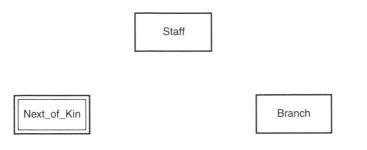

Figure 5.3
Diagrammatic representation of strong and weak entity types.

5.1.2 Attributes

> **Attribute**   A property of an entity or a relationship type.

The particular properties of entities are called attributes. For example, a Branch entity may be described by the branch number (Branch_No), address (Address), phone number (Tel_No) and fax number (Fax_No). The attributes of an entity hold values that describe each entity. The values held by attributes represent the main part of the data stored in the database.

A relationship that associates entities can also have attributes similar to those of an entity type. The characteristics of relationship types are discussed in Section 5.1.3 and attributes associated with relationships are discussed in Section 5.1.4.

> **Attribute domain**   A set of values that may be assigned to a single-valued attribute.

Each attribute is associated with a set of values called a domain. The domain defines the potential values that an attribute may hold. For example, the number of rooms associated with a property is between 1 and 15 for each individual entity. We therefore define the set of values for the number of rooms (Rooms) attribute of the Property_for_Rent entity as the set of integers between 1 and 15.

Attributes may share a domain. For example, the Address attributes of the Staff and Owner entities share the same domain of all possible addresses.

Domains can also be composed of domains. For example, the domain for the date of birth (DOB) attribute of the Staff entity is made up of subdomains: day, month and year.

The domain of the first name (FName) attribute is more difficult to define, as it consists of all first names. It is certainly a character string, but it might consist of not only letters but hyphens or other special characters. A fully developed data model includes the domains of each attribute in the ER model.

We can classify attributes as being: simple or composite; single-valued or multi-valued; or derived.

> **Simple attribute**   An attribute composed of a single component with an independent existence.

Simple attributes cannot be further subdivided. Examples of simple attributes include Sex and Salary. Simple attributes are sometimes called atomic attributes.

> **Composite attribute**   An attribute composed of multiple components, each with an independent existence.

Some attributes can be further divided to yield smaller components with an independent existence of their own. For example, the Address attribute of the Branch entity with the value (163 Main Street, Partick, Glasgow, G11 9QX) can be subdivided into Street (163 Main Street), Area (Partick), City (Glasgow) and Postcode (G11 9QX) attributes.

The decision to model the Address attribute as a simple attribute or to subdivide the attribute into Street, Area, City and Postcode is dependent on whether the user view of the model refers to the Address attribute as a single unit or as individual components.

> **Single-valued attribute**   An attribute that holds a single value for a single entity.

The majority of attributes are single-valued for a particular entity. For example, the Branch entity has a single-value for the branch number (Branch_No) attribute (for example B3), and therefore the Branch_No attribute is referred to as being single-valued.

> **Multi-valued attribute**   An attribute that holds multiple values for a single entity.

Some attributes have multiple values for a particular entity. For example, the Branch entity may have multiple values for the branch telephone number (Tel_No) attribute (for example, 0171-886-1212 and 0171-886-1233) and therefore the Tel_No attribute in this case would be multi-valued. A multi-valued attribute may have a set of numbers with upper and lower limits. For example, the Tel_No attribute of a branch may have between one and ten values. In other words, a branch may have a minimum of a single telephone number or a maximum of ten telephone numbers.

Derived attribute	An attribute that represents a value that is derivable from the value of a related attribute or set of attributes, not necessarily in the same entity.

Some attributes may be related for a particular entity. For example, the age of a member of staff (Age) is derivable from the date of birth (DOB) attribute, and therefore the Age and DOB attributes are related. We refer to the Age attribute as a derived attribute, the value of which is derived from the DOB attribute.

In some cases, the value of an attribute is derived from the entities in the same entity type. For example, the total number of staff (Total_Staff) attribute of the Staff entity can be calculated by counting the total number of Staff entities.

Derived attributes may also involve the association of attributes of different entities. For example, consider an attribute called Deposit of a Rental_Agreement entity. The value of the rental deposit (Deposit) attribute associated with a rental agreement is calculated as twice the monthly rent for the property. Therefore, the value of the Deposit attribute of the Rental_Agreement entity is derived from the Rent attribute of the Property_for_Rent entity.

Keys

We think of a key as a data item that allows us to uniquely identify individual occurrences of an entity type. We now present a more exact definition of the concept of a key.

Candidate key	An attribute or set of attributes that uniquely identifies individual occurrences of an entity type.

A candidate key is one or more attributes, whose value(s) uniquely identify each entity. For example, branch number (Branch_No) is the candidate key for the Branch entity type, and has a distinct value for each branch entity. The candidate key must hold values that are unique for every occurrence of an entity type. For example, each branch has a unique branch number (for example, B3), and there will never be more than one branch with the same branch number.

Primary key	An entity type may have one or more possible candidate keys, one of which is selected to be the primary key.

An entity type may have more than one candidate key. For example, a member of staff has a unique National Insurance Number (NIN) and also a unique company-defined staff number (Staff_No). We therefore have two candidate keys for the Staff entity, one of which must be selected as the primary key.

The choice of primary key for an entity is based on considerations of attribute length, the minimal number of attributes required and the current and future certainty of uniqueness. For example, the company defined staff number (for example, SG14) is smaller in size, and is likely to be preferred to that of the National Insurance Number (for example, WL220658D). Therefore, we select Staff_No as the primary key of the Staff entity and NIN is then referred to as the **alternate key**.

Composite key   A candidate key that consists of two or more attributes.

In some cases, the key of an entity is composed of several attributes, whose values together are unique for each individual entity but not separately. For example, consider the entity called Advert with the following attributes: Property_No, Newspaper_Name, Date_Advert and Cost. Many properties are advertised in many newspapers on a given date. To uniquely identify each occurrence of an advert requires values for the Property_No, Newspaper_Name and Date_Advert attributes. Thus, the Advert entity has a composite primary key made up of the Property_No, Newspaper_Name and Date_Advert attributes.

Diagrammatic representation of attributes

An attribute is shown as an ellipse attached to the relevant entity by a line and labelled with the attribute name. Figure 5.4 displays the attributes associated with the Staff, Branch and Next_of_Kin entities.

The ellipse is dotted if the attribute is derived and has double lines if the attribute is multi-valued. As shown in Figure 5.4, the total number of staff (Total_Staff) attribute of the Staff entity is a derived attribute and the telephone number (Tel_No) attribute of the Branch entity is a multi-valued attribute.

If the attribute is composite, its component attributes are shown as ellipses emanating from the composite attribute. As shown in Figure 5.4, the Name attribute of the Staff entity is a composite attribute consisting of a first (FName) and last name (LName) attributes. Also, the Address attribute of the Branch entity is also a composite attribute including the Street, Area, City and Postcode attributes.

The name of each primary key attribute is underlined. As shown in Figure 5.4, the primary key of the Staff entity is the staff number (Staff_No) attribute and the primary key of the Branch entity is the branch number (Branch_No). We cannot identify a primary key for the weak entity Next_of_Kin until we know the constraints on the relationship between the Next_of_Kin entity and its owner entity, namely the Staff entity. As a weak entity, the primary key of the Next_of_Kin entity will be partially or totally derived from the Staff entity.

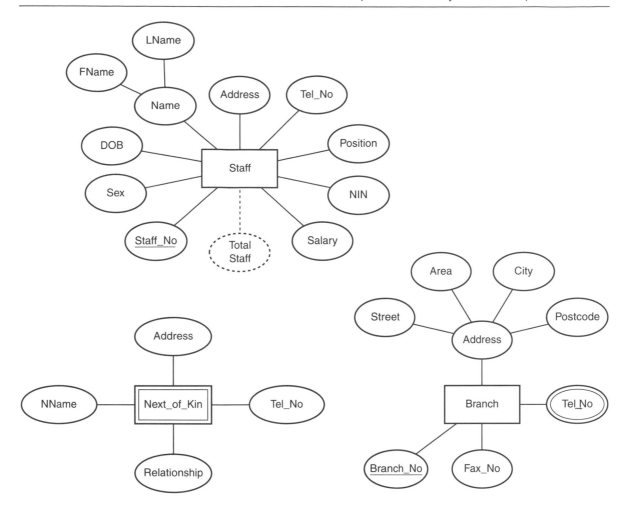

From this diagram, we can determine the attributes associated with the Staff, Branch and Next_of_Kin entity types. The composition of the Staff entity type includes:

Figure 5.4
Diagrammatic representation of Staff, Branch and Next_of_Kin entities and their attributes.

Staff (Staff_No, FName, LName, Address, Tel_No, Sex, DOB, Position, NIN, Salary)

Primary Key Staff_No

Alternate Key FName, LName, DOB

Alternate Key NIN

Composite Attribute Name (FName, LName)

Derived Attribute Total_Staff

The composition of the Branch entity type includes:

Branch (Branch_No, Street, Area, City, Postcode, Tel_No, Fax_No)

Primary Key Branch_No
Alternate Key Fax_No
Composite Attribute Address (Street, Area, City, Postcode)
Multi-valued Attribute Tel_No

The composition of the Next_of_Kin entity type includes:

Next_of_Kin (NName, Address, Tel_No, Relationship)

5.1.3 Relationship Types

> **Relationship type** A meaningful association among entity types.

A relationship type is a set of associations between two (or more) participating entity types. Each relationship type is given a name that describes its function. For example, the Owner entity is associated with the Property_for_Rent entity through the relationship called *Owns*.

As with entities, it is necessary to distinguish between the terms 'relationship type' and 'relationship'.

> **Relationship** An association of entities where the association includes one entity from each participating entity type.

Each uniquely identifiable occurrence of a relationship type is referred to simply as a relationship. A relationship indicates the particular entities that are related. Other authors may refer to our definition of a relationship as a **relationship occurrence** or **relationship instance**. Throughout this chapter, we use only the terms 'relationship type' or 'relationship'. As with the term entity, we use the more general term 'relationship' when the meaning is obvious.

The relationship *IsAllocated* indicates an association between Branch and Staff entities. However, each occurrence of the *IsAllocated* relationship associates one Branch entity with one Staff entity. Figure 5.5 represents individual occurrences of the *IsAllocated* relationship using a diagram called a **semantic net**. The semantic net is an object-level diagram in which the symbol • represents entities and the ◈ symbol represents relationships.

To simplify the semantic net diagram, only some of the attributes of the Branch and Staff entities are represented in Figure 5.5. The Branch entity type is reduced to three attributes: Branch_No, Address and Tel_No and the Staff entity type has three attributes: Staff_No, Address and DOB (Date of Birth). Each attribute holds a value from its associated domain. For example, the value for the Branch_No attribute for Branch entity (b1) is B3.

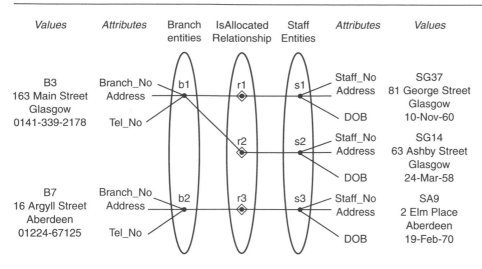

Figure 5.5 A semantic net model illustrating individual occurrences of the *IsAllocated* relationship.

There are three relationships (r1, r2 and r3) that describe the association of the Branch entity with the Staff entity. The relationships are shown by lines, which join each participating Branch entity with the associated Staff entity. For example, relationship r1 describes the association between Branch entity b1 and Staff entity s1.

If we represented an enterprise using semantic nets, it would be difficult to understand due to the level of detail. We can more easily represent the relationships between entities in an enterprise using the concepts of the Entity–Relationship model. The higher-level representation of the *IsAllocated* relationship, using the concepts of the ER model, is shown in Figure 5.6.

Diagrammatic representation of relationships

Each relationship is shown as a diamond, labelled with the name of the relationship. The diamond symbol has double lines if the relationship connects a weak entity to the strong entity on which it depends. Figure 5.6 displays an association between the Branch and Staff entities through a relationship called *IsAllocated*. The Next_of_Kin and Staff entities are related through a relationship called *RelatedTo*. The *RelatedTo* relationship is shown as a double-lined diamond to indicate that it is an association between a weak (Next_of_Kin) and a strong (Staff) entity.

To reduce the level of detail shown in a single ER diagram, often only the attributes that represent the primary key of each entity are displayed, and in some cases, no attributes are shown at all. For example, in Figure 5.6 only the attributes representing the primary key of the strong entities are shown, namely Staff_No and Branch_No.

Degree of a relationship	The number of participating entities in a relationship.

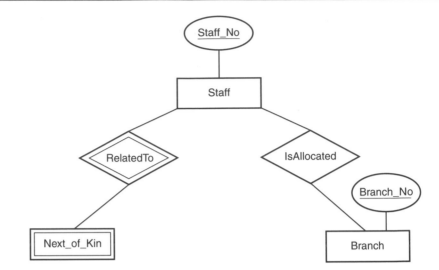

Figure 5.6 A diagrammatic representation of the Branch, Staff and Next_of_Kin entities, relationships and primary key attributes.

The entities involved in a particular relationship are referred to as **participants** in that relationship. The number of participants in a relationship is called the **degree** of that relationship. Therefore, the degree of a relationship indicates the number of entities involved in a relationship. A relationship of degree two is called **binary**. An example of a binary relationship is *Owns*, with two participating entities, namely Owner and Property_for_Rent. Figure 5.7(a) diagrammatically represents the binary relationship *Owns*.

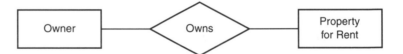

Figure 5.7(a) An example of a binary relationship called *Owns.*

A relationship of degree three is called **ternary**. An example of a ternary relationship is *SetsUp* with three participating entities, namely Renter, Staff and Interview. The purpose of this relationship is to represent the situation where a member of staff is responsible for setting up an interview with potential renters of property. Figure 5.7(b) diagrammatically represents the ternary relationship *SetsUp*.

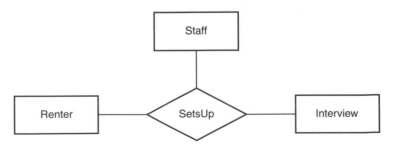

Figure 5.7(b) An example of a ternary relationship called *SetsUp.*

A relationship of degree four is called **quaternary**. An example of a quaternary relationship is *Arranges* with four participating entities, namely Buyer, Solicitor, Financial_Institution and Bid. This relationship represents the situation where a buyer, advised by a solicitor and supported by a financial institution, places a bid for a property. Figure 5.7(c) diagrammatically represents the quaternary relationship *Arranges*.

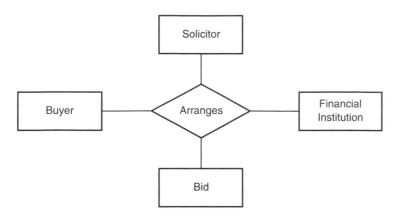

Figure 5.7(c) An example of a quaternary relationship called *Arranges.*

Recursive relationship	A relationship where the *same* entity participates more than once in *different roles*.

Consider a recursive relationship called *Supervises*, which represents an association of staff with a supervisor where the supervisor is also a member of staff. In other words, the Staff entity participates twice in the *Supervises* relationship; the first participation as a supervisor, and the second participation as a member of staff who is supervised (supervisee). Recursive relationships are sometimes called **unary** relationships.

Relationships may be given **role names** to indicate the purpose that each participating entity plays in a relationship. Role names are important for recursive relationships to determine the function of each participation. The use of role names to describe the *Supervises* recursive relationship is shown in Figure 5.8. The first participation of the Staff entity in the *Supervises* relationship is given the role name Supervisor and the second participation is given the role name Supervisee.

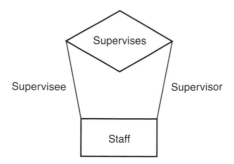

Figure 5.8 An example of a recursive relationship called *Supervises* with role names Supervisor and Supervisee.

Figure 5.9 An example of entities associated through two distinct relationships called *Manages* and *IsAllocated* with role names.

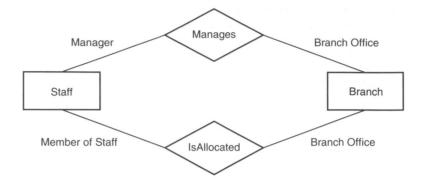

Figure 5.9 An example of entities associated through two distinct relationships called *Manages* and *IsAllocated* with role names.

Role names may also be used when two entities are associated through more than one relationship. For example, the Staff and Branch entities are associated through two distinct relationships called *Manages* and *IsAllocated*. As shown in Figure 5.9, the use of role names clarifies the purpose of each relationship. For example, in the case of the Staff *Manages* Branch, a member of staff (Staff entity) given the role name 'Manager' manages a branch (Branch entity) given the role name 'Branch Office'. Similarly, for Branch *IsAllocated* Staff, a branch office, given the role name 'Branch Office' is allocated staff, given the role name 'Member of Staff'.

Role names are usually not required if the function of the participating entities in a relationship is unambiguous.

5.1.4 Attributes on Relationships

The attributes described in Section 5.1.2 can also be assigned to relationships. For example, consider the relationship *Views*, which associates the Client and Property_for_Rent entities. We may wish to record the date the property was viewed by the client and any comments made by the client regarding the suitability or otherwise of the property. This information is associated with the *Views* relationship rather than the Client or the Property_for_Rent entities. As shown in Figure 5.10, we create attributes called Date_View and Comments to store this information and assign them to the *Views* relationship.

The presence of an attribute or attributes assigned to a relationship may indicate that the relationship conceals an unidentified entity. For example, the presence of the Date_View and Comments attributes on the *Views* relationship may indicate the presence of an entity called Viewing.

Figure 5.10 An example of a relationship called *Views* with attributes (Date_View and Comments).

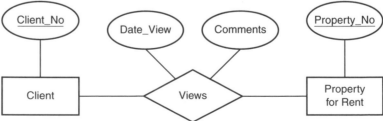

Figure 5.10 An example of a relationship called *Views* with attributes (Date_View and Comments).

5.2 Structural Constraints

We now examine the constraints that may be placed on participating entities in a relationship. The constraints should reflect the restrictions on the relationships as perceived in the 'real world'. Examples of such constraints include the requirements that a property for rent must have an owner and each branch office must be allocated staff. There are two main types of restrictions on relationships called **cardinality** and **participation** constraints.

5.2.1 Cardinality Constraints

Cardinality ratio	Determines the number of possible relationships for each participating entity.

The most common degree for relationships is binary and the cardinality ratios for binary relationships are one-to-one (1:1), one-to-many (1:M) and many-to-many (M:N).

The cardinality ratio between entities is a function of the policies in operation, as determined by an enterprise. The rules defining cardinality are referred to as **business rules**. Ensuring that all appropriate business rules are identified and represented is an important part of modelling an enterprise. Unfortunately, not all business rules can be represented in an ER model. An example of such a business rule is the requirement that a member of staff receives an additional day's holiday for every year of employment with the enterprise.

One-to-one relationships

Consider the binary relationship *Manages*, which relates the Staff and Branch entities. Figure 5.11(a) represents the Staff *Manages* Branch relationship using the concepts of the semantic net model (Section 5.1.3). Note that, to simplify the semantic net models shown in this section, only some of the attributes associated with each entity are shown.

The semantic net model shown in Figure 5.11(a) displays individual occurrences of the *Manages* relationship between the Staff and Branch entities. For example, Susan Brand, Staff entity s1, is the Manager of branch office B3, Branch entity b1 in Glasgow, and John White, Staff entity s3, is the Manager of branch office B5, Branch entity b2 in London.

From Figure 5.11(a), we also note that Ann Beech (s2) is not a Manager, and is therefore not associated with the *Manages* relationship. However, in determining the cardinality ratio of a relationship, we are interested only in entities that are involved in the relationship. The involvement of each entity in a given relationship is called the 'entity participation'. This topic is discussed in more detail in the following section.

We conclude from the semantic net diagram of the *Manages* relationship that a single Staff entity (Manager) is associated with a single Branch entity (branch office), and therefore the *Manages* relationship is a one-to-one

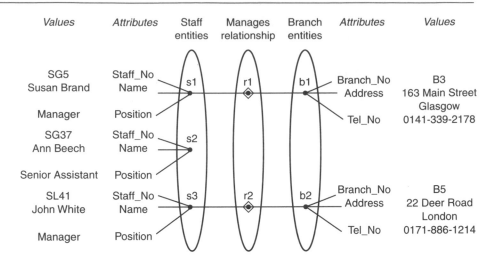

Figure 5.11(a) A semantic net model of a the Staff *Manages* Branch relationship.

(1:1) relationship. In other words, the cardinality ratio for the *Manages* relationship is 1:1.

An ER diagram of the Staff *Manages* Branch relationship is shown in Figure 5.11(b). In general, the participants in each relationship are connected by lines, which are labelled with 1, M or N as determined by the cardinality ratio of the relationship.

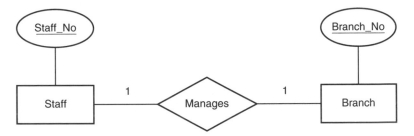

Figure 5.11(b) The Staff *Manages* Branch (1:1) relationship.

One-to-many relationships

Consider the binary relationship *Oversees*, which relates the Staff and Property_for_Rent entities. Figure 5.12(a) represents the Staff *Oversees* Property_for_Rent relationship using the concepts of the semantic net model.

This diagram displays individual occurrences of the *Oversees* relationship between the Staff and Property_for_Rent entities. For example, Ann Beech (s2) manages two properties in Glasgow PG21 and PG36 (p1 and p2), and Mary Howe (s3) manages a single property PA14 (p3) in Aberdeen. Susan Brand (s1) is not involved in the *Oversees* relationship. As we stated above, in determining the cardinality ratio of a relationship, we are interested only in entities that are specifically involved in the relationship. We conclude that a single Staff entity can be associated with one or more Property_for_Rent

Values	Attributes	Staff entities	Oversees relationship	Property_ for_Rent entities	Attributes	Values

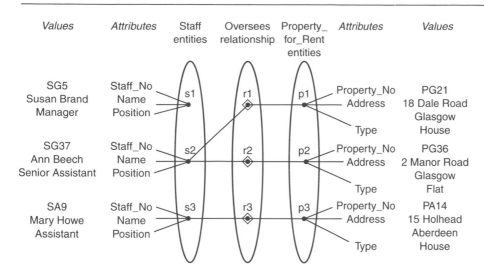

SG5 Susan Brand Manager	Staff_No Name Position	s1	r1	p1	Property_No Address Type	PG21 18 Dale Road Glasgow House
SG37 Ann Beech Senior Assistant	Staff_No Name Position	s2	r2	p2	Property_No Address Type	PG36 2 Manor Road Glasgow Flat
SA9 Mary Howe Assistant	Staff_No Name Position	s3	r3	p3	Property_No Address Type	PA14 15 Holhead Aberdeen House

Figure 5.12(a) A semantic net diagram of the Staff *Oversees* Property_for_Rent relationship.

entities, and therefore the *Oversees* relationship from the viewpoint of the Staff entity is a one-to-many (1:M) relationship.

If we examine the *Oversees* relationship from the opposite direction, we note that property numbers PG21 (p1) and PG36 (p2) located in Glasgow are managed by Ann Beech (s2). Property number PA14 (p3) in Aberdeen is managed by Mary Howe (s3). We conclude that a single Property_for_Rent entity is associated with a single Staff entity, and therefore the *Oversees* relationship from the viewpoint of the Property_for_Rent entity is a one-to-one (1:1) relationship.

In summary, the *Oversees* relationship is 1:M from the viewpoint of the Staff entity and 1:1 from the viewpoint of the Property_for_Rent entity. However, we represent the relationship using the higher cardinality, that is, from the viewpoint of the Staff entity. In other words, the cardinality ratio for the *Oversees* relationships is 1:M. An ER diagram of the Staff *Oversees* Property_for_Rent relationship is shown in Figure 5.12(b).

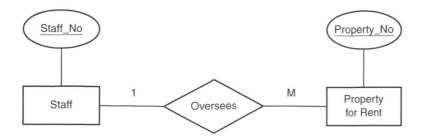

Figure 5.12(b) The Staff *Oversees* Property_for_Rent (1:M) relationship.

Many-to-many relationships

Consider the binary relationship *Advertises*, which relates the Newspaper and Property_for_Rent entities. Figure 5.13(a) represents the Newspaper *Advertises* Property_for_Rent relationship using the concepts of the semantic net model.

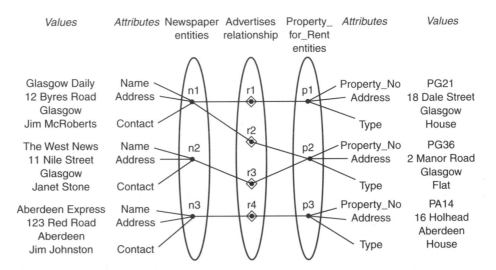

Figure 5.13(a) A semantic net diagram of the Newspaper *Advertises* Property_for_Rent relationship.

This diagram displays individual occurrences of the *Advertises* relationship between the Newspaper and Property_for_Rent entities. For example, the *Glasgow Daily* advertises two properties PG21 and PG36 (p1 and p2), *The West News* advertises a single property PG36 (p2) and the *Aberdeen Express* advertises a single property PA14 (p3).

We conclude that a single Newspaper entity can be associated with one or more Property_for_Rent entities, and therefore the *Advertises* relationship from the viewpoint of the Newspaper entity is a one-to-many (1:M) relationship.

If we examine the *Advertises* relationship from the opposite direction, we note that property number PG21 (p1) is advertised in the *Glasgow Daily* (n1), property number PG36 (p2) is advertised in the *Glasgow Daily* and *The West News* (n1 and n2), and property number PA14 (p3) is advertised in the *Aberdeen Express* (n3).

We conclude that a single Property_for_Rent entity can be associated with one or more Newspaper entities, and therefore the *Advertises* relationship from the viewpoint of the Property_for_Rent entity is a one-to-many (1:M) relationship.

In summary, the *Advertises* relationship is 1:M from the viewpoint of both the Newspaper and Property_for_Rent entities. We represent this relationship as two one-to-many relationships in both directions, which are collectively referred to as a many-to-many (M:N) relationship. In other words, the cardinality ratio for the *Advertises* relationships is M:N. An ER diagram

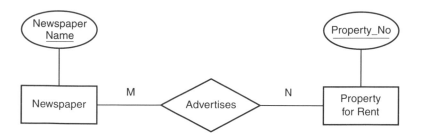

Figure 5.13(b) The Newspaper *Advertises* Property_for_Rent (M:N) relationship.

of the Newspaper *Advertises* Property_for_Rent relationship type is shown in Figure 5.13(b).

5.2.2 Participation Constraints

Participation constraints	Determines whether the existence of an entity depends upon its being related to another entity through the relationship.

There are two types of participation constraints, **total** and **partial**. The participation is total if an entity's existence requires the existence of an associated entity in a particular relationship, otherwise the participation is partial. For example, in the Branch *IsAllocated* Staff relationship, if every branch office is allocated members of staff, then the participation of the Branch entity in the *IsAllocated* relationship is total. However, if some members of staff (for example, Sales Personnel) do not work at a particular branch office, then the participation of the Staff entity in the *IsAllocated* relationship is partial.

The representation of the participation constraints associated with the Branch *IsAllocated* Staff relationship is shown in Figure 5.14. The terms total and partial participation are sometimes referred to as **mandatory** and **optional** participation. The participants in each relationship are connected by lines, which are single if the participation is partial and double if the participation is total.

We may use an alternative notation for displaying the structural constraints of a relationship by displaying the minimum and maximum (Min, Max) values next to the connecting line that represents the participation of the entity in the relationship. For example, this alternative notation to represent the structural constraints associated with the Branch *IsAllocated* Staff

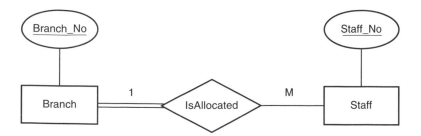

Figure 5.14 The participation constraints of the Branch *IsAllocated* Staff relationship.

relationship is shown in Figure 5.15. The usefulness of this notation is that sometimes more information on the constraints of the relationship is displayed. For example, in Figure 5.15 the (5,N) notation between the Branch entity and the *IsAllocated* relationship indicates that there is a minimum of five members of staff (Min = 5) working at each branch office and an unspecified maximum number (Max = N). Similarly, the (0,1) notation between the Staff entity and the *IsAllocated* relationship means that a member of staff need not work at any particular branch office (Min = 0) or a member of staff may work at a maximum of one branch office (Max = 1). This information is not represented if the simpler values representing cardinality are used, namely 1, M or N.

Figure 5.15 The participation constraints of the Branch *IsAllocated* Staff relationship using the alternative notation (Min, Max).

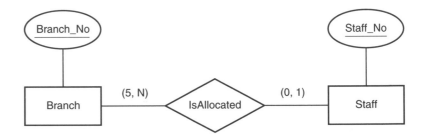

A summary of the conventions introduced in this section to represent the basic concepts of the ER model is shown on the front cover of this book.

5.3 Problems with ER Models

In this section, we examine several problems that may arise when designing a conceptual data model. These problems are referred to as **connection traps**, and normally occur due to a misinterpretation of the meaning of certain relationships. We examine two main types of connection traps, called **fan traps** and **chasm traps**, and illustrate how to identify and resolve such problems in ER models. However, it is worth mentioning that although it is important to check a data model for potential connection traps, some of those found may not be significant to the enterprise whilst others are, and require restructuring the conceptual model.

In general, to identify connection traps, we must ensure that the meaning of a relationship is fully understood and clearly defined. If we do not understand the relationships we may create a model that is not a true representation of the 'real world'.

5.3.1 Fan Traps

Fan trap	When a model represents a relationship between entity types, but the pathway between certain entity occurrences is ambiguous.

A fan trap may exist where two or more 1:M relationships fan out from the same entity. A potential fan trap is illustrated in Figure 5.16(a), which shows two 1:M relationships (*IsAllocated* and *Operates*) emanating from the same entity called Division.

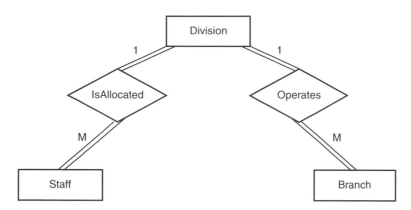

Figure 5.16(a) An example of a fan trap.

We conclude from the ER model shown in Figure 5.16(a) that a single division operates many branch offices and is allocated many staff. However, a problem arises when we want to know what members of staff work at a particular branch office. To appreciate the problem we examine the ER model shown in Figure 5.16(a) at the level of individual occurrences, using the semantic net model, shown in Figure 5.16(b).

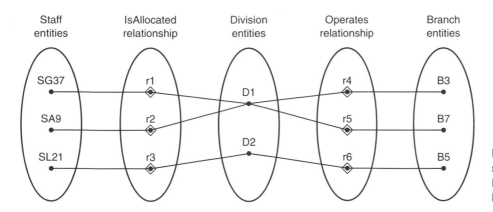

Figure 5.16(b) The semantic net of the ER model shown in Figure 5.16(a).

Using the semantic net model, we attempt to answer the following question: 'At which branch office does staff number SG37 work?'. Unfortunately, with the current structure, it is impossible to give a specific answer. From the semantic model shown in Figure 5.16(b), we can only determine that staff number SG37 works at Branch B3 or B7. The inability to answer this question specifically is the result of a fan trap associated with the misrepresentation of the correct relationships between the Staff, Division and Branch entities. We can resolve this fan trap by restructuring the original ER model to represent the correct association between these entities, as shown in Figure 5.17(a).

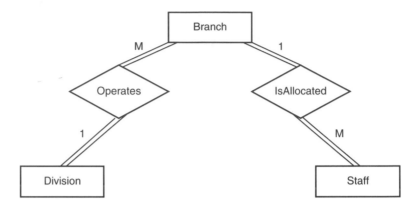

Figure 5.17(a) The ER model shown in Figure 5.16(a) is restructured to remove the fan trap.

If we now examine this structure at the level of individual occurrences, as shown in Figure 5.17(b), we can see that we are now in a position to answer the type of question posed earlier. From this semantic net model, we can determine that staff number SG37 works at branch office number B3, which is part of the division D1.

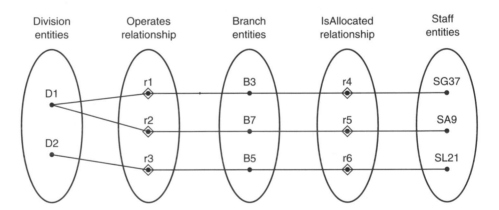

Figure 5.17(b) The semantic net of the ER model shown in Figure 5.17(a).

5.3.2 Chasm Traps

Chasm trap	When a model suggests the existence of a relationship between entity types, but the pathway does not exist between certain entity occurrences.

A chasm trap may occur where there is a relationship with partial participation, which forms part of the pathway between entities that are related. A potential chasm trap is illustrated in Figure 5.18(a), which shows the relationships between the Branch, Staff and Property_for_Rent entities.

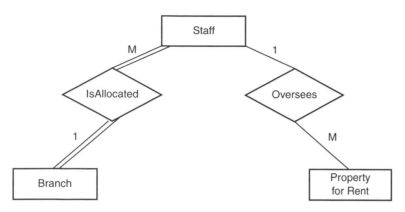

Figure 5.18(a)
An example of a
chasm trap.

We conclude from this ER model that a single branch is allocated many staff who oversee the management of properties for rent. We also note that not all staff oversee property, and not all properties are managed by a member of staff. A problem arises when we want to know what properties are available at each branch office. To appreciate the problem we examine the ER model shown in Figure 5.18(a) at the level of individual occurrences, using a semantic net model, as shown in Figure 5.18(b).

Using this semantic net diagram, we attempt to answer the following question: 'At which branch office is property number PA14 available?'. Unfortunately, we are unable to answer this question as this property is not yet allocated to a member of staff working at a given branch office. The inability to answer this question is considered to be a loss of information (as we know a property must be available at a branch office), and is the result of a chasm trap. The partial participation of Staff and Property_for_Rent in the *Oversees* relationship means that some properties cannot be associated with a branch office through a member of staff. Therefore to solve this problem, it is necessary to identify the missing relationship, which we call *IsAllocated* between the Branch and Property_for_Rent entities. The structure shown in Figure 5.19(a) represents the true association between these entities. This structure ensures that, at all times, the properties associated with each branch office are known, including properties that are not yet allocated to a member of staff.

If we now examine this structure at the level of individual occurrences, as shown in Figure 5.19(b), we see that we are now in a position to answer the type of question posed earlier. We can now determine that property number PA14 is available at branch number B7.

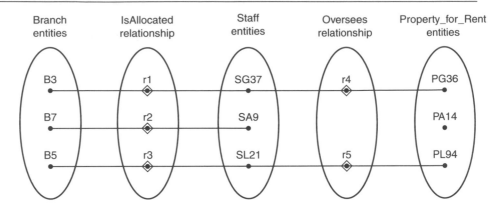

Figure 5.18(b) The semantic net of the ER model shown in Figure 5.18(a).

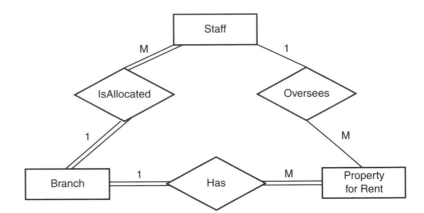

Figure 5.19(a) The ER diagram shown in Figure 5.18(a) is restructured to remove the chasm trap.

5.4 The Enhanced Entity–Relationship Model

The ER modelling concepts discussed in the earlier sections of this chapter are adequate for the representation of the majority of database schema for the traditional, administrative-based database applications. However, since the 1980s there has been a rapid increase in the development of many new database applications, such as Computer Aided Design (CAD), Computer Aided Manufacturing (CAM), Computer Aided Software Engineering (CASE) tools and multimedia applications. These types of applications have more demanding database requirements than those of the traditional administrative applications. The basic concepts of ER modelling are not sufficient to represent the requirements of the newer, more complex applications. This stimulated the need to develop additional 'semantic' modelling concepts. Many distinct semantic data models have been proposed. However, some of the most important semantic concepts have been successfully incorporated into the

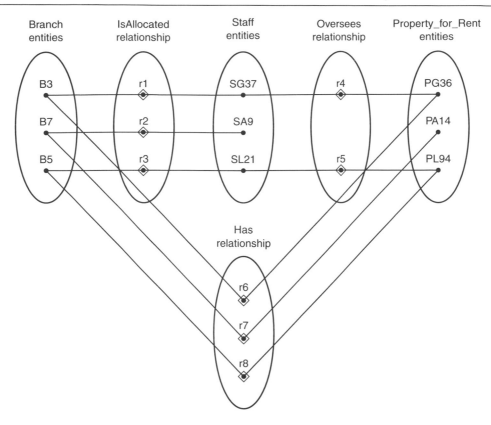

Figure 5.19(b) The semantic net of the ER model shown in Figure 5.19(a).

original ER model. The ER model supported with additional semantic concepts is called the Enhanced Entity-Relationship (EER) model.

The EER model includes all of the concepts of the original ER model together with the additional concepts of specialization/generalization, categorization and aggregation. In this section, we describe only the main concept of the EER model, namely specialization/generalization, and illustrate how this concept is represented in an EER model. For a detailed discussion of the other EER concepts, namely categorization and aggregation, the interested reader is referred to Elmasri and Navathe (1994).

The concept of specialization/generalization is associated with the related concepts of entity types described as superclasses or subclasses, and the process of attribute inheritance. This section begins by introducing these related concepts.

5.4.1 Superclasses and Subclasses of Entity Types

As we discussed in an earlier section, an entity type represents a set of entities of the same type such as the Staff, Branch and Property_for_Rent.

> **Superclass**   An entity type that includes distinct subclasses that require to be represented in a data model.

> **Subclass**   A subclass is an entity type that has a distinct role and is also a member of a superclass.

In some cases, an entity type may have many distinct subclasses. For example, the entities that are members of the Staff entity type may be classified as Manager, Secretary and Sales Personnel. In other words, the Staff entity is referred to as the superclass of the Manager, Secretary and Sales_Personnel subclasses. The relationship between a superclass and any one of its subclasses is called a superclass/subclass relationship. For example, Staff/Manager is a superclass/subclass relationship.

Each member of a subclass is also a member of the superclass. In other words, the subclass member is the same as the entity in the superclass, but has a distinct role. The relationship between a superclass and a subclass is a one-to-one (1:1) relationship. Some superclasses may contain overlapping subclasses, as illustrated by a member of staff who is both a Manager and member of the Sales Personnel. In this example, Manager and Sales_Personnel are overlapping subclasses of the Staff superclass. On the other hand, not every member of a superclass need be a member of a subclass: for example, members of staff without a distinct job role.

The purpose of introducing superclasses and subclasses is to avoid describing, for example, different types of staff with possibly different attributes within a single entity, as this may prove to be very inefficient. For example, Sales Personnel may have special attributes such as Car_Allowance and Sales_Area, and so on. The attributes that specifically describe the Sales Personnel are not required by other staff. If all staff attributes and those specific to particular jobs are described by a single Staff entity, this may result in a lot of nulls for the job specific attributes. Clearly, Sales Personnel have common attributes with other staff, such as Staff_No, Name, Address and DOB (Date of Birth). However, it is the unshared attributes that cause problems when we try to represent all members of staff within a single entity. We can also show relationships that are only associated with particular types of staff (subclasses) and not with staff, in general. For example, Sales Personnel may have distinct relationships that are not appropriate for all staff, such as Sales_Personnel *Requires* Car.

5.4.2   Attribute Inheritance

As mentioned above, an entity in a subclass represents the same 'real world' object as in the superclass, and therefore may possess subclass-specific attributes, as well as those associated with the superclass. For example, the Sales_Personnel subclass has all of the attributes of the Staff superclass such as Staff_No, Name, Address and DOB together with those specifically associated with the Sales_Personnel subclass such as Car_Allowance and Sales_Area.

A subclass is also an entity, and may therefore also have its own sub-classes. An entity and its subclasses and their subclasses, and so on, is called a **type hierarchy**. Type hierarchies are known by a variety of names including: **specialization hierarchy** (for example, Manager is a specialization of Staff), **generalization hierarchy** (for example, Staff is a generalization of Manager) and **IS-A hierarchy** (for example, Manager IS-A (member of) Staff). We describe the process of specialization and generalization in the following sections.

5.4.3 Specialization

Specialization	The process of maximizing the differences between members of an entity by identifying their distinguishing characteristics.

Specialization is a top-down approach to defining a set of superclasses and their related subclasses. The set of subclasses is defined on the basis of some distinguishing characteristics of the entities in the superclass. When we identify a set of subclasses of an entity type, we then associate attributes specific to each subclass (where necessary), and also identify any relationships between each subclass and other entity types or subclasses (where necessary).

For example, consider the specialization that identifies the set of sub-classes including Manager, Secretary and Sales_Personnel of the Staff super-class. This specialization can be represented diagrammatically in an EER model, as illustrated in Figure 5.20. Note that the Staff superclass and the subclasses, being entities, are represented as rectangles. The subclasses of a specialization are attached by lines to a circle, which is also connected to the superclass. The subset symbol (⊂) on each line that connects a subclass to the circle indicates the direction of the superclass/subclass relationship (for example, Manager (⊂) Staff). The 'o' in the specialization circle represents a constraint on the superclass/subclass relationship, which we describe in Section 5.4.5.

Attributes that are only specific to a given subclass are directly attached to the rectangle representing that subclass. For example, the Car_Allowance and Sales_Area attributes, shown in Figure 5.20, are only associated with the Sales_Personnel subclass, and are not applicable to the Manager or the Secretary subclasses. Similarly, we show attributes that are specific to the Manager (Bonus) and Secretary (Typing_Speed) subclasses.

Note that we can also show relationships that are only applicable to specific subclasses. For example, the Manager subclass is related to the Branch entity through the *Manages* relationship, whereas the Staff entity is related to the Branch entity through the *IsAllocated* relationship, as shown in Figure 5.20.

We may have several specializations of the same entity based on dif-ferent distinguishing characteristics. For example, another specialization of the Staff entity may produce the subclasses Full_Time_Permanent and Part_Time_Temporary, which distinguishes between the type of employment contract for members of staff. The specialization of the Staff entity type into job roles and employment contract subclasses is shown in Figure 5.21. In this

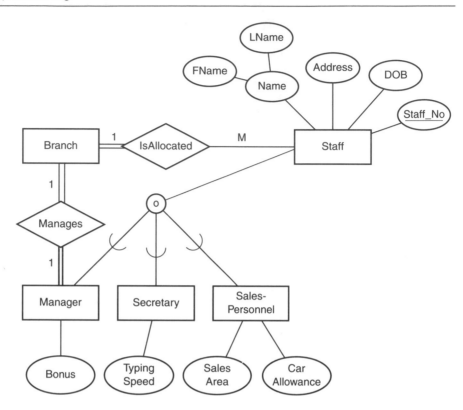

Figure 5.20
Specialization of the
Staff entity into job
roles subclasses.

figure, we also show attributes that are specific to the Full_Time_Permanent (Salary_Scale and Holiday_Allowance) and Part_Time_Temporary (Hourly_Rate) subclasses. The 'd' in the specialization circle represents a constraint on the superclass/subclass relationship, which we describe in Section 5.4.5.

A subclass may also have subclasses, which forms a specialization hierarchy. As shown in Figure 5.22, the Sales_Trainee subclass is a subclass of the Sales_Personnel and Trainee subclasses. A subclass with more than one superclass is called a **shared subclass**. In other words, a member of the Sales_Trainee shared subclass must be a member of the Sales_Personnel and Trainee subclasses. As a consequence, the attributes of the Sales_Personnel (Sales_Area and Car_Allowance) and Trainee (Start_Date) subclasses are inherited by the Sales_Trainee subclass, which also has its own additional attribute called Sales_Target. This process is referred to as **multiple inheritance.**

5.4.4 Generalization

Generalization	The process of minimizing the differences between entities by identifying their common features.

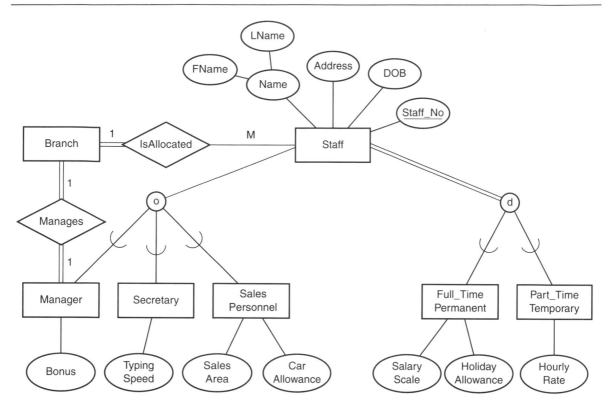

The process of generalization is a bottom-up approach, which results in the identification of a generalized superclass from the original subclasses. The process of generalization can be viewed as the reverse of the specialization process. For example, consider a model where Manager, Secretary and Sales_Personnel are represented as distinct entities. If we apply the process of generalization on these entities, we attempt to identify any similarities between them such as common attributes and relationships. As stated earlier, these entities share attributes common to all staff, and therefore we would identify Manager, Secretary and Sales_Personnel as subclasses of a generalized Staff superclass, as previously shown in Figure 5.20.

Figure 5.21
Specialization of the Staff entity into job roles and contract of employment subclasses.

5.4.5   Constraints on Specialization and Generalization

In this section, we discuss the constraints that may apply to a specialization or a generalization. Although we only describe these constraints in relation to a specialization, they apply equally to a generalization.

The first constraint is called the **disjoint** constraint. This constraint specifies that if the subclasses of a specialization are disjointed, then an entity can be a member of only one of the subclasses of the specialization. To represent a disjointed specialization a '**d**' for disjoint is placed in the circle that connects the subclasses to the superclass. The subclasses of the contract of employment specialization (Full_Time_Permanent, Part_Time_Temporary)

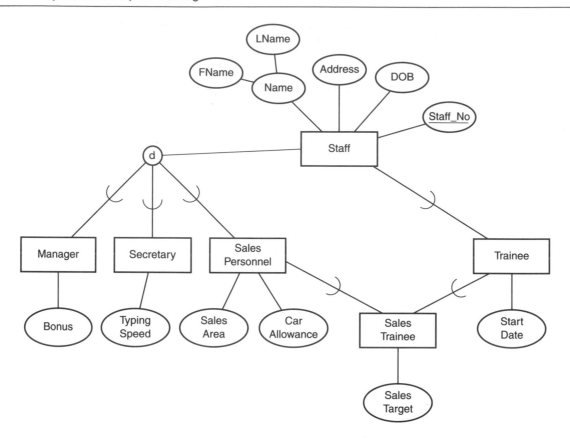

illustrated in Figure 5.21 are disjoint. This means that a member of staff is either on a full-time permanent contract or a part-time temporary contract.

If subclasses of a specialization are not disjoint, then an entity may be a member of more than one subclass of a specialization. To represent a **nondisjoint** specialization, an 'o' for overlapping is placed in the circle that connects the subclasses to the superclass. The subclasses of the job role specialization (Manager, Secretary, Sales_Personnel) illustrated in Figure 5.21 are nondisjoint. This means, for example, that an entity can be a member of both the Manager and Sales_Personnel subclasses.

The second constraint on a specialization is called the **participation** constraint, which may be total or partial. A specialization with a total participation specifies that every entity in the superclass must be a member of a subclass in the specialization. To represent total participation, a double line is drawn between the superclass and the specialization circle. In Figure 5.21, the contract of employment specialization has total participation, which means that every member of staff must be on either a full-time permanent contract or a part-time temporary contract.

A specialization with partial participation specifies that an entity need not belong to any of the subclasses of a specialization. A partial participation is represented as a single line between the superclass and the specialization circle. In Figure 5.21 the job role specialization has partial participation, which means that every member of staff need not have an additional job role such as a Manager, Secretary or Sales_Personnel.

The disjoint and participation constraints of specialization are distinct, and also apply to generalization. There are four categories of specialization or generalization as follows: disjoint, total; disjoint, partial; overlapping, total; and overlapping partial. A summary of the conventions used to represent specialization/generalization in an EER diagram is shown on the back cover of this book.

If we now return to consider Figure 5.1, you should recognize and understand the concepts shown in the model. If this is not the case, you should return and re-read the necessary sections of this chapter. Additionally, the following section may help to clarify the concepts of EER modelling by demonstrating, in a step-by-step fashion, the creation of the EER diagram shown in Figure 5.1.

5.5   The Manager's View of the *DreamHome* Case Study – Building an EER Model

In this section, we demonstrate the creation of an Enhanced Entity-Relationship (EER) model for the Manager's view of the *DreamHome* case study. A description of this case study is given in Section 1.7.

The requirements collection and analysis phase of the database systems lifecycle was carried out at several *DreamHome* branch offices, and involved interviewing members of staff with the job title of Manager and reviewing any documentation used or generated in their day-to-day work. This phase resulted in the production of a requirements specification for the Manager's view of the company, which describes the data to be held in the *DreamHome* database.

Note that when we use the term 'Manager's view', we refer to the view as generally defined by members of staff with the job title of 'Manager'.

5.5.1   The Manager's Requirements Specification

(1)   *DreamHome* has branch offices in various cities throughout the country. Each branch office is allocated members of staff and a manager to manage the operations of the office. The information to be held on the office includes: a unique branch number, address (street, area, city, postcode), telephone number and fax number.

Additional information is held on each manager. This includes the date that a manager assumed his or her position at the current branch office, the car allowance, and the monthly bonus payment based upon his or her performances in the property for rent market.

(2)   The information stored on each member of staff includes: staff number, name (first and last name), address, telephone number, sex, date of birth, national insurance number (NIN), position, salary and the date the member of staff joined the *DreamHome* company. The staff number is unique across all branches of the company.

When possible, the details of the next-of-kin of staff members are stored. The information to be stored on each next-of-kin includes: name, relationship to the member of staff, address and telephone number. Only the details of a single next-of-kin are held for a member of staff.

(3) Members of staff with the role of Supervisor are responsible for day-to-day activities of an allocated group of staff. Not all members of staff are assigned to a supervisor.

(4) Each branch office has property for rent. The information stored on each property includes: property number, address (street, area, city, postcode), type, number of rooms and monthly rent. The property number is unique across all branch offices. Each property for rent is allocated to a member of staff, who oversees the management of the property.

(5) The details of owners of property are also stored. There are two main types of property owner: private owners and business owners. The information stored on private owners includes: owner number, name, address and telephone number. The information stored on business owners includes: owner number, name of business, type of business, address, telephone number and contact name. The owner number is unique for each business or private property owner across all *Dream-Home* branches.

(6) Clients interested in viewing and renting property are called renters by the company. A prospective renter calls at a particular branch office where they may request to view various properties. The information stored on each viewing includes: the date of viewing and any comments made by the renter regarding the suitability or otherwise of the property. A renter may view many properties.

(7) The information stored on renters includes: the renter number, name (first and last name), address, telephone number, preferred type of accommodation and the maximum rent the renter is prepared to pay. The renter number is unique across all *DreamHome* branches.

(8) When a property is rented out, a rental agreement is drawn up between the renter and the property. The information detailed on the rental agreement includes: the rental number, monthly rent and the date the rental period is to start and finish.

(9) When required, the details of properties for rent are placed in adverts, which are displayed in local and national newspapers. The information stored on each advert includes: the date of the advert, the name of the newspaper and the cost of the advert.

The information stored on each newspaper includes: the newspaper name, address, telephone number, fax number and contact name.

5.5.2   Building an EER Model

In this section, we demonstrate the creation of the EER model shown in Figure 5.1. This model represents the Manager's view of the *DreamHome* case study. The steps presented below in the building of this model form part of the logical database design methodology, which will be described in detail in Chapter 7.

Identify entity types

We start by identifying the major entities in the Manager's requirements specification. Entities are normally present as noun or noun expressions, and include:

Branch	Private_Owner
Staff	Business_Owner
Manager	Renter
Next_of_Kin	Viewing
Supervisor	Rental_Agreement
Allocated_Staff	Advert
Property_for_Rent	Newspaper

Identify relationship types

We next identify the major relationships that exist between the main entities identified in the Manager's requirements specification. Relationships are normally present as verb or verb expressions. Table 5.1 lists the major relationships identified in the requirements specification.

Table 5.1 The major relationships identified in the Manager's requirements specification.

Entity type	Relationship type	Entity type
Branch	*IsAllocated*	Staff
	Has	Property_for_Rent
Staff	*Oversees*	Property_for_Rent
	RelatedTo	Next_of_Kin
	AssignedTo	Allocated_Staff
Manager	*Manages*	Branch
Supervisor	*Supervises*	Allocated_Staff
Property_for_Rent	*PlacedIn*	Advert
Private_Owner	*Owns*	Property_for_Rent
Business_Owner	*Owns*	Property_for_Rent
Renter	*CallsAt*	Branch
	Requests	Viewing
	Holds	Rental_Agreement
Viewing	*Of*	Property_for_Rent
Rental_Agreement	*For*	Property_for_Rent
Advert	*PlacedIn*	Newspaper
Newspaper	*Displays*	Advert

We must closely examine each relationship to ensure that each is a true representation of a relationship that exists in the 'real world'. If we discover any ambiguity, we must clarify the situation with the users.

We next identify the cardinality and participation constraints for each relationship type identified in Table 5.1.

Determine cardinality and participation constraints of relationship types

We first consider the cardinality ratio of the Owner *Owns* Property_for_Rent relationship. A single owner may own many properties, and therefore the cardinality of the *Owns* relationship is 1:M. However, if we consider this relationship from the viewpoint of the Property_for_Rent (Property_for_Rent *OwnedBy* Owner), we note that a single property for rent is owned by a single owner. Therefore, the cardinality of the *OwnedBy* relationship is 1:1. As shown in Figure 5.1, we represent this relationship showing the higher cardinality (1:M), namely the Owner *Owns* Property_for_Rent.

We next consider the participation constraints of the Owner *Owns* Property_for_Rent relationship. Using the fact that every owner owns at least one property for rent, then the participation of the Owner entity in the *Owns* relationship is total. If we also consider this relationship from the viewpoint of the Property_for_Rent (Property_for_Rent *OwnedBy* Owner), we note that every property must have an owner, and therefore again the participation of the Property_for_Rent entity in the *OwnedBy* relationship is total. The participation constraint for the Owner *Owns* Property_for_Rent relationship is shown in Figure 5.1 as double lines on either side of the diamond symbol.

The cardinality and participation constraints for the remaining relationships are shown in Figure 5.1. You should examine the constraints on each relationship to ensure that you understand how each was determined.

Note that in some cases the name of a relationship has been changed from that given in Table 5.1. For example, the Viewing *Of* Property_for_Rent (M:1) relationship is changed to Property_for_Rent *Takes* Viewing (1:M) relationship and the Renter *CallsAt* Branch (M:1) relationship is changed to Branch *RefersTo* Renter (1:M) relationship. This change is consistent with the convention that we always name relationships in the 1:M direction.

Identify and associate attributes with entity or relationship types

We now identify attributes that may be present as nouns (or their expressions). An attribute may describe some aspect of an entity or a relationship. Once identified, the attributes are associated with their respective entity or relationship, as shown in Table 5.2.

Table 5.2 Entities and their attributes identified in the Manager's requirements specification.

Entity type	Attribute
Branch	Branch_No
	Address (Street, Area, City, Postcode)
	Tel_No
	Fax_No
Staff	Staff_No
	Name (FName and LName)
	Address
	Tel_No
	Sex
	DOB (Date of Birth)
	NIN (National Insurance Number)
	Salary
	Position
	Date_Joined
Manager	Staff_No
	(Same attributes as
	Staff entity)
	Date_Mgr_Start
	Car_Allowance
	Bonus_Payment
Next_of_Kin	NName
	Relationship
	Address
	Tel_No
Supervisor	Staff_No
	(Same attributes as
	Staff entity)
Property_for_Rent	Property_No
	Address (Street, Area, City, Postcode)
	Tel_No
	Type
	Rooms
	Rent
Private_Owner	Owner_No
	Name (FName and LName)
	Address
	Tel_No
Business_Owner	Owner_No
	BName
	BType
	Address
	Tel_No
	Contact_Name

Table 5.2 *(contd).*

Entity type	Attribute
Renter	Renter_No
	Name (FName and LName)
	Address
	Tel_No
Viewing	Date_View
	Comments
Rental_Agreement	Rental_No
	Rent_Start
	Rent_Finish
Advert	Date_Advert
	Newspaper_Name
	Cost
Newspaper	Newspaper_Name
	Address
	Tel_No
	Fax_No
	Contact_Name

Determine candidate and primary key attributes

We examine Table 5.2 to identify candidate keys for each entity. For entities with more than one candidate key, we must select one to be the primary key. For example, the candidate keys for the Staff entity type include:

- Staff_No,
- FName, LName, DOB (Date of Birth),
- NIN (National Insurance Number).

The simplest candidate key, namely Staff_No, is selected as the primary key for the Staff entity, with the other candidate keys referred to as alternate keys for the entity. Table 5.3 identifies the primary key (and alternate keys, if any) for each entity in Table 5.2.

In Table 5.3, we note that the Next_of_Kin, Allocated_Staff, Viewing and Advert entities do not have a primary key, and are therefore weak entities. The primary keys for these entities will be partially or totally derived from their owner entities. The formation and identification of primary keys for weak entities are discussed as part of the logical database design methodology in Chapter 7.

Table 5.3 Entity types and their primary and alternate keys.

Entity	Primary key	Alternate key(s)
Branch	Branch_No	Tel_No Fax_No
Staff	Staff_No	FName, LName, DOB NIN
Manager	Staff_No	FName, LName, DOB NIN
Next_of_Kin		
Supervisor	Staff_No	FName, LName, DOB NIN
Allocated_Staff		
Property_for_Rent	Property_No	
Private_Owner	Owner_No	
Business_Owner	Owner_No	Tel_No Fax_No
Renter	Renter_No	
Viewing		
Rental_Agreement	Rental_No	
Advert		
Newspaper	Newspaper_Name	Tel_No Fax_No

Specialize/generalize entity types

Finally, we consider the option to specialize or generalize on the entities described in the Manager's requirements specification. This option is, to a certain extent, a subjective decision. However, it is important to follow as closely as possible the requirements specification when deciding how best to represent entities in the data model. In the Manager's requirements specification given in Section 5.5.1, there are several instances where decisions to specialize or generalize on entities are required. For example, the Manager and Supervisor entities are obviously related to the Staff entity. The decision is whether to represent these entities as subclasses of the generalized Staff superclass or leave them as distinct entities.

The decision to specialize or generalize entities may be based on the commonality of attributes and relationships associated with each entity. As shown in Table 5.2, all of the attributes of the Staff entity are represented in the Manager and Supervisor entities, including the same primary key. Furthermore, the Supervisor entity does not have any additional attributes representing this job role. On the other hand, the Manager entity has three additional attributes including: Date_Mgr_Start, Car_Allowance and Bonus_Payment. In addition, both the Manager and Supervisor entities are associated with distinct relationships in that Manager *Manages* Branch and Supervisor *Supervises* Staff. Based on this information, it is clear that Manager and Supervisor represent subclasses of the generalized Staff superclass, as shown in Figure 5.1.

This superclass/subclass relationship is partial and disjointed, as not all members of staff hold the role of Manager or Supervisor, and also a single member of staff cannot be both a manager and a supervisor. This representation is particularly useful for displaying the shared attributes associated with these subclasses and the Staff superclass.

An additional consideration is the relationship between owners of property. The Manager's requirements specification describes two types of owners; namely, Private_Owner and Business_Owner. Based on the information given in Tables 5.1 and 5.2, we note that these entities share some attributes (Owner_No, Address and Tel_No) and have the same relationship type (*Owns* Property_for_Rent). However, both types of owner also have different attributes. In this case, we create a generalized superclass called Owner, with Private_Owner and Business_Owner as subclasses, as shown in Figure 5.1. This superclass/subclass relationship is total and disjointed, as an owner must be either a person or a business but cannot be both.

The examples of specialization/generalization given in this section are relatively straightforward. As we mentioned previously, the generalization process can be taken further. For example, Staff, Manager, Supervisor, Private_Owner and Renter are persons with common characteristics (Name, Address, Tel_No), so we could create a generalized Person superclass. However, in this case, we decide against this approach and leave these entities as they are.

Draw the EER diagram

Based on the requirements specification given in Section 5.5.1, we build the EER data model of the Manager's view of the *DreamHome* case study, as shown in Figure 5.1.

The Manager's view of the *DreamHome* case study will be used in Chapter 8 to demonstrate the process of logical database design and, in particular, the merging of local views to create a global view of the *DreamHome* case study.

5.6 CASE Tools for ER Modelling

In Chapter 4, we described CASE (Computer Aided Software Engineering) tools as an increasingly important component of the database environment. In this section, we briefly demonstrate an example of a CASE tool that supports the process of database design, including ER modelling. We use a CASE tool called Software Through Pictures (StP) produced by Interactive Developments Incorporation (IDE, 1994).

StP is a powerful CASE tool that provides many features to assist the

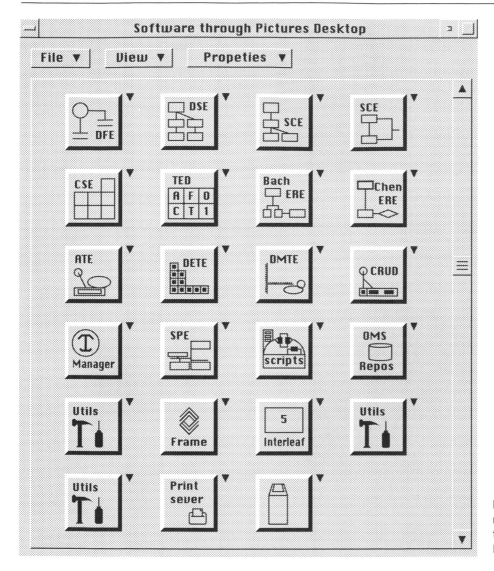

Figure 5.23 The main Software through Pictures (StP) Desktop screen.

software developer. The main StP Desktop screen is shown in Figure 5.23. For the purposes of this section, we will confine our brief examination of this product to the Chen Entity Relationship Editor (ERE). The ERE is an interactive graphical tool for drawing ER models. This tool supports the diagrammatic conventions originally developed by Chen (1976).

The ERE is capable of generating a Data Dictionary (DD) that describes the ER model, and checking the ER model for consistency and completeness. For example, if a data object is used but not defined, or if it has been defined more than once, the DD will indicate an error.

The ERE can also generate schema definitions based on an ER model.

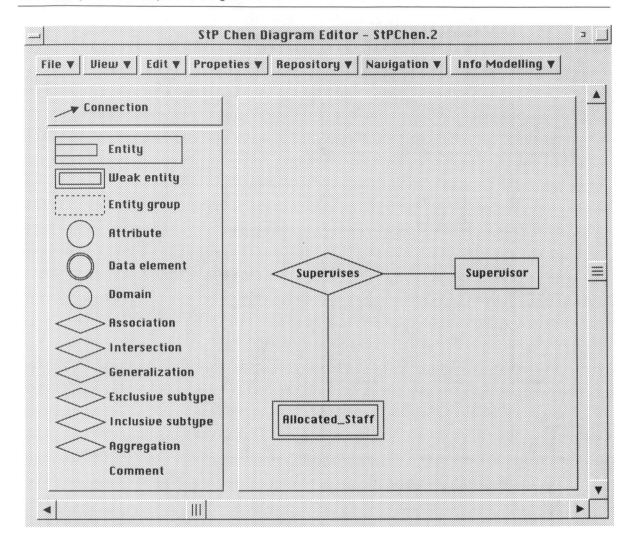

Figure 5.24 An example ER model created using StP.

The schema definitions may be textual representations of the ER diagram or representations of the diagram in a variety of Data Definition Languages (DDLs) for systems such as INGRES, ORACLE, Sybase and Informix. The ERE can also generate programming language code that implements the ER data structures. If required, we may change the DDL specifications or write our own specifications for a language that StP does not support. Figure 5.24 demonstrates the creation of a simple ER model using StP. Note that different CASE tools may support different diagrammatic conventions for ER models. For example, the Chen Diagram Editor represents attributes as circles rather than ellipses, as used throughout this book.

Chapter Summary

- The **Entity–Relationship (ER) model** uses ER diagrams to represent the conceptual schema that is independent of the DBMS.

- An **entity** is an object or concept which is identified by the enterprise as having an independent existence, and is uniquely identifiable. An **entity type** is a set of entities that have the same attributes. An **entity identifier** is a value which uniquely identifies an entity.

- A **weak entity type** is an entity that is existence-dependent on some other entity. A **strong entity** is an entity that is *not* existence-dependent on some other entity.

- An **attribute** is a property of an entity or a relationship.

- A **composite attribute** is an attribute composed of components with an independent existence.

- A **single-valued attribute** is an attribute which represents a single value for the same entity.

- **Attribute domains** represent a set of values that may be assigned to a single-valued attribute.

- A **multi-valued attribute** is an attribute which represents multiple values for the same entity.

- A **derived attribute** is an attribute which represents a value that is derivable from the value of a related attribute.

- A **candidate key** is an entity that may have one or more key attributes, each of which is called a candidate key. A **key attribute** represents values which are unique for each individual entity.

- A **composite key** represents several attributes which together represent values that are unique for each individual entity.

- A **relationship** is a meaningful association between entities. A **relationship type** is a set of associations among entities.

- A **relationship instance** is an association of entities, where the association includes one entity from each participating entity type.

- The **degree of a relationship type** is the number of participating entity types in a relationship.

- A **recursive relationship** is one in which the *same* entity participates more than once in *different* roles.

- **Role names** are used to determine the function of each participating entity type in a relationship.

- The **cardinality ratio** determines the number of possible relationship instances for each participating entity.

- The **participation constraints** determine whether the existence of an entity depends upon its being related to another entity through the relationship type.

- A **fan trap** exists when a model represents a relationship between entity types, but the pathway between certain entity occurrences is ambiguous.

- A **chasm trap** exists when a model suggests the existence of a relationship between entity types, but the pathway does not exist between certain entity occurrences.

- **Specialization** is the process of defining a set of subclasses of an entity type. **Generalization** is the process of minimizing the differences between entity types by identifying their common features.

- A **superclass entity** is an entity type with subclasses that require to be represented in the database. A **subclass entity** is a subclass entity is the same as the superclass entity but also has a distinct role.

REVIEW QUESTIONS

5.1 Describe the purpose of high-level data models in database design.

5.2 Describe the basic concepts of the Entity–Relationship (ER) model. Present the diagrammatic representation of these concepts.

5.3 Describe the constraints that may be placed on participating entities in a relationship.

5.4 Describe the problems that may occur when creating an ER model.

5.5 Why are the concepts of the basic ER model not sufficient to represent the requirements of newly emerging database applications?

5.6 Describe the main concepts associated with the Enhanced Entity–Relationship model. Present the diagrammatic representation of these concepts.

EXERCISES

The University Accommodation Office

The Director of the University Accommodation Office requires you to design and implement a database system to assist with the administration of the office. The requirements collection and analysis phase of the database design process based on the Manager's view has provided the following requirements specification for the accommodation office database system:

(1)   Each hall of residence has a name, number, address, telephone number and a hall manager who supervises the operation of the hall. The halls provide only single rooms which have a room number, place number

and weekly rent rate. The total number of rooms provided by the accommodation office should also be available.

(2) The place number uniquely identifies each room in all of the halls controlled by the accommodation office, and is used when renting a room to a student.

(3) Students may rent rooms throughout the academic year for various periods of time. Each individual rent agreement between a student and the accommodation office is uniquely identified using a lease number.

   The data stored on rooms currently rented includes the lease number, date the student started the rent period and date the student wishes to terminate the rent period (if known).

(4) The data stored on each undergraduate student includes: the matric number, name (first and last name), home address (street, city/town, postcode), date of birth, category of student (for example, first year undergraduate (1UG), postgraduate (PG)) and current status (placed/waiting).

   The student information stored relates to those currently renting a room and those on the waiting list.

   The total number of students records stored by the accommodation office should also be available.

(5) The accommodation office also stores a limited amount of information on the courses run by the university including: course number, course title, course leader and department name. Each student is associated with a single course.

(6) Whenever possible, information on a student's next-of-kin is stored, which includes the name, relationship, address (street, city/town, postcode) and contact telephone number.

5.7 Create a conceptual schema for the University Accommodation Office using the concepts of the Entity–Relationship (ER) model.

5.8 State any assumptions you made when creating the ER model.

6 Normalization

Chapter Objectives

In this chapter you will learn:

- The purpose of normalization.
- The problems associated with redundant information in rows.
- The identification of various types of update anomalies such as insertion, deletion and modification anomalies.
- How to recognize the appropriateness or quality of the design of relations.
- The concept of functional dependency, the main tool for measuring the appropriateness of attribute groupings in relations.
- How functional dependencies can be used to group attributes into relations that are in a known normal form.
- How to define normal forms for relations.
- How to undertake the process of normalization.
- How to identify first (1NF), second (2NF) and third (3NF) normal forms, and Boyce–Codd normal form (BCNF).

6.1   The Purpose of Normalization

When we design a database for a relational system, the main objective in developing a logical data model is to create an accurate representation of the data, its relationships and constraints. To achieve this objective, we must identify a suitable set of relations. A technique that we can use to help identify such relations is called **normalization**.

Normalization	A technique for producing a set of relations with desirable properties, given the data requirements of an enterprise.

The process of normalization was first developed by E. F. Codd (1972b). Normalization is often performed as a series of tests on a relation to determine whether it satisfies or violates the requirements of a given normal form. Three normal forms were initially proposed, called first (1NF), second (2NF) and third (3NF) normal forms. Subsequently, a stronger definition of third normal form was introduced by R. Boyce and E. F. Codd, referred to as Boyce–Codd Normal Form (BCNF) (Codd, 1974). All of these normal forms are based on the functional dependencies among the attributes of a relation. This chapter discusses the concept of functional dependency and its relationship to relational database design (Maier, 1983).

Higher normal forms that go beyond BCNF were introduced later. For example, there are fourth (4NF) and fifth (5NF) normal forms (Fagin, 1977, 1979). However, these later normal forms deal with practical situations that are very rare. This chapter describes only the most commonly used normal forms, which include the normal forms up to BCNF. For a detailed discussion on normal forms that follow BCNF, the interested reader is referred to Elmasri and Navathe (1994).

In Chapter 7, we will demonstrate how normalization can be used in conjunction with the Entity–Relationship (ER) technique, which we described in Chapter 5, to support the logical design of a database. Although normalization can be used to facilitate the development of other logical data models, this chapter considers only the relational data model.

In Chapter 3, we saw that a relation consists of a number of attributes, and a relational schema consists of a number of relations. Attributes may be grouped together to form a relational schema based largely on the common sense of the database designer, or by mapping the relational schema from an ER diagram. Whatever the approach taken, a formal method is often required to help the database designer identify the optimal grouping of attributes for each relation in the schema.

The process of normalization is a formal method that identifies relations based on their primary key (or candidate keys in the case of BCNF) and the functional dependencies among their attributes. Normalization supports database designers by presenting a series of tests, which can be applied to individual relations so that a relational schema can be normalized to a specific form to prevent the possible occurrence of update anomalies.

To illustrate the process of normalization, examples are drawn from the *DreamHome* case study (see Section 1.7). Note that in this chapter, some attribute names are given a fuller description to help the reader's comprehension of the text. For example, staff number is referred to as Staff_No rather than Sno. Also note that in some cases only a subset of the attributes associated with each relation of the *DreamHome* case study are used as examples in this chapter.

6.2 Information Redundancy and Update Anomalies

A major aim of relational database design is to group attributes into relations so as to minimize information redundancy and thereby reduce the file storage space required by the base relations. The problems associated with information redundancy are illustrated by comparing the Staff and Branch relations shown in Figure 6.1 with the Staff_Branch relation shown in Figure 6.2. The Staff_Branch relation is an alternative format of the Staff and Branch relations. The relations have the form:

Staff   (Staff_No, SName, SAddress, Position, Salary, Branch_No)

Branch   (Branch_No, BAddress, Tel_No)

Staff_Branch (Staff_No, SName, SAddress, Position, Salary, Branch_No, BAddress, Tel_No)

In the Staff_Branch relation there is redundant information; the details of a branch are repeated for every member of staff located at that branch. In contrast, the branch information appears only once for each branch in the Branch relation, and only the branch number (Branch_No) is repeated in the Staff relation, to represent where each member of staff is located.

Another serious difficulty using relations that have redundant information is the problem of update anomalies. These can be classified as insertion, deletion or modification anomalies.

6.2.1 Insertion Anomalies

There are two main types of insertion anomalies, which we illustrate using the Staff_Branch relation shown in Figure 6.2.

- To insert the details of new members of staff into the Staff_Branch relation, we must include the details of the branch at which the staff are to be located. For example, to insert the details of new staff located at branch number B7, we must enter the correct details of branch number B7 so that the branch details are consistent with values for

STAFF RELATION

Staff_No	SName	SAddress	Position	Salary	Branch_No
SL21	John White	19 Taylor Street, London	Manager	30000	B5
SG37	Ann Beech	81 George Street, Glasgow	Snr Asst	12000	B3
SG14	David Ford	63 Ashby Street, Glasgow	Deputy	18000	B3
SA9	Mary Howe	2 Elm Place, Aberdeen	Assistant	9000	B7
SG5	Susan Brand	5 Gt Western Road, Glasgow	Manager	24000	B3
SL41	Julie Lee	28 Malvern Street, Kilburn	Assistant	9000	B5

BRANCH RELATION

Branch_No	BAddress	Tel_No
B5	22 Deer Road, London	0171–886–1212
B7	16 Argyll Street, Glasgow	01224–67125
B3	163 Main Street, Glasgow	0141–339–2178

Figure 6.1 Staff and Branch relations.

STAFF_BRANCH RELATION

Staff_No	SName	SAddress	Position	Salary	Branch_No	BAddress	Tel_No
SL21	John White	19 Taylor Street, London	Manager	30000	B5	22 Deer Road, London	0171–886–1212
SG37	Ann Beech	81 George Street, Glasgow	Snr Asst	12000	B3	163 Main Street, Glasgow	0141–339–2178
SG14	David Ford	63 Ashby Street, Glasgow	Deputy	18000	B3	163 Main Street, Glasgow	0141–339–2178
SA9	Mary Howe	2 Elm Place, Aberdeen	Assistant	9000	B7	16 Argyll Street, Aberdeen	01224–67111
SG5	Susan Brand	5 Gt Western Rd, Glasgow	Manager	24000	B3	163 Main Street, Glasgow	0141–339–2178
SL41	Julie Lee	28 Malvern Street, Kilburn	Assistant	9000	B5	22 Deer Road, London	0171–886–1212

branch B7 in other rows of the Staff_Branch relation. The relations shown in Figure 6.1 do not suffer from this potential inconsistency, because we only enter the appropriate branch number for each staff member into the Staff relation. Also, the details of branch number B7 are recorded only once in the database as a single row in the Branch relation.

Figure 6.2
Staff_Branch relation.

- To insert details of a new branch that currently has no members of staff into the Staff_Branch relation. When we attempt to enter the branch details, it is necessary to enter nulls into the attributes for staff, such as Staff_No. However, as Staff_No is the primary key for the Staff_Branch relation, attempting to enter nulls for Staff_No violates entity integrity (see Section 3.3). We therefore cannot enter a row for a new branch into the Branch_Staff relation with a null for the Staff_No. The design of the relations shown in Figure 6.1 avoids this problem because branch details are entered in the Branch relation separately from the staff details. The details of staff ultimately located at that branch are entered at a later date into the Staff relation.

6.2.2 Deletion Anomalies

If we delete a staff row from the Staff_Branch relation that represents the last member of staff located at a branch, the information about that branch is also lost from the database. For example, if we delete the row for staff number SA9 (Mary Howe) from the Staff_Branch relation, the information relating to branch number B7 is lost from the database. The design of the relations in Figure 6.1 avoids this problem, because branch rows are stored separately from staff rows and only the attribute Branch_No relates the two relations. If we delete the row for staff number SA9 from the Staff relation, the information on branch number B7 remains unaffected in the Branch relation.

6.2.3 Modification Anomalies

In the Staff_Branch relation, if we want to change the value of one of the attributes of a particular branch, for example the telephone number for branch number B3, we must update the rows of all staff located at that branch. If this modification is not carried out on all the appropriate rows of the Branch_Staff relation, the database will become inconsistent. For example, branch number B3 may appear to have different telephone numbers in different staff rows.

The above examples illustrate that the Staff and Branch relations of Figure 6.1 have more desirable properties than the Staff_Branch relation of Figure 6.2. Later in this chapter, we discuss how the process of normalization can be used to derive well-formed relations. However, we first introduce the concepts of functional dependencies, which are fundamental to the process of normalization.

6.3 Functional Dependencies

One of the main concepts associated with normalization is functional dependency. A functional dependency describes the relationship between attributes. In this section we describe the concept of functional dependency, and then in the following sections, describe the association of functional dependency with the process of normalizing database relations.

6.3.1 Definition of Functional Dependency

Functional dependency	Describes the relationship between attributes in a relation. For example, if A and B are attributes of relation R, B is functionally dependent on A (denoted A → B), if each value of A in R is associated with exactly one value of B in R.

Functional dependency is a property of the meaning or semantics of the attributes in a relation. The semantics indicate how the attributes relate to one another, and specify the functional dependencies between attributes. When a functional dependency is present, the dependency is specified as a **constraint** between the attributes.

Consider a relation with attributes A and B, where attribute B is functionally dependent on attribute A. (Note that A and B may each consist of one or more attributes.) In other words, if we know the value of A and we examine the relation which holds the dependency, we find only one value of B in all the rows that have a given value of A, at any moment in time. Thus, when two rows have the same value of A, they also have the same value of B. However, for a given value of B there may be several different values of A. The dependency between attributes A and B can be represented diagrammatically, as shown Figure 6.3.

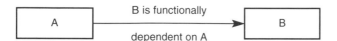

Figure 6.3   A functional dependency diagram.

Determinant	The determinant of a functional dependency refers to the attribute or group of attributes on the left-hand side of the arrow.

When a functional dependency exists, the attribute or group of attributes on the left-hand side of the arrow is called the **determinant**. For example, A is the determinant of B as shown in Figure 6.3.

Throughout this chapter, we ignore **trivial** functional dependencies: that is, dependencies of the type A → B, where B is dependent on a subset of A. To illustrate functional dependencies, consider the following examples.

Example 6.1

Consider the attributes Staff_No and Position of the Staff relation of Figure 6.1. For a specific Staff_No, for example SL21, we can determine the position of that member of staff as Manager. In other words, the Position attribute is functionally dependent on the Staff_No, as shown in Figure 6.4(a). However, Figure 6.4(b) illustrates that the opposite is not true, as Staff_No is not functionally dependent on Position. A member of staff holds one position, however, there may be several members of staff with the same position.

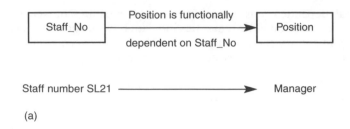

(a)

Figure 6.4 (a)
Position is functionally
dependent on
Staff_No (Staff_No →
Position). (b) Staff_No
is *not* functionally
dependent on
Position (Position
—X→ Staff_No).

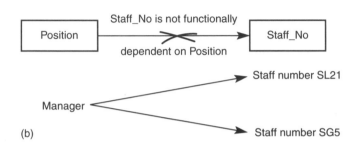

(b)

The relationship between Staff_No and Position is 1:1: for each staff number there is only one position. The relationship between Position and Staff_No is 1:M: there are several staff numbers (members of staff) associated with a position. In this instance, Staff_No is the determinant of this functional dependency.

Example 6.2

We now identify the functional dependencies of the Staff_Branch relation shown in Figure 6.2.

$$Staff\_No \rightarrow SName$$
$$Staff\_No \rightarrow SAddress$$
$$Staff\_No \rightarrow Position$$
$$Staff\_No \rightarrow Salary$$
$$Staff\_No \rightarrow Branch\_No$$
$$Staff\_No \rightarrow BAddress$$
$$Staff\_No \rightarrow Tel\_No$$
$$Branch\_No \rightarrow BAddress$$
$$Branch\_No \rightarrow Tel\_No$$
$$BAddress \rightarrow Branch\_No$$
$$Tel\_No \rightarrow Branch\_No$$

There are 11 functional dependencies in the Staff_Branch relation with Staff_No, Branch_No, BAddress and Tel_No as determinants. An alternative format for displaying such functional dependencies is shown below:

Staff_No → SName, SAddress, Position, Salary, Branch_No, BAddress,
         Tel_No

Branch_No → BAddress, Tel_No

BAddress → Branch_No

Tel_No → Branch_No

To identify the candidate key(s) for the Staff_Branch relation, we must recognize the attribute (or group of attributes) that uniquely identifies each row in this relation. If a relation has more than one candidate key, we identify the candidate key that is to act as the primary key for the relation. All of the attributes that are not part of the primary key (non-primary-key attributes) should be functionally dependent on the key.

The only candidate key of the Staff_Branch relation, and therefore the primary key, is Staff_No, as all other attributes of the relation are functionally dependent on Staff_No. Although Branch_No, BAddress and Tel_No are determinants in this relation, they are not candidate keys for the relation.

The concept of functional dependency is central to the process of normalization, which we discuss in the following sections.

6.4   The Process of Normalization

Normalization is a formal technique for analysing relations based on their primary key (or candidate keys in the case of BCNF) and functional dependencies. The technique involves a series of rules that can be tested against individual relations so that a database can be normalized to any degree. When a requirement is not met, the relation violating the requirement must be decomposed into relations that individually meet the requirements of normalization.

Normalization is often executed as a series of steps. Each step corresponds to a specific normal form, which has known properties. As normalization proceeds, the relations become progressively more restricted (stronger) in format, and also less vulnerable to update anomalies. In relational database design, it is important to recognize that it is only first normal form (1NF) that is critical in creating appropriate relations. All of the subsequent normal forms are optional. However, to avoid the update anomalies discussed in Section 6.2, it is normally recommended that we proceed to BCNF.

The process of normalization is illustrated in Figure 6.5, which demonstrates the relationship between the various normal forms. It shows that some 1NF relations are also in 2NF and that some 2NF relations are also in 3NF, and so on.

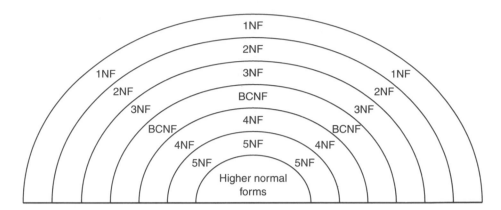

Figure 6.5
Diagrammatic
illustration of the
relationship
between the
normal forms.

In the following sections, we demonstrate the process of normalization by transferring information initially held as a form into table format with columns and rows. We then proceed to normalize this tabular information. It is important to note that, in Chapter 7, we present a logical database design methodology which recommends that we first attempt to understand the relationships between the information shown on the form using the Entity–Relationship (ER) modelling technique described in Chapter 5. However, in this chapter we do not use the ER modelling technique, and simply concentrate on using the process of normalization to help our understanding of the information held on the form.

6.5   First Normal Form (1NF)

Before discussing first normal form, we initially give a definition of the state prior to first normal form.

> **Unnormalized form (UNF)**   A table that contains one or more repeating groups.

> **First normal form (1NF)**   A relation in which the intersection of each row and column contains one and only one value.

In this chapter, we begin the process of normalization by first transferring the information from the source (for example, a standard data entry form) into table format with columns and rows. In this format, the table of information is in unnormalized form (UNF) and is referred to as an **unnormalized table**. To transform the unnormalized table to first normal form (1NF), we identify and remove repeating groups within the table. A repeating group is an attribute or group of attributes within a table that occurs with multiple values for a single occurrence of the nominated key attribute(s) for that table. Note that in this context, the term 'key' refers to the attribute(s) that uniquely identify each row within the unnormalized table. There are two common approaches to removing repeating groups from unnormalized tables.

In the first approach, we remove the repeating groups by entering appropriate data in the empty columns of rows containing the repeating data. In other words, we fill in the blanks by duplicating the non-repeating data, where required. This approach is commonly referred to as 'flattening' the table. The resulting table, now referred to as a relation, contains atomic (or single) values at the intersection of each row and column, and is therefore in first normal form. With this approach, redundancy is introduced into the resulting relation, which is subsequently removed during the normalization process.

In the second approach, we nominate an attribute or group of attributes as a key for the unnormalized table, and then remove the repeating group(s) by placing the repeating data, along with a copy of the original key attribute(s), in a separate relation. Primary keys are identified for the new relations. Sometimes the unnormalized table may contain more than one repeating group, or repeating groups within repeating groups. In such cases, this approach is applied iteratively until no repeating groups remain. A set of relations are in 1NF if they contain no repeating groups.

Both approaches are correct. However, the second approach initially produces relations in at least 1NF with less redundancy. If we choose the first approach, the 1NF relation is decomposed further during subsequent normalization steps into the same relations produced as a result of the second approach. In this section, we demonstrate both approaches using an example from the *DreamHome* case study.

Example 6.3

The *DreamHome* Customer Rental Details form, shown in Figure 6.6, holds the details of property rented by a customer called John Kay. To simplify this example, we assume that a customer rents a given property only once, and cannot rent more than one property at any one time.

The information on properties rented by two customers, namely John Kay and Aline Stewart, is transformed from the Customer Rental Details forms into table format with columns and rows, as shown in Figure 6.7. This is an example of an unnormalized table.

We identify the key attribute for the Customer_Rental unnormalized table as Customer_No. Next, we identify the repeating group in the unnormalized table as the property rented details, which repeats for each customer. The structure of the repeating group is:

Repeating Group = (Property_No, PAddress, RentStart, RentFinish, Rent,
                          Owner_No, OName)

Page 1	**_DreamHome_** Customer Rental Details	Date 7-Oct-95

Customer Name _John Kay_   Customer Number _CR76_

Property Number	Property Address	Rent Start	Rent Finish	Rent	Owner Number	Owner Name
PG4	6 Lawrence Street, Glasgow	1-Jul-93	31-Aug-95	350	CO40	Tina Murphy
PG16	5 Novar Drive, Glasgow	1-Sep-95	1-Sep-96	450	CO93	Tony Shaw

Figure 6.6
Dreamhome Customer Rental Details form.

CUSTOMER RENTAL TABLE

Customer_No	CName	Property_No	PAddress	RentStart	RentFinish	Rent	Owner_No	OName
CR76	John Kay	PG4	6 Lawrence Street, Glasgow	1-Jul-93	31-Aug-95	350	CO40	Tina Murphy
		PG16	5 Novar Drive, Glasgow	1-Sep-95	1-Sep-96	450	CO93	Tony Shaw
CR56	Aline Stewart	PG4	6 Lawrence Street, Glasgow	1-Sep-92	10-June-93	350	CO40	Tina Murphy
		PG36	2 Manor Road, Glasgow	10-Oct-93	1-Dec-94	375	CO93	Tony Shaw
		PG16	5 Novar Drive, Glasgow	1-Jan-95	10-Aug-95	450	CO93	Tony Shaw

Figure 6.7
Customer_Rental unnormalized table.

As a consequence, there are multiple values at the intersection of certain rows and columns. For example, there are two values for Property_No (PG4 and PG16) for the customer named John Kay.

To transform an unnormalized table into 1NF, we must ensure that there is a single value at the intersection of each row and column. This is achieved by removing the repeating group.

In the first approach, we remove the repeating group (property rented details) by entering the appropriate customer data into each row. The resulting first normal form Customer_Rentals relation is shown in Figure 6.8. We identify the primary key for the Customer_Rental relation as being a composite key comprising (Customer_No, Property_No). Note that we have placed the attributes, which make up the primary key together, at the left-hand side of the relation.

The Customer_Rental relation is defined as follows:

> Customer_Rental (Customer_No, Property_No, CName, PAddress,
> RentStart, RentFinish, Rent, Owner_No, OName)

The Customer_Rental relation is in 1NF as there is a single value at the intersection of each row and column. The relation contains data describing customers, property rented and property owners, which is repeated several times. As a result, the Customer_Rental relation contains significant data redundancy. If implemented, the 1NF relation would be subject to the update anomalies described in Section 6.2. To remove some of these, we must transform the relation into second normal form.

In the second approach, we remove the repeating group (property rented details) by placing the repeating data along with a copy of the original key attribute (Customer_No) in a separate relation, as shown in Figure 6.9. We then identify a primary key for each of the new relations. The format of the resulting 1NF relations are as follows:

> Customer   (Customer_No, CName)
>
> Prop_Rental_Owner   (Customer_No, Property_No, PAddress, RentStart,
>   RentFinish, Rent, Owner_No, OName)

The Customer and Prop_Rental_Owner relations are both in 1NF as there is a single value at the intersection of each row and column. The Prop_Rental_Owner relation contains data describing property rented and property owners. However, as we can see from Figure 6.9, this relation also contains some redundancy. As a result, it may suffer from similar update anomalies as described above for the Customer_Rental relation.

Figure 6.8 First Normal Form (1NF) Customer_Rental relation.

CUSTOMER_RENTAL RELATION

Customer_No	Property_No	CName	PAddress	RentStart	RentFinish	Rent	Owner_No	OName
CR76	PG4	John Kay	6 Lawrence Street, Glasgow	1-Jul-93	31-Aug-95	350	CO40	Tina Murphy
CR76	PG16	John Kay	5 Novar Drive, Glasgow	1-Sep-95	1-Sep-96	450	CO93	Tony Shaw
CR56	PG4	Aline Stewart	6 Lawrence Street, Glasgow	1-Sep-92	10-Jun-93	350	CO40	Tina Murphy
CR56	PG36	Aline Stewart	2 Manor Road, Glasgow	10-Oct-93	1-Dec-94	375	CO93	Tony Shaw
CR56	PG16	Aline Stewart	5 Novar Drive, Glasgow	1-Jan-95	10-Aug-95	450	CO93	Tony Shaw

Figure 6.9 Alternative
First Normal Form
(1NF) Customer and
Prop_Rental_Owner
relations.

CUSTOMER RELATION

Customer_No	CName
CR76	John Kay
CR56	Aline Stewart

PROP_RENTAL_OWNER RELATION

Customer_No	Property_No	PAddress	RentStart	RentFinish	Rent	Owner_No	OName
CR76	PG4	6 Lawrence Street, Glasgow	1-Jul-93	31-Aug-95	350	CO40	Tina Murphy
CR76	PG16	5 Novar Drive, Glasgow	1-Sep-95	1-Sep-96	450	CO93	Tony Shaw
CR56	PG4	6 Lawrence Street, Glasgow	1-Sep-92	10-Jun-93	350	CO40	Tina Murphy
CR56	PG36	2 Manor Road, Glasgow	10-Oct-93	1-Dec-94	375	CO93	Tony Shaw
CR56	PG16	5 Novar Drive, Glasgow	1-Jan-95	10-Aug-95	450	CO93	Tony Shaw

To demonstrate the process of normalizing relations from 1NF to 2NF, we use only the Customer_Rental relation shown in Figure 6.8. However, recall that both approaches are correct, and will ultimately result in the production of the same relations as we continue the process of normalization to BCNF.

6.6   Second Normal Form (2NF)

Second normal form (2NF) is based on the concept of full functional dependency, which we describe next.

6.6.1   Full Functional Dependency

Full functional dependency	Indicates that if A and B are attributes of a relation, B is fully functionally dependent on A if B is functionally dependent on A, but not on any proper subset of A.

A functional dependency A → B is a full functional dependency if removal of any attribute from A results in the dependency not being sustained any more. A functional dependency A → B is **partially dependent** if there is some attribute that can be removed from A and the dependency still holds.

For example, consider the following functional dependency:

Staff_No, SName → Branch_No

It is correct to say that each value of (Staff_No, SName) is associated with a single value of Branch_No. However, it is not a full functional dependency because Branch_No is also functionally dependent on a subset of (Staff_No, SName). In other words, Branch_No is fully functionally dependent on only Staff_No. Further examples of full and partial functional dependencies are described in the following sections.

6.6.2 Definition of Second Normal Form

Second normal form applies to relations with composite keys, that is, relations with a primary key composed of two or more attributes. A relation with a single attribute primary key is automatically in at least 2NF. A relation that is not in 2NF may suffer from the update anomalies discussed in Section 6.2. For example, suppose we wish to change the rent of property number PG4. We have to update two rows in the Customer_Rental relation. If only one row is updated with the new rent, this results in an inconsistent state in the database.

Second normal form (2NF)	A relation that is in first normal form and every non-primary-key attribute is fully functionally dependent on the primary key.

The normalization of 1NF relations to 2NF involves the removal of partial dependencies which we demonstrate using the Customer_Rental relation shown in Figure 6.8. If a partial dependency exists, we remove the functionally dependent attributes from the relation by placing them in a new relation along with a copy of their determinant.

Example 6.4

We first identify the functional dependencies in the Customer_Rental relation. The Customer_Rental relation has the following functional dependencies:

Customer_No, Property_No → RentStart, RentFinish

Customer_No → CName

Property_No → PAddress, Rent, Owner_No, OName

Owner_No → OName

Figure 6.10 illustrates the functional dependencies associated with the Customer_Rental relation.

Note that the customer attribute (CName) is partially dependent on the primary key, in other words, on only the Customer_No attribute. The property attributes (PAddress, Rent, Owner_No, OName) are partially dependent on the primary key, that is on only the Property_No attribute. The property rented attributes (RentStart and RentFinish) are fully dependent on the whole primary key, that is the Customer_No and Property_No attributes.

Also note that Figure 6.10 indicates the presence of a **transitive depend-**

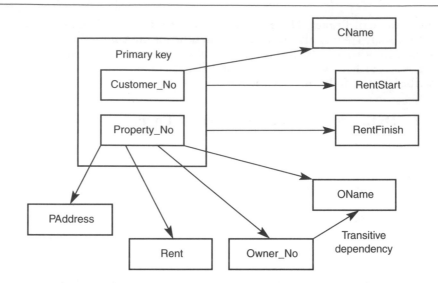

Figure 6.10
Functional
dependencies for the
Customer_Rental
relation.

ency on the primary key. Although a transitive dependency can also cause update anomalies, its presence in a relation does not violate 2NF. Such dependencies are removed when we reach 3NF.

The identification of partial dependencies within the Customer_Rental relation indicates that the relation is not in second normal form. To transform the Customer_Rental relation into 2NF requires the creation of new relations so that the non-primary-key attributes are removed along with a copy of the part of the primary key on which they are fully functionally dependent. This results in the creation of three new relations called Customer, Rental and Property_Owner, shown in Figure 6.11. These three relations are in second

CUSTOMER RELATION

Customer_No	CName
CR76	John Kay
CR56	Aline Stewart

RENTAL RELATION

Customer_No	Property_No	RentStart	RentFinish
CR76	PG4	1-Jul-93	31-Aug-95
CR76	PG16	1-Sep-95	1-Sep-96
CR56	PG4	1-Sep-92	10-Jun-93
CR56	PG36	10-Oct-93	1-Dec-94
CR56	PG16	1-Jan-95	10-Aug-95

PROPERTY_OWNER RELATION

Figure 6.11 Second
Normal Form (2NF)
relations derived from
the Customer_Rental
relation.

Property_No	PAddress	Rent	Owner_No	OName
PG4	6 Lawrence Street, Glasgow	350	CO40	Tina Murphy
PG16	5 Novar Drive, Glasgow	450	CO93	Tony Shaw
PG36	2 Manor Road, Glasgow	375	CO93	Tony Shaw

normal form as every non-primary-key attribute is fully functionally dependent on the primary key of the relation. The relations have the form:

Customer	(<u>Customer_No</u>, CName)
Rental	(<u>Customer_No</u>, <u>Property_No</u>, RentStart, RentFinish)
Property_Owner	(<u>Property_No</u>, PAddress, Rent, Owner_No, OName)

6.7 Third Normal Form (3NF)

Although 2NF relations have less redundancy than those in 1NF, they may still suffer from update anomalies. For example, if we want to update the name of an owner, such as Tony Shaw (Owner_No CO93), we have to update two rows in the Property_Owner relation of Figure 6.11. If we update only one row and not the other, the database would be in an inconsistent state. This update anomaly is caused by a transitive dependency. We need to remove such dependencies by progressing to third normal form. In this section, we discuss transitive dependencies and third normal form.

6.7.1 Transitive Dependency

Transitive dependency	A condition where A, B and C are attributes of a relation such that if A → B and B → C, then C is transitively dependent on A via B (provided that A is not functionally dependent on B or C).

Transitive dependency is a description of a type of functional dependency that occurs when the following functional dependencies hold between attributes A, B and C of a relation:

A → B and B → C

Then the transitive dependency A → C exists via attribute B. This condition holds provided that attribute A is not functionally dependent on B or C.

For example, consider the following functional dependencies within the Staff_Branch relation shown in Figure 6.2.

Staff_No → Branch_No and Branch_No → BAddress

Then the transitive dependency Staff_No → BAddress exists via the Branch_No attribute. This condition holds as Staff_No is not functionally dependent on Branch_No or BAddress. Additional examples of transitive dependencies are described in the following sections.

6.7.2 Definition of Third Normal Form

Third normal form (3NF)	A relation that is in first and second normal form, and in which no non-primary-key attribute is transitively dependent on the primary key.

The normalization of 2NF relations to 3NF involves the removal of transitive dependencies. If a transitive dependency exists, we remove the transitively dependent attribute(s) from the relation by placing the attribute(s) in a new relation along with a copy of the determinant(s).

Example 6.5 _____

First, we examine the functional dependencies for the Customer, Rental and Property_Owner relations.

<u>Customer Relation</u>

Customer_No → CName

<u>Rental Relation</u>

Customer_No, Property_No → RentStart, RentFinish

<u>Property_Owner Relation</u>

Property_No → PAddress, Rent, Owner_No, OName

Owner_No → OName

All of the non-primary-key attributes within the Customer and Rental relations are functionally dependent on only their primary keys. The Customer and Rental relations have no transitive dependencies and are therefore already in third normal form (3NF).

All of the non-primary-key attributes within the Property_Owner relation are functionally dependent on the primary key, with the exception of OName, which is also dependent on Owner_No. This is an example of a transitive dependency, which occurs when a non-primary-key attribute (OName) is dependent on one or more non-primary-key attributes (Owner_No). This transitive dependency was previously identified in Figure 6.10.

To transform the Property_Owner relation into third normal form, we must first remove the transitive dependency identified above by creating two new relations called Property_for_Rent and Owner, as shown in Figure 6.12. The new relations have the form:

Property_for_Rent   (<u>Property_No</u>, PAddress, Rent, Owner_No)

Owner   (<u>Owner_No</u>, OName)

PROPERTY_FOR_RENT RELATION

Property_No	PAddress	Rent	Owner_No
PG4	6 Lawrence Street, Glasgow	350	CO40
PG16	5 Novar Drive, Glasgow	450	CO93
PG36	2 Manor Road Glasgow	375	CO93

OWNER RELATION

Owner_No	OName
CO40	Tina Murphy
CO93	Tony Shaw

Figure 6.12 3NF relations derived from the Property_Owner relation.

The Property_for_Rent and Owner relations are in third normal form as there are no further transitive dependencies on the primary key.

The Customer_Rental relation shown in Figure 6.8 has been transformed by the process of normalization into four relations in third normal form. Figure 6.13 illustrates the process by which the original 1NF relation is decomposed into the 3NF relations.

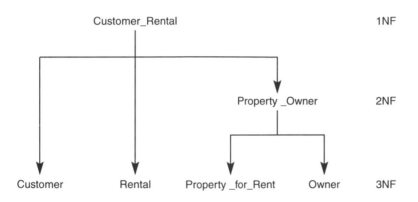

Figure 6.13 The decomposition of the Customer_Rental 1NF relation into 3NF relations.

The resulting 3NF relations have the form:

Customer   (Customer_No, CName)
Rental   (Customer_No, Property_No, RentStart, RentFinish)
Property_for_Rent   (Property_No, PAddress, Rent, Owner_No)
Owner   (Owner_No, OName)

The original Customer_Rental relation shown in Figure 6.8 can be recreated by joining the Customer, Rental, Property_for_Rent and Owner relations. This is achieved through the primary key/foreign key mechanism. For example, the Owner_No attribute is a primary key within the Owner relation, and is also present within the Property_for_Rent relation as a foreign key. The Owner_No attribute acting as a primary key/foreign key allows us to associate the Property_for_Rent and Owner relations to identify the name of property owners.

The Customer_No attribute is a primary key of the Customer relation and is also present within the Rental relation as a foreign key. Note that in this case, the Customer_No attribute in the Rental relation acts both as a

CUSTOMER RELATION

Customer_No	CName
CR76	John Kay
CR56	Aline Stewart

RENTAL RELATION

Customer_No	Property_No	RentStart	RentFinish
CR76	PG4	1-Jul-93	31-Aug-95
CR76	PG16	1-Sep-95	1-Sep-96
CR56	PG4	1-Sep-92	10-Jun-93
CR56	PG36	10-Oct-93	1-Dec-94
CR56	PG16	1-Jan-95	10-Aug-95

PROPERTY_FOR_RENT RELATION

Property_No	PAddress	Rent	Owner_No
PG4	6 Lawrence Street, Glasgow	350	CO40
PG16	5 Novar Drive, Glasgow	450	CO93
PG36	2 Manor Road Glasgow	375	CO93

OWNER RELATION

Owner_No	OName
CO40	Tina Murphy
CO93	Tony Shaw

Figure 6.14 A summary of the 3NF relations derived from the Customer_Rental relation.

foreign key and as part of the primary key of this relation. Similarly, the Property_No attribute is the primary key of the Property_for_Rent relation, and is also present within the Rental relation acting both as a foreign key and as part of the primary key for this relation.

In other words, the normalization process has decomposed the original Customer_Rental relation using a series of relational algebra projections (see Section 3.4). This results in a nonloss (or lossless) decomposition, which is reversible using the natural join operation.

The Customer, Rental, Property_for_Rent and Owner relations are shown in Figure 6.14.

6.8 Boyce–Codd Normal Form (BCNF)

Database relations are designed so that they have neither partial dependencies nor transitive dependencies, because these types of dependencies result in update anomalies, as discussed in Section 6.2. We have so far used definitions of second and third normal forms that identify and disallow partial and transitive dependencies on the primary key. However, these definitions do not consider if such dependencies remain on other candidate keys of a relation, if any exist.

6.8.1 Definition of Boyce–Codd Normal Form

Boyce–Codd Normal Form (BCNF) is based on functional dependencies that take into account all candidate keys in a relation. For a relation with only one candidate key, 3NF and BCNF are equivalent.

| **Boyce–Codd normal** | A relation is in BCNF if and only if every determi- |
| **form (BCNF)** | nant is a candidate key. |

BCNF does not state that the relation must first be in 3NF and then satisfy an additional constraint. Therefore, to test for BCNF, we simply identify all the determinants and make sure they are candidate keys. Recall that a determinant is an attribute or a group of attributes on which some other attribute is fully functionally dependent. Therefore, Boyce–Codd normal form is a stronger form of 3NF, such that every relation in BCNF is also in 3NF. However, a relation in 3NF is not necessarily in BCNF.

Before we consider the next example, let us re-examine the Customer, Rental, Property_for_Rent and Owner relations shown in Figure 6.14. The Customer, Property_for_Rent and Owner relations are all in BCNF, as each relation only has a single determinant which is the candidate key. However, note that the Rental relation in fact has three determinants (Customer_No, Property_No), (Customer_No, RentStart) and (Property_No, RentStart), as shown below:

Customer_No, Property_No → RentStart, RentFinish

Customer_No, RentStart → Property_No, RentFinish

Property_No, RentStart → Customer_No, RentFinish

As the three determinants of the Rental relation are also candidate keys, the Rental relation is also already in BCNF.

Violation of BCNF is quite rare, since it may only happen under specific conditions. The potential to violate BCNF may occur in a relation that:

- contains two (or more) composite candidate keys,
- which overlap and share at least one attribute in common.

In the following example, we present a situation where a relation violates BCNF, and demonstrate the transformation of this relation to BCNF.

Example 6.6

In this example, we present the Client_Interview relation, which contains details of the arrangements for interviews of clients by members of staff of the *DreamHome* company. The members of staff involved in interviewing clients are allocated to a specific room on the day of interview. A client is only interviewed once on a given date, but may be requested to attend further interviews at later dates. This relation has two candidate keys, namely (Client_No, Interview_Date) and (Staff_No, Interview_Date, Interview_Time). We select (Client_No, Interview_Date) to act as the primary key for this relation.

The Client_Interview relation is shown in Figure 6.15 and has the following form:

Client_Interview (Client_No, Interview_Date, Interview_Time, Staff_No, Room_No)

CLIENT_INTERVIEW RELATION

Client_No	Interview_Date	Interview_Time	Staff_No	Room_No
CR76	13-May-95	10.30	SG5	G101
CR56	13-May-95	12.00	SG5	G101
CR74	13-May-95	12.00	SG37	G102
CR56	1-Jul-95	10.30	SG5	G102

Figure 6.15
Client_Interview
relation.

The Client_Interview relation has the following functional dependencies:

Client_No, Interview_Date $\rightarrow$ Interview_Time, Staff_No, Room_No

Staff_No, Interview_Date, Interview_Time $\rightarrow$ Client_No

Staff_No, Interview_Date $\rightarrow$ Room_No

Therefore the (Client_No, Interview_Date) and (Staff_No, Interview_Date, Interview_Time) are composite candidate keys of the Client_Interview relation, which overlap and share the common attribute Interview_Date.

The Client_Interview relation does not have any partial or transitive dependencies on the primary key (Client_No, Interview_Date) and is therefore in 3NF. However, this relation is not in BCNF due to the presence of the (Staff_No, Interview_Date) determinant, which is not a candidate key for the relation. To transform the Client_Interview relation to BCNF, we must remove the violating functional dependency by creating two new relations called Interview and Staff_Room, as shown in Figure 6.16. The Interview and Staff_Room relations have the following form:

Interview (Client_No, Interview_Date, Interview_Time, Staff_No)

Staff_Room (Staff_No, Interview_Date, Room_No)

INTERVIEW RELATION

Client_No	Interview_Date	Interview_Time	Staff_No
CR76	13-May-95	10.30	SG5
CR56	13-May-95	12.00	SG5
CR74	13-May-95	12.00	SG37
CR56	1-Jul-95	10.30	SG5

STAFF_ROOM RELATION

Staff_No	Interview_Date	Room_No
SG5	13-May-95	G101
SG37	13-May-95	G102
SG5	1-Jul-95	G102

Figure 6.16 The
Interview and
Staff_Room BCNF
relations.

We can decompose any relation that is not in BCNF into BCNF as illustrated. However, it may not always be desirable to transform a relation into BCNF: for example, if there is a functional dependency that is not preserved when we perform the decomposition (that is, the determinant and the attributes it determines are placed in different relations). In this situation, it is difficult to enforce the functional dependency in the relation, and an important constraint is lost. When this occurs, it is better to stop at 3NF, which always preserves dependencies.

6.9   Review of Normalization (1NF to BCNF)

The purpose of this section is to review the process of normalization detailed in the previous sections. We again use the *DreamHome* case study to present a second example to enable us to re-examine the process of transforming unnormalized data to Boyce–Codd normal form.

Example 6.7 _____

The *DreamHome* Company manages property on behalf of the owners, and as part of this service the company undertakes regular inspections of the property by members of staff. When staff are required to undertake these inspections, they are allocated a company car for the day. A member of staff may inspect several properties on a given date, and a property is only inspected

Page 1	**DreamHome** Property Inspection Report		Date 1-Oct-95			
Property Number PG4			Property Address 6 Lawrence Street, Glasgow			
Inspection Date	Inspection Time	Comments	Staff Number	Staff Name	Car Regn.	
18-Oct-94	10.00	Need to replace crockery	SG37	Ann Beech	M231 JGR	
22-Apr-95	09.00	In good order	SG14	David Ford	M533 HDR	
1-Oct-95	12.00	Damp rot in bathroom	SG14	David Ford	N721 HFR	

Figure 6.17
DreamHome Property Inspection Report form.

once on a given date. An example of a *DreamHome* Property Inspection Report is shown in Figure 6.17, and displays information on the inspections of property number PG4. Note that the report shown in Figure 6.17 is a simplified version of the Property Inspection Report described in the *Dream-Home* case study in Section 1.7.

First Normal Form (1NF)

We first transfer some sample information held on two property inspection reports for property numbers PG4 and PG16 into table format with columns and rows. This is referred to as the Property_Inspection unnormalized table and is shown in Figure 6.18. We next identify the key attribute(s) for this unnormalized table as Property_No.

PROPERTY_INSPECTION TABLE

Property_No	PAddress	IDate	ITime	Comments	Staff_No	SName	Car_Reg
PG4	6 Lawrence Street, Glasgow	18-Oct-94	10.00	Need to replace crockery.	SG37	Ann Beech	M231 JGR
		22-Apr-95	09.00	In good order.	SG14	David Ford	M533 HDR
		1-Oct-95	12.00	Damp rot in bathroom.	SG14	David Ford	N721 HFR
PG16	5 Novar Drive, Glasgow	22-Apr-95	13.00	Replace living room carpet.	SG14	David Ford	M533 HDR
		24-Oct-95	14.00	Good condition.	SG37	Ann Beech	N721 HFR

Figure 6.18
Property_Inspection
unnormalized table.

We identify the repeating group in the unnormalized table as the property inspection and staff details, which repeats for each property. The structure of the repeating group is listed below:

Repeating Group = (IDate, ITime, Comments, Staff_No, SName, Car_Reg)

As a consequence, there are multiple values at the intersection of certain rows and columns. For example, for Property_No (PG4) there are three values for IDate (18-Oct-94, 22-Apr-95, 1-Oct-95).

We transform the unnormalized form to first normal form using the first approach described in Section 6.5. In the first approach, we transform the unnormalized table to 1NF by removing the repeating group (property inspection and staff details) by entering the appropriate property details (non-repeating data) into each row. The resulting first normal form Property_Inspection relation is shown in Figure 6.19.

The Property_Inspection relation has two candidate keys, namely (Property_No, IDate) and (Staff_No, IDate, ITime). We select (Property_No, IDate) as the primary key for this relation, and refer to the (Staff_No, IDate, ITime) as the alternate key. Note that we have placed the attributes, which

PROPERTY_INSPECTION RELATION

Property_No	IDate	ITime	PAddress	Comments	Staff_No	SName	Car_Reg
PG4	18-Oct-94	10.00	6 Lawrence Street, Glasgow	Need to replace crockery.	SG37	Ann Beech	M231 JGR
PG4	22-Apr-95	09.00	6 Lawrence Street, Glasgow	In good order.	SG14	David Ford	M533 HDR
PG4	1-Oct-95	12.00	6 Lawrence Street, Glasgow	Damp rot in bathroom.	SG14	David Ford	N721 HFR
PG16	22-Apr-95	13.00	5 Novar Drive, Glasgow	Replace living room carpet.	SG14	David Ford	M533 HDR
PG16	24-Oct-95	14.00	5 Novar Drive, Glasgow	Good condition.	SG37	Ann Beech	N721 HFR

Figure 6.19 The First Normal Form (1NF) Property_ Inspection relation.

make up the primary key together, at the left-hand side of the relation. The Property_Inspection relation is defined as follows:

> Property_Inspection   (<u>Property_No</u>, <u>IDate</u>, ITime, PAddress, Comments, Staff_No, SName, Car_Reg)

The Property_Inspection relation is in first normal form (1NF) as there is a single value at the intersection of each row and column. The relation contains data describing the inspection of property by members of staff, with the property and staff details repeated several times. As a result, the Property_Inspection relation contains a lot of data redundancy. If implemented, this 1NF relation would be subject to update anomalies. To remove some of these, we must transform the relation into second normal form.

Second Normal Form (2NF)
The normalization of 1NF relations to 2NF involves the removal of partial dependencies on the primary key. If a partial dependency exists, we remove the functionally dependent attributes from the relation by placing them in a new relation with a copy of their determinant.

We first identify the functional dependencies in the Property_Inspection relation. The functional dependencies for this relation are listed below:

> Property_No, IDate → ITime, Comments, Staff_No, SName, Car_Reg
>
> Property_No → PAddress
>
> Staff_No → SName
>
> Staff_No, IDate → Car_Reg
>
> Staff_No, IDate, ITime → Property_No, PAddress, Comments

Figure 6.20 illustrates the functional dependencies associated with the Property_Inspection relation.

The property attribute (PAddress) is partially dependent on part of the primary key, namely the Property_No. The attributes (ITime, Comments,

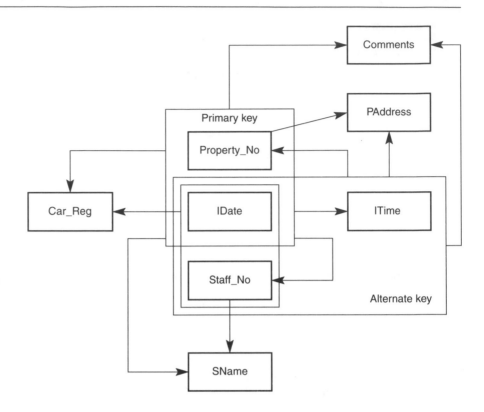

Figure 6.20
Functional
dependencies for the
Property_Inspection
relation.

Staff_No, SName and Car_Reg) are fully dependent on the whole primary key (Property_No and IDate).

The identification of the partial dependency within the Property_ Inspection relation indicates that the relation is not in second normal form. To transform the relation into 2NF requires the creation of new relations so that the attributes that are not fully dependent on the primary key are associated with only the appropriate part of the key.

The Property_Inspection relation is transformed into second normal by removing the partial dependency from the relation and creating two new relations called Prop and Prop_Inspection. The relations are in second normal form, as every non-primary-key attribute is fully functionally dependent on the primary key of the relation. The relations have the form:

Prop	(Property_No, PAddress)
Prop_Inspection	(Property_No, IDate, ITime, Comments, Staff_No, SName, Car_Reg)

Third Normal Form (3NF)

The normalization of 2NF relations to 3NF involves the removal of transitive dependencies. If a transitive dependency exists, we remove the transitively dependent attributes from the relation by placing them in a new relation along with a copy of their determinant.

First, we examine the functional dependencies within the Prop and Prop_Inspection relations, which are as follows:

> Prop Relation
>
> Property_No → PAddress
>
> Prop_Inspection Relation
>
> Property_No, IDate → ITime, Comments, Staff_No, SName, Car_Reg
>
> Staff_No → SName
>
> Staff_No, IDate → Car_Reg
>
> Staff_No, IDate, ITime → Property_No, Comments

As required for 2NF, the non-primary-key attribute within the Prop relation (PAddress) is fully functionally dependent on the primary key (Property_No). Also, this relation does not have transitive dependencies on the primary key, and is therefore already in third normal form (3NF).

However, although all of the non-primary-key attributes within the Prop_Inspection relation are functionally dependent on the primary key, SName is also dependent on Staff_No. This is an example of a transitive dependency, which occurs when a non-primary-key attribute is dependent on another non-primary-key attribute. To transform the Prop_Inspection relation into third normal form, we must first remove the transitive dependency identified above. The transitive dependency is removed by creating two new relations called Staff and Prop_Inspect with the form:

> Staff   (Staff_No, SName)
>
> Prop_Inspect (Property_No, IDate, ITime, Comments, Staff_No, Car_Reg)

The Staff and Prop_Inspect relations are in third normal form as no non-primary-key attribute is functionally dependent on another non-primary-key attribute.

The Property_Inspection relation shown in Figure 6.20 has been transformed by the process of normalization into three relations in third normal form. The resulting 3NF relations have the following form:

> Prop   (Property_No, PAddress)
>
> Staff   (Staff_No, SName)
>
> Prop_Inspect (Property_No, IDate, ITime, Comments, Staff_No, Car_Reg)

Boyce–Codd Normal Form (BCNF)

We now examine the Prop, Staff and Prop_Inspect relations to determine whether they are in BCNF. Recall that a relation is in BCNF if every determinant of a relation is a candidate key. Therefore, to test for BCNF, we simply identify all the determinants and make sure they are candidate keys.

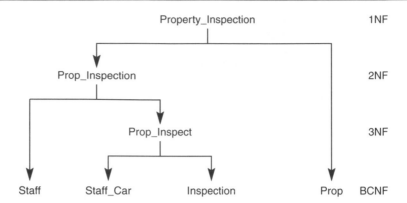

Figure 6.21
Decomposition of the
Property_Inspection
relation into BCNF
relations.

The functional dependencies for the Prop, Staff and Prop_Inspect relations are as follows:

Prop Relation
Property_No → PAddress
Staff Relation
Staff_No → SName
Prop_Inspect Relation
Property_No, IDate → ITime, Comments, Staff_No, Car_Reg
Staff_No, IDate → Car_Reg
Staff_No, IDate, ITime → Property_No, Comments, Car_Reg

We can see that the Prop and Staff relations are already in BCNF as the determinant in each of these relations is also the candidate key. The only 3NF relation that is not in BCNF is Prop_Inspect, because of the presence of the determinant (Staff_No, IDate) which is not a candidate key. To transform the Prop_Inspect relation into BCNF, we must remove the dependency that violates BCNF by creating two new relations called Staff_Car and Inspection with the form:

Staff_Car   (Staff_No, IDate, Car_Reg)
Inspection   (Property_No, IDate, ITime, Comments, Staff_No)

The Staff_Car and Inspection relations are in BCNF as the determinant in each of these relations is also a candidate key.

In summary, the decomposition of the Property_Inspection relation shown in Figure 6.19 into BCNF relations is shown in Figure 6.21.

The resulting BCNF relations have the following form:

Prop (<u>Property_No</u>, PAddress)

Staff (<u>Staff_No</u>, SName)

Inspection (<u>Property_No</u>, <u>IDate</u>, ITime, Comments, Staff_No)

Staff_Car (<u>Staff_No</u>, <u>IDate</u>, Car_Reg)

The original Property_Inspection relation shown in Figure 6.19 can be re-created from the Prop, Staff, Inspection and Staff_Car relations using the primary key/foreign key mechanism. For example, the attribute Staff_No is a primary key within the Staff relation, and is also present within the Inspection relation as a foreign key. The foreign key allows us to associate the Staff and Inspection relations to identify the name of the member of staff undertaking the property inspection.

Chapter Summary

- **Normalization** is a technique for producing a set of relations with desirable properties, given the data requirements of an enterprise.

- Normalization is a formal method that can be used to identify relations based on their keys and the functional dependencies among their attributes.

- The process of normalization takes a relation through the various normal forms. At each stage the process seeks to remove undesirable characteristics from the relation that leave it vulnerable to update anomalies. As the relation is transformed to higher normal forms, it becomes progressively more restricted in format and less vulnerable to disruptive operations. The process of normalization up to BCNF is represented diagrammatically in Figure 6.22.

- Three normal forms were initially proposed, called **first (1NF), second (2NF)** and **third (3NF) normal forms**. A stronger definition of third normal form (3NF) was also introduced, and is referred to as **Boyce–Codd Normal Form (BCNF)**. All these normal forms are dependent on the functional dependencies among the attributes of a relation.

- Relations with data redundancy suffer from **update anomalies**, which can be classified as insertion, deletion and modification anomalies.

- One of the main concepts associated with normalization is **functional dependency**. Functional dependency describes the relationship between attributes in a relation. For example, if A and B are attributes of relation R, B is functionally dependent on A (denoted $A \to B$), if each value of A in R is associated with exactly one value of B in R.

- A **determinant** is any attribute on which some other attribute is fully functionally dependent. The determinant of a functional dependency refers to the attribute or group of attributes on the left-hand side of the arrow.

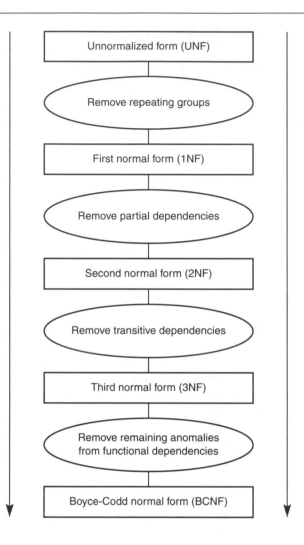

Figure 6.22 The process of normalization.

- **Unnormalized Form (UNF)** is a table that contains one or more repeating groups.
- **First Normal Form (1NF)** is a relation in which the intersection of each row and column contains one and only one value.
- **Second Normal Form (2NF)** is a relation that is in first normal form and every non-primary-key attribute is fully functionally dependent on the primary key.
- **Full functional dependency** indicates that if A and B are attributes of a relation, B is fully functionally dependent on A if B is functionally dependent on A but not on any proper subset of A.
- **Third Normal Form (3NF)** is a relation that is in first and second normal

form in which no non-primary-key attribute is transitively dependent on the primary key.

- **Transitive dependency** is a condition where A, B and C are attributes of a relation such that if A → B and B → C, then C is transitively dependent on A via B (provided that A is not functionally dependent on B or C).

- **Boyce–Codd Normal Form (BCNF)** is a relation in which every determinant is a candidate key.

REVIEW QUESTIONS

6.1   Describe the purpose of normalizing data.

6.2   Describe the problems that are associated with redundant information in rows.

6.3   Describe the concept of functional dependency.

6.4   How is the concept of functional dependency associated with the process of normalization?

6.5   Provide a definition for first, second, third and Boyce–Codd normal forms.

EXERCISES

The table shown in Figure 6.23 lists dentist/patient appointment data. A patient is given an appointment at a specific time and date with a dentist located at a particular surgery. On each day of patient appointments, a dentist is allocated to a specific surgery for that day.

StaffNo	DentistName	PatNo	PatName	Appointment Date	Time	SurgeryNo
S1011	Tony Smith	P100	Gillian White	12-Sep-95	10.00	S15
S1011	Tony Smith	P105	Jill Bell	12-Sep-95	12.00	S15
S1024	Helen Pearson	P108	Ian MacKay	12-Sep-95	10.00	S10
S1024	Helen Pearson	P108	Ian MacKay	14-Sep-95	14.00	S10
S1032	Robin Plevin	P105	Jill Bell	14-Sep-95	16.30	S15
S1032	Robin Plevin	P110	John Walker	15-Sep-95	18.00	S13

Figure 6.23 Lists dentist/patient appointment data.

6.6   The table shown in Figure 6.23 is susceptible to update anomalies. Provide examples of insertion, deletion and update anomalies.

6.7 Describe and illustrate the process of normalizing the table shown in Figure 6.23 to Boyce–Codd normal form. State any assumptions you make about the data shown in this table.

An agency called *Instant Cover* supplies part-time/temporary staff to hotels within Strathclyde region. The table shown in Figure 6.24 lists the time spent by agency staff working at various hotels. The National Insurance Number (NIN) is unique for every member of staff.

Figure 6.24 *Instant Cover's* contracts.

NIN	ContractNo	Hours	EName	H_No	H_Loc
1135	C1024	16	Smith J	H25	East Kilbride
1057	C1024	24	Hocine D	H25	East Kilbride
1068	C1025	28	White T	H4	Glasgow
1135	C1025	15	Smith J	H4	Glasgow

6.8 The table shown in Figure 6.24 is susceptible to update anomalies. Provide examples of insertion, deletion and update anomalies.

6.9 Describe and illustrate the process of normalizing the table shown in Figure 6.24 to Boyce–Codd normal form. State any assumptions you make about the data shown in this table.

7 Methodology – Logical Database Design

Chapter Objectives

In this chapter you will learn:

- The purpose of a design methodology.
- Database design has two main phases: logical database design and physical database design.
- End users play an integral role throughout the process of logical database design.
- How to document the process of logical database design.
- How to decompose the scope of the design into specific user views of the enterprise.
- How to use Entity–Relationship (ER) modelling to build a local conceptual data model based on the information given in the user's view of an enterprise.
- How to map a local conceptual model to a local logical data model.
- How to derive relations from a local logical data model.
- How to validate a logical data model using the technique of normalization and against the transactions it is required to support.
- How to merge local logical data models based on specific user views into a global logical data model of the enterprise.
- How to ensure that the resultant global model is a true and accurate representation of the part of the enterprise we are attempting to model.

In Chapter 4, we described the database development lifecycle as consisting of the main phases: feasibility, requirements collection and analysis, logical and physical design, implementation, validation and testing, and operational maintenance. In this chapter, and in Chapters 8, 9 and 10, we describe and illustrate by example a methodology for the logical and physical design phases of the lifecycle for relational databases.

The database design methodology consists of two main phases: **logical database design**, in which the designer decides on the logical structure of the database (that is, the entity and relationship types), and **physical database design**, in which the designer decides how the logical structure is to be physically implemented on the target Database Management System (DBMS).

In this chapter, we present a step-by-step guide to logical database design for the relational data model. We use the Entity–Relationship (ER) modelling technique described in Chapter 5 to help build local conceptual data models, which represent different user views of the enterprise we are interested in modelling. We then map the conceptual models to local logical data models. We validate these models using the technique of normalization described in Chapter 6, and against the transactions they must support for the users. We finally merge the local data models together to create a global data model for the enterprise.

In Chapter 8, we will demonstrate the logical database design methodology working in practice using an example taken from the *DreamHome* case study (see Section 1.7). In Chapter 9, we continue the database design methodology by presenting a step-by-step guide for physical database design of relational databases. This part of the methodology illustrates that the development of the logical data model alone is insufficient to guarantee the optimum development and implementation of a database application. For example, we may have to consider performance-related issues. In Chapter 10, we will demonstrate the physical database design methodology working in practice. The starting point for this chapter is the logical database design for the *DreamHome* case study created in Chapter 8.

Appendix E presents a summary of the methodology, for those readers who are already familiar with database design and simply require an overview of the main steps.

Throughout this chapter, the terms 'entity' and 'relationship' are used in place of 'entity type' and 'relationship type', where the meaning is obvious; 'type' is generally only added to avoid ambiguity. Also note that in this chapter we mostly use examples from the *DreamHome* case study to illustrate each step of the methodology. However, the examples have been simplified, and are used only to demonstrate the specific point under discussion.

7.1 Database Design Methodology

Before we present the methodology, it may be useful to discuss what a design methodology represents and, in particular, how a methodology for logical database design relates to the physical design of a database.

7.1.1 What is a Design Methodology?

Design methodology	A structured approach that uses procedures, techniques, tools and documentation aids to support and facilitate the process of design.

A design methodology consists of phases that contain steps which guide the designer in the techniques appropriate at each stage of the project, and also helps to plan, manage, control and evaluate database development projects. Furthermore, it is a structured approach for analysing and modelling a set of requirements for a database in a standardized and organized manner.

7.1.2 Logical and Physical Database Design

In presenting a database design methodology, we divide the design process into two main phases: logical database design and physical database design.

Logical database design	The process of constructing a model of the information used in an enterprise based on a specific data model, but independent of a particular DBMS and other physical considerations.

The logical database design phase begins with the creation of a conceptual data model of the enterprise, which is entirely independent of implementation details such as the target DBMS software, application programs, programming languages, hardware platform, or any other physical considerations. The conceptual data model is then mapped to a logical data model of the enterprise, which is influenced by the target data model for the database (for example, the relational data model).

The logical data model of the enterprise is a source of information for the physical design phase. The model provides the physical database designer with a vehicle for making trade-offs that are very important to efficient database design.

Physical database design	The process of producing a description of the implementation of the database on secondary storage; it describes the storage structures and access methods used to gain access effectively.

Physical database design is the second phase of the database design process, during which the designer decides how the database is to be implemented. Therefore, physical design is tailored to a specific DBMS system. There is feedback between physical and logical design, because decisions taken during physical design for improving performance may affect the structure of the logical data model.

7.2 Overview of Methodology

In this section, we present an overview of the database design methodology. The steps in the methodology are as follows:

Logical database design for relational databases

Step 1   Build local conceptual data model from user view
- Step 1.1   Identify entity types
- Step 1.2   Identify relationship types
- Step 1.3   Identify and associate attributes with entity or relationship types
- Step 1.4   Determine attribute domains
- Step 1.5   Determine candidate and primary key attributes
- Step 1.6   Specialize/generalize (optional step)
- Step 1.7   Draw entity–relationship diagram
- Step 1.8   Review local conceptual data model with user

Step 2   Build and validate local logical data model
- Step 2.1   Map local conceptual data model to local logical data model
- Step 2.2   Derive relations from local logical data model
- Step 2.3   Validate model using normalization
- Step 2.4   Validate model against user transactions
- Step 2.5   Draw entity–relationship diagram
- Step 2.6   Define integrity constraints
- Step 2.7   Review local logical data model with user

Step 3   Build and validate global logical data model
- Step 3.1   Merge local logical data models into global model
- Step 3.2   Validate global logical data model
- Step 3.3   Check for future growth
- Step 3.4   Draw final entity–relationship diagram
- Step 3.5   Review global logical data model with users

Physical database design and implementation for relational databases

Step 4   Translate global logical data model for target DBMS
- Step 4.1   Design base relations for target DBMS
- Step 4.2   Design integrity rules for target DBMS

Step 5   Design and implement physical representation
- Step 5.1   Analyse transactions
- Step 5.2   Choose file organization
- Step 5.3   Choose secondary indexes
- Step 5.4   Consider the introduction of controlled redundancy
- Step 5.5   Estimate disk space

Step 6   Design and implement security mechanisms
- Step 6.1   Design user views
- Step 6.2   Design access rules

Step 7   Monitor and tune the operational system

Logical database design is divided into three main steps. The objective of the first step is to decompose the design into more manageable tasks by examining different user perspectives of the enterprise, or **user views**. The output of this step is the building of a local conceptual data model, which should be a complete and accurate representation of the enterprise as seen by that user view. The second step maps the local conceptual model to a local logical data model. In this step, we remove undesirable features from the data model that would be difficult to implement in a relational DBMS. The logical model is then validated using the technique of normalization. Normalization is an effective means of ensuring that the model is structurally consistent, logical and has minimal redundancy. The data model is also validated against the transactions that it is required to support. Validation is the process of ensuring that we are creating the 'correct' model. At the end of the second step, the local logical data model could be used to generate a prototype database implementation for the user view, if necessary. The third and final step is to integrate the user views together to provide a single global logical data model of the enterprise. Throughout this methodology, users play a critical role in continually reviewing and validating the data model and the supporting documentation.

Logical database design is an iterative process, which has a starting point and an almost endless procession of refinements. Although it is presented here as a procedural process, it must be emphasized that this does not imply that it should be performed in this manner. It is likely that knowledge gained in one step may alter decisions made in a previous step. Similarly, we may find it useful to briefly look at a later step to help with an earlier step. The methodology should act as a framework to help guide us through the database design activity effectively.

Although the physical database design steps are shown here for completeness, we will consider these steps in detail in Chapters 9 and 10.

Critical success factors in logical database design

The following guidelines may prove to be critical to the success of the logical database design:

- Work interactively with the users as much as possible.
- Follow a structured methodology throughout the logical data modelling process.
- Employ a data-driven approach.
- Incorporate structural and integrity considerations into the logical data model.
- Combine conceptualization, normalization and transaction validation techniques into the logical data modelling methodology.
- Use diagrams to represent as much of the logical data model as possible.
- Use a Database Design Language (DBDL) to represent additional data semantics.
- Build a data dictionary to supplement the data model diagrams.
- Be willing to repeat steps.

7.3   The Logical Database Design Methodology

This section provides a step-by-step guide for producing a logical database design.

Step 1   Build Local Conceptual Data Model from User View

> **Objective**   To build a local conceptual data model of an enterprise for a specific user view.

The first step in logical database design is the production of conceptual data models for each user view of the enterprise. A **user view** is the data required by a particular user to make a decision or perform some task. Typically, a user view is a functional area of the enterprise such as production, marketing, sales, personnel, accounts or stock control. A user could be an actual person or group of people who may directly use the system. Alternatively, a user may reference a report that is produced by the system, or even request the results of a transaction that must be supported by the system.

We can identify user views using various methods. First, we could examine the data flow diagrams that should have been produced previously to identify functional areas and possibly individual functions. Alternatively, we could interview users, examine procedures, reports, forms and/or observe the enterprise in operation.

We refer to the conceptual data model for each user view that we are attempting to model as the local conceptual model for that view. Each local conceptual data model comprises:

- entity types,
- relationship types,
- attributes,
- attribute domains,
- candidate keys,
- primary keys.

The conceptual data model is supported by documentation, which is produced throughout the development of the model. The tasks involved in Step 1 are:

- Step 1.1   Identify entity types
- Step 1.2   Identify relationship types
- Step 1.3   Identify and associate attributes with entity or relationship types
- Step 1.4   Determine attribute domains
- Step 1.5   Determine candidate and primary key attributes

- Step 1.6   Specialize/generalize entity types (optional step)
- Step 1.7   Draw entity–relationship diagram
- Step 1.8   Review local conceptual data model with user.

Step 1.1   Identify entity types

> **Objective**   To identify the main entity types in the user's view of the enterprise.

The first step in building a local conceptual data model is to define the main objects that the user is interested in. These objects are the entity types for the model. One method of identifying entities is to examine the requirements specification for the user's particular function within the enterprise. From this specification, we identify nouns or noun phrases that are mentioned (for example, staff number, staff name, property number, property address, rent, number of rooms). We also look for major objects such as people, places or concepts of interest, excluding those nouns which are merely qualities of other objects. For example, we could group staff number and staff name with an object or entity called Staff and group property number, property address, rent and number of rooms with an entity called Property. An alternative way of identifying entities is to look for objects that have an existence in their own right. For example, Staff is an entity because Staff exists whether or not we know their names, addresses and telephone numbers. If possible, the user should assist with this activity.

It is sometimes difficult to identify entities because of the way they are presented in the user's requirement specification. Users often talk in terms of examples or analogies. Instead of talking about staff in general, users may mention people's names. In some cases, users talk in terms of job roles, particularly of people and organizations. These roles may be job titles or responsibilities, such as Manager, Deputy Manager, Supervisor or Assistant.

To further confuse matters, users frequently use synonyms and homonyms. Two words are *synonyms* when they have the same meaning, for example, 'branch' and 'office'. *Homonyms* occur when the same word can have different meanings depending on the context. For example, the word 'programme' has several alternative meanings such as course of study, series of events, plan of work and an item on the television.

It is not always obvious whether a particular object is an entity, a relationship or an attribute. For example, how would we classify marriage? In fact, we could classify marriage as any or all of these. Analysis is subjective, and different designers may produce different, but equally valid, interpretations. The activity therefore relies, to a certain extent, on judgement and experience. Database designers must take a very selective view of the world and categorize the things that they observe within the context of the enterprise. Thus, there may be no unique set of entity types deducible from a given requirements specification. However, successive iterations of the analysis process should lead to the choice of entities that are at least adequate for the system required.

Document entity types

As we identify entities, we assign them names that are meaningful and obvious to the user. We record the names and descriptions of entities in a data dictionary. If possible, we document the expected number of occurrences of each entity. If an entity is known by different names (aliases), we also record the aliases in the data dictionary.

Step 1.2 Identify relationship types

> **Objective** To identify the important relationships that exist between the entity types that we have identified.

Having identified the entities, the next step is to identify all the relationships that exist between these entities. When we identify entities, one method is to look for nouns in the user's requirements specification. Again, we can use the grammar of the requirements specification to identify relationships. Typically, relationships are indicated by verbal expressions. For example:

- Branch *Has* Staff.
- Staff *Manages* Property.
- Renter *Views* Property.

The fact that the requirements specification records these relationships suggests that they are important to the enterprise, and should be included in the model.

We are interested only in required relationships between entities. In the previous example, we identified the Staff *Manages* Property and the Renter *Views* Property relationships. We may also be inclined to include a relationship between Staff and Renter (for example, Staff *Assists* Renter). However, although this is a possible relationship, from the requirements specification it is not a relationship that we are interested in modelling.

In most instances, the relationships are binary; in other words, relationships exist between exactly two entities. However, we should be careful to look out for complex relationships that may involve more than two entity types and recursive relationships that involve only one entity type.

Great care must be taken to ensure that all the relationships that are either explicit or implicit in the user's requirements specification are detected. In principle, it should be possible to check each pair of entity types for a potential relationship between them, but this would be a daunting task for a large system comprising hundreds of entity types. On the other hand, it is unwise not to perform some such check, and the responsibility is often left to the analyst/designer. However, missing relationships should become apparent when we validate the model against the transactions that are required to be supported (Step 2.4).

Determine the cardinality and participation constraints of relationship types
Having identified the relationships we wish to model, we next determine the cardinality of each relationship as being either one-to-one (1:1), one-to-many

(1:M) or many-to-many (M:N). If specific values for the cardinality are known, or even upper or lower limits, we document these values as well. In addition, we determine the participation constraints of each entity in a relationship as being either total or partial.

A model with cardinality and participation more explicitly represents the semantics of the relationship. Cardinality and participation are forms of constraints that are used to check and maintain data quality. These constraints are assertions about entity occurrences that can be applied when the database is updated, to determine whether or not the updates violate the stated rules of data semantics.

Document relationship types

As we identify relationship types, we assign them names that are meaningful and obvious to the user. We also record relationship descriptions, cardinality and participation constraints in the data dictionary.

Use Entity–Relationship (ER) modelling

It is often easier to visualize a complex system rather than decipher long textual descriptions of a user's requirements specification. We use Entity–Relationship (ER) diagrams to more easily represent entities and how they relate to one another.

Throughout the logical database design phase, we recommend that ER modelling should be used whenever necessary, to help build up a picture of the part of the enterprise that we are attempting to model.

Step 1.3 Identify and associate attributes with entity or relationship types

Objective	To associate attributes with the appropriate entity or relationship types.

The next step in the methodology is to identify the types of facts about the entity and relationships that we have chosen to be represented in the database. In a similar way to identifying entities, we look for nouns or noun phrases in the user's requirements specification. The attributes can be identified where the noun or noun phrase is a property, quality, identifier or characteristic of one of these entities or relationships.

By far the easiest thing to do when we have identified an entity or a relationship in the requirements specification, is to consider *What information are we required to hold on ...?* The answer to this question should be described in the specification. However, in some cases, it may be necessary to ask the users to clarify the requirement. Unfortunately, they may give answers to this question that also contain other concepts, so that the users' responses must be carefully considered.

Simple/composite attributes

It is important to note whether an attribute is simple or composite. Composite attributes are made up of simple attributes. For example, the Address attribute can be simple and hold all the details of an address as a single value, for example, '115 Dumbarton Road, Partick, Glasgow, G11 6YG'. However, the Address attribute may also represent a composite attribute, made up of simple attributes that hold the address details as separate values in the Street ('115 Dumbarton Road'), Area ('Partick'), City ('Glasgow'), and Postcode ('G11 6YG') attributes. The option to represent address details as a simple or composite attribute is determined by the user's requirements. If the user does not require to access the separate component parts of an address, we should represent the Address attribute as a simple attribute. On the other hand, if the user does require to access the individual component parts of an address, we should represent the Address attribute as being composite, made up of the required simple attributes.

In this step, it is important that we identify all simple attributes to be represented in the conceptual data model including those attributes that make up a composite attribute.

Derived attributes

Attributes, whose value can be found by examining the values of other attributes, are known as **derived** or **calculated** attributes. Examples of derived attributes include:

- the number of staff that work at a particular branch;
- the age of a member of staff;
- the total monthly salaries of all staff at a particular branch;
- the number of properties that a member of staff manages.

Often, these attributes are not shown in the conceptual data model. However, sometimes the value of the attribute or attributes on which the derived attribute is based may be deleted or modified. In this case, the derived attribute must be shown in the data model to avoid this potential loss of information. However, if a derived attribute is shown in the model, we must indicate that it is derived. The representation of derived attributes will be considered during physical database design. Depending on how the attribute is used, new values for a derived attribute may be calculated each time it is accessed or when the value(s) it is derived from changes. However, this issue is not the concern of logical database design, and is discussed in more detail in Chapter 9.

When identifying the attributes for the enterprise, it is not uncommon for it to become apparent that one or more entities have been omitted from the original selection. In this case, we return to the previous steps, document the new entities and re-examine the associated relationships.

It may be useful to produce a list of all attributes given in the user's requirement specification. As we associate an attribute with a particular entity or relationship, we can remove the item from the list. In this way, we ensure that an attribute is associated with only one entity or relationship type and, when the list is empty, that all attributes are associated with some entity or relationship type.

We must also be aware of cases where attributes appear to be associated with more than one entity type. This may indicate that we have identified several entities such as Manager, Supervisor and Secretary that in fact can be represented as a single entity called Staff. In this case, we must decide whether we want to generalize the entities into a single entity such as Staff, or leave them as specialized entities representing distinct staff roles. The consideration of whether to specialize or generalize entities is discussed in more detail in Step 1.6.

Document attributes
As we identify attributes, assign them names that are meaningful and obvious to the user. Record the following information for each attribute:

- attribute name and description;
- any aliases or synonyms that the attribute is known by;
- data type and length;
- default values for the attribute (if specified);
- whether the attribute must always be specified (in other words, whether the attribute allows or disallows nulls);
- whether the attribute is composite and if so, what are the simple attributes that make up the composite attribute;
- whether the attribute is derived and if so, how it should be computed;
- whether the attribute is multi-valued.

Step 1.4   Determine attribute domains

Objective	To determine domains for the attributes in the local conceptual model.

The objective of this step in building the local conceptual data model is to determine attribute domains for the attributes in the model. A **domain** is a pool of values from which one or more attributes draw their values. For example, we may define:

- The attribute domain of valid branch numbers as being a three-character string, with the first character as a letter and the next two characters as digits in the range 01–99.
- The attribute domain for valid telephone and fax numbers as being a 13-digit string.
- The possible values for the Sex attribute of the Staff entity as being either 'M' or 'F'. The domain of this attribute is a single character string consisting of the values 'M' or 'F'.

A fully developed data model specifies the domains for each of the model's attributes and includes:

- the allowable set of values for an attribute;
- the allowable operations on an attribute;
- which attributes can be compared with other attributes or used in combination with other attributes;
- the sizes and formats of the attribute fields.

Document attribute domains

As we identify attribute domains record their names and characteristics in the data dictionary. Update the data dictionary entries for attributes to record their domain.

Step 1.5 Determine candidate and primary key attributes

> **Objective** To identify the candidate key(s) for each entity and, if there is more than one candidate key, to choose one to be the primary key.

Identify candidate keys and choose a primary key

This step is concerned with identifying the candidate key(s) for an entity and then selecting one to be the primary key. A **candidate key** is an attribute or minimal set of attributes of an entity that uniquely identifies each occurrence of that entity. We may identify more than one candidate key. However, in this case, we must choose one to be the **primary key**; the remaining candidate keys are called **alternate keys**. When choosing a primary key from among the candidate keys, use the following guidelines to help make the selection:

- the candidate key with the minimal set of attributes;
- the candidate key that is less likely to have its values changed;
- the candidate key that is less likely to lose uniqueness in the future;
- the candidate key with fewest characters (for those with textual attribute(s));
- the candidate key that is easiest to use from the users' point of view.

In the process of identifying primary keys, we note whether an entity is strong or weak. If we are able to assign a primary key to an entity, the entity is referred to as being 'strong'. On the other hand, if we are unable to identify a primary key for an entity, the entity is referred to as being 'weak'. Recall that a weak entity cannot exist without the owner entity with which it has a relationship (which is referred to as existence dependency), and that its primary key is partially or totally derived from the owner entity.

Therefore, the primary key of a weak entity can only be identified when we map the weak entity and its relationship with its owner entity to a relation, through the placement of a foreign key in that relation. The process of mapping entities and their relationships to relations is described in Step 2.2, and therefore the identification of primary keys for weak entities cannot take place until we reach that step.

Document primary and alternate keys
Record the identification of primary and alternate keys (when available) in the
data dictionary.

Step 1.6 Specialize/generalize entity types (optional step)

Objective	To identify superclass and subclass entity types, where appropriate.

In this step, we have the option to continue the development of the ER model
using the process of specialization or generalization on the entities identified
in Step 1.1. If we select the specialization approach, we attempt to highlight
differences by defining one or more **subclasses** on an entity, which is called
the **specialization superclass**. If we select the generalization approach, we
attempt to identify common features between entities to define a generalizing
entity, called the **generalization superclass**.

As an example, consider the Property_for_Rent and Property_for_Sale
entities shown in Figure 7.1(a). The decision is whether we want to generalize
these entities into subclasses of a generalized superclass, called Property entity,
or leave them as distinct entities. These entities share many common attributes, such as those relating to the type of property (Type), the address (Street,
Area, City, Postcode), and even the primary key (Property_No). However,
they also have distinct attributes such as Rent in the case of Property_for_
Rent and Price in the case of Property_for_Sale. Also, note that Property_
for_Rent and Property_for_Sale entities share a common relationship, Owner
Owns Property. However, each entity also has relationships that are distinct,
such as Renter *Rents* Property_for_Rent and Buyer *Buys* Property_for_Sale.

We choose to generalize the Property_for_Sale and Property_for_Rent
entities based on the commonality of attributes and relationships associated
with each entity. We therefore represent the Property_for_Rent and the Prop-
erty_for_Sale entities as distinct subclasses of a Property superclass, as shown
in Figure 7.1(b). The relationship that the Property superclass has with its
subclasses is total and disjointed, as each member of the Property superclass
must be a member of at least one of the subclasses (Property_for_Rent and
Property_for_Sale), but cannot belong to both. This representation is particularly useful for displaying the shared attributes and relationship associated
with these distinct subclasses.

There are no strict guidelines on when to develop the ER model through
specialization or generalization, as the choice is often subjective and dependent on the particular characteristics of the situation that we are attempting to
model.

As a useful 'rule of thumb' when considering using specialization or
generalization, we should always attempt to represent the important entities
and their relationships as clearly as possible in the ER model. Therefore, the
degree of specialization/generalization displayed in an ER diagram should be
guided by the readability of the diagram and the clarity by which it models
important entity and relationship types.

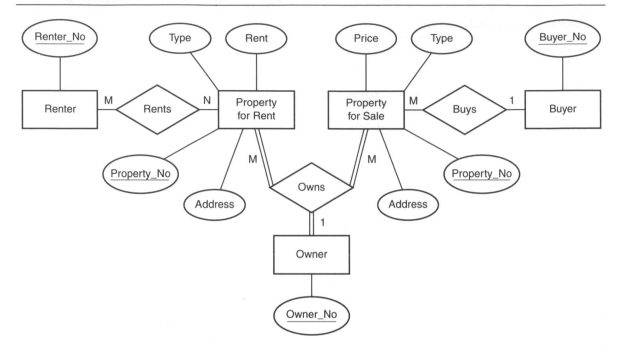

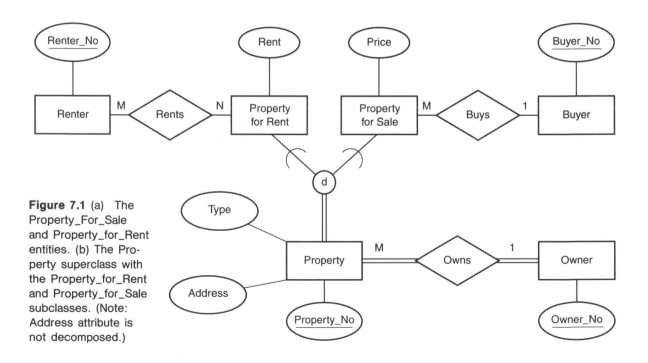

Figure 7.1 (a) The Property_For_Sale and Property_for_Rent entities. (b) The Property superclass with the Property_for_Rent and Property_for_Sale subclasses. (Note: Address attribute is not decomposed.)

The concept of specialization/generalization is associated with enhanced ER modelling. However, as this step is optional, we simply use the term 'ER diagram' or 'ER model' when referring to the diagrammatic representation of data models throughout the rest of this chapter.

Step 1.7   Draw Entity–Relationship diagram

Objective	To draw an Entity-Relationship (ER) diagram that is a conceptual representation of a user view of the enterprise.

We are now able to present an ER diagram that represents the local conceptual data model based on a particular user's view of the enterprise.

Step 1.8   Review local conceptual data model with user

Objective	To review the local conceptual data model with the user to ensure that the model is a 'true' representation of the user's view of the enterprise.

Before completing Step 1, we should review the local conceptual data model with the user. The conceptual data model includes the ER diagram and the supporting documentation that describes the data model. If any anomalies are present in the data model, we must make the appropriate changes, which may require repeating the previous step(s). We repeat this process until the user is prepared to 'sign off' the model as being a 'true' representation of the part of the enterprise that we are attempting to model.

Step 2   Build and Validate Local Logical Data Model

Objective	To build a logical data model based on the conceptual data model of the user's view of the enterprise, and then to validate this model using the technique of normalization and against the required transactions.

In this step, we refine the local conceptual data model created in the previous step, to remove data structures that are difficult to implement using relational Database Management Systems (DBMS). At the end of this process, when we have altered the structure of the conceptual model towards the requirements of the relational data model, we more correctly refer to the model as being a logical data model. We then validate the logical data model using the rules of normalization and against the transactions it is required to support, as given in the user's requirements specification.

On completion of this step, we should have a model of a user view that is correct, comprehensive and unambiguous. At this stage, we will then have a solid foundation to proceed to the next activity, which is to combine the individual local logical data models into a global logical data model of the enterprise. A validated local logical data model may be used as the basis for prototyping, if required.

The activities in this step include:

- Step 2.1 Map local conceptual data model to local logical data model
- Step 2.2 Derive relations from local logical data model
- Step 2.3 Validate model using normalization
- Step 2.4 Validate model against user transactions
- Step 2.5 Draw entity–relationship diagram
- Step 2.6 Define integrity constraints
- Step 2.7 Review local logical data model with user

Step 2.1 Map local conceptual data model to local logical data model

> **Objective** To refine the local conceptual data model to remove undesirable features, and to map this model to a local logical data model.

From Step 1, we now have a local conceptual data model for a user view of the enterprise. However, the data model may contain some data structures that are not easily modelled by conventional database management systems. In this step, we transform such data structures into a form that is more easily handled by such systems. It may be argued that this is not part of logical database design. However, the process makes the designer think more carefully about the meaning of the data and, consequently, leads to a truer representation of the enterprise.

The objectives of this step are to:

(1) Remove M:N relationships.
(2) Remove complex relationships.
(3) Remove recursive relationships.
(4) Remove relationships with attributes.
(5) Re-examine 1:1 relationships.
(6) Remove redundant relationships.

(1) Remove M:N relationships
If a many-to-many (M:N) relationship is represented in the conceptual data model, we should decompose this relationship to identify an intermediate entity. The M:N relationship is replaced with two 1:M relationships to the newly identified entity. For example, consider the M:N relationship, Newspaper *Advertises* Property, as shown in Figure 7.2(a). If we decompose the

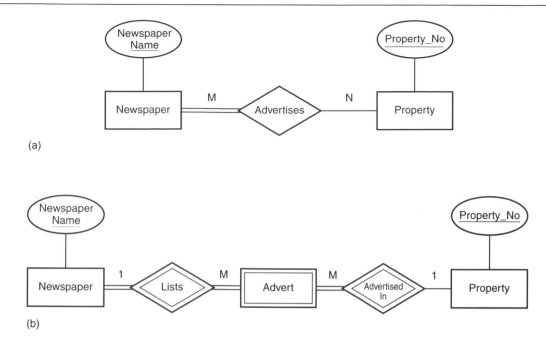

Advertises relationship, we identify the Advert entity and two new 1:M relationships (*Lists* and *AdvertisedIn*). The M:N *Advertises* relationship is now represented as Newspaper *Lists* Advert and Property *AdvertisedIn* Advert, as shown in Figure 7.2(b).

Note that the Advert entity is shown as a weak entity because of its existence dependency on the owner entities, namely Newspaper and Property.

(2) Remove complex relationships

A complex relationship is a relationship between three or more entity types. If a complex relationship is represented in the conceptual data model, we should decompose this relationship to identify an intermediate entity. The complex relationship is replaced with the required number of 1:M (binary) relationships to the newly identified entity. For example, the ternary *Leases* relationship represents the association between the member of staff who organized the leasing of a property by a renter, as shown in Figure 7.3(a). We can simplify this relationship by introducing a new entity and defining (binary) relationships between each of the original entities and the new entity. In this example, we may decompose the *Leases* relationship to identify a new entity called Lease_Agreement. The new entity is associated with the original entities through three new binary relationships: Staff *Organizes* Lease_Agreement, Property *AssociatedWith* Lease_Agreement and Renter *Holds* Lease_Agreement, as shown in Figure 7.3(b).

Figure 7.2 (a) The Newspaper *Advertises* Property M:N relationship. (b) Decomposing the *Advertises* M:N relationship into two 1:M relationships (*Lists* and *AdvertisedIn*) and the Advert entity.

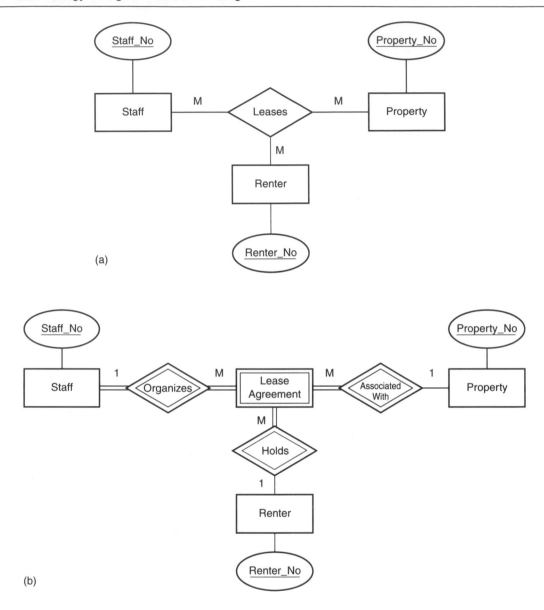

Figure 7.3 (a) The Complex *Leases* relationship. (b) Decomposing the *Leases* complex relationship into three 1:M relationships (*Organizes*, *AssociatedWith* and *Holds*) and the Lease_Agreement entity.

(3) Remove recursive relationships

A recursive relationship is a particular type of relationship in which an entity type has a relationship with itself. If a recursive relationship is represented in the conceptual data model, we should decompose this relationship to identify an intermediate entity. For example, to represent the situation where a member of staff supervises other members of staff, we could define a one-to-many (1:M) recursive relationship Staff *Supervises* Staff, as shown in Figure 7.4(a).

The recursive nature of this relationship requires special consideration to allow its representation in both the logical database design and the physical database implementation. To simplify a 1:M recursive relationship, we replace the relationship with an entity called Allocated_Staff and an additional 1:M relationship called *SupervisedBy*, as shown in Figure 7.4(b).

We decompose M:N recursive relationships in the same way as a binary M:N relationship described in part (1) of this step.

(4) Remove relationships with attributes

If we have a relationship with attributes represented in the conceptual data model, we should decompose this relationship to identify an entity. For example, consider the situation where we wish to record the number of hours

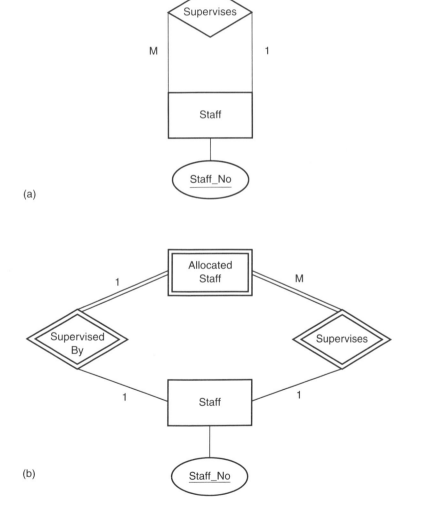

(a)

(b)

Figure 7.4 (a) The *Supervises* recursive relationship. (b) Removing the *Supervises* recursive relationship to create an additional relationship called *SupervisedBy* and an entity called Allocated Staff.

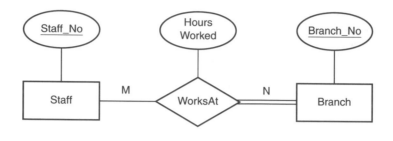

(a)

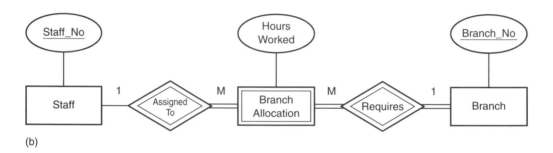

(b)

Figure 7.5 (a) The *WorksAt* relationship with the Hours_Worked attribute. (b) Decomposing the *WorksAt* relationship to create the Branch Allocation entity and two 1:M relationships (*AssignedTo* and *Requires*).

worked by temporary staff at each branch, as shown in Figure 7.5(a). The relationship Staff *WorksAt* Branch has an attribute called Hours_Worked. We decompose the *WorksAt* relationship into an entity called Branch_Allocation, which is assigned the Hours_Worked attribute, and create two new 1:M relationships, as shown in Figure 7.5(b).

(5) Re-examine 1:1 relationships
In the identification of entities, we may have identified two entities that represent the same object in the enterprise. For example, we may have identified two entities Branch and Department that are actually the same; in other words, Branch is a synonym for Department. In this case, the two entities should be merged together. If the primary keys are different, choose one of them to be the primary key and leave the other as an alternate key.

(6) Remove redundant relationships
A relationship is redundant if the same information can be obtained via other relationships. Remember that we are trying to develop a minimal data model and, as redundant relationships are unnecessary, they should be removed. It is relatively easy to identify whether there is more than one path between two entities. However, this does not necessarily imply that one of the relationships is redundant, as they may represent different associations in the enterprise.

The time dimension of relationships is important when assessing redundancy. For example, consider the situation where we wish to model the relationships between the entities Man, Woman and Child, as illustrated in Figure 7.6. Clearly, there are two paths between Man and Child: one via the direct relationship *FatherOf* and the other via the relationships *MarriedTo* and *MotherOf*. Consequently, we may think that the relationship *FatherOf* is unnecessary. However, this would be incorrect for two reasons. Firstly, the father may have children from a previous marriage, and we are modelling only the father's current marriage through a 1:1 relationship. Secondly, the father and mother may not be married, or the father may be married to someone other than the mother (or the mother may be married to someone who is not the father), so again, the required relationship could not be modelled without the *FatherOf* relationship type.

The message is that it is important to examine the meaning of each relationship between entities when assessing redundancy.

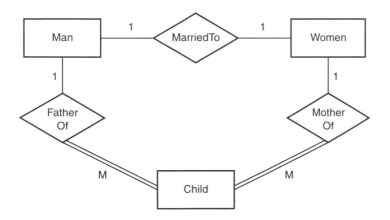

Figure 7.6
Non-redundant
relationship.

At the end of this step, we have simplified the local conceptual data model by removing the data structures that are difficult to implement in relational databases. Therefore at this stage, it is more correct to refer to the refined local conceptual data model as a **local logical data model**.

Step 2.2 Derive relations from local logical data model

Objective   To derive relations from the local logical data model.

In this step, we derive relations from the local logical data model to represent the entities and relationships described in the user's view of the enterprise.

The relationship that an entity has with another entity is represented by the primary key/foreign key mechanism. Recall that a foreign key is an attribute or set of attributes within one entity that is a copy of the primary key of another entity. In deciding where to post or place the foreign key attribute(s), we must first identify the 'parent' and 'child' entities involved in the relationship. The parent entity refers to the entity that posts a copy of its primary key into the relation that represents the child entity, to act as the foreign key.

We now describe how relations representing entities and their relationships are derived from the possible data structures present in the logical data model. We illustrate the process using the logical model shown in Figure 7.7.

We describe the composition of each relation using a Database Definition Language (DBDL) for relational databases. Using the DBDL, we first specify the name of the relation, followed by a list of the names of the relation's simple attributes enclosed in brackets. We then identify the primary key and any alternate and/or foreign key(s) of the relation. Following the identification of a foreign key, the relation containing the referenced primary key is also given.

Figure 7.7 An example logical data model.

Strong entity types
For each strong (regular) entity in the logical data model, create a relation that includes all of the simple attributes of that entity. For composite attributes

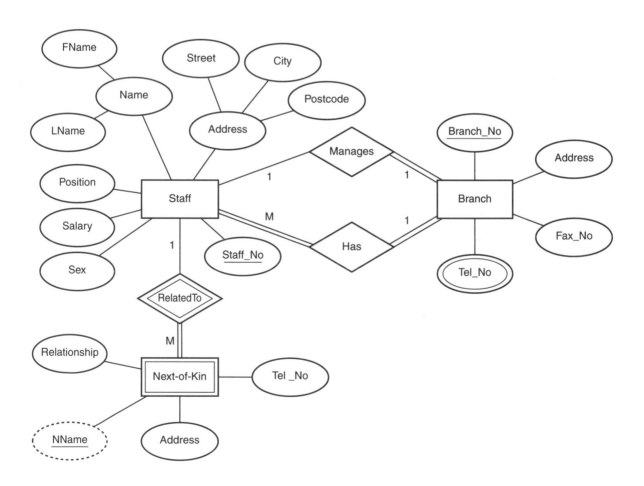

of an entity, such as Address, include only the simple attributes, namely, Street, City, Postcode in the relation. For example, the composition of the Staff relation shown in Figure 7.7 is:

> **Staff** (Staff_No, FName, LName, Street, City, Postcode, Position, Sex, Salary)
>
> **Primary Key** Staff_No

Weak entity types

For each weak entity in the logical data model, create a relation that includes all of the simple attributes of that entity. In addition, include as a foreign key the primary key of the owner entity. The primary key of a weak entity is partially or fully derived from the owner entity. For example, in Figure 7.7, the Staff entity is the owner of the weak entity Next-of-Kin. The composition of the Next-of-Kin relation is:

> **Next-of-Kin** (Staff_No, NName, Address, Tel_No, Relationship)
>
> **Primary Key** Staff_No, NName
>
> **Foreign Key** Staff_No **references** Staff(Staff_No)

Note that the foreign key attribute of the Next-of-Kin relation forms part of the primary key for this entity. In this situation, the primary key for the Next-of-Kin relation could not have been identified until after the foreign key had been posted from the Staff relation to the Next-of-Kin relation. At the end of this step, we should therefore identify any primary key or candidate keys that have been formed in the process of deriving relations from the logical data model.

One-to-one (1:1) binary relationship types

For each binary 1:1 relationship between entities E1 and E2 in the logical data model, we post a copy of the primary key attribute(s) of entity E1 into the relation that represents entity E2, to act as a foreign key. The identification of the parent and child entities is dependent on the participation constraints of E1 and E2 in the relationship. The entity that partially participates in the relationship is designated as the parent entity, and the entity that totally participates in the relationship is designated as the child entity. As described above, a copy of the primary key of the parent entity is placed in the relation representing the child entity. Note that in the case where both entity types totally or partially participate in a 1:1 relationship, the designation of the parent and child entities is arbitrary. Furthermore, when both entities totally participate in a relationship, we have the choice to represent this relationship using the primary key/foreign key link as before or merge the attributes associated with both entities into a single relation. We tend to merge the two entity types when the entities are not involved in other relationships.

The following example illustrates how we may represent a 1:1 relationship in relations derived from a logical data model.

The Staff *Manages* Branch relationship, shown in Figure 7.7, is a 1:1 relationship because a single member of staff manages a single branch. The

Staff entity partially participates in the *Manages* relationship, while the Branch entity totally participates. The entity that partially participates in the relationship (Staff) is designated as the parent entity, and the entity that totally participates in the relationship (Branch) is designated as the child entity. Therefore, a copy of the primary key of the Staff (parent) entity, namely Staff_No, is placed in the Branch (child) relation. The composition of the Staff and Branch relations is:

> **Staff** (Staff_No, FName, LName, Street, City, Postcode, Position, Sex, Salary)
>
> **Primary Key** Staff_No
>
> **Branch** (Branch_No, Address, Fax_No, Manager_Staff_No)
>
> **Primary Key** Branch_No
>
> **Alternate Key** Fax_No
>
> **Foreign Key** Manager_Staff_No **references** Staff(Staff_No)

Note that the Staff_No attribute representing the Manager of a branch has been renamed as Manager_Staff_No, to more clearly indicate the purpose of the foreign key in the Branch relation. Also, note that in the example shown in Figure 7.7, the Tel_No attribute of the Branch entity is multi-valued. The representation of multi-valued attributes is described below.

One-to-many (1:M) binary relationship types

For each binary 1:M relationship between the entities E1 and E2 in the logical data model, we post a copy of the primary key attribute(s) of E1 into the E2 relation, to act as a foreign key. The entity on the 'one side' of the relationship is designated as the parent entity, and the entity on the 'many side' is designated as the child entity. As before, to represent this relationship, a copy of the primary key of the parent entity is placed into the relation representing the child entity, as a foreign key.

The following example illustrates how we may represent a 1:M relationship in relations derived from a logical data model.

The Branch *Has* Staff relationship shown in Figure 7.7 is a 1:M relationship, as a single branch has many members of staff. In this example, Branch is on the 'one side' and represents the parent entity, and Staff is on the 'many side' and represents the child entity. The relationship between these entities is established by placing a copy of the primary key of the Branch (parent) entity, namely Branch_No, into the Staff (child) relation. The composition of the Branch and Staff relations is:

> **Staff** (Staff_No, FName, LName, Street, City, Postcode, Position, Sex, Salary, Branch_No)
>
> **Primary Key** Staff_No
>
> **Foreign Key** Branch_No **references** Branch(Branch_No)
>
> **Branch** (Branch_No, Address, Fax_No, Manager_Staff_No)
>
> **Primary Key** Branch_No

Alternate Key Fax_No

Foreign Key Manager_Staff_No **references** Staff(Staff_No)

Multi-valued attributes

For each multi-valued attribute A of an entity E1 in the logical data model, create a relation that contains the attribute A plus the primary key of E1, to act as a foreign key. The primary key of this new relation is attribute A or if necessary, a combination of attribute A and the primary key of E1.

The following example illustrates how we may represent a multi-valued attribute in relations derived from a logical data model.

As shown in Figure 7.7, the Tel_No attribute of the Branch entity is multi-valued. This means that a single branch may have one or more telephone numbers. We represent this multi-valued attribute by creating a new relation that contains the Tel_No attribute and the primary key of the Branch entity, namely Branch_No, to act as a foreign key. The composition of the Branch_ Tel relation is:

Branch_Tel (Branch_No, Tel_No)

Primary Key Tel_No

Foreign Key Branch_No **references** Branch(Branch_No)

Superclass/subclass relationships

For each superclass/subclass relationship in the logical data model, we identify the superclass entity as the parent entity and the subclass entity as the child entity. There are various options on how we may represent such a relationship as one or more relations. The selection of the most appropriate option is dependent on the disjointness and participation constraints on the superclass/subclass relationship.

For example, examine the Property superclass/subclass relationships previously shown in Figure 7.1(b). There are various ways to represent this relationship as listed below:

(Option 1)
All_Property (Property_No, Street, Area, City, Postcode, Type, Rent, Price)

Primary Key Property_No

(Option 2)
Property_for_Rent (Property_No, Street, Area, City, Postcode, Type, Rent)

Primary Key Property_No

Property_for_Sale (Property_No, Street, Area, City, Postcode, Type, Price)

Primary Key Property_No

(Option 3)
Property (Property_No, Street, Area, City, Postcode, Type)

Primary Key Property_No

Property_for_Rent (Property_No, Rent)

Primary Key Property_No

Foreign Key Property_No **references** Property(Property_No)

Property_for_Sale (Property_No, Price)

Primary Key Property_No

Foreign Key Property_No **references** Property(Property_No)

The options range from placing all of the property attributes into one relation (Option 1), to dividing the attributes into three relations (Option 3). The most appropriate representation of this relationship is determined by the constraints on this relationship. The relationship that the Property superclass has with its subclasses is total and disjointed, as each member of the Property superclass must be a member of at least one of the subclasses (Property_for_Rent and Property_for_Sale), but cannot belong to both. In other words, for a superclass/subclass relationship that is total and disjointed, create a separate relation to represent each subclass, and include a copy of the primary key attribute of the superclass in each. We therefore select Option 2 as the best representation of this relationship. However, there are other factors that may influence the final selection, such as whether the subclasses are involved in distinct relationships.

Document relations and foreign key attributes
Document the composition of the relations derived from the logical data model using the DBDL. Note that the DBDL syntax can be extended to show integrity constraints on the foreign keys (Step 2.6).

The data dictionary should also be updated to reflect any new key attributes that have been identified in this step.

Step 2.3 Validate model using normalization

> **Objective** To validate a local logical data model using the technique of normalization.

We examined the process of normalization in some detail in Chapter 6. Normalization is used to improve the model so that it satisfies various constraints that avoid unnecessary duplication of data. Normalization ensures that the resultant model is a closer model of the enterprise that it serves, it is consistent, and has minimal redundancy and maximum stability.

Normalization is a procedure for deciding which attributes belong together in an entity type (or which fields belong together in a record). One of the basic concepts of relational theory is that attributes are grouped together in a relation because there is a logical relationship between them. It is sometimes argued that a normalized database design does not provide maximum processing efficiency. However, the following points can be argued:

- A normalized design organizes the data according to its functional dependencies. Consequently, the process lies somewhere between conceptual and physical design.

- The logical design may not be the final design. It should represent the designer's best understanding of the nature and the meaning of the data in the enterprise. If there are specific performance criteria, the physical design may be different. One possibility is that some normalized entities are de-normalized. This does not mean that time has been wasted; in fact, the designer has learned more about the data semantics to perform normalization correctly. We will discuss de-normalization in more detail in Chapter 9.

- A normalized design is robust and free of the update anomalies discussed in Chapter 6.

- Modern computers are much more powerful than those that were available a few years ago. It is sometimes reasonable to implement a design which gains ease of use at the cost of additional processing.

- Normalization forces us to completely understand each attribute that has to be represented in the database. This last benefit may be the most important.

- Normalization produces a flexible database design that can be easily extended.

In the previous step, we derived relations from the local logical data model. In this step, we examine the groupings of attributes in each of these relations. In other words, we validate the composition of each relation using the rules of normalization. The process of normalization includes the following major steps:

- First Normal Form (1NF), which removes repeating groups;
- Second Normal Form (2NF), which removes partial dependencies on the primary key;
- Third Normal Form (3NF), which removes transitive dependencies on the primary key;
- Boyce–Codd Normal Form (BCNF), which removes remaining anomalies from functional dependencies.

The objective of this step is to ensure that each relation derived from the logical data model is in at least Boyce–Codd Normal Form (BCNF). If we identify relations that are not in BCNF, this may indicate that part of the logical data model is incorrect, or that we have introduced an error when deriving the relations from the model. If necessary, we must restructure the data model to ensure that it is a 'true' representation of the part of the enterprise that we are interested in modelling.

Step 2.4   Validate model against user transactions

> **Objective**   To ensure that the logical data model supports the transactions that are required by the user view.

The objective of this step is to validate the local logical data model, to ensure that the model supports the transactions required by the user view. The transactions that are required by each user view can be determined from the user's requirements specification. Using the ER diagram, the data dictionary and the primary key/foreign key links shown in the relations, we attempt to perform the operations manually. If we can resolve all transactions in this way, we have validated the logical data model against the transactions. However, if we are unable to perform a transaction manually, there must be a problem with the data model, which has to be resolved. In this case, it is likely that we have omitted an entity, a relationship or an attribute from the data model.

We examine two possible approaches to ensuring that the logical data model supports the required transactions. The first approach requires that we check that all of the information (entities, relationships and their attributes) required by each transaction is provided by the model by providing a textual description of each transaction's requirements.

For example, the transactions for the Manager of a branch may include the following operations:

(a) Insert details for a new member of staff
The primary key of the Staff relation is the Staff_No attribute; first check that the new staff number does not already exist. If it does, prohibit the insertion and abandon the process. Otherwise, insert the new staff details. Check that each detail is represented by an attribute in the Staff relation.

(b) Delete details of a member of staff, given the staff number
Search for the given staff number in the appropriate column of the Staff relation. If it is not found, a user error has occurred and the details cannot be deleted. Otherwise, delete the entity occurrence from the Staff relation and update the foreign keys of occurrences in the Property relation that the member of staff was allocated to manage.

The second approach to validating the data model against the required transactions involves diagrammatically representing the pathway taken by each transaction directly on the ER diagram. A simple example of this approach is shown in Figure 7.8 using transactions (a) and (b).

This approach allows us to visualize areas of the model that are not required by transactions and those areas that are critical to transactions. We are therefore in a position to directly overview the support provided by the data model for the transactions required. If there are areas of the model that do not appear to be used by any transactions, we may question the purpose of representing this information in the data model. On the other hand, if there are areas of the model that are inadequate in providing the correct pathway for a transaction, we may need to investigate the possibility that critical entity or relationship types have been missed.

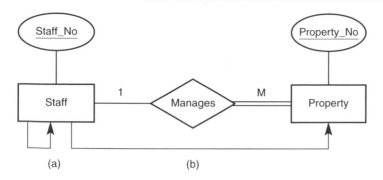

Figure 7.8 A diagrammatic representation of transactions (a) and (b).

Step 2.5 Draw Entity–Relationship diagram

Objective	To draw an Entity–Relationship (ER) diagram that is a logical representation of the data given in the user's view of the enterprise.

We are now in a position to draw an ER diagram of the user's view of the enterprise. This diagram has been validated using the process of normalization and against the transactions it must support.

Step 2.6 Identify integrity constraints

Objective	To identify the integrity constraints given in the user's view of the enterprise.

Integrity constraints are the constraints that we wish to impose in order to protect the database from becoming inconsistent. Note that, although DBMS controls on integrity may or may not exist, this is not the question here. At this stage, we are concerned only with high-level design, that is, specifying what integrity constraints are required, irrespective of how this might be achieved. Having identified the integrity constraints, we will have a logical data model that is a complete and accurate representation of a user view. If necessary, we could produce a physical database design from the local logical data model, for example, to prototype the system for the user.

We consider five types of integrity constraints:

- required data,
- attribute domain constraints,
- entity integrity,
- referential integrity,
- enterprise constraints,

Required data

Some attributes must always contain a valid value; in other words they are not allowed to hold nulls. For example, every member of staff must have an associated job position (such as Manager, Assistant).

These constraints should have been identified when we documented the attributes in the data dictionary (Step 1.3).

Attribute domain constraints

Every attribute has a domain, that is a set of values that are legal for it. For example, the sex of a member of staff is either 'M' or 'F', so the domain of the Sex attribute is a single character string consisting of 'M' or 'F'.

These constraints should have been identified when we chose the attribute domains for the data model (Step 1.4).

Entity integrity

The primary key of an entity cannot hold nulls. For example, each occurrence of the Staff entity must have a value for the primary key attribute, namely Staff_No.

These constraints should have been considered when we identified the primary keys for each entity type (Step 1.5).

Referential integrity

A foreign key links each occurrence in the relation representing a child entity to the occurrence of the parent entity containing the matching candidate key value. Referential integrity means that, if the foreign key contains a value, that value must refer to an existing occurrence in the parent entity. For example, the Branch_No attribute in the Staff relation links the member of staff to the occurrence of the Branch entity where he or she works. If Branch_No is not null, it must contain a valid value that exists in the Branch_No attribute of the Branch entity, or the member of staff will be assigned to a non-existent branch.

There are several issues regarding foreign keys that must be addressed. The first considers whether nulls are allowed for the foreign key. For example, can we store the details for a member of staff without having a branch number for the employee? The issue is not whether the branch number must exist, but whether a branch number must be specified.

In general, if the participation of the child entity in the relationship is total, then the strategy is that nulls are not allowed. On the other hand, if the participation of the child entity is partial, then nulls should be allowed.

The next issue we must address is how to ensure referential integrity. To do this, we specify **existence constraints**. Existence constraints define conditions under which a candidate key or foreign key may be inserted, updated or deleted. Consider the 1:M relationship, Staff *Manages* Property. The primary key of the Staff entity type, namely Staff_No, is a foreign key in the Property entity type. Consider the following cases.

Case 1: Insert occurrence into child entity (Property) To ensure referential integrity, check that the foreign key attribute, namely Staff_No, of the new Property occurrence is set to null or to a value of an existing Staff occurrence.

Case 2: Delete occurrence from child entity (Property)   If an occurrence of a child entity is deleted, this causes no problem as referential integrity is unaffected.

Case 3: Update foreign key of child occurrence (Property)   This is similar to Case 1. To ensure referential integrity, check that the Staff_No of the updated Property occurrence is set to null or to a value of an existing Staff occurrence.

Case 4: Insert occurrence into parent entity (Staff)   Inserting an occurrence into the parent entity type (Staff) does not cause a problem for referential integrity; it simply becomes a parent without any children – in other words, a member of staff without properties to manage.

Case 5: Delete occurrence from parent entity (Staff)   If an occurrence of a parent entity is deleted, referential integrity is lost if there exists a child occurrence referencing the deleted parent occurrence. In other words, if the deleted member of staff currently manages one or more properties. There are several strategies we can consider:

- NO ACTION   Prevent a deletion from the parent entity, if there are any referenced child entities. In our example, 'You cannot delete a member of staff if he or she currently manages any properties'.

- CASCADE   When the parent occurrence is deleted, automatically delete any referenced child occurrences. If any deleted child occurrence acts as the parent entity in another relationship then the delete operation should be applied to the occurrences in this child entity and so on in a cascading manner. In other words, deletions from the parent relation cascade to the child relation. In our example, 'Deleting a member of staff automatically deletes all properties he or she manages'. Clearly, in this situation, this strategy would not be wise.

- SET NULL   When a parent occurrence is deleted, the foreign key values in all of its child occurrences are automatically set to null. Deletions from the parent entity thus cause a 'set to null' update on selected attributes of the child entities. In our example, 'If a member of staff is deleted, indicate that the current assignment of those properties previously managed by that employee is unknown'. We can only consider this strategy if the attributes comprising the foreign key are able to accept nulls.

- SET DEFAULT   When a parent occurrence is deleted, the foreign key values in all of its child occurrences should automatically be set to their default values. Deletions from the parent entity type thus cause a 'set to default' update on selected attributes of the child entities. In our example, 'If a member of staff is deleted, indicate that the current assignment of some properties is being handled by another (default) member of staff such as the Manager'. We can only consider this strategy if the attributes comprising the foreign key have default values.

- NO CHECK   When a parent occurrence is deleted, do nothing to ensure that referential integrity is maintained.

Case 6: Update primary key of parent occurrence (Staff) If the primary key value of a parent entity occurrence is updated, referential integrity is lost if there exists a child occurrence referencing the old primary key value: that is, if the updated member of staff currently manages one or more properties. To ensure referential integrity, the strategies described above can be used. In the case of CASCADE, the updates to the primary key of the parent occurrence are reflected in any referencing child entities and so on in a cascading manner.

Enterprise constraints
Finally, we consider constraints known as enterprise constraints, sometimes called business rules. Updates to entities may be constrained by enterprise rules governing the 'real world' transactions that are represented by the updates. For example, *DreamHome* may have a rule that prevents a member of staff from managing more than 10 properties at the same time.

Document all integrity constraints
Document all integrity constraints in the data dictionary for consideration during physical implementation.

Step 2.7 Review local logical data model with user

Objective	To ensure that the local logical data model is a true representation of the user's view.

The local logical data model for a user view should now be complete and fully documented. However, to finish this step, we should review the logical model and the supporting documentation with the user.

Before we move on to Step 3 of the database design methodology, we briefly consider an additional useful approach to validating the logical data model, using data flow diagrams.

Relationship between logical data model and data flow diagrams
A logical data model reflects the structure of stored data for an enterprise. A Data Flow Diagram (DFD) shows data moving about the enterprise and being stored in datastores. All attributes should appear within an entity type if they are held within the enterprise, and will probably be seen flowing around the enterprise as a dataflow. When these two techniques are being used to model the user's requirements specification, we can use each one to check the consistency and completeness of the other. The rules that control the relationship between the two techniques are:

● Each datastore should represent a whole number of entity types.
● Attributes on dataflows should belong to entity types.

Step 3   Build and Validate Global Logical Data Model

Objective	To combine the individual local logical data models into a single global logical data model that can be used to represent the part of the enterprise that we are interested in modelling.

The third major activity of the logical database design methodology is to build a global logical data model by merging together the individual local logical data models produced for each user view. Having combined the models together, it may be necessary to validate the global model, first against the normalization rules, and secondly against the transactions described in all of the user views. This validation process uses the same techniques as we employed in Steps 2.3 and 2.4. However, we need normalize only if an entity type is changed during the merging process, and also validate the model for those transactions that require access to areas of the model that underwent change. In a large system, this will significantly reduce the amount of re-validation that needs to be performed.

Although each local logical data model should be correct, comprehensive and unambiguous, each model is only a representation of a user's or group of users' perception of their function within the enterprise. In other words, the model is not strictly a model of the function of the enterprise, but it is a model of a user's view of the function of the enterprise, and this view may not be complete. This may mean that there are inconsistencies as well as overlaps when we look at the complete set of user views. Thus, when we merge the local logical data models into a single global model, we must endeavour to resolve conflicts between the views and any overlaps that exist.

This process may be the most important in logical database design because it delivers a representation of the enterprise that is independent of any particular user, business function or application. The activities in this step include:

- Step 3.1   Merge local logical data models into global model
- Step 3.2   Validate global logical data model
- Step 3.3   Check for future growth
- Step 3.4   Draw final Entity–Relationship diagram
- Step 3.5   Review global logical data model with users

Step 3.1   Merge local logical data models into global model

Objective	To merge the individual local logical data models into a single global logical data model of the enterprise.

In a small system with only two or three user views and a small number of entity and relationship types, it is a relatively easy task to compare the local models, merge them together and resolve any differences that exist. However, in a large system, a more systematic approach must be taken. We present one approach that may be used to merge the local models together and resolve any inconsistencies found. Some typical tasks in this approach are as follows:

(1)   Review the names of entities and their primary keys.

(2)   Review the names of relationships.

(3)   Merge entities from the local views.

(4)   Include (without merging) entities unique to each local view.

(5)   Merge relationships from the local views.

(6)   Include (without merging) relationships unique to each local view.

(7)   Check for missing entities and relationships.

(8)   Check foreign keys.

(9)   Check integrity constraints.

(10)   Draw the global logical data model.

(11)   Update the documentation.

Perhaps the easiest way to merge several local data models together is to first merge two of the data models to produce a new model, and then to successively merge the remaining local data models until all the local models are represented in the final global data model. This may prove a simpler approach than trying to merge all the local data models at the same time.

It is important to note that before we begin to create a global view of the enterprise, we must ensure that each of the local models to be included in the merging process has been created following Steps 1 and 2 of the logical database design methodology.

(1) Review the names of entities and their primary keys
It may be worthwhile reviewing the names of entities that appear in the local data models by inspecting the data dictionary. Problems can arise when two or more entities:

- Have the same name but are, in fact, different.
- Are the same but have different names.

It may be necessary to compare the data content of each entity type to resolve the problem. In particular, we may use the primary keys to help us identify equivalent entities, which may be named differently across views.

(2) Review the names of relationships
This activity is the same as described for entities.

(3) Merge entities from the local views
We examine the name and content of each entity type in the models to be merged. Typical activities involved in this task include:

- Merge entities with the same name and the same primary key.

- Merge entities with the same name using different primary keys.
- Merge entities with different names using the same or different primary keys.

Merge entities with the same name and the same primary key   Generally, entities with the same primary key represent the same 'real world' object and should be merged. The merged entity includes the attributes from the original entities with duplicates removed. For example, in Figure 7.9, we list the attributes associated with two entities called Staff defined in two different views (namely, View 1 and View 2). The primary key of both entities is Staff_No. We merge these two entities together by combining their attributes, so that the merged Staff entity now has all of the original attributes associated with both Staff entities. Note that there is conflict between the views on how we should represent the name of a member of staff. In this situation, we should (if possible) consult the users of each view to determine the final representation. Note, in this example, we use the decomposed version of the Name attribute, that is the FName and LName attributes, in the merged Global View.

(View 1)
Staff (Staff_No, Name, Position, Sex, Salary, Branch_No)
Primary Key Staff_No
Foreign Key Branch_No **references** Branch(Branch_No)

(View 2)
Staff (Staff_No, FName, LName, Address, Branch_No)
Primary Key Staff_No
Foreign Key Branch_No **references** Branch(Branch_No)

(Global View)
Staff (Staff_No, FName, LName, Address, Position, Sex, Salary, Branch_No)
Primary Key Staff_No
Foreign Key Branch_No **references** Branch(Branch_No)

Figure 7.9 Merging the Staff entities from View 1 and View 2.

Merge entities with the same name using different primary keys   In some situations, we may find two entities with the same name, which do not use the same primary keys but have similar candidate keys. In this case, the entities should be merged together as described above. However, it is necessary to choose one key to be the primary key, the others becoming alternate keys. For example, in Figure 7.10, we list the attributes associated with two entities called Staff, defined in two different views (namely View 1 and View 2). The primary key of the Staff entity in View 1 is Name and the primary key of the Staff entity in View 2 is Staff_No. However, the alternate key for Staff (View 1) is Staff_No and the alternate key for Staff (View 2) is (FName, LName). Although the primary keys are different, the primary key of Staff in View 1 is the alternate key of Staff in View 2, and vice versa. We merge these two entities together as previously shown in Figure 7.9 and include the (FName, LName) attributes as the alternate key.

(View 1)
Staff (Staff_No, Name, Position, Sex, Salary, Branch_No)
Primary Key Name
Alternate Key Staff_No
Foreign Key Branch_No **references** Branch(Branch_No)

(View 2)
Staff (Staff_No, FName, LName, Address, Branch_No)
Primary Key Staff_No
Alternate Key FName, LName
Foreign Key Branch_No **references** Branch(Branch_No)

Figure 7.10 Merging equivalent entities using different primary keys.

Merge entities with different names using the same or different primary keys   In some cases, we identify entities that have different names but appear to have the same purpose. These equivalent entities may be recognized simply by their name, which indicates their similar purpose, their content and, in particular, their primary key, and also by their association with particular relationships. An obvious example of this occurrence is entities called Staff and Employee, which if found to be equivalent should be merged.

(4) Include (without merging) entities unique to each local view
The previous tasks should identify all entities that are the same. All remaining entities are included in the global model without change.

(5) Merge relationships from the local views
In this step, we examine the name and purpose of each relationship in all user views. Before merging relationships, it is important to resolve any conflicts between the relationships such as the participation and cardinality constraints. The activities in this step include merging relationships with the same name and the same purpose, and then merging relationships with different names but the same purpose.

(6) Include (without merging) relationships unique to each local view
Again, the previous task should identify relationships that are the same (by definition, they must be between the same entities which would be merged together). All remaining relationships are included in the global model without change.

(7) Check for missing entity and relationships
Perhaps one of the most difficult tasks in producing the global model is identifying missing relationships between different user views. If a corporate data model exists for the enterprise, this may show relationships between user views that do not appear in any of the user views. Alternatively, as a preventative measure, when interviewing the users of a specific view, ask them to pay particular attention to the relationships that exist between the other views. Otherwise, examine the attributes of each entity type and look for references to entities in other user views. We may find that we have an attribute associated

with an entity in one user view that corresponds to a primary key, alternate key, or even a non-key attribute of an entity in another view.

(8) Check foreign keys
During this step, entities and relationships may have been merged, primary keys changed and new relationships identified. Check that the foreign keys in child entities are still correct, and make any necessary modifications that are required.

(9) Check integrity constraints
Check that the integrity constraints for the global logical data model do not conflict with those originally specified for each user view. Any conflicts must be resolved in consultation with the users.

(10) Draw the global logical data model
We now draw an ER diagram of the global data model that represents all of the merged local data models.

(11) Update the documentation
Update the documentation to reflect any changes made during the development of the global data model from the individual user views. It is very important that the documentation is up to date and reflects the current data model. If changes are made to the model subsequently, either during database implementation or during maintenance, then the documentation should be updated at the same time. Out-of-date information will cause considerable confusion at a later time.

Step 3.2   *Validate global logical data model*

Objective	To validate the global logical data model using normalization and against the required transactions, if necessary.

This step is equivalent to Steps 2.3 and 2.4, where we validated each local logical data model.

Step 3.3   *Check for future growth*

Objective	To determine whether there are any significant changes likely in the foreseeable future, and to assess whether the global logical data model can accommodate these changes.

It is important that the global logical data model can be easily expanded. If the model can sustain current requirements only, then the life of the model may be relatively short and significant reworking may be necessary. It is important to develop a model that is *extensible*, and has the ability to evolve to support new requirements with minimal affect on existing users.

Consequently, it is worth examining the global model to check that future requirements can be accommodated with minimal impact. However, it is not necessary to incorporate any changes into the data model unless requested by the user.

Step 3.4 Draw final Entity–Relationship diagram

> **Objective**   To draw an Entity–Relationship (ER) diagram that represents the global logical data model of the enterprise.

With the validation of the global logical data model now complete, we can draw the final ER diagram. This diagram represents the global logical data model of the enterprise that we are attempting to model.

Step 3.5 Review global logical data model with users

> **Objective**   To ensure that the global logical data model is a true representation of the enterprise.

The global logical data model for the enterprise should now be complete and fully documented. This step reviews the model with the users to ensure that it is a complete and accurate representation of the enterprise.

The following chapter demonstrates the use of the logical database design methodology described in this chapter. The methodology is illustrated using a worked example taken from the *DreamHome* case study. The steps in this methodology are summarized in Appendix E.

REVIEW QUESTIONS

7.1   Describe the purpose of a design methodology.

7.2   Identify the main phases involved in database design.

7.3   Identify important factors in the success of logical database design.

7.4   Discuss the important role played by users in the process of database design.

7.5   Describe how to break down the scope of a design into manageable pieces.

7.6   Describe the purpose of the main steps in the logical database design methodology presented in this chapter.

8 Logical Database Design Methodology – Worked Example

Chapter Objectives

In this chapter you will learn:

- How to use the logical database design methodology for relational databases, described in Chapter 7.
- How to use this methodology to create a logical database design for the *DreamHome* case study, described in Section 1.7.

In this chapter, we illustrate by example the logical database design methodology for relational databases described in Chapter 7. We use this methodology to create a logical database design for the *DreamHome* case study, described in Section 1.7. To illustrate this methodology, we examine the case study from the perspective of particular users' views of *DreamHome*, namely the Supervisor's and Manager's views. In this chapter, we describe the development of a local logical data model for the Supervisor's view of *DreamHome*. We then merge this model with the local logical data model that represents the Manager's view of *DreamHome*, which was developed previously in Chapter 5. The merging of these models results in the creation of a global logical data model that represents both views of the *DreamHome* case study.

To improve the readability of this chapter, the terms 'entity' and 'relationship' are used in place of 'entity type' and 'relationship type' where the meaning is obvious; 'type' is generally only added to avoid ambiguity.

8.1 The Supervisor's Requirements Specification

The requirements collection and analysis phase of the database development lifecycle was carried out at a *DreamHome* branch office and involved interviewing members of staff with the job title of Supervisor and reviewing any documentation used or generated in their day-to-day work. This phase resulted in the production of a requirements specification for the Supervisor's view of the company, which describes the information to be held in the *DreamHome* database and the required transactions on the database.

Note that when we use the term 'Supervisor's view', we refer to the view as generally defined by members of staff with the job title of 'Supervisor'.

8.1.1 Database Requirements

(1)   Each branch of *DreamHome* has staff who are dedicated to the management of property for rent. The staff work in groups that are supervised by a Supervisor and supported by a Secretary.

(2)   The information stored on each branch office includes a unique branch number, address (street, area, city, postcode), telephone number and fax number.

(3)   The information held on all members of staff includes a staff number, name (first and last name), address, telephone number, sex, date of birth (DOB) and job title. Additional information held on staff with the job title of Secretary is their typing speed. The staff number is unique across all branches of the *DreamHome* company.

(4)   Each Supervisor supervises the day-to-day work of a group of staff (minimum 5 to a maximum of 10 members of staff, at any one time).

(5)   A portfolio of property for rent is available at each *DreamHome* branch. Each property for rent is managed by a particular member of staff. A member of staff may manage a maximum of 10 properties for rent at any one time. The information stored on each property for rent

includes: property number, address (street, area, city, postcode), type, number of rooms and monthly rent. The monthly rent for a property is reviewed annually. Most of the properties rented out by *DreamHome* are flats. Each property is owned by a single owner.

(6) The details of owners of property are also stored. There are two main types of property owner: private owners and business owners. The information stored on private owners includes: owner number, name (first and last name), address and telephone number. The information stored on business owners includes: owner number, name of business, business type, address, telephone number and contact name. Each owner owns at least one property.

(7) The staff responsible for the management of property for rent must undertake the following activities:

(a) To ensure that property is rented out continuously. This may require placing an advert describing a property for rent in an appropriate newspaper. The information stored on each advert includes the advert number, the date the advert was placed in the newspaper, the name of the newspaper and the cost. The advert number is unique across all *DreamHome* branches.

The information stored on each newspaper includes the newspaper name, address, telephone number, fax number and contact name. Properties are only advertised in the newspapers if they prove difficult to rent out.

(b) To set up interviews with clients interested in renting property. The information stored as a result of each interview includes the date of the interview and any general comments about the client.

During the interview, the details of clients are also collected. However, some clients do not attend an interview and simply provide their details by telephone or on their first visit to a *Dream-Home* branch office.

The information stored on clients includes the client number, name (first and last name), current address, telephone number, and some information on the desired property, including the preferred type of accommodation and the maximum rent the client is prepared to pay. The client number is unique across all *DreamHome* branches.

(c) To encourage clients to view properties for rent. The information stored includes the date the client viewed the property, and any comments made by the client regarding the suitability or otherwise of the property. A client may view the same property only once on a given date.

(d) To organize the lease agreement between client and property. Once a client agrees to rent a property, a lease agreement is organized by a member of staff. The information on the lease includes the lease number, the property to be rented identified by property number, the monthly rent, method of payment, deposit (calculated as twice the monthly rent), whether the deposit is paid, the date the rent period starts and finishes, and the duration of the lease. The lease number is unique across all *DreamHome* branches. A client may hold a lease agreement associated with a given property for a minimum of three months to a maximum of 1 year.

(e) To carry out inspections of property on a regular basis to ensure that the property is correctly maintained. Each property is inspected at least once over a six month period. However, *Dream-Home* staff are required to inspect only property that is currently being rented or is available for rent. The information stored on the inspection includes the date of the inspection, and any comments on the condition of the property.

8.1.2 Database Transactions

The main transactions required by Supervisors include:

(a) Produce a list of staff supervised by a Supervisor.

(b) Produce a list of staff supported by a Secretary.

(c) Produce a list of Supervisors at each branch.

(d) Create and maintain records recording the details of property for rent and the owners at each branch.

(e) Produce a report listing the details of property for rent at each branch.

(f) Produce a list of properties for rent managed by a specific member of staff.

(g) Create and maintain records describing the details of clients at each branch.

(h) Produce a list of clients registered at each branch.

(i) Search for properties for rent that satisfy various criteria.

(j) Create and maintain records holding the details of viewings by clients of properties for rent.

(k) Produce a report listing the comments of clients concerning a specific property for rent.

(l) Create and maintain records detailing the adverts placed in newspapers for properties for rent.

(m) Produce a list of all adverts for a specific property.

(n) Produce a list of all adverts placed in a specific newspaper.

(o) Create and maintain records describing the details of lease agreements between a client and a property.

(p) List the details of the lease agreement for a specific property.

(q) Create and maintain records describing the details of inspections of properties for rent.

(r) Produce a list of all inspections of a specific property.

8.2 Using the Logical Database Design Methodology for Relational Databases

Step 1 Build Local Conceptual Data Model based on the Supervisor's View

To begin building the local conceptual data model for the Supervisor's view of the *DreamHome* case study, we must first identify the various component parts of the model, described in the requirements specification. The components of the data model include:

- entity types,
- relationship types,
- attributes,
- attribute domains,
- candidate keys,
- primary keys.

Step 1.1 Identify entity types

We begin by identifying the main entity types in the requirements specification (Section 8.1.1). Entities are normally present as noun or noun expressions. From the requirements specification, the major entities identified include:

Branch	Advert
Staff	Newspaper
Supervisor	Interview
Secretary	Client
Property_for_Rent	Lease_Agreement
Private_Owner	Inspection
Business_Owner	

Document entity types
We document the details of these entity types by providing a fuller description of each entity, indicating whether aliases are used and describing the occurrence of the entity type. This information is provided as Appendix 8.1 of this chapter.

Step 1.2 Identify relationship types

We next identify the major relationship types that exist between the entities. Relationships are normally present as verb or verb expressions. We look again at the requirements specification (Section 8.1.1) to identify potential relationships between entities. The main relationships identified in the requirements specification are shown in Table 8.1.

Table 8.1 The major relationships identified in the Supervisor's requirements specification.

Entity type	Relationship type	Entity type
Branch	*Has*	Staff
Staff	*Manages*	Property_for_Rent
	SupervisedBy	Supervisor
	SupportedBy	Secretary
	SetsUp	Interview
	Organizes	Lease_Agreement
	CarryOut	Inspection
Supervisor	*Supervises*	Staff
Property_for_Rent	*IsAvailableAt*	Branch
	ManagedBy	Staff
	OwnedBy	Owner
Private_Owner	*Owns*	Property_for_Rent
Business_Owner	*Owns*	Property_for_Rent
Advert	*Describes*	Property_for_Rent
	PlacedIn	Newspaper
Interview	*With*	Client
Client	*Views*	Property_for_Rent
	Rents	Property_for_Rent
	Holds	Lease_Agreement
Lease_Agreement	*AssociatedWith*	Property_for_Rent
Inspection	*Of*	Property_for_Rent

If we examine the relationships listed in Table 8.1 we can, in some cases, identify relationships that are obviously the same. For example, the two relationship types Staff *SupervisedBy* Supervisor and Supervisor *Supervises* Staff represent the same relationship. This relationship is listed twice in Table 8.1 as the requirements specification detailed this relationship from both the Staff and the Supervisor's viewpoint.

It is important that we closely examine the Supervisor's requirements specification to ensure that we have identified all of the relationships that we want to represent in the Supervisor's local conceptual model. If there is any ambiguity in the specification regarding a relationship, we must clarify the situation with the user.

Determine the cardinality and participation constraints of relationship types
We next determine the cardinality and participation constraints for each relationship type identified in Table 8.1.

The cardinality constraint on a relationship is specified as being either one-to-one (1:1), one-to-many (1:M) or many-to-many (M:N). If known, specific values for the cardinality, or even upper or lower limits, should be noted. We also identify the participation of each entity in a relationship as either total or partial. Most of the information that describes the cardinality and participation of each relationship is detailed in the requirements specification shown in Section 8.1.1. However, if these constraints cannot be unequivocally determined from the Supervisor's requirements specification, we must approach the user for clarification of the situation.

Listed below are some examples of how we may determine the cardinality and participation constraints for the relationships listed in Table 8.1.

Branch Has *Staff*   In the requirements specification, this relationship is described as 'Each branch of *DreamHome* has staff . . .'. In other words, a single branch has many staff, and therefore the cardinality of this relationship is 1:M. As every branch has staff, the participation of Branch in the *Has* relationship is total.

To fully understand a relationship, we also examine the *Has* relationship from the direction of Staff *WorksAt* Branch direction. The requirements specification does not explicitly describe the *WorksAt* relationship, and we therefore ask the user the following question.

Question: Do all members of staff work at a single branch?

Answer: Yes.

The answer to this question indicates that a single member of staff *WorksAt* a single branch and therefore this relationship has a 1:1 cardinality ratio. As all members of staff are allocated to a branch, the participation of the Staff entity in the *WorksAt* relationship is total.

We may refer to the relationship between the Staff and Branch entities as either Branch *Has* Staff or Staff *WorksAt* Branch. However, when we represent this relationship in an Entity–Relationship (ER) model, we display only the higher ratio, that is 1:M. It is therefore more appropriate to name this relationship in the 1:M direction, namely, Branch *Has* Staff. The cardinality and participation constraints on the Branch *Has* Staff relationship are shown in Figure 8.1.

To improve a user's comprehension of an ER model, it is important that we adopt a consistent approach to naming entities and relationships.

Figure 8.1 The Branch *Has* Staff relationship.

Property_for_Rent ManagedBy *Staff*   In the requirements specification, this relationship is described as 'Each property for rent is managed by a particular member of staff'. This indicates that the cardinality of the Property_for_Rent *ManagedBy* Staff relationship is 1:1.

We must also consider the Property_for_Rent *ManagedBy* Staff relationship from the direction of Staff *Manages* Property_for_Rent. Although the requirements specification does identify the *Manages* relationship, we are still uncertain about certain characteristics of the relationship between the Staff and Property_for_Rent entities, and we are required to ask the user the following questions:

Question (a):   Do all members of staff manage property?

Answer (a):   No. Not all members of staff are responsible for the management of property.

Question (b):   How many properties are associated with those staff responsible for the management of property?

Answer (b):   A member of staff may manage up to a maximum of 10 properties, at any one time.

Question (c):   Are properties associated with a member of staff, at all times?

Answer (c):   No. There are occasions when a property is not specifically allocated to a member of staff, such as when the property is first registered with the company or when a property is not available for rent.

This information has clarified the precise relationship between the Staff and Property_for_Rent entities. The cardinality ratio for the Staff *Manages* Property_for_Rent relationship is 1:M, as a single member of staff manages many properties. Furthermore, we also know that the upper limit for the 'Many' side of this relationship is set at 10. In other words, a single member of staff can manage up to a maximum of 10 properties at any one time. Although this information can be displayed on an ER diagram, such detail may over-complicate a diagram. We therefore simply record this maximum value in the data dictionary.

Based on the answers to Questions (a) and (c), we know that both the Staff and Property_for_Rent entities partially participate in the *Manages* relationship. This is determined from the facts that not all members of staff are responsible for the management of property, and not all properties are allocated to a member of staff.

The cardinality and participation constraints for the relationship between the Staff and Property_for_Rent entities are shown in Figure 8.2. The Staff *Manages* Property_for_Rent relationship displays the higher cardinality 1:M and is given the name that is appropriate in the 1:M direction.

Figure 8.2 The Staff *Manages* Property_for_Rent relationship.

Advert Describes *Property_for_Rent*   In the requirements specification, this relationship is described as '... placing an advert describing a property for rent in an appropriate newspaper.' As a single advert describes a single property, the cardinality of the *Describes* relationship is 1:1. If we consider the *Describes* relationship from the direction of Property_for_Rent, we note that the Property_for_Rent *DescribedIn* Advert is not explicitly specified in the Supervisor's requirements specification. However, after consultation with the user, we learn that a single property may be associated with many adverts, and therefore the cardinality of the *DescribedIn* relationship is 1:M. Following the naming convention, we identify the relationship as Property_for_Rent *DescribedIn* Advert.

The participation of the Advert entity in the *Describes* relationship is total, as the purpose of an advert is to describe a property. However, Property_for_Rent only partially participates in this relationship, as the Supervisor's requirements specification states that properties are advertised only if they prove difficult to rent out.

The cardinality and participation constraints for the Property_for_Rent *DescribedIn* Advert relationship are shown in Figure 8.3.

Figure 8.3 The Property_for_Rent *DescribedIn* Advert relationship.

Client Views *Property_for_Rent*   In the requirements specification, this relationship is described as '... clients to view properties for rent ...'. We clarify the characteristics of this relationship with the users, and learn that a single client *Views* many properties (1:M) and a single property is *ViewedBy* many clients (1:M). Therefore, the cardinality of the *Views* relationship is M:N. We should note that the *ViewedBy* relationship is not explicitly described in the Supervisor's requirements specification. In a M:N relationship, we may select either the *Views* or *ViewedBy* relationship name. We select to use the simpler of the two names, that is Client *Views* Property_for_Rent.

To determine the participation of Client and Property_for_Rent in the *Views* relationship, we must ask the users the following questions:

Question (a):   Does every client view property?

Answer   (a):   No. Some clients only register an interest with the company but do not go on to view property.

Question (b):   Is every property viewed by clients?

Answer   (b):   No. Some properties are registered with the company but are not viewed by clients.

Based on the answers to these questions, we determine that the participation of both Client and Property_for_Rent in the *Views* relationship is partial.

The cardinality and participation constraints for the Client *Views* Property_for_Rent relationship are shown in Figure 8.4.

Figure 8.4 The Client *Views* Property_for_Rent relationship.

Use entity–relationship modelling

As we attempt to understand how the entities relate to one another through their relationships, it is often easier to visualize the situation as an Entity–Relationship (ER) diagram. We therefore present a sketch of an ER model to represent the main entities and relationships described in the Supervisor's requirements specification, as shown in Figure 8.5. However, it is assumed that throughout the logical database design process, the designer is constantly using ER diagrams, when required.

Note that all the 1:M relationships display names that are appropriate in the 1:M direction. In some cases, the relationships are renamed. For example, the Inspection *Of* Property_for_Rent (M:1) relationship is renamed Property_for_Rent *Undergoes* Inspection (1:M), and Property_for_Rent *IsAvailableAt* Branch (M:1) is renamed Branch *Offers* Property_for_Rent (1:M).

Document relationship types

We document the details of the relationships shown in Figure 8.5, and this information is provided as Appendix 8.3 of this chapter.

Step 1.3 Identify and associate attributes with entity or relationship types

We now identify attributes that may be present as nouns (or their expressions) in the Supervisor's requirements specification. An attribute may describe some aspect of an entity or relationship. Once identified, the attributes are associated with their respective entity or relationship, as shown in Tables 8.2(a) and (b).

Document attributes

We document the details of the attributes listed in Tables 8.2(a) and (b). For each attribute we provide a description, data type and length, constraints, default values (if any), aliases (if any), whether the attribute is composite, derived or multi-valued, and whether nulls are allowed. A part of this documentation is provided as Appendix 8.2 of this chapter. Note that the Duration and Deposit_Amount attributes of the Lease_Agreement entity are examples of derived attributes.

Step 1.4 Determine attribute domains

In this step, we determine the domains for the attributes in the Supervisor's local conceptual data model of the *DreamHome* company. A **domain** is a pool of values from which one or more attributes draw their values. For example, the Branch_No attribute of the Branch entity has a domain that includes a three-character string, with values ranging from B1 to B99. Also, the Sex attribute of the Staff entity is a single character consisting of either 'M' or 'F'.

An example of a domain that is shared by many attributes is the domain that holds values for addresses. The Address attributes of the Staff, Client, Private_Owner, Business_Owner and Newspaper entities share the same domain.

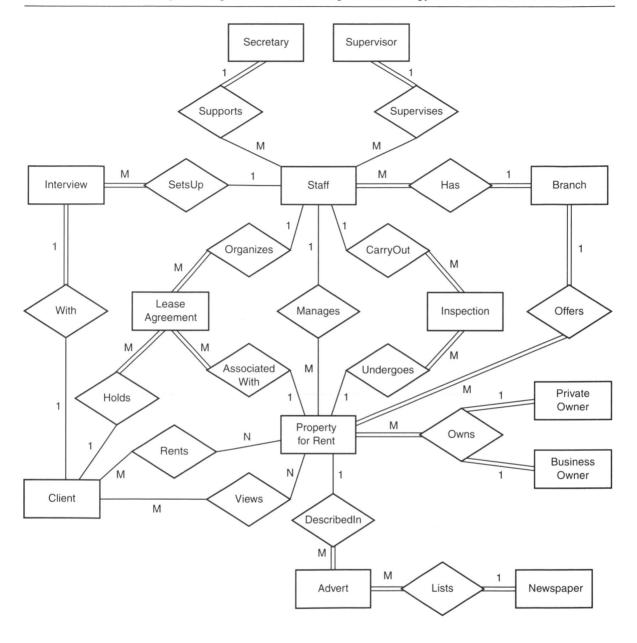

Figure 8.5 Sketch of the Supervisor's local conceptual data model of the *DreamHome* case study.

Table 8.2(a) Attributes associated with entities.

Entity type	Attribute
Branch	Branch_No
	Address (Street, City, Area, Postcode)
	Tel_No
	Fax_No
Staff	Staff_No
	Name (FName and LName)
	Address
	Tel_No
	Sex
	DOB
	Job_Title
Supervisor	(Same attributes as the Staff entity)
Secretary	(Same attributes as the Staff entity)
	Typing_Speed
Property_for_Rent	Property_No
	Address (Street, Area, City, Postcode)
	Type
	Rooms
	Rent
Private_Owner	Owner_No
	Name (FName and LName)
	Address
	Tel_No
Business_Owner	Owner_No
	BName
	BType
	Address
	Tel_No
	Contact_Name
Advert	Advert_No
	Date_Advert
	Newspaper_Name
	Cost
Newspaper	Newspaper_Name
	Address
	Tel_No
	Fax_No
	Contact_Name
Interview	Interview_Date
	Comments
Client	Client_No
	Name (FName and LName)

Table 8.2(a) *continued*

Entity type	Attribute
	Address
	Tel_No
	Pref_Type
	Max_Rent
Lease_Agreement	Lease_No
	Property_No
	Rent
	Payment_Method
	Deposit_Amount
	Deposit_Paid
	Rent_Start
	Rent_Finish
	Duration
Inspection	Date_Inspect
	Comments

Table 8.2(b) Attributes associated with a relationship.

Relationship type	Attribute
Views	Date_View
	Comments

Document attribute domains
Some of the domains for the attributes of the Supervisor's local conceptual data model are described in Appendix 8.4 of this chapter.

Step 1.5   Determine candidate and primary key attributes

Identify candidate keys and choose a primary key
We now examine Table 8.2(a), and identify all possible candidate keys for each entity in the Supervisor's local conceptual data model. From the candidate keys, we select the most appropriate primary key for each entity. For example, the Lease_Agreement entity has two candidate keys, Lease_No and (Property_No, Rent_Start). The candidate key with the minimal set of attributes, namely, Lease_No, is selected as the primary key for the Lease_Agreement entity. The other candidate key, namely (Property_No, Rent_Start), is referred to as the alternate key for the Lease_Agreement entity.

For each entity, we identify the primary key and where available any alternate keys, as shown in Table 8.3.

In this step, we cannot assign primary keys for weak entities as their existence is dependent on their owner (parent) entities. Therefore, primary

Table 8.3 Entities and their primary and alternate keys.

Entity	Primary key	Alternate key(s)
Branch	Branch_No	Tel_No Fax_No
Staff	Staff_No	
Supervisor	Staff_No	
Secretary	Staff_No	
Property_for_Rent	Property_No	
Private_Owner	Owner_No	
Business_Owner	Owner_No	
Advert	Advert_No	
Newspaper	Newspaper_Name	Tel_No Fax_No
Interview		
Client	Client_No	
Lease_Agreement	Lease_No	Property_No, Rent_Start
Inspection		

keys for weak entities are identified in Step 2.2 as part of the process of deriving relations from the ER model to represent entities and their relationships.

For example, the Interview and Inspection entities do not have primary keys, and are therefore weak entities. The primary keys of these entities can be identified only when we map the weak entity and its relationship with the owner entity to a relation, through the placement of a foreign key in that relation. The process of mapping entities and their relationships to relations is described in Step 2.2, and therefore the identification of primary keys for weak entities cannot take place until we reach that step.

Document keys

We document the attribute(s) that represent the primary and alternate keys for each entity in Appendix 8.2 of this chapter.

Step 1.6 Specialize/generalize entity types (optional step)

In this step, we have the option to enhance the ER model using the process of specialization or generalization on the entities (identified in Step 1.1). If we take the specialization approach, we attempt to highlight differences between entities. On the other hand, if we take the generalization approach, we attempt to identify common features between entities.

For example, in Figure 8.5, Supervisor and Secretary are represented as distinct entities. The decision is whether we want to generalize these entities

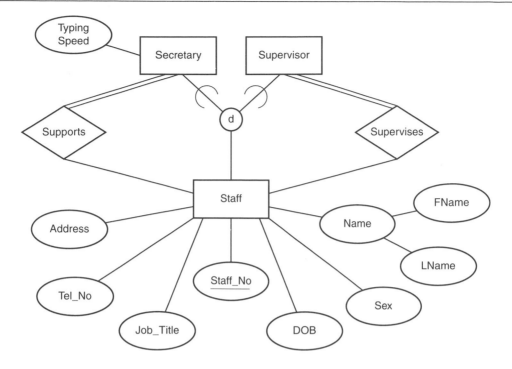

into subclasses of a generalized Staff superclass or leave them as separate entities.

As shown in Table 8.2(a), all of the attributes including the primary key of the Staff entity are represented in the Supervisor and Secretary entities. Furthermore, the Supervisor entity does not have any additional attributes. The Secretary entity has only one additional attribute, namely Typing_Speed. However, both the Supervisor and Secretary entities are associated with distinct relationships: Supervisor *Supervises* Staff and the Secretary *Supports* Staff. Based on this information, we choose to generalize the Supervisor and Secretary entities. We represent these entities as subclasses of the generalized Staff superclass. The relationship that the Staff superclass has with its subclasses is partial and disjointed, as a member of staff cannot be both a Supervisor and a Secretary, and also some members of staff do not hold the position of Supervisor or Secretary. This representation is particularly useful for displaying the shared attributes associated with Supervisor, Secretary and Staff, as shown in Figure 8.6.

An additional example to consider is the relationship between owners of property for rent. The Supervisor's requirements specification describes two types of owners: Private_Owner and Business_Owner. Based on the information given in Tables 8.1 and 8.2(a), we note that these entities share some attributes (Owner_No, Address and Tel_No) and have the same relationship (*Owns* Property_for_Rent), as shown in Figure 8.5. However, there are also attributes that are specific to Private_Owner (FName and LName) and

Figure 8.6 The Staff superclass and the Supervisor and Secretary subclasses.

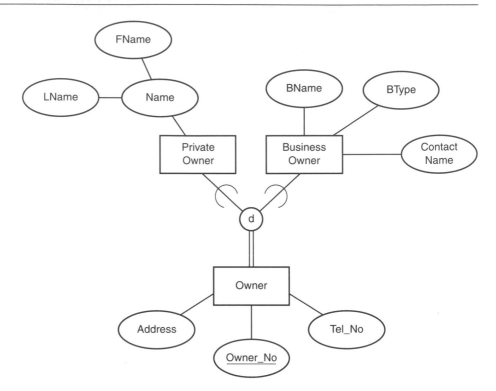

Figure 8.7 The Owner superclass with the Private_ Owner and Business_Owner subclasses.

Business_Owner (BName, BType and Contact_Name). Therefore, the entities represent different types of owners.

We choose to generalize the Private_Owner and Business_Owner entities based on the commonality of attributes and the shared *Owns* relationship. We therefore represent the Private_Owner and Business_Owner entities as distinct subclasses of a generalized Superclass called Owner. The relationship that the Owner superclass has with its subclasses is total and disjointed, as an owner must be either a private owner or a business owner, but cannot be both. This representation is particularly useful for displaying the shared attributes associated with the Private_Owner and Business_Owner and the shared *Owns* relationship as shown in Figure 8.7.

Although the examples given in this section are relatively straightforward, we should note that the process of generalization can be taken further. For example, Staff, Supervisor, Secretary, Private_Owner and Client are persons with common attributes (FName, LName, Address and Tel_No). Although there are no strict guidelines concerning the specialization/generalization process, it is important to represent the important entities and relationships as clearly as possible in a data model. Therefore, the degree of specialization/generalization displayed in a diagram should be guided by the readability of the diagram and the clarity with which it models important entities and relationships found in the 'real world'. With this in mind, we do not represent a Person superclass in the ER model.

Step 1.7 Draw Entity–Relationship diagram

To help us visualize the main entities and relationships described in the Supervisor's requirements specification, we redraw the ER diagram (Figure 8.5), as shown in Figure 8.8. This ER diagram and the documentation created in Step 1 is referred to as the Supervisor's local conceptual data model of the *DreamHome* case study.

Note that, although we use the concept of generalization/specialization of entities, which is associated with Enhanced Entity–Relationship (EER) modelling, we continue to refer to the models presented in this chapter as ER models for simplicity.

Step 1.8 Review local conceptual data model with user

Before completing Step 1, we must review the local conceptual data model with the user(s). If any errors are discovered, we must make the appropriate changes by returning to previous steps. We repeat this process until the user is prepared to 'sign off' the data model as being a 'true' representation of the Supervisor's view of *DreamHome*.

Step 2 Build and Validate Local Logical Data Model

In this step, we refine the Supervisor's local conceptual data model to remove any features of the model that are difficult to implement in relational database systems. We also validate the model against the rules of normalization and against the transactions given in the Supervisor's requirements specification. In altering the structure of the conceptual model to accommodate the requirements of the relational data model, we more correctly refer to the model as a logical data model. At the end of this step, we aim to create a local logical data model of the Supervisor's view of the *DreamHome* case study that is correct, comprehensive and unambiguous.

Step 2.1 Map local conceptual data model to local logical data model

In this step, we refine the conceptual data model by removing data structures that are difficult to implement in relational databases. This is achieved by undertaking the following activities:

(1)   Remove M:N relationships.
(2)   Remove complex relationships.
(3)   Remove recursive relationships.
(4)   Remove relationships with attributes.
(5)   Re-examine 1:1 relationships.
(6)   Remove redundant relationships.

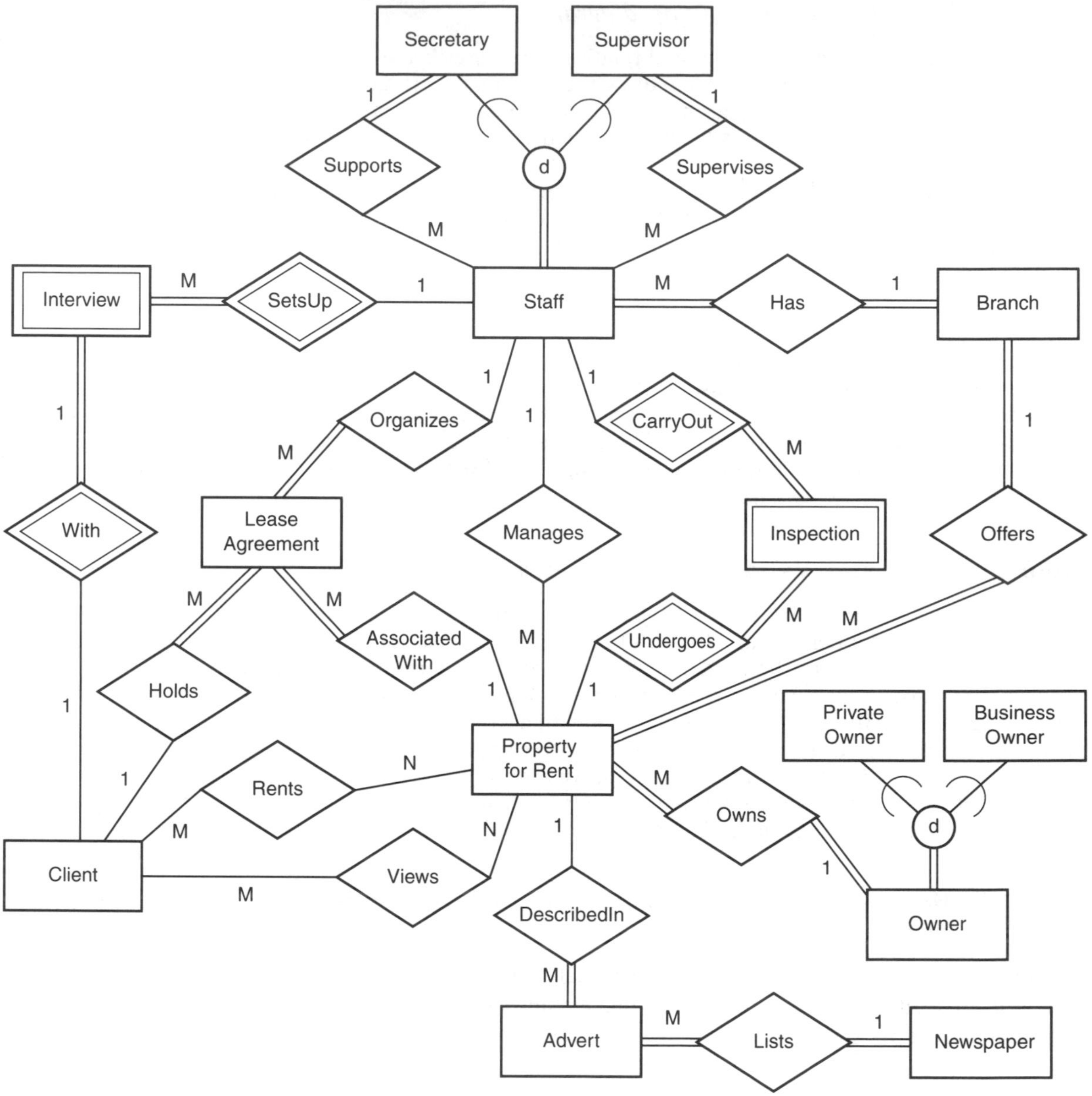

Figure 8.8 The Supervisor's local conceptual data model of the *DreamHome* case study.

(1) Remove M:N relationships

As shown in Figure 8.8, the Client *Views* Property_for_Rent relationship has a many-to-many (M:N) cardinality ratio. We decompose the *Views* relationship into two 1:M relationships (called *Attends* and *Takes*), as shown in Figure 8.9, which results in the identification of a weak entity called Viewing. Note that Viewing is a weak entity because its existence is dependent on its owner entities, namely Client and Property_for_Rent. Also, as a weak entity, the primary key of Viewing is partially or fully derived from the owner entities.

(2) Remove complex relationships

At this stage, we should remove any complex (non-binary) relationships from the ER model. However, there are no such relationships in the ER model shown in Figure 8.8. All of the relationships shown in this model are binary; in other words, each relationship is between two entity types.

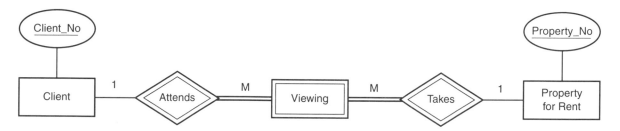

(3) Remove recursive relationships

As shown in Figure 8.8, the Supervisor *Supervises* Staff and the Secretary *Supports* Staff are two examples of recursive relationships. These relationships are recursive because they represent relationships that an entity has with itself. The Supervisor and Secretary entities are simply members of staff with specific job roles that involve relationships with other members of staff. However, the Supervisor and Secretary entities are associated only with specific members of staff and not with all staff.

The *Supervises* and *Supports* recursive relationships are removed by introducing a weak entity called Allocated_Staff, as shown in Figure 8.10. This entity represents those members of staff that are supervised by a Supervisor and supported by a Secretary.

Figure 8.9 Removing the M:N client *Views* Property_for_Rent (M:N) relationship.

(4) Remove relationships with attributes

The presence of relationships with attributes may indicate the presence of an, as yet, unidentified entity. The Client *Views* Property_for_Rent relationship is an example of a relationship with attributes, namely Date_View and Comments. However, the *Views* relationship was already decomposed, when we removed M:N relationships in Step 2.1(1). This resulted in the identification of the Viewing entity.

(5) Re-examine 1:1 relationships

In some cases, entities associated through a one-to-one (1:1) relationship may in fact represent the same entity. It is therefore advisable to re-examine all 1:1

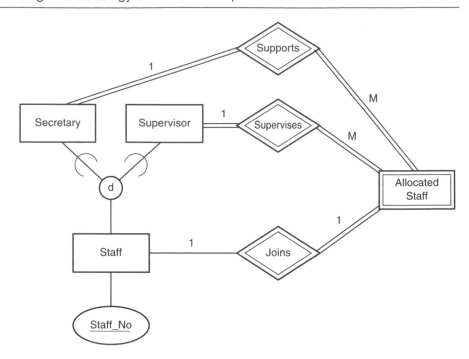

Figure 8.10
Removing the
recursive *Supervises*
and *Supports*
relationships.

relationships in the data model. Although, the Interview *With* Staff is an example of a 1:1 relationship, clearly the Interview and Staff entities represent different entities in the 'real world'.

In Step 2.1(3), we introduced a second 1:1 relationship, when we removed recursive relationships. The Staff *Joins* Allocated_Staff (1:1) relationship is shown in Figure 8.10. In this case, the Staff and Allocated_Staff entities have the same primary key, namely Staff_No, and do in fact represent the same entity. However, the members of staff represented by the Allocated_Staff entity have particular relationships with the Supervisor and Secretary entities, and represent only a subset of all staff. We therefore decide to leave the current representation of the Staff and Allocated_Staff as separate entities, as shown in Figure 8.10.

(6) Remove redundant relationships
In Figure 8.8, the Client *Rents* Property_for_Rent relationship is an example of a redundant relationship. This relationship is already represented through the pathway that includes Client *Holds* Lease_Agreement and Lease_Agreement *AssociatedWith* Property_for_Rent. The *Rents* relationship is redundant, as it does not provide any additional information that is not shown by the pathway that includes the Lease_Agreement entity. Furthermore, a client cannot rent a property without first holding a lease agreement for the property. The Client *Rents* Property_for_Rent relationship is therefore removed from the data model.

Draw Entity–Relationship diagram
The ER diagram representing the local conceptual model of the Supervisor's view of the *DreamHome* company is shown in Figure 8.8. In Step 2.1, we re-examined this model to identify any data structures that are difficult to implement in relational databases. We redraw the data model as shown in Figure 8.11 with the amendments discussed in Step 2.1. With these refinements, we more correctly refer to the model as the local logical model for the Supervisor's view of the *DreamHome* company.

It is important that we update the supporting documentation for this logical data model, to reflect any significant structural changes that may have occurred during the refinement step.

Step 2.2   Derive relations from local logical data model

In this step, we derive relations from the local logical data model, shown in Figure 8.11, to represent the entities and relationships described in the Supervisor's view of *DreamHome*. We represent the relationships between entities using the primary key/foreign key mechanism.

To illustrate this process, we examine the representation of the Client *Attends* Viewing and Property_for_Rent *Takes* Viewing part of the logical data model shown in Figure 8.11. We use a Database Definition Language (DBDL) for relational databases to describe the composition of each relation.

For each strong (regular entity) in the data model, we create a relation that includes all of the simple attributes of that entity. The composition of the Client relation is:

> **Client** (Client_No, FName, LName, Address, Tel_No, Pref_Type, Max_Rent)
> **Primary Key** Client_No

The composition of the Property_for_Rent relation is:

> **Property_for_Rent** (Property_No, Street, Area, City, Postcode, Type,
>   Rooms, Rent)
> **Primary Key** Property_No

For each weak entity in the data model, we create a relation that includes all of the simple attributes of that entity. In addition, we include as a foreign key the primary key of the owner (parent) entities. The Viewing entity has two owner entities, namely Client and Property_for_Rent, and therefore receives a copy of their primary keys to act as foreign keys within that relation.

The primary key of a weak entity is partially or fully derived from the owner entities. Note that the primary key of the Viewing entity, namely (Property_No, Client_No, Date_View) is partially derived from the Client and Property_for_Rent entities, through the posting of foreign keys to the Viewing relation.

The composition of the Viewing relation is:

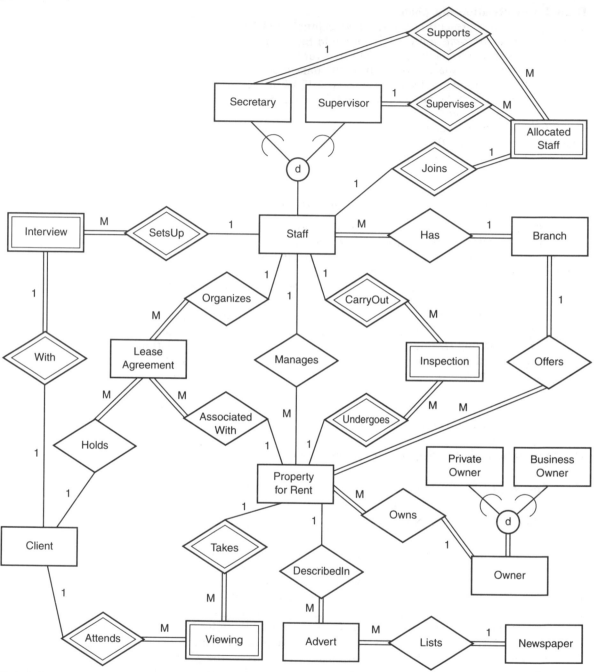

Figure 8.11 The Supervisor's local logical data model of the *DreamHome* case study (Version 1).

Viewing (Property_No, Client_No, Date_View, Comments)

Primary Key Property_No, Client_No, Date_View

Foreign Key Property_No **references** Property_for_Rent(Property_No)

Foreign Key Client_No **references** Client(Client_No)

This process is continued for all of the entities and relationships in the logical data model shown in Figure 8.11. Note that the composition of the Property_for_Rent relation shown here is incomplete, as we have not yet represented all of the relationships that this entity has with other entities in the logical model.

Document relations and foreign key attributes

The set of relations derived from the Supervisor's logical data model is given in Appendix 8.5 of this chapter. The data dictionary is also updated to record all key attributes that have been identified in this step. We should specifically note any new primary or alternate keys formed in the process of posting foreign keys to represent relationships.

Step 2.3   Validate model using normalization

In this step, we validate the composition of the relations that represent the Supervisor's view of the *DreamHome* case study using the technique of normalization. The process of normalization was fully described in Chapter 6, and involves the following major steps:

- First Normal Form (1NF), which removes repeating groups;
- Second Normal Form (2NF), which removes partial dependencies on the primary key;
- Third Normal Form (3NF), which removes transitive dependencies on the primary key;
- Boyce–Codd Normal Form (BCNF), which removes remaining anomalies from all functional dependencies.

We examine the functional dependencies of the relations listed in Appendix 8.5, to ensure that each relation is in at least BCNF. If we identify a relation that is not in BCNF, this may indicate that the logical model is structurally incorrect, or that we have introduced an error in the process of deriving relations from the model. In either case, we must return to earlier steps to correct this error.

To illustrate this process, we examine the functional dependencies of the Client, Lease_Agreement and Property_for_Rent relations, which are listed in Appendix 8.5. (Note that the DBDL notation shown here does not included the references to the foreign key attributes.)

Client (Client_No, FName, LName, Address, Tel_No, Pref_Type, Max_Rent)
Primary Key Client_No

Client_No → FName, LName, Address, Tel_No, Pref_Type, Max_Rent

Lease_Agreement (Lease_No, Client_No, Property_No, Rent,
        Payment_Method, Deposit_Paid, Rent_Start, Rent_Finish, Staff_No)
Primary Key Lease_No
Alternate Key Property_No, Rent_Start

Lease_No → Client_No, Property_No, Rent, Payment_Method,
        Deposit_Amount, Deposit_Paid, Rent_Start, Rent_Finish, Staff_No

Property_No, Rent_Start → Lease_No, Client_No, Rent, Payment_Method,
        Deposit_Amount, Deposit_Paid, Rent_Finish, Staff_No

Property_No → Rent

Property_for_Rent (Property_No, Street, Area, City, Postcode, Type,
        Rooms, Rent, Owner_No, ManagedBy_Staff_No (Staff_No),
        Branch_No)
Primary Key Property_No

Property_No → Street, Area, City, Postcode, Type, Rooms, Rent,
        Owner_No, ManagedBy_Staff_No (Staff_No), Branch_No

From these examples, we note that the Client and Property_for_Rent relations do not contain repeating groups, or have partial or transitive dependencies on their primary keys. Furthermore, both entities have only a single determinant, which is the primary key (candidate key) for that relation. We conclude that the Client and Property_for_Rent relations are therefore in BCNF.

However, if we examine the functional dependencies of the Lease_Agreement relation, we identify a transitive dependency, namely Property_No → Rent, on the primary key (Lease_No) of this relation. This type of dependency violates 3NF, and must therefore be removed from the Lease_Agreement relation. However, it is not necessary to create a separate relation for this functional dependency, as it is already represented within the Property_for_Rent relation. Also, this anomaly does not require any redrawing of the ER model shown in Figure 8.11, but simply requires the documentation to be updated.

On removing the Rent attribute from the Lease_Agreement relation, we now confirm that this relation is in 3NF. We also note that the determinants, namely Lease_No and (Property, Rent_Start), of this relation are also candidate keys, and therefore the Lease_Agreement relation is also in BCNF.

This process is continued for all of the relations described in Appendix 8.5. When we are satisfied that all of the relations are in BCNF, we may proceed to the next step.

Step 2.4 Validate model against user transactions

The purpose of this step is to validate the Supervisor's logical data model against the transactions that are required for this user view (Section 8.1.2). To validate the data model for transactions, we use the ER model shown in Figure 8.11 and the supporting documentation. With this information we attempt to perform the transaction operations manually. If we confirm support for all transactions in this way, we have validated the logical data model against the transactions. However, if we are unable to perform a transaction manually, there must be a problem with the data model, which has to be resolved. In this case, it is likely that we have omitted a relationship or an attribute from the data model. On the other hand, if there is some portion of the model that is not required to support current or future transactions, we must consider whether this part of the model is redundant and should be removed from the final logical data model.

We consider two possible approaches to ensure that the logical data model shown in Figure 8.11 supports the transactions described in the Supervisor's view. We illustrate both approaches using examples taken from the database transactions given in Section 8.1.2. The first approach requires that we ensure that the information (entities, relationships and attributes) required by each transaction is supported by the model by providing a description of how we may achieve the transaction. To illustrate this approach, we examine two typical operations associated with transaction (d) given in the Supervisor's requirements specification.

Create and maintain records recording the details of property for rent and the owner at each branch

- To update details of an existing property for rent, given a property number, we first search for the given property number in the appropriate attribute of the Property_for_Rent relation. If it is not found, a user error has occurred and the details cannot be updated. Otherwise, we check that each detail to be updated is represented by an attribute in the Property_for_Rent relation.

- To delete details of an owner, given the owner number and any associated property for rent, we first search for the given owner number in the appropriate foreign key attribute of the Property_for_Rent relation. If found, we delete the occurrence(s) from the Property_for_ Rent relation. We then search for the given owner number in the appropriate column of the Owner relation, and delete the occurrence from the Owner relation. If the owner number is not found, a user error has occurred and the required details cannot be deleted.

The second approach to validating the transactions requires diagrammatically representing each transaction on the Supervisor's local logical data model, as shown in Figure 8.12.

The pathway required by each transaction (a) to (r), described in Section 8.1.2, is represented on the model. The transaction pathway is depicted as

Figure 8.12 The Supervisor's local logical data model of the *DreamHome* case study displaying the transactions supported by this model.

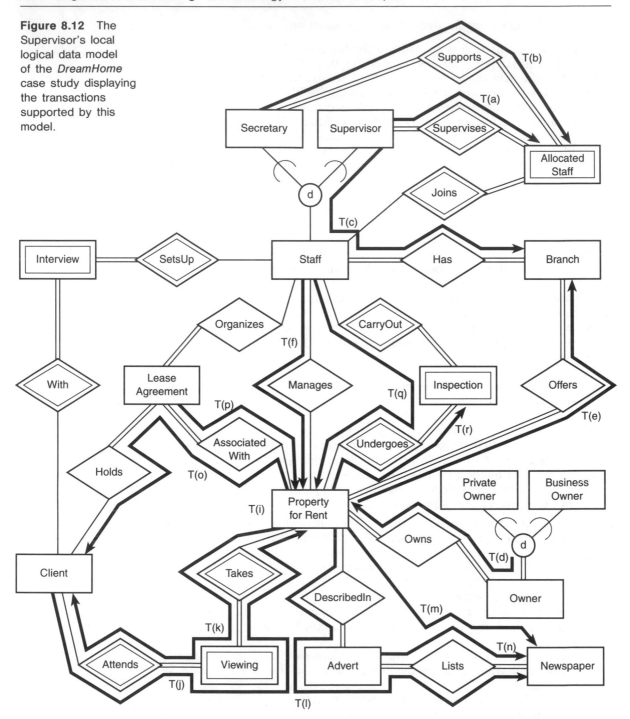

a line, with an arrow indicating the direction of the transaction and identifying the entities and relationships required by the transaction. Each transaction is labelled with a T(x), where x identifies the transaction given in the list of database transactions. The specific attributes required for each transaction are also checked in the supporting documentation and found to be satisfactory.

Step 2.5   Draw entity–relationship diagram

The diagrammatic representation of transactions directly on the ER model, as shown in Figure 8.12, helps to identify areas of the model that are critical to transactions, and those areas that do not appear to be required by transactions. For example, as shown in Figure 8.12, the data model does not provide the pathway required by transactions (g) and (h), described in Section 8.1.2, as both require a direct link between the Client and Branch entities to identify clients associated with a branch. We therefore conclude that a critical relationship between Branch and Client has been overlooked, and must be introduced into the data model. We learn that a single client registers with a single branch. We represent this relationship Branch *Registers* Client, as shown in Figure 8.13, and introduce Branch_No as a foreign key into the Client relation.

We note that there are no transactions associated with the Staff *SetsUp* Interview and Interview *With* Client part of the ER model, as shown in Figure 8.12. This calls into question the requirement to hold this information in the database. After consultation with the user(s), it is agreed that this part of the model should be removed from the Supervisor's local logical data model. Although it is still current practice to interview potential clients (when possible), the details of an interview (Date_Interview and Comments) are rarely, if ever, accessed after the event. The user(s) confirm that we should remove the Interview entity and the associated relationships from the data model.

Similarly, there are no transactions associated with the Staff *Organizes* Lease_Agreement part of the model. After consultation with the user(s) it is agreed that, although a particular member of staff does organize the lease agreement between a client and a property, this information is not required after the event. The Staff *Organizes* Lease_Agreement relationship does not need to be represented in the data model, and is therefore removed.

We redraw the Supervisor's logical data model with the amendments discussed in this step, as shown in Figure 8.13.

Step 2.6   Define integrity constraints

In this step, we identify integrity constraints that we wish to impose on the Supervisor's local logical data model, to ensure that once implemented as a database, the data remains consistent over time. At this stage, we specify only what integrity constraints are required, and need not state how this is to be achieved. We consider five types of integrity constraints:

- required data,
- attribute domain constraints,

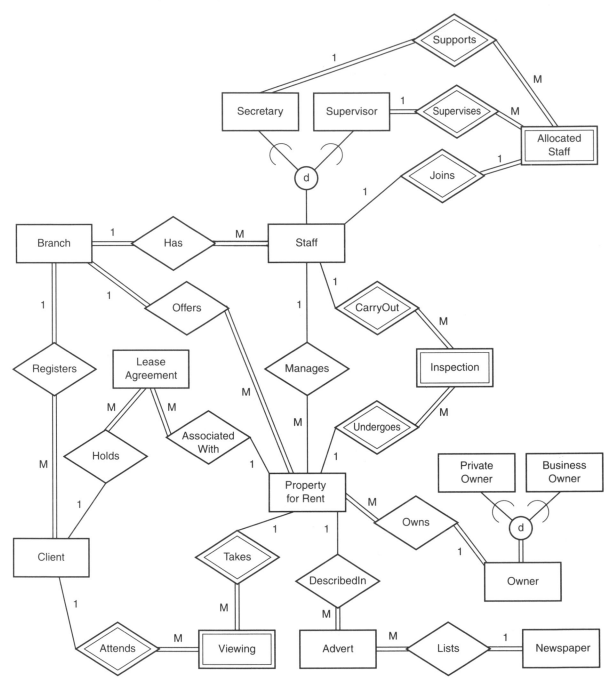

Figure 8.13 The Supervisor's local logical data model of the *DreamHome* case study (final version).

- entity integrity,
- referential integrity,
- enterprise constraints.

Required data

We identify the attributes that must contain a valid value at all times: in other words, attributes that are not allowed to contain missing information or nulls. For example, the Staff_No and Name (FName and LName) attributes of the Staff entity must always hold a value, and cannot hold nulls. However, the Tel_No of the Staff entity does not always need to hold a value, and may therefore hold nulls that can represent missing, unknown or not applicable information.

The details of the attributes of the Supervisor's data model were described in Step 1.3, and are documented in Appendix 8.2 of this chapter. This appendix provides examples of attributes that allow or disallow nulls.

Attribute domain constraints

The domain for an attribute identifies the set of legal values that an attribute may hold. For example, the set of values for the Client_No attribute of the Client entity is a five-character variable string containing the values ranging from CR1 to CR999. Examples of the domains for the attributes of the Supervisor's local logical data model were described in Step 1.4, and are documented in Appendix 8.4 of this chapter.

Entity integrity

The primary key of an entity must not allow nulls. For example, each occurrence of the Branch entity must have a value for the primary key attribute, Branch_No. The attribute(s) that constitute the primary key for each entity were identified in Steps 1.5 and 2.2, and are listed in Appendix 8.5.

Referential integrity

Relationships between entities are represented by placing a copy of the primary key of the parent relation in the child relation. Referential integrity means that if the foreign key of a child relation contains a value, that value must refer to an existing valid occurrence in the parent relation. For example, if the Branch_No (foreign key) attribute of the Staff (child) relation contains the value B3, this value must be an existing value in the Branch_No (primary key) attribute of the Branch (parent) relation. The attributes that constitute the primary and foreign keys of entities are described in Appendix 8.5.

We must identify the constraints that are to be placed on primary and foreign keys to ensure that referential integrity is maintained between parent and child relations. Note that the Database Definition Language (DBDL) used to describe the composition of the relations that represent the Supervisor's logical data model can be extended to describe the constraints on the foreign key(s) in each relation.

We first consider whether nulls are allowed for foreign keys. In general, if the participation of the child entity in the relationship is total, then we do not allow nulls. For example, consider the relationships that the Property_ for_Rent entity is associated with, in the role of the child entity in Figure 8.13, such as the Owner *Owns* Property_for_Rent relationship: the Property_for_Rent entity (child) totally participates in this relationship, and we therefore do not allow nulls for the Owner_No (foreign key) in this relation. Following this reasoning, we also decide to disallow nulls for the Branch_No (foreign key), which represents the Branch *Offers* Property_for_Rent relationship.

On the other hand, if the participation of the child entity in the relationship is partial, then we allow nulls. For example, in the Staff *Manages* Property_for_Rent relationship, the Property_for_Rent entity (child) partially participates in this relationship, and we therefore do allow nulls for the ManagedBy_Staff_No (foreign key) in this relation.

We represent the constraints on the foreign keys of the Property_for_Rent relation by extending the notation of the DBDL:

> **Property_for_Rent** (Property_No, Street, Area, City, Postcode, Type, Rooms, Rent, Owner_No, ManagedBy_Staff_No, Branch_No)
>
> **Primary Key** Property_No
>
> **Foreign Key** Owner_No is **NOT NULL references** Private_Owner(Owner_No) and Business_Owner(Owner_No)
>
> **Foreign Key** ManagedBy_Staff_No is **NULL references** Staff(Staff_No)
>
> **Foreign Key** Branch_No is **NOT NULL references** Branch(Branch_No)

We next consider how to ensure referential integrity by specifying existence constraints on primary and foreign keys. These constraints define the conditions under which occurrences of a primary key are updated or deleted, and occurrences of a foreign key are inserted or updated. Note that inserting a new occurrence of a primary key or deleting an occurrence of a foreign key does not cause any problems for referential integrity.

For each foreign key of a relation we must define the conditions for updating or deletion of the referencing primary key. In these conditions there are several strategies to select from, namely NO ACTION, CASCADE, SET NULL and SET DEFAULT. We represent the existence constraints on the foreign keys of the Property_for_Rent relation by extending the notation of the DBDL:

> **Property_for_Rent** (Property_No, Street, Area, City, Postcode, Type, Rooms, Rent, Owner_No, ManagedBy_Staff_No, Branch_No)
>
> **Primary Key** Property_No
>
> **Foreign Key** Owner_No is **NOT NULL references** POwner(Owner_No) and BOwner(Owner_No) on delete **NO ACTION** on update **CASCADE**
>
> **Foreign Key** ManagedBy_Staff_No is **NULL references** Staff(Staff_No) on delete **SET NULL** on update **CASCADE**
>
> **Foreign Key** Branch_No is **NOT NULL references** Branch(Branch_No) on delete is **NO ACTION** on update is **CASCADE**

This process is continued for all of the relations described in Appendix 8.5.

Enterprise constraints
These constraints are defined by enterprise rules that control the transactions in the 'real world'. For example, the *DreamHome* company specifies that a Supervisor should supervise a minimum of 5 and a maximum of 10 members of staff at any one time. The enterprise rules given in the Supervisor's requirements specification are listed in Appendix 8.6.

Document integrity constraints
We document the details of all integrity constraints in the Supervisor's logical data model.

Step 2.7   Review local logical data model with user

In this step, we validate the Supervisor's local logical data model by reviewing the model with the user(s). It is critical that the model is a 'true' representation of the 'real world', as viewed by the Supervisors. The ER diagram acts as a communication tool between the developer(s) of the model and the user(s). However, it is also important that the users examine the documentation supporting the model. If the user(s) find a flaw in the model or documentation, we must repeat the necessary step(s).

The Supervisor's local logical data model of the *DreamHome* case study includes the ER model, shown in Figure 8.13, and the documentation that describes the components of the model.

Step 3   Build and Validate Global Logical Data Model

In this section, we merge the local logical data model for the Supervisor's view with the local logical data model for the Manager's view that we created in Chapter 5, to form a global logical data model. The global logical data model will represent both views of the *DreamHome* case study. In this step, we illustrate one possible approach to the process of merging local logical data models into a single global logical data model.

The logical data models to be merged in this step are shown in Figure 8.13 (Supervisor's view) and Figure 5.1 (Manager's view).

Step 3.1   Merge local logical data models into global model

In this step, we merge the two individual local logical data models to form a global logical data model; in other words, a global view of the *DreamHome* company. We begin the process of merging the data models by first identifying similarities between the models, then identifying and resolving areas of conflict between the models, and finally including those areas of each model that are unique to each view. Some of the typical tasks involved in the merging process are illustrated below.

Table 8.4 A comparison of the names of entities and their primary keys in the Supervisor's and Manager's views.

Entity type (Supervisor's view)	Primary key	Entity type (Manager's view)	Primary key
Branch	**Branch_No**	**Branch**	**Branch_No**
Staff	**Staff_No**	**Staff**	**Staff_No**
Supervisor	**Staff_No**	**Supervisor**	**Staff_No**
Secretary	Staff_No		
Allocated_Staff	**Staff_No**	**Allocated_Staff**	**Staff_No**
		Manager	Staff_No
		Next_of_Kin	Staff_No, NName
Property_for_Rent	**Property_No**	**Property_for_Rent**	**Property_No**
Private_Owner	**Owner_No**	**Private_Owner**	**Owner_No**
Business_Owner	**Owner_No**	**Business_Owner**	**Owner_No**
Advert	**Advert_No**	**Advert**	**Property_No, Date_Advert, Newspaper_Name**
Newspaper	**Newspaper_Name**	**Newspaper**	**Newspaper_Name**
Client	Client_No		
		Renter	Renter_No
Viewing	**Property_No, Client_No, Date_View**	**Viewing**	**Property_No, Renter_No, Date_View**
Lease_Agreement	Lease_No		
		Rental_Agreement	Rental_No
Inspection	Property_No, Staff_No, Date_Inspect		

(1) Review names of entities and their primary keys

We compare the names of entities and their primary keys in the two local data models, as shown in Table 8.4.

This initial comparison of the names of entities and their primary keys in each view gives some indication as to the extent to which the views overlap. The entities that appear to be common to both views are highlighted in bold. Note that despite the fact that both views have an Advert and Viewing entity, the composition of their primary keys differs in each view. The resolution of this conflict is discussed below in part (3).

(2) Review the names of relationships

We now compare the names of the relationships associated with the Supervisor's and the Manager's views. The names of the relationships in both views

Table 8.5 Comparison of relationships present in the Supervisor's and Manager's views.

Entity type (Supervisor's view)	Relationship type	Entity type (Supervisor's view)	Entity type (Manager's view)	Relationship type	Entity type (Manager's view)
Branch	*Has*	Staff	Branch	*Has*	Staff
	Offers	Property_for_Rent		*Offers*	Property_for_Rent
	Registers	Client		*RefersTo*	Renter
Staff	*Manages*	Property_for_Rent	Staff	*Oversees*	Property_for_Rent
	CarryOut	Inspection		*RelatedTo*	Next_of_Kin
	Joins	Allocated_Staff		*Joins*	Allocated_Staff
Supervisor	*Supervises*	Allocated_Staff	Supervisor	*Supervises*	Allocated_Staff
Secretary	*Supports*	Allocated_Staff			
			Manager	*Manages*	Branch
Property_for_Rent	*AssociatedWith*	Lease_Agreement	Property_for_Rent	*LinkedTo*	Rental_Agreement
	DescribedIn	Advert		*PlacedIn*	Advert
	Undergoes	Inspection		*Takes*	Viewing
	Takes	Viewing			
Private_Owner	*Owns*	Property_for_Rent	Private_Owner	*Owns*	Property_for_Rent
Business_Owner	*Owns*	Property_for_Rent	Business_Owner	*Owns*	Property_for_Rent
Newspaper	*Lists*	Advert	Newspaper	*Displays*	Advert
Client	*Attends*	Viewing			
	Holds	Lease_Agreement			
			Renter	*Requests*	Viewing
				Holds	Rental_Agreement

are listed in Table 8.5. Each relationship is listed only once in the table in association with the parent entity.

This initial comparison of the relationship names in each view again gives some indication as to the extent to which the views overlap. However, it is important to recognize that we should not rely too heavily on the fact that entities or relationships with the same name play the same role in both views. However, comparing the names of entities and relationships is a good starting point when searching for overlap between the views, as long as we are aware of the pitfalls.

We must be careful of entities or relationships that have the same name, but in fact represent different concepts (also called homonyms). An example of this occurrence is the Staff *Manages* Property_for_Rent (Supervisor's view) and Manager *Manages* Branch (Manager's view). Obviously, the *Manages* relationship in this case means something different in both views.

We must also be aware of entities or relationships that have different names, but actually represent the same concept (also called synonyms). An example of this occurrence is the Client (Supervisor's view) and Renter (Manager's view) entities. Examination of the attributes (and in particular the domains of the keys) associated with these entities suggests that these entities are the same. The primary keys of the Client and Renter entities also have different names, namely Client_No and Renter_No, respectively. However, the domain for these primary keys is the same, being a five-digit variable string holding values ranging from CR1 to CR999.

We must therefore ensure that entities or relationships that have the same name represent the same concept in the 'real world', and that the names that differ in each view represent different concepts. To achieve this, we compare the attributes (and, in particular, the keys) associated with each entity and also their associated relationships with other entities. We should also be aware that entities or relationships in one view may be represented simply as attributes in another view. For example, consider the scenario where the Branch entity has an attribute called Manager_Name in one view, which is represented as an entity called Manager in another view.

(3) Merge entities from the local views

In this step, we examine the name and content of each entity in both views. In particular, we use the primary keys to help us identify equivalent entities, which may be named differently in both views. Typically, this step includes the following activities:

- Merge entities with the same name and the same primary key.
- Merge entities with the same name but with different primary keys.
- Merge entities with different names but with the same or different primary keys.

Merge entities with the same name and the same primary key   Entities in both views with the same primary key normally represent the same concept in the 'real world', and should be easily identified and combined. These entities are highlighted in Table 8.4, and include Branch, Staff, Allocated_Staff, Property_for_Rent, Private_Owner, Business_Owner and Newspaper.

The combined entities include the attributes from both entities with duplicates removed. For example, the merging of the Staff entity for both views is shown in Figure 8.14. The majority of attributes for the Staff entity are common to both views, with the exception of the Salary, Date_Joined and NIN (National Insurance Number) attributes, which are only required in the Manager's view. Also, the Job_Title (Supervisor's View) and Position (Manager's View) attributes differ in name but not in purpose. The merged Staff entity for the global view contains all of the common attributes, and also those required only by the Manager's view.

Merge entities with the same name using different primary keys   In some cases, we may identify entities that are the same but use different primary keys. For example, the Advert entities in both views have common attributes but use different primary keys. The Supervisor's view of the Advert entity uses the Advert_No as the primary key and the Manager's view; the Advert entity uses Property_No, Date_Advert and Name_of_Newspaper. Both primary keys are candidate keys of the Advert entity. We merge the Advert entities from

(Supervisor's View)

Staff (Staff_No, FName, LName, Address, Tel_No, Sex, DOB (Date_of_Birth),
     Job_Title, Typing_Speed, Branch_No)
Primary Key Staff_No
Foreign Key Branch_No **references** Branch(Branch_No)

(Manager's View)

Staff (Staff_No, FName, LName, Address, Tel_No, Sex, DOB (Date_of_Birth),
     Position, **Salary, Date_Joined, NIN (National Insurance Number),**
     Typing_Speed, Branch_No)
Primary Key Staff_No
Alternate Key NIN
Foreign Key Branch_No **references** Branch(Branch_No)

(Global View)

Staff (Staff_No, FName, LName, Address, Tel_No, Sex, DOB (Date_of_Birth),
     Position, Salary, Date_Joined, NIN (National Insurance Number),
     Typing_Speed, Branch_No)
Primary Key Staff_No
Alternate Key NIN
Foreign Key Branch_No **references** Branch(Branch_No)

Figure 8.14 Merging the Staff entities from the Supervisor's and Manager's views.

(Supervisor's View)

Advert (**Advert_No**, Property_No, Cost, Date_Advert, Newspaper_Name)
Primary Key Advert_No
Alternate Key Property_No, Date_Advert, Newspaper_Name
Foreign Key Property_No **references** Property_for_Rent(Property_No)
Foreign Key Newspaper_Name **references** Newspaper(Newspaper_Name)

(Manager's View)

Advert (Property_No, Cost, Date_Advert, Newspaper_Name)
Primary Key Property_No, Date_Advert, Newspaper_Name
Foreign Key Property_No **references** Property(Property_No)
Foreign Key Newspaper_Name **references** Newspaper(Newspaper_Name)

(Global View)

Advert (Advert_No, Property_No, Cost, Date_Advert, Newspaper_Name)
Primary Key Advert_No
Alternate Key Property_No, Date_Advert, Newspaper_Name
Foreign Key Property_No **references** Property_for_Rent(Property_No)
Foreign Key Newspaper_Name **references** Newspaper(Newspaper_Name)

Figure 8.15 Merging the Advert entities from the Supervisor's and Manager's views.

both views, and select one of the candidate keys to be the primary key, as shown in Figure 8.15.

The merged Advert entity for the global view contains all of the common attributes, and also those attributes representing the primary keys in each view. The Advert_No is selected as the primary key for the Advert entity in the global view.

Merge entities with different names using the same or different primary keys   In some cases, we identify entities that have different names but appear to have the same purpose. These equivalent entities may be recognized simply by their name, which indicates the similar purpose, and also by their association with particular relationships. For example, does the Client (Supervisor's view) and Renter (Manager's view) represent the same entity in both views? These entities certainly appear to be very similar based on their similar attributes and relationships, such has *Holds* Lease/Rental_Agreement and *Attends* Viewing. After checking with the users, we learn that the Client and Renter entities represent the same entity.

(4) Include (without merging) entities unique to each local view
So far we have identified the entities that are the same in both views. This leaves the entities that are unique to each view, which are included in the global data model without change. These include the Manager and Next_of_Kin entities from the Manager's view, and the Secretary and Inspection entities from the Supervisor's view.

(5) Merge relationships from the local views
In this step, we examine the name and purpose of each relationship in both views. Before merging relationships, it is important to resolve any conflicts such as participation and cardinality constraints. The names of the relationships in both views are listed in Table 8.5.

Typical activities in this step include merging relationships with the same name and the same purpose, and then merging relationships with different names but the same purpose.

Merge relationships with the same name and the same purpose   From Table 8.5, we identify the relationships that are common to both views. For example, Private/Business_Owner *Owns* Property_for_Rent.

We also note that there are some examples of relationships with the same name but with different constraints. For example, although Branch *Has* Staff appears in both views, the participation constraint for the Staff entity in this relationship is different. In this case, we must clarify the situation with the users. On consultation with the users, they state that the Supervisor's view of the relationship is more correct, and that all staff work at a branch. The participation of Staff in the *Has* relationship is therefore total, as shown in the Supervisor's view (Figure 8.13).

As mentioned earlier, we must be careful of relationships that have the same name but have a different purpose. For example, in the Staff *Manages* Property_for_Rent (Supervisor's view) and Manager *Manages*

Branch (Manager's view), the *Manages* relationship clearly plays a different role in both views.

Merge relationships with different names but the same purpose   From Table 8.5, we identify the relationships that have different names but appear to have the same purpose in both views. This may be evident by the fact that two relationships in different views are associated with the same entities. Also, the cardinality and participation constraints on each relationship should be the same or similar. For example, the *Manages* (Supervisor's view) and *Oversees* (Manager's view) relationships are associated with the same entities, namely Staff *Manages/Oversees* Property_for_Rent. Also, the cardinality and participation constraints on both relationships are the same. We therefore conclude that the *Manages* and *Oversees* relationships are the same.

(6) Include (without merging) relationships unique to each local view
From Table 8.5, we identify the relationships that are unique to the Supervisor's or Manager's views. These relationships are added to the global data model without change. For example, Staff *CarryOut* Inspection and Secretary *Supports* Allocated_Staff relationships of the Supervisor's view, and the Manager *Manages* Branch and the Staff *RelatedTo* Next_of_Kin relationships of the Manager's view.

(7) Check for missing entities and relationships
Checking for missing entities and relationships between different user views is an important activity in creating a global data model. However, this activity can be a very difficult task. Entities and relationships can be left out of local views when there is uncertainty about the responsibility for certain activities. Each user may assume that a given activity is the responsibility of another user, and therefore the required data and transactions for this activity are absent from all local views. This problem occurs particularly at the interface of one view with another.

(8) Check foreign keys
In this step, we check that all child entities contain the appropriate foreign keys. We should be particularly careful of entities and relationships directly involved in the merging of the views. For example, the Branch entity in the Supervisor's view did not contain any foreign keys, but in the global view it has Staff_No (re-named Manager_Staff_No) to represent the Staff *Manages* Branch relationship.

(9) Check integrity constraints
We check all integrity constraints for the global data model, and ensure that any conflicts between different local views are resolved.

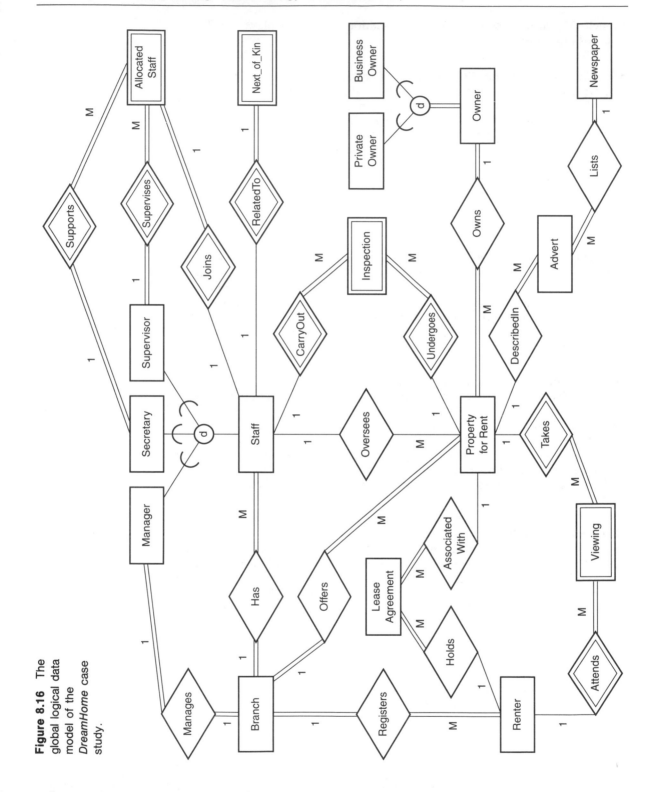

Figure 8.16 The global logical data model of the *DreamHome* case study.

(10) Draw the global logical data model
We now draw the global logical data model that represents the merged views of both the Supervisor and Manager. The global logical data model of the *DreamHome* case study is shown in Figure 8.16.

The global data model contains all the entities and relationships previously represented in the individual local views. In the cases where there was a choice of name for an entity or relationship, the users are asked to indicate a preference for representation in the data model. However, the original user preference for the name of an entity or relationship can be re-established when the views are implemented.

(11) Update the documentation
We must continually update the documentation to reflect any changes made during the development of the global data model from the individual user views. It is very important that the documentation is up to date and reflects the current data model.

Appendix 8.7 describes the relations that represent the global logical data model of the *DreamHome* case study shown in Figure 8.16. The Database Design Language (DBDL) specifies constraints on foreign keys.

Step 3.2   Validate global logical data model

Although we validated the Supervisor's and Manager's data models before we started to build the global logical data model for the *DreamHome* case study, we may have introduced errors during the process of merging the data models. It is particularly important to validate the global logical data model using the rules of normalization and against the required transactions.

Step 3.3   Check for future growth

It is important that a global logical data model is capable of being extended at a later stage as the users' requirements change. For example, the Managing Director of *DreamHome* is considering expanding the property maintenance side of *DreamHome*. Currently, *DreamHome* subcontracts repair and maintenance work to external companies. However, the Managing Director would like to offer this service to owners of property in the near future. The current global view of the *DreamHome* company should be capable of expansion to account for such changes in the profile of services offered by *DreamHome*.

Step 3.4   Draw final Entity–Relationship diagram

In this worked example, we find that there are no revisions to the ER diagram previously shown in Figure 8.16. This final ER diagram represents the global view of the *DreamHome* company.

Step 3.5 Review global logical data model with users

It is important to review the global logical data model with the users of each view. If the model contains any errors we must repeat the appropriate step(s) in the methodology. This process of review is repeated until all the users are satisfied with the global logical data model. When the data model is 'signed off' by the users, we proceed to the next stage of the database design process, which concerns the physical design of the database.

The phase of the methodology that describes physical database design for relational databases is given in Chapter 9, and illustrated by example in Chapter 10, using the Paradox for Windows DBMS. The logical database design for the *DreamHome* case study created in this chapter is used as the starting point for Chapter 10.

EXERCISES

The *Wellmeadows Hospital* case study

8.1 Identify user views for the Medical Director and Charge Nurse in the *Wellmeadows Hospital* case study, described in Section 1.8.

8.2 List the users' requirements specification for each of these views.

8.3 Create and validate the local logical data models for each of the user views. State any assumptions necessary to support your design.

8.4 Merge the local data models to create a global logical data model of the *Wellmeadows Hospital* case study. State any assumptions necessary to support your design.

8.5 Validate the global logical data model.

8.6 Where necessary, create or update the supporting documentation for the global data model.

Appendix 8.1: Document Entity Types for the Supervisor's View of the *DreamHome* Company

Entity name	*Description*	*Aliases*	*Occurrence*
Branch	Place of work	Office and Branch Office	One or more *DreamHome* branches are located in main cities throughout the UK.
Staff	General term describing all staff employed by *DreamHome*.		Each member of staff works at a particular branch.
Supervisor	Supervises the work of staff responsible for the management of property for rent.		Each branch has several Supervisors. Each Supervisor supervises a specific group of staff (min 5 and max 10 members of staff, at any one time).
Secretary	Responsible for providing secretarial support to staff.		Each branch has several secretaries. Each secretary provides support to a specific group of staff.
Property_for_Rent	General term describing all property for rent.		Each property has a single owner. Each property is available at a specific branch, where the property is managed by a member of staff. Each property is rented by a single client, at any one time. Each property is viewed by clients and inspected by staff.
Private_Owner	Private owner of property for rent.	Owner	Each private owner owns one or more properties for rent.
Business_Owner	Business owner of property for rent.	Owner	Each business owner owns one or more properties for rent.
Advert	Describes a property for rent.		A single advert describing a single property is placed in a newspaper.
Newspaper	Contains adverts describing property for rent.		Properties are described in adverts, placed in local and national newspapers.
Interview	A meeting to assess the suitability of potential clients to rent property. Also to note the property requirements of client.		Staff interview clients wishing to rent property. Not all clients are interviewed.
Client	General term describing all clients interested in viewing and renting property.		A single client may rent one or more properties at any given time.
Lease_Agreement	Contains details of the lease agreement between a client and a property.	Lease	Each lease agreement is held by a single client for a single property.
Inspection	Contains details of property inspection carried out by staff.	Property Inspection	Each inspection is carried out by a single member of staff on a single property.

Appendix 8.2: Document Attributes for the Supervisor's View

Entity	Names of attributes	Description	Data type and length
Branch	Branch_No	Uniquely identifies branch office.	3 variable character
	Address	Address (composed of Street, Area, City and Postcode attributes)	
	Street	Street of branch address	25 variable character
	Area	Area of branch address	15 variable character
	City	City of branch address	15 variable character
	Postcode	Postcode of branch address	8 variable character
	Tel_No	Telephone number of branch	13 fixed character
	Fax_No	Fax number of branch	13 fixed character
Staff	Staff_No	Uniquely identifies a member of staff	5 variable character
	Name	Name (composed of FName and LName attributes)	
	FName	First name of staff	15 variable character
	LName	Last name of staff	15 variable character
	Address	Full home address of member of staff	50 variable character
	Tel_No	Home telephone number of staff	13 fixed character
	Sex	Gender of staff	1 fixed character
	DOB	Date of birth of staff	Date
	Job_Title	Job title of staff	20 variable character
Supervisor	Same as the Staff entity type	Identifies a member of staff with the job title 'Supervisor'.	(Same as Staff entity)
Secretary	Same as the Staff entity type and Typing_Speed	Identifies a member of staff with the job title 'Secretary'.	(Same as Staff entity)
Property _for_Rent	Property_No	Uniquely identifies each property.	5 variable characters
	Address	Address (composed of Street, Area, City and Postcode attributes)	
	Street	Street of property address.	25 variable characters
	Area	Area of property address.	15 variable character
	City	City of property address.	15 variable character
	Postcode	Postcode of property address.	8 variable character
	Type	Type of property.	1 character
	Rooms	The number of rooms in a property (excluding bathroom).	Integer
	Rent	The monthly rent.	Currency

† Only part of the data dictionary for the Supervisor's view is shown.

of the *DreamHome* Company[†]

Constraint	Default value	Alias	Null value (Yes or No?)	Derived?
Primary key			No	No
			No	No
			No	No
			No	No
			Yes	No
Alternate key			No	No
Alternate key			No	No
Primary key			No	No
			No	No
			No	No
			No	No
			Yes	No
			No	No
			Yes	No
			Yes	No
(Same as Staff entity)			(Same as Staff entity)	(Same as Staff entity)
(Same as Staff entity)			(Same as Staff entity)	(Same as Staff entity)
Primary key			No	No
			No	No
			No	No
			No	No
			Yes	No
			No	No
	4		Yes	No
	600.00		Yes	No

Appendix 8.3: Document Relationship Types for the Supervisor's View of the *DreamHome* Company

Entity type	Relationship type	Entity type	Cardinality ratio	Participation[†]
Branch	*Has*	Staff	1:M	T:T
	Offers	Property_for_Rent	1:M	T:T
Staff	*Manages*	Property_for_Rent	1:M	P:P
	SetsUp	Interview	1:M	P:T
	CarryOut	Inspection	1:M	P:T
	Organizes	Lease_Agreement	1:M	
Supervisor	*Supervises*	Staff	1:M	T:P
Secretary	*Supports*	Staff	1:M	T:P
Property_for_Rent	*DescribedIn*	Advert	1:M	P:T
	Undergoes	Inspection	1:M	P:T
	AssociatedWith	Lease_Agreement	1:M	P:T
Private_Owner	*Owns*	Property_for_Rent	1:M	T:T
Business_Owner	*Owns*	Property_for_Rent	1:M	T:T
Newspaper	*Lists*	Advert	1:M	T:T
Interview	*With*	Client	1:1	T:P
Client	*Views*	Property_for_Rent	M:N	P:P
	Rent	Property_for_Rent	M:N	P:P
	Holds	Lease_Agreement	1:M	P:T
Inspection	*Of*	Property_for_Rent	1:1	T:P

[†] P represents partial participation and T represents total participation.

Appendix 8.4 Document Attribute Domains for the Supervisor's View of the *DreamHome* Company (examples)

Domain name	Domain characteristics	Examples of allowable values
Property_No	5-character variable length string	PA14, PL94, PG4
Street	25-character variable length string	2 Manor Road, 5 Novar Drive
Tel_No and Fax_No	13-character variable length string	0141–339–4439, 01224–67111
Sex	1-character string ('M' or 'F')	M, F
Rooms	Integer value (Range 1 to 15)	5, 8, 12

Appendix 8.5:   The Supervisor's View of the *DreamHome* Case Study

Branch (Branch_No, Street, Area, City, Postcode, Tel_No, Fax_No)
Primary Key Branch_No
Alternate Key Tel_No
Alternate Key Fax_No

Staff (Staff_No, FName, LName, Address, Tel_No, Sex, DOB (Date of Birth), Job_Title, Typing_Speed, Branch_No)
Primary Key Staff_No
Foreign Key Branch_No **references** Branch(Branch_No)

Allocated_Staff (Supervisee_Staff_No, Supervisor_Staff_No, Secretary_Staff_No)
Primary Key Supervisee_Staff_No
Foreign Key Supervisee_Staff_No **references** Staff(Staff_No)
Foreign Key Supervisor_Staff_No **references** Staff(Staff_No)
Foreign Key Secretary_Staff_No **references** Staff(Staff_No)

Property_for_Rent (Property_No, Street, Area, City, Postcode, Type, Rooms, Rent, Owner_No, ManagedBy_Staff_No, Branch_No)
Primary Key Property_No
Foreign Key Owner_No **references** Private_Owner(Owner_No) and Business_Owner(Owner_No)
Foreign Key ManagedBy_Staff_No **references** Staff(Staff_No)
Foreign Key Branch_No **references** Branch(Branch_No)

Private_Owner (Owner_No, FName, LName, Address, Tel_No)
Primary Key Owner_No

Business_Owner (Owner_No, BName, BType, Address, Tel_No, Contact_Name)
Primary Key Owner_No
Alternate Key Tel_No

Client (Client_No, FName, LName, Address, Tel_No, Pref_Type, Max_Rent)
Primary Key Client_No

Lease_Agreement (Lease_No, Client_No, Property_No, Rent, Payment_Method, Deposit_Paid, Rent_Start, Rent_Finish, Staff_No)
Primary Key Lease_No
Alternate Key Property_No, Rent_Start
Foreign Key Client_No **references** Client(Client_No)
Foreign Key Property_No **references** Property_for_Rent(Property_No)
Foreign Key Staff_No **references** Staff(Staff_No)

Advert (Advert_No, Property_No, Date_Advert, Newspaper_Name, Cost)
Primary Key Advert_No
Alternate Key Property_No, Date_Advert, Newspaper_Name
Foreign Key Property_No **references** Property_for_Rent(Property_No)

Foreign Key Newspaper_Name **references** Newspaper(Newspaper_Name)

Newspaper (Newspaper_Name, Address, Tel_No, Fax_No, Contact_Name)
Primary_Key Newspaper_Name
Alternate Key Tel_No
Alternate Key Fax_No

Viewing (Property_No, Client_No, Date_View, Comments)
Primary Key Property_No,Client_No, Date_View
Foreign Key Property_No **references** Property_for_Rent(Property_No)
Foreign Key Client_No **references** Client(Client_No)

Inspection (Property_No, Staff_No, Date_Inspect, Comments)
Primary Key Property_No, Staff_No, Date_Inspect
Foreign Key Property_No **references** Property_for_Rent(Property_No)
Foreign Key Staff_No **references** Staff(Staff_No)

Appendix 8.6: Enterprise Constraints for the Supervisor's View of *DreamHome* Case Study

(1) A member of staff may only manage a maximum of 10 properties for rent, at any one time.

(2) The minimum and maximum duration for a single lease period is three months and one year, respectively.

(3) The monthly rent for a property should be reviewed annually.

(4) Supervisors should supervise a minimum of five and a maximum of 10 members of staff, at any one time.

(5) Property for rent should be inspected at least once over a six month period.

Appendix 8.7: The Global View of the *DreamHome* Case Study

Branch (Branch_No, Street, Area, City, Postcode, Tel_No, Fax_No, Manager_Staff_No, Manager_Start_Date, Bonus_Payment, Car_Allowance)
Primary Key Branch_No
Alternate Key Tel_No
Alternate Key Fax_No
Foreign Key Manager_Staff_No is **NOT NULL references** Staff(Staff_No) on delete **SET DEFAULT** on update **CASCADE**

Staff (Staff_No, FName, LName, Address, Tel_No, Sex, DOB (Date_of_Birth), Position, Salary, Date_Joined, NIN (National Insurance Number), Typing_Speed, Branch_No)

Primary Key Staff_No
Alternate Key NIN
Foreign Key Branch_No is **NOT NULL references** Branch(Branch_No) on
    delete **SET DEFAULT** on update **CASCADE**

Next_of_Kin (Staff_No, NName, Relationship, Address, Tel_No)
Primary Key Staff_No, NName
Foreign Key Staff_No is **NOT NULL references** Staff(Staff_No) on delete
    CASCADE on update **CASCADE**

Allocated_Staff (Supervisee_Staff_No, Supervisor_Staff_No,
    Secretary_Staff_No)
Primary Key Supervisee_Staff_No
Foreign Key Supervisee_Staff_No is **NOT NULL references**
    Staff(Staff_No) on delete **CASCADE** on update **CASCADE**
Foreign Key Supervisor_Staff_No is **NOT NULL references** Staff(Staff_No)
    on delete **SET DEFAULT** on update **CASCADE**
Foreign Key Secretary_Staff_No is **NOT NULL references** Staff(Staff_No)
    on delete **SET DEFAULT** on update **CASCADE**

Property_for_Rent (Property_No, Street, Area, City, Postcode, Type,
    Rooms, Rent, Owner_No, ManagedBy_Staff_No, Branch_No)
Primary Key Property_No
Foreign Key Owner_No is **NOT NULL references**
    Private_Owner(Owner_No) and Business_Owner(Owner_No) on
    delete **NO ACTION** on update **CASCADE**
Foreign Key ManagedBy_Staff_No is **NULL references** Staff(Staff_No) on
    delete **SET NULL** on update **CASCADE**
Foreign Key Branch_No is **NOT NULL references** Branch(Branch_No) on
    delete **SET DEFAULT** on update **NO ACTION**

Private_Owner (Owner_No, FName, LName, Address, Tel_No)
Primary Key Owner_No

Business_Owner (Owner_No, BName, BType, Address, Tel_No,
    Contact_Name)
Primary Key Owner_No
Alternate Key Tel_No
Renter (Renter_No, FName, LName, Address, Tel_No, Pref_Type,
    Max_Rent, Branch_No)
Primary Key Renter_No
Foreign Key Branch_No is **NOT NULL references** Branch(Branch_No) on
    delete **NO ACTION** on update **CASCADE**

Lease_Agreement (Lease_No, Renter_No, Property_No, Payment_Method,
    Deposit_Amount, Deposit_Paid, Rent_Start, Rent_Finish)
Primary Key Lease_No
Alternate Key Property_No, Rent_Start
Foreign Key Renter_No is **NOT NULL references** Renter(Renter_No) on
    delete **NO ACTION** on update **CASCADE**

Foreign Key Property_No is **NOT NULL references** Property_for_Rent (Property_No) on delete **NO ACTION** on update **CASCADE**

Advert (Advert_No, Property_No, Cost, Date_Advert, Newspaper_Name)
Primary Key Advert_No
Alternate Key Property_No, Date_Advert, Newspaper_Name
Foreign Key Property_No is **NOT NULL references** Property(Property_No) on delete **CASCADE** on update **CASCADE**
Foreign Key Newspaper_Name is **NOT NULL references** Newspaper(Newspaper_Name) on delete **NO ACTION** on update **CASCADE**

Newspaper (Newspaper_Name, Address, Contact_Name, Tel_No, Fax_No)
Primary Key Newspaper_Name
Alternate Key Tel_No
Alternate Key Fax_No

Viewing (Property_No, Renter_No, Date_View, Comments)
Primary Key Property_No, Renter_No
Foreign Key Property_No is **NOT NULL references** Property_for_Rent (Property_No) on delete **CASCADE** on update **CASCADE**
Foreign Key Renter_No is **NOT NULL references** Renter(Renter_No) on delete **NO ACTION** on update **CASCADE**

Inspection (Property_No, Staff_No, Date_Inspect, Comments)
Primary Key Property_No, Staff_No, Date_Inspect
Foreign Key Property_No is **NOT NULL references** Property_for_Rent (Property_No) on delete **CASCADE** on update **CASCADE**
Foreign Key Staff_No is **NOT NULL references** Staff(Staff_No) on delete **NO ACTION** on update **CASCADE**

9 Methodology – Physical Database Design

Chapter Objectives

In this chapter you will learn:

- The purpose of physical database design.
- How to map the logical database design to a physical database design.
- How to design base relations for the target DBMS.
- How to design integrity rules for the target DBMS.
- How to select an appropriate file organization based on analysis of transactions.
- When to use secondary indexes to improve performance.
- When to denormalize to improve performance.
- How to estimate the size of the database.
- How to design security mechanisms to satisfy user requirements.
- The importance of monitoring and tuning the operational system.

9.1 Introduction

In Chapter 7, we presented a step-by-step methodology for **logical database design** for the **relational model**. During logical database design, the designer produces a global logical data model, which represents the logical structure of the database (that is, the entities, attributes, relationships and constraints). Now, we concentrate on the second part of the database design methodology: **physical database design**. In physical database design, the designer decides how the logical structure is to be physically realized using the global logical data model as the starting point.

As many parts of physical database design are highly dependent on the target DBMS, there may be more than one way of implementing any given part of the database. Consequently, the designer must be fully aware of the functionality of the target DBMS, and must understand the advantages and disadvantages of each alternative for a particular implementation. The designer must be capable of selecting a suitable storage strategy that takes account of usage.

In this chapter, we show how to convert the relations derived from the global logical data model into a specific database implementation. We provide guidelines on choosing storage structures for the base relations, deciding when to create indexes and when to denormalize the logical data model and introduce redundancy. In places, we show physical implementation details to clarify the discussion. Before we present the methodology for physical database design, we briefly review the design process.

9.1.1 The Database Design Process

For the purposes of the methodology presented in this book, we have divided the database design process into two phases: logical database design and physical database design.

Logical database design	The process of constructing a model of the information use in an enterprise based on one model of data, but independent of a particular DBMS and other physical aspects.

The logical database design methodology for the relational model presented in Chapter 7 is largely independent of implementation details, such as the specific functionality of the target DBMS, application programs, programming languages or any other physical considerations. The output of this process is a global logical data model supplemented by a data dictionary that describes the details of the model. Together, these represent the sources of information for the physical design process, and they provide the physical database designer with a vehicle for making trade-offs that are so important to an efficient database design.

> **Physical** The process of producing a description of the implementation
> **database** of the database on secondary storage; it describes the storage
> **design**   structures and access methods used to gain access effectively.

Physical database design is the second main phase of the database design process, in which the designer decides how the database is to be realized. It involves:

- designing the base relations and integrity constraints for the target DBMS;
- selecting specific storage structures and access methods for the data to achieve good performance for the database activities;
- designing any security measures required on the data.

Whereas logical database design is concerned with the *what*, physical database design is concerned with the *how*. It requires different skills that are often found in different people. In particular, the physical database designer must know how the computer system hosting the DBMS functions, and must be fully aware of the functionality of the target DBMS. As the functionality provided by current systems varies widely, physical design must be tailored to a specific DBMS system. However, physical database design is not an isolated activity – there is often feedback between physical, logical and application design. For example, decisions taken during physical design for improving performance might affect the structure of the logical schema.

9.1.2   Overview of Physical Database Design Methodology

The physical database design methodology presented in this book is divided into four main subphases, numbered consecutively from 4 to fit in with the three subphases of the logical database design methodology. The first subphase of physical database design (Step 4) involves the design of the base relations and integrity constraints using the available functionality of the target DBMS.

The second subphase (Step 5) involves choosing the storage structures and access methods for the base relations. Typically, DBMSs provide a number of alternative storage structures for data, with the exception of PC DBMSs which tend to have a fixed storage structure. From the user's viewpoint, the internal storage representation for relations should be transparent – the user should be able to access relations and tuples without having to specify where or how the tuples are stored. This requires that the DBMS provides **physical data independence**, so that users are unaffected by changes to the physical structure of the database, as discussed in Section 2.1.5. The mapping between the logical data model and physical data model is defined in the internal schema, as shown in Figure 4.5. The designer must provide the physical design details to both the DBMS and the operating system. For the DBMS, the designer must specify the file structures that are to be used to represent each relation; for the operating system, the designer must specify details such as the location and protection for each file. Step 5 also considers relaxing the normalization constraints imposed on the logical data model to improve the overall performance of the system. This is a step that should be undertaken only if necessary, because of the inherent problems involved in introducing redundancy while still maintaining consistency.

The third subphase (Step 6) involves designing the security measures to protect data from unauthorized access. This involves deciding how each local logical data model should be implemented, and the access controls that are required on the base relations. The final subphase (Step 7) is an ongoing process of monitoring the operational system to identify and resolve any performance problems resulting from the design, and to implement new or changing requirements. The steps in the methodology are summarized in Figure 9.1. For easy reference, an overview of the steps in both the logical and physical database design phases is given in Appendix E. We recommend that the reader reviews Appendix A on file organization and storage structures before Step 5 of the methodology.

Figure 9.1 Summary of steps in physical database design.

Logical Database Design for Relational Databases
    Step 1   Build local conceptual data model from user view
    Step 2   Build and validate local logical data model
    Step 3   Build and validate global logical data model

Physical Database Design and Implementation for Relational Databases
    Step 4   Translate global logical data model for target DBMS
            Step 4.1   Design base relations for target DBMS
            Step 4.2   Design integrity rules for target DBMS
    Step 5   Design and implement physical representation
            Step 5.1   Analyse transactions
            Step 5.2   Choose file organizations
            Step 5.3   Choose secondary indexes
            Step 5.4   Consider the introduction of controlled redundancy
            Step 5.5   Estimate disk space
    Step 6   Design and implement security mechanisms
            Step 6.1   Design and implement user views
            Step 6.2   Design and implement access rules
    Step 7   Monitor and tune the operational system

9.2 Physical Database Design and Implementation for Relational Databases

This section provides a step-by-step guide to producing a physical database design and implementation for relational databases. We show how to design and implement base relations from the target DBMS from information gained during logical database design. We provide guidelines on choosing storage structures for the base relations, deciding when to create indexes, and deciding when to denormalize the logical data model and introduce redundancy.

Step 4   Translate Global Logical Data Model for Target DBMS

> **Objective**   To produce a basic working relational database schema from the global logical data model.

The first subphase of physical database design involves the translation of the relations derived from the global logical data model into a form that can be implemented in the target relational DBMS. The first part of this process entails collating the information gathered during logical data modelling and documented in the data dictionary. The second part of the process uses this information to produce the design of the base relations. This process requires intimate knowledge of the functionality offered by the target DBMS. For example, the designer will need to know:

- whether the system supports the definition of primary keys, foreign keys and alternate keys;
- whether the system supports the definition of required data (that is, whether the system allows attributes to be defined as NOT NULL);
- whether the system supports the definition of domains;
- whether the system supports the definition of enterprise constraints;
- how to create base relations.

The two steps in this subphase are:

- Step 4.1   Design base relations for target DBMS
- Step 4.2   Design integrity rules for target DBMS

Step 4.1 Design base relations for target DBMS

> **Objective**   To decide how to represent the base relations we have identified in the global logical data model in the target DBMS.

To start the physical design process, we first need to collate and assimilate the information about relations produced during logical data modelling. The information can be obtained from the data dictionary and the definition of the relations defined using the Database Design Language (DBDL). For each relation identified in the global logical data model, we have a definition consisting of:

- the name of the relation;
- a list of simple attributes in brackets;
- the primary key and, where appropriate, alternate keys (AK) and foreign keys (FK);
- integrity constraints for any foreign keys identified.

```
domain property_number:    variable length character string length 5
domain street:             variable length character string maximum length 25
domain area:               variable length character string maximum length 15
domain city:               variable length character string maximum length 15
domain post_code:          variable length character string maximum length 8
domain property_type:      single character, must be one of 'B', 'C', 'D', 'E', 'F', 'M', 'S'
domain property_rooms:     integer, in the range 1 to 15
domain property_rent:      monetary value, in the range 0.00–9999.00
domain owner_number:       variable length character string length 5
domain staff_number:       variable length character string length 5
domain branch_number:      variable length character string length 3

property_for_rent(
           pno:      property_number        NOT NULL,
           street:   street                 NOT NULL,
           area:     area,
           city:     city                   NOT NULL,
           pcode:    post_code,
           type:     property_type          NOT NULL      DEFAULT: 'F',
           rooms:    property_rooms         NOT NULL      DEFAULT: 4,
           rent:     property_rent          NOT NULL      DEFAULT: 600,
           ono:      owner_number           NOT NULL,
           sno:      staff_number,
           bno:      branch_number          NOT NULL)
           PK pno
           FK sno REFERENCES staff(sno) ON DELETE SET NULL ON UPDATE
                      CASCADE
           FK ono REFERENCES owner(ono) ON DELETE NO ACTION ON UPDATE
                      CASCADE
           FK bno REFERENCES branch(bno) ON DELETE NO ACTION ON
                      UPDATE CASCADE
```

Figure 9.2 DBDL for the Property_for_Rent relation.

From the data dictionary, we also have for each attribute:

- its domain, consisting of a data type, length and any constraints on the domain;
- an optional default value for the attribute;
- whether the attribute can hold nulls;
- whether the attribute is derived and, if so, how it should be computed.

To represent the design of the base relations, we use the DBDL to define domains, default values and null indicators. For example, for the Property_for_Rent relation of the *DreamHome* case study, we may produce the design shown in Figure 9.2.

The next step is to decide how to implement the base relations. This decision is dependent on the target DBMS; some systems provide more facilities than others for defining base relations and integrity constraints. To illustrate this process, we show four particular ways to create relations and integrity constraints using:

(1)   the 1993 ISO SQL standard (SQL2),

(2)   triggers,

(3)   INGRES 6.4,

(4)   unique indexes.

(1) The 1993 ISO SQL Standard (SQL2)

If the target DBMS is compliant with the 1993 ISO SQL standard, which we discuss in Chapters 11 and 12, then it is relatively easy to design the base implementation. For example, to create the Property_for_Rent relation we could use the SQL statements shown in Figure 9.3.

The relation has the same attribute names and domain types as identified in the DBDL in Figure 9.2. The primary key of the relation is the property number, Pno. SQL automatically enforces uniqueness on this attribute. Three foreign keys have been identified with appropriate referential constraints. For example, the staff number, Sno, is a foreign key referencing the Staff relation. A deletion rule has been specified (ON DELETE SET NULL) such that, if a staff number in the Staff relation is deleted, then the corresponding value(s) for the Sno attribute in the Property_for_Rent relation are set to NULL. The owner number, Ono, is a foreign key referencing the Owner relation. An update rule has been specified (ON UPDATE CASCADE), such that, if an owner number in the Owner relation is updated, then the corresponding value(s) in the Ono attribute in the Property_for_Rent relation are set to the new value (that is, the update **cascades**). In addition, we have set up some default values: for example, we have assigned a default value of 'F' to attribute Type.

(2) Triggers

Some systems, such as Sybase, provide **triggers**. A trigger is an action associated with an event that causes a change in the content of a relation. The three events that can trigger an action are attempts to INSERT, UPDATE or DELETE tuples of a relation. Triggers can be used to enforce referential integrity, as the following example shows:

```
CREATE TRIGGER property_update
ON property_for_rent
FOR INSERT, UPDATE
AS IF ((SELECT COUNT(*) FROM branch,INSERTED WHERE
branch.bno = INSERTED.bno)=0)
BEGIN
        PRINT "Invalid branch number specified"
        ROLLBACK TRANSACTION
END
```

This creates a trigger that is invoked whenever a tuple is inserted into the Property_for_Rent relation or an existing tuple is updated. It checks that the branch number in the Property_for_Rent relation (INSERTED.bno) exists in the branch relation (branch.bno), displaying a message and aborting

```
CREATE DOMAIN owner_number AS VARCHAR(5)
        CHECK (VALUE IN (SELECT ono FROM owner))
CREATE DOMAIN staff_number AS VARCHAR(5)
        CHECK (VALUE IN (SELECT sno FROM staff))
CREATE DOMAIN branch_number AS VARCHAR(3)
        CHECK (VALUE IN (SELECT bno FROM branch))
CREATE DOMAIN property_number AS VARCHAR(5)
CREATE DOMAIN street AS VARCHAR(25)
CREATE DOMAIN area AS VARCHAR(15)
CREATE DOMAIN city AS VARCHAR(15)
CREATE DOMAIN post_code AS VARCHAR(8)
CREATE DOMAIN property_type AS CHAR(1)
        CHECK(VALUE IN ('B', 'C', 'D', 'E', 'F', 'M', 'S'))
CREATE DOMAIN property_rooms AS SMALLINT
        CHECK(VALUE BETWEEN 1 AND 15)
CREATE DOMAIN property_rent AS DECIMAL(6,2)
        CHECK(VALUE BETWEEN 0 AND 9999)

CREATE TABLE property_for_rent (
    pno          PROPERTY_NUMBER   NOT NULL,
    street       STREET            NOT NULL,
    area         AREA,
    city         CITY              NOT NULL,
    pcode        POST_CODE,
    type         PROPERTY_TYPE     NOT NULL    DEFAULT 'F',
    rooms        PROPERTY_ROOMS    NOT NULL    DEFAULT 4,
    rent         PROPERTY_RENT     NOT NULL    DEFAULT 600,
    ono          OWNER_NUMBER      NOT NULL,
    sno          STAFF_NUMBER,
    bno          BRANCH_NUMBER     NOT NULL,
    PRIMARY KEY (pno),
    FOREIGN KEY (sno) REFERENCES staff ON DELETE SET NULL ON UPDATE
                CASCADE,
    FOREIGN KEY (ono) REFERENCES owner ON DELETE NO ACTION ON UPDATE
                CASCADE,
    FOREIGN KEY (bno) REFERENCES branch ON DELETE NO ACTION ON UPDATE
                CASCADE
)
```

Figure 9.3 SQL to create Property_for_Rent relation.

the transaction if it does not. It is also possible to create a trigger that **cascades** modifications to primary keys through associated foreign keys. For example, we could create the following trigger to cascade updates to the branch number through the Property_for_Rent relation:

```
CREATE TRIGGER cascade_branch_update
ON branch
FOR UPDATE
AS IF UPDATE (BRANCH)
BEGIN
```

```
        UPDATE property_for_rent SET property_for_rent.bno = INSERTED.bno
        FROM property_for_rent, INSERTED, DELETED
        WHERE property_for_rent.bno = DELETED.bno
     END
```

The references DELETED.bno and INSERTED.bno in the trigger refer, respectively, to the values of the Bno attribute before and after the UPDATE statement.

(3) INGRES Version 6.4

In some systems that do not comply with the new SQL standard, there is no support for one or more of the clauses PRIMARY KEY, FOREIGN KEY, DEFAULT. Similarly, many systems do not support domains. For example in INGRES Version 6.4, the Property_for_Rent relation would be created in SQL as follows:

```
     CREATE TABLE property_for_rent(
             pno      VARCHAR(5)      NOT NULL,
             street   VARCHAR(25)     NOT NULL,
             area     VARCHAR(15),
             city     VARCHAR(15)     NOT NULL,
             pcode    VARCHAR(8),
             type     CHAR(1)         NOT NULL,
             rooms    SMALLINT        NOT NULL,
             rent     MONEY           NOT NULL,
             ono      VARCHAR(5)      NOT NULL,
             sno      VARCHAR(5),
             bno      VARCHAR(3)      NOT NULL);
```

In this case, we have to build key constraints, default values and domain constraints into the application and design for this accordingly. The exception to this is primary key constraints, which can be implemented through unique indexes, as described below, or alternatively, we could specify the storage structure for the relation as either B-Tree or ISAM (see Appendix A).

(4) Unique indexes

An index is an access mechanism that speeds up retrieval of data from a relation, similar to the index of a book (see Appendix A). A unique index is one in which no two tuples of a relation are permitted to have the same index value. The system checks for duplicate values when the index is created (if data already exists), and each time data is added. Many RDBMSs support the creation of indexes. A unique index can be used to support the uniqueness constraint of primary and alternate keys. For example, the INGRES Create Table statement above does not prevent two records being inserted into the Property_for_Rent relation with the same primary key value. To overcome this, we can create a unique index on the primary key field Pno using the INGRES SQL statement:

CREATE UNIQUE INDEX property_no_index ON property_for_rent(pno);

Similarly, we can create a composite index for the Viewing relation for the composite primary key consisting of the attributes (Cno, Pno) using the INGRES SQL statement:

CREATE UNIQUE INDEX viewing_index ON viewing(cno, pno);

If the target DBMS does not support the definition of primary and alternate keys, unique indexes should be created to provide this functionality.

Document design of base relations

The design of the base relations should be fully documented along with the reasons for selecting the proposed design. In particular, document the reasons for selecting one approach where many alternatives exist.

Step 4.2 Design enterprise constraints for target DBMS

> **Objective**   To design the enterprise constraints for the target DBMS.

Updates to relations may be constrained by enterprise rules governing the 'real world' transactions that are represented by the updates. The design of such constraints is again dependent on the choice of DBMS; some systems provide more facilities than others for defining enterprise constraints. As in the previous step, if the system is compliant with the new SQL2 standard, some constraints may be easy to implement. For example, *DreamHome* may have a rule that prevents a member of staff from managing more than 10 properties at the same time. We could design this constraint into the SQL Create Table statement for Property_for_Rent, using the following clause:

```
CONSTRAINT staff_not_handling_too_much
        CHECK (NOT EXISTS   (SELECT sno
                             FROM property_for_rent
                             GROUP BY sno
                             HAVING COUNT(*) > 10))
```

Alternatively, a trigger could be used to enforce some constraints. For the previous example, we could write:

```
CREATE TRIGGER staff_property_check
ON property_for_rent
FOR INSERT, UPDATE
AS IF ((SELECT COUNT(*) FROM property_for_rent p, WHERE
p.sno = INSERTED.sno) > 10)
BEGIN
    PRINT "Staff member already managing 10 properties"
    ROLLBACK TRANSACTION
END
```

This creates a trigger that is invoked whenever a tuple is inserted into the Property_for_Rent relation or an existing tuple is updated. It checks that the number of properties the staff member is managing is not greater than 10, and if greater, displays a message and aborts the transaction.

In some systems, there will be no support for some or all of the enterprise constraints and it will be necessary to design the constraints into the application. For example, there are very few DBMSs (if any) that would be able to handle a time constraint such as 'at 17.30 on the last working day of each year, archive the records for all properties sold that year and delete the associated records'.

Document design of enterprise constraints
The design of enterprise constraints should be fully documented. In particular, document the reasons for selecting one approach where many alternatives exist.

Step 5 Design and Implement Physical Representation

Objective	To determine the file organizations and access methods that will be used to store the base relations: that is, the way in which relations and tuples will be held on secondary storage.

One of the main objectives of physical database design is to store data in an efficient way (see Appendix A). There are a number of factors that we may use to measure efficiency:

- *Transaction throughput* This is the number of transactions that can be processed in a given time interval. In some systems, such as airline reservations, high transaction throughput is critical to the overall success of the system.

- *Response time* This is the elapsed time for the completion of a single transaction. From a user's point of view, we would want to minimize response time as much as possible. However, there are some factors that influence response time that the designer may have no control over, such as system loading or communication times.

- *Disk storage* This is the amount of disk space used by the database files. The designer may wish to minimize the amount of disk storage used.

However, there is no one factor that is always correct. Typically, the designer has to trade off one factor against another to achieve a reasonable balance. For example, increasing the amount of data stored may increase the response time or transaction throughput. The initial physical database design should not be regarded as static, but should be considered as an estimate of operational performance. Once the initial design has been implemented, it will be necessary to monitor the system and tune it as a result of observed performance and changing requirements (Step 7). Many DBMSs provide the Database Administrator (DBA) with utilities to monitor the operation of the system and tune it. We will see that there are some storage structures that are efficient for bulk loading data into the database but inefficient after that. In other words, we may choose to use an efficient storage structure to set up the database and then change it for operational use.

Again, the types of file organization available are dependent on the target DBMS; some systems provide more choice of storage structures than others. It is extremely important that the physical database designer fully understands the storage structures that are available, and how the target system uses these structures. This may require that the designer knows how the system's query optimizer functions. For example, there may be circumstances where the query optimizer would not use a secondary index, even if one was available. Thus, adding a secondary index would not improve the performance of the query, and the resultant overhead would be unjustified. Some systems allow users to inspect the optimizer's strategy for executing a particular query or update, the **Query Execution Plan (QEP)**. For example, DB2 has an EXPLAIN utility, Oracle has an EXPLAIN PLAN diagnostic utility and INGRES has an online QEP-viewing facility. When a query runs slower than expected, it is worth using such a facility to determine the reason for the slowness, and to find an alternative strategy that may improve the performance of the query.

Understanding system resources

To improve performance, the physical database designer must be aware of how the four basic hardware components interact and affect system performance:

- *Main memory* Main memory accesses are significantly faster than secondary storage accesses, sometimes tens or even hundreds of thousands of times faster. In general, the more main memory available to the system and the applications, the faster the applications will run. However, it is sensible to always have a minimum of 5% of main memory available. Equally well, it is advisable not to have any more than 10% available, otherwise main memory is not being used optimally. When there is insufficient memory to accommodate all processes, the operating system transfers pages of processes to disk to free up memory. When one of these pages is next required, the operating system has to transfer it back from disk. Sometimes, it is necessary to swap entire processes from memory to disk, and back again, to free up memory. Problems occur with main memory when paging or swapping becomes excessive.

- *CPU* The CPU controls the tasks of the other system resources and executes user processes. The main objective for this component is to prevent CPU contention in which processes are waiting for the CPU. CPU bottlenecks occur when either the operating system or user programs make too many demands on the CPU. This is often a result of excessive paging or swapping.

- *Disk I/O* With any large DBMS, there is a significant amount of disk I/O involved in storing and retrieving data. Disks usually have a recommended I/O rate. When this rate is exceeded, I/O bottlenecks occur. The way in which data is organized on disk can have a major impact on the overall disk performance. It is recommended that storage should be evenly distributed across available drives to reduce the likelihood of performance problems occurring. Figure 9.4 illustrates the basic principles of distributing the data across disks:

- The operating system files should be separated from the database files.
- The main database files should be separated from the index files.
- The recovery log file should be separated from the rest of the database.

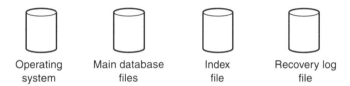

				Figure 9.4 Typical
Operating	Main database	Index	Recovery log	disk configuration.
system	files	file	file

- *Network* When the amount of traffic on the network is too great, or when the number of network collisions is large, network bottlenecks occur.

Each of these resources may affect other system resources. Equally well, an improvement in one resource may effect an improvement in other system resources. For example:

- Procuring more main memory should result in less paging and swapping. This should help avoid CPU bottlenecks.
- More effective use of main memory may result in less disk I/O.

With these objectives in mind, we now discuss the activities in this step:

- Step 5.1 Analyse transactions
- Step 5.2 Choose file organizations
- Step 5.3 Add secondary indexes
- Step 5.4 Consider the introduction of controlled redundancy
- Step 5.5 Estimate disk space

Step 5.1 Analyse transactions

| **Objective** | To understand the functionality of the transactions that will run on the database and to analyse the important transactions. |

To carry out physical database design effectively, it is necessary to have knowledge of the transactions or queries that will run on the database. This includes both qualitative and quantitative information. For each *transaction*, we should determine:

- The expected frequency at which the transaction will run.
- The relations and attributes accessed by the transaction and the type of access; that is, query, insert, update or delete.
  - For an update transaction, note the attributes that are updated, as these attributes may be candidates for avoiding an access structure, such as a secondary index.
- The attributes used in any predicates (in SQL, the predicates are the conditions specified in the WHERE clause). Check whether the predicates involve pattern matching, range searches or exact-match key retrieval.
  - These attributes may be candidates for access structures.
- For a query, the attributes that are involved in the join of two or more relations.
  - Again, these attributes may be candidates for access structures.
- The time constraints imposed on the transaction; for example, the transaction must complete within 1 second.
  - The attributes used in any predicates for critical transactions should have a higher priority for access structures.

Transaction usage maps

In many situations, however, it is not possible to analyse all the expected transactions, so we should at least investigate the most 'important' ones. It has been suggested that the most active 20% of user queries account for 80% of the total data access (Wiederhold, 1983). This 80/20 rule may be used as a guideline in carrying out the analysis. To help identify which transactions to investigate, we could use a transaction usage map that shows which relations each transaction accesses, and diagrammatically indicates which of these relations are potentially heavily used. To focus on areas that may be problematic, one way to proceed is to:

- Map all transaction paths to relations.
- Determine which relations are most frequently accessed by transactions.
- Analyse selected transactions that involve these relations.

For example, suppose that the following transactions operate on the *Dream-Home* database:

(A) Insert details for a new member of staff, given the branch address.

(B) List rental properties handled by each staff member at a given branch address.

(C)   Assign a rental property to a member of staff, checking that a staff member does not manage more than 10 properties already.

(D)   List rental properties handled by each branch office.

Figure 9.5(a) shows the expected number of occurrences for the Staff, Branch and Property_for_Rent relations, and the average and maximum numbers of occurrences in each relationship. For example, we expect there to be about 1500 members of staff and 50 branch offices, with an average of 20 members of staff per branch. Mapping the transaction paths to relations produces the transaction usage map shown in Figure 9.5(b). This figure shows that Property_for_Rent and Staff relations are required most often, and so a closer analysis of transactions involving these relations would be useful.

In considering each transaction, it is important not only to know the average and maximum numbers of executions per hour, but also to know the day and time that the transaction is run, including when the maximum load is likely. For example, some transactions may run at the average rate for most of the time, but have a peak loading between 14.00 and 16.00 on a Thursday prior to a meeting on Friday morning. Other transactions may run only at specific times, for example 9.00–10.00 on Mondays, which is also their peak loading.

Where transactions require frequent access to particular relations, then their pattern of operation is very important. If these transactions operate in a mutually exclusive manner, the risk of likely performance problems is diminished. However, if their operating patterns conflict, potential problems may be alleviated by examining the transactions more closely to determine how they can be changed to improve performance, as we discuss in Step 5.4. As an illustration, we select the first three transactions given above for closer analysis.

In our analysis, we look at how each relation is accessed, for example, whether it is an Insert (I), Read (R), Update (U) or Delete (D), and which attribute or attributes are used to gain access. This is signified as an **entry point** (E). We assume that all transactions can gain immediate access to the required relation through the indicated attributes. Transactions that scan through a number set of records are asterisked. Where such scans occur, a measure of how many times **one execution** of the transaction accesses particular relations is given by using the average and maximum values of the likely relationship occurrences. For update transactions, there are two accesses made on a relation: one to Read and one to Update. It is unnecessary in most cases to list all attributes for each relation, but where values are obtained to subsequently access other relations, these should be shown. The analysis tables for each of the selected transactions are shown in Figure 9.6.

Step 5.2   *Choose file organizations*

Objective	To determine an efficient file organization for each base relation.

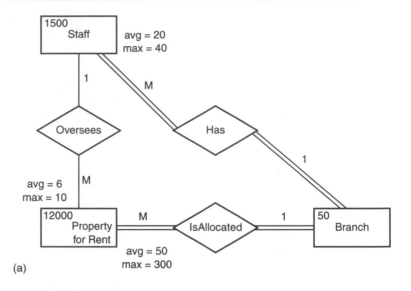

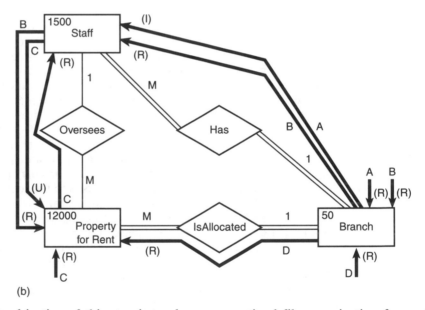

Figure 9.5 Example transaction usage map for sample transactions: (a) simplified ER model for sample transactions showing expected occurrences; (b) transaction usage map.

The objective of this step is to choose an optimal file organization for each relation. We provide guidelines for selecting a file organization based on the following types of files:

- heap
- hash
- Indexed Sequential Access Method (ISAM)
- B^+-Tree.

Transaction A				
	Day	Time	Number of runs per hour	
Peak	–	–	–	
Ave.	–	–	occasionally only	
From relation	To relation	Attributes	Access	No. of times accessed
–	Branch			1
		Address	R(E)	
		Bno	R	
Branch	Staff		I	1
		(all)		

Transaction B				
	Day	Time	Number of runs per hour	
Peak	Mon	9–10 am	2	
	Wed	2–4 pm	2	
Ave.	–	–	–	
From relation	To relation	Attributes	Access	No. of times accessed
–	Branch			1
		Address	R(E)	
		Bno	R	
Branch	Staff			8–20
		Bno	R(E)*	
		Sno	R	
		FName	R	
		LName	R	
		•		
Staff	Property_for_Rent			48–200
		Sno	R(E)*	
		Pno	R	
		Address	R	
		•		

Transaction C				
	Day	Time	Number of runs per hour	
Peak	Mon	9–11 am	4	
Ave.	rest of week		1	
From relation	To relation	Attributes	Access	No. of times accessed
–	Property_for_Rent			2
		Pno	R(E)	
		Address	R	
		•		
		Bno	R	
		Sno	U	
Property_for_Rent	Staff			8–20
		Sno	R	
		FName	R	
		LName	R	
		•		
		Bno	R(E)*	
Staff	Property_for_Rent			6–200
		Sno	R(E)*	

Figure 9.6
Analysis of selected transactions.

Heap

The heap file organization is discussed in Appendix A.2. Heap is a good storage structure in the following situations:

(1) When data is being bulk-loaded into the relation. For example, to populate a relation after it has been created, a batch of records may have to be inserted into the relation. If heap is chosen as the initial file organization, it may be more efficient to restructure the file after the insertions have been completed.

(2) The relation is only a few pages long. In this case, the time to locate any record is short, even if the entire relation has to be searched serially.

(3) When every tuple in the relation has to be retrieved (in any order) every time the relation is accessed. For example, retrieve the addresses of all properties for rent.

(4) When the relation has an additional access structure, such as an index key, heap storage can be used to conserve space.

Heap files are inappropriate when only selected tuples of a relation are to be accessed.

Hash

The hash file organization is discussed in Appendix A.4. Hash is a good storage structure when tuples are retrieved based on an exact match on the hash field value. For example, if the Property_for_Rent relation is hashed on Pno, retrieval of the tuple with Pno equal to SG37 is efficient. Hash is not a good storage structure in the following situations:

(1) When tuples are retrieved based on a pattern match of the hash field value. For example, retrieve all properties whose property number, Pno, begins with the characters 'SG'.

(2) When tuples are retrieved based on a range of values for the hash field. For example, retrieve all properties with a rent in the range 300–500.

(3) When tuples are retrieved based on a field other than the hash field. For example, if the Staff relation is hashed on Sno, then hashing could not be used to search for a tuple based on the LName attribute. In this case, it would be necessary to perform a linear search to find the tuple, or add LName as a secondary index (see Step 5.3).

(4) When tuples are retrieved based on only part of the hash field. For example, if the Property_for_Rent relation is hashed on Rooms and Rent, then hashing could not be used to search for a tuple based on the Rooms attribute alone. Again, it would be necessary to perform a linear search to find the tuple.

Indexed Sequential Access Method (ISAM)

The indexed sequential file organization is discussed in Appendix A.5.1. ISAM is a more versatile storage structure than hash; it supports retrievals based on exact key match, pattern matching, range of values and part key specification.

However, the ISAM index is static, created when the file is created. Thus, the performance of an ISAM file deteriorates as the relation is updated. Updates also cause an ISAM file to lose the access key sequence, so that retrievals in order of the access key will become slower. These two problems are overcome by B^+-Tree file organization. However, unlike B^+-Tree, because the index is static, concurrent access to the index can be easily managed.

B^+-Tree

The B^+-Tree file organization is discussed in Appendix A.5.4. Again, B^+-Tree is a more versatile storage structure than hashing. It supports retrievals based on exact key match, pattern matching, range of values and part key specification. The B^+-Tree index is dynamic, growing as the relation grows. Thus, unlike ISAM, the performance of a B^+-Tree file does not deteriorate as the relation is updated. The B^+-Tree also maintains the order of the access key even when the file is updated, so retrieval of tuples in the order of the access key is more efficient than ISAM. However, if the relation is not frequently updated, the ISAM structure may be more efficient as it has one less level of index than the B^+-Tree, whose leaf nodes contain record pointers.

Document choice of file organization

The choice of file organization should be fully documented, along with the reasons for the choice. In particular, document the reasons for selecting one approach where many alternatives exist.

Step 5.3 Choose secondary indexes

Objective	To determine whether adding secondary indexes will improve the performance of the system.

Secondary indexes provide a mechanism for specifying an additional key for a base relation that can be used to retrieve data more efficiently. For example, the Property_for_Rent relation may be hashed on the property number, Pno, the **primary index**. However, there may be frequent access to this relation based on the Rent attribute. In this case, we may decide to add Rent as a **secondary index**. This may be implemented using the SQL statement:

```
CREATE INDEX property_rent_index ON property_for_rent(rent);
```

However, there is an overhead involved in the maintenance and use of secondary indexes that has to be balanced against the performance improvement gained when retrieving data. This overhead includes:

- adding an index record to every secondary index whenever a record is inserted in the relation;
- updating a secondary index when the corresponding record in the relation is updated;
- additional increase in disk space needed to store the secondary index;

- possible performance degradation during query optimization, as the query optimizer may consider all secondary indexes before selecting an optimal execution strategy.

We provide the following guidelines to help with the selection of indexes:

(1) In general, index the primary key of a relation if it is not a key of the file organization. It should be noted that, although the SQL2 standard provides a clause for the specification of primary keys as discussed in Step 4.1, this does not guarantee that the primary key will be indexed.

(2) Do not index small relations. It may be more efficient to search the relation in memory than to store an additional index structure.

(3) Add a secondary index to any attribute that is heavily used as a secondary key (for example, add a secondary index to the Property_for_Rent relation based on the attribute Rent, as discussed above).

(4) Add a secondary index to a foreign key if there is frequent access based on it. For example, we may frequently join the Property_for_Rent relation and the Owner relation on the attribute Ono, the owner number. Therefore, it may be more efficient to add a secondary index to the Property_for_Rent relation based on the attribute Ono.

(5) Avoid indexing an attribute or relation that is frequently updated.

(6) Avoid indexing an attribute if the query will retrieve a significant proportion of the tuples in the relation. In this case, it may be more efficient to search the entire relation than to search using an index.

(7) Avoid indexing attributes that consist of long character strings.

If a large number of tuples are being inserted into a relation with one or more indexes, it may be more efficient to drop the indexes first, perform the inserts, and then recreate the indexes afterwards. As a rule of thumb, if the insert will increase the relation by at least 10%, drop the indexes temporarily.

Document choice of secondary indexes
The choice of indexes should be fully documented, along with the reasons for the choice. In particular, if there are performance reasons why some attributes should not be indexed, these should also be documented.

Step 5.4 Consider the introduction of controlled redundancy

Objective	To determine whether introducing redundancy in a controlled manner by relaxing the normalization rules will improve the performance of the system.

Normalization is a procedure for deciding which attributes belong together in a relation. One of the basic concepts of relational theory is that we group attributes together in a relation because there is a functional dependency between them. The result of normalization is a logical database design that is structurally consistent and has minimal redundancy. However, it is sometimes argued that a normalized database design does not provide maximum processing efficiency. Consequently, there may be circumstances where it may be necessary to accept the loss of some of the benefits of a fully normalized design in favour of performance. This should be considered only when it is estimated that the system will not be able to meet its performance requirements. We are not advocating that normalization should be omitted from logical database design: normalization forces us to completely understand each attribute that has to be represented in the database. This may be the most important factor that contributes to the overall success of the system. In addition, the following factors have to be considered:

- Denormalization makes implementation more complex.
- Denormalization often sacrifices flexibility.
- Denormalization may speed up retrievals but it slows down updates.

Formally, the term **denormalization** refers to a refinement to the relational schema, such that the degree of normalization for a modified relation is less then the degree of at least one of the original relations. We also use the term more loosely to refer to the situations where we combine two relations into one new relation, where the new relation is still normalized but contains more nulls than the original relations. Denormalization is also called **usage refinement**.

Cross-reference transactions and relations

As a general rule of thumb, if performance is unsatisfactory and a relation has a low update rate and a very high query rate, denormalization may be a viable option. A transaction/relation cross-reference matrix provides useful information for this step. The matrix shows the transactions that are required and the relations they access, as illustrated in Table 9.1. The matrix summarizes, in a visual way, the access patterns of the transactions that will run on the database. It can be used to highlight possible candidates for denormalization, and to assess the effects this would have on the rest of the model. To be more useful, we could indicate the number of accesses over some time interval (for example, hourly, daily, weekly) in each cell. However, to keep the table simple, we do not show this information.

Table 9.1 Cross-referencing transactions and relations.

Transaction/ relation	Maintain properties				List properties for for each branch				List viewings with comments			
	I	R	U	D	I	R	U	D	I	R	U	D
Branch		X				X				X		
Staff		X										
Property_for_Rent	X	X	X	X		X				X		
Owner	X	X	X	X		X						
Viewing	X	X	X	X						X		
Renter		X	X	X						X		

I = Insert; R = Read; U = Update; D = Delete

In this section, we consider the following main steps:

- Step 5.4.1   Consider derived data
- Step 5.4.2   Consider duplicating attributes or joining relations together

We use the sample instance of the *DreamHome* database shown in Figure 3.3 to help illustrate this step.

Step 5.4.1   Consider derived data

Attributes whose value can be found by examining the values of other attributes are known as **derived** or **calculated attributes**. For example, the following are all derived attributes:

- the number of staff that work in a particular branch;
- the total monthly salaries of all staff;
- the number of properties that a member of staff handles.

Often, derived attributes will not appear in the logical data model, but should be documented in the data dictionary. If a derived attribute has been kept in the model, there should be an indication that it is derived. The first step, then, is to examine the logical data model and the data dictionary, and produce a list of all derived attributes.

From a physical database design perspective, whether a derived attribute is stored in the database or calculated every time it is needed is a trade-off. The designer should calculate:

- the additional cost to store the derived data and keep it consistent with operational data from which it is derived, and
- the cost to calculate it each time it is required,

and choose the less expensive option subject to performance constraints. For the last of the examples cited above, we would need to store an additional attribute in the Staff relation representing the number of properties that each member of staff currently manages. A simplified Staff relation with the new derived attribute is shown in Figure 9.7.

The additional storage overhead for this new derived attribute is not particularly significant. The field would be updated every time a member of staff was assigned to or deassigned from managing a property, or the property was removed from the list of available properties. In each case, the No_of_Properties attribute for the appropriate member of staff would be incremented or decremented by 1. It would be necessary to ensure that this change was made consistently to maintain the correct count, and consequently ensure the integrity of the database. When a query accesses this attribute, the value is immediately available, and does not have to be calculated. On the other hand, if the attribute is not stored directly in the Staff relation, it must be calculated each time it is required. This involves a join of the Staff and Property_for_Rent relations. Thus, if this type of query is frequent or is

PROPERTY_FOR_RENT

Pno	Street	Area	City	Pcode	Type	Rooms	Rent	Ono	Sno	Bno
PA14	16 Holhead	Dee	Aberdeen	AB7 5SU	House	6	650	CO46	SA9	B7
PL94	6 Argyll St	Kilburn	London	NW2	Flat	4	400	CO87	SL41	B5
PG4	6 Lawrence St	Partick	Glasgow	G11 9QX	Flat	3	350	CO40	SG14	B3
PG36	2 Manor Rd		Glasgow	G32 4QX	Flat	3	375	CO93	SG37	B3
PG21	8 Dale Rd	Hyndland	Glasgow	G12	House	5	600	CO87	SG37	B3
PG16	5 Novar Dr	Hyndland	Glasgow	G12 9AX	Flat	4	450	CO93	SG14	B3

STAFF

Sno	FName	LName	Address	NIN	Bno	No_of_Properties
SL21	John	White	19 Taylor St, Cranford, London	WK442011B	B5	0
SG37	Ann	Beech	81 George St, Glasgow PA1 2JR	WL432514C	B3	2
SG14	David	Ford	63 Ashby St, Partick, Glasgow G11	WL220658D	B3	2
SA9	Mary	Howe	2 Elm Pl, Aberdeen AB2 3SU	WM532187D	B7	1
SG5	Susan	Brand	5 Gt Western Rd, Glasgow G12	WK588932E	B3	0
SL41	Julie	Lee	28 Malvern St, Kilburn NW2	WA290573K	B5	1

Figure 9.7 Simplified Staff relation with the derived attribute No_of_Properties.

considered to be critical for performance purposes, it may be more appropriate to store the derived attribute rather than calculate it each time.

It may also be more appropriate to store derived attributes whenever the system's query language cannot easily cope with the algorithm to calculate the derived attribute. For example, SQL has a limited set of aggregate functions and cannot easily handle recursive queries, as we will see in Chapter 11.

Step 5.4.2 Consider duplicating attributes or joining relations together

The next step is to consider duplicating certain attributes or joining relations together to reduce the number of joins required to perform a query. Indirectly, we have encountered an implicit example of denormalization when dealing with address attributes. For example, consider the definition of the Branch relation:

Branch (<u>Bno</u>, Street, Area, City, Pcode, Tel_No, Fax_No)

Strictly speaking, this relation is not in third normal form: Pcode, the post or zip code, functionally determines Area and City. Therefore, to normalize the relation, it would be necessary to split the relation into two, as follows:

Branch (<u>Bno</u>, Street, Pcode, Tel_No, Fax_No)

Post_Code (<u>Pcode</u>, Area, City)

However, we rarely wish to access the branch address without the area and city attributes. This would mean that we would have to perform a join whenever we want a complete address for a branch. As a result, we settle for the second normal form and implement the original Branch relation.

Unfortunately, there are no fixed rules for determining when to denormalize relations. We discuss some of the more common situations for considering denormalization. For additional information, the interested reader is referred to Rogers (1989) and Fleming and Von Halle (1989). In particular, we consider denormalization in the following situations, specifically to speed up frequent or critical requests:

- combining one-to-one (1:1) relationships;
- duplicating nonkey attributes in one-to-many (1:M) relationships to reduce joins;
- reference tables;
- duplicating foreign key attributes in one-to-many (1:M) relationships to reduce joins;
- duplicating attributes in many-to-many (M:N) relationships to reduce joins;
- introducing repeating groups;
- creating extract tables.

Combining one-to-one (1:1) relationships   Re-examine one-to-one (1:1) relationships to determine the effects of combining the relations into a single relation. Combination should only be considered for relations that are frequently referenced together and infrequently referenced separately. Consider, for example, the 1:1 relationship between Renter and Interview in Figure 8.12. The Renter relation contains information on renters and potential renters of property; the Interview relation contains the date of the interview and comments made by a member of staff about a renter, as shown in Figure 9.8. The relationship between Renter and Interview is 1:1; the participation is partial. Since the participation is partial, there may be a significant number of nulls in the combined relation, depending on the proportion of tuples involved in the participation, as shown in Figure 9.9. If the Renter relation is large and the proportion of tuples involved in the participation is small, there will be a significant amount of wasted space.

Duplicating nonkey attributes in one-to-many (1:M) relationships   With the specific aim of reducing or removing joins from frequent or critical queries, consider the benefits that may result in duplicating one or more nonkey attributes of the parent relation in the child relation in a 1:M relationship. For example, whenever the Property_for_Rent relation is accessed, it is very common for the owner's name to be accessed at the same time. A typical SQL query would be:

```
SELECT p.*, o.lname
FROM property_for_rent p, owner o
WHERE p.ono = o.ono AND bno = 'B3';
```

based on the original relations shown in Figure 9.10.

RENTER

Rno	FName	LName	Pref_Type	Max_Rent
CR76	John	Kay	Flat	425
CR56	Aline	Stewart	Flat	350
CR74	Mike	Ritchie	House	750
CR62	Mary	Tregear	Flat	600

INTERVIEW

Rno	Sno	Date	Comment
CR62	SA9	14–May–95	needs property urgently
CR56	SG37	28–Apr–95	current lease ends in June

Figure 9.8 Original Renter and Interview relations.

RENTER

Rno	FName	LName	Pref_Type	Max_Rent	Sno	Date	Comment
CR76	John	Kay	Flat	425	null	null	null
CR56	Aline	Stewart	Flat	350	SG37	28–Apr–95	current lease ends in June
CR74	Mike	Ritchie	House	750	null	null	null
CR62	Mary	Tregear	Flat	600	SA9	14–May–95	needs property urgently

Figure 9.9 Combined Renter and Interview relation.

PROPERTY_FOR_RENT

Pno	Street	Area	City	Pcode	Type	Rooms	Rent	Ono	Sno	Bno
PA14	16 Holhead	Dee	Aberdeen	AB7 5SU	House	6	650	CO46	SA9	B7
PL94	6 Argyll St	Kilburn	London	NW2	Flat	4	400	CO87	SL41	B5
PG4	6 Lawrence St	Partick	Glasgow	G11 9QX	Flat	3	350	CO40	SG14	B3
PG36	2 Manor Rd		Glasgow	G32 4QX	Flat	3	375	CO93	SG37	B3
PG21	8 Dale Rd	Hyndland	Glasgow	G12	House	5	600	CO87	SG37	B3
PG16	5 Novar Dr	Hyndland	Glasgow	G12 9AX	Flat	4	450	CO93	SG14	B3

OWNER

Ono	FName	LName	Address	Tel_No
CO46	Joe	Keogh	2 Fergus Dr, Banchory, Aberdeen AB2 7SX	01224–861212
CO87	Carol	Farrel	6 Achray St, Glasgow G32 9DX	0141–357–7419
CO40	Tina	Murphy	63 Well St, Shawlands, Glasgow G42	0141–943–1728
CO93	Tony	Shaw	12 Park Pl, Hillhead, Glasgow G4 0QR	0141–225–7025

Figure 9.10 Original Property_for_Rent and Owner relations.

If we duplicate the LName attribute in the Property_for_Rent relation, we can remove the Owner relation from the query, which in SQL would now be:

```
SELECT p.*
FROM property_for_rent p
WHERE bno = 'B3';
```

based on the revised relation shown in Figure 9.11.

PROPERTY_FOR_RENT

Pno	Street	Area	City	Pcode	Type	Rooms	Rent	Ono	LName	Sno	Bno
PA14	16 Holhead	Dee	Aberdeen	AB7 5SU	House	6	650	CO46	Keogh	SA9	B7
PL94	6 Argyll St	Kilburn	London	NW2	Flat	4	400	CO87	Farrel	SL41	B5
PG4	6 Lawrence St	Partick	Glasgow	G11 9QX	Flat	3	350	CO40	Murphy	SG14	B3
PG36	2 Manor Rd		Glasgow	G32 4QX	Flat	3	375	CO93	Shaw	SG37	B3
PG21	8 Dale Rd	Hyndland	Glasgow	G12	House	5	600	CO87	Farrel	SG37	B3
PG16	5 Novar Dr	Hyndland	Glasgow	G12 9AX	Flat	4	450	CO93	Shaw	SG14	B3

Figure 9.11
Duplicating LName attribute in the Property_for_Rent relation.

The benefits that result from this change have to be balanced against the problems that may arise. For example, if the duplicated data is changed in the parent relation, it must be updated in the child relation. Further, for a 1:M relationship, there may be multiple occurrences of each data item in the child relation (for example, the names Farrel and Shaw both appear twice in the revised Property_for_Rent relation). Thus, it is necessary to maintain consistency of multiple copies. If the update of the LName attribute in the Owner and Property_for_Rent relation cannot be automated, the potential for loss of integrity is considerable. An associated problem with duplication is the additional time that will be required to automatically maintain consistency every time a record is inserted, updated or deleted. In our case, it is unlikely that the name of the owner of a property will change, so the duplication may be warranted.

Another problem to consider is the increase in storage space resulting from the duplication. Again, with the relatively low cost of secondary storage nowadays, this may not be so much of a problem. However, this is not a justification for arbitrary duplication.

Reference tables Reference tables, sometimes called lookup tables or pick lists, are a special case of 1:M relationships. Typically, a lookup table contains a code and a description. For example, we may define a lookup table for property type and modify the Property_for_Rent table, as shown in Figure 9.12.

The advantages of using a lookup table are:

- Reduction in the size of the child relation; the type code occupies 1 byte as opposed to 5 bytes for the type description.

PROPERTY_TYPE

Type	Description
1	House
2	Flat

PROPERTY_FOR_RENT

Pno	Street	Area	City	Pcode	Type	Rooms	Rent	Ono	Sno	Bno
PA14	16 Holhead	Dee	Aberdeen	AB7 5SU	1	6	650	CO46	SA9	B7
PL94	6 Argyll St	Kilburn	London	NW2	2	4	400	CO87	SL41	B5
PG4	6 Lawrence St	Partick	Glasgow	G11 9QX	2	3	350	CO40	SG14	B3
PG36	2 Manor Rd		Glasgow	G32 4QX	2	3	375	CO93	SG37	B3
PG21	8 Dale Rd	Hyndland	Glasgow	G12	1	5	600	CO87	SG37	B3
PG16	5 Novar Dr	Hyndland	Glasgow	G12 9AX	2	4	450	CO93	SG14	B3

- If the description can change (which would not be the case in this particular example), it is easier changing it once in the lookup table as opposed to changing it many times in the child relation.
- The lookup table can be used to validate user input.

Figure 9.12
Lookup table for Property_Type with modified Property_ for_Rent relation.

If lookup tables are used in frequent or critical queries, and the description is unlikely to change, consideration should be given to duplicating the description field in the child relation, as shown in Figure 9.13. The original lookup table is not redundant – it can still be used to validate user input. However, by duplicating the description in the child relation, we have eliminated the need to join the child relation to the lookup table.

PROPERTY_FOR_RENT

Pno	Street	Area	City	Pcode	Type	Description	Rooms	Rent	Ono	Sno	Bno
PA14	16 Holhead	Dee	Aberdeen	AB7 5SU	1	House	6	650	CO46	SA9	B7
PL94	6 Argyll St	Kilburn	London	NW2	2	Flat	4	400	CO87	SL41	B5
PG4	6 Lawrence St	Partick	Glasgow	G11 9QX	2	Flat	3	350	CO40	SG14	B3
PG36	2 Manor Rd		Glasgow	G32 4QX	2	Flat	3	375	CO93	SG37	B3
PG21	8 Dale Rd	Hyndland	Glasgow	G12	1	House	5	600	CO87	SG37	B3
PG16	5 Novar Dr	Hyndland	Glasgow	G12 9AX	2	Flat	4	450	CO93	SG14	B3

Duplicating foreign key attributes in one-to-many (1:M) relationships   Again, with the specific aim of reducing or removing joins from frequent or critical queries, consider the benefits that may result in duplicating one or more of the foreign key attributes in a relationship. For example, a frequent query for *DreamHome* is to list all the property owners at a branch, using an SQL query of the form:

Figure 9.13 Modified Property_for_Rent relation with duplicated Description attribute.

```
SELECT o.lname
FROM property_for_rent p, owner o
WHERE p.ono = o.ono AND p.bno = 'B3';
```

based on the original relations shown in Figure 9.10.

In other words, to get the list of owners we have to use the Property_for_Rent relation that has the required branch number, Bno (see Figure 8.17). We can remove the need for this join by duplicating the foreign key Bno in the Owner relation; that is, we introduce a direct relationship between the Branch and Owner relations. In this case, we can simplify the SQL query to:

```
SELECT o.lname
FROM owner o
WHERE bno = 'B3';
```

based on the new Owner relation shown in Figure 9.14.

OWNER

Ono	FName	LName	Address	Tel_No	Bno
CO46	Joe	Keogh	2 Fergus Dr, Banchory, Aberdeen AB2 7SX	01224–861212	B7
CO87	Carol	Farrel	6 Achray St, Glasgow G32 9DX	0141–357–7419	B5
CO40	Tina	Murphy	63 Well St, Shawlands, Glasgow G42	0141–943–1728	B3
CO93	Tony	Shaw	12 Park Pl, Hillhead, Glasgow G4 0QR	0141–225–7025	B3

Figure 9.14
Duplicating foreign key Bno in the Owner relation.

If this change is made, it will be necessary to introduce additional foreign key constraints, as discussed in Step 2.3.

If an owner could rent properties through many branches, the above change would not work. In this case, it would be necessary to model a many-to-many relationship between Branch and Owner. Note also that the only reason the Property_for_Rent relation has the Bno attribute is that it is possible for a property not to have a member of staff allocated to it, particularly at the start when the property is first taken on by the agency. If the Property_for_Rent relation did not have the branch number, it would be necessary to join the Property_for_Rent relation to the Staff relation based on the Sno attribute to get the required branch number. The original SQL query would then become:

```
SELECT o.lname
FROM staff s, property_for_rent p, owner o
WHERE s.sno = p.sno AND p.ono = o.ono AND s.bno = 'B3';
```

Removing two joins from the query may provide greater justification for duplicating the foreign key in the Owner relation.

Duplicating attributes in many-to-many (M:N) relationships During the logical data modelling process, we transformed each M:N relationship into two 1:M relationships. This transformation introduced a third, intermediate relation. Now, if we wish to produce information from the M:N relationship, we have to join three entities: the two original entities and the new intermediate relation. In some circumstances, it may be possible to reduce the number of tables to be joined by duplicating attributes from one of the original entities in the intermediate relation.

For example, the M:N relationship between Renter and Property_for_Rent has been decomposed by introducing the intermediate Viewing relation. Consider the requirement that the *DreamHome* sales staff wish to contact renters who have viewed properties, but have still to make a comment on the property. However, the sales staff need only the Street attribute of the property when talking to the renters. The required SQL query is:

SELECT p.street, r.*, v.date
FROM renter r, viewing v, property_for_rent p
WHERE v.pno = p.pno AND r.rno = v.rno AND comment IS NULL;

based on the original relations shown in Figure 9.15.

PROPERTY_FOR_RENT

Pno	Street	Area	City	Pcode	Type	Rooms	Rent	Ono	Sno	Bno
PA14	16 Holhead	Dee	Aberdeen	AB7 5SU	House	6	650	CO46	SA9	B7
PL94	6 Argyll St	Kilburn	London	NW2	Flat	4	400	CO87	SL41	B5
PG4	6 Lawrence St	Partick	Glasgow	G11 9QX	Flat	3	350	CO40	SG14	B3
PG36	2 Manor Rd		Glasgow	G32 4QX	Flat	3	375	CO93	SG37	B3
PG21	8 Dale Rd	Hyndland	Glasgow	G12	House	5	600	CO87	SG37	B3
PG16	5 Novar Dr	Hyndland	Glasgow	G12 9AX	Flat	4	450	CO93	SG14	B3

RENTER

Rno	FName	LName	Address	Tel_No	Pref_Type	Max_Rent
CR76	John	Kay	56 High St, Putney, London SW1 4EH	0171–774–5632	Flat	425
CR56	Aline	Stewart	64 Fern Dr, Pollock, Glasgow G42 0BL	0141–848–1825	Flat	350
CR74	Mike	Ritchie	18 Tain St, Gourock PA1G 1YQ	01475–392178	House	750
CR62	Mary	Tregear	5 Tarbot Rd, Kildary, Aberdeen AB9 3ST	01224–196720	Flat	600

VIEWING

Rno	Pno	Date	Comment
CR56	PA14	24–May–95	too small
CR76	PG4	20–Apr–95	too remote
CR56	PG4	26–May–95	
CR62	PA14	14–May–95	no dining room
CR56	PG36	28–Apr–95	

Figure 9.15 Original Property_for_Rent, Renter and Viewing relations.

If we duplicate the Street attribute in the intermediate Viewing relation, we can remove the Property_for_Rent relation from the query, giving the SQL query:

SELECT r.*, v.street, v.date
FROM renter r, viewing v
WHERE r.rno = v.rno AND comment IS NULL;

based on the revised relations shown in Figure 9.16.

RENTER

Rno	FName	LName	Address	Tel_No	Pref_Type	Max_Rent
CR76	John	Kay	56 High St, Putney, London SW1 4EH	0171–774–5632	Flat	425
CR56	Aline	Stewart	64 Fern Dr, Pollock, Glasgow G42 0BL	0141–848–1825	Flat	350
CR74	Mike	Ritchie	18 Tain St, Gourock PA1G 1YQ	01475–392178	House	750
CR62	Mary	Tregear	5 Tarbot Rd, Kildary, Aberdeen AB9 3ST	01224–196720	Flat	600

VIEWING

Rno	Pno	Street	Date	Comment
CR56	PA14	16 Holhead	24–May–95	too small
CR76	PG4	163 Main Street	20–Apr–95	too remote
CR56	PG4	163 Main Street	26–May–95	
CR62	PA14	16 Holhead	14–May–95	no dining room
CR56	PG36	2 Manor Rd	28–Apr–95	

Figure 9.16
Duplicating Street
attribute in the
Viewing relation.

Introducing repeating groups Repeating groups were eliminated from the logical data model as a result of the requirement that all entities be in first normal form. Repeating groups were separated out into a new relation, forming a 1:M relationship with the original (parent) relation. Occasionally, reintroducing repeating groups is an effective way to improve system performance. For example, each *DreamHome* branch office may have a number of company cars that can be used by staff when visiting properties. Not all offices have a company car pool; the ones that do have a maximum of four cars in the pool. Typically, the company car data would be separated out to form a new child relation with the primary key as the car registration number and a foreign key as the branch number Bno, as shown in Figure 9.17.

If the access to this information is an important or frequent query, it may be more efficient to combine the relations and store the car details in the original Branch relation, with one column for each car, as shown in Figure 9.18.

In general, this type of denormalization should be considered only in the following circumstances:

- The absolute number of items in the repeating group is known (in this example, there are four cars).

BRANCH

Bno	Street	Area	City	Pcode	Tel_No	Fax_No
B5	22 Deer Rd	Sidcup	London	SW1 4EH	0171–886–1212	0171–886–1214
B7	16 Argyll St	Dyce	Aberdeen	AB2 3SU	01224–67125	01224–67111
B3	163 Main St	Partick	Glasgow	G11 9QX	0141–339–2178	0141–339–4439
B4	32 Manse Rd	Leigh	Bristol	BS99 1NZ	0117–916–1170	0117–776–1114
B2	56 Clover Dr		London	NW10 6EU	0181–963–1030	0181–453–7992

BRANCH_CARS

Bno	Registration_No
B5	M109 ABG
B5	M670 BFT
B5	N64 SAB
B7	M536 XRT
B7	N90 BDC

Figure 9.17
Original Branch
and Branch_Cars
relations.

BRANCH

Bno	Street	Area	City	Pcode	Tel_No	Car1	Car2	Car3	Car4	Fax_No
B5	22 Deer Rd	Sidcup	London	SW1 4EH	0171–886–1212	M109 ABG	M670 BFT	N64 SAB	null	0171–886–1214
B7	16 Argyll St	Dyce	Aberdeen	AB2 3SU	01224–67125	M536 XRT	N90 BDC	null	null	01224–67111
B3	163 Main St	Partick	Glasgow	G11 9QX	0141–339–2178	...	...	...	...	0141–339–4439
B4	32 Manse Rd	Leigh	Bristol	BS99 1NZ	0117–916–1170	...	...	...	...	0117–776–1114
B2	56 Clover Dr		London	NW10 6EU	0181–963–1030	...	...	...	...	0181–453–7992

Figure 9.18 Revised
Branch relation with
repeating group.

- The number is static and will not change over time (the number of cars in a pool is fixed by the company).
- The number is not very large, typically not greater than 12, although this is not as important as the first two conditions.

Sometimes, it may be only the most recent or current value in a repeating group, or just the fact that there is a repeating group, that is needed most frequently. In the above example, we may need store only the fact that an office has a company car pool. In this case, we could consider storing just one extra column in the Branch relation representing this information.

Creating extract tables There may be situations where reports have to be run at peak times during the day. These reports access derived data and perform multi-relation joins on the same set of base relations. However, the data the report is based on may be relatively static or, in some cases, may not have to be current (that is, if the data were a few hours old, the report would be perfectly acceptable). In this case, it may be possible to create a single, highly denormalized extract table based on the relations required by the reports, and allow the users to access the extract table directly instead of the base relations. The most common technique for producing extract tables is to create and populate the tables in an overnight batch run when the system is lightly loaded.

Step 5.4.3 Document introduction of redundancy

The introduction of redundancy should be fully documented, along with the reasons for introducing it. In particular, document the reasons for selecting one approach where many alternatives exist. Update the logical data model to reflect any changes made as a result of denormalization.

Step 5.5 Estimate disk space

> **Objective**   To estimate the amount of disk space that will be required by the database.

It may be a requirement that the physical database implementation can be handled by the current hardware configuration. Even if this is not the case, the designer still has to estimate the amount of disk space that is required to store the database, in the event that new hardware has to be procured. The objective of this step is to estimate the amount of disk space that is required to support the database implementation on secondary storage. As with the previous steps in this subphase, estimating the disk usage is very dependent on the target DBMS and the hardware used to support the database. In general, the estimate is based on the size of each tuple and the number of tuples in the relation. The latter estimate should be a maximum number, but it may also be worth considering how the relation will grow, and modifying the resulting disk size by this growth factor to determine the potential size of the database in the future.

We illustrate this process using the file organizations discussed in Step 5.2 with the INGRES DBMS. The formulae are based on newly populated relations before data has been deleted or added. In general, calculations for the amount of space required by a relation involve multiplying the number of tuples by the size of a tuple and adding on the size for any indexes required. The size of a tuple is a sum of the attribute size plus any overhead introduced by the system. The size of an attribute is partly determined by its size and type. In INGRES, the size of a tuple is calculated as the total number of bytes per tuple, including 2 bytes overhead for variable length character strings and an additional byte for nullable fields.

Heap

An INGRES page is 2048 bytes, of which 40 bytes are used as a page header and the remaining 2008 bytes are available to store user data. The total space required for a heap file can be calculated as follows:

$$\text{rows\_per\_page} = 2008/(\text{row\_width} + 2) \quad \text{rounded down to nearest integer}$$

$$\text{total\_heap\_pages} = \text{num\_rows}/\text{rows\_per\_page} \quad \text{rounded up to nearest integer}$$

where row_width is the size of a tuple. For example, to determine the size for the Property_for_Rent relation with 10 000 records stored as a heap file, we have:

$$\text{rows\_per\_page} \quad = 2008/(111 + 2) = 17$$
$$\text{total\_heap\_pages} = 10000/17 \qquad = 589$$

Therefore, the Property_for_Rent relation would require 589 INGRES pages to be stored as a heap file. On a system with a block size of 512 bytes, the Property_for_Rent relation would require 589*2048/512 = 2356 disk blocks.

Hash

The formula for a hash file is the same as that for a heap file. In addition, the number of pages must be adjusted to take account of the **fillfactor**, which is the percentage of a page that will be used before the page is considered full. In INGRES, the default fillfactor for hash is 50%, unless the record width is greater than 1000 bytes, in which case the fillfactor is 100%. The calculation becomes:

$$\text{rows\_per\_page} \quad = (\text{fillfactor}*2008)/(\text{row\_width} + 2) \qquad \text{rounded down}$$
$$\text{total\_hash\_pages} = \text{num\_rows}/\text{rows\_per\_page}*(1/\text{fillfactor}) \quad \text{rounded up}$$

For example, to determine the size for the Property_for_Rent relation with 10 000 records stored as a hash file with a 50% fillfactor, we have:

$$\text{rows\_per\_page} \quad = 0.5*2008/(111 + 2) = 8$$
$$\text{total\_hash\_pages} = (10000/8)*2 \qquad\quad = 2501$$

Therefore, the Property_for_Rent relation would require 2501 INGRES pages to be stored as a hash file with a 50% fillfactor. On a system with a block size of 512 bytes, the Property_for_Rent relation would require 2501*2048/512 = 10 004 disk blocks.

ISAM

Like a hash file, an ISAM file also has to take account of the fillfactor but, in addition, it has to make an allowance for the amount of space the ISAM index will require. In INGRES, the default fillfactor for ISAM is 80%. The calculation for the size of the relation is:

$$\text{rows\_per\_page} \quad = (\text{fillfactor}*2008)/(\text{row\_width} + 2) \qquad\qquad \text{rounded down}$$
$$\text{free} \qquad\qquad = 2008 - (\text{rows\_per\_page} * (\text{row\_width} + 2))$$
$$\text{if free} > ((2048 - (\text{fillfactor}*2048)) \text{ and row\_width} \leqslant \text{free}$$
$$\qquad \text{rows\_per\_page} = \text{rows\_per\_page} + 1 \qquad\qquad\qquad \text{maximum value 512}$$
$$\text{total\_data\_pages} = \text{num\_rows}/\text{rows\_per\_page} \qquad\qquad \text{rounded up}$$

The calculation for the size of the index is:

$$keys\_per\_page \quad = 2008/(key\_width + 2) \qquad \text{rounded down}$$
$$total\_index\_pages = total\_data\_pages/keys\_per\_page + 1 \quad \text{rounded up}$$

where key_width is the size of the key columns. The overall space required by an ISAM file is then:

$$total\_isam\_pages = total\_data\_pages + total\_index\_pages$$

For example, to determine the size for the Property_for_Rent relation with 10 000 records stored as an ISAM file indexed on the Pno attribute using an 80% fillfactor, we have:

$$rows\_per\_page \quad = 0.8*2008/(111 + 2) = 15$$
$$total\_data\_pages \, = 10000/15 \qquad = 667$$
$$keys\_per\_page \quad = 2008/(5 + 2) \qquad = 286$$
$$total\_index\_pages = 770/286 + 1 \qquad = 4$$
$$total\_isam\_pages = 667 + 4 \qquad \quad = 671$$

Therefore, the Property_for_Rent relation would require 671 INGRES pages to be stored as an ISAM file, with an index on the Pno attribute using an 80% fillfactor. On a system with a block size of 512 bytes, the Property_for_Rent relation would require 671*2048/512 = 2684 disk blocks.

B^+-Tree

A B^+-Tree file includes index pages, intermediate *sprig* pages that point to leaf pages, leaf pages that point to data pages, and the data pages themselves. In addition, data, index and leaf pages can use different fillfactors. In INGRES, the default fillfactors are 80% for data and index pages and 70% for leaf pages. The calculation for the size of the relation is:

$$rows\_per\_page \quad = (data\_fill*2010)/(row\_width + 2) \qquad \text{rounded down}$$
$$free \qquad \qquad = 2008 - (rows\_per\_page * (row\_width + 2))$$
$$\text{if } free > ((2048 - (data\_fill*2048)) \text{ and } row\_width \leqslant free$$
$$\qquad rows\_per\_page = rows\_per\_page + 1 \qquad \text{maximum value 512}$$
$$max\_keys \qquad = (1964 / (key\_width + 6)) - 2 \qquad \text{rounded down}$$
$$keys\_per\_leaf \quad = max\_keys * leaf\_fill \qquad \text{rounded down, minimum value 2}$$
$$keys\_per\_index = max\_keys * index\_fill \qquad \text{rounded down, minimum value 2}$$

$$num\_leaf\_pages \quad = (num\_rows/keys\_per\_leaf) + 1 \qquad \text{rounded up}$$
$$num\_data\_pages \; = num\_leaf\_pages*(keys\_per\_leaf/rows\_per\_page) +$$
$$\qquad \qquad MODULO(num\_rows/keys\_per\_leaf)/rows\_per\_page \quad \text{both divisions rounded up}$$

$$num\_sprig\_pages \; = 0 \qquad \qquad \text{if } num\_leaf\_pages \leqslant keys\_per\_index$$
$$num\_sprig\_pages \; = (num\_leaf\_pages/keys\_per\_index) \quad \text{otherwise} \qquad \text{rounded up}$$

```
num_index_pages  = 0
                    if (num_sprig_pages > keys_per_index) then
                        x = num_sprig_pages
                        do
                            x = x/keys_per_index
                            num_index_pages = num_index_pages + x
                        while (x > keys_per_index)
```

The overall space required by a B^+-Tree file is then:

$$\text{total\_btree\_pages} = \text{num\_data\_pages} + \text{num\_leaf\_pages} +$$
$$\text{num\_sprig\_pages} + \text{num\_index\_pages} + 2$$

For example, to determine the size for the Property_for_Rent relation with 10 000 records stored as a B^+-Tree file indexed on the Pno attribute using the default fillfactors, we have:

rows_per_page	= (.8*2010)/(111 + 2)	= 15
max_keys	= (1964 / (5 + 6)) − 2	= 176
keys_per_leaf	= 176 * .7	= 123
keys_per_index	= 176 * .8	= 140
num_leaf_pages	= (10000/123) + 1	= 83
num_data_pages	= 83*(123/15) + 3	= 750
num_sprig_pages	= 0	
num_index_pages	= 0	
total_btree_pages	= 750 + 83 + 0 + 0 + 2	= 835

Therefore, the Property_for_Rent relation would require 835 INGRES pages to be stored as a B^+-Tree file, with an index on the Pno attribute using default fillfactors. On a system with a block size of 512 bytes, the Property_for_Rent relation would require 835*2048/512 = 3340 disk blocks.

Table 9.2 shows the disk space requirements (in 512 byte blocks) for the Property_for_Rent relation as the number of records in the file increases.

Table 9.2 Comparison of space requirements for Property_for_Rent relation.

	10 000	20 000	30 000	40 000	50 000
Heap	2 356	4 708	7 060	9 412	11 768
Hash	10 004	20 004	30 004	40 004	50 004
ISAM	2 684	5 360	8 032	10 712	13 388
B^+-Tree	3 340	6 592	9 844	13 100	16 352

Step 6 Design and Implement Security Mechanisms

> **Objective** To design and implement the security measures for the database as specified by the users.

A database represents an essential corporate resource, and so security of this resource is extremely important. There should be specific security requirements documented during logical database design. The objective of this subphase is to decide how these security measures will be realized. Some systems offer different security facilities than others. Again, the database designer must be aware of the facilities offered by the target DBMS. We will discuss security in detail in Chapter 14. The steps in this subphase are:

- Step 6.1 Design and implement user views
- Step 6.2 Design and implement access rules

Step 6.1 Design and implement user views

> **Objective:** To design and implement the user views that were identified in Step 1 of the logical database design methodology.

The first part of the logical database design methodology presented in Chapter 7 involved the production of local logical data models for each of the user views. These local logical data models were merged subsequently into one global logical data model. The objective of this step is to design the user views, based on the local logical data models. In a standalone DBMS on a personal computer, views are usually a convenience, defined to simplify database requests. However, in a multi-user DBMS, views play a central role in defining the structure of the database and enforcing security. We will discuss the major advantages of views, such as data independence, reduced complexity and customization, in Section 12.1.7.

Normally, views are created using SQL. For example, we could create a view for the staff details at branch B3 that excludes salary information, so that only the manager at that branch can access the salary details for staff who work in his or her office. The SQL statement in this case would be:

```
CREATE VIEW staff3
AS   SELECT sno, fname, lname, address, tel_no, position, sex
     FROM staff
     WHERE bno = 'B3';
```

This creates a view called Staff3 with the same attributes as the Staff relation, but excluding the Salary, NIN and Bno attributes. If we list this view we would get the data given in Figure 9.19.

To ensure that only the branch manager can see the Salary attribute, staff should not be given access to the base relation Staff. Instead, they should

Sno	FName	LName	Address	Tel_no	Position	Sex
SG37	Ann	Beech	81 George St, Glasgow PA1 2JR	0141–848–3345	Snr Asst	F
SG14	David	Ford	63 Ashby St, Partick, Glasgow G11	0141–339–2177	Deputy	M
SG5	Susan	Brand	5 Gt Western Rd, Glasgow G12	0141–334–2001	Manager	F

Figure 9.19 Staff3 view listing.

be given **access permission** to the view Staff3, thereby denying them access to sensitive salary data. Access permissions are discussed further in Step 6.2.

Step 6.2   Design and implement access rules

> **Objective**   To design and implement the access rules to the base relations and user views.

One way to provide security is to use the access control facilities of SQL, which we will describe in Section 12.4. Typically, users should not be given access to the base relations. Instead, they should be given access to the base relations through the user views designed in Step 6.1. This provides a large degree of data independence and insulates users from changes in the database structure. We briefly review the access control mechanisms of SQL2.

Each database user is assigned an **authorization identifier** by the DBA; usually, the identifier has an associated password, for obvious security reasons. Every SQL statement that is executed by the DBMS is performed on behalf of a specific user. The authorization identifier is used to determine which database objects that user may reference, and what operations may be performed on those objects. Each object that is created in SQL has an owner. The owner is identified by the authorization identifier. The owner is the only person who may know of the existence of the object and, consequently, perform any operations on the object.

Privileges are the actions that a user is permitted to carry out on a given base relation or view. For example, SELECT is the privilege to retrieve data from a table. When a user creates a relation using the SQL Create Table statement, he or she automatically becomes the owner of the relation and receives full privileges for the relation. Other users initially have no privileges on the newly created relation. To give them access to the relation, the owner must explicitly grant them the necessary privileges using the GRANT statement. A WITH GRANT OPTION clause can be specified with the GRANT statement to allow the receiving user(s) to pass the privilege(s) on to other users. Privileges can be revoked using the REVOKE statement.

When a user creates a view with the Create View statement, he or she automatically becomes the owner of the view, but does not necessarily receive full privileges on the view. To create the view, a user must have SELECT privilege to all the relations that make up the view. However, the owner will only get other privileges if he or she holds those privileges for every relation in the view.

For example, to allow the user MANAGER to retrieve rows from the Staff relation and to insert, update and delete data from the Staff relation, we use the following SQL statement:

```
GRANT ALL PRIVILEGES
ON staff
TO manager WITH GRANT OPTION;
```

In this case, MANAGER will also be able to reference the relation and all the attributes in any relation he or she creates subsequently. We specified the keyword WITH GRANT OPTION so that MANAGER can pass these privileges on to other users that he or she sees fit. As another example, we could give the user with authorization identifier ADMIN the privilege SELECT on the Staff relation using the following SQL statement:

```
GRANT SELECT
ON staff
TO admin;
```

We have omitted the keyword WITH GRANT OPTION so that ADMIN will not be able to pass this privilege on to other users.

Document design of security measures and user views
The design of the individual user views and associated security mechanisms should be fully documented. If the physical design affects the individual local logical data models, these diagrams should also be updated.

Step 7   Monitor and Tune the Operational System

Objective	To monitor the operational system and improve the performance of the system to correct inappropriate design decisions or reflect changing requirements.

As mentioned earlier, the initial physical database design should not be regarded as static, but should be considered as an estimate of operational performance. Once the initial design has been implemented, it is necessary to monitor the system and **tune** it as a result of observed performance and changing requirements. Many DBMSs provide the DBA with utilities to monitor the operation of the system and tune it.

There are many benefits to be gained from tuning the database:

- It can avoid the procurement of additional hardware.
- It may be possible to downsize the hardware configuration. This results

in less, and cheaper, hardware and consequently less expensive maintenance.

- A well-tuned system produces faster response times and better throughput, which in turn makes the users, and hence the organization, more productive.
- Improved response times can improve staff morale.
- Improved response times can increase customer satisfaction.

These last two benefits are more intangible than the others. However, we can certainly state that slow response times demoralize staff and potentially lose customers.

Tuning is an activity that is never complete. Throughout the life of the system, it will be necessary to monitor performance, particularly to account for changes in the environment and user requirements. However, making a change to one area of an operational system to improve performance may have an adverse effect on another area. For example, adding an index to a relation may improve the performance of one application, but it may adversely affect another, perhaps more important, application. Therefore, care must be taken when making changes to an operational system. If possible, test the changes either on a test database, or alternatively, when the system is not being fully used (for example, out of working hours).

Chapter Summary

- **Physical database design** is the process of producing a description of the implementation of the database on secondary storage. It describes the base relations and the storage structures and access methods used to access this data effectively. The design of the base relations can be undertaken only once the designer is fully aware of the facilities offered by the target DBMS.

- The first subphase of physical database design is the translation of the global logical data model into a form that can be implemented in the target relational DBMS.

- The second subphase designs the file organization and access methods that will be used to store the base relations. This involves analysing the transactions that will run on the database, choosing a suitable file organization based on this analysis, adding secondary indexes, introducing controlled redundancy to improve performance, and finally estimating the disk space that will be required by the implementation.

- **Heap** files are good for inserting a large number of records into the file. They are inappropriate when only selected records are to be retrieved. **Hash** files are good when retrieval is based on an exact key match. They are not good when retrieval is based on pattern matching, range of values, part keys, or when retrieval is based on an attribute other than the hash field.

- **ISAM** is a more versatile storage structure than hashing. It supports retrievals based on exact key match, pattern matching, range of values and part key specification. However, the ISAM index is static, created when the file is created. Thus, the performance of an ISAM file will deteriorate as the relation is updated. Updates also cause the ISAM file to lose the access key sequence, so that retrievals in order of the access key will become slower. These two problems are overcome by B^+-**Tree** file organization, which has a dynamic index. However, unlike B^+-Tree, because the index is static, concurrent access to the index can be easily managed. If the relation is not frequently updated or not very large nor likely to be, the ISAM structure may be more efficient as it has one less level of index than the B^+-Tree, whose leaf nodes contain record pointers.

- **Secondary indexes** provide a mechanism for specifying an additional key for a base relation that can be used to retrieve data more efficiently. However, there is an overhead involved in the maintenance and use of secondary indexes that has to be balanced against the performance improvement gained when retrieving data.

- There may be circumstances where it may be necessary to accept the loss of some of the benefits of a fully normalized design in favour of performance. This should be considered only when it is estimated that the system will not be able to meet its performance requirements. As a rule of thumb, if performance is unsatisfactory and a relation has a low update rate and a very high query rate, **denormalization** may be a viable option.

- A database represents an essential corporate resource, and so security of this resource is extremely important. The objective of the third subphase is to design how the security measures identified during logical database design will be realized. This may include the creation of user views and the use of SQL access control. The final subphase of physical database design is the ongoing process of monitoring and tuning the operational system to achieve maximum performance.

REVIEW QUESTIONS

9.1 Explain the difference between logical and physical database design. Why might these tasks be carried out by different people?

9.2 Describe the inputs and outputs of physical database design.

9.3 Describe the purpose of the main steps in the physical design methodology presented in this chapter.

9.4 'One of the main objectives of physical database design is to store data in an efficient way.' How might we measure efficiency in this context?

9.5 Under what circumstances would we want to denormalize a logical data model? Use examples to illustrate your answer.

EXERCISES

9.6   Produce a physical database design for the global logical data model presented in Figure 8.17 from the worked example of Chapter 8. Use any DBMS that you have access to as the basis for the design. State any assumptions necessary to support your design.

9.7   Produce a physical database design for the global logical data model that you developed in the Exercises at the end of Chapter 8. Use any DBMS that you have access to as the basis for the design. State any assumptions necessary to support your design.

10 Physical Database Design Methodology – Worked Example

Chapter Objectives

In this chapter you will learn:

- How to use the physical database design methodology for relational databases, described in Chapter 9.
- How to use this methodology to translate the logical database design for the *DreamHome* case study, created in Chapter 8, into the physical design for the database.
- How to use the physical database design for the *DreamHome* case study to implement a working database system using the Paradox for Windows DBMS.

In this chapter, we illustrate by example the physical database design methodology for relational databases which was described in detail in Chapter 9. We use this methodology to create a physical database design based on the logical data model for the *DreamHome* case study created in Chapter 8. (An overview of this case study was given in Section 1.7.) We then use this physical database design to demonstrate the implementation of the working *DreamHome* database using the Paradox for Windows Database Management System (DBMS). We use the implementation of the working database to provide feedback on the success or otherwise of the physical database design.

We selected Paradox for Windows as the target DBMS for this chapter to illustrate how to use the guidelines described in Chapter 9 to implement a correct and efficient system. One of the main reasons for selecting a PC-based DBMS rather than a larger system is to emphasize that the usefulness and applicability of each guideline is governed by the functionality provided by the target DBMS. In other words, we must adapt the physical database design methodology to the target DBMS. For example, in this chapter we do not use Step 5.2 of the methodology, as this step involves selecting an appropriate file organization for database tables, and this option is not available to users of the Paradox for Windows DBMS.

Therefore, before we begin the physical design for the *DreamHome* database, it is important that we are aware of the functionality of the Paradox for Windows DBMS.

10.1 Paradox for Windows DBMS

There are literally many hundreds of PC-based DBMSs currently on the marketplace. For many users, the process of selecting the best DBMS package can be a difficult task. In Chapter 4, we reviewed the main features that should be considered when selecting a DBMS package. Some of the most popular PC-based DBMS packages are produced by Borland International, including Paradox, Paradox for Windows and dBase. In this chapter, we use Paradox for Windows Version 5.0 as the target DBMS for the *DreamHome* case study.

Paradox for Windows is a typical PC-based DBMS capable of storing, sorting and retrieving data for a variety of applications. This DBMS package provides the tools to create tables, forms and reports, and to develop customized database applications using a high-level object-oriented programming language called ObjectPAL. Paradox for Windows can be used as a standalone system on a single PC, or as a multiuser system on a PC network.

10.2 Using the Physical Database Design and Implementation Methodology for Relational Databases

Step 4 Translate Global Logical Data Model for Target DBMS

In this step, we translate the global logical data model of the *DreamHome* case study into a form that can be implemented in the target relational DBMS, namely Paradox for Windows. The first part of this process involves collating the information created during the logical design phase. The second part of this process uses this information to produce the physical design for the base relations of the *DreamHome* case study, which are to be implemented using Paradox for Windows.

Step 4.1 Design base relations for target DBMS

We first identify the relations that represent the global logical data model for the *DreamHome* case study. This information was described in Chapter 8, and includes the global logical data model shown in Figure 8.16, and the documentation that describes this model. Examples of this documentation were given as appendices at the end of Chapter 8. This logical database design is the starting point for this chapter, where we convert the logical design into a physical design, which is to be implemented using the Paradox for Window DBMS.

The composition of each relation of the *DreamHome* case study was described using a Database Design Language (DBDL) for relational databases, and is given in Appendix 8.7. The DBDL specifies the name of the relation, followed by a list of the names of the simple attributes of the relation, enclosed in brackets. Listed below this information is the primary key and, where appropriate, the alternate key(s) and foreign key(s) of the relation. We also list any constraints on the foreign key(s).

The details of each attribute of the global logical model are described in the data dictionary, part of which was given in Appendix 8.3. For each attribute, the data dictionary describes the attribute domain, which includes the data type, length and any constraints on the domain, a default value (if any), whether the attribute can hold nulls, and whether the attribute is derived (and, if so, how it should be computed).

When we are satisfied that we have gathered together the necessary information that describes the relations of the *DreamHome* case study, we may now design the base relations for the database implementation. The design of each base relation must take into account the functionality of the target DBMS.

We document the design of the base relations, using an extended form of the DBDL used in Chapter 8, to include the definition of domains, default values and null indicators. For example, the extended DBDL for the Property_for_Rent base relation of the *DreamHome* case study for implemen-

```
domain Property_Number: Alpha (A) length 5   PICTURE: P&#[#][#]
domain Street:          Alpha (A) length 25
domain Area:            Alpha (A) length 15
domain City:            Alpha (A) length 15
domain Postcode:        Alpha (A) length 8
domain Property_Type:   Alpha (A) length 1
domain Property_Rooms:  Number                RANGE: 1 to 15
domain Property_Rent:   Money                 RANGE: 0.00–9999.00
domain Owner_Number:    Alpha (A) length 5   PICTURE: CO#[#][#]
domain Staff_Number:    Alpha (A) length 5   PICTURE: S&#[#][#]
domain Branch_Number:   Alpha (A) length 3   PICTURE: B#[#]

PROPRENT(
        Property_No:    Property_Number   REQUIRED,
        Street:         Street            REQUIRED,
        Area:           area,
        City:           city              REQUIRED,
        Postcode:       Postcode,
        Type:           Property_Type     REQUIRED   VALUES: 'B','C','D','E','F','M' or 'S',
        Rooms:          Property_Rooms    REQUIRED   DEFAULT: 4,
        Rent:           Property_Rent     REQUIRED   DEFAULT: 600.00,
        POwner_No:      Owner_Number      REQUIRED,
        BOwner_No:      Owner_Number      REQUIRED
        Staff_No:       Staff_Number,
        Branch_No:      Branch_Number     REQUIRED)
        Primary Key Property_No
        Foreign Key POwner_No references POWNER(POwner_No) on delete RESTRICT on update CASCADE
        Foreign Key BOwner_No references BOWNER(BOwner_No) on delete RESTRICT on update CASCADE
        Foreign key Staff_No references STAFF(Staff_No) on delete RESTRICT on update CASCADE
        Foreign Key Branch_No references BRANCH(Branch_No) on delete RESTRICT on update CASCADE
```

Figure 10.1 Extended DBDL for the Property_for_Rent relation (to be implemented as the PROPRENT table).

tation using Paradox for Windows, is shown in Figure 10.1. Note that the information shown in this figure is explained at various stages throughout this chapter.

Owing to a restriction on the length of Paradox for Windows table names, the Property_for_Rent relation is to be implemented as a table called PROPRENT. Also, the Private_Owner and Business_Owner relations are to be implemented as tables called POWNER and BOWNER, respectively.

In designing the Property_for_Rent base relation, the original logical design for the relation is altered to accommodate the functionality of the target DBMS. We provide some examples of changes to the logical design of the Property_for_Rent relation to illustrate this process:

- The logical design for the Property_No attribute given in Appendix 8.3 was described as being a variable character string of maximum length 5. However, as Paradox for Windows does not distinguish between fixed and variable length character strings, this attribute is simply defined as data type Alpha (A), length 5.

- The logical design given in Appendix 8.7 indicates that the Property_for_Rent relation is related to the Private_Owner, Business_Owner,

Staff and Branch relations through the foreign key/primary key mechanism. If we examine the relationship between properties for rent and property owners more closely, we note that an owner (being either a private or business owner) is associated with a property through the Owner_No foreign key of the Property_for_Rent relation. However, Paradox for Windows does not allow a single foreign key in a table to reference more than one master (parent) table, and therefore it is necessary to create a separate foreign key for each type of owner. As a consequence, we must alter the logical design of the Property_for_Rent relation by introducing two foreign keys, called POwner_No and BOwner_No, which reference the POWNER and BOWNER tables, respectively, as shown in Figure 10.1.

- In the logical design, we described how referential integrity is to be maintained between related tables. The update and delete rules for each foreign key in a relation is specified as being either **NO ACTION**, **CASCADE, SET NULL** or **SET DEFAULT**. These options determine what is to happen if a record in a parent table is updated or deleted, while a referencing record in the child table exists. For example, the update rule for the Branch_No foreign key of the Property_for_Rent relation is set to CASCADE and for the delete rule is SET NULL. However, Paradox for Windows only provides a choice for the update

Figure 10.2 The Paradox for Windows desktop.

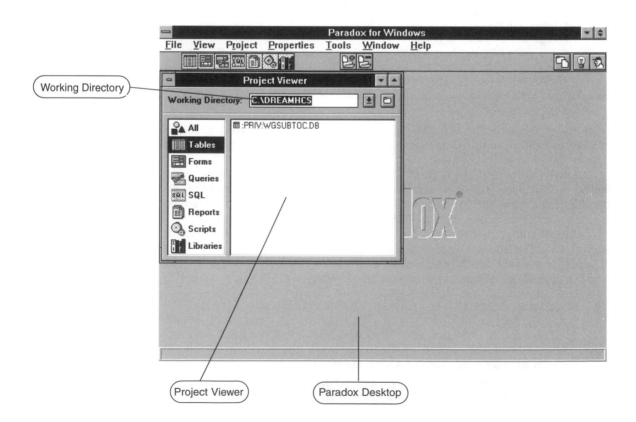

rule of CASCADE or RESTRICT (NO ACTION), and does not provide any options for the delete rule, with it being permanently set at RESTRICT (NO ACTION). We must therefore alter the logical design of the Property_for_Rent relation to reflect the fact that Paradox for Windows does not support the SET NULL option for the delete rule. As shown in Figure 10.1, the delete rule for the Branch_No foreign key is set to RESTRICT rather than to the SET NULL option, as given in Appendix 8.7.

On completion of the design of the base relations of the *DreamHome* case study, we are now ready to implement each relation as a Paradox for Windows table. To demonstrate this process, we implement the PROPRENT table as described in Figure 10.1.

When we start the Paradox for Windows DBMS, we see the Paradox Desktop, as shown in Figure 10.2. Using the Desktop, we can manage files, define defaults and preferences while working with the system and control all Paradox objects such as tables, forms, queries and reports. Note that the Project Viewer is opened to the working directory called DREAMHCS, which is to hold all of the components of the *DreamHome* database.

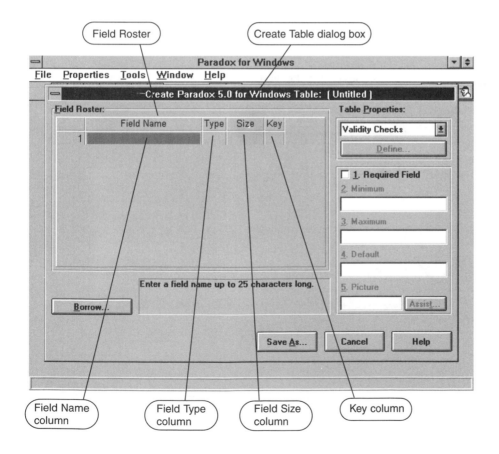

Figure 10.3 The Create Paradox for Windows table dialog box.

(1) Specifying the fields for the PROPRENT table

We create a Paradox for Windows table using the **File**, **New** and **Table** options, which results in the display of the dialog box, shown in Figure 10.3.

We fill in the required information of the Create Table dialog box for each field of the PROPRENT table as given in Figure 10.1, including the **Field Name**, **Type**, **Size** and whether a field is all or part of the **Primary Key** for the table. Each field name must be unique within a table.

Figure 10.4 displays the creation of the PROPRENT table. Paradox for Windows supports various data types for storing different types of information. We select the appropriate data type for each field of the PROPRENT table to ensure the most efficient storage of the information to be held by each field. Most of the fields in this table are specified as being alphanumeric (A), including the Property_No, Street, Area, City, Postcode, Type, POwner_No, BOwner_No, Staff_No and Branch_No fields. Note that in the original description of the Property_for_Rent relation in Appendix 8.7, these attributes were variable character. However, as mentioned earlier, Paradox for Windows does not distinguish between fixed and variable length character strings. The Rooms field is specified as Number (N) and the Rent field is specified as Money ($). Note that only the first eleven fields of the PROPRENT table are shown in the **Field Roster** of Figure 10.4. As a consequence, Branch_No, the last field of this table, is hidden from view.

Figure 10.4 The PROPRENT table structure.

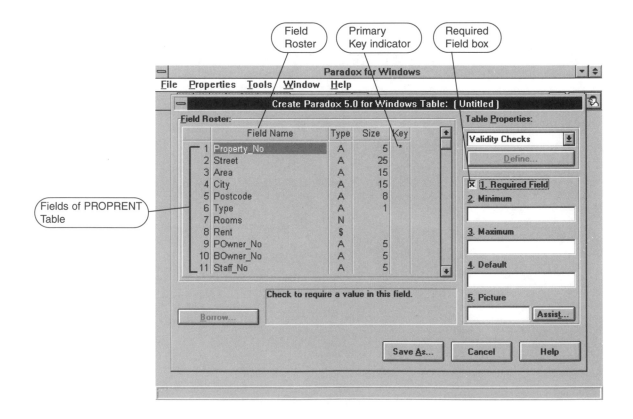

(2) Specifying the primary key for the PROPRENT table
The primary key for the PROPRENT table is the Property_No field and, as such, must be positioned as the first field in the table. We then enter the **key indicator (*)** in the **Key** column of this field, as shown in Figure 10.4. The primary key ensures that each property number in the PROPRENT table is unique. It also establishes the primary index and sort order for the table.

For those tables in the *DreamHome* database that have a composite primary key made up of two or more fields, these fields must be located at the top of the table with the key indicator (*) placed in the Key column for each of the component fields. For example, the Viewing table, described in Appendix 8.7, has a composite key made up of the (Property_No, Renter_No and Date_View) fields.

We continue the process of creating the PROPRENT table to include the other constraints on the table, as described in Figure 10.1. Paradox for Windows provides facilities for adding constraints to a table through the **Table Properties** section of the Create Paradox for Windows Table dialog box, as shown in Figure 10.5. (These facilities are also available through the Restructure Paradox for Windows Table dialog box.)

We begin by placing data validation checks on the appropriate fields of the PROPRENT table, as described in Figure 10.1.

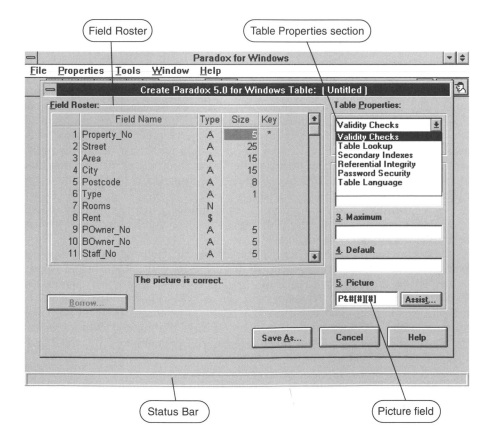

Figure 10.5 The Table Properties menu.

(3) Specifying validity checks for the PROPRENT table

To improve the quality of the data held in tables, Paradox for Windows provides various facilities to ensure that the values entered into a table meet certain conditions. There are five types of validity checks, including:

- required field (whether a value is required in a field for every record in the table);
- minimum (the minimum value for a field);
- maximum (the maximum value for a field);
- default (the default value for a field, which is automatically entered);
- picture (the template for the values that can be entered in this field, which are automatically formatted).

When we attempt to enter data of the wrong format or value into the fields with validation checks, the data will not be accepted and a warning message will be displayed informing the user of the data entry error. The error message appears in the Status bar area along the bottom of the screen.

The validity checks required for each attribute of the Property_for_Rent relation are shown in Figure 10.1. We use examples to demonstrate the implementation of these validity checks on the fields of the PROPRENT table.

To place one or more validity checks on a field, we first select the field in the **Field Roster**, and then choose the **Validity Checks** from the **Table Properties** list, shown in Figure 10.5.

Field requirement   Required fields are fields that must hold a value in every record. The field requirement facility is equivalent to allowing or disallowing nulls. The extended DBDL for the Property_for_Rent relation, shown in Figure 10.1, indicates whether each field in the PROPRENT table should or should not allow nulls. For example, each property must be associated with a branch: therefore Branch_No is a required field and must not allow nulls. However, in the case of the Postcode field, for some properties we may not know the postcode: therefore this field is not a required field and should allow nulls.

As key fields play an important part in uniquely identifying each record in a table, it is critical that key fields should not allow nulls, and must always be implemented as required fields.

When creating a table, the default setting for each field (including key fields) is set to not required. As shown in Figure 10.4, the **Required Field** box is located on the right-hand side of the Create Table dialog box under the Table Properties section. As we move down each field in the **Field Roster**, we indicate whether the field is required by clicking the Required Field box. For example, Figure 10.4 shows the Property_No field highlighted with a cross in the Required Field box. As Property_No is the primary key for the PROPRENT table, it should not allow nulls.

Minimum and maximum values   We may set a range of allowable values for numeric or date fields. This reduces the number of errors that may occur when the records are being entered into the table. The minimum and maximum values for the range of allowable values are entered into the **Minimum** and **Maximum** fields in the Table Properties section of the Create Table dialog box. For example, for a single property the possible range of rooms ranges from a minimum of 1 to a maximum of 15. The validation check for the Rooms field of the PROPRENT table is shown in Figure 10.6.

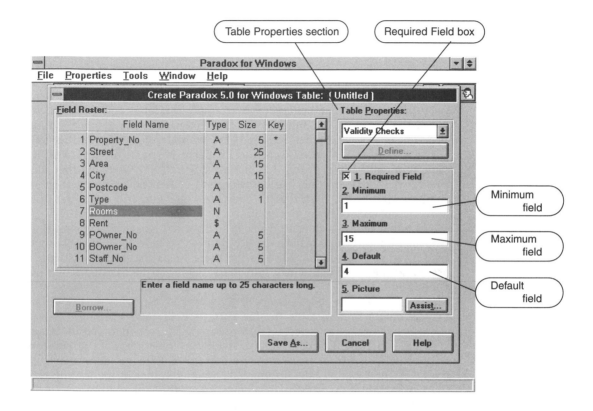

Additional fields with similar validation checks include the Rent field, which requires that the possible range of rent associated with a single property ranges from a minimum of £0.00 to a maximum of £9999.00.

Figure 10.6 Validation checks for Rooms field.

Default values   To speed up and reduce possible errors in data entry, we may assign default values for each field in a table. The default value for a field is entered into the **Default** field in the Table Properties section of the Create Table dialog box. The default values for the attributes of the Property_ for_Rent relation are shown in Figure 10.1. For example, the average number of rooms in a single property is four: we therefore set '4' as the default value for the Rooms field of the PROPRENT table, as shown in Figure 10.6.

As another example, the average monthly rent for a single property is £600.00: we therefore set 600.00 as the default value for the Rent field of the PROPRENT table.

Picture templates Picture templates can assist the process of data entry by controlling the format of the data as it is entered into the table. A picture establishes the type of character that is allowed for each position of a field. Picture templates simplify data entry by automatically entering special formatted characters where required, and generating error messages when incorrect entries are attempted.

The picture function for a field is entered into the **Picture** field in the Table Properties section of the Create Table dialog box, as shown in Figure 10.5. Paradox for Windows provides a range of picture characters to control data entry.

For example, the values to be entered into the Property_No field of the PROPRENT table have a specific format, as described in Appendix 8.4, which documents examples of allowable values for this field. The first character is 'P' for property, the second character is an uppercase letter and the third, fourth and fifth characters are numeric. The fourth and fifth characters are optional, and will only be used when required (for example, property number PG21).

As shown in Figure 10.4, the Property_No field of the PROPRENT table represents the Property_No picture as P&#[#][#], meaning that the first character 'P' is a constant letter, the second character is converted to uppercase, the third, fourth and fifth characters are numeric, with the last two numeric characters being optional.

Other fields, such as POwner_No, BOwner_No, Staff_No and Branch_No, also have formats which require data to be entered in a consistent and specific way. The specific formats for these fields may prove difficult for a user, and therefore data entry into these fields can be assisted using picture validation.

(4) Creating a lookup table for the PROPRENT table

An alternative way to speed up and reduce the errors involved in data entry is to use the Table Lookup facility. A lookup table acts as a reference table that displays a list of acceptable values for a field on data entry. When required, the lookup table automatically copies values in the lookup table to the target table. As shown in Figure 10.5, the Table Lookup facility is available as one of the choices in the Table Properties section of the Create Table dialog box.

The Type field of the PROPRENT table has a limited selection of possible values, as described in Figure 10.1. The full description of each property type according to the abbreviated value is shown in Table 10.1. This list of property types is implemented as a Paradox for Windows table called PROPTYPE, which has two fields, Type and Prop_Description. The Type field (key field) has the same name and structure as the original Type field in the PROPRENT table and holds the property type codes. The Prop_Description field provides a description of the codes to remind the user what the codes represent. In this way, the PROPTYPE table acts as the reference lookup table for the Type field of the PROPRENT table.

To define the PROPTYPE table, we use the Table Lookup dialog box shown in Figure 10.7, which displays the fields of the PROPRENT table on the left-hand side and the list of possible lookup tables on the right-hand side. (Note that, at this stage, only the PROPTYPE table is implemented, and

Table 10.1   The PROPTYPE table
contains possible values for the Type
Field of the PROPRENT table.

Type	Prop_Description
B	Bungalow
C	Cottage
D	Detached
E	End-Terrace
F	Flat
M	Mid-Terrace
S	Semi-Detached

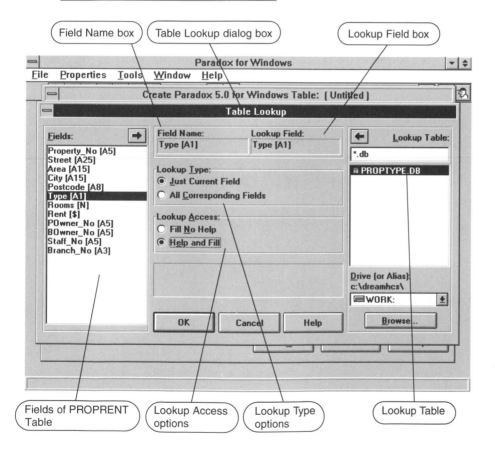

Figure 10.7   The
Table Lookup dialog
box: creating the
Lookup Table for the
Type field of the
PROPRENT table.

therefore appears on the right-hand side.) The Type field is highlighted, and automatically placed in the **Field Name** box. The PROPTYPE table is highlighted and the Type field of this table is automatically placed in the **Lookup Field** box. The other options in this dialog box includes the **Lookup Type** and **Lookup Access** options, which control the way in which the lookup table enters values into the PROPRENT table.

When we attempt to enter data into the Type field of the PROPRENT table, we will see a message displayed in the Status bar area informing us that this field has a lookup table. On accessing the lookup table, we simply highlight the required value in the table and it is automatically entered into the PROPRENT table. The lookup table for the Type field of the PROPRENT table in operation is shown in Figure 10.8.

The major difference between the table lookup facility and referential integrity is that table lookup is primarily a data entry tool. Unlike referential integrity, table lookup does not track or control changes we make to the lookup table. Table lookup ensures that values are copied accurately from one table to another. Referential integrity ensures that the relationships between data in separate tables is not violated.

We continue the process of implementing the relations of the *Dream-Home* case study, originally listed in Appendix 8.7. Once all of the tables are

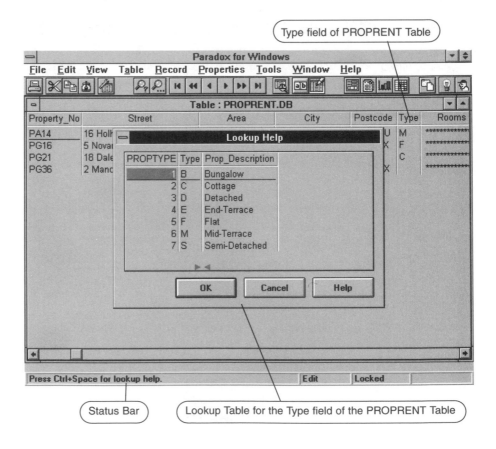

Figure 10.8 Using Lookup Table for the Type field of the PROPRENT table.

created, we begin the process of implementing the referential integrity constraints between these tables.

(5) Defining referential integrity for the PROPRENT table

Referential integrity is an important facility provided by Paradox for Windows, which ensures consistency between related tables. Referential integrity establishes a link between a parent table and a child table through a field that is present in both tables.

We illustrate the process of implementing referential integrity between related tables, again using the PROPRENT table. From Figure 10.1, we see that the PROPRENT table is related to the POWNER, BOWNER, STAFF and BRANCH tables. For example, the PROPRENT (child) table contains a field called Staff_No, which is also present in the STAFF (parent) table, as the primary key. The Staff_No field in the PROPRENT table is the foreign key, which allows these two tables to be joined.

To define referential integrity between two tables, we first open the PROPRENT (child) table and select **Referential Integrity** from the Table Properties section of the Restructure (Create) Table dialog box, as shown in Figure 10.5.

Figure 10.9 shows the Referential Integrity dialog box, which displays

Figure 10.9 The Referential Integrity dialog box: creating referential integrity between the PROPRENT (child) and STAFF (parent) tables.

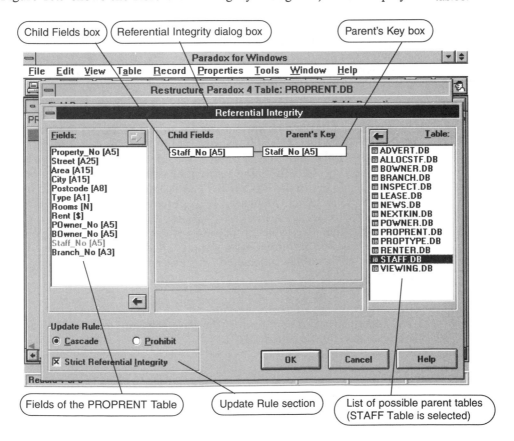

the fields of the PROPRENT table on the left-hand side and the list of possible parent tables on the right-hand side. The Staff_No field is selected and automatically placed in the box below the **Child Fields** label. The STAFF table is selected as the parent table and then the Staff_No field is designated as the linking field, which is placed in the box below the **Parent's Key** label.

Figure 10.1 also describes the update and deletion rules to be implemented on each foreign key of the Property_for_Rent relation. Paradox for Windows has an **Update Rule** section for foreign keys that offers **Cascade** and **Prohibit** options to control the effects of changing the data held in tables associated through referential integrity. The Cascade option causes changes in the parent table to be reflected in the child table. The Prohibit option prevents any changes to the key field of the parent table when there are records in the child table that are dependent on the record that is being altered. Paradox for Windows does not provide options for deletion rules, but simply restricts all deletions from the parent table when there any referencing records in the child table.

We use the Staff_No field of the Property_for_Rent relation to illustrate the process of implementing constraints on a foreign key. Note that the deletion rule for the Staff_No foreign key of this relation was originally **SET NULL**, as shown in Appendix 8.7. However, as mentioned earlier, Paradox for Windows does not provide options for deletion rules, and therefore the logical database design was altered to indicate that this option is not available and has been replaced with the mandatory **RESTRICT** rule, as shown in Figure 10.1.

Although there are no options for the deletion rule, we can select options for the update rule. As described in Figure 10.1, the update rule for the Staff_No field is set to Cascade, as shown in Figure 10.9. This means that if we changed the Staff_No field in the STAFF table, the change is automatically reflected in the appropriate records in the Staff_No field of the PROPRENT table. When we are finished defining the referential integrity between the PROPRENT and STAFF tables, we select OK to name and save it.

The process of defining referential integrity is repeated for the other three foreign keys in the PROPRENT table, namely POwner_No (referencing the POWNER table), BOwner_No (referencing the BOWNER table) and Branch_No (referencing the BRANCH table).

Note that the Table Properties section of the Create Table dialog box shown in Figure 10.5 provides an option called **Dependent Table**. This option lists any child tables associated with a parent table through referential integrity.

Document design of base relations
We document the description of the base relations of the *DreamHome* case study, using the extended DBDL.

Step 4.2 Design enterprise constraints for target DBMS

In this step, we design the enterprise constraint rules for the *DreamHome* case study. Examples of these constraints were given in Appendix 8.6. Most current

DBMSs do not provide support for the implementation of enterprise constraints on tables. Therefore, it is no surprise that Paradox for Windows does not provide this support. To implement such constraints on the *Dream-Home* tables, we must use the Paradox for Windows application language ObjectPAL.

An example of an enterprise constraint for the *DreamHome* case study is that 'The minimum and maximum duration for a single lease period is 3 months to 1 year'. We design and then implement this enterprise rule using ObjectPAL.

We attach the ObjectPAL code shown in Figure 10.10 to a derived field called Lease_Duration. This field is displayed on a customized form for the Lease table, shown in Figure 10.10. The Lease_Duration field calculates and displays the duration of each lease based on the values in the Rent_Start and Rent_Finish fields. The ObjectPAL code implements the enterprise constraint by monitoring the value stored in the Lease_Duration field. If the derived value for the Lease_Duration field is less than three months or greater than one year, an error message will be displayed on screen, warning the user that an enterprise constraint has been violated (Figure 10.11).

We continue the process of designing and implementing enterprise con-

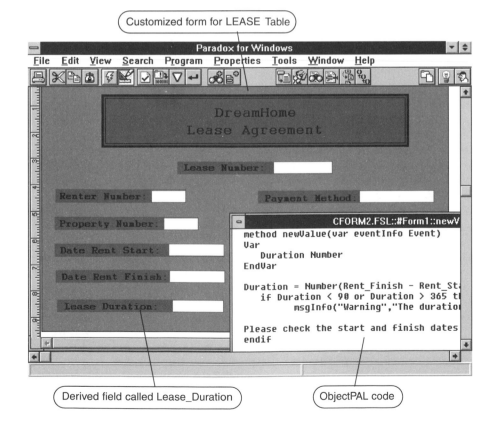

Figure 10.10
Implementing an enterprise constraint using ObjectPAL.

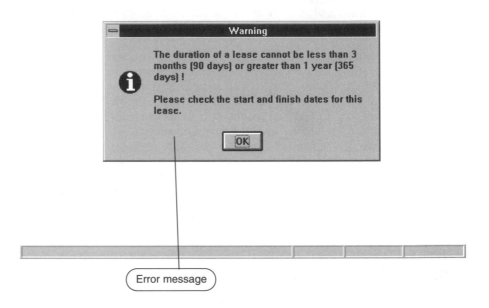

Figure 10.11 Violating an enterprise constraint.

Error message

straints for all of the enterprise constraints specified in the *DreamHome* case study.

Document design of enterprise constraints
We document the design of the enterprise constraints of the *DreamHome* case study, implemented using the Paradox for Windows application language ObjectPAL.

Step 5 Design and Implement Physical Representation

The purpose of this step is to determine the optimal file organizations and access methods for the tables of the *DreamHome* database. In other words, to determine the most efficient way in which to store the tables and records on secondary storage. Most PC-based DBMSs provide only limited facilities to make such alterations to the database structure.

Despite using a PC-based DBMS such as Paradox for Windows, we can still make slight alterations to the database structure (if necessary) to accommodate the demands of the most frequently run transactions. Any decision to change the database structure should be based on analysis of the predicted behaviour of transactions on the database.

There are several ways to determine whether the structure of the

DreamHome database is likely to be sufficient to support all of the required transactions. These include estimating the transaction throughput over a given period of time, the response time for a given transaction, and the amount of disk storage required for the database. We demonstrate some of the approaches to analysing transactions on the database to identify the factors that may influence the performance of the *live* (in other words, operational) *DreamHome* database.

Step 5.1   Analyse transactions

We examine the behaviour of transactions required by *DreamHome*. To demonstrate this process, we use some examples of transactions including:

(A)   Produce a report listing the details of property for rent at each branch office.

(B)   Create and maintain records describing the details of prospective renters at each branch office.

(C)   List the details of viewings by prospective renters to properties for rent, given the details of the property address.

Transaction usage maps
We record the frequency that transactions run on the *DreamHome* database using a transaction usage map. We illustrate the production of such a map using transactions A, B and C, as shown in Figure 10.12.

The number given in the top left-hand corner of each entity is an estimation of the total number of occurrences for each entity. The values assigned to 'avg' and 'max' indicate the estimated average and maximum occurrences of an entity associated with a single occurrence of a related entity.

We can also record the average and maximum numbers of executions over a given period of time for each transaction, and also note the day and time that the transaction is run, including when the maximum load is likely.

For those transactions that needed to access the *DreamHome* database frequently, we continue to examine and document their pattern of operation. To illustrate this approach, we use another example transaction:

(D)   Search for properties for rent at a specific branch office that satisfy a prospective renter's requirements for a particular type of property.

In Figure 10.13, we document the Insert (I), Read (R), Update (U) or Delete (D) activities for transaction D, and also note which attribute or attributes are used to gain access. This is signified as an entry point (E).

Based on the results of the analysis of transactions to run on the *DreamHome* database, we note that many transactions require frequent access to the PROPRENT table.

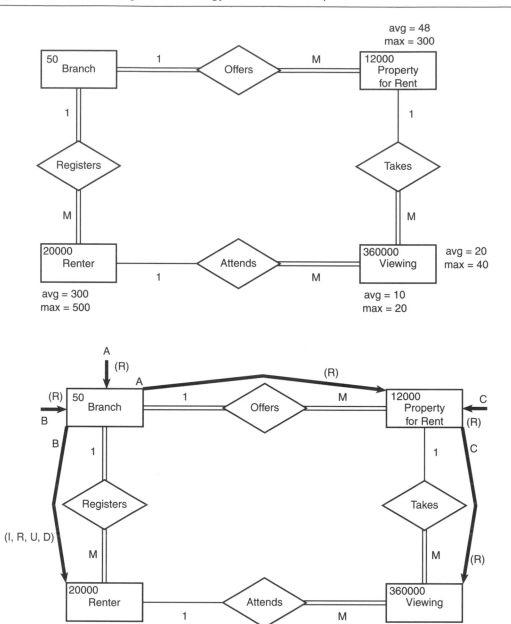

Figure 10.12
Transaction usage
map for transactions
A, B and C.

Step 5.2 Choose file organization

In most cases, PC-based DBMSs such as Paradox for Windows do not provide facilities to enable the designer to alter the file organization of base tables. We are therefore unable to alter the file organization of the *DreamHome* base tables to improve performance or storage space.

Transaction D				
	Day	Time	Load/Hour	
Peak	Every Day	11–14.00	40	
Avg.	Every Day		10	
From entity	To entity	Attributes	Access	No. of times accessed
	Branch			1
		Branch_No	R(E)	
Branch	Property_for_Rent			48–300
		Type (E)*	R	
		Property_No	R	
		Address	R	
		Street	R	
		Area	R	
		Postcode	R	
		Type	R	
		Rooms	R	
		Rent	R	

Figure 10.13
Analysis of
transaction D.

Step 5.3   Choose secondary indexes

Following the analysis of transactions on the *DreamHome* database, we decide to create secondary indexes to improve the performance of the system. The creation of indexes allows Paradox for Windows faster access to tables. We may define indexes when creating or restructuring a table.

Paradox for Windows automatically creates and maintains indexes for fields used as primary keys. We can also define **secondary indexes** for fields that relate tables together, and also to allow various sort orders for the tables. However, we only create secondary indexes that are predicted to improve system performance, as maintaining indexes has resource implications and may have the opposite effect to that sought, by slowing the system down. We therefore decide to create indexes only on fields that are frequently accessed for purposes such as maintaining referential integrity or for specific sorting requirements to answer frequently run queries on the database.

To illustrate the process of creating secondary indexes, we examine the requirements of transactions that access the PROPRENT table. Based on the results of the analysis of the transactions in Step 5.1, we note that the joining of the PROPRENT and STAFF tables is required frequently. To speed up the joining of these tables, we create a secondary index on the Staff_No field (foreign key) of the PROPRENT table.

We create an index by selecting the Secondary Index option from the Table Properties section of the Restructure (Create) Table dialog box, as shown in Figure 10.5.

Figure 10.14 displays the Define Secondary Index dialog box, which lists the fields of the PROPRENT table on the left-hand side of the box. We select the field(s) that we wish to index on, and those fields appear in the **Indexed Fields** box. For example, as shown in Figure 10.14, the Staff_No field is selected and automatically appears in the Indexed Fields box.

There are two **Index Options** for a secondary index: The **Maintained** option requests that Paradox for Windows automatically indexes the table when changes are made to the records; the **Case Sensitive** option allows the index to ignore or differentiate between upper and lowercase letters. As shown in Figure 10.14, we select only the Maintained option for the Staff_No secondary index.

To improve system performance, we repeat the process of defining secondary indexes for the other three foreign keys in the PROPRENT table, namely POwner_No (referencing the POWNER table), BOwner_No (referencing the BOWNER table) and Branch_No (referencing the BRANCH table).

We also decide to create secondary indexes for the PROPRENT table to improve the search and retrieval of property records according to property type or property rent in answering frequently requested customer queries.

We continue the process of examining the transactions on the relations of the *DreamHome* case study to assess whether the creation of secondary indexes is likely to improve the system performance.

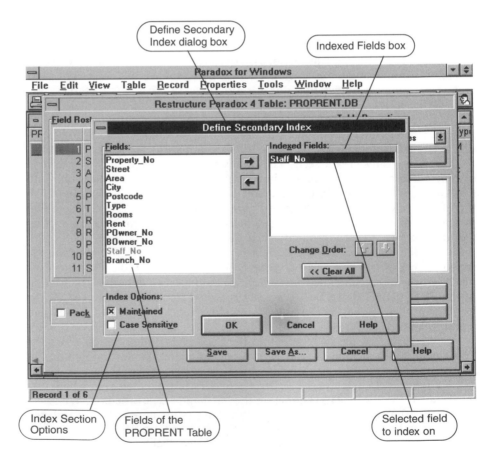

Figure 10.14 The Define Secondary Index dialog box: creating a secondary index for the PROPRENT table on the Staff_No field.

Document choice of secondary indexes
We document the creation of secondary indexes on the tables of the *Dream-Home* database, together with an explanation of why each secondary index was considered to be necessary.

Step 5.4   Consider the introduction of controlled redundancy

After some months, the live *DreamHome* database begins to show performance problems. These problems are particularly acute in transactions that require access to the PROPRENT table. The demand for access to this table has been underestimated, and as a result the performance of the database has begun to fall. A diagrammatic overview of the transactions that require access to the PROPRENT table was previously shown in Figure 8.12. To improve performance of the *DreamHome* database, we consider introducing controlled redundancy into the PROPRENT table, particularly for those transactions that require high levels of access. To illustrate the process of introducing controlled redundancy into a database, we examine the following transactions:

(E)   List property details including the rental deposit for properties at a given branch.

(F)   List property details with the last name of the member of staff responsible for the management of each property.

Step 5.4.1   Consider derived data
Transaction E accesses the PROPRENT table to retrieve the Property_No, City, Type and Rent fields and to display a derived field called Deposit. The deposit for each property is based on twice the value of the rent held in the Rent field. Figure 10.15 shows the implementation of transaction E using the Query-By-Example (QBE) facility of the Paradox for Windows DBMS and also the result of running this query.

We introduce controlled redundancy into the PROPRENT table by restructuring the base table to include an additional field called Deposit, to permanently hold the value of the rental deposit for each property. This removes the requirement to calculate the deposit for each property, every time transaction E is run.

Step 5.4.2   Consider duplicating attributes or joining relations together
Transaction F accesses the STAFF and PROPRENT tables to retrieve the Staff_No and LName fields of the STAFF table and the Property_No, Street, City and Staff_No fields of the PROPRENT table. To achieve this transaction requires joining the STAFF and PROPRENT tables on the Staff_No field. Transaction F is implemented using the QBE shown in Figure 10.16.

We introduce controlled redundancy into the PROPRENT table by placing a copy of the LName field of the STAFF table into the PROPRENT table, to permanently hold the last name of the member of staff responsible for the management of each property. This removes the requirement to join the PROPRENT and STAFF tables every time transaction F is run.

To ensure that the database remains consistent, despite the introduction

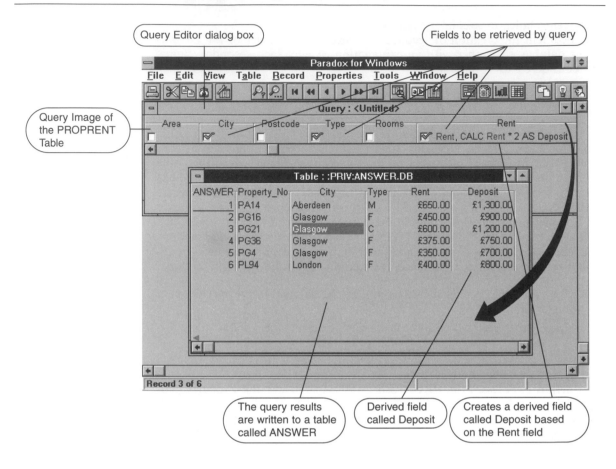

Figure 10.15
Transaction E: QBE
and Answer Table.

of controlled redundancy, we design and implement application programs using ObjectPAL to monitor any change of values in the parent table (STAFF), and to transmit this change to the second copy in the child table (PROPRENT).

The Query-By-Example (QBE) facility of Paradox for Windows will be discussed in detail in Chapter 13.

Step 5.4.3   Document introduction of redundancy

We document the introduction of controlled redundancy into the base relations of the *DreamHome* database, together with the reasons for introducing it. We also update the logical data model to reflect any changes made as a result of denormalization.

Step 5.5   Estimate disk space

In this step, we must estimate the amount of disk space that the *DreamHome* database requires. In Chapter 9, we described in detail the calculation to

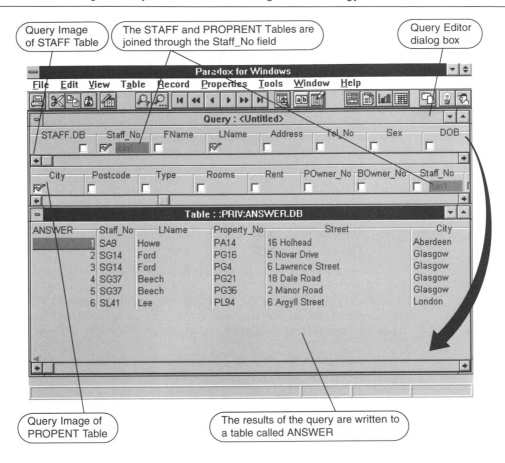

Figure 10.16
Transaction F: QBE
and Answer Table.

estimate the disk space required for the Property_for_Rent relation. To estimate the size of the entire database, we need to repeat the process for all of the tables in the *DreamHome* database. This calculation is important to ensure that we have sufficient disk space for the database when it goes live, and during the lifetime of the system.

Step 6   Design and Implement Security Mechanisms

We design security measures for the *DreamHome* database as specified by the users. This includes creating user views of the database as detailed in Step 1 of the logical database design methodology. In Chapters 5 and 8, we created a local logical data model for the Manager's and Supervisor's view of the *DreamHome* case study, respectively. In this step, we also design access rules for the base relations of the database.

Step 6.1 Design and implement user views

To illustrate the process of creating user views of the *DreamHome* database, we use the Supervisor's view of the Staff relation. Note that this view only requires access to some of the attributes of the Staff base relation, as shown below.

The global view of the Staff relation contains all the attributes required by all user views of this relation. The composition of the global view of the Staff relation (taken from Appendix 8.7) includes:

> **Staff** (Staff_No, FName, LName, Address, Tel_No, Sex, DOB (Date_of_Birth), Position, Salary, Date_Joined, NIN (National Insurance Number), Typing_Speed, Branch_No)
>
> **Primary Key** Staff_No
>
> **Alternate Key** FName, LName, DOB
>
> **Alternate Key** NIN
>
> **Foreign Key** Branch_No **references** Branch(Branch_No)

The Supervisor's view of the Staff relation requires access to only a subset of the attributes of the Staff base relation. The composition of the Supervisor's view of the Staff base relation (taken from Appendix 8.5) includes:

> **Staff** (Staff_No, FName, LName, Address, Tel_No, Sex, DOB (Date of Birth), Job_Title, Typing_Speed, Branch_No)
>
> **Primary Key** Staff_No
>
> **Alternate Key** FName, LName, DOB
>
> **Alternate Key** NIN
>
> **Foreign Key** Branch_No **references** Branch(Branch_No)

The Supervisor's view of the Staff relation requires access to most of the attributes of this relation with the exception of the Salary, Date_Joined and NIN attributes. Also, this view should enable the users (Supervisors) to update the information held in the Staff relation through the view.

We can limit the view of data in a Paradox for Windows table using a live query view from a query to generate an answer set that can be edited. Paradox for Windows writes the edits to the table being queried. We create a live query view for the Supervisor's view of the Staff relation by first selecting the table to be queried, namely the STAFF table, and placing CheckPlus marks in the fields to be included in the live query view. Note that we have also changed the title of the field called Position to Job Title to support the Supervisor's view. We then choose the **Properties, Answer Options, Live Query View**, and then name and save the query. The creation of this live query view, and the result of running this query, is shown in Figure 10.17.

We could have created the Supervisor's view of the Staff relation using the QBE facility. However, the Answer table generated by a QBE query does not maintain a relationship with the original table queried. This means that

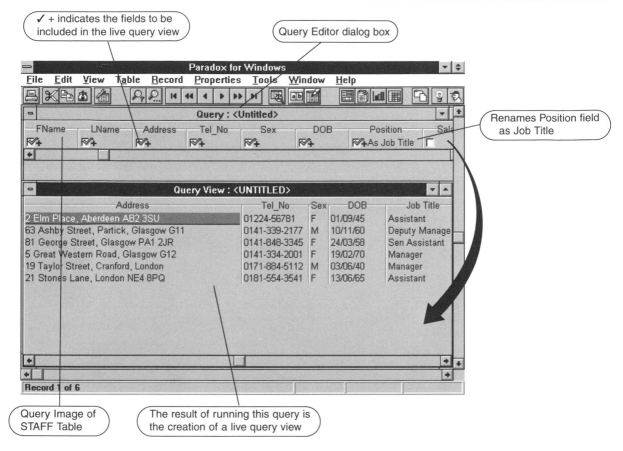

✓ + indicates the fields to be included in the live query view

Query Editor dialog box

Renames Position field as Job Title

Query Image of STAFF Table

The result of running this query is the creation of a live query view

the Supervisor would not be able to edit the contents of the STAFF table using this method.

Figure 10.17
Supervisor's live query view of the Staff relation.

Step 6.2   Design and implement access rules

Similar to most PC DBMSs, Paradox for Windows provides a password facility to restrict access to base tables of the *DreamHome* database. However, there is no facility to protect the database through the implementation of user views.

We illustrate the process of setting up password security to prevent unauthorized access to the tables of the *DreamHome* database by considering the security requirements for the LEASE table. The only users of this table include the Manager and Supervisors at each branch office.

Paradox for Windows provides several levels of access, or *rights* for each table. As shown in Figure 10.5, the **Password Security** facility is available through the Table Properties section of the Restructure (Create) Table dialog box. Once selected, a Password Protection dialog box for the LEASE table is displayed, as shown in Figure 10.18. We simply enter and then verify the

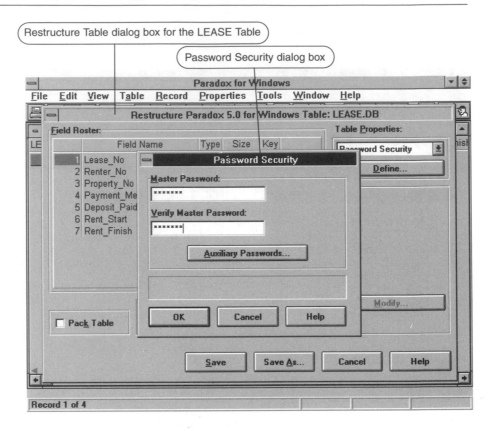

Restructure Table dialog box for the LEASE Table

Password Security dialog box

Figure 10.18
Password security
dialog box: creating a
password for access
to the LEASE table.

password for the table. This level allows an authorized user to view, modify and delete the table.

We continue the process of establishing password security for all the tables of the *DreamHome* database to the level specified by the users.

Step 6.3 Document design of security measures and user views

We document the design of the individual user views and security mechanisms of the *DreamHome* database.

Step 7   Monitor and Tune the Operational System

We continue to monitor the operational *DreamHome* database to ensure that the performance is optimal, and to correct inappropriate design decisions or reflect changing requirements. After some months as a fully operational database, a new requirement is raised by several users of the system. This requirement proposes that the database holds pictures of the properties for rent, together with comments that describe the main features of the property.

We are able to accommodate this request, as the Paradox for Windows DBMS can store non-standard types of information such as graphics and text in binary large object (BLOB) files. We restructure the PROPRENT table to include a field called View specified as a Graphic data type, and a field called Comments specified as a formatted Memo data type. A customized form of the PROPRENT table including the new fields is shown in Figure 10.19.

The View field holds graphical images of properties, created by scanning photographs of the properties for rent and saving the images as BMP (Bit Mapped) graphic files. However, the main problem associated with the storage of graphic images is the large amount of disk space required to store the image files. We will therefore continue to monitor the performance of the *DreamHome* database to ensure that satisfying this new requirement does not compromise the system's performance.

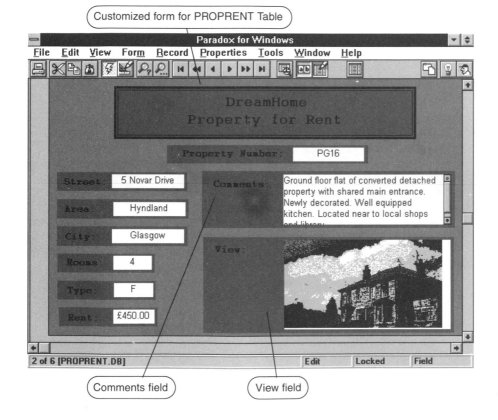

Figure 10.19
PROPRENT
customized form.

Part Three

Database Languages

11 SQL

Chapter Objectives

In this chapter you will learn:

- The purpose and importance of the Structured Query Language (SQL).
- The history and development of SQL.
- How to write an SQL command.
- How to retrieve data from the database using the SELECT statement.
- How to build SQL statements that:
  - Use compound WHERE conditions.
  - Sort query results using ORDER BY.
  - Use the aggregate functions of SQL.
  - Group data using GROUP BY and HAVING.
  - Use subqueries.
  - Join tables together.
  - Perform set operations (UNION, INTERSECT, EXCEPT).
- How to perform database updates using INSERT, UPDATE and DELETE.
- The data types supported by the SQL–92 standard.
- How to create and delete tables and indexes using SQL.
- How Query-By-Example (QBE) compares with SQL.

11.1 Introduction to SQL

In Chapter 3, we described the relational data model and relational languages in some detail. A particular language that has emerged from the development of the relational model is the Structured Query Language, or SQL as it is commonly called. Over the last few years, SQL has become the standard relational database language. In 1986, a standard for SQL was defined by the American National Standards Institute (ANSI), which was subsequently adopted as an international standard by the International Standards Organization (ISO) in 1987 (ISO, 1987). More than 100 database management systems now support SQL, running on various hardware platforms from personal computers to mainframes.

SQL can be used in two ways. The first way is to use SQL *interactively* by entering the statements at a terminal. The second way is to *embed* the SQL statements in a procedural language. Due to the current importance of SQL, we devote two chapters of this book to examining the language in detail, providing a comprehensive, in-depth treatment for both technical and non-technical users including programmers, database professionals and managers. In this chapter, we examine the basics of the language. We concentrate on how to create relations using SQL, how to insert, update and delete data from the relations and perhaps what is more important, how to retrieve data from the relations. In the next chapter, we will examine the more advanced features of the language, including views, integrity constraints, access control and embedded SQL. In the following sections, we outline the objectives of SQL, provide a short history of the language, and discuss why the language is so important to current database applications. In this and the following chapter, we largely concentrate on the ISO definition of the SQL language. However, due to the complexity of this standard, we do not attempt to cover all parts of the language.

11.1.1 Objectives of SQL

Ideally, a database language should allow a user to create the database and relation structures; it should allow a user to perform basic data management tasks, such as the insertion, modification and deletion of data from the relations; and it should allow a user to perform both simple and complex queries to transform the raw data into information. In addition, a database language must perform these tasks with minimal user effort, and its command structure and syntax must be relatively easy to learn. Finally, it must be portable: that is, it must conform to some recognized standard so that we can use the same command structure and syntax when we move from one DBMS to another. SQL is intended to satisfy these requirements.

SQL is an example of a **transform-oriented language**, or a language designed to use relations to transform inputs into required outputs. As a language, SQL has two major components[†]:

[†] The ANSI categorization of SQL divides DDL into two: a DDL for defining the database structure, and a DCL (Data Control Language) for controlling access to the data.

- a Data Definition Language (DDL) for defining the database structure;
- a Data Manipulation Language (DML) for retrieving and updating data.

SQL contains only these definitional and manipulative commands; it does not contain flow control commands. In other words, there are no IF ... THEN ... ELSE, GO TO, DO ... WHILE or other commands to provide a flow of control. These must be implemented using a programming or job-control language, or interactively by the decisions of the user.

SQL is a relatively easy language to learn:

- It is a non-procedural language: you specify *what* information you require, rather than *how* to get it. In other words, SQL does not require you to specify the access methods to the data.
- Like most modern languages, SQL is essentially free-format, which means that parts of statements do not have to be typed at particular locations on the screen.
- The command structure consists of standard English words such as CREATE TABLE, INSERT, SELECT. For example:

      CREATE TABLE staff(sno VARCHAR(5), lname VARCHAR(15),
      salary DECIMAL(7,2));

      INSERT INTO staff
      VALUES ('SG16', 'Brown', 8300);

      SELECT sno, lname, salary
      FROM staff
      WHERE salary > 10000;

- SQL can be used by a range of users including Database Administrators (DBA), management personnel, application programmers, and many other types of end-users.

An international standard now exists for the SQL language (ISO, 1992), making it both the formal and *de facto* standard language for defining and manipulating relational databases.

11.1.2 History of SQL

As stated in Chapter 3, the history of the relational model (and indirectly SQL) started with the publication of the seminal paper by E. F. Codd (1970), while working at IBM's Research Laboratory in San Jose. In 1974, D. Chamberlin, also from the IBM San Jose Laboratory, defined a language called the 'Structured English Query Language', or SEQUEL. A revised version SEQUEL/2 was defined in 1976, but the name was subsequently changed to SQL for legal reasons (the acronym SEQUEL was found to have been used previously by someone else) (Chamberlin and Boyce, 1974; Chamberlin *et al.*, 1976). Today, many people still pronounce SQL as 'see-quel', though the official pronunciation is 's-q-l'.

IBM subsequently produced a prototype DBMS called *System R*, based on SEQUEL/2 (Astrahan *et al.*, 1976). The purpose of this prototype was to validate the feasibility of the relational model. Besides its other successes, one of the most important results that has been attributed to this project was the development of SQL. However, the roots of SQL are in the language SQUARE (Specifying Queries as Relational Expressions), which predates the System R project. SQUARE was designed as a research language to implement relational algebra with English sentences (Boyce *et al.*, 1975).

In the late 1970s, the database system ORACLE was produced by what is now called the ORACLE Corporation, and was probably the first commercial implementation of a relational DBMS based on SQL. INGRES followed shortly afterwards, with a query language called QUEL, which although more 'structured' than SQL, was less English-like. When SQL emerged as the standard database language, INGRES was converted to an SQL-based DBMS. IBM produced its first commercial RDBMS, called SQL/DS, for the DOS/VSE and VM/CMS environments in 1981 and 1982, respectively, and subsequently as DB2 for the MVS environment in 1983.

In 1982, the American National Standards Institute (ANSI) began work on a Relational Database Language (RDL) based on a concept paper from IBM. ISO joined in this work in 1983, and together they defined a standard for SQL. (The name RDL was dropped in 1984, and the draft standard reverted to a form that was more like the existing implementations of SQL.)

The initial ISO standard published in 1987 attracted a considerable degree of criticism. Date, an influential researcher in this area, claimed that important features such as referential integrity rules and certain relational operators had been omitted. He also pointed out that the language was extremely redundant; in other words, there was more than one way to write the same query (Date, 1986, 1987, 1990, 1992). Much of the criticism was valid, and had been recognized by the standards bodies before the standard was published. It was decided, however, that it was more important to release a standard as early as possible to establish a common base from which the language and the implementations could develop than to wait until all the features that people felt should be present could be defined and agreed.

In Section 12.7, we will describe the facilities that were felt to be missing in the earlier versions of the standard and have now been included. We will also list the features that are being considered for inclusion in future versions of the standard. In 1989, ISO published an addendum that defined an 'Integrity Enhancement Feature' (ISO, 1989). In 1992, the first major revision to the ISO standard occurred, sometimes referred to as SQL2 or SQL-92 (ISO, 1992). Although some features have been defined in the standard for the first time, many of these have already been implemented, in part or in a similar form, in one or more of the many SQL implementations.

Features that are added to the standard by the vendors are called **extensions**. For example, the standard specifies six different data types for data in an SQL database. Many implementations supplement this list with a variety of extensions. Each implementation is called a **dialect**. No two dialects are exactly alike, and currently no dialect exactly matches the ISO standard. Moreover, as database vendors introduce new functionality, they are expanding their SQL dialects and moving them even further apart. However, the central core of the SQL language is showing signs of becoming more standardized.

Although SQL was originally an IBM concept, its importance soon motivated other vendors to create their own implementations. Today there are literally hundreds of SQL-based products available, with new products being introduced.

11.1.3 Importance of SQL

SQL is the first and, so far, only standard database language to gain wide acceptance. The only other standard database language, the Network Database Language (NDL), based on the CODASYL network model, has few followers. Nearly every major current vendor provides database products based on SQL or with an SQL interface, and most are represented on at least one of the standard-making bodies. There is a huge investment in the SQL language both by vendors and by users. It has become part of application architectures such as IBM's Systems Application Architecture (SAA), and is the strategic choice of many large and influential organizations, for example, the X/OPEN consortium for UNIX standards. SQL has also become a Federal Information Processing Standard (FIPS), to which conformance is required for all sales of DBMSs to the US Government. The SQL Access Group, a consortium of vendors, is attempting to define a set of enhancements to SQL that will support interoperability across disparate systems.

The SQL standard language is used in other standards, and even influences the development of other standards as a definitional tool. Examples include ISO's Information Resource Dictionary System (IRDS) standard (see Section 2.7.1) and Remote Data Access (RDA) standard. The development of the language is supported by considerable academic interest, providing both a theoretical basis for the language and the techniques needed to implement it successfully. This is especially true in query optimization, distribution of data and security. Hardware support is developing with the availability of database machines. Specialized implementations of SQL are beginning to appear that are directed at new markets, such as On-Line Transaction Processing (OLTP). There are plans for future enhancements including, for example, support for distributed processing, object-oriented programming and user-defined extensions (see Section 12.7).

11.1.4 Terminology

The ISO SQL standard does not use the formal terms of relations, attributes and tuples, instead using the terms tables, columns and rows. In our presentation of SQL we mostly use the ISO terminology. It should also be noted that SQL does not adhere strictly to the definition of the relational model described in Chapter 3. For example, SQL allows the table produced as the result of the SELECT operation to contain duplicate rows; it imposes an ordering on the columns; and it allows the user to order the rows of a table.

11.2 Writing SQL Commands

In this section, we briefly describe the structure of an SQL statement and the notation we use to define the format of the various SQL constructs. An SQL statement consists of **reserved words** and **user-defined words**. Reserved words are a fixed part of the SQL language and have a fixed meaning. They must be spelt *exactly* as required, and cannot be split across lines. User-defined words are made up by the user (according to certain syntax rules), and represent the names of various database objects such as relations, columns, views, indexes, and so on. The words in a statement are also built according to a set of syntax rules. Although the standard does not require it, many dialects of SQL require the use of a statement terminator to mark the end of each SQL statement (usually the semicolon ';' is used).

Most components of an SQL statement are **case insensitive**, which means that letters can be typed in either upper or lower case. The one important exception to this rule is that literal character data must be typed *exactly* as it appears in the database. For example, if we store a person's surname as 'SMITH' and then search for it using the string 'Smith', the record will not be found.

Although SQL is free-format, an SQL statement or set of statements is more readable if indentation and lineation are used. For example:

- Each clause in a statement should begin on a new line.
- The beginning of each clause should line up with the beginning of other clauses.
- If a clause has several parts, they should each appear on a separate line and be indented under the start of the clause to show the relationship.

Throughout this and the next chapter, we use the following extended form of the Backus Naur Form (BNF) notation to define SQL statements:

- Upper case letters are used to represent reserved words and must be spelt exactly as shown.
- Lower case letters are used to represent user-defined words.
- A vertical bar (|) indicates a **choice** among alternatives; for example, a | b | c.
- Curly braces indicate a **required element**: for example, {a}.
- Square brackets indicate an **optional element**: for example, [a].
- An ellipsis (...) is used to indicate **optional repetition** of an item zero or more times. For example:

     {a|b} [,c ...]

  means either a or b followed by zero or more repetitions of c separated by commas.

In practice, the DDL statements are used to create the database structure (that is, the tables), and then the DML statements are used to populate and query the tables. However, in this chapter we present the DML before the DDL statements to reflect the relative importance of DML statements to the general user.

11.3 Data Manipulation

This section looks at the available SQL DML statements, namely:

- SELECT   To query data in the database.
- INSERT   To insert data into a table.
- UPDATE   To update data in a table.
- DELETE   To delete data from a table.

Due to the complexity of the SELECT statement and the relative simplicity of the other DML statements, we devote most of this section to the SELECT statement and its various formats. We begin by considering simple queries, and successively add more complexity to show how more complicated queries that use sorting, grouping, aggregates and also queries on multiple tables can be generated. We end the section by considering the INSERT, UPDATE and DELETE statements.

We illustrate the SQL statements using the instance of the *DreamHome* case study shown in Figure 3.3, which consists of the following tables:

Branch	(Bno, Street, Area, City, Pcode, Tel_No, Fax_No)
Staff	(Sno, FName, LName, Address, Tel_No, Position, Sex, DOB, Salary, NIN, Bno)
Property_for_Rent	(Pno, Street, Area, City, Pcode, Type, Rooms, Rent, Ono, Sno, Bno)
Renter	(Rno, FName, LName, Address, Tel_No, Pref_Type, Max_Rent)
Owner	(Ono, FName, LName, Address, Tel_No)
Viewing	(Rno, Pno, Date, Comment)

Literals

Before we discuss the SQL DML statements, it is necessary to understand the concept of **literals**. Literals are **constants** that are used in SQL statements. There are different forms of literals for every data type supported by SQL (see Section 11.4.2). However, for simplicity, we can distinguish between literals that are enclosed in single quotes and those that are not. All non-numeric data values must be enclosed in single quotes; all numeric data values must not be enclosed in single quotes. For example, we could use literals to insert data into a table:

INSERT INTO property_for_rent(pno, street, area, city, pcode, type,
                              rooms, rent, ono, sno, bno)

VALUES ('PA14', '16 Holhead', 'Dee', 'Aberdeen', 'AB7 5SU', 'House', 6,
650.00, 'CO46', 'SA9', 'B7');

The value in column Rooms is an integer literal and the value in column Rent
is a decimal number literal; they are not enclosed in single quotes. All other
columns are character strings and are enclosed in single quotes.

11.3.1 Simple Queries

The purpose of the SELECT statement is to retrieve and display data from
one or more database tables. It is an extremely powerful command capable
of performing the equivalent of the relational algebra's *selection*, *projection* and *join* in a single statement (see Section 3.4.1). SELECT is the most
frequently used SQL command. The general form of the SELECT statement
is:

SELECT   [DISTINCT | ALL] {* | [column_expression [AS new_name]] [, ...]}

FROM   table_name [alias] [, . . .]

[WHERE   condition]

[GROUP BY column_list]   [HAVING condition]

[ORDER BY column_list]

Column_expression represents a column name or an expression; *table_name* is the name of an existing database table or view that you have access to; and *alias* is an optional abbreviation for *table_name*. The sequence of processing in a SELECT statement is:

FROM	Specifies the table or tables to be used.
WHERE	Filters the rows subject to some condition.
GROUP BY	Forms groups of rows with the same column value.
HAVING	Filters the groups subject to some condition.
SELECT	Specifies which columns are to appear in the output.
ORDER BY	Specifies the order of the output.

The order of the clauses in the SELECT statement *cannot* be changed. The
only two mandatory clauses are the first two: SELECT and FROM; the
remainder are optional. The SELECT operation is **closed**: the result of a query
on a table is another table (see Section 3.4.1). There are many variations of
this command; however, the following examples illustrate the main variations
of this statement.

Retrieve all rows

Example 11.1:   Retrieve all columns, all rows _____

List full details of all staff.

Since there are no restrictions specified in this query, the WHERE clause is unnecessary and all columns are required. We write this query as:

      SELECT sno, fname, lname, address, tel_no, position, sex, dob, salary,
                nin, bno
      FROM   staff;

Since many SQL retrievals require all columns of a table, there is a quick way of expressing 'all columns' in SQL, using an asterisk (*) in place of the column names. The following statement is an equivalent and shorter way of expressing this query:

      SELECT *

      FROM staff;

The result table in either case is shown in Table 11.1.

Table 11.1   Result table for Example 11.1.

sno	fname	lname	address	tel_no	position	sex	dob	salary	nin	bno
SL21	John	White	19 Taylor St, Cranford, London	0171–884–5112	Manager	M	1–Oct–45	30000.00	WK442011B	B5
SG37	Ann	Beech	81 George St, Glasgow PA1 2JR	0141–848–3345	Snr Asst	F	10–Nov–60	12000.00	WL432514C	B3
SG14	David	Ford	63 Ashby St, Partick, Glasgow G11	0141–339–2177	Deputy	M	24–Mar–58	18000.00	WL220658D	B3
SA9	Mary	Howe	2 Elm Pl, Aberdeen AB2 3SU		Assistant	F	19–Feb–70	9000.00	WM532187D	B7
SG5	Susan	Brand	5 Gt Western Rd, Glasgow G12	0141–334–2001	Manager	F	3–Jun–40	24000.00	WK588932E	B3
SL41	Julie	Lee	28 Malvern St, London NW2	0181–554–3541	Assistant	F	13–Jun–65	9000.00	WA290573K	B5

(6 rows)

Example 11.2:   Retrieve specific columns, all rows _____

Produce a list of salaries for all staff, showing only the staff number, Sno, the first and last names and the salary details.

      SELECT sno, fname, lname, salary

      FROM staff;

In this example, a new table is created from Staff containing only the designated columns Sno, FName, LName and Salary, in the specified order. The result of this operation is shown in Table 11.2.

Table 11.2 Result table for Example 11.2.

sno	fname	lname	salary
SL21	John	White	30000.00
SG37	Ann	Beech	12000.00
SG14	David	Ford	18000.00
SA9	Mary	Howe	9000.00
SG5	Susan	Brand	24000.00
SL41	Julie	Lee	9000.00

(6 rows)

Example 11.3:   Use of DISTINCT

Table 11.3 (a) Result table for Example 11.3 with duplicates.

pno
PA14
PG4
PG4
PA14
PG36

(5 rows)

List the property numbers of all properties that have been viewed.

    SELECT pno
    FROM viewing;

The result table is shown in Table 11.3.

Notice that there are several duplicates because, unlike the relational algebra *projection* operation, SELECT does not eliminate duplicates when it projects over a column or columns. To eliminate the duplicates, we use the DISTINCT keyword. Rewriting the query as:

    SELECT DISTINCT pno
    FROM viewing;

we get the result table shown in Table 11.3 (b) with the duplicates eliminated:

Table 11.3 (b) Result table for Example 11.3 with duplicates eliminated.

pno
PA14
PG4
PG36

(3 rows)

Example 11.4   Calculated fields _____

Produce a list of monthly salaries for all staff, showing the staff number, the first and last names and the salary details.

    SELECT sno, fname, lname, salary/12
    FROM staff;

This query is almost identical to Example 11.2, with the exception that monthly salaries are required. In this case, the desired result can be obtained by simply dividing the salary by 12, giving the result table in Table 11.4.

This is an example of the use of a **calculated**, **computed** or **derived** field. In general, to use a calculated field, you specify an SQL expression in the SELECT list. An SQL expression can involve addition, subtraction, multiplication and division, and parentheses can be used to build complex expressions. More than one table column can be used in a calculated column; however, the columns referenced in an arithmetic expression must have a numeric type.

Table 11.4   Result table for Example 11.4.

sno	fname	lname	col4
SL21	John	White	2500.00
SG37	Ann	Beech	1000.00
SG14	David	Ford	1500.00
SA9	Mary	Howe	750.00
SG5	Susan	Brand	2000.00
SL41	Julie	Lee	750.00

(6 rows)

The fourth column of this result table has been output as *col4*. Normally, a column in the result table takes its name from the corresponding column of the database table from which it has been retrieved. However, in this case, SQL does not know how to label the column. Some dialects give the column a name corresponding to its position in the table (for example, col4); some may leave the column name blank or use the expression entered in the SELECT list. The ISO standard allows the column to be named using an AS clause. In the previous example, we could have written:

    SELECT sno, fname, lname, salary/12 AS monthly_salary
    FROM staff;

In this case, the column heading of the result table would be *monthly_salary* rather than *col4*.

Row selection (WHERE clause)

The above examples show the use of the SELECT statement to retrieve all rows from a table. However, we often need to restrict the rows that are retrieved. This can be achieved with the WHERE clause, which consists of the keyword WHERE followed by a search condition that specifies the rows to be retrieved. The five basic search conditions (or **predicates** using the ISO terminology) are as follows:

- *Comparison.* Compare the value of one expression to the value of another expression.
- *Range.* Test whether the value of an expression falls within a specified range of values.
- *Set membership.* Test whether the value of an expression equals one of a set of values.
- *Pattern match.* Test whether a string matches a specified pattern.
- *Null.* Test whether a column has a null (unknown) value.

We now present examples of each of these types of search conditions.

Example 11.5:   Comparison search condition

List all staff with a salary greater than £10,000.

```
SELECT sno, fname, lname, position, salary
FROM staff
WHERE salary > 10000;
```

Here, the table is Staff and the predicate is salary > 10000. The selection creates a new table containing only those Staff rows with a salary greater than £10,000. The result of this operation is shown in Table 11.5.

Table 11.5   Result table for Example 11.5.

sno	fname	lname	position	salary
SL21	John	White	Manager	30000.00
SG37	Ann	Beech	Snr Asst	12000.00
SG14	David	Ford	Deputy	18000.00
SG5	Susan	Brand	Manager	24000.00

(4 rows)

In SQL, the following simple comparison operators are available:

=	equals
<	is less than
>	is greater than
< =	is less than or equal to
> =	is greater than or equal to
< >	is not equal to (ISO standard)
! =	is not equal to (allowed in some dialects)

More complex predicates can be generated using the logical operators **AND**, **OR** and **NOT,** with parentheses (if needed or desired) to show the order of evaluation. The rules for evaluating a conditional expression are:

- An expression is evaluated left to right.
- Subexpressions in brackets are evaluated first.
- NOTs are evaluated before ANDs and ORs.
- ANDs are evaluated before ORs.

The use of parentheses is always recommended to remove any possible ambiguities.

Example 11.6:   Compound comparison search condition _____

List the addresses of all branch offices in London or Glasgow.

        SELECT bno, street, area, city, pcode
        FROM branch
        WHERE city = 'London' OR city = 'Glasgow';

In this example, the logical operator OR is used in the WHERE clause to find the branches in London (city = 'London') *or* in Glasgow (city = 'Glasgow'). The result table is shown in Table 11.6.

Table 11.6   Result table for Example 11.6.

bno	street	area	city	pcode
B5	22 Deer Rd	Sidcup	London	SW1 4EH
B3	163 Main St	Partick	Glasgow	G11 9QX
B2	56 Clover Dr		London	NW10 6EU

(3 rows)

Example 11.7: Range search condition (BETWEEN/NOT BETWEEN) _____

List all staff with a salary between £20,000 and £30,000.

```
SELECT sno, fname, lname, position, salary
FROM staff
WHERE salary BETWEEN 20000 AND 30000;
```

The BETWEEN test includes the endpoints of the range, so any members of staff with a salary of £20,000 or £30,000 would be included in the result. The result table is shown in Table 11.7.

Table 11.7 Result table for Example 11.7.

sno	fname	lname	position	salary
SL21	John	White	Manager	30000.00
SG5	Susan	Brand	Manager	24000.00

(2 rows)

There is also a negated version of the range test (NOT BETWEEN) which checks for values outside the range. The BETWEEN test does not add much to the expressive power of SQL, because it can be expressed equally well using two comparison tests. We could have expressed the above query as:

```
SELECT sno, fname, lname, position, salary
FROM staff
WHERE salary > = 20000 AND salary < = 30000;
```

However, you may find the BETWEEN test is a simpler way to express a search condition when you are considering a range of values.

Example 11.8: Set membership search condition (IN/NOT IN) ___

List all Managers and Deputy Managers.

```
SELECT sno, fname, lname, position
FROM staff
WHERE position IN ('Manager', 'Deputy');
```

The set membership test (IN) tests whether a data value matches one of a list of values, in our case either 'Manager' or 'Deputy'. The result table is shown in Table 11.8.

Table 11.8   Result table for Example 11.8.

sno	fname	lname	position
SL21	John	White	Manager
SG14	David	Ford	Deputy
SG5	Susan	Brand	Manager

(3 rows)

There is a negated version (NOT IN) which can be used to check for data values that do not lie in a specific list of values. Like BETWEEN, the IN test does not add much to the expressive power of SQL. We could have expressed the above query as:

SELECT sno, fname, lname, position
FROM staff
WHERE position = 'Manager' OR position = 'Deputy';

However, the IN test provides a more efficient way of expressing the search condition, particularly if the set contains many values.

Example 11.9:   Pattern match search condition (LIKE/NOT LIKE) _____

Find all staff with the string 'Glasgow' in their address.

For this query, we must search for the string 'Glasgow' appearing somewhere within the Address column of the Staff table. SQL has two special pattern matching symbols:

%	percent character represents any sequence of zero or more characters (*wildcard*);
_	underscore character represents any single character.

All other characters in the pattern represent themselves. For example:

- address LIKE 'H%' means the first character must start with *H*, but the rest of the string can be anything.
- address LIKE 'H___' means that there must be exactly four characters in the string, the first of which must be an *H*.
- address LIKE '%e' means any sequence of characters, of length at least 1, with the last character an *e*.

- address LIKE '%Glasgow%' means a sequence of characters of any length containing *Glasgow*.
- address NOT LIKE 'H%' means the name cannot start with an *H*.

If the search string can include the pattern-matching character itself, we can use an **escape character** to represent the pattern-matching character. For example, to check for the string '15%', we can use the predicate:

LIKE '15#%' ESCAPE '#'

Using the pattern-matching search condition of SQL, we can find all staff with the string 'Glasgow' in their address using the following query:

SELECT sno, fname, lname, address, salary

FROM staff

WHERE address LIKE '%Glasgow%';

The result table is shown in Table 11.9.

Table 11.9 Result table for Example 11.9.

sno	fname	lname	address	salary
SG37	Ann	Beech	81 George St, Glasgow PA1 2JR	12000.00
SG14	David	Ford	63 Ashby St, Partick, Glasgow G11	18000.00
SG5	Susan	Brand	5 Gt Western Rd, Glasgow G12	24000.00

(3 rows)

Example 11.10: NULL search condition (IS NULL/IS NOT NULL)

List the details of all viewings on property PG4 where a comment has not been supplied.

From the Viewing table of Figure 3.3, we can see that there are two viewings for property PG4: one with a comment, the other without a comment. In this simple example, you may think that the latter record could be accessed by using one of the search conditions:

(pno = 'PG4' AND comment = '   ') *or*
(pno = 'PG4' AND comment 〈 〉 'too remote')

However, neither of these conditions would work. A null comment is considered to have an unknown value, so we cannot test whether it is equal or not equal to another string. If we tried to execute the SELECT statement using either of these compound conditions, we would get an empty result table. Instead, we have to test for the null explicitly using the special keyword IS NULL:

Table 11.10   Result table for Example 11.10.

> SELECT rno, date
> FROM viewing
> WHERE pno = 'PG4' AND comment IS NULL;

rno	date
CR76	20–May–95

The result table is shown in Table 11.10.

(1 row)

The negated version (IS NOT NULL) can be used to test for values that are not null.

11.3.2   Sorting Results (ORDER BY Clause)

In general, the rows of an SQL query result table are not arranged in any particular order. However, we can sort the results of a query using the ORDER BY clause in the SELECT statement. The ORDER BY clause consists of a list of **column identifiers** that the result is to be sorted on, separated by commas. A column identifier may be either a column name or a column number[†] that identifies an element of the SELECT list by its position within the list, 1 being the first (left-most) element in the list, 2 the second element in the list, and so on. Column numbers could be used if the column to be sorted on is an expression and no AS clause is specified to assign the column a name that can subsequently be referenced. The ORDER BY clause allows us to order the retrieved records in ascending (ASC) or descending (DESC) order on any column or combination of columns, regardless of whether that column appears in the result. However, some dialects insist that the ORDER BY elements appear in the SELECT list. In either case, the ORDER BY clause must always be the last clause of the SELECT statement.

Example 11.11:   Single column ordering

Produce a list of salaries for all staff, arranged in descending order of salary.

> SELECT sno, fname, lname, salary
> FROM staff
> ORDER BY salary DESC;

This example is very similar to Example 11.2. The difference in this case is that the output is to be arranged in descending order of salary. This is achieved by adding the ORDER BY clause to the end of the SELECT statement, specifying Salary as the column to be sorted and DESC to indicate that the order is to be descending. In this case, we get the result table shown in Table 11.11.

[†] Column numbers are a deprecated feature of the ISO standard, and should not be used.

Table 11.11 Result table for Example 11.11.

sno	fname	lname	salary
SL21	John	White	30000.00
SG5	Susan	Brand	24000.00
SG14	David	Ford	18000.00
SG37	Ann	Beech	12000.00
SA9	Mary	Howe	9000.00
SL41	Julie	Lee	9000.00

(6 rows)

Note that we could have expressed the ORDER BY clause as: ORDER BY 4 DESC. The 4 relates to the fourth column name in the SELECT list, namely Salary.

It is possible to include more than one element in the ORDER BY clause. The **major sort key** determines the overall order of the result table. In the previous example, the major sort key is Salary. If the major sort key is unique, there is no need for additional keys to control the sort. However, if the major sort key is not unique, there may be multiple rows in the result table with the same value for the major sort key. In this case, it may be desirable to order rows with the same value for the major sort key by some additional sort key. If a second element appears in the ORDER BY clause, it is called a **minor sort key**.

Example 11.12: Multiple column ordering

Produce an abbreviated list of properties arranged in order of property type.

```
SELECT pno, type, rooms, rent
FROM property_for_rent
ORDER BY type;
```

In this case, we get the result table shown in Table 11.12(a).

Table 11.12 (a) Result table for Example 11.12 with one sort key.

pno	type	rooms	rent
PL94	Flat	4	400
PG4	Flat	3	350
PG36	Flat	3	375
PG16	Flat	4	450
PA14	House	6	650
PG21	House	5	600

(6 rows)

There are four flats in this list. As we did not specify any minor sort key, the system arranges these rows in any order it chooses. To arrange the properties in order of rent, we specify a minor order, as follows:

> SELECT pno, type, rooms, rent
>
> FROM property_for_rent
>
> ORDER BY type, rent DESC;

Now, the result is ordered first by property type, in ascending alphabetic order (ASC being the default setting), and within property type, in descending order of Rent. In this case, we get the result table shown in Table 11.12(b).

Table 11.12(b)   Result table for Example 11.12 with two sort keys.

pno	type	rooms	rent
PG16	Flat	4	450
PL94	Flat	4	400
PG36	Flat	3	375
PG4	Flat	3	350
PA14	House	6	650
PG21	House	5	600

(6 rows)

The ISO standard specifies that nulls in a column or expression sorted with ORDER BY should be treated as either less than all non-null values or greater than all non-null values. The choice is left to the DBMS implementor.

11.3.3   Using the SQL Aggregate Functions

The ISO standard defines five **aggregate functions**:

COUNT	Returns the number of values in a specified column.
SUM	Returns the sum of the values in a specified column.
AVG	Returns the average of the values in a specified column.
MIN	Returns the smallest value in a specified column.
MAX	Returns the largest value in a specified column.

These functions operate on a single column of a table and return a single value. COUNT, MIN and MAX apply to both numeric and non-numeric fields, but SUM and AVG may be used on numeric fields only. Apart from COUNT(*), each function eliminates nulls first and operates only on the remaining non-null values. COUNT(*) is a special use of COUNT. Its purpose is to count all the rows of a table, regardless of whether nulls or duplicate values occur.

If we want to eliminate duplicates before the function is applied, we use the keyword DISTINCT before the column name in the function. The ISO standard allows the keyword ALL to be specified if we do not want to eliminate duplicates, although ALL is assumed if nothing is specified. DISTINCT has no effect with the MIN and MAX functions. However, it may have an effect on the result of SUM or AVG, so consideration must be given to whether duplicates should be included or excluded in the computation. In addition, DISTINCT can be specified only once in a query.

It is important to note that an aggregate function can be used only in the SELECT list and in the HAVING clause (see Section 11.3.4). It is incorrect to use it elsewhere. If the SELECT list includes an aggregate function and no GROUP BY clause is being used to group data together (see Section 11.3.4), then no item in the SELECT list can include any reference to a column unless that column is the argument to an aggregate function. For example, the following query is illegal:

    SELECT sno, COUNT(salary)
    FROM staff;

because the SELECT list contains both a column name (Sno) and a separate aggregate function (COUNT), without a GROUP BY clause being used.

Example 11.13: Use of COUNT(*)

How many properties cost more than £350 per month to rent?

    SELECT COUNT(*) AS count
    FROM property_for_rent
    WHERE rent > 350;

The result table is shown in Table 11.13.

Table 11.13 Result table for Example 11.13.

count
5

(1 row)

Example 11.14: Use of COUNT(DISTINCT)

How many different properties were viewed in May 1995?

    SELECT COUNT(DISTINCT pno) AS count
    FROM viewing
    WHERE date BETWEEN '1-May-95' AND '31-May-95';

The result table is shown in Table 11.14.

Table 11.14   Result table
for Example 11.14.

count
2

(1 row)

Example 11.15:   Use of COUNT and SUM _____

Find the total number of Managers and the sum of their salaries.

    SELECT COUNT(sno) AS count, SUM(salary) AS sum
    FROM staff
    WHERE position = 'Manager';

Restricting the query to Managers is achieved using the WHERE clause. The
number of Managers and the sum of their salaries can be found by using the
COUNT and the SUM functions respectively on this restricted set. The result
table is shown in Table 11.15.

Table 11.15   Result table
for Example 11.15.

count	sum
2	54000.00

(1 row)

Example 11.16:   Use of MIN, MAX, AVG _____

Find the minimum, maximum and average staff salary.

    SELECT MIN(salary) AS min, MAX(salary) AS max, AVG(salary) AS avg
    FROM staff;

In this example, we wish to consider all staff, and therefore do not require
a WHERE clause. The required values can be calculated using the MIN, MAX
and AVG functions based on the Salary column. The result table is shown in
Table 11.16.

Table 11.16 Result table for Example 11.16.

min	max	avg
9000.00	30000.00	17000.00

(1 row)

11.3.4   Grouping Results (GROUP BY Clause)

The above summary queries are similar to the totals at the bottom of a report. They condense all of the detailed data in the report into a single summary row of data. However, it is often useful to have subtotals in reports. We can use the GROUP BY clause of the SELECT statement to do this. A query that includes the GROUP BY clause is called a **grouped query**, because it groups the data from the SELECT table(s) and produces a single summary row for each group. The columns named in the GROUP BY clause are called the **grouping columns**. The ISO standard requires that the SELECT clause and the GROUP BY clause be closely integrated. When GROUP BY is used, each item in the SELECT list must be **single-valued per group**. Further, the SELECT clause may only contain:

- column names,
- aggregate functions,
- constants,
- an expression involving combinations of the above.

All column names in the SELECT list must appear in the GROUP BY clause unless the name is used only in an aggregate function. The contrary is not true: there may be column names in the GROUP BY clause that do not appear in the SELECT list. When the WHERE clause is used with GROUP BY, the WHERE clause is applied first, then groups are formed from the remaining rows that satisfy the search condition.

   The ISO standard considers two nulls to be equal for purposes of the GROUP BY clause. If two rows have nulls in the same grouping columns and identical values in all of the non-null grouping columns, they are combined into the same group.

Example 11.17:   Use of GROUP BY _____

Find the number of staff working in each branch and the total of their salaries.

    SELECT bno, COUNT(sno) AS count, SUM(salary) AS sum
    FROM staff
    GROUP BY bno
    ORDER BY bno;

It is not necessary to include the column names Sno and Salary in the GROUP BY list because they appear only in the SELECT list within aggregate functions. On the other hand, Bno is not associated with an aggregate function and so must appear in the GROUP BY list. The result table is shown in Table 11.17.

Table 11.17 Result table for Example 11.17.

bno	count	sum
B3	3	54000.00
B5	2	39000.00
B7	1	9000.00

(3 rows)

Conceptually, SQL performs the query as follows:

1. SQL divides the staff into groups according to their respective branch numbers. Within each group, all staff have the same branch number. In this example, we get three groups:

bno	sno	salary		COUNT(sno)	SUM(salary)
B3	SG37	12000.00			
B3	SG14	18000.00		3	54000.00
B3	SG5	24000.00			
B5	SL21	30000.00			
B5	SL41	9000.00		2	39000.00
B7	SA9	9000.00		1	9000.00

2. For each group, SQL computes the number of staff members and sums the values in the Salary column to get the total of their salaries. SQL generates a single summary row in the query result for each group.

3. Finally, the result is sorted in ascending order of branch number, Bno.

The SQL2 standard allows the SELECT list to contain nested queries (see Section 11.3.5). Therefore, we could also express the above query as:

```
SELECT bno,   (SELECT COUNT(sno) AS count
              FROM staff s
              WHERE s.bno = b.bno),
              (SELECT SUM(salary) AS sum
              FROM staff s
              WHERE s.bno = b.bno)
FROM branch b
ORDER BY bno;
```

With this version of the query, however, the two aggregate values are produced for each branch office in Branch, in some cases possibly with zero values.

Restricting grouping (HAVING clause)

The HAVING clause is designed for use with the GROUP BY clause to restrict the **groups** that appear in the final result table. Although similar in syntax, HAVING and WHERE serve different purposes. The WHERE clause filters individual **rows** going into the final result table, whereas HAVING filters **groups** going into the final result table. The ISO standard requires that column names used in the HAVING clause must also appear in the GROUP BY list or be contained within an aggregate function. In practice, the search condition in the HAVING clause always includes at least one aggregate function, otherwise the search condition could be moved to the WHERE clause and applied to individual rows. (Remember that aggregate functions cannot be used in the WHERE clause.)

The HAVING clause is not a necessary part of SQL – any query expressed using a HAVING clause can always be rewritten without the HAVING clause.

Example 11.18:   Use of HAVING

For each branch office with more than one member of staff, find the number of staff working in each branch and the sum of their salaries.

    SELECT bno, COUNT(sno) AS count, SUM(salary) AS sum
    FROM staff
    GROUP BY bno
    HAVING COUNT(sno) > 1
    ORDER BY bno;

This is similar to the previous example with the additional restriction that we want to consider only those groups (that is, branches) with more than one member of staff. This restriction applies to the groups and so the HAVING clause is required. The result table is shown in Table 11.18.

Table 11.18   Result table for Example 11.18.

bno	count	sum
B3	3	54000.00
B5	2	39000.00

(2 rows)

11.3.5   Subqueries

Some SQL statements can have a complete SELECT statement embedded within them. The results of this **inner** SELECT statement (or **subselect**) are used in the **outer** statement to help determine the contents of the final result. A subselect can be used in the WHERE and HAVING clauses of an outer SELECT statement, where it is called a **subquery** or **nested query**. Subselects may also appear in INSERT, UPDATE and DELETE statements (see Section 11.3.10).

Example 11.19:   Using a subquery with equality _____

List the staff who work in the branch at '163 Main St'.

        SELECT sno, fname, lname, position
        FROM staff
        WHERE bno =
                    (SELECT bno
                    FROM branch
                    WHERE street = '163 Main St');

The inner SELECT statement (SELECT bno FROM branch ...) finds the branch number that corresponds to the branch with street name '163 Main St' (there will be only one such branch number). Having obtained this branch number, the outer SELECT statement then retrieves the details of all staff who work at this branch. In other words, the inner SELECT returns a result table containing a single value 'B3', corresponding to the branch at '163 Main St'. The outer SELECT then becomes:

        SELECT sno, fname, lname, position
        FROM staff
        WHERE bno = 'B3';

The result table is shown in Table 11.19.

Table 11.19   Result table for Example 11.19.

sno	fname	lname	position
SG37	Ann	Beech	Snr Asst
SG14	David	Ford	Deputy
SG5	Susan	Brand	Manager

(3 rows)

We can think of the subquery as producing a temporary table with results that can be accessed and used by the outer statement. A subquery can be used immediately following a relational operator (that is, $=$, $<$, $>$, $<=$, $>=$, $<>$) in a WHERE clause or a HAVING clause. The subquery itself is always enclosed in parentheses.

Example 11.20:   Using a subquery with an aggregate function

List all staff whose salary is greater than the average salary.

```
SELECT sno, fname, lname, position, salary
FROM staff
WHERE salary >
              (SELECT avg(salary)
              FROM staff);
```

First, note that we cannot write 'WHERE salary > avg(salary)' because aggregate functions cannot be used in the WHERE clause. Instead, we use a subquery to find the average salary, and then use the outer SELECT statement to find those staff with a salary greater than this average. In other words, the subquery returns the average salary as £17,000. The outer query is reduced then to:

```
SELECT sno, fname, lname, position, salary
FROM staff
WHERE salary > 17000;
```

The result table is shown in Table 11.20.

Table 11.20   Result table for Example 11.20.

sno	fname	lname	position	salary
SL21	John	White	Manager	30000.00
SG14	David	Ford	Deputy	18000.00
SG5	Susan	Brand	Manager	24000.00

(3 rows)

The following rules apply to subqueries:

(1)   The ORDER BY clause may not be used in a subquery (although it may be used in the outermost SELECT statement).

(2)   The subquery SELECT list must consist of a single column name or expression, except for subqueries that use the keyword EXISTS (see Section 11.3.8).

(3)   By default, column names in a subquery refer to the table name in the FROM clause of the subquery. It is possible to refer to a table in a

FROM clause in an outer query by qualifying the column name (see below).

(4)   When a subquery is one of the two operands involved in a comparison, the subquery must appear on the right-hand side of the comparison. For example, it would be incorrect to express the last example as:

>   SELECT sno, fname, lname, position, salary
>
>   FROM staff
>
>   WHERE (SELECT avg(salary) FROM staff) < salary;

because the subquery appears on the left-hand side of the comparison with Salary.

(5)   A subquery may not be used as an operand in an expression.

Example 11.21:   Nested subqueries; use of IN _____

List the properties that are handled by staff that work at the branch at '163 Main St'.

>   SELECT pno, street, area, city, pcode, type, rooms, rent
>
>   FROM property_for_rent
>
>   WHERE sno IN
>   (SELECT sno
>   FROM staff
>   WHERE bno =
>   (SELECT bno
>   FROM branch
>   WHERE street = '163 Main St'));

Working from the innermost query outwards, the first query selects the number of the branch at '163 Main St'. The second query then selects those staff that work at this branch number. In this case, there may be more than one such row found, and so we cannot use the equality condition (=) in the outermost query. Instead, we use the IN keyword. The outermost query then retrieves the details of the properties that are managed by each member of staff identified in the middle query. The result table is shown in Table 11.21.

Table 11.21   Result table for Example 11.21.

pno	street	area	city	pcode	type	rooms	rent
PG4	6 Lawrence St	Partick	Glasgow	G11 9QX	Flat	3	350
PG16	5 Novar Dr	Hyndland	Glasgow	G12 9AX	Flat	4	450
PG36	2 Manor Rd		Glasgow	G32 4QX	Flat	3	375
PG21	18 Dale Rd	Hyndland	Glasgow	G12	House	5	600

(4 rows)

11.3.6 ANY and ALL

The words ANY and ALL may be used with subqueries that produce a single column of numbers. If the subquery is preceded by the keyword ALL, the condition will only be true if it is satisfied by all values produced by the subquery. If the subquery is preceded by the keyword ANY, the condition will be true if it is satisfied by any (one or more) values produced by the subquery. If the subquery is empty, the ALL condition returns true, the ANY condition returns false. The ISO standard allows the qualifier SOME to be used in place of ANY.

Example 11.22:   Use of ANY/SOME

Find staff whose salary is larger than the salary of at least one member of staff at branch B3.

```
SELECT sno, fname, lname, position, salary
FROM staff
WHERE salary > SOME
        (SELECT salary
        FROM staff
        WHERE bno = 'B3');
```

While this query can be expressed using a subquery that finds the minimum salary of the staff at branch B3, and then an outer query that finds all staff whose salary is greater than this number (see Example 11.20), the alternative approach uses the SOME/ANY keyword. The inner query produces the set {12000, 18000, 24000} and the outer query selects those staff whose salaries are greater than any of the values in this set (that is, greater than the minimum value, 12000). This alternative method may seem more natural than finding the minimum salary in a subquery. In either case, the result table is shown in Table 11.22.

Table 11.22   Result table for Example 11.22.

sno	fname	lname	position	salary
SL21	John	White	Manager	30000.00
SG14	David	Ford	Deputy	18000.00
SG5	Susan	Brand	Manager	24000.00

(3 rows)

Example 11.23:   Use of ALL _____

Find staff whose salary is larger than the salary of every member of staff at branch B3.

        SELECT sno, fname, lname, position, salary

        FROM staff

        WHERE salary > ALL
                (SELECT salary
                FROM staff
                WHERE bno = 'B3');

This is very similar to the last example. Again, we could use a subquery to find the maximum salary of staff at branch B3 and then use an outer query to find all staff whose salary is greater than this number. However, this approach uses the ALL keyword. The result table is shown in Table 11.23.

Table 11.23   Result table for Example 11.23.

sno	fname	lname	position	salary
SL21	John	White	Manager	30000.00

(1 row)

11.3.7   Multi-Table Queries

All of the examples we have considered so far have a major limitation: the columns that are to appear in the result table must all come from a single table. In many cases, this is not sufficient. To combine columns from several tables into a result table, we need to use a **join** operation. The SQL join operation combines information from two tables by forming pairs of related rows from the two tables. The row pairs that make up the joined table are those where the matching columns in each of the two tables have the same value.

If we need to obtain information from more than one table, the choice is between using a subquery and using a join. If the final result table is to contain columns from different tables, then we must use a join. To perform a join, we simply include more than one table name in the FROM clause, using a comma as a separator and typically including a WHERE clause to specify the join column(s). It is also possible to use an **alias** for a table named in the FROM clause. In this case, the alias is separated from the table name with a space. An alias can be used to qualify column names whenever there is ambiguity regarding the source of the column name. It can also be used as a shorthand notation for the table name. If an alias is provided it must be used everywhere the table name would have been specified.

Example 11.24: Simple join _____

List the names of all renters who have viewed a property along with any comment supplied.

> SELECT r.rno, fname, lname, pno, comment
> FROM renter r, viewing v
> WHERE r.rno = v.rno;

We want to display the details from both the Renter table and the Viewing table, and so we have to use a join. The SELECT clause lists the columns to be displayed. Note that it is necessary to qualify the renter number, Rno, in the SELECT list: Rno could come from either table, and we have to indicate which one. (We could equally well have chosen the Rno column from the Viewing table.) The qualification is achieved by prefixing the column name with the appropriate table name (or its alias). In this case, we have used *r* as the alias for the Renter table.

To obtain the correct rows, we include only those rows from both tables that have identical values in the Rno columns. We do this by the search condition (r.rno = v.rno). We call these two columns the **matching columns** for the two tables. This is equivalent to the **equi-join** we discussed in Section 3.4.1. The result table is shown in Table 11.24.

Table 11.24   Result table for Example 11.24.

rno	fname	lname	pno	comment
CR56	Aline	Stewart	PG36	
CR56	Aline	Stewart	PA14	too small
CR56	Aline	Stewart	PG4	
CR62	Mary	Tregear	PA14	no dining room
CR76	John	Kay	PG4	too remote

(5 rows)

The most common multi-table queries involve two tables that have a 1:M (or a parent/child) relationship. The previous query involving renters and viewings is an example of such a query. Each viewing (child) has an associated renter (parent), and each renter (parent) can have many associated viewings (children). The pairs of rows that generate the query results are parent/child row combinations. In Section 3.2.5, we described how primary key and foreign keys create the parent/child relationship in a relational database. The table containing the foreign key is the child table; the table containing the primary key is the parent table. To use the parent/child relationship in an SQL query, we specify a search condition that compares the foreign key and the primary key. In Example 11.24, we compared the primary key in the Renter table, r.rno, with the foreign key in the Viewing table, v.rno.

The SQL2 standard provides the following alternative ways to specify this join:

FROM renter r JOIN viewing v ON r.rno = v.rno

FROM renter JOIN viewing USING rno

FROM renter NATURAL JOIN viewing

In each case, the FROM clause replaces the original FROM and WHERE clauses. However, the first alternative produces a table with two identical Rno columns; the remaining two produce a table with a single Rno column.

Example 11.25:   Sorting a join

For each branch office, list the names of staff who manage properties.

SELECT s.bno, s.sno, fname, lname, pno
FROM staff s, property_for_rent p
WHERE s.sno = p.sno;

The result table is shown in Table 11.25(a).

Table 11.25(a)   Result table for Example 11.25 without sorting.

bno	sno	fname	lname	pno
B3	SG14	David	Ford	PG4
B3	SG14	David	Ford	PG16
B5	SL41	Julie	Lee	PL94
B3	SG37	Ann	Beech	PG21
B3	SG37	Ann	Beech	PG36
B7	SA9	Mary	Howe	PA14

(6 rows)

To make the results more readable, we may want to order the output using the branch number as the major sort key and the staff number and property number as the minor keys. In this case, the query becomes:

SELECT s.bno, s.sno, fname, lname, pno
FROM staff s, property_for_rent p
WHERE s.sno = p.sno
ORDER BY s.bno, s.sno, pno;

and the result table becomes as shown in Table 11.25(b).

Table 11.25(b) Result table for Example 11.25 sorted on bno, sno, pno.

bno	sno	fname	lname	pno
B3	SG14	David	Ford	PG4
B3	SG14	David	Ford	PG16
B3	SG37	Ann	Beech	PG21
B3	SG37	Ann	Beech	PG36
B5	SL41	Julie	Lee	PL94
B7	SA9	Mary	Howe	PA14

(6 rows)

Example 11.26: Three-table join

For each branch, list the staff who manage properties, including the city in which the branch is located and the properties they manage.

```
SELECT b.bno, b.city, s.sno, fname, lname, pno
FROM branch b, staff s, property_for_rent p
WHERE b.bno = s.bno AND s.sno = p.sno
ORDER BY b.bno, s.sno, pno;
```

The result table requires columns from three tables: Branch, Staff and Property_for_Rent, so a join must be used. The Branch and Staff details are joined using the condition (b.bno = s.bno), to link each branch to its corresponding staff. The Staff and Property_for_Rent details are joined using the condition (s.sno = p.sno), to link staff to the properties they manage. The result table is shown in Table 11.26.

Table 11.26 Result table for Example 11.26.

bno	city	sno	fname	lname	pno
B3	Glasgow	SG14	David	Ford	PG16
B3	Glasgow	SG14	David	Ford	PG4
B3	Glasgow	SG37	Ann	Beech	PG21
B3	Glasgow	SG37	Ann	Beech	PG36
B5	London	SL41	Julie	Lee	PL94
B7	Aberdeen	SA9	Mary	Howe	PA14

(6 rows)

Note, again, that the SQL2 standard provides alternative formulations for the FROM and WHERE clauses, for example:

        FROM (branch b JOIN staff s USING bno) AS
                bs JOIN property_for_rent p USING sno

Example 11.27:   Multiple grouping columns _____

Find the number of properties handled by each staff member in each branch.

        SELECT s.bno, s.sno, COUNT(*) AS count

        FROM staff s, property_for_rent p

        WHERE s.sno = p.sno

        GROUP BY s.bno, s.sno

        ORDER BY s.bno, s.sno;

To list the required numbers, we first need to find out which staff actually manage properties. This can be found by joining the Staff and Property_ for_Rent tables on the Sno column, using the FROM/WHERE clause. Next, we need to form groups consisting of the branch number and staff number, using the GROUP BY clause. Finally, we sort the output using the ORDER BY clause. The result table is shown in Table 11.27.

Table 11.27(a)   Result table for Example 11.27.

bno	sno	count
B3	SG14	2
B3	SG37	2
B5	SL41	1
B7	SA9	1

(4 rows)

Computing a join

A join is a subset of a more general combination of two tables known as the **Cartesian product** of two tables (see Section 3.4.1). The Cartesian product of two tables is another table consisting of all possible pairs of rows from the two tables. The columns of the product table are all the columns of the first table followed by all the columns of the second table. If we specify a two-table query without a WHERE clause, SQL produces the Cartesian product of the two tables as the query result. In fact, the ISO standard provides a special format of the SELECT statement for the Cartesian product:

SELECT	[DISTINCT	ALL]	{*	column_list}
FROM	table_name1 CROSS JOIN table_name2	

Consider again Example 11.24, where we joined the Renter and Viewing tables using the matching column, Rno. The Cartesian product of these two tables would contain 20 rows (4 renters * 5 viewings = 20 rows). It is equivalent to the query used in Example 11.24 without the WHERE clause.

The procedure for generating the results of a SELECT with a join are as follows:

(1)   Form the Cartesian product of the tables named in the FROM clause.

(2)   If there is a WHERE clause, apply the search condition to each row of the product table, retaining those rows that satisfy the condition. In terms of the relational algebra, this operation yields a **restriction** of the Cartesian product.

(3)   For each remaining row, determine the value of each item in the SELECT list to produce a single row in the result table.

(4)   If SELECT DISTINCT has been specified, eliminate any duplicate rows from the result table. In relational algebra, Steps 3 and 4 are equivalent to a **projection** of the restriction over the columns mentioned in the SELECT list.

(5)   If there is an ORDER BY clause, sort the result table as required.

Outer joins

The join operation combines data from two tables by forming pairs of related rows where the matching columns in each table have the same value. If one row of a table is unmatched, the row is omitted from the result table. This has been the case for the joins we examined above. The ISO standard provides another set of join operators called **outer joins** (see Section 3.4.1). The outer join retains rows that do not satisfy the join condition. To understand the outer join operators, consider the following two simplified Branch and Property_for_Rent tables:

BRANCH1

bno	bcity
B3	Glasgow
B4	Bristol
B2	London

PROPERTY_FOR_RENT1

pno	pcity
PA14	Aberdeen
PL94	London
PG4	Glasgow

The (inner) join of these two tables:

>   SELECT b.*, p.*
>   FROM branch1 b, property_for_rent1 p
>   WHERE b.bcity = p.pcity;

produces the result table shown in Table 11.27(b).

Table 11.27(b)   Result table for inner join of simplified Branch and Property_for_Rent.

bno	bcity	pno	pcity
B3	Glasgow	PG4	Glasgow
B2	London	PL94	London

(2 rows)

The result table has two rows where the cities are the same. In particular, note that there is no row corresponding to the branch office in Bristol and there is no row corresponding to the property in Aberdeen. If we want to include the unmatched rows in the result table, we can use an outer join. There are three types of outer join: **left**, **right** and **full outer** joins. We illustrate their functionality in the following examples.

Example 11.28:   Left outer join _____

List the branch offices and properties that are in the same city along with any unmatched branches.

The left outer join of these two tables:

>   SELECT b.*, p.*
>   FROM branch1 b LEFT JOIN property_for_rent1 p
>   ON b.bcity = p.pcity;

produces the result table shown in Table 11.28.

Table 11.28   Result table for Example 11.28

bno	bcity	pno	pcity
B3	Glasgow	PG4	Glasgow
B4	Bristol	NULL	NULL
B2	London	PL94	London

(3 rows)

In this example, the left outer join includes those rows of the first (left) table that are unmatched with rows from the second (right) table. The columns from the second table are filled with NULLs.

Example 11.29: Right outer join

List the branch offices and properties in the same city and any unmatched properties.

The right outer join of these two tables:

```
SELECT b.*, p.*
FROM branch1 b RIGHT JOIN property_for_rent1 p
ON b.bcity = p.pcity;
```

produces the result table shown in Table 11.29.

Table 11.29 Result table for Example 11.29.

bno	bcity	pno	pcity
NULL	NULL	PA14	Aberdeen
B3	Glasgow	PG4	Glasgow
B2	London	PL94	London

(3 rows)

In this example, the right outer join includes those rows of the second (right) table that are unmatched with rows from the first (left) table. The columns from the first table are filled with NULLs.

Example 11.30: Full outer join

List the branch offices and properties in the same city and any unmatched branches or properties.

The full outer join of these two tables:

```
SELECT b.*, p.*
FROM branch1 b FULL JOIN property_for_rent1 p
ON b.bcity = p.pcity;
```

produces the result table shown in Table 11.30.

Table 11.30   Result table for Example 11.30.

bno	bcity	pno	pcity
NULL	NULL	PA14	Aberdeen
B3	Glasgow	PG4	Glasgow
B4	Bristol	NULL	NULL
B2	London	PL94	London

(4 rows)

In this case, the full outer join includes those rows that are unmatched in both tables. The unmatched columns are filled with NULLs. At the time of writing, there are very few systems that provide outer joins.

11.3.8   EXISTS and NOT EXISTS

The keywords EXISTS and NOT EXISTS are designed for use only with subqueries. They produce a simple true/false result. EXISTS is true if and only if there exists at least one row in the result table returned by the subquery; it is false if the subquery returns an empty result table. NOT EXISTS is the opposite of EXISTS. Since EXISTS and NOT EXISTS check only for the existence or non-existence of rows in the subquery result table, the subquery can contain any number of columns. For simplicity, it is common for subqueries following one of these keywords to be of the form:

(SELECT * ...)

Example 11.31: Query using EXISTS

Find all staff who work in a London branch.

```
SELECT sno, fname, lname, position
FROM staff s
WHERE EXISTS
        (SELECT *
        FROM branch b
        WHERE s.bno = b.bno AND city = 'London');
```

This query could be rephrased as 'Find all staff such that there exists a Branch record containing their branch number, Bno, and City equal to London'. The test for inclusion is the existence of such a record. If it exists, the *EXISTS subquery* evaluates to true. Notice that we need to use the name/alias of the main query table Staff in the subquery to qualify the branch number. The result table is shown in Table 11.31.

Table 11.31   Result table for Example 11.31.

sno	fname	lname	position
SL21	John	White	Manager
SL41	Julie	Lee	Assistant

(2 rows)

Note that the first part of the search condition s.bno = b.bno is necessary to ensure that we consider the correct branch record for each member of staff. If we omitted this part of the search query, we would get all staff records listed out because the subquery (SELECT * FROM branch WHERE city = 'London') would always be true and the query would be reduced to:

SELECT sno, fname, lname, position FROM staff WHERE true;

which is equivalent to:

SELECT sno, fname, lname, position FROM staff;

We could also have written this query using the join construct:

SELECT sno, fname, lname, position
FROM staff s, branch b
WHERE s.bno = b.bno AND city = 'London';

11.3.9   Combining Result Tables (UNION, INTERSECT, EXCEPT)

In SQL, we can use the normal set operations of union, intersection and difference to combine the results of two or more queries into a single result table. The **union** of two tables, A and B, is a table containing all rows that are in either the first table A or the second table B or both. The **intersection** of two tables, A and B, is a table containing all rows that are common to both tables A and B. The **difference** of two tables, A and B, is a table containing all rows that are in table A but are not in table B. The set operations are illustrated in Figure 11.1.

There are restrictions on the tables that can be combined using the set operations. The most important is that the two tables are **union compatible**; that is, they have the same structure. This implies that the two tables must contain the same number of columns, and that their corresponding columns have the same data types and lengths. It is the user's responsibility to ensure that data values in corresponding columns come from the same **domain**. For example, it would be nonsensical to combine a column containing the age of staff with the number of rooms in a property,

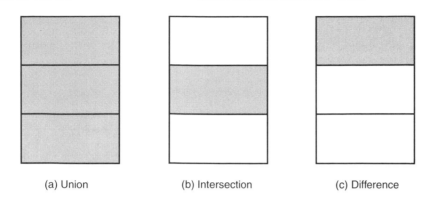

(a) Union   (b) Intersection   (c) Difference

Figure 11.1 Union, intersection and difference set operations.

even though both columns may have the same data type: for example, SMALLINT.

The three set operators in the ISO standard are called UNION, INTERSECT and EXCEPT. The format of the set operator clause in each case is:

<u>operator</u> [ALL] [CORRESPONDING [BY { column1 [, ...] }]]

If CORRESPONDING BY is specified, then the set operation is performed on the named column(s); if CORRESPONDING is specified but not the BY clause, the set operation is performed on the columns that are common to both tables. If ALL is specified, the result can include duplicate rows.

Some dialects of SQL do not support INTERSECT and EXCEPT; others use MINUS in place of EXCEPT.

Example 11.32:   Use of UNION

Construct a list of all areas where there is either a branch office or a rental property.

(SELECT area	or	(SELECT *
FROM branch		FROM branch
WHERE area IS NOT NULL)		WHERE area IS NOT NULL)
UNION		UNION CORRESPONDING BY area
(SELECT area		(SELECT *
FROM property_for_rent		FROM property_for_rent
WHERE area IS NOT NULL);		WHERE area IS NOT NULL);

Table 11.32
Result table for
Example 11.32.

area
Sidcup
Dyce
Partick
Leigh
Dee
Kilburn
Hyndland

(7 rows)

This query is executed by producing a result table from the first query and a result table from the second query, and then merging both tables into a single result table consisting of all the rows from both result tables with the duplicate rows removed. The final result table is shown in Table 11.32.

Example 11.33: Use of INTERSECT

Construct a list of all cities where there is both a branch office and a rental property.

```
(SELECT city           or    (SELECT *
FROM branch)                 FROM branch)
INTERSECT                    INTERSECT CORRESPONDING BY city
(SELECT city                 (SELECT *
FROM property_for_rent);     FROM property_for_rent);
```

This query is executed by producing a result table from the first query and a result table from the second query, and then creating a single result table consisting of those rows that are common to both result tables. The final result table is shown in Table 11.33.

We could rewrite this query without the INTERSECT operator, for example:

```
(SELECT city                    or    SELECT distinct city
FROM branch b property_for_rent p     FROM branch b
WHERE b.city = p.city;                WHERE EXISTS
                                        (SELECT *
                                        FROM property_for_rent p
                                        WHERE p.city = b.city);
```

Table 11.33
Result table for
Example 11.33.

city
Aberdeen
Glasgow
London

(3 rows)

The ability to write a query in several equivalent forms illustrates one of the disadvantages of the SQL language.

Example 11.34: Use of EXCEPT

Construct a list of all cities where there is a branch office but no rental properties.

```
(SELECT city           or    (SELECT *
FROM branch)                 FROM branch)
EXCEPT                       EXCEPT CORRESPONDING BY city
(SELECT city                 (SELECT *
FROM property_for_rent);     FROM property_for_rent);
```

This query is executed by producing a result table from the first query and a result table from the second query, and then creating a single result table consisting of those rows that appear in the first result table but not in the second one. The final result table is shown in Table 11.34.

We could rewrite this query without the EXCEPT operator, for example:

Table 11.34
city
Bristol
(1 row)

```
SELECT distinct city          or      SELECT distinct city
FROM branch                           FROM branch b
WHERE city NOT IN                     WHERE NOT EXISTS
    (SELECT city                          (SELECT *
    FROM property_for_rent);              FROM property_for_rent p
                                          WHERE p.city = b.city);
```

11.3.10 Database Updates

SQL is a complete data manipulation language that can be used for modifying the data in the database as well as querying the database. The commands for modifying the database are not as complex as the SELECT statement. In this section, we describe the three SQL statements that are available to modify the contents of the tables in the database:

- INSERT   Adds new rows of data to a table.
- UPDATE   Modifies existing data in a table.
- DELETE   Removes rows of data from a table.

Adding data to the database (INSERT)

There are two forms of the INSERT statement. The first allows a single row to be inserted into a named table. The format of the INSERT statement is:

```
INSERT INTO table_name [ (column_list) ]
VALUES (data_value_list)
```

Table_name may be either a base table or an updatable view (see Section 12.1), and *column_list* represents a list of one or more column names separated by commas. *Column_list* is optional; if omitted, SQL assumes a list of all columns in their original CREATE TABLE order. If specified, then any columns that are omitted from the list must have been declared as NULL columns when the table was created, unless the DEFAULT option was used when creating the column (see Section 12.3.1). The *data_value_list* must match the *column_list* as follows:

- The number of items in each list must be the same.
- There must be a direct correspondence in the position of items in the two lists, so that the first item in the *data_value_list* applies to the first

item in the *column_list*, the second item in the *data_value_list* applies to the second item in the *column_list*, and so on.

- The data type of each item in the *data_value_list* must be compatible with the data type of the corresponding column.

Example 11.35: INSERT ... VALUES

Insert a new record into the Staff table supplying data for all columns.

INSERT INTO staff

VALUES ('SG16', 'Alan', 'Brown', '67 Endrick Rd, Glasgow G32 8QX', '0141–211–3001', 'Assistant', 'M', DATE '1957–05–25', 8300, 'WN848391H', 'B3');

As we are inserting data into each column in the order the table was created, there is no need to specify a column list. Note that character literals such as 'Alan' must be enclosed in single quotes.

Example 11.36: INSERT using defaults

Insert a new record into the Staff table supplying data for all mandatory columns: Sno, FName, LName, Position, Salary and Bno.

INSERT INTO staff (sno, fname, lname, position, salary, bno)

VALUES ('SG44', 'Anne', 'Jones', 'Assistant', 8100, 'B3');

As we are inserting data only into certain columns, we must specify the names of the columns that we are inserting data into. The order for the column names is not significant, but it is more normal to specify them in the order they appear in the table. We could also express the INSERT statement as:

INSERT INTO staff

VALUES ('SG44', 'Anne', 'Jones', NULL, NULL, 'Assistant', NULL, NULL, 8100, NULL, 'B3');

In this case, we have explicitly specified that the columns Address, Tel_No, Sex, DOB and NIN should be set to NULL.

The second form of the INSERT statement allows multiple rows to be copied from one or more tables to another. The format is:

```
INSERT INTO table_name [ (column_list) ]
    SELECT ...
```

Table_name and *column_list* are defined as before when inserting a single row. The SELECT clause can be any valid SELECT statement. The rows inserted into the named table are identical to the result table produced by the subselect. The same restrictions that apply to the first form of the INSERT statement also apply here.

Example 11.37: INSERT ... SELECT _____

Assume that there is a table Staff_Prop_Count that contains the names of staff and the number of properties they manage:

Staff_Prop_Count(sno, fname, lname, prop_cnt)

Populate the Staff_Prop_Count table using details from the Staff and Property_for_Rent tables.

```
INSERT INTO staff_prop_count
    (SELECT s.sno, fname, lname, COUNT(*)
    FROM staff s, property_for_rent p
    WHERE s.sno = p.sno
    GROUP BY s.sno, fname, lname)
    UNION
    (SELECT sno, fname, lname, 0
    FROM staff
    WHERE sno NOT IN
        (SELECT DISTINCT sno
        FROM property_for_rent));
```

This example is complex because we want to count the number of properties that staff manage. If we omit the second part of the UNION, then we get only a list of those staff who currently manage at least one property; in other words, we exclude those staff who currently do not manage any properties. Therefore, to include the staff who do not manage any properties, we need to use the UNION statement and a second SELECT statement to add in such staff, using a 0 value for the count attribute. The Staff_Prop_Count table will now be as shown in Table 11.35.

Table 11.35   Result table for Example 11.37.

sno	fname	lname	prop_cnt
SG14	David	Ford	2
SL21	John	White	0
SG37	Ann	Beech	2
SA9	Mary	Howe	1
SG5	Susan	Brand	0
SL41	Julie	Lee	1

(6 rows)

Note that with some dialects of SQL, we may not be allowed to use the UNION operator within a subselect for an INSERT.

Modifying data in the database (UPDATE)

The UPDATE statement allows you to change the contents of existing rows in a named table. The format of the command is:

```
UPDATE table_name
SET column_name1 = data_value1 [, column_name2 = data_value2 ... ]
[WHERE search_condition]
```

The *table_name* can be the name of a base table or an updatable view (see Section 12.1). The SET clause specifies the names of one or more columns that are to be updated. The WHERE clause is optional. If omitted, the named columns are updated for *all* rows in the table. If a WHERE clause is specified, only those rows that satisfy the *search_condition* are updated. The new *data_value(s)* must be compatible with the data type for the corresponding column.

Example 11.38:   UPDATE all rows

Give all staff a 3% pay increase.

```
UPDATE staff
SET salary = salary*1.03;
```

The update is applied to all rows in the Staff table, therefore the WHERE clause is not required.

Example 11.39:   UPDATE specific rows

Give all Managers a 5% pay increase.

```
UPDATE staff
SET salary = salary*1.05
WHERE position = 'Manager';
```

The WHERE clause finds the rows that contain data for Managers. The update salary = salary*1.05 is applied only to these particular rows.

Example 11.40:   UPDATE multiple columns _____

Promote David Ford (Sno = 'SG14') to Manager and change his salary to £18,000.

    UPDATE staff
    SET position = 'Manager', salary = 18000
    WHERE sno = 'SG14';

Deleting data from the database (DELETE)

The DELETE statement allows you to delete rows from a named table. The format of the command is:

> DELETE FROM table_name
> [WHERE search_condition]

As with the INSERT and UPDATE statements, *table_name* can be the name of a base table or an updatable view (see Section 12.1). The *search_condition* is optional; if omitted, *all* rows are deleted from the table. This does not delete the table itself – if you want to delete the table contents and the table definition, you must use the DROP TABLE statement instead (see Section 11.4.5). If a *search_condition* is specified, only those rows that satisfy the condition are deleted.

Example 11.41:   DELETE specific rows _____

Delete all viewings that relate to property PG4.

    DELETE FROM viewing
    WHERE pno = 'PG4';

The WHERE clause finds the rows for property PG4. The delete operation applies only to these particular rows.

Example 11.42:   DELETE all rows _____

Delete all records from the Viewing table.

    DELETE FROM viewing;

No WHERE clause has been specified, so the delete operation applies to all rows in the table. This removes all rows from the table, leaving only the table definition, so that we are still able to insert data into the table at a later stage.

11.4 Data Definition

The SQL Data Definition Language (DDL) allows us to create and destroy database objects (schemas, domains, tables, views and indexes). In this section, we briefly examine how to create and destroy schemas, tables and indexes. In the next chapter, we will examine the creation and removal of domains and views, and how to specify integrity constraints when creating or altering tables. The ISO standard also allows the creation of assertions, character sets, collations and translations. However, we will not consider these database objects in this book. The interested reader is referred to Cannan and Otten (1993).

The main SQL data definition language statements are:

CREATE SCHEMA		DROP SCHEMA
CREATE DOMAIN	ALTER DOMAIN	DROP DOMAIN
CREATE TABLE	ALTER TABLE	DROP TABLE
CREATE VIEW		DROP VIEW

Although not covered by the SQL2 standard, the following two statements are provided by many DBMS:

CREATE INDEX	DROP INDEX

These statements are used to create, change and destroy the structures that make up the conceptual schema. Additional commands are available to the DBA to specify the physical details of data storage; however we do not discuss them here, as these commands are system-specific. Before we consider the DDL statements, we discuss the syntax of SQL identifiers and the SQL data types that can be used to define table columns.

11.4.1 SQL Identifiers

SQL identifiers are used to identify objects in the database, such as table names, view names and columns. The characters that can be used in a user-defined SQL identifier must appear in a **character set**. The ISO standard provides a default character set, which consists of the upper-case letters A ... Z, the lower-case letters a ... z, the digits 0 ... 9 and the underscore (_) character. It is also possible to specify an alternative character set. The following restrictions are imposed on an identifier:

- An identifier can be no longer than 128 characters (most dialects have a much lower limit than this).
- An identifier must start with a letter.
- An identifier cannot contain spaces.

Table 11.36 ISO SQL data types.

Data type	Declarations			
character	CHAR,	VARCHAR		
bit	BIT,	BIT VARYING		
exact numeric	NUMERIC,	DECIMAL,	INTEGER,	SMALLINT
approximate numeric	FLOAT,	REAL,	DOUBLE PRECISION	
datetime	DATE,	TIME,	TIMESTAMP	
interval	INTERVAL			

11.4.2 The ISO SQL Data Types

There are six SQL scalar data types defined in the ISO standard, which are shown in Table 11.36.

Sometimes for manipulation and conversion purposes, the data types *character* and *bit* are collectively referred to as **string** data types, and *exact numeric* and *approximate numeric* are referred to as **numeric** data types, as they share similar properties.

Character data

Character data consists of a sequence of characters from an implementor-defined character set; that is, it is defined by the vendor of the particular SQL dialect. Thus, the exact characters that can appear as data values in a character type column will vary. ASCII and EBCDIC are two sets in common use today. The format for specifying a character data type is:

CHARACTER [VARYING] [length]

CHARACTER can be abbreviated to CHAR and
CHARACTER VARYING to VARCHAR.

When a character string column is defined, a length can be specified to indicate the maximum number of characters that the column can hold (default length is 1). A character string may be defined as having a **fixed** or **varying** length. If the string is defined to be a fixed length, and we enter a string with fewer characters than this length, the string is padded with blanks on the right to make up the required size. If the string is defined to be of a varying length and we enter a string with fewer characters than this length, only those characters entered are stored, thereby using less space. For example, the staff number column Sno of the Staff table, which has a fixed length of five characters, is declared as:

    sno   CHAR(5)

The column Address of the Staff table, which has a variable number of characters up to a maximum of 30, is declared as:

> address   VARCHAR(30)

Bit data

The bit data type is used to define bit strings: that is, a sequence of binary digits (bits), each having either the value 0 or 1. The format for specifying the bit data type is similar to that of the character data type:

BIT [VARYING] [length]

For example, to hold the fixed length binary string '0011', we declare a column *bit_string*, as:

> bit_string   BIT(4)

Exact numeric data

The exact numeric data type is used to define numbers with an exact representation. The number consists of digits, an optional decimal point and an optional sign. An exact numeric data type consists of a **precision** and a **scale**. The precision gives the total number of significant decimal digits: that is, the total number of digits, including decimal places but excluding the point itself. The scale gives the total number of decimal places. For example, the exact numeric value -12.345 has precision 5 and scale 3. A special case of exact numeric occurs with integers. There are several ways of specifying an exact numeric data type:

NUMERIC [precision [, scale]]
DECIMAL [precision [, scale]]
INTEGER
SMALLINT

INTEGER can be abbreviated to INT and DECIMAL to DEC

NUMERIC and DECIMAL store numbers in decimal notation. The default scale is always 0; the default precision is implementation-defined. INTEGER is used for large positive or negative whole numbers. SMALLINT is used for small positive or negative whole numbers. By specifying this data type, less storage space can be reserved for the data. For example, the maximum absolute value that can be stored in this type of data might be 32 767. The column Rooms of the Property_for_Rent table, which represents the number of rooms in a property, is obviously a small integer and can be declared as:

> rooms   SMALLINT

The column Salary of the Staff table can be declared as:

     salary   DECIMAL(7,2)

which can handle a value up to £99,999.99.

Approximate numeric data

The approximate numeric data type is used for defining numbers that do not
have an exact representation, such as real numbers. Approximate numeric, or
floating point, is similar to scientific notation in which a number is written
as a *mantissa* times some power of ten (the *exponent*). For example, 10E3,
+5.2E6, −0.2E−4. There are several ways of specifying an approximate
numeric data type:

```
FLOAT [ precision ]
REAL
DOUBLE PRECISION
```

The *precision* controls the precision of the mantissa. The precision of REAL
and DOUBLE PRECISION is implementation-defined.

Datetime data

The datetime data type is used to define points in time to a certain degree of
accuracy. Examples are dates, times and times of day. The ISO standard
subdivides the datetime data type into YEAR, MONTH, DAY, HOUR,
MINUTE, SECOND, TIMEZONE_HOUR and TIMEZONE_MINUTE. The
latter two fields specify the hour and minute part of the time zone offset from
Universal Coordinated Time (which used to be called Greenwich Mean Time).
Three types of datetime data type are supported:

```
DATE
TIME [time_precision] [WITH TIME ZONE]
TIMESTAMP [time_precision] [WITH TIME ZONE]
```

DATE is used to store calendar dates using the YEAR, MONTH and DAY
fields. TIME is used to store time using the HOUR, MINUTE and SECOND
fields. TIMESTAMP is used to store date and times. The *time_precision* is
the number of decimal places of accuracy to which the SECOND field is kept.
If not specified, TIME defaults to a precision of 0 (that is, whole seconds),
and TIMESTAMP defaults to 6 (that is, microseconds). The WITH TIME
ZONE keyword controls the presence of the TIMEZONE_HOUR and
TIMEZONE_MINUTE fields. For example, the column Date of the Viewing
table, which represents the date (year, month and day) that a renter viewed
a property, can be declared as:

     date   DATE

Interval data

The interval data type is used to represent periods of time. Every interval data type consists of a contiguous subset of the fields: YEAR, MONTH, DAY, HOUR, MINUTE, SECOND. There are two classes of interval data type: **year-month** intervals and **day-time** intervals. The year-month class may contain only the YEAR and/or the MONTH fields; the day-time class may contain only a contiguous selection from DAY, HOUR, MINUTE, SECOND. The format for specifying the interval data type is:

```
INTERVAL { {start_field TO end_field}│single_datetime_field}

start_field = YEAR│MONTH│DAY│HOUR│MINUTE
                 [(interval leading field precision)]
end_field   = YEAR│MONTH│DAY│HOUR│MINUTE│SECOND
                 [(fractional seconds precision)]
single_datetime_field = start_field│SECOND
                 [(interval leading field precision [,fractional seconds
                 precision])]
```

In all cases, *start_field* has a leading field precision that defaults to 2. For example:

    INTERVAL YEAR(2) TO MONTH

represents an interval of time with a value between 0 years 0 months and 99 years 11 months, and:

    INTERVAL HOUR TO SECOND(4)

represents an interval of time with a value between 0 hours 0 minutes 0 seconds

Table 11.37 ISO SQL scalar operators.

Operator	Meaning
BIT_LENGTH	Returns the length of a string in bits. For example, BIT_LENGTH(X'FFFF') returns 16.
OCTET_LENGTH	Returns the length of a string in octets (bit length divided by 8). For example, OCTET_LENGTH(X'FFFF') returns 2.
CHAR_LENGTH	Returns the length of a string in characters (or octets, if the string is a bit string). For example, CHAR_LENGTH('Beech') returns 5.
CAST	Converts a value expression of one data type into a value in another data type. For example, CAST(5E3 AS INTEGER).
||	Concatenates two character strings or bit strings. For example, fname || lname.

Table 11.37   *contd.*

Operator	Meaning
CURRENT_USER or USER	Returns a character string representing the current authorization identifier (informally, the current user name).
SESSION_USER	Returns a character string representing the SQL-session authorization identifier.
SYSTEM_USER	Returns a character string representing the identifier of the user who invoked the current module.
LOWER	Converts upper-case letters to lower-case. For example, LOWER(SELECT fname FROM staff WHERE sno = 'SL21')
UPPER	Converts lower-case letters to upper-case. For example, UPPER(SELECT fname FROM staff WHERE sno = 'SL21')
TRIM	Removes leading (LEADING), trailing (TRAILING) or both leading and trailing (BOTH) characters from a string. For example, TRIM(BOTH '*' FROM '*** Hello World ***')
POSITION	Returns the position of one string within another string. For example, POSITION('ee' IN 'Beech') returns 2.
SUBSTRING	Returns a substring selected from within a string. For example, SUBSTRING('Beech' FROM 1 TO 3) returns the string 'Bee'.

CASE	Returns one of a specified set of values, based on some condition. For example,
	
	CASE type
	  WHEN 'House' THEN 1
	  WHEN 'Flat' THEN 2
	  ELSE 0
	END

CURRENT_DATE	Returns the current date in the time zone that is local to the user.
CURRENT_TIME	Returns the current time in the time zone that is the current default for the session. For example, CURRENT_TIME(6) gives time to microsecond precision.
CURRENT_TIME_STAMP	Returns the current date and time in the time zone that is the current default for the session. For example, CURRENT_TIMESTAMP(0) gives time to second precision.
EXTRACT	Returns the value of a specified field from a datetime or interval value. For example, EXTRACT(YEAR FROM staff.dob).

and 99 hours 59 minutes 59.9999 seconds (leading field precision defaults to 2; the fractional precision of second is 4).

Scalar operators

SQL provides a number of built-in scalar operators and functions that can be used to construct a scalar expression: that is, an expression that evaluates to a scalar value. Apart from the obvious arithmetic operators $(+, -, *$ and $/)$, the operators shown in Table 11.37 are available.

11.4.3 Creating a Database

The process of creating a database differs significantly from product to product. In multi-user systems, the authority to create a database is usually reserved for the DBA. In a single-user system, a default database may be established when the system is installed and configured. The ISO standard does not specify how databases are created, and each dialect generally has a different approach. The techniques used by INGRES and ORACLE are:

- INGRES includes a special utility program called CREATEDB, which creates a new INGRES database. A companion program, DESTROY-DB, removes a database.

- ORACLE creates a database as part of the installation process. For the most part, user tables are always placed in this single, system-wide database.

According to the ISO standard, relations and other database objects exist in an **environment**. Among other things, each environment consists of one or more **catalogs**, and each catalog consists of a set of **schemas**. A schema is a named collection of database objects that are in some way related to one another (all the objects in the database are described in one schema or another). The objects in a schema can be tables, views, domains, assertions, collations, translations and character sets. All the objects in a schema have the same owner and share a number of defaults.

The standard leaves the mechanism for creating and destroying catalogs as implementation-defined, but provides mechanisms for creating and destroying schemas. The schema definition statement has the following (simplified) form:

CREATE SCHEMA [name | AUTHORIZATION creator-identifier]

Therefore, if the creator of a schema sql_tests is Smith, the SQL statement is:

CREATE SCHEMA sql_tests AUTHORIZATION Smith;

The ISO standard also indicates that it should be possible to specify within this statement the range of facilities available to the users of the schema, but the details of how these privileges are specified are implementation-dependent.

A schema can be destroyed using the DROP SCHEMA statement, which has the following form:

DROP SCHEMA name [RESTRICT | CASCADE]

If RESTRICT is specified, which is the default if neither qualifier is specified, the schema must be empty or the operation fails. If CASCADE is specified, the operation cascades to drop all objects associated with the schema in the order defined above. If any of these drop operations fail, the DROP

SCHEMA fails. The total effect of a DROP SCHEMA with CASCADE can be very extensive, and should be carried out only with extreme caution.

At present, the CREATE and DROP SCHEMA statements are not yet widely implemented. In some implementations, the following statement is used instead of CREATE SCHEMA:

CREATE DATABASE database_name

11.4.4   Creating a Table (CREATE TABLE)

Having created the database structure, we may now create the base table structures for the relations to be located in the database. This is achieved using the CREATE TABLE command, which has the following basic syntax:

CREATE TABLE table_name
(column_name data_type [NULL | NOT NULL] [, . . .])

This creates a table called *table_name* consisting of one or more columns of the specified *data_type*. The set of permissible data types is described in Section 11.4.2. The NULL specifier is used to indicate whether a column is allowed to contain *nulls*. A null is distinct from blank or zero, and is used to represent data that is either not available, missing or not applicable (see Section 3.3.1). When NOT NULL is specified, the system rejects any attempt to insert a null in the column. If NULL is specified, the system accepts nulls. The ISO default is NULL.

 Primary keys should *always* be specified as NOT NULL to ensure that the primary key of a relation cannot accept nulls, thereby enforcing entity integrity. If the NOT NULL specification is not used, the relation may accept null entries, and we either accept this lack of entity integrity or write programs to enforce entity integrity. Foreign keys are often (but not always) candidates for NOT NULL.

Example 11.43:   CREATE TABLE _____

To illustrate the table creation process, we create the structures for the two tables Staff and Property_for_Rent:

```
CREATE TABLE staff(
        sno         VARCHAR(5)    NOT NULL,
        fname       VARCHAR(15)   NOT NULL,
        lname       VARCHAR(15)   NOT NULL,
        address     VARCHAR(50),
        tel_no      VARCHAR(13),
        position    VARCHAR(10)   NOT NULL,
        sex         CHAR,
```

dob	DATETIME,	
salary	DECIMAL(7,2)	NOT NULL,
nin	CHAR(9),	
bno	VARCHAR(3)	NOT NULL);

CREATE TABLE property_for_rent(

pno	VARCHAR(5)	NOT NULL,
street	VARCHAR(25)	NOT NULL,
area	VARCHAR(15),	
city	VARCHAR(15)	NOT NULL,
pcode	VARCHAR(8),	
type	CHAR(1)	NOT NULL,
rooms	SMALLINT	NOT NULL,
rent	DECIMAL(6,2)	NOT NULL,
ono	VARCHAR(5)	NOT NULL,
sno	VARCHAR(5),	
bno	VARCHAR(3)	NOT NULL);

In the case of the Property_for_Rent table, although the staff number Sno is a foreign key, we have not specified the NOT NULL keyword, because there may be periods of time when there is no member of staff allocated to manage the property (for example, when the property is first registered). However, the other foreign keys – Ono, the owner number, and Bno, the branch number – must be specified. This is a simplified version of the ISO CREATE TABLE statement. We will consider the full version of the statement in Section 12.3.1.

11.4.5 Removing a Table (DROP TABLE)

Over time the structure of a database will change; new tables will be created and some old ones will no longer be needed. We can remove a redundant table from the database using the DROP TABLE statement, which has the format:

```
DROP TABLE table_name [RESTRICT | CASCADE]
```

For example, to remove the Property_for_Rent table we use the command:

```
DROP TABLE property_for_rent;
```

Note, however, that this command removes not only the named table, but also all the rows within it. If you simply want to remove the rows from the table but retain the table structure, use the DELETE statement instead (see Section 11.3.10).

The DROP TABLE statement allows you to specify whether the DROP action is to be cascaded or not. If RESTRICT is specified and there are any other objects that depend for their existence upon the continued existence of the table to be dropped, SQL does not allow the DROP TABLE request to proceed. If CASCADE is specified, SQL automatically drops all dependent objects (and objects dependent on these objects). The total effect of a DROP TABLE with CASCADE can be very extensive, and should be carried out only with extreme caution.

One common use of DROP TABLE is to correct mistakes made when creating a table. If you create a table with an incorrect structure, you can use DROP TABLE to delete the newly created table and start again.

11.4.6 Creating an Index (CREATE INDEX)

An index is a structure that provides rapid access to the rows of a table based on the values of one or more columns (see Appendix A for a discussion of indexes and how they may be used to improve the efficiency of data retrievals). The presence of an index can significantly improve the performance of a query. However, since indexes may be updated by the system every time the underlying tables are updated, additional overheads may be incurred. Indexes are usually created to satisfy particular search criteria after the table has been in use for some time and has grown in size. The creation of indexes is *not* standard SQL. However, most dialects support at least the following capabilities:

CREATE [UNIQUE] INDEX index_name
ON table_name (column [ASC | DESC] [, ...])

The specified columns constitute the index key, and should be listed in major to minor order. Indexes can be created only on base tables *not* on views. If the UNIQUE clause is used, uniqueness of the indexed column or combination of columns will be enforced by the system. This is certainly required for the primary key, and possibly for other columns as well (for example, for alternate keys). Although indexes can be created at any time, we may have a problem if we try to create a unique index on a table with records in it, because the values stored for the indexed column(s) may already contain duplicates. Therefore, it is good practice to create unique indexes, at least for primary key columns, when the base table is created and the system does not automatically enforce primary key uniqueness.

For the Staff and Property_for_Rent tables, we should create at least the following indexes:

    CREATE UNIQUE INDEX sno_ind ON staff (sno);

    CREATE UNIQUE INDEX pno_ind ON property_for_rent (pno);

For each column, we may specify that the order is ascending (ASC) or descending (DESC), with ASC being the default setting. For example, if we create an index on the Property_for_Rent table as:

    CREATE INDEX rent_ind on property_for_rent (area, rent);

then an index file called *rent_ind* is created for the Property_for_Rent table. Entries will be in alphabetical order by area and then by rent within each area.

11.4.7   Removing an Index (DROP INDEX)

If you create an index for a base table and later decide that it is no longer needed, the DROP INDEX statement removes the index from the database. DROP INDEX has the format:

```
DROP INDEX index_name
```

The following statement will remove the index created in the previous example:

DROP INDEX rent_ind;

11.5   Comparison with QBE

In Chapter 13, we will examine an alternative, graphical-based way of querying the database using **QBE** (**Q**uery **b**y **E**xample) (Zloof, 1977). QBE has acquired the reputation of being one of the easiest ways for non-technical computer users to obtain information from the database (Greenblatt and Waxman, 1978). QBE provides a visual means for querying the data through the use of templates. Querying the database is achieved by illustrating the query to be answered. The screen display is used instead of typing in column names and formats; however, we must indicate the columns we want to see and specify data values that we want to use to restrict the query. Languages like QBE can be a highly productive way to interactively query or update the database.

Unfortunately, unlike SQL, there is no official standard for these languages. However, the functionality provided by vendors is generally very similar and the languages are usually more intuitive to use than SQL.

Chapter Summary

- SQL is a non-procedural language, consisting of standard English words such as SELECT, INSERT, DELETE, that can be used by professionals and non-professionals alike. It is both the formal and *de facto* standard language for defining and manipulating relational databases.

- The **SELECT** statement is used to express a query, and is the most important statement in the language. It combines the three fundamental relational operations of *selection*, *projection* and *join*. Every SELECT statement produces a query result table consisting of one or more columns and zero or more rows.

- The SELECT clause identifies the columns and/or calculated data to appear in the result table. All column names that appear in the SELECT clause must have their corresponding tables or views listed in the FROM clause.

- The WHERE clause selects rows to be included in the result table by applying a search condition to the rows of the named table(s). The ORDER BY clause allows the result table to be sorted on the values in one or more columns. Each column can be sorted in ascending or descending order. If specified, the ORDER BY clause must be the last clause in the SELECT statement.

- SQL supports five aggregate functions (COUNT, SUM, AVG, MIN and MAX) that take an entire column as an argument and compute a single value as the result. It is illegal to mix aggregate functions with column names in a SELECT clause, unless the GROUP BY clause is used.

- The GROUP BY clause allows summary information to be included in the result table. Rows that have the same value for one or more columns can be grouped together and treated as a unit for using the aggregate functions. In this case, the aggregate functions take each group as an argument and compute a single value for each group as the result. The HAVING clause acts as a WHERE clause for groups, restricting the groups that appear in the final result table. However, unlike the WHERE clause, the HAVING clause can include aggregate functions.

- A **subquery** is a complete SELECT statement embedded in another query. Subqueries may appear within the WHERE or HAVING clauses. Conceptually, a subquery produces a temporary table whose contents can be accessed by the outer query. A subquery can be embedded in another subquery.

- If the columns of the result table come from more than one table, a **join** must be used, by specifying more than one table in the FROM clause and typically including a WHERE clause to specify the join column(s). The ISO standard allows **outer joins** to be defined. It also allows the set operations of union, intersection and difference to be used with the **UNION**, **INTERSECT** and **EXCEPT** set operations.

- As well as SELECT, the SQL DML includes the **INSERT** statement to insert a single row of data into a named table or to insert an arbitrary number of rows from another table using a **subselect**; the **UPDATE** statement to update one or more values in a specified column of a named table; the **DELETE** statement to delete one or more rows from a named table.

- The ISO standard provides six base data types: character, bit, exact numeric, approximate numeric, datetime and interval.

- The SQL DDL statements allow database objects to be defined. The CREATE and DROP SCHEMA statements allow schemas to be created and destroyed; the CREATE, ALTER and DROP TABLE statements allow tables to be created, modified and destroyed; the

CREATE and DROP INDEX statements allow indexes to be created and destroyed.

REVIEW QUESTIONS

11.1 What are the two major components of SQL and what function do they serve?

11.2 What are the advantages and disadvantages of SQL?

11.3 Explain the function of each of the clauses in the SELECT statement. What restrictions are imposed on these clauses?

11.4 What restrictions apply to the use of the aggregate functions within the SELECT statement? How do nulls affect the aggregate functions?

11.5 Explain how the GROUP BY clause works. What is the difference between the WHERE and HAVING clauses?

11.6 What is the difference between a subquery and a join? Under what circumstances would you not be able to use a subquery?

EXERCISES

The following tables form part of a database held in a relational DBMS:

Hotel	(Hotel_No, Name, Address)
Room	(Room_No, Hotel_No, Type, Price)
Booking	(Hotel_No, Guest_No, Date_From, Date_To, Room_No)
Guest	(Guest_No, Name, Address)

where Hotel contains hotel details and Hotel_No is the primary key
Room contains room details for each hotel and Hotel_No/Room_No forms the primary key
Booking contains details of the bookings and the primary key comprises Hotel_No, Guest_No and Date_From
and   Guest contains guest details and Guest_No is the primary key.

Simple queries
11.7 List full details of all hotels.

11.8 List full details of all hotels in London.

11.9 List the names and addresses of all guests in London, alphabetically ordered by name.

11.10 List all double or family rooms with a price below £40.00 per night, in ascending order of price.

11.11 List the bookings for which no date_to has been specified.

Aggregate functions
11.12 How many hotels are there?

11.13 What is the average price of a room?

11.14 What is the total revenue per night from all double rooms?

11.15 How many different guests have made bookings for August?

Subqueries and joins
11.16 List the price and type of all rooms at the Grosvenor Hotel.

11.17 List all guests currently staying at the Grosvenor Hotel.

11.18 List the details of all rooms at the Grosvenor Hotel, including the name of the guest staying in the room, if the room is occupied.

11.19 What is the total income from bookings for the Grosvenor Hotel today?

11.20 List the rooms that are currently unoccupied at the Grosvenor Hotel.

11.21 What is the lost income from unoccupied rooms at the Grosvenor Hotel?

Grouping
11.22 List the number of rooms in each hotel.

11.23 List the number of rooms in each hotel in London.

11.24 What is the average number of bookings for each hotel in August?

11.25 What is the most commonly booked room type for each hotel in London?

11.26 What is the lost income from unoccupied rooms at each hotel today?

Creating and populating tables
11.27 Using the CREATE TABLE statement, create the Hotel, Room, Booking and Guest tables.

11.28 Insert records into each of these tables.

11.29 Update the price of all rooms by 5%.

11.30 Create a separate table with the same structure as the Booking table to hold archive records. Using the INSERT statement, copy the records from the Booking table to the archive table relating to bookings before 1 January 1990. Delete all bookings before 1 January 1990 from the Booking table.

General

11.31 Investigate the SQL dialect on any DBMS that you are currently using. Determine the compliance of the DBMS with the ISO standard. Investigate the functionality of any extensions the DBMS supports. Are there any functions not supported?

11.32 Show that a query using the HAVING clause has an equivalent formulation without a HAVING clause.

11.33 Show that SQL is relationally complete.

12 Advanced SQL

Chapter Objectives

In this chapter you will learn:

- The purpose of views.
- How to create and delete views using SQL.
- How the DBMS performs operations on views.
- Under what conditions views are updatable.
- The advantages and disadvantages of views.
- The purpose of the integrity enhancement feature of SQL.
- How to define integrity constraints using SQL including:
  - Required data.
  - Domain constraints.
  - Entity integrity.
  - Referential integrity.
  - Enterprise constraints.
- How to use the integrity enhancement feature in the CREATE and ALTER TABLE statements.
- How the ISO transaction model works.
- How to use the GRANT and REVOKE statements as a level of security.
- That SQL statements can be embedded in high-level programming languages.
- The difference between static and dynamic embedded SQL.
- How to write programs that use embedded DML and DDL statements.
- The enhancements introduced in the SQL 1992 standard and future enhancements.

In the previous chapter, we discussed in some detail the Structured Query Language (SQL) and, in particular, the data manipulation and data definition facilities. In this chapter, we continue our presentation of SQL and examine more advanced features of the language. In Section 12.1, we discuss views, which we introduced in Section 3.5. We show how views can be created using SQL, and how the DBMS converts operations on views into equivalent operations on the base tables. We also discuss the restrictions that the ISO SQL standard places on views in order for them to be updatable.

The 1989 ISO standard introduced an Integrity Enhancement Feature (IEF), which provides facilities for defining referential integrity and other constraints (ISO, 1989). Prior to this standard, it was the responsibility of each application program to ensure compliance with these constraints. The provision of an IEF greatly enhances the functionality of SQL, and allows constraint checking to be centralized and standardized. We consider the integrity enhancement feature in Section 12.2 and advanced data definition in Section 12.3.

Views provide a certain degree of database security. SQL also provides a separate access control subsystem, containing facilities to allow users to share database objects or, alternatively, restrict access to database objects. We discuss the access control subsystem in Section 12.4.

In Section 11.1, we mentioned that SQL can be used in two ways: it can be used **interactively** by entering the statements at a terminal; it can also be **embedded** in a high-level procedural language. We examine how SQL statements can be embedded in high-level languages in Sections 12.5 and 12.6. We conclude the discussion on SQL with a brief review of the features that were added to the 1989 ISO standard, and the features that are being considered for inclusion in future versions of the standard. As in the previous chapter, we present the features of SQL using examples drawn from the *DreamHome* case study introduced in Section 1.7. We use the same notation for specifying the format of SQL statements as defined in Section 11.2.

12.1 Views

Recall from Section 3.5 the definition of a view:

View	A view is the dynamic result of one or more relational operations operating on the base relations to produce another relation. A view is a **virtual relation** that does not actually exist in the database but is produced upon request by a particular user, at the time of request.

To the database user, a view appears just like a real table, with a set of named columns and rows of data. However, unlike a base table, a view does not exist in the database as a stored set of data values. Instead, the rows and columns of data visible through the view are the results produced by the query that defines the view. The DBMS stores the definition of the view in the database. When the DBMS encounters a reference to a view, it looks up this definition and translates the request into an equivalent request against the source tables of the view and then performs the request. This merging process, called **view resolution**, is discussed in Section 12.1.4. First, we examine how to create and use views.

12.1.1 Creating a View (CREATE VIEW)

The format of the CREATE VIEW statement is:

CREATE VIEW view_name [(column_name [, ...])]
AS subselect [WITH [CASCADED | LOCAL] CHECK OPTION]

You can optionally assign a name to each column in the view. If a list of column names is specified, it must have the same number of items as the number of columns produced by the *subselect*. If the list of column names is omitted, each column in the view takes the name of the corresponding column in the *subselect*. The list of column names must be specified if there is any ambiguity in the name for a column. This may occur if the *subselect* includes calculated columns, and the AS subclause has not been used to name such columns, or it produces two columns with identical names as a result of a join.

The *subselect* is known as the **defining query**. If WITH CHECK OPTION is specified, SQL ensures that if a row fails to satisfy the WHERE clause of the defining query of the view, it is not added to the underlying base table of the view (see Section 12.1.6). It should be noted that to create a view successfully, you must have SELECT privilege on all of the tables referenced in the subselect and USAGE privilege on any domains used in referenced columns. These privileges are discussed further in Section 12.4. Although all views are created in the same way, in practice different types of views are used for different purposes. We illustrate the different types of views with examples.

Example 12.1: Create a horizontal view _____

A horizontal view allows you to restrict a user's access to selected rows of a table.

Create a view so that the manager at branch B3 can see only the details for staff who work in his or her office.

> CREATE VIEW manager3_staff
> AS SELECT *
>   FROM staff
>   WHERE bno = 'B3';

This creates a view called Manager3_Staff with the same column names as the

Staff table but containing only those rows where the branch number is B3. (Strictly speaking, the Bno column is unnecessary and could have been omitted from the definition of the view, as all entries have *bno = 'B3'*.) If we now execute the statement:

SELECT * FROM manager3_staff;

we would get the result table shown in Table 12.1.

Table 12.1 Data for view Manager3_Staff

sno	fname	lname	address	tel_no	position	sex	dob	salary	nin	bno
SG37	Ann	Beech	81 George St, Glasgow PA1 2JR	0141–848–3345	Snr Asst	F	10–Nov–60	12000.00	WL432514C	B3
SG14	David	Ford	63 Ashby St, Partick, Glasgow G11	0141–339–2177	Deputy	M	24–Mar–58	18000.00	WL220658D	B3
SG5	Susan	Brand	5 Gt Western Rd, Glasgow G12	0141–334–2001	Manager	F	3–Jun–40	24000.00	WK588932E	B3

(3 rows)

To ensure that the branch manager can see only these rows, the manager should not be given access to the base table Staff. Instead, the manager should be given access permission to the view Manager3_Staff. This effectively gives the branch manager a customized view of the Staff table, showing only the staff at his or her branch. Access permissions are discussed in Section 12.4.

Example 12.2: Create a vertical view

A vertical view allows you to restrict a user's access to selected columns of a table.

Create a view of the staff details at branch B3 that excludes salary information, so that only the manager at that branch can access the salary details for staff who work in his or her office.

    CREATE VIEW staff3
    AS SELECT sno, fname, lname, address, tel_no, position, sex
        FROM staff
        WHERE bno = 'B3';

Note that we could rewrite this statement to use the Manager3_Staff view instead of the Staff table, thus:

    CREATE VIEW staff3
    AS SELECT sno, fname, lname, address, tel_no, position, sex
        FROM manager3_staff;

This creates a view called Staff3 with the same columns as the Staff table, but excluding the Salary, DOB, NIN and Bno columns. If we list this view we would get the result table shown Table 12.2.

Table 12.2 Data for view Staff3.

sno	fname	lname	address	tel_no	position	sex
SG37	Ann	Beech	81 George St, Glasgow PA1 2JR	0141–848–3345	Snr Asst	F
SG14	David	Ford	63 Ashby St, Partick, Glasgow G11	0141–339–2177	Deputy	M
SG5	Susan	Brand	5 Gt Western Rd, Glasgow G12	0141–334–2001	Manager	F

(3 rows)

To ensure that only the branch manager can see the salary details, staff at branch office B3 should not be given access to the base table Staff or the view Manager3_Staff. Instead, they should be given access permission to the view Staff3, thereby denying them access to sensitive salary data.

A view where we omit specific columns is often called a 'vertical view' because it fragments the Staff table vertically to create the view. Vertical views are commonly used where the data stored in a table is used by various users or groups of users. They provide a private table for each user or group of users, composed only of the columns needed by that user.

Example 12.3:   Grouped and joined views _____

Create a view of staff who manage properties for rent, including the branch number they work at, the staff number and the number of properties they manage.

> CREATE VIEW staff_prop_cnt (branch_no, staff_no, cnt)
> AS   SELECT s.bno, s.sno, COUNT(*)
>   FROM staff s, property_for_rent p
>   WHERE s.sno = p.sno
>   GROUP BY s.bno, s.sno;

giving the data shown in Table 12.3.

Table 12.3   Data for view Staff_Prop_Cnt.

branch_no	staff_no	cnt
B3	SG14	2
B3	SG37	2
B5	SL41	1
B7	SA9	1

(4 rows)

This example illustrates the use of a subselect containing a GROUP BY clause (giving a view called a **grouped view**) and containing multiple tables (giving a view called a **joined view**). One of the most frequent reasons for using views is to simplify multi-table queries. Once a multi-joined view has been defined, you can often use a simple single-table query against the view for queries that would otherwise require a multi-table join. Note that we have to include the names of the columns in the definition of the view because of the use of the unqualified aggregate function COUNT in the subselect.

12.1.2   Removing a View (DROP VIEW)

A view is removed from the database with the DROP VIEW statement:

> DROP VIEW view_name [RESTRICT | CASCADE]

DROP VIEW causes the definition of the view to be deleted from the database. For example, we could remove the Manager3_Staff view using the statement:

> DROP VIEW manager3_staff;

If CASCADE is specified, DROP VIEW deletes all related dependent objects; in other words, all objects that reference the view. This means that DROP VIEW also deletes any views that are defined on the view being dropped. If RESTRICT is specified and there are any other objects that depend for their existence on the continued existence of the view being dropped, the command is rejected. The default setting is RESTRICT.

12.1.3   Restrictions on Views

The ISO standard imposes several important restrictions on the creation and use of views, although there is considerable variation among dialects.

- If a column in the view is based on an aggregate function, then the column may appear only in SELECT and ORDER BY clauses of queries that access the view. In particular, such a column may not be used in a WHERE clause and may not be an argument to an aggregate function in any query based on the view. For example, consider the view Staff_Prop_Cnt of Example 12.3, which has a column *cnt* based on the aggregate function COUNT. The following query would fail:

  > SELECT COUNT(cnt)
  > FROM staff_prop_cnt;

  because we are using an aggregate function on the column *cnt*, which is itself based on an aggregate function. Similarly, the following query would also fail:

    SELECT *

    FROM staff_prop_cnt

    WHERE cnt > 2;

because we are using the view column, *cnt*, derived from an aggregate function in a WHERE clause.

- A grouped view may never be joined with a base table or a view. For example, the Staff_Prop_Cnt view is a grouped view, so that any attempt to join this view with another table or view fails.

12.1.4 View Resolution

Having considered how to create and use views, we now look more closely at how a query on a view is handled. To illustrate the process of **view resolution**, consider the following query, which counts the number of properties managed by each member of staff at branch office B3. This query is based on the Staff_Prop_Cnt view of Example 12.3:

    SELECT staff_no, cnt

    FROM staff_prop_cnt

    WHERE branch_no = 'B3'

    ORDER BY staff_no;

View resolution merges the above query with the defining query of the Staff_Prop_Cnt view. View resolution proceeds as follows:

(1)   The view column names in the SELECT list are translated into their corresponding column names in the defining query. This gives:

    SELECT s.sno, COUNT(*)

(2)   View names in the FROM clause are replaced with the corresponding FROM lists of the defining query:

    FROM staff s, property_for_rent p

(3)   The WHERE clause from the user query is combined with the WHERE clause of the defining query using the logical operator AND, thus:

    WHERE s.sno = p.sno AND bno = 'B3'

(4)   The GROUP BY and HAVING clauses are copied from the defining query. In this example, we have only a GROUP BY clause:

    GROUP BY s.sno, s.bno

(5)   Finally, the ORDER BY clause is copied from the user query with the view column name translated into the defining query column name:

    ORDER BY s.sno

(6)   The final merged query is now executed to produce the result:

SELECT s.sno, COUNT(*)

FROM staff s, property_for_rent p

WHERE s.sno = p.sno AND bno = 'B3'

GROUP BY s.sno, s.bno

ORDER BY s.sno;

giving the result table shown in Table 12.4.

Table 12.4 Result table
after view resolution.

staff_no	cnt
SG14	2
SG37	2

(2 rows)

12.1.5 View Updatability

All updates to a base table are immediately reflected in all views that encompass that base table. Similarly, we may expect that if a view is updated then the base table(s) will reflect that change. However, consider again the view Staff_Prop_Cnt of Example 12.3:

CREATE VIEW staff_prop_cnt (branch_no, staff_no, cnt)

AS   SELECT s.bno, s.sno, COUNT(*)

FROM staff s, property_for_rent p

WHERE s.sno = p.sno

GROUP BY s.bno, s.sno;

giving the data shown in Table 12.5.

Table 12.5 The view Staff_Prop_Cnt.

branch_no	staff_no	cnt
B3	SG14	2
B3	SG37	2
B5	SL41	1
B7	SA9	1

(4 rows)

Consider what would happen if we tried to insert a record that showed that at branch B3, staff member SG5 manages two properties, using the following insert:

INSERT INTO staff_prop_cnt

VALUES ('B3', 'SG5', 2);

We have to insert two records into the Property_for_Rent table showing which properties staff member SG5 manages. However, we do not know which properties they are; all we know is that this member of staff manages two properties. In other words, we do not know the primary keys for the Property_ for_Rent table. If we change the definition of the view and replace the count with the actual property numbers:

CREATE VIEW staff_prop_list (branch_no, staff_no, property_no)

AS   SELECT s.bno, s.sno, p.pno

        FROM staff s, property_for_rent p

        WHERE s.sno = p.sno;

and we try to insert the record:

INSERT INTO staff_prop_list

VALUES ('B3', 'SG5', 'PG19');

then there is still a problem with this insertion, because in the definition of the Property_for_Rent table, we specified that all columns except Area, Pcode and Sno were not allowed to have nulls (see Example 11.43). However, as the Staff_Prop_List view excludes all columns from the Property_for_Rent table except the property number, we have no way of providing the remaining non-null columns with values.

The ISO standard specifies the views that must be updatable in a system that conforms to the standard. The definition given in the ISO standard is that a view is updatable if and only if:

- DISTINCT is not specified: that is, duplicate rows must not be eliminated from the query results.

- Every element in the SELECT list of the defining query is a column name (rather than a constant, expression or aggregate function) and no column appears more than once.

- The FROM clause specifies only one table: that is, the view must have a single source table for which the user has the required privileges. If the source table is itself a view, then that view must satisfy these conditions. This, therefore, excludes any views based on a join, union (UNION), intersection (INTERSECT) or difference (EXCEPT).

- The WHERE clause does not include any nested SELECTs that reference the table in the FROM clause.

- There is no GROUP BY or HAVING clause in the defining query.

In addition, every row that is added through the view must not violate the integrity constraints of the base table. For example, if a new row is added through a view, columns that are not included in the view must be set to null, but this must not violate a NOT NULL integrity constraint of the base table. The basic concept behind these restrictions is as follows:

Updatable view	For a view to be updatable, the DBMS must be able to trace any row or column back to its row or column in the source table.

12.1.6 WITH CHECK OPTION

Rows exist in a view because they satisfy the WHERE condition of the defining query. If a row is altered such that it no longer satisfies this condition, then it will disappear from the view. Similarly, new rows will appear within the view when an insert or update on the view cause them to satisfy the WHERE condition. The rows that enter or leave a view are called **migrating rows**.

Generally, the WITH CHECK OPTION of the CREATE VIEW statement allows us to prohibit a row migrating out of the view. The optional qualifiers LOCAL/CASCADED are applicable to view hierarchies: that is, a view that is derived from another view. In this case, if the WITH LOCAL CHECK OPTION is specified, then any row insert or update on this view and on any view directly or indirectly defined on this view must not cause the row to disappear from the view, unless the row also disappears from the underlying derived view/table. If the WITH CASCADED CHECK OPTION is specified (the default if neither LOCAL nor CASCADED is specified), then any row insert or update on this view and on any view directly or indirectly defined on this view must not cause the row to disappear from the view.

This feature is so useful that it can make working with views more attractive than working with the base tables. When an INSERT or UPDATE statement on the view violates the WHERE condition of the defining query, the operation is rejected. This enforces constraints on the database and helps preserve database integrity. The WITH CHECK OPTION can be specified only for an updatable view.

Example 12.4: WITH CHECK OPTION

Consider again the view created in Example 12.1:

```
CREATE VIEW manager3_staff
AS SELECT *
    FROM staff
    WHERE bno = 'B3'
WITH CHECK OPTION;
```

with the conceptual table shown in Table 12.1.

If we now tried to update the branch number of one of the rows from B3 to B5, for example:

> UPDATE manager3_staff
>
> SET bno = 'B5'
>
> WHERE sno = 'SG37';

then the specification of the keyword WITH CHECK OPTION in the definition of the view prevents this from happening, as this would cause the row to migrate from this horizontal view. Similarly, if we tried to insert the following row through the view:

> INSERT INTO manager3_staff
>
> VALUES('SL15', 'Mary' , 'Black', '2 Hillcrest, London, NW2',
>
> '0181–554–3426', 'Assistant', 'F', '1967–06–21', 8000, 'WM787850T', 'B2');

then the specification of WITH CHECK OPTION would prevent the row from being inserted into the underlying Staff table and immediately disappearing from this view.

Now consider the situation where Manager3_Staff is defined not on Staff directly but on another view of Staff:

CREATE VIEW low_salary   CREATE VIEW high_salary   CREATE VIEW manager3_staff
AS SELECT *   AS SELECT *   AS SELECT *
  FROM Staff   FROM low_salary   FROM high_salary
  WHERE salary > 9000;   WHERE salary > 10000   WHERE bno = 'B3';
                               WITH LOCAL CHECK OPTION;

If we now tried the following update on Manager3_Staff:

> UPDATE manager3_staff
>
> SET salary = 9500
>
> WHERE sno = 'SG37';

then this update would fail: although the update would cause the row to disappear from the view High_Salary, the row would not disappear from the table Low_Salary that High_Salary is derived from. However, if instead the update tried to set the salary to 8000, then the update would succeed as the row would no longer be part of Low_Salary. If, instead, the view High_Salary had specified a WITH CASCADED CHECK OPTION, then setting the salary to either 9500 or 8000 would be rejected because the row would disappear from High_Salary. Therefore, to ensure that anomalies like this do not arise, each view should be created using the WITH CASCADED CHECK OPTION.

12.1.7 Advantages and Disadvantages of Views

Advantages

In the case of a DBMS run on a standalone personal computer, views are usually a convenience, defined to simplify database requests. However, in a multi-user DBMS, views play a central role in defining the structure of the database and enforcing security. The major advantages of views are as follows:

Data independence

A view can present a consistent, unchanging picture of the structure of the database, even if the underlying source tables are changed (for example, columns added or removed, relationships changed, tables split, restructured or renamed). If columns are added or removed from a table, and these columns are not required by the view, the definition of the view need not change. If an existing table is rearranged or split up, a view may be defined so that users can continue to see the old table. In the case of splitting up a table, the old table can be recreated by defining a view from the join of the new tables, provided that the split allows the reconstruction of the table. We can ensure that this is possible by placing the primary key in both of the new tables. Thus, if we originally had a Renter table of the form:

> Renter   (Rno, FName, LName, Address, Tel_No, Pref_Type, Max_Rent)

we could reorganize it into two new tables:

> Renter_Details (Rno, FName, LName, Address, Tel_No)
>
> Renter_Reqts   (Rno, Pref_Type, Max_Rent)

Users and applications could still access the data using the old table structure, which would be recreated by defining a view called Renter as the natural join of Renter_Details and Renter_Reqts, with Rno as the join column:

```
CREATE VIEW renter
AS SELECT rd.rno, fname, lname, address, tel_no, pref_type, max_rent
   FROM renter_details rd, renter_reqts rq
   WHERE rd.rno = rq.rno;
```

Currency

Changes to any of the base tables in the defining query are immediately reflected in the view.

Security

Each user can be given the privilege to access the database only through a small set of views that contain the data appropriate for that user, thus restricting and controlling each user's access to the database.

Reduced complexity
A view can simplify queries, by drawing data from several tables into a single table and, in this way, transforming multi-table queries into single-table queries.

Convenience
Views can provide greater convenience to users; users are presented with only that part of the database that they need to see. This also reduces the complexity from the user's point of view.

Customization
Views provide a method to customize the appearance of the database, so that the same underlying base tables can be seen by different users in different ways.

Data integrity
If the WITH CHECK OPTION of the CREATE VIEW statement is used, SQL ensures that no row that fails to satisfy the WHERE clause of the defining query is ever added to any of the underlying base table(s) through the view, thereby ensuring the integrity of the view.

Disadvantages

Although views provide many significant benefits, there are also some disadvantages with SQL views:

Update restriction
In Section 12.1.6 we showed that, in some cases, a view cannot be updated.

Structure restriction
The structure of a view is determined at the time of its creation. If the defining query was of the form SELECT * FROM . . . , then the * refers to the columns of the base table present when the view is created. If columns are subsequently added to the base table, then these columns will not appear in the view, unless the view is dropped and recreated.

Performance
There is a performance penalty to be paid when using a view. In some cases, this will be negligible; in other cases, it may be more problematic. For example a view defined by a complex, multi-table query may take a long time to process as the view resolution must join the tables together *every time the view is accessed*. View resolution requires additional computer resources.

12.2 Integrity Enhancement Feature (IEF)

In this section, we examine the facilities provided by the 1992 ISO SQL standard for integrity control (ISO, 1992). Integrity control consists of constraints that we wish to impose in order to protect the database from becoming inconsistent. In Section 7.3, we considered five types of integrity constraints:

- required data,
- domain constraints,
- entity integrity,
- referential integrity,
- enterprise constraints.

Most of these constraints can be defined in the CREATE and ALTER TABLE statements. The version of the CREATE TABLE statement that we considered in the previous chapter was greatly simplified, and did not include specification of integrity constraints. In the next section, we examine the CREATE and ALTER TABLE statements in more detail, following a discussion of these five integrity constraints.

Required data

Some columns must contain a valid value; they are not allowed to contain missing values or nulls. For example, every member of staff must have an associated job position (for example, Manager, Assistant, and so on). The ISO standard provides the NOT NULL column specifier in the CREATE and ALTER TABLE statements to provide this type of constraint. For example, to specify that the column Position of the Staff table cannot be null, we define the column as:

    position   VARCHAR(10) NOT NULL

Domain constraints

Every column has a domain, in other words a set of legal values (see Section 3.2.1). For example, the sex of a member of staff is either 'M' or 'F', so the domain of the column Sex of the Staff table is a single character string consisting of either 'M' or 'F'. The ISO standard provides two mechanisms for specifying domains in the CREATE and ALTER TABLE statements. The first is the CHECK clause, which allows a constraint to be defined on a column or the whole table. The format of the CHECK clause is:

```
CHECK   (search_condition)
```

In a column constraint, the CHECK clause can reference only the column being defined. Thus, to ensure that the column Sex can only be specified as 'M' or 'F', we could define the column as:

    sex CHAR NOT NULL CHECK (sex IN ('M', 'F'))

However, the ISO standard allows domains to be defined more explicitly using the CREATE DOMAIN statement:

CREATE DOMAIN domain_name [AS] data_type
[DEFAULT default_option]
[CHECK (search_condition)]

A domain is given a name, *domain_name*, a data type, as described in Section 11.4.2, a default value and a CHECK constraint. This is not the complete definition, but it is sufficient to demonstrate the basic concept. Thus, for the above example, we could define a domain for Sex as:

    CREATE DOMAIN sex_type AS CHAR
        CHECK (VALUE IN ('M', 'F'));

This creates a domain Sex_Type that consists of a single character with either the value 'M' or 'F'. When defining the column Sex, we can now use the domain name Sex_Type in place of the data type CHAR:

    sex SEX_TYPE NOT NULL

The *search_condition* can involve a table lookup. For example, we can create a domain Branch_Number that ensures that the values entered correspond to an existing branch number in the Branch table, with the statement:

    CREATE DOMAIN branch_number AS VARCHAR(3)
        CHECK (VALUE IN (SELECT bno FROM branch));

Domains can be removed from the database using the DROP DOMAIN statement:

DROP DOMAIN domain_name [RESTRICT | CASCADE]

The drop behaviour, RESTRICT or CASCADE, was discussed in Section 11.4.5. Note that, in the case of CASCADE, any table column that is based on the domain is automatically changed to use the domain's underlying data type, and any constraint or default clause for the domain is replaced by a column constraint or column default clause, if appropriate. The preferred method of defining domain constraints is using the CREATE DOMAIN statement.

Entity integrity

The primary key of a table must contain a unique, non-null value for each row. For example, each row of the Staff table has a unique value for the staff number Sno, which uniquely identifies the member of staff represented by that row. The ISO standard supports entity integrity with the PRIMARY KEY clause in the CREATE and ALTER TABLE statements. For example, to define the primary key of the Staff table, we include the clause:

    PRIMARY KEY(sno)

With a composite primary key, for example the primary key of the Viewing table consists of both the columns Rno and Pno, we include the clause:

    PRIMARY KEY(rno, pno)

The PRIMARY KEY clause can be specified only once per table. However, it is still possible to ensure uniqueness for the alternate keys in the table using the keyword UNIQUE. We would also recommended that you use the keyword NOT NULL when defining alternate keys. For example, with the Viewing table, we could also have written:

    rno   CHAR(5)   NOT NULL,
    pno   CHAR(5)   NOT NULL,
    UNIQUE (rno, pno)

Referential integrity

A foreign key is a column or set of columns that links each row in the child table containing the foreign key to the row of the parent table containing the matching candidate key value. Referential integrity means that, if the foreign key contains a value, that value must refer to an existing, valid row in the parent table (see Section 3.3.3). For example, the branch number column Bno in the Staff table links the member of staff to that row in the Branch table where he or she works. If the branch number is not null, it must contain a valid value from the column Bno of the Branch table, or the member of staff is assigned to an invalid branch office.

The ISO standard supports the definition of foreign keys with the FOREIGN KEY clause in the CREATE and ALTER TABLE statements. For example, to define the foreign key Bno of the Staff table, we include the clause:

    FOREIGN KEY(bno) REFERENCES branch

SQL rejects any INSERT or UPDATE operation that attempts to create a foreign key value in a child table without a matching candidate key value in the parent table. The action SQL takes for any UPDATE or DELETE operation that attempts to update or delete a candidate key value in the parent table that has some matching rows in the child table is dependent on the **referential action** specified using the ON UPDATE and ON DELETE subclauses of the FOREIGN KEY clause. When the user attempts to delete a row from a parent table, and there are some matching rows in the child table, SQL supports four options regarding the action to be taken:

- CASCADE: Delete the row from the parent table and automatically delete the matching rows in the child table. Since these deleted rows may themselves have a candidate key that is used as a foreign key in another table, the foreign key rules for these tables are triggered, and so on in a cascading manner.

- SET NULL: Delete the row from the parent table and set the foreign key column(s) in the child table to NULL. This is only valid if the foreign key columns do not have the NOT NULL qualifier specified.

- SET DEFAULT: Delete the row from the parent table and set each component of the foreign key in the child table to the specified default value. This is valid only if the foreign key columns have a DEFAULT value specified.

- NO ACTION: Reject the delete operation from the parent table. This is the default setting if the ON DELETE rule is omitted.

SQL supports the same options when the candidate key in the parent table is updated. With CASCADE, the foreign key column(s) in the child table are set to the new value(s) of the candidate key in the parent table. In the same way, the updates cascade if the updated column(s) in the child table reference foreign keys in another table. For example, in the Property_for_Rent table, the staff number Sno is a foreign key referencing the Staff table. We can specify a deletion rule, such that if a staff number is deleted from the Staff table, the corresponding column(s) in the Property_for_Rent table are set to NULL:

> FOREIGN KEY (sno) REFERENCES staff ON DELETE SET NULL

Similarly, the owner number Ono in the Property_for_Rent table is a foreign key referencing the Owner table. We can specify an update rule, such that if an owner number is updated in the Owner table, the corresponding column(s) in the Property_for_Rent table are set to the new value:

> FOREIGN KEY (ono) REFERENCES owner ON UPDATE CASCADE

Enterprise constraints

Updates to tables may be constrained by enterprise rules governing the real-world transactions that are represented by the updates. For example, *Dream-Home* may have a rule that prevents a member of staff from managing more than 10 properties at the same time. The ISO standard allows enterprise constraints to be specified using the CHECK and UNIQUE clauses of the

CREATE and ALTER TABLE statements and the CREATE ASSERTION statement. We have already discussed the CHECK and UNIQUE clauses earlier in this section. The CREATE ASSERTION statement is an integrity constraint that is not directly linked with a table definition. The format of the statement is:

> CREATE ASSERTION assertion_name
> CHECK (search_condition)

This statement is very similar to the CHECK clause discussed above. However, when an enterprise constraint involves more than one table, it may be preferable to use an ASSERTION rather than duplicate the check in each table or place the constraint in an arbitrary table. For example, to define the enterprise constraint that prevents a member of staff from managing more than 10 properties at the same time, we could write:

> CREATE ASSERTION staff_not_handling_too_much
> CHECK (NOT EXISTS (SELECT sno
> FROM property_for_rent
> GROUP BY sno
> HAVING COUNT(*) > 10))

12.3 Advanced Data Definition

12.3.1 Integrity in CREATE TABLE

In Section 11.4.4, we showed a simplified version of the CREATE TABLE statement. The definition of the CREATE TABLE statement in the ISO standard consists of several variations, but the basic format of the statement is:

> CREATE TABLE table_name
> {(column_name data_type [NOT NULL] [UNIQUE]
> [DEFAULT default_option] [CHECK (search_condition)] [,...] }
> [PRIMARY KEY (list_of_columns),]
> {[UNIQUE (list_of_columns),] [,...] }
> {[FOREIGN KEY (list_of_foreign_key_columns)
> REFERENCES parent_table_name [(list_of_candidate_key_columns)],
> [MATCH {PARTIAL | FULL}
> [ON UPDATE referential_action]
> [ON DELETE referential_action]] [,...] }
> {[CHECK (search_condition)] [, . . .] })

As we discussed in the previous section, this version of the CREATE TABLE statement incorporates facilities for defining referential integrity and other constraints. There is significant variation in the support provided by different SQL dialects for this version of the statement. However, when it is supported, the facilities should be used.

The basic elements of the statement (that is, *table_name*, *column_name*, *data_type* and the NOT NULL specifier) are as discussed in Section 11.4.4. The optional DEFAULT clause can be specified to provide a default value for a particular column. SQL uses this default value whenever an INSERT statement fails to specify a value for the column. Among other values, the *default_option* includes literals. The UNIQUE and CHECK clauses were discussed in the previous section. The remaining clauses are known as **table constraints** and can optionally be preceded with the clause:

CONSTRAINT constraint_name

which allows the constraint to be dropped by name using the ALTER TABLE statement (see below).

The **PRIMARY KEY** clause specifies the column or columns that form the primary key for the table. If this clause is available, it should be specified for every table created. By default, NOT NULL is assumed for each column that comprises the primary key. Only one PRIMARY KEY clause is allowed per table. SQL rejects any INSERT or UPDATE operation that attempts to create a duplicate row within the PRIMARY KEY column(s). In this way, SQL guarantees the uniqueness of the primary key.

The **UNIQUE** clause identifies the remaining candidate keys (that is, a set of one or more columns that uniquely identify each row of the table). Again, every column that appears in the UNIQUE clause must also be declared as NOT NULL. There may be as many UNIQUE clauses per table as required. SQL rejects any INSERT or UPDATE operation that attempts to create a duplicate value within each candidate key.

The **FOREIGN KEY** clause specifies a foreign key in the (child) table and the relationship it has to another (parent) table. This clause implements referential integrity constraints. The clause specifies:

- A *list_of_foreign_key_columns*, the column or columns from the table being created that form the foreign key.

- A REFERENCES subclause, giving the parent table: that is, the table holding the matching candidate key. If the *list_of_candidate_key_ columns* is omitted, the foreign key is assumed to match the primary key of the parent table. In this case, the parent table must have a PRIMARY KEY clause in its CREATE TABLE statement.

- An optional update rule (ON UPDATE) for the relationship that specifies the action to be taken when a candidate key is updated in a parent table that matches a foreign key in the child table. The **referential_action** can be CASCADE, SET NULL, SET DEFAULT or NO ACTION. If the ON UPDATE clause is omitted, the default NO ACTION is assumed (see Section 12.2).

- An optional delete rule (ON DELETE) for the relationship that specifies the action to be taken when a row is deleted from a parent table that has a candidate key that matches a foreign key in the child table. The **referential_action** can be CASCADE, SET NULL, SET DEFAULT or NO ACTION. If the ON DELETE clause is omitted, the default NO ACTION is assumed (see Section 12.3).

- By default, the referential constraint is satisfied if any component of the foreign key is null or there is a matching row in the parent table. The MATCH option provides additional constraints relating to nulls within the foreign key. If MATCH FULL is specified, the foreign key components must all be null or must all have values. If MATCH PARTIAL is specified, the foreign key components must all be null, or there must be at least one row in the parent table that could satisfy the constraint if the other nulls were correctly substituted. Some authors argue that referential integrity should imply MATCH FULL.

There can be as many FOREIGN KEY clauses as required. The **CHECK** and **CONSTRAINT** clauses allow additional constraints to be defined. If used as a column constraint, the CHECK clause can reference only the column being defined. Constraints are effectively checked after every SQL statement has been executed, although this check can be deferred until the end of the enclosing transaction (see Section 12.3.4). Example 12.5 demonstrates the potential of this version of the CREATE TABLE statement.

Example 12.5: CREATE TABLE

Consider again the creation of the Property_for_Rent table as shown in Example 11.43. Using the complete version of the CREATE TABLE statement, we could create this table as follows:

```
CREATE DOMAIN owner_number AS VARCHAR(5)
        CHECK (VALUE IN (SELECT ono FROM owner));
CREATE DOMAIN staff_number AS VARCHAR(5)
        CHECK (VALUE IN (SELECT sno FROM staff));
CREATE DOMAIN branch_number AS VARCHAR(3)
        CHECK (VALUE IN (SELECT bno FROM branch));
CREATE DOMAIN property_number AS VARCHAR(5);
CREATE DOMAIN street AS VARCHAR(25);
CREATE DOMAIN area AS VARCHAR(15);
CREATE DOMAIN city AS VARCHAR(15);
CREATE DOMAIN post_code AS VARCHAR(8);
CREATE DOMAIN property_type AS CHAR(1)
        CHECK(VALUE IN ('B', 'C', 'D', 'E', 'F,' 'M', 'S'));
CREATE DOMAIN property_rooms AS SMALLINT;
        CHECK(VALUE BETWEEN 1 AND 15);
CREATE DOMAIN property_rent AS DECIMAL(6,2)
        CHECK(VALUE BETWEEN 0 AND 9999);
```

```
CREATE TABLE property_for_rent (
        pno             PROPERTY_NUMBER   NOT NULL,
        street          STREET            NOT NULL,
        area            AREA,
        city            CITY              NOT NULL,
        pcode           POST_CODE,
        type            PROPERTY_TYPE     NOT NULL   DEFAULT 'F',
        rooms           PROPERTY_ROOMS    NOT NULL   DEFAULT 4,
        rent            PROPERTY_RENT     NOT NULL   DEFAULT 1600,
        ono             OWNER_NUMBER      NOT NULL,
        sno             STAFF_NUMBER
                        CONSTRAINT staff_not_handling_too_much
                            CHECK (NOT EXISTS (SELECT sno
                                               FROM property_for_rent
                                               GROUP BY sno
                                               HAVING COUNT(*) > 10)),
        bno             BRANCH_NUMBER     NOT NULL,
        PRIMARY KEY (pno),
        FOREIGN KEY (sno) REFERENCES staff ON DELETE SET NULL ON
        UPDATE CASCADE,
        FOREIGN KEY (ono) REFERENCES owner ON DELETE NO ACTION
        ON UPDATE CASCADE,
        FOREIGN KEY (bno) REFERENCES branch ON DELETE NO ACTION
        ON UPDATE CASCADE);
```

The table has the same column names and underlying data types as in Example 11.43. In addition, a default value of 'F' for 'Flat' has been assigned to column Type. A CONSTRAINT for the staff number column has been specified to ensure that a member of staff does not handle too many properties. The constraint checks that the number of properties the staff member currently handles is not greater than 10.

The primary key is the property number, Pno. SQL automatically enforces uniqueness on this column. The staff number, Sno, is a foreign key referencing the Staff table. A deletion rule has been specified, such that if a staff number is deleted from the Staff table, the corresponding column(s) in the Property_for_Rent table are set to NULL. Additionally, an update rule has been specified, such that if a staff number is updated in the Staff table, the corresponding column(s) in the Property_for_Rent table are updated accordingly. The owner number, Ono, is a foreign key referencing the Owner table. A delete rule of NO ACTION has been specified to prevent deletions from the Owner table if there are matching Ono columns in the Property_for_Rent table. An update rule of CASCADE has been specified, so that if an owner number is updated, the corresponding column(s) in the Property_ for_Rent table are set to the new value. Similarly for the Bno column. In all FOREIGN KEY constraints, because the *list_of_primary_key_columns* has been omitted, SQL assumes that the foreign keys match the primary keys of the respective parent tables.

12.3.2 Changing a Table Definition (ALTER TABLE)

The ISO standard provides an ALTER TABLE statement for changing the structure of a table once it has been created. The definition of the ALTER TABLE statement in the ISO standard consists of six options to:

- Add a new column to a table.
- Drop a column from a table.
- Add a new table constraint.
- Drop a table constraint.
- Set a default for a column.
- Drop a default for a column.

The basic format of the statement is:

```
ALTER TABLE table_name
  [ADD [COLUMN] column_name data_type [NOT NULL] [UNIQUE]
    [DEFAULT default_option ] [CHECK (search_condition) ] ]
  [DROP [COLUMN] column_name [RESTRICT | CASCADE] ]
  [ADD [CONSTRAINT [constraint_name]] table_constraint_definition ]
  [DROP CONSTRAINT constraint_name [RESTRICT | CASCADE] ]
  [ALTER [COLUMN] SET DEFAULT default_option ]
  [ALTER [COLUMN] DROP DEFAULT ]
```

where the parameters are as defined for the CREATE TABLE statement in the previous section. A *table_constraint_definition* is one of the clauses: PRIMARY KEY, UNIQUE, FOREIGN_KEY or CHECK. The ADD COLUMN clause is similar to the definition of a column in the CREATE TABLE statement. The DROP COLUMN clause specifies the name of the column to be dropped from the table definition. It has an optional qualifier that allows you to specify whether the DROP action is to cascade or not:

- RESTRICT: The DROP operation is rejected if the column is referenced by another database object (for example, in a view definition). The default setting is RESTRICT.
- CASCADE: The DROP operation proceeds and automatically drops the column from any database objects it is referenced by. This operation

cascades, so that if a column is dropped from a referencing object, SQL checks whether *that* column is referenced by any other object and drops it from there if it is, and so on.

This is the same concept as the RESTRICT/CASCADE qualifier of the DROP TABLE statement (see Section 11.4.5).

Example 12.6: ALTER TABLE

Change the Staff table by removing the default of 'Assistant' for the Position column and setting the default for the Sex column to female ('F').

    ALTER TABLE staff
        ALTER position DROP DEFAULT;
    ALTER TABLE staff
        ALTER sex SET DEFAULT 'F';

Change the Property_for_Rent table by removing the constraint that staff are not allowed to handle more than 10 properties at a time. Change the Renter table by adding a new column representing the preferred area for accommodation.

    ALTER TABLE property_for_rent
        DROP CONSTRAINT staff_not_handling_too_much;
    ALTER TABLE renter
        ADD pref_area VARCHAR(15);

The ALTER TABLE statement is not available in all dialects of SQL. In some dialects, the ALTER TABLE statement cannot be used to remove an existing column from a table. In such cases, if a column is no longer required, the column could simply be ignored but kept in the table definition. If, however, you wish to remove the column from the table you must:

- Unload all the data from the table.
- Remove the table definition using the DROP TABLE statement.
- Redefine the new table using the CREATE TABLE statement.
- Reload the data back into the new table.

The bulk load and unload steps are typically performed with special-purpose utility programs supplied with the DBMS. However, it is possible to create a temporary table and use the INSERT ... SELECT statement to load the data from the old table into the temporary table and then from the temporary table into the new table.

12.3.3   Transactions

The ISO standard defines a transaction model based on two SQL statements: COMMIT and ROLLBACK. Most, but not all, commercial implementations of SQL conform to this model, which is based on IBM's DB2 DBMS. A transaction is a logical unit of work consisting of one or more SQL statements that is guaranteed to be atomic with respect to recovery. The standard specifies that an SQL transaction automatically begins with a **transaction-initiating** SQL statement executed by a user or program (for example, SELECT, INSERT, UPDATE). Changes made by a transaction are not visible to other concurrently executing transactions until the transaction completes. A transaction can complete in one of four ways:

- A COMMIT statement ends the transaction successfully, making the database changes permanent. A new transaction starts after COMMIT with the next transaction-initiating statement.

- A ROLLBACK statement aborts the transaction, backing out any changes made by the transaction. A new transaction starts after ROLLBACK with the next transaction-initiating statement.

- For programmatic SQL, successful program termination ends the final transaction successfully, even if a COMMIT statement has not been executed.

- For programmatic SQL, abnormal program termination aborts the transaction.

SQL transactions cannot be nested. The SET TRANSACTION statement allows the user to configure certain aspects of the transaction. The basic format of the statement is:

```
SET TRANSACTION
  [READ ONLY | READ WRITE] |
  [ISOLATION LEVEL READ UNCOMMITTED |
     READ COMMITTED | REPEATABLE READ | SERIALIZABLE ]
```

The READ ONLY and READ WRITE qualifiers indicate whether the transaction is read only or involves both read and write operations. The default is READ WRITE if neither qualifier is specified (unless the isolation level is READ UNCOMMITTED). Perhaps confusingly, READ ONLY allows a transaction to issue INSERT, UPDATE and DELETE statements against temporary tables (but only temporary tables). The isolation level indicates the degree of interaction from other transactions that is allowed during the execution of the transaction. Table 12.6 shows the violations of serializability allowed by each isolation level.

Only the SERIALIZABLE isolation level is safe: that is, generates serializable schedules. The remaining isolation levels require a mechanism to be provided by the DBMS that can be used by the programmer to ensure

Table 12.6 Violations of serializability permitted by isolation levels.

Isolated level	Dirty read	Non-repeatable read	Phantom read
READ UNCOMMITTED	Y	Y	Y
READ COMMITTED	N	Y	Y
REPEATABLE READ	N	N	Y
SERIALIZABLE	N	N	N

serializability. Chapter 15 discusses the meaning of the dirty read, non-repeatable read and phantom reads, and provides additional information on transactions and serializability.

12.3.4 Immediate and Deferred Integrity Constraints

In some situations, we do not want integrity constraints to be checked immediately, that is, after every SQL statement has been executed, but instead at transaction commit. A constraint may be defined as INITIALLY IMMEDIATE or INITIALLY DEFERRED, indicating which mode the constraint assumes at the start of each transaction. In the former case, it is also possible to specify whether the mode can be changed subsequently using the qualifier [NOT] DEFERRABLE. The default mode is INITIALLY IMMEDIATE.

The SET CONSTRAINTS statement is used to set the mode for specified constraints for the current transaction. The format of this statement is:

```
SET CONSTRAINTS
  {ALL | constraint_name [, ...] } {DEFERRED | IMMEDIATE}
```

12.4 Access Control

In Section 2.4, we stated that a DBMS should provide a mechanism to ensure that only authorized users can access the database. SQL provides the GRANT and REVOKE statements to allow security to be set up on the tables in the database. The security mechanism is based on the concepts of **authorization identifiers**, **ownership** and **privileges**.

Authorization identifiers and ownership

An authorization identifier is a normal SQL identifier that is used to establish the identity of a user. Each database user is assigned an authorization identifier by the Database Administrator (DBA). Usually, the identifier has an associated password, for obvious security reasons. Every SQL statement that is executed by the DBMS is performed on behalf of a specific user.

The authorization identifier is used to determine which database objects that user may reference and what operations may be performed on those objects.

Each object that is created in SQL has an owner. The owner is identified by the authorization identifier defined in the AUTHORIZATION clause of the schema to which the object belongs (see Section 11.4.3). The owner is initially the only person who may know of the existence of the object and, consequently, perform any operations on the object.

Privileges

Privileges are the actions that a user is permitted to carry out on a given base table or view. The privileges defined by the ISO standard are:

- SELECT: The privilege to retrieve data from a table.
- INSERT: The privilege to insert new rows into a table.
- UPDATE: The privilege to modify rows of data in a table.
- DELETE: The privilege to delete rows of data from a table.
- REFERENCES: The privilege to reference columns of a named table in integrity constraints.
- USAGE: The privilege to use domains, collations, character sets and translations. We do not discuss collations, character sets and translations in this book. The interested reader is referred to Cannan and Otten (1993).

The INSERT and UPDATE privileges can be restricted to specific columns of the table, allowing changes to these columns but disallowing changes to any other column. Similarly, the REFERENCES privilege can be restricted to specific columns of the table, allowing these columns to be referenced in constraints, such as check constraints and foreign key constraints when creating another table, but disallowing others from being referenced.

When a user creates a table using the CREATE TABLE statement, he or she automatically becomes the owner of the table and receives full privileges for the table. Other users initially have no privileges on the newly created table. To give them access to the table, the owner must explicitly grant them the necessary privileges using the GRANT statement.

When a user creates a view with the CREATE VIEW statement, he or she automatically becomes the owner of the view, but does not necessarily receive full privileges on the view. To create the view, a user must have SELECT privilege on all the tables that make up the view and REFERENCES privilege on the named columns of the view. However, the view owner gets INSERT, UPDATE and DELETE privileges only if he or she holds this privilege for every table in the view.

12.4.1 Granting Privileges to Other Users (GRANT)

The GRANT statement is used to grant privileges on database objects to specific users. Normally the GRANT statement is used by the owner of a table to give other users access to the data. The format of the GRANT statement is:

```
GRANT    {privilege_list | ALL PRIVILEGES}
ON       object_name
TO       {authorization_id_list | PUBLIC }
[WITH GRANT OPTION]
```

The *privilege_list* consists of one or more of the following privileges separated by commas:

SELECT

DELETE

INSERT   [(column_name [, . . .])]

UPDATE   [(column_name [, . . .])]

REFERENCES   [(column_name [, . . .])]

USAGE

For convenience, the GRANT statement allows the keyword ALL PRIVI-LEGES to be used to grant all privileges to a user instead of having to specify the six privileges individually. It also provides the keyword PUBLIC to allow access to be granted to all present and future authorized users, not just to the users currently known to the DBMS. The *object_name* can be the name of a base table, view, domain, character set, collation or translation.

The WITH GRANT OPTION keyword allows the user(s) in *authorization_id_list* to pass the privileges they have been given for the named object on to other users. If these users pass a privilege on specifying WITH GRANT OPTION, the users receiving the privilege may in turn grant it to still other users. If this keyword is not specified, the receiving user(s) will not be able to pass the privileges on to other users. In this way, the owner of the object maintains very tight control over who has permission to use the object and what forms of access are allowed.

Example 12.7:   GRANT all privileges _____

Give the user with authorization identifier Manager full privileges to the Staff table.

GRANT ALL PRIVILEGES

ON staff

TO manager WITH GRANT OPTION;

The user identified as Manager can now retrieve rows from the Staff table, and also insert, update and delete data from this table. Manager can also reference the Staff table, and all the Staff columns in any table he or she creates subsequently. We also specified the keyword WITH GRANT OPTION, so that Manager can pass these privileges on to other users that he or she sees fit.

Example 12.8:   GRANT specific privileges _____

Give the user with authorization identifier Admin the privileges SELECT and UPDATE on column Salary of the Staff table.

> GRANT SELECT, UPDATE (salary)
> ON staff
> TO admin;

We have omitted the keyword WITH GRANT OPTION, so that user Admin cannot pass either of these privileges on to other users.

Example 12.9:   GRANT specific privileges to multiple users _____

Give users Personnel and Deputy the privilege SELECT on the Staff table.

> GRANT SELECT
> ON staff
> TO personnel, deputy;

Example 12.10:   GRANT specific privileges to PUBLIC _____

Give all users the privilege SELECT on the Branch table.

> GRANT SELECT
> ON branch
> TO PUBLIC;

The use of the keyword PUBLIC means that all users (now and in the future) are able to retrieve all the data in the Branch table. Note that it does not make sense to use WITH GRANT OPTION in this case: as every user has access to the table, there is no need to pass the privilege on to other users.

12.4.2   Revoking Privileges from Users (REVOKE)

The REVOKE statement is used to take away privileges that were granted with the GRANT statement. A REVOKE statement can take away all or some of the privileges that were previously granted to a user. The format of the statement is:

```
REVOKE [GRANT OPTION FOR] {privilege_list | ALL PRIVILEGES}
ON       object_name
FROM     {authorization_id_list | PUBLIC} [RESTRICT | CASCADE]
```

The keyword ALL PRIVILEGES refers to all the privileges granted to a user by the user revoking the privileges. The GRANT OPTION FOR optional keyword allows privileges passed on via the WITH GRANT OPTION of the GRANT statement to be revoked separately from the privileges themselves. The RESTRICT and CASCADE keywords operate exactly like the same keywords in the DROP TABLE statement (see Section 11.4.5).

Since privileges are required to create certain objects, revoking a privilege can remove the authority that allowed the object to be created (such an object is said to be **abandoned**). The REVOKE statement fails if it results in an abandoned object, such as a view, unless the CASCADE keyword has been specified. If CASCADE is specified, an appropriate DROP statement is issued for any abandoned views, domains, constraints or assertions.

The privileges that were granted to this user by other users are not affected by this REVOKE statement. Therefore, if another user has granted the user the privilege being revoked, the other user's grant still allows the user to access the table. For example, in Figure 12.1, User A grants User B INSERT privilege on the Staff table WITH GRANT OPTION (step 1). User B passes this privilege on to User C (step 2). Subsequently, User C gets the same privilege from User E (step 3). User C then passes the privilege on to User D (step 4). When User A revokes the INSERT privilege from User B (step 5), the privilege cannot be revoked from User C, because User C has also received the privilege from User E. If User E had not given User C this privilege, the revoke would have cascaded to User C and User D.

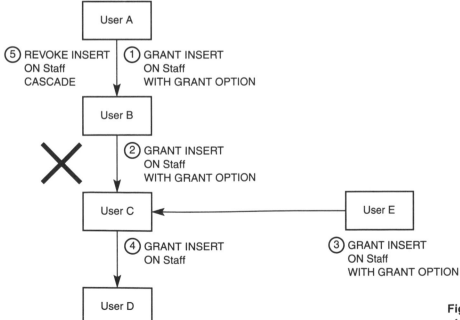

Figure 12.1 Effects of REVOKE.

Example 12.11:   REVOKE specific privileges from PUBLIC _____

Revoke the privilege SELECT on the Branch table from all users.

REVOKE SELECT
ON branch
FROM PUBLIC;

Example 12.12:   REVOKE specific privileges from named user ____

Revoke all privileges you have given to Deputy on the Staff table.

REVOKE ALL PRIVILEGES
ON staff
FROM deputy;

This is equivalent to REVOKE SELECT ... , as this was the only privilege that has been given to Deputy.

12.5   Embedded SQL

In the previous chapter, we mentioned that SQL can be used in two ways. In the preceding discussions, we have concentrated on the **interactive** use of SQL. However, SQL can also be **embedded** in a high-level procedural language. In many cases, the SQL language is identical, although the SELECT statement, in particular, requires more extensive treatment in embedded SQL. In fact, we can distinguish between two types of programmatic SQL:

- *Embedded SQL statements.*   SQL statements are embedded directly into the program source code and mixed with the host language statements. This approach allows users to write programs that access the database directly. A special precompiler modifies the source code to replace SQL statements with calls to DBMS routines. The source code can then be compiled and linked in the normal way. The ISO standard specifies embedded support for Ada, C, COBOL, Fortran, MUMPS, Pascal and PL/1 programming languages.

- *Application Program Interface (API)*   An alternative technique is to provide the programmer with a standard set of functions that can be invoked from the software. An API can provide the same functionality as embedded statements and removes the need for any precompilation. It may be argued that this approach provides a cleaner interface and generates more manageable code.

Most DBMS vendors provide some form of embedded SQL, including INGRES, ORACLE, Informix and DB2; ORACLE also provides an API; Sybase and SQLBase only provide an API. In this section, we concentrate on embedded SQL. To make the discussions more concrete, we demonstrate the use of the INGRES (Version 6.4) dialect of embedded SQL using the 'C' programming language. At the end of this section, we discuss the differences between INGRES embedded SQL and the ISO standard and conclude with a brief overview of APIs. In Section 12.6, we discuss an extended form of embedded SQL called **dynamic SQL** that provides increased flexibility and helps produce more general-purpose software.

12.5.1   Simple Embedded SQL Statements

The simplest type of embedded SQL statements are those that do not produce any query results: that is, non-selects.

Example 12.13: CREATE TABLE _____

We can create the Viewing table interactively using the following SQL statement:

```
CREATE TABLE viewing  (pno       VARCHAR(5)   NOT NULL,
                       rno       VARCHAR(5)   NOT NULL,
                       date      DATE         NOT NULL,
                       comment   VARCHAR(40));
```

However, we could also write the 'C' program listed in Figure 12.2 to create the table.

This is a trivial example of an embedded program, but it is nevertheless useful to illustrate some basic concepts:

- Embedded SQL statements start with an identifier, usually the keywords EXEC SQL, as defined in the ISO standard ['@SQL(' in MUMPS]. This indicates to the precompiler that the statement is an embedded SQL statement.

- Embedded SQL statements end with a terminator that is dependent on the host language. In Ada, 'C' and PL/1 the terminator is a semicolon (;); in COBOL, the terminator is the keywords END-EXEC; in Fortran, the embedded statement ends when there are no more continuation lines.

- Embedded SQL statements can continue over more than one line, using the continuation marker of the host language.

- An embedded SQL statement can appear anywhere that an executable host language statement can appear.

- The embedded statements (CONNECT, CREATE TABLE, COMMIT and DISCONNECT), in this case, are the same as would be entered interactively.

```
/* Program to create the VIEWING table */
#include ⟨stdio.h⟩
#include ⟨stdlib.h⟩
EXEC SQL INCLUDE sqlca;

main( )
{
/* Connect to database */
EXEC SQL CONNECT 'estatedb';
if (sqlca.sqlcode < 0) exit(-1);

/* Display message for user and create the table */
printf("Creating VIEWING table\n");
EXEC SQL CREATE TABLE viewing (pno varchar(5) not null,
                               rno varchar(5) not null,
                               date date not null,
                               comment varchar(40));
if (sqlca.sqlcode >= 0)                         /* Check success */
    printf("Creation successful\n");
else
    printf("Creation unsuccessful\n");

/* Commit the transaction */
EXEC SQL COMMIT;

/* Finally, disconnect from the database */
EXEC SQL DISCONNECT;
}
```

Figure 12.2
Embedded program
to create Viewing
table.

12.5.2 SQL Communications Area (SQLCA)

The DBMS uses an SQL Communications Area (SQLCA) to report runtime errors to the application program. The SQLCA is a data structure that contains error variables and status indicators. An application program can examine the SQLCA to determine the success or failure of each SQL statement. Figure 12.3 shows the definition of the SQLCA for INGRES. To use the SQLCA, at the start of the program we include the line:

EXEC SQL INCLUDE sqlca;

This tells the precompiler to include the SQLCA data structure in the program. In INGRES, the precompiler generates a data structure called *sqlca* using the statement:

extern IISQLCA sqlca;

The most important part of this structure is the SQLCODE variable, which we use to check for errors. The SQLCODE is set by the DBMS as follows:

```
/*
** SQLCA – Structure to hold the error and status information returned
**          by INGRES runtime routines
*/

typedef struct {
    char        sqlcaid[8];     /* contains fixed text "SQLCA    " */
    long        sqlcabc;        /* length of SQLCA structure */
    long        sqlcode;        /* SQL return code */
    struct {
        short   sqlerrm1;       /* length of error message */
        char    sqlerrcm[70];   /* text of error message */
    } sqlerrm;
    char        sqlerrp[8];     /* unused */
    long        sqlerrd[6];     /* sqlerrd[3] – number of rows processed */
    struct   {
        char sqlwarn0;          /* set to "W" on warning */
        char sqlwarn1;          /* set to "W" if character string truncated */
        char sqlwarn2;          /* set to "W" if NULLs eliminated from aggregates */
        char sqlwarn3;          /* set to "W" if mismatch in columns/host variables */
        char sqlwarn4;          /* set to "W" when preparing an update/delete without a where-clause */
        char sqlwarn5;          /* unused */
        char sqlwarn6;          /* set to "W" when error caused abnormal end to open */
        char sqlwarn7;          /* unused */
    } sqlwarn;
    char        sqlext[8];      /* unused */
} IISQLCA;
```

Figure 12.3 SQL Communications Area (SQLCA).

- An SQLCODE of zero indicates that the statement executed successfully (although there may be warning messages in *sqlwarn*).
- A negative SQLCODE indicates that an error occurred. The value in SQLCODE indicates the specific error that occurred.
- A positive SQLCODE indicates that the statement executed successfully, but an exceptional condition occurred, such as no more rows returned by a SELECT statement (see below).

In the previous example, we checked for a negative SQLCODE (sqlca.sqlcode < 0) for unsuccessful completion of the CONNECT and CREATE TABLE statements.

The WHENEVER statement

Every embedded SQL statement can potentially generate an error. Clearly, checking for success after every SQL statement would be quite laborious, so SQL provides an alternative method to simplify error handling. The WHENEVER statement is a directive to the precompiler to automatically generate code to handle errors after every SQL statement. The format of the WHEN-EVER statement is:

EXEC SQL WHENEVER ⟨condition⟩ ⟨action⟩

The WHENEVER statement consists of a condition and an action to be taken if the condition occurs. The **condition** can be one of the following:

- SQLERROR tells the precompiler to generate code to handle errors (SQLCODE < 0).
- SQLWARNING tells the precompiler to generate code to handle warnings (SQLCODE > 0).
- NOT FOUND tells the precompiler to generate code to handle the specific warning that a retrieval operation has found no more records (SQLCODE = 100).

The **action** can be:

- CONTINUE, to ignore the condition and proceed to the next statement;
- GOTO *label* or GO TO *label*, to transfer control to the specified *label*.

For example, the WHENEVER statement in the code segment:

EXEC SQL WHENEVER SQLERROR GOTO error1;
EXEC SQL INSERT INTO viewing VALUES ('CR76', 'PA14', DATE '1995–05–12', 'Not enough space');
EXEC SQL INSERT INTO viewing VALUES ('CR77', 'PA14', DATE '1995–05–13', 'Quite like it');

would be converted by the precompiler to:

EXEC SQL INSERT INTO viewing VALUES ('CR76', 'PA14', DATE '1995–05–12', 'Not enough space');
if (sqlca.sqlcode < 0) goto error1;
EXEC SQL INSERT INTO viewing VALUES ('CR77', 'PA14', DATE '1995–05–13', 'Quite like it');
if (sqlca.sqlcode < 0) goto error1;

12.5.3 Host Language Variables

A host language variable is a program variable declared in the host language. Host language variables can be used in embedded SQL statements to transfer data from the database into the program, and vice versa. They can also be used within the WHERE clause of SELECT statements. In fact, they can be used anywhere that a constant can appear. However, they cannot be used to represent database objects, such as table names or column names.

To use a host variable in an embedded SQL statement, the variable name is prefixed by a colon (:). For example, suppose we have a program variable, *increment*, representing the salary increase for staff member SL21, then we could update the member's salary using the statement:

EXEC SQL UPDATE staff SET salary = salary + :increment
        WHERE sno = 'SL21';

Host language variables must be declared to SQL, as well as being declared in the syntax of the host language. All host variables must be declared to SQL in a BEGIN DECLARE SECTION ... END DECLARE SECTION block. This block must appear before any of the variables are used in an embedded SQL statement. Using the previous example, we would have to include a declaration of the form:

EXEC SQL BEGIN DECLARE SECTION;
    float increment;
EXEC SQL END DECLARE SECTION;

A host language variable must be compatible with the SQL value it represents. Table 12.7 shows the INGRES SQL data types and the corresponding data types in 'C'. This mapping may differ from product to product. Note that the 'C' data types for character and date strings require an extra character to allow for the null terminator for 'C' strings. Host variables can be single variables or structures.

Table 12.7 INGRES and 'C' types.

INGRES SQL type	*'C' type*
char(n), varchar(n)	char[n + 1]
integer1, integer2, smallint	short
integer	int
integer	long
float4	float
float	double
date	char[26]
money	double

Indicator variables

Most programming languages do not provide support for unknown or missing values, as represented in the relational model by null (see Section 3.3.1). This causes a problem when a null has to be inserted or retrieved from a table. Embedded SQL provides *indicator variables* to resolve this problem. Each host variable has an associated indicator variable that can be set or examined. The meaning of the indicator variable is as follows:

* An indicator value of zero means that the associated host variable contains a valid value.
* A negative indicator value means that the associated host variable

should be assumed to contain a null; the actual contents of the host variable are irrelevant.

- A positive indicator value means that the associated host variable contains a valid value, which may have been rounded or truncated (that is, the host variable was not large enough to hold the value returned).

In an embedded statement, indicator variables are used immediately following the associated host variable with a colon (:) separating the two variables. For example, to set the Address column of staff member 'SL21' to NULL, we could write:

```
EXEC SQL  BEGIN DECLARE SECTION;
    char      address[51];
    short     address_ind;
EXEC SQL  END DECLARE SECTION;
address_ind = −1;

EXEC SQL   UPDATE staff SET address = :address :address_ind
            WHERE sno = 'SL21';
```

An indicator variable is a two-byte integer variable, so we declare *address_ind* as type short within the BEGIN DECLARE SECTION. We set *address_ind* to a negative value (-1) to indicate that the associated host variable, *address*, should be interpreted as NULL. The indicator variable is then placed in the update statement immediately following the host variable, *address*.

If we retrieve data from the database and it is possible that a column in the query result may contain a null, then we must use an indicator variable for that column; otherwise, the DBMS generates an error and sets SQLCODE to some negative value.

12.5.4 Retrieving Data Using Embedded SQL and Cursors

In Section 12.5.1, we discussed simple embedded statements that do not produce any query results. We can also retrieve data using the SELECT statement, but the processing may be more complicated if the query produces more than one row. The complication results from the fact that most high-level programming languages can process only individual data items or individual rows of a structure, whereas SQL processes multiple rows of data. Consequently, SQL provides a mechanism for allowing the host language to access the rows of a query result one at a time. SQL divides queries into two groups:

- single-row queries, where the query result contains at most one row of data;
- multi-row queries, where the query result may contain an arbitrary number of rows, which may be zero, one or more.

Single-row queries

In embedded SQL, single-row queries are handled by the **singleton select** statement, which has the same format as the SELECT statement presented in Section 11.3, with an extra INTO clause specifying the names of the host variables to receive the query result. The INTO clause follows the SELECT list. There must be a one-to-one correspondence between expressions in the SELECT list and host variables in the INTO clause. For example, to retrieve the details of staff member SL21, we write:

```
EXEC SQL SELECT fname, lname, address, tel_no, position, sex, dob,
            salary, nin, bno
         INTO :first_name, :last_name, :address :address_ind, :tel_no
            :telno_ind, :position, :sex :sex_ind, :dob :dob_ind, :salary,
            :nin :nin_ind, :branch_no
         FROM staff
         WHERE sno = 'SL21';
```

In this example, the value for column FName is placed into the host variable *first_name*, the value for LName into *last_name*, the value for Address into *address* (together with the null indicator into *address_ind*), and so on. We have to declare all host variables beforehand using a BEGIN DECLARE SECTION.

If the singleton select works successfully, the DBMS sets SQLCODE to zero; if there are no rows that satisfies the WHERE clause, the DBMS sets SQLCODE to NOT FOUND. If an error occurs or there is more than one row that satisfies the WHERE clause, or a column in the query result contains a null and no indicator variable has been specified for that column, the DBMS sets SQLCODE to some negative value depending on the particular error encountered. We illustrate some of the previous points concerning host variables, indicator variables and singleton select in the next example.

Example 12.14:   Single-row query ―――――――――――――――――――――

Produce a program that asks the user for a staff number and prints out the corresponding staff details.

The program is shown in Figure 12.4. Clearly, this is a single-row query. We ask the user for a staff number, select the corresponding row from the Staff table, check that the data has been successfully returned, and finally, print out the corresponding columns. When we retrieve the data, we have to use an indicator variable for the Address column, as this column may contain nulls.

```
/* Program to print out STAFF details */
#include <stdio.h>
#include <stdlib.h>
EXEC SQL INCLUDE sqlca;

main( )
{
EXEC SQL BEGIN DECLARE SECTION;
    char    staff_no[6];        /* input staff number */
    char    first_name[16];     /* returned first name */
    char    last_name[16];      /* returned last name */
    char    address[51];        /* returned address */
    char    branch_no[4];       /* returned branch number */
    short   address_ind;        /* NULL indicator */
EXEC SQL END DECLARE SECTION;

/* Connect to database */
EXEC SQL CONNECT 'estatedb';
if (sqlca.sqlcode < 0) exit (−1);
/* Prompt for staff number */
    printf("Enter staff number: ");
    scanf("%s", staff_no);

EXEC SQL SELECT fname, lname, address, bno
        INTO :first_name, :last_name, :address :address_ind, :branch_no
        FROM staff
        WHERE sno = :staff_no;

/* Check success and display data*/
    if (sqlca.sqlcode == 0) {
        printf("First name:     %s\n", first_name);
        printf("Last name:      %s\n", last_name);
        if (address_ind < 0)
            printf("Address:            NULL\n");
        else
            printf("Address:        %s\n", address);
        printf("Branch number:  %s\n", branch_no);
    }
    else if (sqlca.sqlcode == 100)
        printf("No staff member with specified number\n");
    else
        printf("SQL error %d\n", sqlca.sqlcode);

/* Finally, disconnect from the database */
EXEC SQL DISCONNECT;
}
```

Figure 12.4 Single-row query.

Multi-row queries

When a database query can return an arbitrary number of rows, SQL provides a different process for returning the data that uses **cursors**. A cursor allows a host language to access the rows of a query result one at a time. In effect, the cursor acts as a pointer to a particular row of the query result. The cursor can be advanced by one to access the next row. A cursor must be **declared** and **opened** before it can be used, and it must be **closed** to deactivate it after it is no longer required. Once the cursor has been opened, the rows of the query result can be retrieved one at a time using a FETCH statement, as opposed to a SELECT statement.

The DECLARE CURSOR statement defines the specific SELECT to be performed and associates a cursor name with the query. The format of the statement is:

> EXEC SQL DECLARE cursor_name CURSOR FOR select_statement

For example, to declare a cursor to retrieve all properties for staff member SL41, we write:

> EXEC SQL DECLARE property_cursor CURSOR FOR
> SELECT pno, street, area, city, pcode
> FROM property_for_rent
> WHERE sno = 'SL41';

The OPEN statement opens a specified cursor and positions it before the first row of the query result table. Usually, either the DECLARE CURSOR or, more normally, the OPEN statement actually executes the SELECT statement. If the SELECT statement contains an error, for example a specified column name does not exist, an error is generated at this point. The format of the OPEN statement is:

> EXEC SQL OPEN cursor_name [FOR READONLY]

The optional FOR READONLY keyword indicates that the data will not be updated while the rows are being fetched from the database. For example, to open the cursor for the above query, we write:

> EXEC SQL OPEN property_cursor FOR READONLY;

The FETCH statement retrieves the next row of the query result table. The format of the FETCH statement is:

> EXEC SQL FETCH cursor_name INTO host_variable [, ...]

where *cursor_name* is the name of a cursor that is currently open. The number of host variables in the INTO clause must match the number of columns in the SELECT clause of the corresponding query in the DECLARE CURSOR statement. For example, to fetch the next row of the query result in the previous example, we write:

EXEC SQL FETCH property_cursor

  INTO :property_no, :street, :area :area_ind, :city, :post_code :postcode_ind;

The FETCH statement puts the value in the Pno column into the host variable *property_no*, the value in the Street column into the host variable *street*, and so on. Since the FETCH statement operates on a single row of the query result, it is usually placed into a loop in the program. When there are no more rows to be returned from the query result table, SQLCODE is set to NOT FOUND, as discussed above for single-row queries. Note that, if there are no rows in the query result table, the OPEN statement still positions the cursor ready to start the successive fetches, and returns successfully. In this case, it is the first FETCH statement that detects there are no rows and returns an SQLCODE of NOT FOUND.

    The format of the CLOSE statement is very similar to the OPEN statement:

EXEC SQL CLOSE cursor_name

---

where *cursor_name* is the name of a cursor that is currently open. For example,

    EXEC SQL CLOSE property_cursor;

Once the cursor has been closed, the query result table is no longer accessible. All cursors are automatically closed at the end of the containing transaction. We illustrate some of these points in the next example.

Example 12.15: Multi-row query

Produce a program that asks the user for a staff number and prints out the properties managed by this member of staff.

The program is shown in Figure 12.5. In this example, the query result table may contain more than one row of data. Consequently, we must treat this as a multi-row query and use a cursor to retrieve the data. We ask the user for a staff number, and set up a cursor to select the corresponding rows from the Property_for_Rent table. After opening the cursor, we loop over each row of the result table and print out the corresponding columns. When there are no more rows to be processed, we close the cursor and terminate. If an error occurs at any point, we generate a suitable error message and stop. As in the previous example, we have to use indicator variables for those columns that may contain nulls.

```
/*
** Program to print out properties managed by a specified member of staff
*/
#include ⟨stdio.h⟩
#include ⟨stdlib.h⟩
EXEC SQL INCLUDE sqlca;

main( )
{
EXEC SQL BEGIN DECLARE SECTION;
    char    staff_no[6];                /* input staff number */
    char    property_no[6];             /* returned property number */
    char    street[26];                 /* returned street of property address */
    char    area[16];                   /* returned area of property address */
    char    city[16];                   /* returned city of property address */
    char    post_code[9];               /* returned post code of property address */
    short   area_ind, postcode_ind;     /* NULL indicators */
EXEC SQL END DECLARE SECTION;

/* Connect to database */
EXEC SQL CONNECT 'estatedb';
if (sqlca.sqlcode < 0) exit (−1);
/* Prompt for staff number */
    printf("Enter staff number: ");
    scanf("%s", staff_no);

/* Establish SQL error handling */
EXEC SQL WHENEVER SQLERROR GOTO error;
EXEC SQL WHENEVER NOT FOUND GOTO done;

/* Declare cursor for selection */
EXEC SQL DECLARE property_cursor CURSOR FOR
        SELECT pno, street, area, city, pcode
        FROM property_for_rent
        WHERE sno = :staff_no
        ORDER by pno;

/* Open the cursor to start of selection */
EXEC SQL OPEN property_cursor;

/* Loop to fetch each row of the result table */
for ( ; ; ) {
/* Fetch next row of the result table */
EXEC SQL FETCH property_cursor
    INTO :property_no, :street, :area :area_ind, :city, :post_code :postcode_ind;

/* Display data */
    printf("Property number: %s\n", property_no);
    printf("Street:         %s\n", street);
    if (area_ind < 0)
        printf("Area:        NULL\n");
    else
```

Figure 12.5 Multi-row query

```
                        printf("Area:        %s\n", area);
                printf("City:        %s\n", city);
                if (postcode_ind < 0)
                    printf("Post code: NULL\n");
                else
                    printf("Post code: %s\n", post_code);
        }
        /* Error condition - print out error */
        error:
                printf("SQL error %d\n" sqlca.sqlcode);
        done:
        /* Close the cursor before completing */
        EXEC SQL WHENEVER SQLERROR continue;
        EXEC SQL CLOSE property_cursor;
        EXEC SQL DISCONNECT;
        }
```

Figure 12.5
Continued.

12.5.5 Using Cursors to Modify Data

A cursor is either **readonly** or **updatable**. If the table identified by a cursor is not updatable (see Section 12.1.5) or if READONLY has been specified in the open cursor statement, then the cursor is readonly; otherwise, the cursor is updatable, and the UPDATE and DELETE CURRENT statements can be used. Rows can always be inserted directly into the base table. If rows are inserted after the current cursor and the cursor is readonly, the effect of the change is not visible through that cursor before it is closed. If the cursor is updatable, the ISO standard specifies that the effect of such changes is implementation-dependent. INGRES makes the newly inserted row visible to the application.

To update data through a cursor in INGRES requires a minor extension to the DECLARE CURSOR statement:

```
EXEC SQL DECLARE cursor_name CURSOR FOR select_statement
    FOR UPDATE OF column_name [, ...]
```

The FOR UPDATE OF clause must list any columns in the database table named in the *select_statement* that may require updating; furthermore, the listed columns must appear in the SELECT list. The format of the cursor-based UPDATE statement is:

```
EXEC SQL UPDATE table_name
    SET column_name = data_value [, ...]
    WHERE CURRENT OF cursor_name
```

where *cursor_name* is the name of an open, updatable cursor. The WHERE clause serves only to specify the row to which the cursor currently points. The update affects only data in that row. Each column name in the SET clause must have been identified for update in the corresponding DECLARE CURSOR statement. For example, the statement:

> EXEC SQL UPDATE property_for_rent
>> SET sno = 'SL22'
>> WHERE current of property_cursor;

updates the staff number, Sno, of the current row of the table associated with the cursor *property_cursor*. The update does not advance the cursor, and so another FETCH must be performed to move the cursor forward to the next row.

It is also possible to delete rows through an updatable cursor. The format of the cursor-based DELETE statement is:

EXEC SQL DELETE FROM table_name
    WHERE CURRENT OF cursor_name

---

where *cursor_name* is the name of an open, updatable cursor. Again, the statement works on the current row, and a FETCH must be performed to advance the cursor to the next row. For example, the statement:

> EXEC SQL DELETE FROM property_for_rent
>> WHERE current of property_cursor;

deletes the current row from the table associated with the cursor, *property_cursor*. Note that to delete rows, the FOR UPDATE OF clause of the DECLARE CURSOR statement need not be specified.

12.5.6 ISO Standard for Embedded SQL

In this section, we briefly describe the differences between the INGRES embedded SQL dialect and the ISO standard.

The WHENEVER statement

The ISO standard does not recognize the SQLWARNING condition of the WHENEVER statement.

The SQL communications area

The ISO standard does not mention an SQL communications area as defined in this section. It does, however, recognize the integer variable SQLCODE, although this is a deprecated feature that is supported only for compatibility with earlier versions of the standard. Instead, it defines a character string SQLSTATE parameter, comprising a two-character class value followed by a three-character subclass value.

Cursors

The ISO standard specifies the definition and processing of cursors slightly differently from INGRES Version 6.4. The ISO standard does not allow the optional clause READONLY in the OPEN statement; instead, this attribute is specified in DECLARE CURSOR. The ISO DECLARE CURSOR statement is as follows:

```
EXEC SQL DECLARE cursor_name [INSENSITIVE] [SCROLL]
CURSOR FOR select_statement
    [FOR { READ ONLY | UPDATE [OF column_name_list] } ]
```

If the optional INSENSITIVE keyword is specified, the effects of changes to the underlying base table are not visible to the user. If the optional keyword SCROLL is specified, the user can access the rows in a random way. The access is specified in the FETCH statement:

```
EXEC SQL FETCH [ [fetch_orientation] FROM ] cursor_name
    INTO host_variable [, ...]
```

where the *fetch_orientation* can be one of the following:

- NEXT: Retrieve the next row of the query result table immediately following the current row of the cursor.
- PRIOR: Retrieve the row of the query result table immediately preceding the current row of the cursor.
- FIRST: Retrieve the first row of the query result table.
- LAST: Retrieve the last row of the query result table.
- ABSOLUTE: Retrieve a specific row by its row number.
- RELATIVE: Move the cursor forward or backward a specific number of rows relative to its current position.

Without this functionality, to move backward through a table, we have to close the cursor, reopen it and FETCH the rows of the query result until the required one is reached.

12.5.7 Application Program Interface (API)

An alternative approach taken by some DBMS vendors is to provide programmers with a library of functions that are invoked from the application software. For many programmers, the use of library routines is standard practice, and they consequently find an API a relatively straightforward way to use SQL. Although not covered by the ISO standard, some important systems provide APIs, and we consider it worthwhile to briefly review the basic concepts, which are not too dissimilar to embedded SQL. We illustrate the concepts using the SQL Server API.

Example 12.16:   Program using an SQL API _____

Produce a program that prints out the properties managed by staff member 'SL41'. For simplicity, assume that all columns are defined as NOT NULL, so that no indicator variables are required.

The program, shown in Figure 12.6, has similar functionality to that of the previous example.

This example illustrates the basic operation of a typical program that uses an SQL API:

- Connect the program to the DBMS, using a function call (call to dbopen()).
- Build up the SQL statement in a buffer (for example, dbcmd()) and pass the buffer to the DBMS for execution (call to dbsqlexec()).
- Check for successful completion of SQL statement (call to dbresults()).
- For a query, retrieve each row of the result table (call dbnextrow()).
- Disconnect the program from the DBMS (call dbexit()) and terminate.

Unfortunately, the APIs offered by the various vendors differ significantly and there has been no attempt by a standard body to agree on a common interface.

12.6   Dynamic SQL

In the previous section, we discussed embedded SQL, or more accurately, **static embedded SQL**. Static SQL provides significant functionality for the application programmer by allowing access to the database using the normal interactive SQL statements, with some minor modifications in some cases. This type of SQL is adequate for many data processing applications. For example, it allows the developer to write programs to handle customer maintenance, order entry, customer enquiries and the production of reports. In each of these examples, the pattern of database access is fixed and can be 'hard-coded' into the program.

However, there are many situations where the pattern of database access is not fixed, and is known only at run time. For example, the production of a front-end that allows users to graphically define their queries or reports, and then generates the corresponding interactive SQL statements, requires more flexibility than static SQL. The ISO standard defines an alternative approach for such programs, called **dynamic SQL**. The basic difference between the two types of embedded SQL is that static SQL does not allow host variables to be used in place of table names or column names. For example, in static SQL, we cannot write:

```
/* Program to print out properties managed by a member of staff */
#include <stdio.h>
main()
{
    LOGINREC      *loginrec;        /* data structure for login information */
    DBPROCESS     *dbproc;          /* data structure for connection */
    int           status;
    char          property_no[6];   /* returned pno */
    char          street[26];       /* returned street */
    char          area[16];         /* returned area */
    char          city[16];         /* returned city */
    char          post_code[9];     /* returned pcode */

/* Get a login structure and login using specified user name and password */
    loginrec = dblogin();
    DBSETLUSER(loginrec, "manager");
    DBSETLPWD(loginrec, "pterodactyl");
    dbproc = dbopen(loginrec, " ");

/* Set up query and execute it */
    dbcmd(dbproc, "SELECT pno, street, area, city, pcode from property_for_rent");
    dbcmd(dbproc, "where sno = 'SL41' order by pno");
    dbsqlexec(dbproc);

/* Get to first statement in batch */
    status = dbresults(dbproc);

/* Set up (bind) variables to receive results and fetch each row of the query result table */
    dbbind(dbproc, 1, NTBSTRINGBIND, 5,  &property_no);
    dbbind(dbproc, 2, NTBSTRINGBIND, 25, &street);
    dbbind(dbproc, 3, NTBSTRINGBIND, 15, &area);
    dbbind(dbproc, 4, NTBSTRINGBIND, 15, &city);
    dbbind(dbproc, 5, NTBSTRINGBIND, 8,  &post_code);

    while (status = dbnextrow(dbproc) == SUCCEED)
    {
        printf("Property number: %s\n", property_no);
        printf("Street:          %s\n", street);
        printf("Area:            %s\n", area);
        printf("City:            %s\n", city);
        printf("Post code:       %s\n", post_code);
    }

/* Check for success before closing connection to database */
    if (status == FAIL)
        printf("SQL error\n");
    dbexit(dbproc);
}
```

Figure 12.6 Sample SQL API program.

```
EXEC SQL BEGIN DECLARE SECTION;
     char table_name[20];
EXEC SQL END DECLARE SECTION;
EXEC SQL INSERT INTO :table_name VALUES ('CR76', 'PA14',
DATE '1995-05-12', 'Not enough space');
```

as static SQL is expecting the name of a database table in the INSERT state-ment and not the name of a host variable. Even if this were allowed, there would be an additional problem associated with the declaration of cursors. Consider the following statement:

```
EXEC SQL DECLARE cursor1 CURSOR FOR
     SELECT *
     FROM :table_name;
```

The '*' indicates that all columns from the table, *table_name*, are required in the result table, but the number of columns may vary with the choice of table. Furthermore, the data types of the columns will vary between tables as well. For example, the Branch and Staff tables have a different number of columns; the Branch and Renter tables have the same number of columns but different underlying data types. If we do not know the number of columns and we do not know their data types, we cannot use the FETCH statement described in the previous section, which requires the number and the data types of the host variables to match the corresponding types of the table columns. In this section, we describe the facilities provided by dynamic SQL to overcome these problems and allow more general-purpose software to be developed.

12.6.1   Basic Concepts of Dynamic SQL

The basic idea of dynamic SQL is to place the complete SQL statement to be executed in a host variable. The host variable is then passed to the DBMS to be executed. The simplest way to do this for statements that do not involve multi-row queries is to use the EXECUTE IMMEDIATE statement, which has the format:

```
EXEC SQL EXECUTE IMMEDIATE host_variable
```

This command allows the SQL statement stored in the buffer, *host_variable*, to be executed. For example, we could replace the static SQL statement:

```
EXEC SQL BEGIN DECLARE SECTION;
     float increment;
EXEC SQL END DECLARE SECTION;
EXEC SQL UPDATE staff SET salary = salary + :increment WHERE
sno = 'SL21';
```

with the following dynamic SQL statement:

```
EXEC SQL BEGIN DECLARE SECTION;
    char buffer[100];
EXEC SQL END DECLARE SECTION;
sprintf(buffer, "update staff set salary = salary + %f where sno =
'SL21'", increment);
EXEC SQL EXECUTE IMMEDIATE :buffer;
```

In the second case, the UPDATE statement is placed in a buffer that is passed to the EXECUTE IMMEDIATE statement. Note that, in the second case, the Increment variable does not have to be declared to SQL, as it is no longer used in an embedded SQL statement.

The PREPARE and EXECUTE statements

Every time an EXECUTE IMMEDIATE statement is processed, the DBMS must parse, validate and optimize the statement, build an execution plan for the statement and finally execute this plan, as illustrated in Figure 12.7. The EXECUTE IMMEDIATE statement is most useful if the SQL statement is executed only once in the application program. However, if the SQL statement is executed many times, then this command is not particularly efficient. Dynamic SQL provides an alternative approach for SQL statements that may be executed more than once, involving the use of two complementary statements: PREPARE and EXECUTE.

The PREPARE statement instructs the DBMS to ready the dynamically built statement for later execution. The prepared statement is assigned a specified statement name. The statement name is an SQL identifier, like a cursor name. When the statement is subsequently executed, the program need only specify the name of the statement to execute it. The format of the PREPARE statement is:

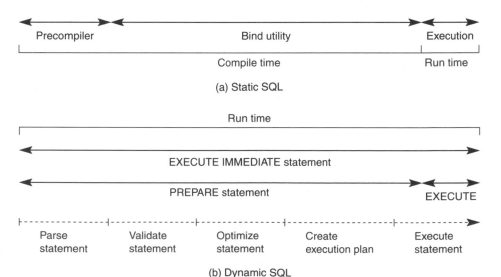

Figure 12.7
Comparison of SQL
processing by DBMS.

EXEC SQL PREPARE statement_name FROM host_variable

The format of the EXECUTE statement is:

EXEC SQL EXECUTE statement_name
[USING host_variable [, ..] | USING DESCRIPTOR descriptor_name]

These two statements used together not only improve the performance of executing an SQL statement that is used more than once, but also provide additional functionality through the provision of the USING clause of the EXECUTE statement. The USING clause allows portions of the prepared statement to be unspecified, replaced instead by **parameter markers** indicated by a question mark (?). A parameter marker can appear anywhere in the *host_variable* of the PREPARE statement that a constant can appear. It signals to the DBMS that a value will be supplied later, in the EXECUTE statement. The program can supply different parameter values each time the dynamic statement is executed. For example, we could prepare and execute an UPDATE statement that has the values for the SET and WHERE clause unspecified:

```
EXEC SQL BEGIN DECLARE SECTION;
    char buffer[100];
    float new_salary;
    char staff_no[6];
EXEC SQL END DECLARE SECTION;
sprintf(buffer, "update staff set salary = ? where sno = ?");
EXEC SQL PREPARE stmt FROM :buffer;
do {
    printf("Enter staff number: ");
    scanf("%s", staff_no);
    printf("Enter new salary: ");
    scanf("%f", new_salary);
    EXEC SQL EXECUTE stmt USING :new_salary, :staff_no;
    printf("Enter another (Y/N)? ");
    scanf("%c", more);
}
until (more != 'Y');
```

The DBMS parses, validates and optimizes the statement, and builds an application plan for the statement once when the PREPARE statement is performed, as illustrated in Figure 12.7. This plan can then be used for every subsequent invocation of the EXECUTE statement. This is similar to the way in which static embedded SQL works.

12.6.2 The SQL Descriptor Area (SQLDA)

Parameter markers are one way to pass parameters to the EXECUTE statement. An alternative is through a dynamic data structure called the SQL Descriptor Area (SQLDA). The SQLDA is used when the number of parameters and their data types are not known when the statement is formulated. We also note that the SQLDA can be used to dynamically retrieve data when we do not know the number of columns to be retrieved or the types of the columns. The structure of the SQLDA for INGRES is shown in Figure 12.8. To use the SQLDA, we include the line:

EXEC SQL INCLUDE sqlda;

```
/*
** SQLDA - Structure to hold data descriptions, used by embedded programs and INGRES
**         runtime during execution of dynamic SQL statements.
*/
typedef struct sqlvar_ {
    short       sqltype;            /* type of column or variable */
    short       sqllen;            /* length of column of variable */
    char        *sqldata;          /* pointer to variable described by type and length */
    short       *sqlind;           /* pointer to indicator variable associated with host variable */
    struct {
        short       sqlname1;      /* length of name */
        char        sqlnamec[34];  /* name of result column from describe */
    } sqlname;
} IISQLVAR;

#define     IISQLDA_TYPE(sq_struct_tag, sq_sqlda_name, sq_num_vars) \
struct sq_struct_tag {                 \
    char        sqldaid[8];       \    /* contains fixed text "SQLDA    " */
    long        sqldabc;          \    /* length of SQLDA structure */
    short       sqln;             \    /* number of allocated sqlvar elements */
    short       sqld;             \    /* number of results columns associated with statement */
    IISQLVAR    sqlvar[sqln];     \    /* array of data */
} sq_sqlda_name;

#define IISQ_MAX_COLS      300
typedef IISQLDA_TYPE(sqda_, IISQLDA, IISQ_MAX_COLS);
#define IISQDA_HEAD_SIZE   16
#define IISQDA_VAR_SIZE    sizeof(IISQLVAR)
```

Figure 12.8 SQL Descriptor Area (SQLDA).

The SQLDA is divided into two parts:

- A **fixed part,** which identifies the structure as an SQLDA and specifies the size of this particular instantiation of the SQLDA. This part is only significant if the statement being prepared is a SELECT statement, as shown below.

- A **variable part,** which contains data relating to each parameter that is passed to or received from the DBMS.

The fields in the variable part of the SQLDA are:

- SQLTYPE: A code corresponding to the data type of the parameter being passed in. The codes for INGRES are shown in Table 12.8. A positive code indicates the column cannot contain nulls; a negative code indicates that the column can contain nulls.
- SQLLEN: The length of the associated data type in bytes.
- *SQLDATA: A pointer to a data area within the application program that contains the parameter value.
- *SQLIND: A pointer to an indicator variable associated with the parameter value. The indicator variable should be set by the application as described in Section 12.5.

The remaining fields are not used to pass parameter values to the EXECUTE statement. They are used when retrieving data from the database, as we see shortly.

Table 12.8 INGRES data type codes.

INGRES SQL type	INGRES code	Value
char	IISQ_CHA_TYPE	20
varchar	IISQ_VCH_TYPE	21
integer	IISQ_INT_TYPE	30
float	IISQ_FLT_TYPE	31
date	IISQ_DTE_TYPE	3
money	IISQ_MNY_TYPE	5

12.6.3 Retrieving Data using Dynamic SQL and Dynamic Cursors

In Section 12.5.3, we distinguished between two types of queries: single-row and multi-row queries. Dynamic SQL is similar. If the result table consists of one row, the PREPARE and EXECUTE statements are used to perform the query. If the result table consists of an arbitrary number of rows, the ISO standard specifies that a cursor must be used to retrieve the data, although INGRES provides an extension to the EXECUTE IMMEDIATE statement. If the columns and data types to be retrieved are known, a list of host variables can be used to receive the results. If the columns are not known, an SQL Descriptor Area must be used.

SQLDA for dynamic SELECT statements

When retrieving data, the two most important fields in the fixed part of the SQLDA are:

- SQLN: The number of elements allocated to the variable part of the structure: that is, an upper limit on the number of columns in the SELECT statement. This must be set by the application program before using the SQLDA.
- SQLD: The actual number of columns in the SELECT statement. This field is set by the DBMS and can be examined using the DESCRIBE statement, as shown below. If DESCRIBE returns a value of zero for the SQLD, this implies that the statement is not a SELECT statement.

The fields in the variable part of the SQLDA are used when retrieving data and are as follows:

- SQLTYPE: A code corresponding to the data type of the column being retrieved (see Table 12.8).
- SQLLEN: The length of the associated data type in bytes.
- *SQLDATA: A pointer to a data area within the application program that will receive the column result.
- *SQLIND: A pointer to an indicator variable associated with the column result.
- SQLNAME: The name of the associated column, consisting of a length in bytes, and a character string for the name itself.

DESCRIBE *statement*

The DESCRIBE statement returns descriptive information about a prepared SQL statement. With a prepared SELECT statement, DESCRIBE returns the names, data types and lengths of columns specified in the query into an SQLDA. With a non-select statement, DESCRIBE sets the SQLD field of the fixed part of an SQLDA to zero. The format of the DESCRIBE statement is:

EXEC SQL DESCRIBE statement_name USING descriptor_name

where *statement_name* is the name of a prepared statement and *descriptor_ name* is the name of an initialized SQLDA. For example, if we prepare and describe the following SELECT statement:

> sprintf(query, "select pno, comment from viewing");
>
> EXEC SQL PREPARE stmt FROM :query;
>
> EXEC SQL DESCRIBE stmt INTO :sqlda;

the *sqldo* will be filled in, as shown in Figure 12.9.

The pointer fields *sqldata* and *sqlind* are not filled in by the DESCRIBE statement, but by the application program. A potential problem with the use of the DESCRIBE statement, and the SQLDA in general, is knowing how much allocated space it requires. If the application deals with a fixed set of

sqld	= 2			
sqlvar[0].sqltype	= 20	sqlvar[1].sqltype	=	−21
sqlvar[0].sqllen	= 5	sqlvar[1].sqllen	=	40
sqlvar[0].sqlname.sqlname1	= 3	sqlvar[1].sqlname.sqlname1	=	7
sqlvar[0].sqlname.sqlnamec	= PNO	sqlvar[1].sqlname.sqlnamec	=	COMMENT

Figure 12.9 Example of data filled in SQLDA by DESCRIBE.

tables with a known number of columns, for example, *max_col*, then we can initialize the SQLDA based on *max_col* SQLVAR elements and set SQLN to *max_col*. If the application deals with an arbitrary set of tables, we can initialize the SQLDA based on some standard or common value; if the DESCRIBE statement returns a value of SQLD that is larger than the area allocated, we then have to allocate an SQLDA based on the value of SQLD returned and re-execute the DESCRIBE statement again. There is no limit to the number of times that a prepared statement can be described.

Multi-row selects

In Section 12.5, we used cursors to retrieve data from a query result table that has an arbitrary number of rows. The basic principle in dynamic SQL is still the same, although some of the statements are slightly different. We still use the DECLARE, OPEN, FETCH and CLOSE statements, but the format is now:

```
EXEC SQL DECLARE cursor_name CURSOR FOR select_statement

EXEC SQL OPEN cursor_name [FOR READONLY]
[USING host_variable [, ...] | USING DESCRIPTOR descriptor_name ]

EXEC SQL FETCH cursor_name USING DESCRIPTOR descriptor_name

EXEC SQL CLOSE cursor_name
```

The dynamic OPEN statement allows values for the parameter markers to be substituted using one or more *host_variables* in a USING clause or passing the values via a *descriptor_name* (that is, an SQLDA) in a USING DESCRIPTOR clause. The main difference is with the FETCH statement which, in dynamic form, uses *descriptor_name* to receive the rows of the query result table. Before the dynamic FETCH statement is called, the application program must provide data areas to receive the retrieved data and indicator variables, and set up the SQLLEN, SQLDATA and SQLIND fields of the SQLDA structure accordingly. If no indicator variable is needed for a particular column, the SQLIND field for the corresponding SQLVAR structure should be set to zero. When the application program closes a cursor, it may also wish to deallocate the SQLDA used by the query and the data areas reserved for the results of the query.

Example 12.17: Using the SQLDA to retrieve data _____

Produce a program that takes an arbitrary statement from the user and executes it.

The program is shown in Figure 12.10. To distinguish between a SELECT statement and a non-SELECT statement, the program uses the DESCRIBE statement and checks the SQLD field of the SQLDA. If SQLD = 0, the statement is a non-SELECT statement and can be processed easily using the EXECUTE IMMEDIATE statement. In the case of a SELECT statement, the program uses the data set up in the SQLDA by DESCRIBE to set up the length and type of each column in the result table and allocate dynamic memory for the data and indicator variable for each column. The program then declares and opens a cursor for the SELECT statement and within a loop, fetches each row of the query result table and prints it out, until all the rows in the result table have been processed. At this point, it closes the cursor and finishes.

12.6.4 Using Dynamic Cursors to Modify Data

In Section 12.5.4, we discussed how data can be modified through cursors, using extensions to the interactive UPDATE and DELETE statements. These extensions can also be used in dynamic SQL.

12.6.5 ISO Standard for Dynamic SQL

In this section, we briefly describe the differences between INGRES dynamic SQL and the ISO standard.

SQLDA

The SQL descriptor area in the ISO standard is treated very much like a variable of an abstract data type in the object-oriented sense. The programmer has access only to the SQLDA via a set of methods (or functions). An SQLDA is allocated and deallocated using the statements:

> ALLOCATE DESCRIPTOR descriptor_name [WITH MAX occurrences]
> DEALLOCATE DESCRIPTOR descriptor_name

The SQLDA can be accessed via the statements:

> GET DESCRIPTOR descriptor_name get_descriptor_info
> SET DESCRIPTOR descriptor_name set_descriptor_info

For example, to get the maximum number of allocated elements of the descriptor, we write:

> EXEC SQL GET DESCRIPTOR :sqlda :count = COUNT;

```
/* Program to process a user-specified select statement */
#include <stdio.h>
EXEC SQL INCLUDE sqlca;
EXEC SQL INCLUDE sqlda;

void init_sqlda(num_items)
short int num_items;
{
/* Procedure to dynamically allocate the area for the SQLDA and initialize the number of elements */
/* If the SQLDA is allocated, deallocate it first of all. */
    if (sqlda)
        free((char *)sqlda):
    sqlda = (IISQLDA *)calloc(1, IISQDA_HEAD_SIZE + (num_items*IISQDA_VAR_SIZE));
    sqlda->sqln = num_items;
}
void setup_sqlda()
{   /* Procedure to set up the dynamic part of SQLDA to receive data from FETCH */
    /* based on information set up in the SQLDA by DESCRIBE */
int         i, base_type;
IISQLVAR    *sqv;

for (i = 0; i < sqlda->sqld; i++) {
    sqv = &sqlda->sqlvar[i];
    base_type = (sqv->sqltype < 0) ? -sqv->sqltype : sqv->sqltype;

    switch (base_type) {
        case IISQ_INT_TYPE:
            sqv->sqllen = sizeof(long);
            break;

        case IISQ_FLT_TYPE:
        case IISQ_MNY_TYPE:
            sqv->sqllen = sizeof(double);
            break;

        case IISQ_DTE_TYPE:
            sqv->sqllen = IISQ_DTE_LEN;

        case IISQ_CHA_TYPE:
        case IISQ_VCH_TYPE:
/* add one byte for null terminator and set data type for DATE, VARCHAR TO CHAR */
            sqv->sqllen = sqv->sqllen + 1;
            sqv->sqltype = (sqv->sqltype < 0) ? -IISQ_CHA_TYPE : IISQ_CHA_TYPE;
            break;
    }
/* Now allocate memory for data and indicator variable, if necessary; first free memory */
/* from any previous usage */
```

Figure 12.10 Using
the SQLDA to
execute an arbitrary
SQL statement

```
                       if (sqv→sqldata) free( (char *)sqv→sqldata);
                       if (sqv→sqlind) free( (short *)sqv→sqlind);
                       sqv→sqldata = (char *)calloc(1, sqv→sqllen);
                       if (sqv→sqltype < 0)
                           sqv→sqlind = (short *)calloc(1, sizeof(short));
                       else
                           sqv→sqlind = (short *)0;
               }   /* next column */
               }   /* end of setup_sqlda */

        void print_row()
        {   /* Procedure to print out a row of data from the query result table */
        int          i, base_type;
        IISQLVAR   *sqv;

        for (i = 0; i < sqlda→sqld; i++) {
            sqv = &sqlda→sqlvar[i];
            base_type = if (sqv→sqltype < 0) ? -sqv→sqltype : sqv→sqltype;

            switch (base_type) {
                case IISQ_INT_TYPE:
                    if ( (sqv→sqlind == 0) or (*sqv→sqlind >= 0) )
                        printf("%d    ", sqv→sqldata);
                    else
                        printf("NULL    ");
                    break;
                case IISQ_FLT_TYPE:
                case IISQ_MNY_TYPE:
                    if ( (sqv→sqlind == 0) or (*sqv→sqlind >= 0) )
                        printf("%f    ", sqv→sqldata);
                    else
                        printf("NULL    ");
                    break;

                case IISQ_DTE_TYPE:
                case IISQ_CHA_TYPE:
                case IISQ_VCH_TYPE:
                    if ( (sqv→sqlind == 0) or (*sqv→sqlind >= 0) )
                        printf("%c    ", sqv→sqldata);
                    else
                        printf("NULL    ");
                    break;
            }
        }   /* next column */
            printf("\n");
        }   /* end of print_row */

        short int get_statement(statement)
        char *statement;
        {   /* Procedure to get statement from user; return 1 if statement given; 0, otherwise */
            char *p;
            int c;
```

Figure 12.10
continued.

```
        p = statement;
        printf("Enter statement: ");
        while ( ( c = getchar() ) > 0 ) {
         if (c = = '\n') {
             *p = 0;
             return 1;
         }
         else
             *p++;
    }
    return 0;
}


main()
{
EXEC SQL BEGIN DECLARE SECTION;
    char    query[100];                     /* query buffer */
EXEC SQL END DECLARE SECTION;

IISQLDA *sqlda = (IISQLDA *)0;        /* pointer to the SQLDA dynamic area */
    init_sqlda(10);                 /* initialize the SQLDA */
/* Connect to database */
EXEC SQL CONNECT 'estatedb';
if (sqlca.sqlcode < 0) exit(-1);

/* Get next statement */
    while (get_statement(query)) {
/* Establish SQL error handling */
        EXEC SQL WHENEVER SQLERROR GOTO error1;
        EXEC SQL WHENEVER NOT FOUND GOTO close_csr;

/* Prepare and describe the query */
        EXEC SQL PREPARE stmt FROM :query;
        EXEC SQL DESCRIBE stmt INTO :sqlda;

/* Check if the statement is a non-select */
        if (sqlda→sqld = = 0)
            EXEC SQL EXECUTE IMMEDIATE :query;
        else {
/* Check if the SQLDA is big enough; if not, reinitialize and DESCRIBE statement again */
            if (sqlda→sqld > sqlda→sqln) {
                init_sqlda(sqlda→sqld);
                EXEC SQL DESCRIBE stmt INTO :sqlda;
            }
/* SQLDA now big enough; setup data area and declare cursor for query */
        setup_sqlda();
        EXEC SQL DECLARE select_cursor CURSOR FOR stmt;
/* Open the cursor to start of selection */
        EXEC SQL OPEN select_cursor;
/* Loop to fetch each row of the result table */
        for ( ; ; ) {
/* Fetch next row of the result table */
                EXEC SQL FETCH select_cursor USING DESCRIPTOR :sqlda;
```

Figure 12.10
continued.

```
/* Display data */
        print_row();
    }    /* end for */
    }    /* end else */
/* Close the cursor before completing */
close_csr:
    EXEC SQL CLOSE select_cursor;
    }        /* end while */
    GOTO finish;
/* Error conditions - print out error */
error1:
    printf("SQL error %d \ n", sqlca.sqlcode);
finish:
EXEC SQL DISCONNECT;
}
```

Figure 12.10
Continued.

To set up the first element of the descriptor, we write:

> EXEC SQL SET DESCRIPTOR :sqlda VALUES 1 LENGTH 4,
> DATA 'ABCD', INDICATOR 0;

The DESCRIBE statement

The DESCRIBE statement is divided into two statements in the ISO standard to distinguish between the description of input and output parameters. The DESCRIBE INPUT statement provides a description of the input parameters for a prepared statement; the DESCRIBE OUTPUT provides a description of the resultant columns of a dynamic select statement. The format, in both cases, is similar to the DESCRIBE statement used above.

12.7 SQL-92 and Beyond

In this section, we review the new features added to the 1992 standard and the features that are being considered for inclusion in a future version of SQL, SQL3. In Section 17.4.4, we briefly discuss the planned object-oriented features of SQL3.

12.7.1 New Features in SQL-92

The main features in the 1992 standard are as follows:

- support for additional data types (VARCHAR, DATETIME and INTERVAL);
- support for multiple character sets;

- support for schema manipulation capabilities;
- additional privilege capabilities (USAGE and INSERT ⟨column_name_list⟩);
- additional integrity features (for example, domains, ASSERTION and extended referential constraints);
- definition of the Information Schema (which gives users access to a standard data dictionary);
- improved diagnostic facilities;
- facilities to support Remote Data Access (RDA) (for example, session statements and schema name qualification);
- additional relational operators (JOIN operators, INTERSECT, EXCEPT);
- support for dynamic SQL;
- definition of direct SQL;
- standardization of support for embedded SQL;
- support for additional language bindings;
- support for increased orthogonality.

12.7.2 Future Features for SQL

ISO has specified the following areas to be considered for inclusion in any revision of the standard:

- additional requirements of Remote Data Access (RDA) standardization;
- additional requirements of Information Resource Dictionary System (IRDS) standardization;
- enhanced schema and constraint definitions;
- additional data manipulation capabilities;
- database services interface;
- additional programming language interfaces;
- support for database utilities;
- interfaces for database distribution;
- support for object-oriented database systems;
- support for knowledge-based systems;
- support for other high-level tools of modern information management.

The following features have already been drafted for inclusion in the next standard:

- an enumerated data type;
- an abstract data type definition capability;

- primitive object management;
- a new form of referential action, PENDANT;
- enhanced assertions;
- triggers;
- multiple null states;
- subtables and generalizations;
- external functions;
- recursive UNION;
- a SIMILAR predicate;
- asynchronous SQL;
- relaxed update rules;
- persistent modules.

Chapter Summary

- A **view** is a virtual table representing a subset of columns and/or rows and/or column expressions from one or more base tables or views. A view is created using the CREATE VIEW statement by specifying a **defining query**. It is not a physically stored table, but is recreated each time it is referenced.

- Views can be used to simplify the structure of the database and make queries easier to write. They can also be used to protect certain columns and/or rows from unauthorized access. Not all views are updatable.

- The ISO SQL standard provides clauses in the **CREATE** and **ALTER TABLE** statements to define **integrity constraints** that handle: required data, domain constraints, entity integrity, referential integrity and enterprise constraints. Required data can be specified using NOT NULL. Domain constraints can be specified using the CHECK clause or by defining domains, using the CREATE DOMAIN statement. **Primary keys** should be defined using the PRIMARY KEY clause and alternate keys using the combination of NOT NULL and UNIQUE. **Foreign keys** should be defined using the FOREIGN KEY clause and update and delete rules using the subclauses ON UPDATE and ON DELETE. Enterprise constraints can be defined using the CHECK and UNIQUE clauses.

- The COMMIT statement signals successful completion of a transaction and all changes to the database are made permanent. The ROLLBACK statement signals that the transaction should be aborted and all changes to the database are undone.

- SQL access control is built around the concepts of authorization identifiers, ownership and privileges. **Authorization identifiers** are assigned to database users by the DBA and identify a user. Each object that is created in SQL has an **owner**. The owner can pass **privileges** on to other users using the GRANT statement and can revoke the privileges passed on using the REVOKE statement. The privileges that can be passed on are USAGE, SELECT, DELETE, INSERT, UPDATE and REFERENCES; the latter three can be restricted to specific columns. A user can allow a receiving user to pass privileges on using the WITH GRANT OPTION clause and can revoke it using the GRANT OPTION FOR clause.

■ SQL statements can be **embedded** in high-level programming languages. The embedded statements are converted into function calls by a vendor-supplied precompiler. Host language variables can be used in embedded SQL statements wherever a constant can appear. The simplest type of embedded SQL statements are those that do not produce any query results and the format of the embedded statement is almost identical to the equivalent interactive SQL statement.

■ A SELECT statement can be embedded in a host language provided the result table consists of a single row. Otherwise, **cursors** have to be used to retrieve the rows from the result table. A cursor acts as a pointer to a particular row of the result table. The DECLARE CURSOR statement defines the query, the OPEN statement opens the cursor to start query processing, the FETCH statement retrieves successive rows of the result table, and the CLOSE statement closes the cursor to end query processing. The positioned UPDATE and DELETE statements can be used to update or delete the row currently selected by a cursor.

■ **Dynamic SQL** is an extended form of embedded SQL that allows more general-purpose application programs to be produced. Dynamic SQL is used when part or all of the SQL statement is unknown at compile-time, and the part that is unknown is not a constant. The EXECUTE IMMEDIATE statement can be used to execute SQL statements that do not involve multi-row queries. If the statement is going to be run more than once, the PREPARE and EXECUTE statements can be used to improve performance. **Parameter markers** can be used to pass values to the EXECUTE statement.

■ The SQL Descriptor Area (SQLDA) is a data structure that can be used to pass or retrieve data from dynamic SQL statements. The DESCRIBE statement returns a description of a dynamically prepared statement into an SQLDA. If the SQLD field of the SQLDA is zero, the statement is a non-select statement. **Dynamic cursors** are used to perform SELECTs that return an arbitrary number of rows.

REVIEW QUESTIONS

12.1 Discuss the advantages and disadvantages of views.

12.2 Describe how the process of view resolution works.

12.3 What restrictions are necessary to ensure that a view is updatable?

12.4 Discuss the functionality and importance of the Integrity Enhancement Feature (IEF).

12.5 Discuss how the access control mechanism of SQL works.

12.6 Discuss the difference between interactive SQL, static embedded SQL and dynamic embedded SQL.

EXERCISES

Answer the following questions using the relational schema from the Exercises of Chapter 11:

12.7 Create a view containing the hotel name and the names of the guests staying at the hotel.

12.8 Create a view containing the account for each guest at the Grosvenor Hotel.

12.9 Give the users Manager and Deputy full access to these views, with the privilege to pass the access on to other users.

12.10 Give the user Accounts SELECT access to these views. Now revoke the access from this user.

12.11 Create the Hotel table using the integrity enhancement features of SQL.

12.12 Now create the Room, Booking and Guest tables using the integrity enhancement features of SQL with the following constraints:
- (a) Type must be one of Single, Double or Family.
- (b) Price must be between £10 and £100.
- (c) Rid must be between 1 and 100.
- (d) Date_From and Date_To must be greater than today's date.
- (e) The same room cannot be double booked.
- (f) The same guest cannot have overlapping bookings.

12.13 Investigate the embedded SQL functionality of any DBMS that you use. Determine the compliance of the DBMS with the ISO standard. Investigate the functionality of any extensions the DBMS supports. Are there any functions not supported?

12.14 Write a small program that prompts the user for guest details and inserts the record into the guest table.

12.15 Write a small program that prompts the user for booking details, checks that the specified hotel, guest and room exists, and inserts the record into the booking table.

12.16 Write a program that increases the price of every room by 5%.

12.17 Write a program that calculates the account for every guest checking out of the Grosvenor Hotel today.

12.18 Write a program that allows the user to insert data into any user-specified table.

13 Query-By-Example (QBE)

Chapter Objectives

In this chapter you will learn:

- The main features of the Paradox for Windows Query-By-Example (QBE) facility.
- How to build a query using QBE.
- How to select fields using QBE.
- How to select rows using QBE.
- How to create multi-table queries using QBE.
- How to perform calculations using QBE.
- How to change the content of tables using QBE.

In this chapter, we provide an overview of the major features of the Query-By-Example (QBE) facility of the Paradox for Windows Database Management System (DBMS). QBE represents a visual approach for accessing information in a database through the use of query templates (Zloof, 1977). We use QBE by entering example values directly into the query template to represent what the access to the database is to achieve, such as the answer to a query.

QBE was originally introduced in an early version of the Paradox for DOS DBMS, to help users in their retrieval of information from the database. The QBE facility provided by Paradox for Windows is easy to use and has very powerful capabilities.

We can use QBE to ask questions about information held in one or more tables, and to specify the fields we want to appear in the answer. We can select records according to specific or non-specific criteria and perform calculations on the information held in tables. We can also use QBE to perform useful operations on tables such as inserting and deleting records, modifying the values of fields or creating new fields. In this chapter, we demonstrate how to use the facilities of QBE using simple examples.

In Chapter 10, we illustrated by example the physical database design methodology presented in this book, using Paradox for Windows as the target DBMS. An overview of the functionality of Paradox for Windows DBMS is given in Section 10.1. We used the physical database design created in Chapter 10 to implement a working database for the *DreamHome* case study. In this chapter, we use the tables of the *DreamHome* database to illustrate the features of the QBE facility of Paradox for Windows.

13.1   Building a Query Using Query-By-Example (QBE)

When we start the Paradox for Windows DBMS, we see the Paradox Desktop, as previously shown in Figure 10.2. Note that the Project Viewer is opened to the working directory called DREAMHCS, which holds all of the components of the *DreamHome* database.

To begin QBE, we select the **File**, **New**, **Query** options, and then select the table to be queried, which in this case is the PROPRENT table created in Chapter 10. The PROPRENT table holds the details of property for rent. The Query Editor dialog box for the PROPRENT table is shown in Figure 13.1.

13.2   Selecting Fields using QBE

The table window called Query shown in Figure 13.2 demonstrates a simple query to retrieve the Street, Area and City fields of the PROPRENT table. A check mark ($\checkmark$) in the square box below the column name indicates the fields that are to be retrieved and represented in the answer. There are various

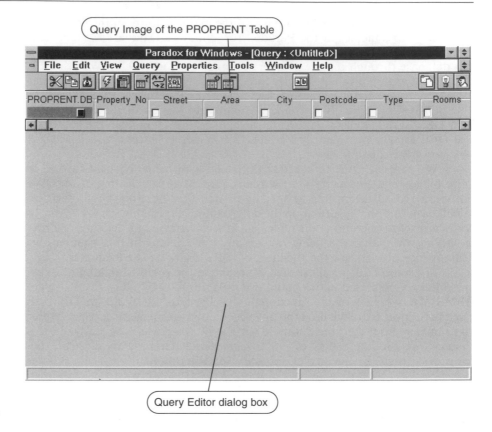

Figure 13.1
The Query Editor
dialog box for
the PROPRENT table.

types of check marks that have different effects on the data in the retrieved field. A check mark is entered by clicking the check box in the selected field and selecting the type of check.

On executing the query shown in Figure 13.2, the results are temporarily written to a table window called ANSWER. The ANSWER table contains only those fields checked in the query. Records are listed in ascending order according to the selected fields.

Every time we run a query, we generate a table called ANSWER. Therefore, if we wish to save the results of a query, we must rename the ANSWER table or it will be overwritten by the next query.

13.3   Selecting Rows using QBE

The query described in the preceding section retrieved specific columns from all rows in the PROPRENT table. It is also possible to retrieve selected rows from the table by specifying various search criteria in one or more fields.

The search criterion is entered into the region to the right of the check box in each field called the **Statement Area**. The search criterion can be an exact match or an inexact match. An inexact match can be constructed using

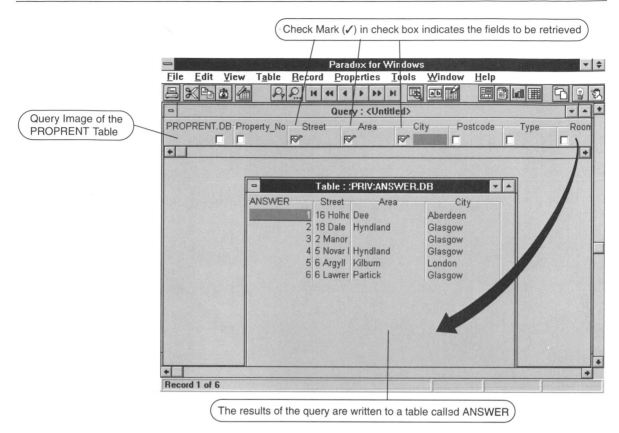

Figure 13.2 An example query to retrieve selected fields of the PROPRENT table and the resulting ANSWER table.

the LIKE operator, wildcard characters, comparison operators such as greater than (>) or less than (<) and logical operators such as AND, NOT or OR.

Listed below are examples of exact and inexact search criteria used to perform specific queries.

13.3.1 Using Exact Match Criteria

An example of a query using an exact match criterion is shown in the Query table of Figure 13.3. The purpose of this query is to search for property for rent in the city of Glasgow, retrieving only the Street, Area and City fields of the PROPRENT table.

When we run this query, the ANSWER table shown in Figure 13.3 is generated. The ANSWER table contains only the Street, Area and City fields for property for rent in Glasgow.

Note that in this example, it is not necessary to represent the field(s) in the ANSWER table that contain the search criteria. For example, we need not have retrieved the City field of the PROPRENT table as shown in Figure 13.3, as all the properties are located in Glasgow. However, in this example and those that follow, we have included fields that more clearly demonstrate the results of each query.

We may enter exact match criteria in one or more fields of a Query

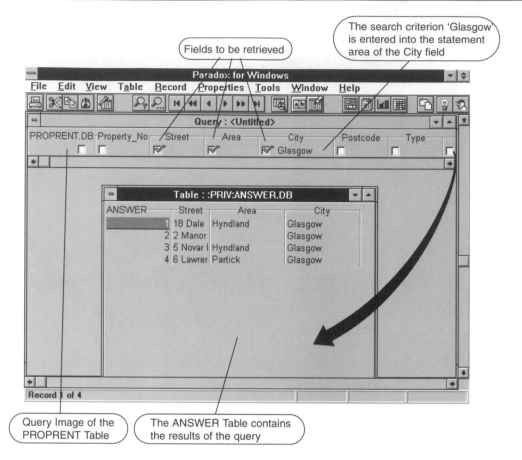

Figure 13.3 An example query using exact match criteria to retrieve selected fields and rows of the PROPRENT table, and the resulting ANSWER table.

table, as shown in Figure 13.4. The purpose of this query is to search for property for rent in the city of Glasgow and also in the Hyndland area retrieving only the Street, Area and City fields of the PROPRENT table.

When we run this query, the ANSWER table shown in Figure 13.4 is generated. The ANSWER table contains only the Street, Area and City fields of property for rent in the Hyndland area of Glasgow.

13.3.2   Using the LIKE Operator and Wildcard Characters

An example of a query using the LIKE operator is shown in the Query table of Figure 13.5. The purpose of this query is to search for property for rent in the city of Glasgow, retrieving only the Property_No, Street and City fields of the PROPRENT table. However, as you can see, we are unsure of the exact spelling for 'Glasgow'. We therefore decide to use the LIKE operator and enter 'LIKE Glasgoe' into the City field of the Query table.

When we run this query, the ANSWER table shown in Figure 13.5 is generated. The ANSWER table contains only the Property_No, Street and City fields for the property for rent in Glasgow.

Alternatively, we could have used wildcard characters to perform the

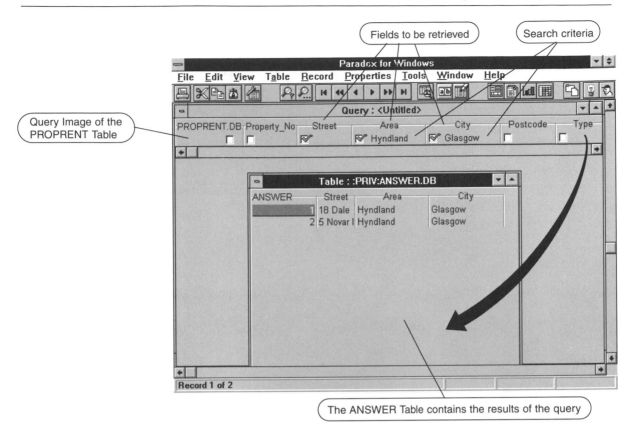

Figure 13.4 An example query using exact match criteria in more than one field.

same search. For example, if we were unsure about the number of characters in the correct spelling of 'Glasgow', we could enter 'Glasg..' in the City field of the Query table. The wildcard .. specifies an unknown number of characters. On the other hand, if we did know the number of characters in the correct spelling of 'Glasgow', we could enter 'Glasg@@'. The wildcard @ specifies a single unknown character.

13.3.3 Using the AND Operator and the Comparison Operators

When we enter search criteria in more than one field on the same row of a Query table, the ANSWER table must contain records that meet all of the search conditions. This type of query was demonstrated in the example shown in Figure 13.4. We can enter several search criteria into a single field using the AND operator, which can also be represented by a comma (,), as shown in the Query table of Figure 13.6. The purpose of this query is to search for property for rent in the city of Glasgow with a monthly rent that is greater than £350 and less than £650, retrieving only the Property_No, City and Rent fields of the PROPRENT table. To run this query, we enter 'Glasgow' into the City field and '>350, <650' into the Rent field of the Query table. The rows retrieved by this query must satisfy all of these criteria.

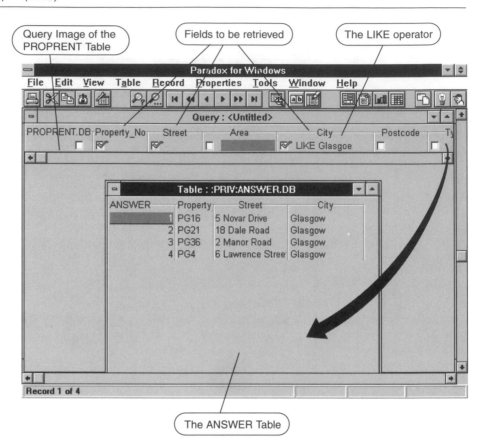

Figure 13.5 An example query using the LIKE operator, and the resulting ANSWER table.

When we run this query, the ANSWER table shown in Figure 13.6 is generated. The ANSWER table contains only the Property_No, City and Rent fields for property in Glasgow with monthly rents that are greater than £350 and less than £650.

13.3.4 Using the OR and NOT Operators

We can enter several search criteria into a single field using the OR operator, as shown in the Query table of Figure 13.7. The purpose of this query is to search for property for rent in the city of London or Glasgow. We also want property with rent that is not more than £500, retrieving only the Property_No, City and Rent fields of the PROPRENT table. To answer this query, we enter the criteria 'London OR Glasgow' into the City field and 'NOT >500' into the Rent field of the Query table.

When we run this query, the ANSWER table shown in Figure 13.7 is generated. The ANSWER table contains only the Property_No, City and Rent fields for property in London or Glasgow with monthly rents that are not more than £500.

Alternatively, we could have specified the OR operation of this query over two lines of the Query table as shown in Figure 13.8.

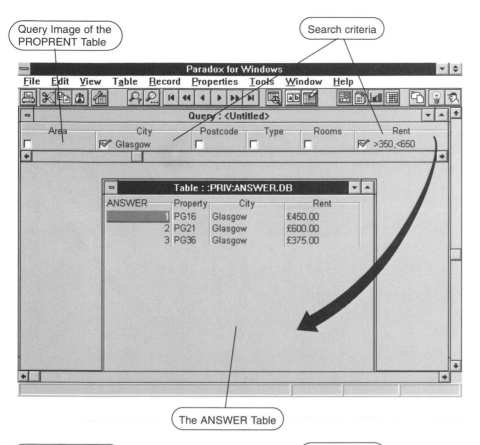

Figure 13.6 An example query using the AND (,) and comparison operators, and the resulting ANSWER table.

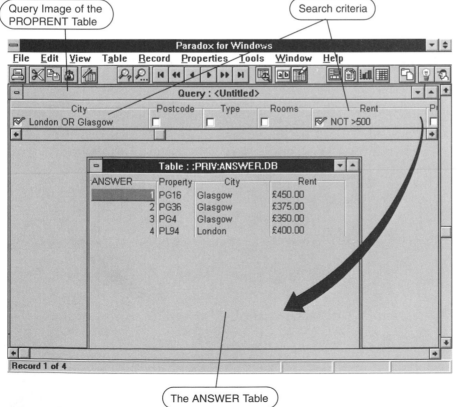

Figure 13.7 An example query using the OR and NOT operators, and the resulting ANSWER table.

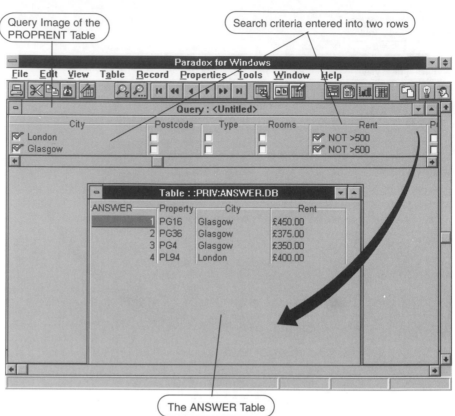

Figure 13.8 An example query using criteria on more than one line of the Query table, and the resulting ANSWER table.

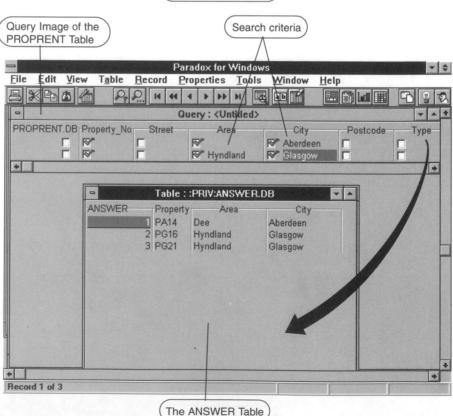

Figure 13.9 A second example query using criteria on more than one line of the Query table, and the resulting ANSWER table.

A further example of entering search criteria across more than one line of the Query table is shown in Figure 13.9. The purpose of this query is to search for all property for rent in Aberdeen and only those located in the Hyndland area of Glasgow, retrieving only the Property_No, Area and City fields.

When we run this query, the ANSWER table shown in Figure 13.9 is generated. The ANSWER table contains the Property_No, Area and City for all the property for rent in Aberdeen and those in the Hyndland area of Glasgow.

13.4   Creating Multi-Table Queries

In a database that is correctly normalized, related data may be stored in several tables. It is therefore essential that in answering a query, the DBMS is capable of joining related information stored in different tables.

In Section 13.3, we constructed single-table queries using one or more example elements to represent particular values in a table. In this section, we construct multi-table queries using **example elements** to join tables by common fields.

There are two ways to join tables. We can either place our own example elements in the tables to be joined, or let Paradox for Windows automatically place them for us. We demonstrate both approaches using the following query.

Which properties are owned by owner number CO93?

The answer should include the owner's full name and the number and address of the properties.

13.4.1   Manually Place Example Elements

To answer this query we need to link information held in two separate tables, namely, the PROPRENT and POWNER tables. To link the tables, we first open the query editor for the POWNER table and then select the **Query, Add Table** menu options and choose the PROPRENT table. These tables contain the common field POwner_No, which will be used to perform the required join. We move to the POwner_No field of the POWNER table, press the **F5** key and enter the characters we want to use as the example element, for example **OWNERX**. We repeat this operation for the POwner_No field of the PROPRENT table, as shown in Figure 13.10. The example element OWNERX indicates the fields to be used in joining the tables. We also enter the owner number value 'CO93' into the POwner_No field of the POWNER table as shown in Figure 13.10. Finally, we select the fields we wish to see in the ANSWER table, which includes the FName and LName fields of the POWNER table and the Property_No, Street and City fields of the PRO-PRENT table.

When we run this query, the ANSWER table shown in Figure 13.10 is created. The records shown are the two properties owned by 'Tony Shaw',

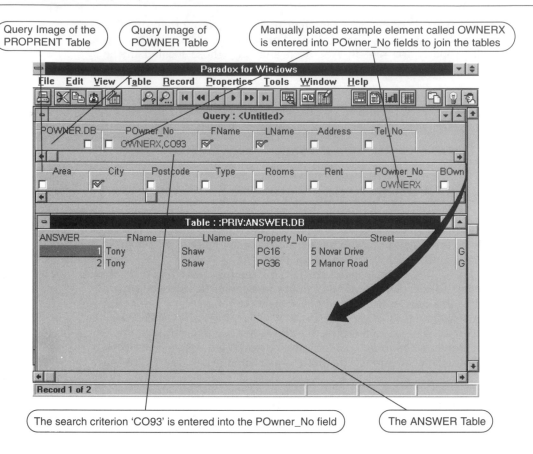

Query Image of the PROPRENT Table

Query Image of POWNER Table

Manually placed example element called OWNERX is entered into POwner_No fields to join the tables

The search criterion 'CO93' is entered into the POwner_No field

The ANSWER Table

Figure 13.10 Joining the POWNER and PROPRENT tables by manually placing example elements, and the resulting ANSWER table.

owner number CO93. Only the ticked fields are shown in the ANSWER table including FName, LName, Property_No, Street and City. As mentioned earlier, we may save the result of this query by renaming the ANSWER table.

Alternatively, we can construct the query described above using a facility provided by Paradox for Windows, which automatically places example elements.

13.4.2 Automatically Place Example Elements

We again repeat all of the steps given in the example described above. However, in this instance, we automatically enter the example element into the POwner_No field of both tables by first selecting the **Join Tables** tool (represented as an icon shown as two overlapping tables) in the speedbar. We move to the POwner_No fields of the POWNER and PROPRENT tables and place the automatically generated example element **Join1**, as shown in Figure 13.11. The Join1 example element indicates the fields to be used in joining the tables. When we run this query, the ANSWER table in Figure 13.11 is generated, which contains the same results as shown in Figure 13.10.

Note that the first automatically generated example element is named Join1. However, if we were required to use additional example elements

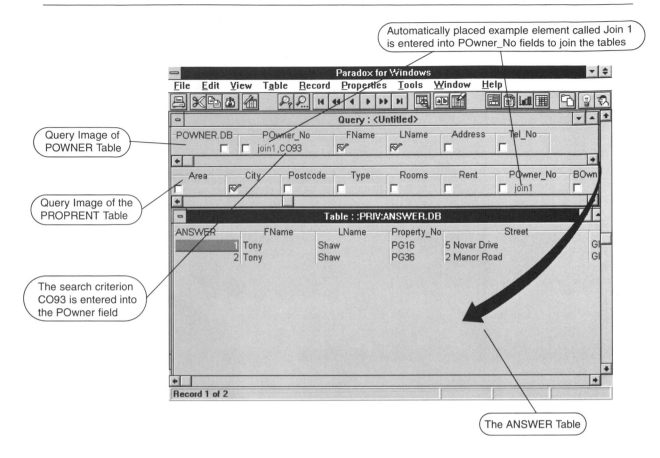

Automatically placed example element called Join 1 is entered into POwner_No fields to join the tables

Query Image of POWNER Table

Query Image of the PROPRENT Table

The search criterion CO93 is entered into the POwner field

The ANSWER Table

Figure 13.11 Joining the POWNER and PROPRENT tables by placing automatically generated example elements, and the resulting ANSWER table.

in joining tables, the names of these elements are incremented by 1: for example, Join2 followed by Join3 and so on. Note that example elements can be used to link up to 24 tables together.

It is important to note that the fields used to link tables must have compatible field types and contain the data values necessary to perform the join.

13.5   Calculating Using QBE

In this section, we demonstrate how QBE performs calculations on the data held in tables using the CALC function. When we use this function, the ANSWER table that is generated contains a new field for the calculated result.

For example, we can use the CALC function to calculate the yearly rent for each property in the PROPRENT table, retrieving only the Property_No and Rent fields, as shown in Figure 13.12. The yearly rent is calculated as 12 times the monthly rent for each property. To run this query, we enter '**Rent**, CALC **Rent** * 12 AS Yearly Rent' into the Rent field of the PROPRENT

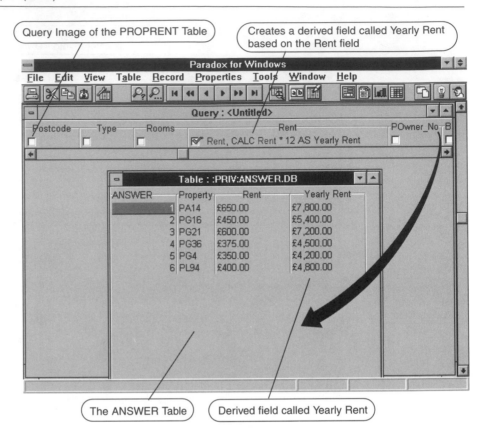

Figure 13.12 An example query using the CALC function, and the ANSWER table.

Query table. Note that we press the F5 key before entering the example element **Rent** into the calculation. The AS operator is used to rename the new calculated field as 'Yearly Rent' otherwise the default name 'Rent * 12' is used.

When we run this query, the ANSWER table shown in Figure 13.12 is generated. The ANSWER table contains the Property_No and Rent fields and the newly created Yearly Rent field.

13.6 Changing Tables Using QBE

In this section, we demonstrate some other useful operations that we may perform on tables using QBE. These operations include inserting or deleting records and modifying table values.

13.6.1 Inserting Records

We use an INSERT query to insert records from one or more source tables into a single target table. For example, we require to insert the details of new owners of property into the POWNER table. The details of these new owners

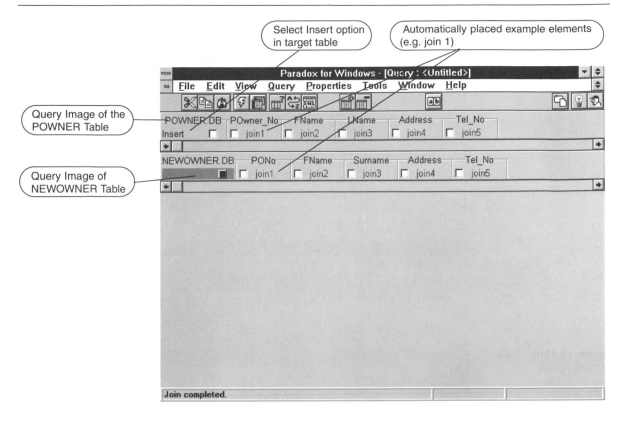

Select Insert option in target table

Automatically placed example elements (e.g. join 1)

Query Image of the POWNER Table

Query Image of NEWOWNER Table

are contained in a table called NEWOWNER. In this example, the POWNER table is the target table and the NEWOWNER table is the source table.

To perform the INSERT query we add the source and target tables to the query window and then link these tables using example elements in all fields, as described in Section 13.4. Note that the field names need not be the same in both tables. For example, the POwner_No field of the POWNER table is equivalent to the PONo field of the NEWOWNER table. We then place the word 'Insert' in the target table (POWNER) as shown in Figure 13.13(a).

When we run this query, a changed POWNER table and an INSERTED table is generated, as shown in Figure 13.13(b). The POWNER table contains all the records contained in the original POWNER table together with the new records. The INSERTED table contains all of the records that were inserted from the source target table. Note that we specifically opened the POWNER table to display its contents after the completion of the insert operation, as this does not occur automatically when we run an INSERT query.

Note that the source and target tables need not be of the same type: for example, we can insert dBase records into a Paradox for Windows table.

Figure 13.13(a) An example of an INSERT query.

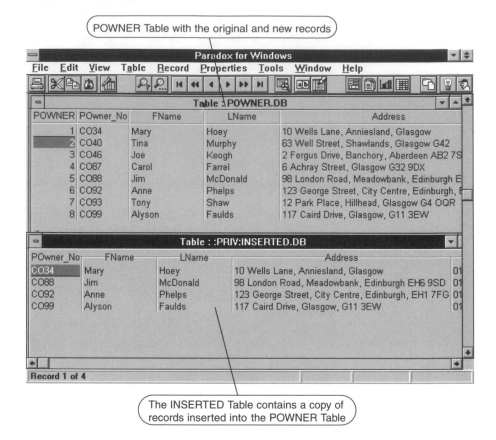

Figure 13.13(b) The POWNER and INSERTED tables for the INSERT query shown in Figure 13.13(a).

13.6.2   Deleting Records

We use a DELETE query to delete selected records from a table. For example, we want to delete the details of owners located in Edinburgh from the POWNER table. To perform the DELETE query we open the POWNER table and enter the required selection criterion '..Edinburgh..' into the Address field of the Query table. Note that we use the wildcard .. to specify an unknown number of characters before and after 'Edinburgh'. We then place the word 'Delete' in the table as shown in Figure 13.14.

When we run this query, a changed POWNER table and a DELETED table are generated. The POWNER table contains the records contained in the original POWNER table minus the deleted records (that is, owners located in Edinburgh). The DELETED table contains all of the records that were deleted as shown in Figure 13.14.

13.6.3   Modifying Records

We use the CHANGETO query to modify field values of selected records in a table. For example, we want to increase the rent of properties in Glasgow

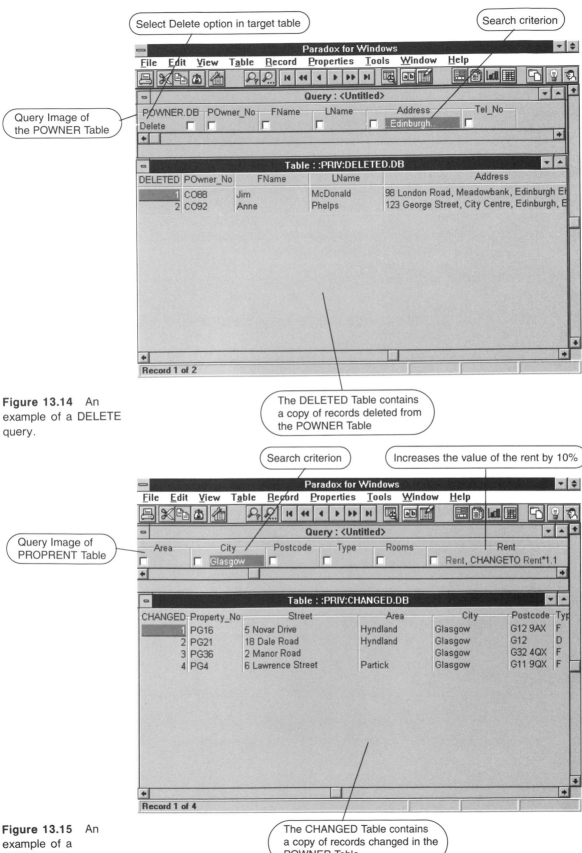

Figure 13.14 An example of a DELETE query.

Figure 13.15 An example of a CHANGETO query.

by 10%. To perform this CHANGETO query, we open the PROPRENT table and enter the required selection criteria, as shown in Figure 13.15. We then enter **'Rent**, CHANGETO **Rent** * 1.1' into the Rent field.

When we run this query, a changed PROPRENT table and a CHANGED table is generated. The PROPRENT table contains all the original records including those that were changed. The CHANGED table contains those records that were changed as shown in Figure 13.15.

Part Four

Selected Database Issues

14 Integrity and Security

Chapter Objectives

In this chapter you will learn:

- What data integrity means and why integrity constraints are important.
- The different types of integrity constraint.
- That integrity and security are closely associated.
- The scope of database security.
- Why security should be taken seriously.
- The type of threats that could affect a database system.
- How to safeguard a system using computer-based controls.
- How to safeguard a system using non-computer-based controls.
- What risk analysis is and how it could be undertaken.
- What privacy and data protection mean.

In Chapter 2 we discussed the database environment and, in particular, the typical functions that should be provided by a DBMS. These functions include integrity and security, both areas of concern to the administration roles discussed in Chapter 4, but which are discussed in more depth in this chapter. Some aspects of integrity have been discussed in Chapter 3 because they are fundamental to the understanding of the relational model, and in Chapter 12 with respect to SQL. However, in the first part of this chapter, we discuss all types of integrity controls that can be used to ensure consistent data. Subsequently we discuss security, and, although acknowledging the security facilities that a DBMS can provide, we take a broader perspective on security to encompass the database environment, not simply the DBMS alone. This is important, because corporate data is a vital resource, parts of which may be of strategic importance to an organization and therefore need to be kept confidential. The type of security controls needed should also take account of any legal obligations that must be observed by an organization. Finally, we discuss privacy. Privacy is also associated with security and is addressed by both Privacy and Data Protection Acts that seek to protect individual rights. As increasing amounts of personal data are stored in DBMSs it is important that all users are aware both of their individual rights and of their legal obligations when dealing with such data. In this context, we look at the issues of data protection and privacy, and the need for safeguards. The examples in this chapter are taken from the *DreamHome* case study.

14.1   Integrity

Data integrity	The data is consistent with all the stated constraints that apply to it, and hence can be considered to be valid.

Data integrity is closely associated with data security or database security, and to properly safeguard a system both sets of controls are essential. If security controls exist without any integrity controls, the reliability and validity of the data rely entirely on the authorized users' correct use of the system. Furthermore, if a breach in security occurs, an unauthorized user could wreak havoc with the data, even if there was no ulterior motive to destroy it. If, on the other hand, only integrity controls exist, data is guaranteed to be consistent although susceptible to the dangers that result from having no security. There are several aspects in considering how to ensure a database maintains data integrity, and we will look at each of these. However, an important point to bear in mind is that although data integrity may be preserved, *it does not absolutely guarantee that the data is correct*. It is very difficult to check data correctness automatically, unless there is a simultaneous checking mechanism, such as a dual data entry system. For example, the number of hours worked by an employee may fall within stated constraints, but may still be incorrect.

To maintain data integrity, it is necessary to have appropriate constraints on the manipulation of the data, particularly on insert, update and delete. In many instances, these constraints may be stored in the DBMS. Ideally, the DBMS would facilitate the handling of all required controls, but to what extent this is possible depends upon the DBMS being used. We have already described some types of integrity constraints in previous chapters, but for completeness we will reiterate these along with further types of integrity.

14.1.1 Entity Integrity (see Section 3.3.2)

> **Entity integrity**   In a base relation, no attribute of a primary key can be null.

This constraint applies to the primary key value of an entity, which is not permitted to be wholly or partially null. For example, let us look at the Branch relation of the *DreamHome* database, a subset of which is as follows:

BRANCH

Bno	Street	Area	City	Postcode	Tel_No	Fax_No
B5	22 Deer Rd	Sidcup	London	SW1 4EH	0171–886–1212	0171–886–1214
B7	16 Argyll St	Dyce	Aberdeen	AB2 3SU	01224–67125	01224–67111
B3	163 Main St	Partick	Glasgow	G11 9QX	0141–339–2178	0141–339–4439

We know that Branch number (Bno) is the primary key, and so has a constraint that it must be unique. The entity integrity constraint also ensures that it cannot be null. This is also the case where the primary key comprises more than one attribute, as in the following Viewing relation:

VIEWING

Rno	Pno	Date	Comment
CR56	PA14	24–May–95	too small
CR76	PG4	20–Apr–95	too remote
CR56	PG4	26–May–95	
CR62	PA14	14–May–95	no dining room
CR56	PG36	28–Apr–95	

Here, the primary key comprises both Renter number (Rno) and Property number (Pno), neither of which is permitted to be null under the entity integrity constraint. We can see, from looking at the data, the likely problems that could arise if either attribute was null, assuming the primary key value is still unique:

- If some values of Pno were null, we would be unable to determine which property was visited, nor to which property the comment applies.

- If some values of Rno were null, we would not know who had visited the property on the date and made the comments (if any).

- If the value of both Rno and Pno were null, the remaining information would be totally meaningless.

Most DBMSs automatically enforce the entity integrity constraint and the key value's uniqueness provided the attribute(s) can be designated a **primary key**. This would be specified through the data definition language, or the specific procedure for defining the schema if a data definition language is not used.

14.1.2 Referential Integrity (see Section 3.3.3)

Referential integrity	If a foreign key exists in a relation, either the foreign key value must match a candidate key value of some tuple in its home relation, or the foreign key value must be wholly null.

This constraint states that if a value exists as a foreign key in a relation, then it must match the value of an existing primary key in another relation, or else be wholly null. For example, if we look at the Staff relation, a subset of which follows, we can see that Branch number (Bno) is a foreign key that refers to the Branch relation:

STAFF

Sno	Fname	Lname	Address	Tel_No	Position	Sex	Salary	NIN	Bno
SL21	John	White	19 Taylor St, Cranford, London	0171–884–5112	Manager	M	30000	WK442011B	B5
SG37	Ann	Beech	81 George St, Glasgow PA1 2JR	0141–848–3345	Snr Asst	F	12000	WL432514C	B3
SG14	David	Ford	63 Ashby St, Partick, Glasgow G11	0141–339–2178	Deputy	M	18000	WL220658D	B3

The referential integrity constraint ensures that any value of Bno that occurs in the Staff relation matches an existing value of Bno in the Branch relation. We can see this is true by referring to the values in the Branch relation given above. However, it is neither feasible nor desirable to check the data visually, so we need to know there is some mechanism whereby it is enforced. Note that under the referential integrity constraint it is possible for values of Bno in the Staff relation to be null, although this may not always be desirable in practice. We present the possible options on handling foreign key values when the matching primary key value changes later in this section.

A number of problems can arise with respect to referential integrity, not least of which is the mechanism to use in enforcing it. This can be a problem with some DBMSs because ideally the enforcement mechanism should be specified in the DBMS, and not externally enforced within an application. We again use the Branch and Staff relations to illustrate the problems. First, suppose the value of Bno changes for the Branch office in Glasgow. Currently, it is B3. If we change only the Branch relation, this will violate the referential integrity of the Staff relation, which will contain obsolete values of Bno that no longer reference an existing value in Branch. Or worse, the Bno value in the Staff relation will reference the wrong branch if another branch is subsequently given the original number. Consequently, it is important that a change such as this is propagated to the Staff relation to ensure that referential integrity is maintained. Alternatively, if values of Bno are found to occur as foreign keys in other relations, any attempt to update Bno could be disallowed to avoid these problems.

Another similar problem arises if a tuple of the Branch relation is deleted. Again, this will lead to violation of referential integrity of the Staff relation if the deleted tuple is referenced. It also raises the question of how such an event should be handled, if at all, by the system. For instance, do we delete all the corresponding tuples in the Staff relation that have an identical value of Bno? A related problem concerns the properties for rent being handled by the Branch, and more specifically, by the member of staff at that Branch. If we look at a subset of the Property_for_Rent relation, we see that both the attributes Sno and Bno occur as foreign keys:

PROPERTY_FOR_RENT

Pno	Street	Area	City	Postcode	Type	Rooms	Rent	Ono	Sno	Bno
PG4	6 Lawrence St	Partick	Glasgow	G11 9QX	Flat	3	350	CO40	SG14	B3
PG36	2 Manor Rd		Glasgow	G32 4QX	Flat	3	375	CO93	SG37	B3
PG21	18 Dale Rd	Hyndland	Glasgow	G12	House	5	600	CO87	SG37	B3
PG16	5 Novar Dr	Hyndland	Glasgow	G12 9AX	Flat	4	450	CO93	SG14	B3

If the value of Bno changes, then it should also be updated in this relation. However, if a Branch occurrence is deleted along with the corresponding staff occurrences, then the values of both foreign keys need to be correctly handled. If we assume that the properties will be retained on the database, the immediate solution that retains referential integrity is to set the values of Bno and Sno to null. This example illustrates how one seemingly simple change to the database could have a ripple effect, requiring a significant number of changes in order to maintain referential integrity.

Clearly, the way that update and delete operations are handled will depend upon how the database designer interprets the application requirements, but broadly the options can be stated as follows. If a primary key is to be updated or the entire tuple is to be deleted and;

(1) The primary key value **does not** occur anywhere as a foreign key:

    (a) *Allow the operation to take place.*

(2) The primary key value **does** occur elsewhere as a foreign key:

    (a) *Do not allow the operation to take place.*

    (b) *Allow the operation to take place, **and also***

        Set the foreign key occurrences either *to null or to a default value* if one has been specified.

(c) *Allow the operation to take place, **and also***

(i) in the case of update

propagate the changed value to the foreign key occurrences, and where the foreign key forms part of the primary key of this relation, propagate the changes where this primary key is also a foreign key in another relation.

(ii) in the case of delete

propagate the deletion, that is, delete the tuples that have a foreign key value matching the primary key, and where the primary key of these deleted tuples is also a foreign key in another relation.

(d) *Enter into dialogue with the user.*

These are general rules, and it can be appreciated that various permutations will result depending on the application. If we look at our two examples again, we can see the possible effects where foreign key values do exist. The first example involved updating the primary key Bno of the Branch relation. If we knew, for example, that this change would be effected only for administrative purposes, with no other alterations to be made, we could enforce referential integrity by simply propagating the changes to the foreign key occurrences. Our second example involved deleting a Branch tuple, which illustrated that the situation may not be straightforward when the primary key of the relation containing the foreign key is also a foreign key in another relation.

We can see from these examples that the database designer will need to specify the action to be taken in each particular case, and have the appropriate action invoked when either an update or delete takes place. This was explained more fully in Chapter 7. As mentioned previously, these situations may be handled within the application itself, but it may be possible to build them into the DBMS using trigger mechanisms. For example, several DBMSs allow database procedures to be created and stored, and these procedures can be invoked (that is, triggered) when particular events occur, such as update or delete of specific attributes. In order for the system to know when to invoke a particular procedure, a rule must be created that activates on, for example, an update of a primary key, and subsequently calls the associated procedure. The SQL standard provides referential integrity control in its table creation statements (see Section 12.2).

14.1.3   Entity Participation in a Relationship (see Chapter 5)

Entity participation is also referred to as **existence dependency** or obligatory/non-obligatory membership of a relationship. During the analysis and subsequent design of a database, the designer needs to determine how entity occurrences exist in relation to others. In particular, the designer should note entities whose occurrences are always associated with occurrences of the corresponding entities through specific relationships. Conversely, the designer should also discover for which entities this is not the case. For example, if we consider the Branch and Staff entities, we may determine that if there is an occurrence of a member of staff, there will always be an associated occurrence of the Branch entity. This knowledge can be shown on the resulting data model by various techniques, and influences the design by helping determine the required physical tables from the logical data model.

This aspect is connected to referential integrity discussed above because the appropriate option(s) given in the previous section can be used to enforce existence dependencies. For example, consider the Property_for_Rent and Staff entities with respect to the relationship between them. Information from the users will determine one of the following situations to be valid:

- A property for rent may exist independently: that is, it need not be associated with a member of staff.
- A property for rent may not exist independently; it must always be associated with some member of staff.

In the first situation, three relations may be required, one for each entity and one for the relationship, Property_Staff, say. Relationship occurrences would exist only where members of staff and properties for rent were associated. Consequently, inserting new Staff and Property_for_Rent occurrences does not affect the other relations, but the update and delete of a Staff tuple, say, may possibly also affect the Property_Staff relation. If, however, only a few occurrences of Property_for_Rent are likely to exist independently, the relationship can be expressed by having the staff number Sno as a foreign key in the Property_for_Rent relation. In this case, to allow properties to be unassigned to members of staff, the foreign key is allowed to be null.

The second situation requires only two relations, one for each entity with the relationship expressed by having Sno as a foreign key in the Property_for_Rent relation. In this case, the foreign key is not permitted to be null. If we also know that properties are not deleted when a staff tuple is deleted from the database, appropriate steps must be taken to reassign the properties such that referential integrity is maintained.

These examples illustrate how entity participation in relationships can influence the resulting relations, which in turn affect the way the referential integrity constraints may be applied. The resulting characteristics of the relations may also indicate where periodic exception reporting would be useful to management: for example, in the first situation, reporting on properties that are not currently assigned to a member of staff.

14.1.4 **Domain Constraint** (see Section 3.2.1)

> **Domain** A domain is the set of allowable values for one or more attributes.

A domain defines a pool of legitimate values. If a DBMS does not support the concept of domains, then specific native data types, such as character or integer, are used to define each attribute of a database. Fundamentally, a native data type comprises its own domain, together with a set of legitimate operations that can be carried out on the values of the domain. The domain of the native data type is determined by the characteristics of the system. For example, a character data type will be able to assume all the available characters present in an implementation-defined character set, such as ASCII or EBCDIC. The legitimate operations that can be carried out on these values may include comparison but exclude operations such as addition and subtraction, which usually belong to numeric data types.

The database domain is at a higher level than the available native data type domain because, although currently a database domain is defined on a native data type, it defines a subset of the available values of the native data type domain. Ideally, a DBMS should permit user-defined data types to be specified, each with its own domain and legitimate operations. Current relational DBMSs provide a range of native data types, and some also permit database domains to be defined on these. The flexibility permitted by the underlying domains of the native data types may not be desirable, because some attributes may only be allowed to take a very restricted range of values. For example, the attribute *Sex* may only need either the value M or F, if it was designated a single character. It may be further constrained to being only an uppercase character. However, not all attributes will have definable ranges of values: for example, names and addresses, in which cases the native data type domains may suffice. Specifying domains helps to ensure that attribute values are legitimate values, but does not guarantee that the values will be the correct ones.

The database designer should have acquired sufficient information on the values that attributes can take to be able to identify the associated domains. The method of specification will vary depending on the DBMS, and is normally part of the data definition language. When a DBMS permits the creation of named domains, these are assigned a native data type with a range of legitimate values. They must be defined first, followed by the table structures, the attributes of which, instead of being assigned a data type, are assigned a domain. In this situation, for example, a domain Branch_numbers can be defined and *all* attributes that take their values from this domain can be defined over the domain named Branch_numbers. Other DBMSs require a domain specification to be defined for each attribute, even if some of the domains are identical. For example, the domain for the Branch number (Bno) in the Branch relation would be distinct from the domain for the Branch number (Bno) in the Staff relation.

14.1.5 Enterprise Constraints (see Section 3.3.4)

> **Enterprise constraints** Additional rules specified by the users or database administrators of a database.

These constraints may also be referred to as application constraints, business rules or assertions, and generally would be enforced either by an application or by the use of a trigger-type mechanism. The ISO SQL standard contains the Assert statement, which would be used for integrity constraints of this nature, although it is not implemented in all systems. Examples of this type of integrity constraint are:

- A member of staff can manage only a maximum of 20 properties for rent.
- There are no more than 20 employees at a Branch.
- An ordinary member of staff's salary shall not exceed that of the Branch manager.
- A clerical staff member's salary shall not exceed £12,000.

This last constraint is, of course, more limiting than the specification of a domain for salary, and is dependent on the value of the attribute *Position*. Hence, it is a conditional domain constraint, which again could be enforced using a trigger mechanism, as discussed above. If these integrity constraints can be built into the DBMS, they will subsequently reduce the effort involved in the development of applications, by removing the need to build the constraints into each application.

14.1.6 Other Semantic Integrity Constraints

One obvious problem mentioned at the beginning of this section is that of data input. An end-user could easily mistype input data that may be acceptable to all the system constraints, but is still incorrect, and therefore undesirable. The only likely way that this sort of problem might be overcome is to have someone else check the data entered against the source documents, or have a dual entry system, the results of which are compared for discrepancies.

The ability to prevent invalid operations being carried out on the data would also enhance the robustness of the database system. For example, multiplying a member of staff's salary by the rental price should not be allowed, even if both attributes were of numeric data type. One way of avoiding this possibility, without resorting to triggers, would be to define attributes as character data types *provided* they were not required to take part in any arithmetical operations.

However, this solution does not cover all types of invalid operation. The fundamental problem is that attribute values, whether or not taken from a domain, are all ultimately influenced by the characteristics of the native data types: that is, even if a domain has been specified, the allowable operations permitted on the values are still those of the native data type. For example, if a domain *Position* is defined as being 10 characters long, a user can compare attributes taking their values from this domain with attributes that are simply defined as 10 characters long. The comparison should be invalid even if there are no matches. In the same manner, it is not sensible to compare values of Renter number (Rno) and Staff number (Sno), because the attributes are unrelated. Unfortunately, DBMSs only have a limited range of native data types and lack a full implementation of domains, which is the cause of the problem. The new SQL3 Standard may help to alleviate these problems (see Chapter 17).

14.2 Database Security

Database security	The protection of the database against threats using both technical and administrative controls.

Security considerations do not only apply to the **database**: that is, the data itself. Breaches of security could affect other parts of the system, which in turn could also affect the database. Consequently, database security encompasses hardware, software, people and data. To effectively implement security requires appropriate controls, and these controls should implement specific policy statements that have been dictated by the requirements of the system, the needs of the organization and any legal constraints. This need for security, while having often been neglected or overlooked in the past, is now increasingly recognized by organizations. It is easy to understand why, because as greater amounts of crucial data are stored on computer systems, the consequence of any loss or unavailability could be disastrous. A database now represents an essential corporate resource, and accordingly, security of this resource is an important goal.

We consider database security in relation to the following situations:

- theft and fraud,
- loss of confidentiality (secrecy),
- loss of privacy,
- loss of integrity,
- loss of availability.

These broadly represent areas in which management should seek to reduce risk: that is, the possibility of incurring loss or damage. There is, of course, some interrelation between these situations. It is often the case that an activity which leads to loss in one area, can also lead to loss in another. In addition, events such as loss of privacy or fraud may arise because of either intentional or unintentional acts, and do not necessarily result in any detectable changes to the database or the system.

Theft and fraud are not limited to only the database environment; the entire organization is susceptible to this risk. However, activities resulting in theft and fraud are perpetrated by people, and consequently, in the database environment, attention should focus on reducing the opportunities for this occurring: for example, keeping salary payment stationery secure, recording exactly the amount used in a pay cheque print run, and ensuring proper recording and subsequent destruction of any payment stationery used in incorrect print runs. It should also not be possible for staff salaries to be altered immediately prior to and after the printing of pay cheques. Theft and fraud do not necessarily alter data, as is the case for activities that result in either loss of confidentiality or loss of privacy.

Confidentiality refers to the need to maintain secrecy over data, usually only that which is critical to the organization, whereas privacy refers to the need to protect data about individuals. Breaches of security resulting in loss

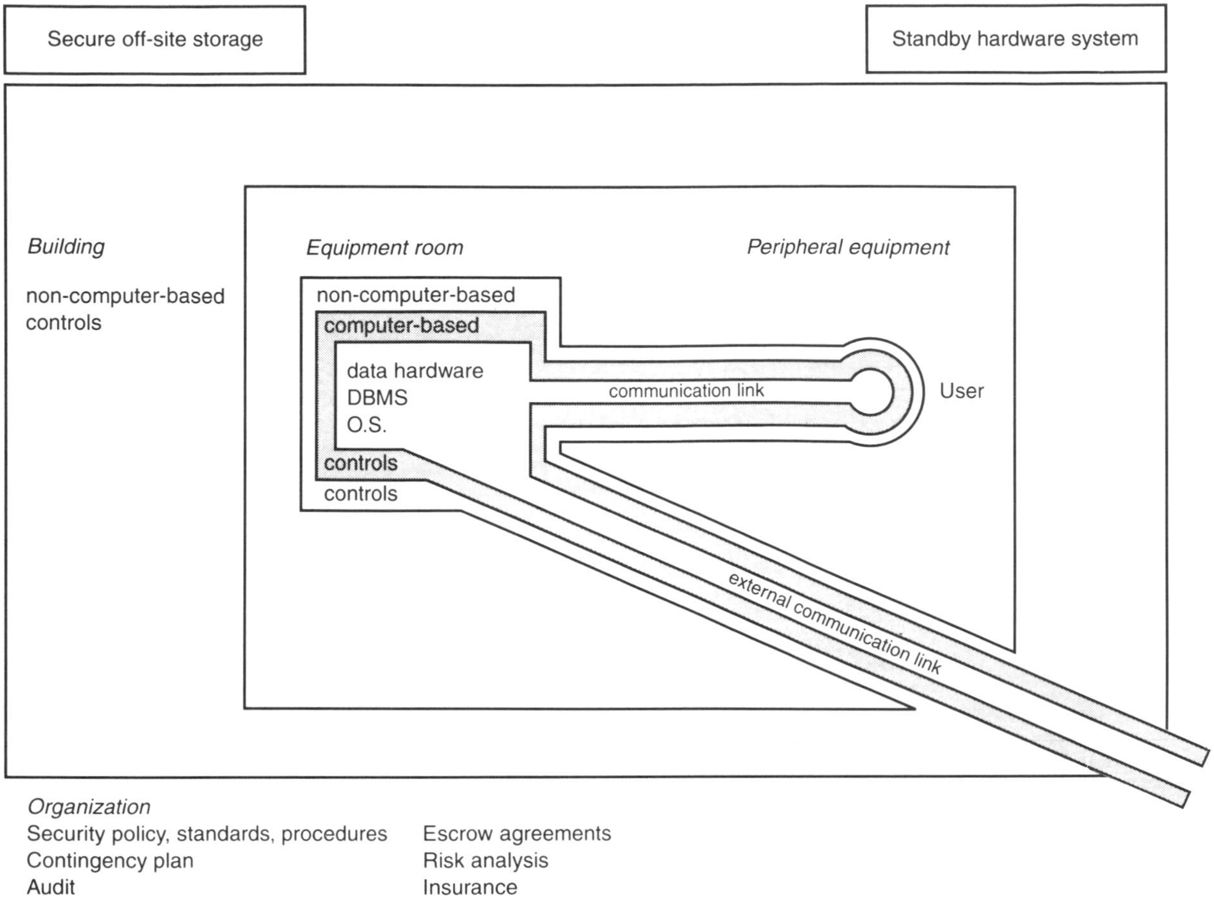

| Secure off-site storage | | Standby hardware system |

Building

non-computer-based
controls

Equipment room

non-computer-based

computer-based

data hardware
DBMS
O.S.

communication link   User

controls

controls

Peripheral equipment

external communication link

Organization
Security policy, standards, procedures   Escrow agreements
Contingency plan   Risk analysis
Audit   Insurance

Figure 14.1
Summary of possible
security control
measures in the
DBMS environment.

of confidentiality could, for instance, lead to loss of competitiveness, and loss of privacy could lead to legal action being taken against an organization.

Loss of data integrity results in invalid or corrupt data, which will seriously affect the operation of an organization. Loss of availability means that the data or system or neither could be accessed, which could jeopardize an organization's existence. In some cases, events that cause a system to be unavailable may also cause data corruption. We examine some of the types of threat that could affect an organization's database systems in Section 14.2.1. Countermeasures are discussed in Sections 14.3 and 14.4. Figure 14.1 illustrates the overall environment in which a DBMS may operate and indicates the security control measures that could be applied to various parts.

We consider security in relation to the database environment, not just in relation to the DBMS, because simply focusing on DBMS security measures alone will not guarantee secure data. All the other parts of the system (that is, the hardware, the software such as the operating system, and the users) are vulnerable to threats, and consequently could directly affect the database, the database systems or the organization.

This wider perspective also considers protection of the buildings and other personnel, and focuses more on physical security controls, some of which are also appropriate to database security. Security, therefore, should apply to the whole organization, which ideally should have a security policy that encompasses DBMS security. It is suggested that organizations should have an IT security team or a security team of which the IT security team is a subset responsible for determining the policy and associated procedures concerned with the IT environment. We also discuss aspects of this in Section 14.4.

It should be recognized that in an organization some loss is inevitable, because at the very least, mistakes do happen. For example, having to reprint a complete set of reports represents a sustained loss in the costs of the materials and power used and time taken to do the reprinting. Database security aims to minimize losses caused by anticipated events in a cost-effective manner without unduly constraining the users. We should also recognize that computer-based criminal activities are increasing, with the forecast that this will be a major growth area during the 1990s and into the next century. Computer-based crime can threaten all parts of a system, and so adequate security measures are vital.

14.2.1 Threats

Threat	Any situation or event, whether intentional or unintentional, that will adversely affect a system and consequently an organization.

A threat may be represented by a person, action or circumstance that is likely to bring harm to an organization. The harm may be tangible, such as loss of hardware, software or data, or intangible, such as loss of credibility or client confidence. The problem facing any organization is in identifying all possible threats, not all of which will be obvious. Consequently, it can take a lot of time and lateral thinking to identify at least the major threats that ought to be considered. We have identified areas of loss in the previous section which may result from intentional (deliberate) or unintentional (accidental) activities. Intentional threats involve people, and may be perpetrated by both authorized users and unauthorized users, some of whom may be external to the organization.

Any threat must be viewed as a potential breach of security which, if successful, will have a certain impact. Table 14.1 presents examples of various types of threat listed under the areas where they would have an impact. We see that some types of threat can have a wide effect, such as inadequate staff training. Some types of threat could be either intentional or unintentional, but the impact remains the same.

To what extent an organization suffers as a result of a threat succeeding depends upon a number of factors. These include the resulting impact that the successful threat makes, balanced against any existing countermeasures and contingency plans. For example, if a hardware failure occurs corrupting

Table 14.1 Examples of threats.

Theft and fraud	Loss of confidentiality	Loss of privacy	Loss of integrity	Loss of availability
Unauthorized amendment of data	Wire tapping	Wire tapping	Electronic interference and radiation	Electronic interference and radiation
Wire tapping	Illegal entry by hacker	Acquiring and using another person's identifier and password to gain access	Data corruption due to power loss or surge	Arson
Program alteration	Acquiring and using another person's identifier and password to gain access			Bomb attack
Illegal entry by hacker		Blackmail	Fire (electrical fault/ lightning strike)	Fire (electrical fault/ lightning strike)
Acquiring and using another person's identifier and password to gain access	Blackmail	Software failure giving greater access than normal	Inadequate staff training	Flood
	Inadequate or ill-thought-out procedures that allow confidential output to be mixed with normal output	Inadequate staff training	Physical damage to equipment	Debris from aircraft
Blackmail			Breaking cables or disconnection of cables	Hardware failures such as disk head crash
Intent to commit fraud	Software failure giving greater access than normal	Viewing unauthorized data and disclosing it	Introduction of viruses	Physical damage to equipment
Developing programs or routines that bypass the security mechanisms, thus forming a 'trapdoor' into the system	Staff shortage or strikes			Breaking cables or disconnection of cables
	Inadequate staff training			Introduction of viruses
Unauthorized access using privileged knowledge, and other anti-social behaviour	Viewing unauthorized data and disclosing it			
Theft				
Software failure giving greater access than normal				
Staff shortage or strikes				
Inadequate staff training				

secondary storage, all processing activity must cease until the problem has been resolved. How long this period of inactivity is and how adequately the database is recovered will depend upon a number of factors, some of which are:

- whether or not alternative hardware and software can be used;

- when the last backups were taken;
- the time needed to restore the system;
- whether or not the lost data can be recovered and recaptured.

Other management concerns would include any likely economic effect, and whether and how any customers might be inconvenienced. For example, a customer may have filled his or her car with petrol expecting to pay by credit card, only to find the computer system has failed. If the customer has an alternative method of payment, he or she may not be inconvenienced very much, but if not how is it handled? Alternatively, a customer may have filled two trolleys at a supermarket and then find, along with several hundred other customers, that all the checkout systems have failed. How is this immediate problem handled, and how is the lost information recovered? These effects impinge upon restocking and purchasing procedures amongst others.

Although both of these situations cause inconvenience, neither one is life-threatening. However, we can appreciate that with increasing reliance on computerized information systems, the possibility of life-threatening situations arising from errors or failures is very real. The 1993 malfunction of the London ambulance scheduling system is one example. In this incident, a new vehicle scheduling system was introduced that was supposed to optimize the scheduling of ambulances, taking into account their location in the city. Consequently, the result should have been a more efficient service. Unfortunately, the system did not work as intended, and quickly caused unacceptable delays to patients. Eventually, the system was abandoned, with control reverting to a manual system. This happened within the first 24 hours of operation. There were, of course, other factors involved in this fiasco, including bringing an untested system online too quickly with inadequately trained staff, but this does not detract from the point that the failure of some computerized information systems can produce life-threatening situations.

Managers, therefore, do need to consider what types of threat their organization may be subject to and initiate appropriate plans and countermeasures, bearing in mind the costs of implementing them. Obviously, it may not be cost-effective to spend considerable time, effort and money on potential threats that may result only in minor inconveniences. The organization's business may also influence the types of threat that should be considered, some of which may be very rare occurrences. However, rare events should be taken account of, particularly if their impact is significant. For example, in 1971 a Milan bank was blown up by the Red Brigade as a political act of terrorism. While undoubtedly a rare event, the effect was catastrophic. More recently, an IRA terrorist bomb attack in the City of London business area has caused business managers to think more carefully about protecting their systems. An organization may not be the direct target of an event, but may suffer from the subsequent effects. For example, in March 1993, a serious fire in the basement of a building in Glasgow adversely affected small businesses in the adjacent building. The reason was that firemen had to tackle the blaze from the adjacent building, causing flooding, amongst other damage, and preventing access to the building (pers. comm.).

These examples demonstrate that no matter how secure computer systems are, it is advisable to take a wider perspective of security. The objective is to achieve a balance between a reasonably secure operation, which does not unduly hinder users, and the costs of maintaining it. We have already identified examples of threats in Table 14.1, noting that some may be accidental. Accidental threats probably result in the most losses for the majority of organizations (Moulton, 1986). Any accidental incident that breaches security should be recorded, together with details of the person or persons involved where appropriate. Periodically, these records should be checked for the frequencies of occurrence of similar incidents involving the same people, to see if any patterns are revealed, or areas where policies or procedures could be improved. For example, repeated disconnection or breaking of a cable should lead to a reappraisal of its location and routeing. Similarly, the introduction of viruses, and similar undesirable software, may be viewed as a serious threat, but it may not be possible to determine whether it is accidental or not after examining the working environment. However, if there are procedures that check all new software and media that enter the premises, coupled with a policy that states employees are not authorized to load their own software, the appearance of a virus is less likely to be unintentional. It may be stupidity on the part of an employee, but there is less opportunity for excuses.

Types of threat identified range from those such as fire and flood, which may directly affect all parts of a system, to those that may directly affect only part of a system: for example, an accidental break in a cable may only affect one user and not affect any software or data. Nevertheless, although some events may not seem to directly affect much, the repercussions on the rest of the system may be severe. Consequently, in considering threats various questions may be raised in order to try to evaluate the impact. If we consider the previous example of a hardware failure corrupting secondary storage, some likely questions may be:

- Does alternative hardware exist that can be used?

- Is this alternative hardware secure?

- Can we legally run our software on this hardware?

- If no alternative hardware exists, how quickly can the problem be fixed?

- When were the last backups taken of the database and log files?

- Are the backups in a fireproof safe or offsite?

- If the most current database needs to be recreated by restoring the backup with the log files, how long will it take?

- How much processing activity has been lost, and are we able to recover the data?

- Can the business continue to function while the system is inactive, and if so, for how long?

- Will there be any immediate effects on our clients?

- If we restore the system, will the same or similar breach of security occur again unless we do something to prevent it happening?

- Could our contingency planning be improved in this instance?

We can see that if one event provokes so many questions a great many more will result when considering all possible threats. Underlying the questions is a need to attempt to quantify the likely effects, such as data lost, time lost, possible costs involved, and the more intangible ones such as inconvenience and possible loss of goodwill, and so on. To evaluate all potential threats as effectively as possible, a risk analysis or assessment should be carried out. There are various ways in which this could be done, either manually or using a software package or using a combination of both (Fernandez *et al.*, 1981; Moulton, 1986; Elbra, 1992). We give an overview of risk analysis in Section 14.7, but first we consider countermeasures to threats.

14.3 Countermeasures – Computer-Based Controls

Table 14.1 shows some of the types of threat that may affect a system, some of which clearly require physical controls or administrative procedures or both, whereas others require different kinds of control, as illustrated in Figure 14.1. Despite the range of computer-based controls that are available, it is worth noting that, generally, the security of a DBMS is only as good as that of the operating system, due to their close association. In this section, we focus on computer-based security controls, with the assumption that we are dealing with a multi-user environment. Typically, not all of these controls will be available in the PC environment. We consider:

- authorization,
- views,
- backing-up,
- journaling,
- checkpointing,
- integrity,
- encryption,
- associated procedures.

14.3.1 Authorization

Authorization	The granting of a right or privilege which enables a subject to legitimately have access to a system or object.

Authorization controls can be built into the software, and govern not only what system or object a specified user can have access to, but also what the user may do with it. For this reason, authorization controls may sometimes be referred to as 'access controls', although access tends to be used specifically in relation to database objects. We shall cover this in more detail later on. The term *subject* in the definition means a user or program. The term *object*, however, can mean database table, view, application, procedure, or any other object that can be created within the system. On some systems, authorization may have to be explicitly granted for each object used. The process of authorization involves authentication of subjects requesting access to objects.

Authentication	A mechanism by which a subject is determined to be the genuine subject that they claim to be.

DBMSs and associated application programs reside on computer systems 'managed' by operating systems. Therefore, in order to gain access to the DBMS, access first has to be gained to the computer system by using the operating system. A system administrator is usually responsible for permitting users to have access to a computer system by creating individual user accounts. Each user is given a unique identifier which the operating system uses to determine who they are. Associated with each identifier is a password, chosen by the user and known to the operating system, which must be supplied to enable the operating system to verify or authenticate who the user claims to be.

This procedure allows authorized use of a computer system, but does not necessarily authorize access to the DBMS or any of the associated application programs. A separate, similar procedure may have to be undertaken to give a user the right to use the DBMS. The responsibility to authorize use of the DBMS usually rests with the Database Administrator (DBA), who must also set up individual user identifiers, but this time on the DBMS itself. Each user identifier is again associated with a password that should be known only to the user, and the DBMS uses this information to authenticate the user. Consequently, authentication is part of authorization control.

As we have described, a password mechanism is the most popular method used to authenticate a user. Unfortunately, this mechanism cannot absolutely guarantee that the real user is who the system acknowledges him or her to be. We discuss methods to reduce this risk in the section on associated procedures. One further point should be mentioned with respect to DBMSs. We have stated that a password is associated with a valid DBMS user. Some DBMSs maintain their own list of valid user identifiers and associated passwords, which can be distinct from the operating system's list. However, others maintain a list whose entries are validated against the operating system's list based on the current user's login identifier. This prevents a user from logging in to the DBMS with one name, after having logged in to the operating system using a different name. Similarly, a DBMS checks whether an external program that accesses the database is valid. Consequently, users can be authorized to execute a program rather than be authorized to use the DBMS.

Privileges

Most DBMSs provide a facility to create a named **database** within which users can create and store tables, views, indexes, and so on. Different users may use different databases. This facility allows collections of related objects to be kept separately from others. Once the right has been granted to use a DBMS, various other privileges may also be automatically associated with it: for example, the right to have access to certain databases, including tables, the right to create databases, tables, views and indexes, and the right to run various DBMS utility programs. Some DBMSs operate as **closed systems** so that users may be authorized to use the DBMS, but unless they are authorized to have access to required objects they will not be able to do anything. This authorization is given by either the DBA or owners of particular objects. The opposite is an **open system**, in which all users have complete access to all objects. In this case, privileges have to be explicitly removed from users to control access.

The types of privilege that an authorized subject may be given include:

- use of specific named databases;
- selection or retrieval of data;
- creation of tables and other objects;
- update of data (may be restricted to certain columns);
- deletion of data (may be restricted to certain columns);
- insertion of data (may be restricted to certain columns);
- unlimited result set from a query (that is, a user is not restricted to a specified number of rows);
- execution of specific procedures and utility programs;
- creation of databases;
- creation (and modification) of DBMS user identifiers and other types of authorized identifiers;
- membership of a group or groups of users, and consequent inheritance of the group's privileges.

Ownership and privileges

Some objects in the DBMS are owned by the DBMS itself, usually in the form of a specific super-user or DBA. Accordingly, ownership of objects gives the owner all appropriate privileges on the objects owned. The same situation applies to other authorized users if they own objects. Any newly created objects are automatically owned by their creator who gains the appropriate privileges for the object. For example, a user may own a view, but only have Select privilege on it because he or she does not have more than Select privilege on the base tables. These privileges can be passed on to other authorized users. For example, an owner of several tables may authorize other users to select data from them, but not to carry out any amendments. In some DBMSs, whenever a user passes on a privilege, he or she can indicate whether the recipient can pass the privilege on. Needless to say, the DBMS needs to keep track of all privileges granted to users, and by whom, in order to maintain the correct set of privileges. This is especially important when a privilege is revoked, which could entail several amendments involving the need to propagate or cascade changes through the database system tables. For further information regarding cascading amendments, see Section 12.4.

Where a DBMS supports several different types of authorization identifiers, including ordinary user identifiers, there may be different priorities associated with each type. For example, a DBMS may permit both individual user identifiers and group identifiers to be created, with the user identifier having a higher priority than the group identifier. In such a DBMS, the user and group identifiers shown in Table 14.2 may be defined.

Table 14.2   User and group identifiers.

Users		Group members	
Identifier	*Type*	*Group*	*Identifier*
SG37	user	sales	SG37
SG14	user	sales	SG14
SG5	user		
sales	group		

The Users table lists each user identifier on the system, together with the user type, which distinguishes individuals from groups. The Group members table shows which users belong to a particular group. Certain privileges may be associated with specific identifiers, which indicate what may be done with certain database objects. Each privilege has a binary value associated with it, as indicated below:

READ	**UPDATE**	**INSERT**	**DELETE**	**ALL**
0001	0010	0100	1000	1111

The values are summed as appropriate, and this final value indicates what a specific user can do with a particular object. The table below, known as an **access control matrix**, illustrates different privileges for different users:

User identifier	Pno	Type	Price	Ono	Sno	Bno	Query row limit
SG5	1111	1111	1111	1111	1111	1111	none
SG37	0101	0101	0111	0101	0111		100
sales	0001	0001	0001				15

This shows the group identifier *sales* only having read access to three attributes, and a limit of 15 rows in a query result set. As user SG14 (David Ford) is a member of this group and has no specific privileges of his own, these are the restrictions that apply to him. On the other hand, user SG37 (Ann Beech) has Read and Insert privilege on Pno, Type and Ono and Read, Insert and Update on Price and Sno. Her query row limit is also greater than for the group identifier.

DBMSs use similar matrices to implement access control, although the precise details of implementation vary from one system to another. On some DBMSs, a user has to tell the system under which identifier he or she is operating, especially if he or she could be a member of more than one group. It is essential to become familiar with the available authorization and other control mechanisms provided by the DBMS, particularly where priorities may be applied to different authorization identifiers and where privileges can be passed on. This will enable the correct types of privileges to be granted to users based on their requirements and those of the application programs that many of them will use.

14.3.2   Views (Subschemas)

> **View**   A view is the dynamic result of one or more relational operations operating on the base relations to produce another relation. A view is a **virtual relation** that does not actually exist in the database, but is produced upon request by a particular user, at the time of request.

Views were discussed in Sections 3.5 and 12.1. The view mechanism is extremely useful, as it can be used to present only the data which is relevant to a user, by effectively hiding other fields. A view can be defined over several tables with a user being granted the appropriate privilege to use it, but not to use the base tables. In this way, using a view is more restrictive than simply having certain privileges granted to a user on the base table(s). For example, if we take the *DreamHome* database table Property_for_Rent, a view may be defined on it to select only those properties handled by a particular member of staff. If the view is for David Ford, and is called DF_Prop, the contents of this view would be as follows:

DF_Prop

Pno	Street	Area	City	Postcode	Type	Rooms	Rent	Ono	Sno
PG4	6 Lawrence St	Partick	Glasgow	G11 9QX	Flat	3	350	CO40	SG14
PG16	5 Novar Dr	Hyndland	Glasgow	G12 9AX	Flat	4	450	CO93	SG14

The only property for rent data that David Ford is permitted to view relates to the properties that he is handling. The view prevents any other data from being retrieved.

14.3.3   Backing-up

> **Backing-up**   The process of periodically taking a copy of the database and journals (and possibly programs) onto offline storage media.

It is always advisable to have backup copies of the database and journals taken at regular intervals and kept in a secure location. In the event of hardware failure that renders the original system unusable, the backup copies can be restored and the database recreated to the latest possible consistent state using the journal entries, as explained in Section 15.3. Many DBMSs provide a backup facility that enables the DBA or other designated person to take backups; others assume backups are performed using the operating system commands.

It is relatively simple to make backup copies when the database is not very large, but in dealing with very large databases (such as those that occupy more than one disk pack), the time that would be required to make the backup may be impractical. Consequently, the backups taken may be of selected data only. Some data may remain relatively unchanged over the life of the database, and so do not require regular backing up. On the other hand, important data may change regularly and must be backed up frequently. Some operating systems facilitate the handling of large databases by allowing incremental backups to be taken regularly, with a full backup taken less frequently, such as every week or month. The net result is that, depending on the data involved and the DBMS, there may be a different backing-up cycle, and consequently, the backing-up routine should be carefully controlled.

14.3.4 Journaling

Journaling	The process of keeping and maintaining a journal or log of all changes made to the database to enable recovery to be undertaken effectively in the event of a failure.

Journaling is an important mechanism that is used by many DBMSs to facilitate recovery procedures. Sometimes it must be explicitly invoked, for example when creating tables, to ensure the DBMS records all changes that are made to the database. The advantage of this is that, in the event of a failure, the database can be reconstructed using the information contained in the journal to amend the database to its last known consistent state. If a media failure occurs and the database becomes corrupted, the database is restored using the journal with a backup copy of the database. If no journaling is enabled on the system, then if the tables become corrupted they may not be accessible, and the only means of recovery will be to restore a backup of the database, which may mean that a considerable amount of time is lost. Some DBMSs have the facility to maintain copies of the journal on other disks in case the first journal becomes corrupted and unusable. For further details about journaling, see Section 15.3.

In addition to the normal journal entries maintained by the DBMS, a record may also be kept of all security violations that take place. These entries may be kept in a separate security log, and could trigger messages or alarms that alert the Database Administrator (DBA) to the violations.

14.3.5 Checkpointing

Checkpointing	The point of synchronization between the database and the transaction log file. All buffers are force-written to secondary storage.

Checkpointing can be used in conjunction with journaling to enable a more efficient recovery process to take place. When a checkpoint is taken, the DBMS ensures that all the data in main memory is written out to disk and a special checkpoint record is written to the journal, which is also on disk. It guarantees that, if successful, all changes made up to that point in time have been written to the database. There are several methods of carrying out checkpoints, which will be determined by the DBMS implementation. The benefit of checkpointing is that it greatly reduces the amount of processing that has to be carried out when effecting a recovery. For further details about checkpointing and recovery, see Section 15.3 on Recovery Control.

14.3.6 Integrity

Integrity controls also contribute to maintaining a secure database system by preventing data from becoming invalid, and hence giving misleading or incorrect results. We have already covered integrity controls in the previous section.

14.3.7 Encryption

Encryption	The encoding of the data by a special algorithm that renders the data unreadable by any program without the decryption key.

If a database system holds particularly sensitive data, it may be deemed necessary to encode it as a precaution against possible external (that is, external to the DBMS) threats or attempts to access it. Some DBMSs provide an encryption facility for this purpose. The DBMS can access the data (after decoding it), although there is a degradation in performance because of the time taken to decode it. Encryption also protects data transmitted over communication lines. There are a number of techniques for coding data to conceal the information; some are termed irreversible and others reversible. Irreversible techniques, as the name implies, do not permit the original data to be known. However, the data can be used to obtain valid statistical information. Reversible techniques are probably of greater interest than irreversible ones.

To transmit data securely over insecure networks requires a **cryptosystem** to be used. Normally this comprises:

- an **encryption key** to be used to encrypt the data (plain text);

- an **encryption algorithm** that, with the key, transforms the plain text into ciphertext;
- a **decryption key** to be used to decrypt the ciphertext;
- a **decryption algorithm** that, with the key, transforms the ciphertext back into plain text.

Some systems use the same key for both encryption and decryption (symmetric encryption) and rely on safe communication lines for exchanging the key. However, most users would not have access to a secure communication line and, to be really secure, the keys need to be as long as the message (Leiss, 1982). However, practical systems are based on user keys shorter than the message. One scheme used for encryption is the Data Encryption Standard (DES), which is a standard encryption algorithm developed by IBM. This uses one key for encryption and decryption, which must be kept secret, although the algorithm need not be. The algorithm transforms each 64-bit block of plaintext using a 56-bit key. The DES is not universally regarded as being very secure, and some authors maintain that a larger key would be better (Denning and Denning, 1979).

Another type of cryptosystem is one that uses different keys for encryption and decryption, and is referred to as an **asymmetric encryption system**. One example is public key cryptosystems, which use two keys, one of which is public but the other must be kept secret. The encryption algorithm may also be public, so that anyone wishing to send a user a message can use the user's publicly known key in conjunction with the algorithm to encrypt it. Only the owner of the private key can then decipher the message. Public Key cryptosystems can also be used to send a 'digital signature' with a message and prove that the message came from the person who claimed to have sent it.

14.3.8 Associated Procedures

Although we have described various mechanisms available to protect the data in a DBMS, on their own they do not guarantee it, and they can be ineffective unless they are properly used and controlled. For this reason, we need to identify associated procedures that should also be initiated in conjunction with the above mechanisms.

Authorization and authentication

We described how a password mechanism is a common method used to verify users. It is important in maintaining security that all passwords are kept secret and are changed at regular intervals. Passwords should not be displayed during the login procedure, and all user identifiers and passwords maintained by the system should be in an encrypted form. The organization may also determine a password standard: for example, all passwords must be of a minimum length, must contain digits as well as characters, and must be changed regularly (for example, every five weeks). Software may also be run on the system to determine whether passwords are too obvious (for example, the real name of a person or place), and when they were last changed. Any users whose passwords breach the standards will have their accounts frozen.

Another aspect of authorization is in establishing procedures whereby specific users are granted access to various objects. Keeping track of authorizations is important, particularly if users' job functions change and they no longer need access to certain areas of the database, but may need access to other areas. In particular, if users leave employment, it is vital that their accounts and authorizations are removed to prevent any possible violations in security.

Backup

Specific procedures should be determined for the backup process, which will be influenced by the nature and size of the database and the facilities that are available with the DBMS. These procedures should also include the actual steps involved in making a backup. As we indicated previously, large databases may only have a backup taken weekly or monthly, but incremental backups will be taken more frequently. The day and time for taking the backup may be specified along with the responsible personnel.

It must also be remembered that all parts of the database system should be backed up. This includes all software from the operating system to the application programs, in addition to the data. Depending on the frequency of change in the system, there may be several backups a day which must be stored safely. There should be a fireproof data safe on site in which to store immediate backups, and there may also be an off-site store for another set of backups. All these details should be clearly specified in the procedures to be followed by personnel.

Recovery

In the same way that the backup procedure needs to be clearly specified, the recovery procedure also needs to be well defined. The recovery procedure depends upon the nature of the crash that has occurred: that is, whether it is a media failure, a software failure or a hardware failure. It will also depend upon the method of recovery used by the DBMS, as described above. The recovery procedure should always be tested to ensure it works properly prior to having to deal with the real event. Ideally, the procedure should be tested at regular intervals.

Audit

One of the purposes of an audit is to check that all the proper controls are in place, and that the level of security is adequate for the installation. In carrying out an audit, the auditors will observe manual procedures, investigate the computer systems, and inspect all the documentation for the systems. In particular, they will be interested in controls for:

- ensuring accuracy of input data;

- ensuring accuracy of data processing;
- prevention and detection of errors during program execution;
- properly testing and documenting program development and maintenance;
- avoiding unauthorized program alteration;
- granting and monitoring access to data;
- ensuring documentation is up to date.

All controls must be effective, otherwise they will need to be redefined. The journals will be inspected to look at the activity that has taken place on the database and identify anything unusual. A regularly undertaken audit, especially if it is known that all journals are regularly inspected for any unusual activity, often acts as a deterrent against any would-be security violations.

Installation of new application software

If new applications are developed in-house, they should be properly tested before authorization is given to install and run them on the live data. If proper testing is not undertaken there is a risk of corruption to the database. Prior to installation, a backup should be taken, and after installation the system should be monitored for a period of time. If software is developed by a third party, greater care should be taken prior to installation. It may be wise to assume that thorough testing has not been undertaken and, if possible, the software should be run on the organization's test data prior to acceptance. Unfortunately this is often not possible, in which case after ensuring backups are complete, very close monitoring will need to be carried out while the system is used. A separate issue which ought to be resolved when third parties or contract staff develop software is the question of ownership. This should be settled prior to development, and is important if there is any likelihood of the organization needing to have amendments made at some later date. The risk associated with this situation is the threat that the organization may not legally be able to run the software or be able to upgrade it. This could cause substantial loss to an organization.

Installation/upgrading of system software

The DBA periodically receives upgrades to the DBMS software from the vendor. Sometimes these upgrades may be quite minor, and may not involve all modules of the system, but at other times there may be a full revision that has to be installed. Accompanying each upgrade there should normally be documentation that details the changes that have taken place in addition to installation details. If missing, the documentation should be requested from the vendor. It may be tempting to assume that the existing databases and applications will automatically function correctly in any upgrade, particularly if workloads are high and documentation appears lengthy to read. However, the overall security of the data and applications are of paramount importance and must take priority. No new upgrades should be installed without first assessing the likely impact on the existing data and software, even if it means delaying the upgrade until a later date when staff have time to properly assess it.

In reviewing any upgrade documentation a plan of action should be drawn up. This will note all changes that affect the databases and applications and the solutions to be implemented. This may necessitate programmers having to search through the programs for particular constructs, and so on. Some changes may be easy to implement: for example, an upgrade may simply require some application programs to be recompiled for them to operate on the upgraded system. Others will be more time-consuming: for example, where data type conversions have altered. Whatever the change, they will all have to be noted together with an estimate of the time involved to effect the changes in each application. The goal of the DBA is to have a smooth changeover with no problems resulting.

In working environments where the system must be available during working hours, the installation of any upgrade has to take place out of hours, usually over a weekend. In this time, the existing system must be fully backed up in case of disasters, the upgrade installed, and all databases and applications amended as necessary and tested before being run on live data.

Changes introduced in the DBMS upgrade may affect the application programmers for any subsequent programs they may write. Therefore, a list of these changes should either be distributed or put on-line for programmer reference. Some of these will be of particular interest if they fix previously known errors, and may facilitate the removal of workarounds that had to be implemented. It is also likely that the upgrade documentation will include a list of known bugs or errors with perhaps suggested workarounds, and again this information should be distributed or put on-line.

14.4 Countermeasures – Non-Computer-Based Controls

Figure 14.1 shows non-computer-based controls in the general database environment, in conjunction with the computer-based controls, which we have previously discussed. The non-computer-based controls are mainly concerned with matters such as policies, agreements and other administrative controls, which are distinct from those that support the computer-based controls. In this section we consider:

- establishment of a security policy and contingency plan,
- personnel controls,
- secure positioning of equipment,
- secure data and software,
- escrow agreements,
- maintenance agreements,
- physical access controls,
- building controls,
- emergency arrangements.

14.4.1   Establishment of a Security Policy and Contingency Plan

A security policy is quite distinct from a contingency plan. The former defines comprehensively how an organization is to maintain a secure system, while the latter defines how an organization is to continue functioning in any given emergency situation. An organization should have both a security policy document and a contingency plan document.

To be able to maintain a secure system requires a written **security policy** (contained in the security policy document), and establishing this policy should be of prime importance to senior management. A security team under the leadership of a member of senior management should be established, and drafting a security policy should be one of their first tasks. Details contained in a security policy should include:

- the area of the business it covers,
- responsibilities and obligations of employees,
- the disciplinary action that will result from breaches of the policy,
- procedures that must be followed.

This final point will give rise to other specific procedures that explicitly refer to particular parts of an information system, but which are not part of a security policy statement. For example, the policy may state that only authorized personnel shall use the DBMS's application systems, but will not state how this is to be achieved. A separate set of procedures needs to be defined that explicitly states how personnel are authorized. There may also be a standard associated with the authorization procedure, for example, governing the format of passwords if these are used. In this way, the policy document remains generally applicable, although it will be reviewed periodically, while the operational procedures which implement the policy need to change more often as systems change and technology improves. An example of a security policy can be found in Herbert (1990). Note that, although we have discussed there being only one security policy document, there may in fact be several depending on the size of the organization, each one dealing with a different part of the organization.

On the other hand, a **contingency plan** is established to deal with unusual events that are not part of the normal daily routine. Again, there may be one contingency plan for the whole organization or several, each covering different areas. Contingency plans detail the response necessary to deal with the types of event that may occur: for example, a fire in the building. It is essential that any contingency plan also takes into account people as well as equipment and such like. This is because in some situations, key personnel may not be available. A contingency plan should include:

- Who the key personnel are and how they can be contacted.
- If key personnel are unavailable, a list of alternative personnel and how they can be contacted.
- Who decides that a contingency exists and how that is decided.

- The technical requirements of transferring operations elsewhere, for example:
  - the additional equipment that will be needed;
  - whether any communication lines will have to be installed.
- The operational requirements of transferring operations elsewhere, for example:
  - whether staff need to work away from home;
  - whether staff need to work unusual hours;
  - how staff will be compensated.
- Any outside contacts who may help, for example:
  - equipment manufacturers.
- Whether any insurance exists to cover the situation.

Senior staff should be familiar with the contingency plan, of which there should be several copies stored safely in different locations. Any plan should also be periodically reviewed and tested as far as practicable.

14.4.2 Personnel Controls

Commercial DBMSs and information systems rely on people to operate them effectively. Consequently, in considering the security of a system, the attitudes and conduct of the people involved are of significance. This is especially so when we consider that the greatest risks faced by an organization involve internal threats rather than external threats. It follows that adequate controls regarding personnel are required in order to minimize the risks.

Assessing and monitoring employees

Proper procedures should exist for the recruitment of staff, for current employees who are being considered for different posts, and for temporary staff who are being considered for permanent positions. These procedures should include how references are obtained, and whether any more stringent vetting is required if the post is of a sensitive nature. Conversely, where staff employment is being terminated, a set of procedures should define the steps to be followed. Variation will occur depending on whether the termination is a result of resignation or dismissal. For example, a person in a key post may be required to leave immediately, irrespective of whether they have resigned or been dismissed. In other situations, where a resignation is involved, they may be moved to a different area until they leave. In both cases, it is important that all authorizations are subsequently removed, and other personnel notified.

Employees should also be monitored during the course of their work to ensure, for example, that they are following procedures. Any unusual behaviour, such as change in lifestyle, not taking holidays, or taking an unusual interest in someone else's work, should be investigated. Inspection of the database recovery journals may also highlight any unusual activity. It is also advisable not to allow employees to work alone, both from a health and safety aspect as well as security, although this is not always practical.

Staff training

Adequate training should be given to both new and existing staff as part of a staff development policy. Training should not just cover the job functions, but should include, as appropriate, aspects of security, quality, health and safety, and any legal requirements and responsibilities. It should also be made clear what disciplinary action may be taken if procedures are not observed. The objective is to make staff aware of their responsibilities and gain their commitment to carrying out procedures. Often, positive feedback can be gained from staff who may suggest improvements to procedures or identify possible weaknesses in them.

Separation of duties/splitting job functions

To prevent any possibility of collusion, employees should have specific duties to perform in carrying out their jobs and, ideally, these should not overlap. It should also not be possible for one person to have complete responsibility for an entire process; for example, the person receiving invoices and payments should not be responsible for entering the same data into the system. For examples of the kinds of fraud that can be perpetrated by this and other lack of controls, see Hearnden (1990).

In small organizations, it may not be possible to separate duties. Insufficient cover in times of absences may be more of a problem. However, this situation can be alleviated, to some extent, by rotating staff to ensure more than one person could undertake the job if necessary. This can also be carried out in larger organizations, and may prevent staff from becoming bored with their job. Staff boredom may result in errors being made.

Other job controls

It may be difficult to separate duties in some cases, a prime example being that of application developers, or systems programmers. In such cases, these people normally should not have access to live data. If this is necessary on occasion, then they should be carefully monitored. Generally, they should not require any access to the live systems, and there should be adequate testing and approval controls in place before any application or program becomes active. All users should have access only to that data which they require in order to carry out their job: that is, organizations should operate a 'Need to know' policy. We have already described mechanisms by which this can be achieved in Section 14.3.2.

Split responsibilities

The control of important functions should not be the responsibility of one individual. A prime example of this is when cheques are issued. If they are above a certain amount it should not be possible for just one person to authorize them. This idea can be extended, for example, to cover access to sensitive parts of a system, whereby two passwords or tokens, such as keys, are required, each held by different people.

14.4.3 Secure Positioning of Equipment

Essential equipment, including printers if they are used to print sensitive information, should be kept in a locked room with access restricted to key personnel. Other equipment, especially if portable, should be fastened securely to surfaces and/or alarmed. It may not be feasible or desirable to keep other rooms locked requiring employees to carry the means of access to the rooms on them. This reduces the ability to move equipment easily, but this is not necessarily a drawback. If equipment is continually moved about there is a greater risk of damage. The siting of computer terminal screens (VDUs) needs to be considered, especially where users are accessing confidential information. There should be no danger of them being overlooked, either by another person in the same room or through a window, even if the equipment is on the fourth floor. Remember that telephoto lenses can be used to look from one building to another. All cabling should be sited so that it does not pose a hazard to employees nor run the risk of being accidentally damaged.

14.4.4 Secure Data and Software

We have already assumed the existence of a secure storage area when discussing the procedures associated with backup. It is vitally important that there is a secure area in which to store copies, backups, archival material and documentation, which preferably should be in a different location from the computer. It is not unknown for some organizations that meticulously maintain backups to store them in the computer area and have them easily accessible. The risks posed in this situation include susceptibility to accidental damage and destruction, fire and theft, with the resulting loss of security and possible inability to recover the system.

It is recommended that all computer media such as disks and tapes are stored in a fireproof data safe that can resist higher temperatures than an ordinary fireproof safe. All documentation should be stored similarly, and there should be an index of all the contents of the store including date of deposit. The frequency with which material is placed in the store will be specified in the procedures. Organizations may also have an off-site storage area, to which backups and copies will be periodically transported. Again, the frequency will be specified in the procedures. Some companies specialize in off-site storage, and may hold material for many organizations. In smaller organizations the off-site store may be the owner's house, but the material should still be kept securely. Some of the store's contents will comprise archived material, which may need to be retained for a number of years to satisfy legal obligations.

We have mentioned the need to keep an index in the secure storage areas to facilitate retrieval and to check that everything is present. In this case, it is important that all material is correctly labelled and indexed to know what is contained on the media, or what the documentation refers to. The date and time should be recorded on the labels and index, to enable old material to be clearly distinguished. Procedures for dealing with out-of-date material also need to be established. For example, confidential paper may need to be shredded and/or burnt, with a similar process for magnetic media. Sometimes the magnetic media can be reused, in which case the media should be cleaned before reuse.

14.4.5 Escrow Agreements

These are agreements concerning software made between developers and their clients, whereby a third party holds the source code for the client's applications. It is a form of insurance for the client who can acquire the source code if the developer goes out of business, and means they will not be left with non-maintainable systems. This area is considered to be one that is most often overlooked and undermanaged (Revella, 1993). In Revella's opinion, 95% of all software escrow agreements will not work as intended, and this emphasizes the need to carefully negotiate over the following issues:

- the type of contents deposited;
- the update process and the timing of this;
- the details of any third party software used;
- whether verification of the deposit is required;
- the conditions governing the release of the deposit;
- the details of the release process.

If the software concerned is critical for an organization's information systems, then it is very important to be aware of the potential pitfalls in this area.

14.4.6 Maintenance Agreements

There should be adequate current maintenance agreements operating for all external hardware and software used by the organization. The speed of response to any failure or error will depend upon how essential that area is to the normal operation of the system. For example, if a computer hardware failure occurs, an immediate response is required to get the system operational again as fast as possible. However, if a fault develops on a printer, it may be acceptable to have an agreement whereby it is fixed within a day or two, because there are other printers available for use. In some cases, replacement equipment may be provided temporarily until the original can be repaired.

14.4.7 Physical Access Controls

In this section, we will briefly consider how security can be enforced by controlling the physical access to equipment and so on. Broadly, we can divide these controls into internal and external controls.

Internal controls

These controls apply within a building, and can be used to govern who has access to particular areas of the building. To protect sensitive areas, such as the computer room, a door entry system can be installed. These can be operated in different ways: for example, by using card readers, by requiring a code or password to be entered, or by the use of keys. More sophisticated techniques include fingerprint or eyeprint recognition, voice recognition and handwriting recognition, although few commercial companies use these types of control at present because of the high costs currently involved.

Ideally, the system installed should not cause employees any difficulties in operating it. For example, if employees regularly need to carry material with them, they may find it awkward to use keys or punch codes, and operate the door handle. This leads to another potential problem, sometimes referred to as 'tailgating'. If an employee has just opened a security door, there is a temptation to hold it open for a following person, especially if their hands are full making it difficult to operate the door mechanism. This sort of activity should be discouraged with a clear statement in the general procedures regarding the operation of any security door.

Another potential problem area lies in the ease of access to and from loading bays or delivery points. If goods are regularly delivered, it will be common to see strangers in and around these points, which are often within the building itself. Consequently, it should not be possible for any unauthorized person to gain access to the rest of the building from these places.

External controls

These controls apply outside a building and control access to the site or building itself. If the building has its own grounds and car parking areas, it may be necessary to protect these. Car parks can be fenced in with a barrier system installed to prevent unauthorized access, and legitimate employees could have a swipe card that gives them entry. Additional security is obtained if a security guard is employed who would then be able to deal with visitors and check that they are legitimate.

Security guards can also be used to check people entering buildings. Legitimate employees may, for example, use a swipe card or display an authorized badge to gain access. Visitors will have essential details recorded including who they are visiting and be required to display some token that identifies them as a visitor. The token could indicate that they have to be accompanied at all times. Requirements such as these will arise from the security policy and the associated procedures. A fundamental objective of any physical access control mechanism is that it should be cost-effective, yet not impede employees in the course of their work, otherwise there is the danger that controls may be circumvented.

14.4.8 Building Controls

The risk of fire and flood probably poses the commonest threat to buildings. Reasonable precautions can be taken against the threat of fire damage by installing an adequate fire detection system and, where necessary, a system to tackle any fire. This system can be either automatic or manual: for example, water sprinkler systems can be automatic, but may not be ideal for computer rooms. Other types of system, for example carbon dioxide systems, may be harmful to people, and are best triggered manually once the area has been evacuated. The proper use of fire doors will also help to contain any fire that occurs. In both cases, adequate insurance policies should exist that compensate for loss of, or damage to, equipment as a result of fire or flood.

To a lesser extent, other problems that may require resolution include rooms overheating in the summer, especially where equipment is housed, and spikes in the electricity supply, which can adversely affect equipment. Sometimes electrical spikes are caused by the operation of other equipment, for example elevators, but whatever the cause, it may be necessary to install devices for smoothing out the current. Electrical security may be very important, especially if there are critical systems that must be maintained at all times. To keep these functioning, despite power loss, requires special arrangements, which we discuss next.

14.4.9 Emergency Arrangements

These are needed for situations where normal operation is not possible and should be specified in the contingency plan. For example, if a serious fault occurs in the hardware, it may be possible to have the use of another system as a temporary measure. However, it is important that this other system is compatible and as secure as the original system, especially if it is actively being used for other purposes. To guarantee the availability of another system could involve a fee being paid on a regular basis to the other company which has the system.

If a serious contingency arises, such as a major fire that prevents use of the premises, alternative arrangements are essential. One of these could be another empty building or room elsewhere (**a cold site**), which could be set up to run the computing operations. Obviously, equipment and any necessary communications would have to be installed, but any contingency plan should have allowed for this. The contents of the off-site store will also be required. A variation of having a spare empty room or building is to have a spare fully equipped room or building (**a warm site**), so continuing operations should only require access to the off-site storage contents. Another variation is having the fallback system operating concurrently, so if one system fails, operations are automatically switched to the other system (**a hot site**). In this case, users may not even notice anything has occurred. Obviously, the costs of maintaining one of these types of sites means that only large organizations could consider having them, although several organizations with similar computing requirements could collectively maintain one. In the aftermath of a fire, if access is needed to the contents of the on-site safe, it is recommended that a proper safe specialist is called in to open it, otherwise damage to the contents could result if non-specialized people attempt to open it.

The ability to continue functioning may be paramount even if a loss of power occurs, such as when a power cut arises due to industrial action, or as a result of bad weather. There are various devices (uninterruptible power supplies) available, depending upon the length of time required to keep the systems functioning. For example, it may only be necessary to maintain power in order to shut the system down properly. In other cases, the system may be needed for several hours, after which it is assumed normal power would have been restored. In addition to considering the computer systems, the arrangements would need to ensure that adequate heating and lighting would be available.

14.5　PC Security

Unlike large machines, personal computer equipment can pose particular problems for security, because it can be moved about quite easily. Indeed, a personal computer has been described as 'a filing cabinet with a built-in photocopier ... [and] often with no lock on it' (Catterell, 1990). The usual controls that can be employed in the mainframe and mini computing environments are inappropriate in the PC environment. One of the key differences is that PCs occur widely on employees' desks, and do not need to be housed in a separate room and looked after by special operators. Consequently, there can be no special physical access controls other than those that apply to the building or area.

　　Most PCs now have a keyboard lock, which although not very secure does act as a deterrent to casual attempts at using a machine. More protection can now be supplied, either by using software or hardware, whereby a user needs to enter an identifier and/or password to gain access. This provides greater protection unless, as with other terminals and workstations, the user leaves the machine for long periods in an accessible state. Again, procedures should stipulate this does not happen.

　　If no data is stored on the PC, but instead is kept on floppy disk, then the data will be secure provided the disks are locked away. In this respect, the PC user is responsible for maintaining all copies and backups of data and possibly software, and keeping them secure. They should also label and index their disks carefully to avoid, for example, a backup disk being inadvertently used for normal processing work. It is therefore important that all staff working in a PC environment have adequate training to equip them with the necessary knowledge of techniques and procedures that should be adhered to.

Infections

A major problem, particularly with PCs, is the risk of infection with unwelcome and possibly pernicious software such as viruses. Careless and lax use of equipment can easily introduce this type of infection: for example, employees bringing in games to run on their machines. The transfer of disks from one machine to another then facilitates the spread of the infection, although some types can spread across networks.

　　The security policy should clearly state that certain procedures must be followed before any software can be transferred onto a system, even if it is from a vendor. It should also state that only authorized software can be used on the computer systems. The resulting procedures should enforce the policy statement and help prevent such situations occurring. Likewise, proper procedures for validating and testing new or amended software will also guard against this sort of threat.

14.6   Security in Statistical Databases

Typically, a statistical database is a collection of information on individuals, each item of which is confidential. However, access is permitted in order to obtain statistical information about these items, such as averages and sums. The general problem with these databases is whether the answers to legal queries can be used to infer the answer to illegal queries. To resolve this problem, various strategies can be used, such as:

- preventing queries from operating on only a few database entries;
- randomly adding in additional entries to the original query result set, which produces a certain error but approximates to the true response;
- using only a random sample of the database to answer the query;
- maintaining a history of the query results and rejecting queries that use a high number of records identical to those used in previous queries.

In general, smaller statistical databases are potentially more prone to security breaches than larger databases.

14.7   Risk Analysis

We only give a brief overview of this process, as it is a subject in its own right. More detailed information can be obtained from the references and bibliography, in particular Sieber (1986), Fernandez *et al.* (1981) and Elbra (1992). The following list summarizes the main stages in undertaking a risk analysis, which we go on to explain:

(1)   Establish a security team.
(2)   Define the scope of the analysis and obtain system details.
(3)   Identify all existing countermeasures.
(4)   Identify and evaluate all assets.
(5)   Identify and assess all threats and risks.
(6)   Select countermeasures, undertake a cost/benefit analysis and compare with existing countermeasures.
(7)   Make recommendations.
(8)   Test security system.

14.7.1   Establish a Security Team

Any large organization that is concerned about security needs to establish a team responsible for managing security. The size and membership of the team responsible for IT security will be dictated, to some extent, by the size and complexity of the organization, but likely candidates for team membership would be representatives from the IT, personnel, legal, audit and buildings departments. It is unlikely that many organizations will have security specialists, so it is recommended that any security team is also aided by a security consultant. The team should be led by a senior manager with appropriate authority. Objectives of the security team are:

- to produce a security policy coupled with standards and procedures for appropriate staff to follow;
- to undertake risk analysis;
- to select, recommend and ensure implementation of countermeasures;
- to monitor and maintain the security system;
- to obtain a balance between system security and system usability.

Small organizations are unlikely to be able to set up a security team, but this does not preclude them from having a security policy and managing the environment effectively. In these situations, it is advisable to have one or two persons designated responsible for the overall security of the organization. This responsibility, however, may only extend to the system(s) operated in specific rooms if the company is very small and shares a building with other organizations. Building security, consequently, would be outside such a company's control, although the effects of breaches in this security should not be neglected, as a previous example of a basement fire indicates.

14.7.2   Define the Scope of the Analysis and Obtain System Details

Unless it is a small organization, it is advisable to focus on one specific area at a time, such as one particular system, rather than try to cover everything in one go. Specific details of the system or even a proposed system need to be documented so that its functionality is understood.

14.7.3   Identify all Existing Countermeasures

The countermeasures currently in place for the system undergoing risk analysis should be listed. Subsequently, these can be compared with any proposed countermeasures and traded off against them when determining susceptibility to risks of threat.

14.7.4   Identify and Evaluate all Assets

Every asset associated with the system undergoing risk analysis should be identified and valued. Assets cover all hardware, all software such as operating system programs and application programs, all data required and used, personnel involved, the buildings, and other items such as power, documentation and supplies. In determining a value, some estimation is unavoidable. For assets such as hardware, the value will be the replacement cost. However, where data is concerned the evaluation task is not easy, unless the data has been bought in from an external source, in which case it is the replacement cost.

Generally, data can be considered to be affected by various **types** of loss, which range from total destruction through unavailability for given time periods to unauthorized disclosure. A value can be assigned to each data asset for each type of loss depending on factors such as personal privacy, commercial confidentiality and legal aspects amongst others. In all instances, the **highest** value is chosen, which represents the maximum loss. Once each asset has been evaluated separately, it is then necessary to establish dependencies between the assets; for example, data depends upon certain hardware and software. The results are correlated, again with the highest values being chosen to represent the worst case scenario for each type of loss.

14.7.5   Identify and Assess all Threats and Risks

Every potential threat should be listed, from obvious ones that may occur often, to exceptional ones that may rarely occur, but could be potentially disastrous. The threats should be considered in terms of the type of loss that they may cause. For each type of asset, a value is determined for each threat producing each type of loss. This value is the probability of the threat occurring. In a similar manner, a value is also determined for the probability of the threat succeeding (vulnerability). All these figures are then collated and correlated to give an indication of the risk of each threat.

14.7.6   Select Countermeasures, Undertake Cost/Benefit Analysis and Compare with Existing Countermeasures

Once the risks have been evaluated, appropriate countermeasures need to be selected and then analysed in cost/benefit terms. There may well be various choices available, and the aim is to achieve maximum effectiveness for minimum cost provided there is an overall benefit in implementing the countermeasure. Comparisons also must be made with any existing countermeasures, as there may well be a high degree of protection in some parts of the system.

14.7.7   Make Recommendations

After finalizing the selection of countermeasures, the security team should produce a report detailing the recommendations resulting from the investigation. Included in the report should be actual costs of the countermeasures and suppliers as appropriate. Senior management have to approve any proposed countermeasures, but once approval has been given, the security team are responsible for overseeing their implementation.

14.7.8 Test Security System

It is strongly recommended that any security measures put in place should be tested to ensure they are able to withstand the identified threats. The overall purpose in doing this is to try to anticipate the measures that the potential perpetrators may develop in response to the installed countermeasures, and thereby ensure continued protection for the system by a process of adaptation. In some instances, special teams may be set up with the consent of senior management, to try to break the security system without the knowledge of other staff.

Risk analysis therefore should consider system security in its widest context, and not simply focus on one part alone, for example a DBMS. A DBMS, however, does provide various controls that can protect the data assets to some extent, and we have seen that these assets should be evaluated according to the type of loss they may be subject to. For some organizations, though, simply regarding all the data as being equal in importance is inadequate. Although a risk analysis should indicate how particular data should be protected, in terms of forming a security policy with its attendant standards and procedures and subsequent guidelines to staff, more information may be needed. To this end, an **information classification** exercise may be undertaken, so that, for example, some data may be classed as 'strictly confidential' while other data may have a 'no restriction' classification. Generally, an organization can decide on a classification scheme to suit itself, although schemes have been proposed for various purposes. Undoubtedly, having information classified in some way can aid in determining the types of controls to enforce on a DBMS. If information is to be classified, this should be undertaken before assessing the risks to any particular system, and again is the responsibility of the security team.

14.8 Data Protection and Privacy Laws

Data protection and privacy laws are all concerned with personal data and the rights of individuals with respect to their personal data. This type of legislation attempts on the one hand to protect individuals from abuse, and on the other hand to enable organizations (both public and private) to carry out their lawful activities or duties.

Privacy	Concerns the right of an individual not to have personal information collected, stored and disclosed either wilfully or indiscriminately.

There has been concern over inadequate privacy controls for a long time, although this concern has increased particularly since the rapid developments in computer technology, coupled with the rapid rise in the volumes of data now stored on this technology and consequent changes in record-keeping practices. Many such practices involve the exchange or correlation of information between different systems, and are not necessarily covered by any legislation. Some have arisen out of administrative decisions or convenience. For example, in the 1970s, Project Match was undertaken by the US Department of Health, Education and Welfare (now the Health and Human Services Department) to catch people defrauding the welfare system. Subsequent Federal laws have imposed matching on state administrations. Another example occurs in the UK, where information supplied when applying for a vehicle licence is automatically passed to the central police computer, Inland Revenue and Home Office, with access also available to Customs and Excise.

In the years before rapid developments began to take place, data collection and processing were limited because they were mainly manual processes. Such infringements of privacy that did occur and were able to be prosecuted generally served as a deterrent against other infringements. However, since the 1960s the technical developments and amount of data stored have created other threats on a much wider scale: for example, record matching across systems, and the ability to transfer data across borders. Consequently, many countries began to consider how to safeguard personal data both within and without national borders, which subsequently led to international cooperation. To some extent, this cooperation has led to a certain degree of harmonization of legislation. Nevertheless, there are variations in how the legislation was and is being developed and in the legislation itself. It has been the concern over privacy that has led to laws concerning data protection.

Data protection	The protection of personal data from unlawful acquisition, storage and disclosure, and the provision of the necessary safeguards to avoid the destruction or corruption of the legitimate data held.

We have defined data protection quite broadly, without specifying, for example, how the data is stored. While it is true that some data protection legislation covers only personal data stored on a computer system, the pattern of legislation is changing, and in general it is likely that a wider remit may apply in future. It is for this reason that we choose a definition that ignores how the data is stored.

It is worth considering the social implications of the increasing usage of personal data and IT. One of the obvious consequences of organizations using personal data is that both systems developers and end users need to be aware of relevant legislation, and how it affects their work. In particular, systems developers need to ensure that there are adequate provisions to satisfy the legal obligations, such as access to specific personal data, which may be additional to normal system requirements. One other consequence of the potential availability of such data is that it could be used in the surveillance of either individuals or groups, which may or may not be undesirable in purpose. In some of the early discussions about privacy and the type of controls needed, some criticism was made about the irresponsible attitude of some parts of the computer industry. In a relatively recent article, Clarke (1988) points out that there has been little discussion about the benefits and dangers of surveillance in the computing literature. He further states that information privacy laws are inadequate, and although IT professionals may not be held responsible for decisions regarding the application of any technology, they do have a responsibility to appreciate the power of the technology, and the need for effective and efficient safeguards.

Generally, whether in North America or Europe, the state of legislation at a national level gives an individual some basic rights, such as the right to know what data is held and the right to have incorrect data amended. There are, of course, exceptions made: for example, where issues of national security arise, or where disclosure might prejudice legal investigations. However, there are differences in national laws; for instance, some cover both manual data and computer-held data, and further variations arise where states have a federal system, such as Germany and the USA. Nevertheless, with the continuing growth of data exchange between countries and the need to protect data from unscrupulous use, there is likely to be a harmonizing of basic legislation in this area.

Chapter Summary

- **Data integrity** ensures that data is consistent with all the stated constraints that apply to it, and hence is considered to be valid. There are several different types of integrity constraints that apply to data. Some, like **entity integrity**, are influenced by the structure of the data, whereas others, like **user defined integrity**, are influenced by the business.

- Integrity controls are needed to ensure data integrity is maintained, and hence are a form of data security. However, preserving data integrity is not an absolute guarantee that the data are correct.

- **Database security** involves protecting a database against potential threats using both technical and administrative controls. Consequently, the scope of database security is wider than simply the DBMS itself, and it affects hardware, software, people, data and the location of DBMS activities.

- Some security measures are essential to ensure the protection of data from either accidental threats or malicious threats. Some threats are obviously malicious, but others may be either accidental or malicious depending upon the context in which they occur.

- **Computer-based controls** form one set of countermeasures that can safeguard a database system. Such controls include proper **authorization** and **authentication** of users, **views** and **backing-up**, **journaling** and **checkpointing**, which all support system recovery in the event of a failure. **Encryption** is also a useful control, particularly where data is transmitted over communication lines.

- **Computer-based controls** alone do not necessarily enforce or maintain a secure system. They need to be supported by **associated procedures** which inform users of what they must or must not do, together with any standards that also must be observed.

- **Non-computer-based controls** are mainly oriented towards the administrative controls that are required to support and maintain a secure system. These controls include **personnel controls**, siting of **equipment**, essential **agreements, physical access controls** and **emergency arrangements**.

- Evaluating the potential threats that may affect a system is accomplished by undertaking a **risk analysis**. To do this effectively requires the establishment of a security team, whose responsibilities include drafting a security policy, identifying existing countermeasures, evaluating assets, identifying all potential threats, then determining any further countermeasures needed.

- **Privacy** concerns the right of an individual not to have personal information collected, stored and disclosed either wilfully or indiscriminately. **Data protection** is the protection of personal data from unlawful acquisition, storage and disclosure, and the provision of the necessary safeguards to avoid the destruction or corruption of the legitimate data held. Since the 1970s, different countries have instituted various laws that deal with these issues. Some legislation only applies to data held on computer, but other legislation applies to all data irrespective of the storage medium.

- In the future, it is expected that the legislation will evolve as technology develops. There is also likely to be further harmonizing of laws between countries. IT professionals should be aware of the implications of the law on system development and use, and should appreciate the potential uses of the developing technology, and be proactive in advocating effective safeguards in the public interest.

REVIEW QUESTIONS

14.1 Explain what is meant by data integrity and describe three types of integrity constraint giving examples.

14.2 Explain the purpose and scope of database security.

14.3 List six different types of threat that could affect a database system, and for each, describe the controls that you would use to counteract each of them.

14.4 Explain the following:

(a) authorization

(b) backing-up

(c) encryption

(d) contingency plan

(e) personnel controls

(f) excrow agreement

(g) privacy

(h) data protection.

14.5 Outline the stages of risk analysis, and provide a brief explanation of each stage.

EXERCISES

14.6 Identify an important computer-based application in your computing environment and determine:

(a) the type of data the application uses and produces;

(b) the integrity checks that are required;

(c) how the system performs the integrity checks.

14.7 Select a DBMS used within your computing environment, and evaluate how well it supports all the integrity controls described in the chapter.

14.8 Carry out an investigation of your computing environment and:

(a) List all potential threats and breaches of security you can identify.

(b) List all examples you find of countermeasures against potential threats.

(c) Determine whether or not any risk assessment is undertaken and, if not, how security breaches are dealt with.

14.9 Determine the nature and extent of the personal data used by your computing environment and:

(a) Identify who has responsibility for setting guidelines for its collection and usage.

(b) Determine which staff handle personal data, and whether they receive any special training regarding the handling of this type of data. Is the training regularly updated?

(c) Give details of the arrangements for access to personal data.

14.10 Discover what legislation exists that applies to data of a personal nature. Does it apply to *all* data, or just that held on computer?

14.11 Consider the *Wellmeadows Hospital* case study introduced in Section 1.8. List the potential threats that should be considered in this environment, and propose countermeasures to overcome them.

15 Transaction Management

Chapter Objectives

In this chapter you will learn:

- The purpose of concurrency control.
- The purpose of database recovery.
- The function and importance of transactions.
- The properties of a transaction.
- The meaning of serializability and how it applies to concurrency control.
- How locks can be used to ensure serializability.
- How the two-phase locking protocol works.
- The meaning of deadlock and how it can be resolved.
- How timestamps can be used to ensure serializability.
- How optimistic concurrency control techniques work.
- How different levels of locking may affect concurrency.
- Some causes of database failure.
- The purpose of the transaction log file.
- The purpose of checkpoints during transaction logging.
- How to recover following database failure.

In Chapter 2, we discussed the functions that a Database Management System (DBMS) should provide. Among these are three closely related functions that are intended to ensure that the database is reliable and remains in a consistent state. This reliability and consistency must be maintained in the presence of failures of both hardware and software components, and when multiple users are accessing the database. In this chapter, we concentrate on these three functions, namely transaction support, concurrency control services, and recovery services.

Each function can be discussed separately, although they are mutually dependent. Both concurrency and recovery control are required to protect the database from data inconsistencies and data loss. Many DBMSs allow users to undertake simultaneous operations on the database. If these operations are not controlled, the accesses will interfere with one another and the database may become inconsistent. To overcome this, the DBMS implements a **concurrency control** protocol that prevents database accesses from interfering with one another. We discuss concurrency control in Section 15.2.

Database recovery is the process of restoring the database to a correct state following a failure. The failure may be a result of a system crash due to hardware or software errors; it may be a media failure, such as a head crash; it may be an application software error, such as a logical error in the program that is accessing the database; it may also be a result of unintentional or intentional corruption or destruction of data or facilities by operators or users. Whatever the underlying cause of the failure, the DBMS must be able to recover from the failure and restore the database to a consistent state. We discuss recovery control in Section 15.3.

Central to an understanding of both concurrency control and recovery is the notion of a **transaction**, which we consider in Section 15.1. In this chapter, we consider concurrency and recovery control for a centralized DBMS: that is, a DBMS that consists of a single database. In Chapter 16, we consider these services for a distributed DBMS: that is, a DBMS that consists of multiple databases distributed across a network.

15.1 Transaction Support

Transaction	An action or series of actions, carried out by a single user or application program, which accesses or changes the contents of the database.

A transaction is a **logical unit of work** on the database. It may be an entire program, a part of a program or a single command (for example, the SQL command INSERT or UPDATE), and it may involve any number of operations on the database. In the database context, the execution of an application program can be thought of as a series of transactions with non-database processing taking place in between. To illustrate the concepts of a transaction, we examine two of the relations of the *DreamHome* rental database shown in Figure 3.3:

Staff	(<u>Sno</u>, FName, LName, Address, Tel_No, Position, Sex, DOB, Salary, NIN, Bno)
Property_for_Rent	(<u>Pno</u>, Street, Area, City, Pcode, Type, Rooms, Rent, Ono, Sno, Bno)

A simple transaction against this database is to update the salary of a particular member of staff given the staff number, x. At a high level, we could write this transaction as shown in Figure 15.1(a). In this chapter, we denote a database read or write operation on a data item x as read(x) or write(x). Additional qualifiers may be added as necessary; for example, in Figure 15.1(a), we have used the notation read(Sno = x, salary) to indicate that we want to read the data item salary for the record with primary key value x. In this example, we have a **transaction** consisting of two database operations (read and write) and a non-database operation (salary = salary*1.1).

A more complicated transaction is to delete the member of staff with a given staff number x, as shown in Figure 15.1(b). In this case, as well as having to delete the tuple in the Staff relation, we also need to find all the Property_for_Rent tuples that this member of staff managed and reassign them to a different member of staff, *new_sno* say. If all these updates are not made, the database will be in an **inconsistent state**: a property will be managed by a member of staff who no longer exists in the database.

```
                                    delete(Sno = x)
                                    for all Property_for_Rent records, pno
                                    begin
  read(Sno = x, salary)                   read(Pno = pno, sno)
  salary = salary * 1.1                   if (sno = x) then
  write(Sno = x, new_salary)              begin
                                                sno = new_sno
                                                write(Pno = pno, sno)
                                          end
                                    end

            (a)                                   (b)
```

Figure 15.1
Example transactions.

A transaction should always transform the database from one consistent state to another, although we accept that consistency may be violated while the transaction is in progress. For example, during the transaction in Figure 15.1(b), there may be some moment when one occurrence of the Property_for_Rent contains the new *new_sno* value and another still contains the old one, x. However, at the end of the transaction, all occurrences should agree. A transaction can have one of two outcomes. If it completes successfully, the transaction is said to have **committed** and the database reaches a new consistent state. On the other hand, if the transaction does not execute successfully, the transaction is **aborted**. If a transaction is aborted, the database must be restored to the consistent state it was in before the transaction started. Such a transaction is **rolled back** or **undone**. A committed transaction cannot be aborted. If we decide that the committed transaction was a mistake, we must perform another transaction to reverse its effects. However, an aborted transaction that is rolled back can be restarted later and, depending on the cause of the failure, may successfully execute and commit at that time.

The DBMS has no inherent way of knowing which updates are grouped together to form a single logical transaction. It must therefore provide a method to allow the user to indicate the boundaries of a transaction. The keywords BEGIN TRANSACTION, COMMIT and ROLLBACK (or their equivalent[†]) are available in most data manipulation languages to delimit transactions. If these delimiters are not used, the entire program is usually regarded as a single transaction, with the DBMS automatically performing a COMMIT when the program terminates correctly and a ROLLBACK if it does not.

15.1.1 Properties of Transactions

There are properties that all transactions should possess. The four basic, or so-called **ACID**, properties of a transaction are (Haerder and Reuter, 1983):

- **Atomicity** The 'all or nothing' property. A transaction is an indivisible unit that is either performed in its entirety or it is not performed at all.

- **Consistency** A transaction must transform the database from one consistent state to another consistent state.

- **Independence** Transactions execute independently of one another. In other words, the partial effects of incomplete transactions should not be visible to other transactions.

- **Durability** The effects of a successfully completed (committed) transaction are permanently recorded in the database and must not be lost because of subsequent failure.

15.1.2 Database Architecture

In Chapter 2, we presented an architecture for a DBMS. Figure 15.2 represents an extract from Figure 2.8 identifying four high-level database modules that handle transactions, concurrency and recovery control. The **transaction manager** coordinates transactions on behalf of application programs. It communicates with the **scheduler**, the module responsible for implementing a particular strategy for concurrency control. The objective of the scheduler is to maximize concurrency without allowing concurrently executing transactions to interfere with one another, and so to compromise the integrity or consistency of the database.

If a failure occurs during the transaction, then the database could be inconsistent. It is the task of the **recovery manager** to ensure that the database is restored to the state it was in before the start of the transaction, and

---

[†] With the SQL2 standard, BEGIN TRANSACTION is implied by the first *transaction-initiating* SQL statement (see Section 12.3.3).

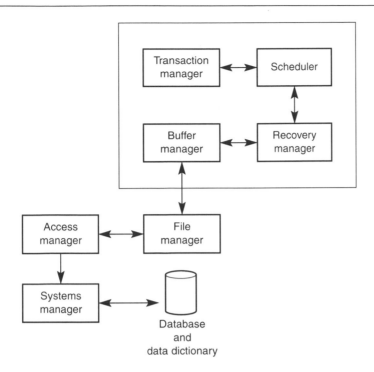

Figure 15.2
DBMS transaction
subsystem.

therefore a consistent state. Finally, the **buffer manager** is responsible for the transfer of data between disk storage and main memory.

15.2 Concurrency Control

In this section, we look at the problems of concurrency control and the techniques that can be used to avoid these problems. We start with the following working definition of concurrency control:

Concurrency control	The process of managing simultaneous operations on the database without having them interfere with one another.

15.2.1 The Need for Concurrency Control

A major objective in developing a database is to enable many users to access shared data concurrently. Concurrent access is relatively easy if all users are only reading data, as there is no way that they can interfere with one another. However, when two or more users are accessing the database simultaneously and at least one is updating data, there may be interference that can result in inconsistencies.

This objective is similar in many respects to the objective of multiuser computer systems. Here, many users can carry out operations simultaneously due to the concept of **multiprogramming**, which allows two or more programs (or transactions) to execute at the same time. For example, many systems have input/output (I/O) subsystems that can handle I/O operations independently, while the main central processing unit (CPU) performs other operations. Such systems can allow two or more transactions to execute simultaneously. The system begins executing the first transaction until it reaches an I/O operation. While the I/O is being performed, the CPU suspends the first transaction and executes commands from the second transaction. When the second transaction reaches an I/O operation, control then returns to the first transaction and its operations are resumed from the point at which it was suspended. The first transaction continues until it again reaches another I/O operation. In this way, the operations of the two transactions are **interleaved** to achieve concurrent execution. In addition, throughput – the amount of work that is accomplished in a given time interval – is improved as the CPU is executing other transactions instead of being in an idle state waiting for I/O operations to complete.

However, although two transactions may be perfectly correct in themselves, the interleaving of operations in this way may produce an incorrect result, thus compromising the integrity and consistency of the database. We examine three examples of potential problems caused by concurrency: the **lost update problem**, the **uncommitted dependency problem** and the **inconsistent analysis problem**. To illustrate these problems, we use a simple bank account relation, which contains the *Dreamhome* staff account balances. Note that we are using the transaction as the unit of concurrency control.

Example 15.1: The lost update problem

An apparently successfully completed update operation by one user can be overridden by another user. This is known as the **lost update problem**, and is illustrated in Figure 15.3, in which transaction T_1 is executing concurrently with transaction T_2. T_1 is withdrawing £10 from an account with balance bal_x, initially £100, and T_2 is depositing £100 into the same account. If these transactions are executed **serially**, one after the other with no interleaving of operations, the final balance would be £190 no matter which transaction is performed first.

Time	T_1	T_2	bal_x
t_1		begin_transaction	100
t_2	begin_transaction	read(bal_x)	100
t_3	read(bal_x)	$bal_x = bal_x + 100$	100
t_4	$bal_x = bal_x - 10$	write(bal_x)	200
t_5	write(bal_x)	commit	90
t_6	commit		90

Figure 15.3 The lost update problem.

Transactions T_1 and T_2 start at nearly the same time, and both read the balance as £100. T_2 increases bal_x by £100 to £200 and stores the update in the database. Meanwhile, transaction T_1 decrements its copy of bal_x by £10 to £90 and stores this value in the database, overwriting the previous update, and thereby 'losing' the £100 previously added to the balance.

The loss of T_2's update is avoided by preventing T_1 from reading the value of bal_x until after T_2's update has been completed.

Example 15.2:   The uncommitted dependency problem _____

The uncommitted dependency problem occurs when one transaction is allowed to see the intermediate results of another transaction before it has committed. Figure 15.4 shows an example of an uncommitted dependency that causes an error, using the same initial value as in the previous example. Here, transaction T_4 updates bal_x to £200, but it aborts the transaction so that bal_x should be back at the original value of £100. However, by this time, transaction T_3 has read the new value of bal_x (£200), and is using this value as the basis of the £10 reduction, giving a new incorrect balance of £190, instead of £90.

Time	T_3	T_4	bal_x
t_1		begin_transaction	100
t_2		read(bal_x)	100
t_3		$bal_x = bal_x + 100$	100
t_4	begin_transaction	write(bal_x)	200
t_5	read(bal_x)		200
t_6	$bal_x = bal_x - 10$	**rollback**	100
t_7	write(bal_x)		190
t_8	commit		190

Figure 15.4
The uncommitted
dependency problem.

The reason for the rollback is unimportant; it may be that the transaction was in error, perhaps crediting the wrong account. The effect is the assumption by T_3 that T_4's update completed successfully, although the update was subsequently rolled back. The problem is avoided by preventing T_3 from reading bal_x until after the decision has been made to either commit or abort T_4's effects.

Example 15.3:   The inconsistent analysis problem _____

The above two problems concentrate on transactions that are updating the database and their interference may corrupt the database. However, transactions that only read the database can also produce inaccurate results, if they are allowed to read partial results of incomplete transactions that are simultaneously updating the database. This is sometimes referred to as a **dirty read** or **unrepeatable read**.

The problem of inconsistent analysis occurs when a transaction reads several values but a second transaction updates some of them during the execution of the first. For example, a transaction that is summarizing data in a database (for example, totalling balances) will obtain inaccurate results if, while it is executing, other transactions are updating the database. One example is illustrated in Figure 15.5, in which a summary transaction, T_6, is executing concurrently with transaction T_5. Transaction T_6 is totalling the balances of account x (£100), account y (£50) and account z (£25). However, in the meantime, transaction T_5 has transferred £10 from bal_x to bal_z, so that T_6 now has the wrong result (£10 too high).

Time	T_5	T_6	bal_x	bal_y	bal_z	sum
t_1		begin_transaction	100	50	25	
t_2	begin_transaction	sum = 0	100	50	25	0
t_3	read(bal_x)	read(bal_x)	100	50	25	0
t_4	$bal_x = bal_x - 10$	sum = sum + bal_x	100	50	25	100
t_5	write(bal_x)	read(bal_y)	90	50	25	100
t_6	read(bal_z)	sum = sum + bal_y	90	50	25	150
t_7	$bal_z = bal_z + 10$		90	50	25	150
t_8	write(bal_z)		90	50	35	150
t_9	commit	read(bal_z)	90	50	35	150
t_{10}		sum = sum + bal_z	90	50	35	185
t_{11}		commit	90	50	35	185

Figure 15.5 The inconsistent analysis problem.

This problem may be avoided by preventing transaction T_6 from reading bal_x and bal_z until after T_5 has completed its updates.

15.2.2 Serializability

The main problems associated with allowing transactions to execute concurrently have been shown above. The objective of a concurrency control protocol is to schedule transactions in such a way as to avoid any interference. One obvious solution would be to allow only one transaction to execute at a time: one transaction is *committed* before the next transaction is allowed to *begin*. However, the aim of a multiuser DBMS is also to maximize the degree of concurrency or parallelism in the system, so that transactions that can execute without interfering with one another can run in parallel. For example, transactions that access different parts of the database can be scheduled together without interference. In this section, we look briefly at serializability as a means of helping to identify those executions of transactions that are *guaranteed* to ensure consistency (Papadimitriou, 1979). First, we give some definitions.

Schedule	A transaction consists of a sequence of reads and writes to the database. The sequence of reads and writes by a set of concurrent transactions taken together is known as a schedule.

Serial schedule	A schedule where the operations of each transaction are executed consecutively without any interleaved operations from other transactions.

In a serial schedule, the entire set of transactions are performed in serial order: T_1 then T_2 or T_2 then T_1. Thus, in serial execution, there is no interference between transactions, since only one is executing at any given time. However, there is no guarantee that the results of all serial executions of a given set of transactions will be identical. In banking, for example, it matters whether interest is calculated on an account before a large deposit is made or after.

Nonserial schedule	A schedule where the operations from a set of concurrent transactions are interleaved.

The three problems described above resulted from the mismanagement of concurrency, leaving the database in an inconsistent state in the first two examples, and the user with the wrong result in the inconsistent analysis example. Serial execution prevents such problems occurring. No matter which serial schedule is chosen, serial execution never leaves the database in an inconsistent state, so every serial execution is considered correct, although different results may be produced. The objective of serializability is to find nonserial schedules that allow transactions to execute concurrently without interfering with one another, and thereby produce a database state that could be produced by a serial execution.

If a set of transactions executes concurrently, we say that the (nonserial) schedule is correct if it *produces the same results as some serial execution*. Such a schedule is called **serializable**. To prevent inconsistency from transactions interfering with one another, it is essential to guarantee serializability of concurrent transactions. In serializability, the ordering of read and write operations is important:

- If two transactions only read a data item, they do not conflict and order is not important.
- If two transactions either read or write completely separate data items, they do not conflict and order is not important.
- If one transaction writes a data item and another either reads or writes the same data item, the order of execution is important.

A serializable schedule orders any conflicting operations in the same way as some serial execution. In general, testing whether a schedule is serializable is NP-complete: that is, it is highly improbable that an efficient algorithm can be found (Ullman, 1988). However, under the **constrained write rule** (that is, a transaction updates a data item based on its old value, which is first read by the transaction), a **precedence graph** can be produced to test for serializability. A precedence graph consists of a node for each transaction and a directed edge $T_i \rightarrow T_j$, if T_j reads the value of an item written by T_i, or T_j writes a value into an item after it has been read by T_i. If the precedence graph contains a cycle the schedule is not serializable.

Example 15.4: Non-serializable schedule

Consider the two transactions shown in Figure 15.6. Transaction T_7 is transferring £100 from one account with balance bal_x to another account with balance bal_y, while T_8 is increasing the balance of these two accounts by 10%. The precedence graph for this schedule, shown in Figure 15.7, has a cycle and so is not serializable.

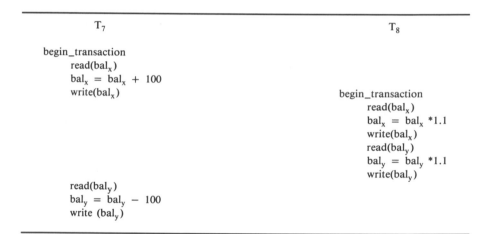

T_7	T_8
begin_transaction	
read(bal_x)	
$bal_x = bal_x + 100$	
write(bal_x)	
	begin_transaction
	read(bal_x)
	$bal_x = bal_x *1.1$
	write(bal_x)
	read(bal_y)
	$bal_y = bal_y *1.1$
	write(bal_y)
read(bal_y)	
$bal_y = bal_y - 100$	
write (bal_y)	

Figure 15.6 Two concurrent update transactions.

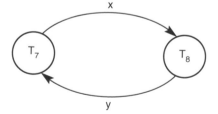

Figure 15.7 Precedence graph for Figure 15.6.

In practice, a DBMS does not test for the serializability of a schedule. This would be impractical, as the interleaving of operations from concurrent transactions is determined by the operating system. Instead, the approach taken is to use protocols that are known to produce serializable schedules. Two such protocols are discussed in the next section.

15.2.3 Concurrency Control Techniques

Serializability can be achieved in several ways. There are two basic concurrency control techniques that allow transactions to execute safely in parallel subject to certain constraints: locking and timestamp methods.

Locking and timestamping are essentially **conservative** (or **pessimistic**) approaches in that they cause transactions to be delayed in case they conflict with other transactions at some time in the future. **Optimistic** methods (as we shall see later) are based on the premise that conflict is rare and allow transactions to proceed unsynchronized and only check for conflicts at the end, when a transaction commits.

Locking

Locking	A procedure used to control concurrent access to data. When one transaction is accessing the database, a lock may deny access to other transactions to prevent incorrect updates.

Locking methods are the most widely used approach to ensure serializability of concurrent transactions. There are several variations, but all share the same fundamental characteristic, namely that a transaction must claim a **read** (*shared*) or **write** (*exclusive*) lock on a data item before the corresponding database read or write operation. The **lock** prevents another transaction from modifying the item or even reading it, in the case of a write lock. Data items of various sizes, ranging from the entire database down to a field, may be locked. The size of the item determines the fineness or **granularity** of the lock. The actual lock might be implemented by setting a bit in the data item to indicate that portion of the database is locked, or by keeping a list of locked parts of the database, or by other means. We examine lock granularity further in Section 15.2.7. In the meantime, we continue to use the term 'data item' to refer to the lock granularity. The basic rules for locking are as follows:

Read lock	If a transaction has a read lock on a data item, it can read the item but not update it.

Write lock	If a transaction has a write lock on a data item, it can both read and update the item.

Since read operations cannot conflict, it is permissible for more than one transaction to hold read locks simultaneously on the same item. On the other hand, a write lock gives a transaction exclusive access to that item. Thus, as long as a transaction holds the write lock on the item, no other transactions can read or update that data item. Locks are used in the following way:

- Any transaction that needs to access a data item must first lock the item, requesting a read lock for read only access or a write lock for both read and write access.

- If the item is not already locked by another transaction, the lock will be granted.
- If the item is currently locked, the DBMS determines whether the request is compatible with the existing lock. If a read lock is requested on an item that already has a read lock on it, the request will be granted; otherwise, the transaction must **wait** until the existing write lock is released.
- A transaction continues to hold a lock until it explicitly releases it either during execution or when it terminates (aborts or commits). It is only when the write lock has been released that the effects of the write operation will be made visible to other transactions.

In addition to these rules, some systems permit a transaction to issue a read lock on an item and then later to **upgrade** the lock to a write lock. This effectively allows a transaction to examine the data first and *then* decide whether it wishes to update it. If upgrading is not supported, a transaction must hold write locks on *all* data items that it may update at some time during the execution of the transaction, thereby potentially reducing the level of concurrency in the system. For the same reason, some systems also permit a transaction to issue a write lock and then later to **downgrade** the lock to a read lock.

Using locks in transactions, as described above, does not guarantee serializability of schedules by themselves, as the following example shows.

Example 15.5: Incorrect locking schedule

Consider again the two transactions shown in Figure 15.6. A valid schedule that may be employed using the above locking rules is:

$$S = \{ \text{write\_lock}(T_7, bal_x), \text{read}(T_7, bal_x), \text{write}(T_7, bal_x), \text{unlock}(T_7, bal_x),$$
$$\text{write\_lock}(T_8, bal_x), \text{read}(T_8, bal_x), \text{write}(T_8, bal_x), \text{unlock}(T_8, bal_x),$$
$$\text{write\_lock}(T_8, bal_y), \text{read}(T_8, bal_y), \text{write}(T_8, bal_y), \text{unlock}(T_8, bal_y),$$
$$\text{commit}(T_8), \text{write\_lock}(T_7, bal_y), \text{read}(T_7, bal_y), \text{write}(T_7, bal_y),$$
$$\text{unlock}(T_7, bal_y), \text{commit}(T_7) \}$$

If prior to execution, $bal_x = 100$, $bal_y = 400$, the result should be $bal_x = 220$, $bal_y = 330$, if T_1 executes before T_2, or $bal_x = 210$ and $bal_y = 340$, if T_2 executes before T_1. However, the result of executing schedule S would give $bal_x = 220$ and $bal_y = 340$. (S is not a serializable schedule.)

The problem in this example is that the schedule releases the locks that are held by a transaction as soon as the associated read/write is executed and that lock unit (say bal_x) no longer needs to be accessed. However, the transaction itself is locking other items (bal_y), after it releases its lock on bal_x. Although this may seem to allow greater concurrency, it permits transactions to interfere with one another, resulting in the loss of total independence and atomicity.

To guarantee serializability, we must follow an additional protocol concerning the positioning of the lock and unlock operations in every transaction. The best known protocol is **two-phase locking (2PL)**.

Two-phase locking (2PL)

> **2PL**   A transaction follows the two-phase locking protocol if all locking operations precede the first unlock operation in the transaction.

According to the rules of this protocol, every transaction can be divided into two phases: first a **growing phase**, in which it acquires all the locks needed but cannot release any locks, and then a **shrinking phase**, in which it releases its locks but cannot acquire any new locks. There is no requirement that all locks be obtained simultaneously. Normally, the transaction acquires some locks, does some processing and goes on to acquire additional locks as needed. However, it never releases any lock until it has reached a stage where no new locks are needed. The rules are:

- A transaction must acquire a lock on an item before operating on the item. The lock may be read or write, depending on the type of access needed.
- Once the transaction releases a single lock, it can never acquire any new locks.

If upgrading of locks is allowed, upgrading can take place only during the growing phase and may require that the transaction wait until another transaction releases a read lock on the item. Downgrading can take place only during the shrinking phase. Let us now look at how two-phase locking is used to resolve the three problems identified in Section 15.2.1.

Example 15.6:   Preventing the lost update problem using 2PL _____

A solution to the lost update problem is shown in Figure 15.8. To prevent the lost update problem occurring, T_2 first requests a write lock on bal_x. It can then proceed to read the value of bal_x from the database, increment it by £100 and write the new value back to the database. When T_1 starts, it also requests a write lock on bal_x. However, because the data item bal_x is currently write locked by T_2, the request is not immediately granted and T_1 has to **wait** until the lock is released by T_2.

Time	T_1	T_2	bal_x
t_1		begin_transaction	100
t_2	begin_transaction	write_lock(bal_x)	100
t_3	write_lock(bal_x)	read(bal_x)	100
t_4	**WAIT**	$bal_x = bal_x + 100$	100
t_5	**WAIT**	write(bal_x)	200
t_6	**WAIT**	unlock(bal_x)	200
t_7	read(bal_x)	commit	200
t_8	$bal_x = bal_x - 10$		200
t_9	write(bal_x)		190
t_{10}	unlock(bal_x)		190
t_{11}	commit		190

Figure 15.8
Preventing the lost
update problem.

Example 15.7: Preventing the uncommitted dependency problem using 2PL

A solution to the uncommitted dependency problem is shown in Figure 15.9. To prevent this problem occurring, T_4 first requests a write lock on bal_x. It can then proceed to read the value of bal_x from the database, increment it by £100, and write the new value back to the database. When the rollback is executed, the updates of transaction T_4 are undone and the value of bal_x in the database is returned to its original value of £100. When T_3 starts, it also requests a write lock on bal_x. However, because the data item bal_x is currently write locked by T_4, the request is not immediately granted and T_3 has to wait until the lock is released by T_4. This only occurs once the rollback of T_4 has been completed.

Time	T_3	T_4	bal_x
t_1		begin_transaction	100
t_2		write_lock(bal_x)	100
t_3		read(bal_x)	100
t_4	begin_transaction	$bal_x = bal_x + 100$	100
t_5	write_lock(bal_x)	write(bal_x)	200
t_6	**WAIT**	unlock(bal_x)	100
t_7	**WAIT**	**rollback**	100
t_8	read (bal_x)		100
t_9	$bal_x = bal_x - 10$		100
t_{10}	write(bal_x)		90
t_{11}	unlock(bal_x)		90
t_{12}	commit		90

Figure 15.9
Preventing the
uncommitted
dependency problem.

**Example 15.8:   Preventing the inconsistent analysis problem
                               using 2PL** _____

A solution to the inconsistent analysis problem is shown in Figure 15.10. To
prevent this problem occurring, T_5 must precede its reads by write locks and
T_6 must precede its reads with read locks. Therefore, when T_5 starts it
requests a write lock on bal_x. Now, when T_6 tries to read lock bal_x the request
is not immediately granted and T_6 has to wait until the lock is released, which
is when T_5 commits.

It can be proved that, if *every* transaction in a schedule follows the two-
phase locking protocol, then the schedule is guaranteed to be serializable
(Eswaran *et al.*, 1976). However, while the two-phase protocol guarantees
serializability, problems can occur with the interpretation of when locks can
be released, as the next example shows.

Time	T_5	T_6	bal_x	bal_y	bal_z	sum
t_1		begin_transaction	100	50	25	
t_2	begin_transaction	sum = 0	100	50	25	0
t_3	write_lock(bal_x)		100	50	25	0
t_4	read(bal_x)	read_lock(bal_x)	100	50	25	0
t_5	$bal_x = bal_x - 10$	WAIT	100	50	25	0
t_6	write(bal_x)	WAIT	90	50	25	0
t_7	write_lock(bal_z)	WAIT	90	50	25	0
t_8	read(bal_z)	WAIT	90	50	25	0
t_9	$bal_z = bal_z + 10$	WAIT	90	50	25	0
t_{10}	write(bal_z)	WAIT	90	50	35	0
t_{11}	unlock(bal_x, bal_z)	WAIT	90	50	35	0
t_{12}	commit	WAIT	90	50	35	0
t_{13}		read(bal_x)	90	50	35	0
t_{14}		sum = sum + bal_x	90	50	35	90
t_{15}		read_lock(bal_y)	90	50	35	90
t_{16}		read(bal_y)	90	50	35	90
t_{17}		sum = sum + bal_y	90	50	35	140
t_{18}		read_lock(bal_z)	90	50	35	140
t_{19}		read(bal_z)	90	50	35	140
t_{20}		sum = sum + bal_z	90	50	35	175
t_{21}		unlock(bal_x, bal_y, bal_z)	90	50	35	175
t_{22}		commit	90	50	35	175

Figure 15.10
Preventing the
inconsistent analysis
problem.

Example 15.9: Cascading rollback

Consider the three transactions shown in Figure 15.11, which conform to the two-phase locking protocol. Transaction T_7 write locks bal_x then updates it using bal_y, which has been obtained with a read lock, and writes the value of bal_x back to the database before releasing the lock on bal_x. Transaction T_8 then write locks bal_x, reads the value of bal_x from the database, updates it and writes the new value back to the database before releasing the lock. Finally, T_9 read locks bal_x and reads it from the database. At this point, T_7 fails and has to be rolled back. However, since T_8 is dependent on T_7 (it has read an item that has been updated by T_7), T_8 must also be rolled back. Similarly, T_9 is dependent on T_8, so it too must be rolled back. This situation, in which a single transaction leads to a series of rollbacks, is called **cascading rollback**.

Cascading rollbacks are undesirable, since they potentially lead to the undoing of a significant amount of work. Clearly, it would be useful if we could design protocols that prevent cascading rollbacks. One way to achieve this with two-phase locking is to leave the release of *all* locks until the end of the transaction. In this way, the problem illustrated here would not occur, as T_8 would not obtain its write lock until after T_7 had completed the rollback.

Time	T_7	T_8	T_9
t_1	begin_transaction		
t_2	write_lock(bal_x)		
t_3	read(bal_x)		
t_4	read_lock(bal_y)		
t_5	$bal_x = bal_y + bal_x$		
t_6	write(bal_x)		
t_7	unlock(bal_x)	begin_transaction	
t_8	⋮	write_lock(bal_x)	
t_9	⋮	read(bal_x)	
t_{10}	⋮	$bal_x = bal_x + 100$	
t_{11}	⋮	write(bal_x)	
t_{12}	⋮	unlock(bal_x)	
t_{13}	⋮	⋮	
t_{14}	**rollback**	⋮	
t_{15}		**rollback**	begin_transaction
t_{16}			read_lock(bal_x)
t_{17}			⋮
t_{18}			**rollback**

Figure 15.11
Cascading rollback
with 2PL.

Another problem with two-phase locking, which applies to all locking-based schemes, is that it can cause deadlock, since transactions can wait for locks on data items. If two transactions wait for locks on items held by the other, deadlock will occur and the deadlock detection and recovery scheme described next is needed. It is also possible for transactions to be in **livelock**, that is, left in a wait state indefinitely, unable to acquire any new locks, although the DBMS is not in deadlock. This can happen if the waiting algorithm for transactions is unfair and does not take account of the time transactions have been waiting. To avoid livelock, a priority system can be used, whereby the longer a transaction has to wait, the higher its priority. Alternatively, a *first-come-first-served* queue can be used for waiting transactions.

15.2.4 Deadlock

Deadlock	An impasse that may result when two (or more) transactions are each waiting for locks held by the other to be released.

Figure 15.12 shows two transactions, T_{10} and T_{11}, that are deadlocked because each is waiting for the other to release a lock on an item it holds. At time t_2, transaction T_{10} requests and obtains a write lock on item bal_x, and at time t_3 transaction T_{11} obtains a write lock on item bal_y. Then at t_6, T_{10} requests a write lock on item bal_y. Since T_{11} holds a lock on bal_y, transaction T_{10} waits. Meanwhile, at time t_7, T_{11} requests a lock on item bal_x, which is held by transaction T_{10}. Neither transaction can continue because each is waiting for a lock it cannot obtain until the other completes. Once deadlock occurs, the applications involved cannot resolve the problem. Instead, the DBMS has to recognize that deadlock exists and break the deadlock in some way.

Unfortunately, there is only one way to break deadlock: abort one or more of the transactions. This involves undoing all the changes made by the transaction(s). In Figure 15.12, we may decide to abort transaction T_{11}. Once

Time	T_{10}	T_{11}
t_1	begin_transaction	
t_2	write_lock(bal_x)	begin_transaction
t_3	read(bal_x)	write_lock(bal_y)
t_4	$bal_x = bal_x - 10$	read(bal_y)
t_5	write(bal_x)	$bal_y = bal_y + 100$
t_6	write_lock(bal_y)	write(bal_y)
t_7	**WAIT**	write_lock(bal_x)
t_8	**WAIT**	**WAIT**
t_9	**WAIT**	**WAIT**
t_{10}	⋮	**WAIT**
t_{11}	⋮	⋮

Figure 15.12
Deadlock between two transactions.

this is complete, the locks held by transaction T_{11} are released and T_{10} is able to continue again. Deadlock should be transparent to the user, so the DBMS should automatically restart the aborted transaction(s).

There are two general techniques for handling deadlock: deadlock prevention and deadlock detection and recovery. Using **deadlock prevention**, the DBMS looks ahead to see if a transaction would cause a deadlock and never allows deadlock to occur. Using **deadlock detection and recovery**, the DBMS allows deadlock to occur but recognizes occurrences of deadlock and breaks it. Since it is easier to test for deadlock and break it when it occurs than to prevent it, many systems use the detection and recovery method.

One possible approach to deadlock prevention is to order transactions using transaction timestamps, which we discuss next. Two algorithms were proposed by Rosenkrantz *et al.* (1978). One algorithm, *Wait-Die*, allows only an older transaction to wait for a younger one, otherwise the transaction is aborted (*dies*) and restarted with the same timestamp, so that eventually it will become the oldest active transaction and will not die. The second algorithm, *Wound-Wait*, uses a symmetrical approach: only a younger transaction can wait for an older one. If an older transaction requests a lock held by a younger one, the younger one is aborted (*wounded*).

Deadlock detection is usually handled by the construction of a **wait-for graph (WFG)**, showing the transaction dependencies: that is, transaction T_i is dependent on T_j, if transaction T_j holds the lock on a data item that T_i is waiting for. The wait-for-graph is constructed as follows:

- Create a node for each transaction.
- Create a directed edge $T_i \rightarrow T_j$, if transaction T_i is waiting to lock an item that is currently locked by T_j.

Deadlock exists if and only if the wait-for-graph contains a cycle (Holt, 1972). Figure 15.13 shows the wait-for-graph for the transactions in Figure 15.12. Clearly, the graph has a cycle in it ($T_{10} \rightarrow T_{11} \rightarrow T_{10}$), so we can conclude that the system is in deadlock.

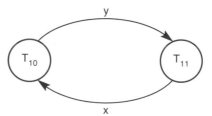

Figure 15.13
WFG showing deadlock between two transactions.

Since a cycle in the wait-for graph is a necessary and sufficient condition for deadlock to exist, the deadlock detection algorithm generates the wait-for graph at regular intervals and examines it for a cycle. The choice of time interval between execution of the algorithm is important. If the interval chosen is too small, deadlock detection will add considerable overhead; if the interval is too large, deadlock may not be detected for a long period. A dynamic deadlock detection algorithm could start with an initial interval size. Each time no deadlock is detected, the detection interval could be increased, for example, to twice the previous interval, and every time deadlock is detected, the interval could be reduced, for example, to half the previous interval, subject to some upper and lower limits.

15.2.5 Timestamping

The use of locks, combined with the two-phase locking protocol, allows us to guarantee serializability of schedules. The order of transactions in the equivalent serial schedule is based on the order in which executing transactions lock the items they require. If a transaction needs an item that is already locked, it may be forced to wait until the item is released. A different approach that also guarantees serializability is that of using transaction timestamps to order transaction execution for an equivalent serial schedule.

Timestamp methods of concurrency control are quite different from locking methods. No locks are involved, and therefore there can be no deadlock. Locking methods generally involve transactions that make conflicting requests wait. With timestamp methods, there is no waiting; transactions involved in conflict are simply rolled back and restarted.

Timestamp	A unique identifier created by the DBMS that indicates the relative starting time of a transaction.

Timestamps can be generated by simply using the system clock at the time the transaction started, or by incrementing a logical counter every time a new transaction starts.

Timestamping	A concurrency control protocol in which the fundamental goal is to order transactions globally in such a way that older transactions, transactions with *smaller* timestamps, get priority in the event of conflict.

With timestamping, if a transaction attempts to read or write a data item, then the read or write is only allowed to proceed if the *last update on that data item* was carried out by an older transaction; otherwise, the transaction requesting the read/write is restarted and given a new timestamp. New timestamps must be assigned to restarted transactions to prevent them from being continually aborted and restarted. Without new timestamps, a transaction with an old timestamp might not be able to commit due to younger transactions having already committed.

Besides timestamps for transactions, there are timestamps for data items. Each data item contains a **read-timestamp**, giving the timestamp of the last transaction to read the item and a **write-timestamp**, giving the timestamp of the last transaction to write (update) the item. Three problems can arise with timestamping. Let us consider a transaction T with timestamp $ts(T)$:

- The transaction asks to read an item (x) that has already been updated by a younger (later) transaction; that is, $ts(T) <$ write_timestamp(x).

   This means that an earlier transaction is trying to read a value of an item that has been updated by a later transaction. The earlier transaction is too late to read the previous outdated value, and any other values it has acquired are likely to be inconsistent with the updated value of the data item. In this situation, the transaction must be aborted and restarted with a new timestamp.

- The transaction asks to write an item (x) whose value has already been read by a younger transaction; that is, $ts(T) <$ read_timestamp(x).

   This means that a later transaction is already using the current value of the item and it would be an error to update it now. In this situation, the transaction must be aborted and restarted with a new timestamp. This problem occurs when a transaction is late in doing a write and a younger transaction has already read the old value or written a new one. In this case, the only solution is to roll back the current transaction and restart it using a later timestamp.

- The transaction asks to write an item (x) whose value has already been written by a younger transaction; that is, $ts(T) <$ write_timestamp(x).

   This means that a later transaction has already updated the value of the item, and the value that the older transaction is writing must be based on an obsolete value of the item. In this case, the write operation can safely be ignored. This is sometimes known as the **ignore obsolete write rule**, and allows for greater concurrency.

In all other cases, the operation is accepted and executed. This scheme guarantees that transactions are serializable, and the results are equivalent to a serial schedule in which the transactions are executed in chronological order by the timestamps. That is, the results will be as if all of transaction one were executed, then all of transaction two, and so on, with no interleaving. The next example shows how these rules can be used to generate a schedule using timestamping.

Example 15.10: Timestamping

Three transactions are executing concurrently, as illustrated in Figure 15.14. Transaction T_{12} has a timestamp of $ts(T_{12})$, T_{13} has a timestamp of $ts(T_{13})$ and T_{14} has a timestamp of $ts(T_{14})$, such that $ts(T_{12}) < ts(T_{13}) < ts(T_{14})$.

15.2.6 Optimistic Techniques

In some environments, conflicts between transactions are rare, and the additional processing required by locking or timestamping protocols is unnecessary for many of the transactions. **Optimistic techniques** are based

Time	Op	T_{12}	T_{13}	T_{14}
t_1		begin_transaction		
t_2	read(bal_x)	read(bal_x)		
t_3	$bal_x = bal_x + 10$	$bal_x = bal_x + 10$		
t_4	write(bal_x)	write(bal_x)	begin_transaction	
t_5	read(bal_y)		read(bal_y)	
t_6	$bal_y = bal_y + 20$		$bal_y = bal_y + 20$	begin_transaction
t_7	read(bal_y)			read(bal_y)
t_8	write(bal_y)		write(bal_y)[†]	
t_9	$bal_y = bal_y + 30$			$bal_y = bal_y + 30$
t_{10}	write(bal_y)			write(bal_y)
t_{11}	$bal_z = 100$			$bal_z = 100$
t_{12}	write(bal_z)			write(bal_z)
t_{13}	$bal_z = 50$	$bal_z = 50$		commit
t_{14}	write(bal_z)	write(bal_z)[‡]	begin_transaction	
t_{15}	read(bal_y)	commit	read(bal_y)	
t_{16}	$bal_y = bal_y + 20$		$bal_y = bal_y + 20$	
t_{17}	write(bal_y)		write(bal_y)	
t_{18}			commit	

[†] At time t_8, the write by transaction T_{13} violates the second timestamping rule described above and therefore is aborted and restarted at time t_{14}.
[‡] At time t_{14}, the write by transaction T_{12} can safely be ignored using the third rule above, as it would have been overwritten by the write of transaction T_{14} at time t_{12}.

Figure 15.14
Timestamping example.

on the assumption that conflict is rare, and that it is more efficient to allow transactions to proceed without imposing delays to ensure serializability (Kung and Robinson, 1981). When a transaction wishes to commit, a check is performed to determine whether conflict has occurred. If there is a conflict, the transaction must be rolled back and restarted. Since the premise is that conflict rarely occurs, rollback will be rare. The overhead involved in restarting a transaction may be considerable, since it effectively means redoing the entire transaction. This could be tolerated only if it happened very infrequently, in which case the majority of transactions will be processed without being subjected to any delays. These techniques potentially allow greater concurrency than traditional protocols, since no locking is required.

There are three phases to an optimistic concurrency control protocol, depending on whether it is a read-only or an update transaction:

- *Read phase* This extends from the start of the transaction until immediately before the commit. The transaction reads the values of all data items it needs from the database and stores them in local variables.

Updates are applied to a local copy of the data, not to the database itself.

- *Validation phase* This follows the read phase. Checks are performed to ensure serializability is not violated if the transaction updates are applied to the database. For a read-only transaction, this consists of checking to see that the data values read are still the current values for the corresponding data items. If no interference occurred, the transaction is committed. If interference occurred, the transaction is aborted and restarted. For a transaction that has updates, validation consists of determining whether the current transaction leaves the database in a consistent state, with serializability maintained. If not, the transaction is aborted.

- *Write phase* This follows the successful validation phase for update transactions. During this phase, the updates made to the local copy are applied to the database.

The validation phase examines the reads and writes of transactions that may cause interference. Each transaction T is assigned a timestamp at the start of its execution, *Start(T)*, one at the start of its validation phase, *Validation(T)*, and one at its finish time, *Finish(T)* (including its write phase, if any). To pass the validation test, one of the following must be true:

(1) All transactions S with earlier timestamps must have finished before transaction T started; that is, *Finish(S) < Start(T)*.

(2) If transaction T starts before an earlier one S finishes, then:

    (a) The set of data items written by the earlier transaction are not the ones read by the current transaction.

and (b) The earlier transaction completes its write phase before the current transaction enters its validation phase; that is, *Start(T) < Finish(S) < Validation(T)*.

Rule 2(a) guarantees that the writes of the earlier transaction are not read by the current transaction; rule 2(b) guarantees that the writes are done serially, ensuring no conflict.

Although optimistic techniques are very efficient when there are few conflicts, they can result in rollback of individual transactions. Note that the rollback involves only a local copy of the data, so there are no cascading rollbacks, since the writes have not actually reached the database. However, if the aborted transaction is a long one, valuable processing time will be lost, since the transaction must be restarted. If rollback occurs often, it is an indication that the optimistic method is a poor choice for concurrency control in that particular environment.

15.2.7   Granularity of Data Items

> **Granularity**   The size of data items chosen as the unit of protection by a concurrency control protocol.

All the concurrency control protocols that we have discussed assume that the database consists of a number of 'data items', without explicitly defining the term. Typically, a data item is chosen to be one of the following, ranging from coarse to fine, where fine granularity refers to small item sizes and coarse granularity refers to large item sizes:

- the entire database;
- a file;
- a page (sometimes called an area or database space – a section of physical disk in which relations are stored);
- a record;
- a field value of a record.

Several trade-offs have to be considered in choosing the data item size. We discuss granularity in the context of locking, although similar arguments can be made for other concurrency control techniques.

The size or granularity of the data item that can be locked in a single operation has a significant effect on the overall performance of the concurrency control algorithm. Consider a transaction that updates a single tuple of a relation. The concurrency control algorithm might allow the transaction to lock only that single tuple, in which case, the granule size for locking is a single record. On the other hand, it might lock the entire database, in which case, the granule size is the entire database. In the second case, the granularity would prevent any other transactions from executing until the lock is released. This would clearly be undesirable. On the other hand, if a transaction updates 95% of the records in a file, then it would be more efficient to allow it to lock the entire file rather than forcing it to lock each individual record separately.

Thus, the coarser the data item size, the lower the degree of concurrency permitted. On the other hand, the finer the item size, the more locking information that is needed to be stored. The best item size depends upon the types of transactions. If a typical transaction accesses a small number of records, it is advantageous to have the data item granularity at the record level. On the other hand, if a transaction typically accesses many records of the same file, it may be better to have area or file granularity so that the transaction considers all those records as one (or a few) data items.

Some techniques have been proposed that have dynamic data item sizes. With these techniques, depending on the types of transactions that are currently executing, the data item size may be changed to the granularity that best suits these transactions. Ideally, the DBMS should support mixed granularity with record, page and file level locking. Some systems automatically upgrade locks from record or page to file if a particular transaction is locking more than a certain percentage of the records or pages in the file.

Hierarchy of granularity

We could represent the granularity of locks in a hierarchical structure where each node represents data items of different sizes, as shown in Figure 15.15. Here, the root node represents the entire database, the level 1 nodes represent files, the level 2 nodes represent pages, the level 3 nodes represent records and the level 4 leaves represent individual fields. Whenever a node is locked, all its descendants are also locked. For example, if a transaction locks a page, $Page_2$, all its records as well as all their fields are also locked. If another transaction requests an incompatible lock on the *same* node, the DBMS clearly knows that the lock cannot be granted.

If another transaction requests a lock on any of the *descendants* of the locked node, the DBMS should check the hierarchical path from the root to the requested node to see if any of its ancestors are locked before deciding whether to grant the lock. Thus, if the request is for a write lock on record $Record_1$, the DBMS should check its parent ($Page_2$), its grandparent ($File_2$) and the database itself to see if any of them are locked. When it finds that $Page_2$ is already locked, it denies the request.

Additionally, a transaction may request a lock on a node and a descendant of the node is already locked. For example, if a lock is requested on $File_2$, the DBMS checks every page in the file, every record in those pages and every field in those records to determine if any of them are locked. To reduce the searching involved in locating locks on descendants, the DBMS can use another type of lock called an **intention lock** (Gray *et al.*, 1975). When any node is locked, an intention lock is placed on all the ancestors of the node. Thus, if some descendant of $File_2$ (in our example, $Page_2$) is locked and a request is made for a lock on $File_2$, the presence of an intention lock on $File_2$ would indicate that some descendant of that node is already locked.

Intention locks may be either read or write. To ensure serializability with locking levels, a two-phase locking protocol is used as follows:

- No lock can be granted once any node has been unlocked.
- No node may be locked until its parent is locked by an intention lock.
- No node may be unlocked until all its descendants are unlocked.

In this way, locks are applied from the root down, using intention locks until the node requiring an actual read or write lock is reached, and locks are released from the bottom-up. However, deadlock is still possible and must be handled as discussed previously.

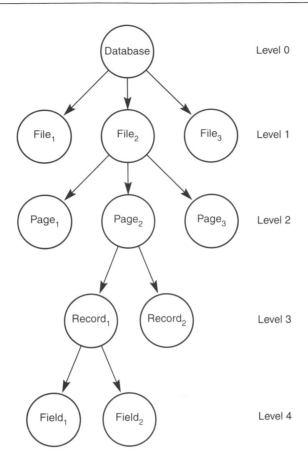

Figure 15.15 Levels of locking.

15.3   Recovery Control

Database recovery	The process of restoring the database to a correct state in the event of a failure.

At the start of this chapter, we introduced the concept of database recovery as a service that should be provided by the DBMS to ensure that the database is reliable and remains in a consistent state in the presence of failures. In this context, reliability refers to both the resilience of the DBMS to various types of failure and its capability to recover from them. In this section, we look more closely at how this service can be provided. To gain a better understanding of the potential problems we may encounter in providing a reliable system, we start by looking at the need for recovery control and the types of failure that can occur in a database environment.

15.3.1 The Need for Recovery Control

The storage of data generally includes four different types of media with an increasing degree of reliability: main memory, magnetic disk, magnetic tape and optical disk. Main memory is **volatile** storage that usually does not survive system crashes. Magnetic disks provide **online non-volatile** storage. Compared with main memory, disks are more reliable and much cheaper, but slower by three to four orders of magnitude. Magnetic tape is an **offline non-volatile** storage medium, which is far more reliable than disk and fairly inexpensive, but slower, providing only sequential access. Optical disk is more reliable than tape, generally cheaper, faster and providing random access. Main memory is also referred to as **primary storage** and disks and tape as **secondary storage**. **Stable storage** represents information that has been replicated in several nonvolatile storage media (usually disk) with independent failure modes.

There are many different types of failures that can affect database processing, each of which has to be dealt with in a different manner. Some failures affect main memory only, while others involve nonvolatile (secondary) storage. Among the causes of failure are:

- **system crashes** due to hardware or software errors, resulting in loss of main memory;
- **media failures**, such as head crashes or unreadable media, resulting in the loss of parts of secondary storage;
- **application software errors**, such as logical errors in the program that is accessing the database, which cause one or more transactions to fail;
- **natural physical disasters**, such as fires, floods, earthquakes or power failures;
- **carelessness** or unintentional destruction of data or facilities by operators or users;
- **sabotage** or intentional corruption or destruction of data, hardware or software facilities.

Whatever the cause of the failure, there are two principal effects that we need to consider: the loss of main memory, including database buffers; and the loss of the disk copy of the database.

In the remainder of this chapter, we discuss the concepts and techniques that can minimize these effects and allow recovery from failure.

15.3.2 Transactions and Recovery

Transactions represent the basic unit of recovery in a database system. It is the role of the recovery manager to guarantee two of the four *ACID* properties of transactions, namely *atomicity* and *durability*, in the presence of failures. The recovery manager has to ensure that, on recovery from failure, either all the effects of a given transaction are permanently recorded in the database or none of them. The situation is complicated by the fact that database writing is not an atomic (single step) action, and it is therefore possible for a transaction to have committed, but for its effects not to have been permanently recorded in the database simply because they have not yet reached the database.

Consider again the first example of this chapter, where the salary of a member of staff was being increased, as shown at a high level in Figure 15.1(a). To implement the read operation, the DBMS carries out the following steps:

- Find the address of the disk block that contains the record with primary key value *sno*.
- Transfer the disk block into a database buffer in main memory.
- Copy the salary data from the database buffer into the variable *salary*.

For the write operation, the DBMS carries out the following steps:

- Find the address of the disk block that contains the record with primary key value *sno*.
- Transfer the disk block into a database buffer in main memory.
- Copy the salary data from the variable *salary* into the database buffer.
- Write the database buffer back to disk.

The database buffers occupy an area in main memory from which data is transferred to and from secondary storage. It is only once the buffers have been **flushed** to secondary storage that any update operations can be regarded as permanent. This flushing of the buffers to the database can be triggered by a specific command (for example, transaction commit), or automatically when the buffers become full. The explicit writing of the buffers to secondary storage is known as **force-writing**.

If a failure occurs between writing to the buffers and flushing the buffers to secondary storage, the recovery manager must determine the status of the transaction that performed the write at the time of failure. If the transaction had issued its commit, then to ensure durability, the recovery manager would have to **redo** that transaction's updates to the database (also known as **rollforward**).

On the other hand, if the transaction had not committed at the time of failure, then the recovery manager would have to **undo (rollback)** any effects of that transaction on the database to guarantee transaction atomicity. If only one transaction has to be undone, this is referred to as **partial undo**. A partial undo can be triggered by the scheduler when a transaction is rolled back and restarted as a result of the concurrency control protocol, as described in the previous section. A transaction can also be aborted unilaterally: for example, by the user or by an exception condition in the application program. When all active transactions have to be undone, this is known as **global undo**.

Example 15.11: Use of UNDO/REDO

Figure 15.16 illustrates a number of concurrently executing transactions T_1 ... T_6. The DBMS starts at time t_0, but fails at time t_f. We assume that the data for transactions T_2 and T_3 have been written to secondary storage.

Clearly, T_1 and T_6 had not committed at the point of the crash; therefore, at restart, the recovery manager must undo transactions T_1 and T_6. However, it is not clear to what extent the changes made by the other (committed) transactions have been propagated to the database on nonvolatile storage. The reason for this uncertainty is the fact that the volatile database buffers may or may not have been written to disk. In the absence of any other information, the recovery manager would be forced to redo transactions T_2, T_3, T_4 and T_5.

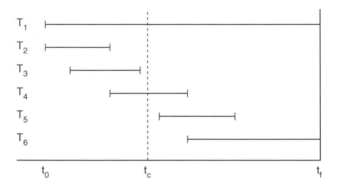

Figure 15.16
Example of
UNDO/REDO.

15.3.3 Recovery Facilities

A DBMS should provide the following facilities to assist with recovery:

- a backup mechanism, which makes periodic backup copies of the database;
- logging facilities, which keep track of the current state of transactions and database changes;
- a checkpoint facility, which enables updates to the database which are in progress to be made permanent;
- a recovery manager, which allows the system to restore the database to a consistent state following a failure.

Backup mechanism

The DBMS should provide a mechanism to allow backup copies of the database and the log file to be made at regular intervals without necessarily having to first stop the system. The backup copy of the database can be used in the event that the database has been damaged or destroyed. Typically, the backup is stored on offline storage, such as magnetic tape.

Log file

To keep track of database transactions, the DBMS maintains a special file called a **log** (or **journal**) that contains information about all updates to the database. The log may contain the following data:

- **Transaction records**, containing:
  - Transaction identifier.
  - Type of log record (transaction start, insert, update, delete, abort, commit).
  - Identifier of data item affected by the database action (insert, delete and update operations).
  - **Before-image** of the data item: that is, its value before change (update and delete operations only).
  - **After-image** of the data item: that is, its value after change (update and insert operations only).
  - Log management information, such as a pointer to previous and next log records for that transaction (all operations).
- **Checkpoint records**, which we describe shortly.

The log is often used for purposes other than recovery (for example, for performance monitoring and auditing). In this case, additional information may be recorded in the log (for example, database reads, user logons, logoffs, and so on), but these are not relevant to recovery and therefore are omitted from this discussion. Figure 15.17 illustrates a segment of a log file, which shows three concurrently executing transactions T1, T2 and T3. The columns PPtr and NPtr represent pointers to the previous and next log records for that transaction.

Tid	Time	Operation	Object	Before image	After image	PPtr	NPtr
T1	10:12	START				0	2
T1	10:13	UPDATE	STAFF SL21	(old value)	(new value)	1	8
T2	10:14	START				0	4
T2	10:16	INSERT	STAFF SG37		(new value)	3	5
T2	10:17	DELETE	STAFF SA9	(old value)		4	6
T2	10:17	UPDATE	PROPERTY PG16	(old value)	(new value)	5	9
T3	10:18	START				0	11
T1	10:18	COMMIT				2	0
	10:19	CHECKPOINT	T2, T3				
T2	10:19	COMMIT				6	0
T3	10:20	INSERT	PROPERTY PG4	(old value)	(new value)	7	12
T3	10:21	COMMIT				11	0

Figure 15.17 A segment of a log file.

Due to the importance of the transaction log file in the recovery process, the log may be duplexed or triplexed (that is, two or three separate copies are maintained) so that if one copy is damaged, another can be used. In the past, log files were stored on magnetic tape because tape was more reliable and cheaper than magnetic disk. However, nowadays, DBMSs are expected to be able to recover quickly from minor failures. This requires that the log file be stored online on a fast direct-access storage device.

In some environments where a vast amount of logging information is generated every day (a daily logging rate of 10^4 megabytes is not uncommon), it is not possible to hold *all* this data online all the time. The log file is needed online for quick recovery following minor failures (for example, rollback of a transaction following deadlock). Major failures, such as disk head crashes, obviously take longer to recover from and may require access to a large part of the log. In these cases, it would be acceptable to wait for parts of the log file to be brought back online from offline storage.

One approach to handling the offlining of the log is to divide the online log into two separate random-access files. Log records are written to the first file until it reaches a high-water mark: for example, 70% full. A second log file is then opened and all log records for *new* transactions are written to the second file. *Old* transactions continue to use the first file until they have finished, at which time the first file is closed and transferred to offline storage. This simplifies the recovery of a single transaction as all the log records for that transaction are either on offline or online storage. It should be noted that the log file is a potential bottleneck, and the speed of the writes to the log file can be critical in determining the overall performance of the database system.

Checkpointing

The information in the log file is used to recover from a database failure. One difficulty with this scheme is that when a failure occurs, we may not know how far back in the log to search and we may end up redoing transactions that have been safely written to the database. To limit the amount of searching and subsequent processing that we need to carry out on the log file, we can use a technique called **checkpointing**.

Checkpoint	The point of synchronization between the database and the transaction log file. All buffers are force-written to secondary storage.

Checkpoints are scheduled at predetermined intervals and involve the following operations:

- Writing all log records in main memory out to secondary storage.
- Writing the modified blocks in the database buffers out to secondary storage.
- Writing a checkpoint record to the log file. This record contains the identifiers of all transactions that are active at the time of the checkpoint.

If transactions are performed serially, when a failure occurs we check the log file to find the last transaction that started before the last checkpoint. Any earlier transactions would have committed previously, and would have been written to the database at the checkpoint. Therefore, we need only redo the one that was active at the checkpoint and any subsequent transactions for which both start and commit records appear in the log. If a transaction is active at the time of failure, the transaction must be undone. If transactions are performed concurrently, we redo all transactions that have committed since the checkpoint and undo all transactions that were active at the time of the crash.

Example 15.12:   Use of UNDO/REDO with checkpointing _____

Referring to Example 15.11, if we now assume that a checkpoint occurred at point t_c, then we would know that the changes made by transactions T_2 and T_3 had been written to secondary storage. In this case, the recovery manager would be able to omit the redo for these two transactions. However, the recovery manager would have to redo transactions T_4 and T_5, which have committed since the checkpoint, and undo transactions T_1 and T_6, which were active at the time of the crash.

Generally, checkpointing is a relatively inexpensive operation, and it is often possible to take three or four checkpoints an hour. In this way, no more than 15–20 minutes of work will need to be recovered.

15.3.4   Recovery Techniques

The particular recovery procedure to be used is dependent on the extent of the damage that has occurred to the database. We consider two cases:

- If the database has been extensively damaged, for example a disk head crash has occurred and destroyed the database, then it is necessary to restore the last backup copy of the database and reapply the update operations of committed transactions using the log file. This assumes, of course, that the log file has not been damaged as well.

- If the database has not been physically damaged but has become inconsistent, for example the system crashed while transactions were executing, then it is necessary to undo the changes that caused the inconsistency. It may also be necessary to redo some transactions to ensure that the updates they performed have reached secondary storage. Here, we do not need to use the backup copy of the database, but can restore the database to a consistent state using the **before-** and **after-images** held in the log file.

We now look at two techniques for recovery from the latter situation: that is, the case where the database has not been destroyed but is in an inconsistent state. The techniques, known as **deferred update** and **immediate update**, differ in the way that updates are written to secondary storage. We also look briefly at an alternative technique called **shadow paging**.

Recovery techniques using deferred update

Using this protocol, updates are not written to the database until after a transaction has reached its commit point. If a transaction fails before it reaches this point, it will not have modified the database and so no undoing of changes will be necessary. However, it may be necessary to redo the updates of committed transactions as their effect may not have reached the database. In this case, we use the log file to protect against system failures in the following way:

- When a transaction starts, write a *transaction start* record to the log.
- When any write operation is performed, write a log record containing all the data specified previously (excluding the before-image of the update). Do not actually write the update to the database buffers or the database itself.
- When a transaction is about to commit, write a *transaction commit* log record, write all the log records for the transaction to disk and then commit the transaction. Use the log records to perform the actual updates to the database.
- If a transaction aborts, ignore the log records for the transaction and do not perform the writes.

Note that we write the log records to disk before the transaction is actually committed, so that if a system failure occurs while the actual database updates are in progress, the log records will survive and the updates can be applied later. In the event of a failure, we examine the log to identify the transactions that were in progress at the time of failure. Starting at the last entry in the log file, we go back to the most recent checkpoint record:

- Any transaction with *transaction start* and *transaction commit* log records should be **redone**. The redo procedure performs all the writes to the database using the **after-image** log records for the transactions, *in the order in which they were written to the log*. If this writing has been done already, before the failure, the write has no effect on the data item, so there is no damage done if we write the data again (that is, the operation is **idempotent**). However, this method guarantees that we will update any data item that was not properly updated prior to the failure.
- For any transactions with *transaction start* and *transaction abort* log records, we do nothing, since no actual writing was done to the database, so these transactions do not have to be undone.

If a second system crash occurs during recovery, the log records are used again to restore the database. With the form of the write log records, it does not matter how many times we redo the writes.

Recovery techniques using immediate update

Using this protocol, updates are applied to the database as they occur without waiting to reach the commit point. As well as having to redo the updates of committed transactions following a failure, it may now be necessary to undo the effects of transactions that had not committed at the time of failure. In this case, we use the log file to protect against system failures in the following way:

- When a transaction starts, write a *transaction start* record to the log.
- When a write operation is performed, write a record containing the necessary data to the log file.
- Once the log record is written, write the update to the database buffers.
- The updates to the database itself are written when the buffers are next flushed to secondary storage.
- When the transaction commits, write a *transaction commit* record to the log.

It is essential that log records (or at least certain parts of them) are written *before* the corresponding write to the database. This is known as the **write-ahead log protocol**. If updates were made to the database first, and failure occurred before the log record was written, then the recovery manager would have no way of undoing (or redoing) the operation. Under the write-ahead log protocol, the recovery manager can safely assume that, if there is no *transaction commit* record in the log file for a particular transaction, then that transaction was still active at the time of failure, and must therefore be undone.

   If a transaction aborts, the log can be used to undo it, since it contains all the old values for the updated fields. As a transaction may have performed several changes to an item, the writes are undone in reverse order. Regardless of whether the transaction's writes have been applied to the database itself, writing the before-images guarantees that the database is restored to its state prior to the start of the transaction.

   If the system fails, recovery involves using the log to undo or redo transactions. For any transaction, T, for which both a *transaction start* and *transaction commit* record appear in the log, we redo by using the log records to write the after-image of updated fields, as described above. Note that if the new values have already been written to the database, these writes, though unnecessary, will have no effect. However, any write that did not actually reach the database will now be performed. For any transaction, S, for which the log contains a *transaction start* record, but not a *transaction commit* record, we need to undo that transaction. This time the log records are used to write the before-image of the affected fields, and thus restore the database to its state prior to the transaction's start. The undo operations are performed *in the reverse order in which they were written to the log*.

Shadow paging

An alternative to the log-based recovery schemes described above is **shadow paging** (Lorie, 1977). The main idea of this scheme is to maintain two page tables during the life of a transaction, a *current* page table and a *shadow* page table. When the transaction starts, the two page tables are the same. The shadow page table is never changed thereafter, and is used to restore the database in the event of a system failure. During the transaction, the current page table is used to record all updates to the database. When the transaction completes, the current page table becomes the shadow page table. Shadow paging has several advantages to the log-based schemes: the overhead of maintaining the log file is eliminated; and recovery is significantly faster, since there is no need for undo or redo operations. However, it has disadvantages as well, such as data fragmentation and the need for periodic garbage collection to reclaim inaccessible blocks.

Chapter Summary

- **Concurrency control** is the process of managing simultaneous operations on the database without having them interfere with one another. Database recovery is the process of restoring the database to a correct state after a failure. Both protect the database from inconsistencies and data loss.

- A **transaction** is a logical unit of work that takes the database from one consistent state to another. Transactions can terminate successfully (**commit**) or unsuccessfully (**abort**). Aborted transactions must be **undone** or rolled back. The transaction is the unit of recovery.

- Concurrency control is needed when multiple users are allowed to access the database simultaneously. Without it, problems of *lost update*, *uncommitted dependency* and *inconsistent analysis* can arise. Serial execution means executing one transaction at a time, with no interleaving of operations. A **schedule** shows the sequence of the operations of transactions. A schedule is **serializable** if it produces the same results as some serial schedule.

- Two methods that guarantee serializability are **locking** and **timestamping**. Locks may be read or write. In **two-phase locking**, a transaction acquires all its locks before releasing any. With timestamping, transactions are ordered in such a way that older transactions get priority in the event of conflict.

- **Deadlock** occurs when two or more transactions are waiting to access data the other transaction has locked. The only way to break deadlock once it has occurred is to abort one or more of the transactions.

- A tree may be used to represent the granularity of locks in a system that allows locking of data items of different sizes. When an item is locked, all its descendants are also locked. When a new transaction requests a lock, it is easy to check all the ancestors of the object to see whether they are already locked. To show whether any of the node's descendants are locked, an **intention lock** is placed on all the ancestors of any node being locked.

- Causes of failure are system crashes, media failures, application software errors, carelessness, natural physical disasters, sabotage and others. They can result in the loss of main memory and/or the disk copy of the database. Recovery techniques minimize these effects.

- To facilitate recovery, the system maintains a **log file** containing transaction records that identify the start/end of transactions and detail write operations. Using **deferred updates**, writes are done initially to the log only and the log records are used to perform actual updates to the database. If the system fails, it examines the log to determine which transactions it needs to **redo**, but there is no need to **undo** any writes. Using **immediate updates**, an update may be made to the database itself any time after a log record is written. The log can be used to undo and redo transactions in the event of failure.

- **Checkpoints** are used to improve database recovery. At a checkpoint, all modified buffer blocks, all log records and a checkpoint record identifying all active transactions are written to disk. If a failure occurs, the checkpoint record identifies which transactions need to be redone.

REVIEW QUESTIONS

15.1 Explain what is meant by a transaction. Why are transactions important units of operation in a DBMS?

15.2 The consistency and reliability aspects of transactions are due to the 'ACIDity' properties of transactions. Discuss each of these properties and how they relate to the concurrency control and recovery mechanisms. Give examples to illustrate your answer.

15.3 Discuss, with examples, the types of problems that can occur in a multiuser environment when concurrent access to the database is allowed.

15.4 Give full details of a mechanism for concurrency control that can be used to ensure the types of problems discussed in Question 15.3 cannot occur. Show how the mechanism prevents the problems illustrated from occurring. Discuss how the concurrency control mechanism interacts with the transaction mechanism.

15.5 Discuss the types of problems that can occur with locking-based mechanisms for concurrency control and the actions that can be taken by a DBMS to prevent them.

15.6 Explain the concepts of serial, non-serial and serializable schedules. State the rules for equivalence of schedules.

15.7 Discuss the types of failure that may occur in a database environment. Explain why it would be unreasonable for a multiuser DBMS not to provide a recovery mechanism.

15.8 Discuss how the log file (or journal) is a fundamental feature in any recovery mechanism. Explain what is meant by forward and backward recovery and describe how the log file is used in forward and backward recovery. What is the significance of the write-ahead log protocol? How do checkpoints affect the recovery protocol?

EXERCISES

15.9 (a) Explain what is meant by the constrained write rule, and explain how to test whether a schedule is serializable under the constrained write rule. Using the above method, determine whether the following schedule is serializable:

$$S = [R_1(Z), R_2(Y), W_2(Y), R_3(Y), R_1(X), W_1(X), W_1(Z),$$
$$W_3(Y), R_2(X), R_1(Y), W_1(Y), W_2(X), R_3(W), W_3(W)]$$

where $R_i(Z)/W_i(Z)$ indicates a read/write by transaction i on data item Z.

(b) Would it be sensible to produce a concurrency control algorithm based on serializability? Give justification for your answer. How is serializability used in standard concurrency control algorithms?

15.10 Produce a wait-for-graph for the following transaction scenario, and determine whether deadlock exists.

Transaction	Data items locked by transaction	Data items transaction is waiting for
T_1	X_2	X_1, X_3
T_2	X_3, X_{10}	X_7, X_8
T_3	X_8	X_4, X_5
T_4	X_7	X_1
T_5	X_1, X_5	X_3
T_6	X_4, X_9	X_6
T_7	X_6	X_5

15.11 Write an algorithm for shared and exclusive locking. How does granularity affect this algorithm?

15.12 Write an algorithm that checks whether the concurrently executing transactions are in deadlock.

15.13 Explain why stable storage cannot really be implemented. How would you simulate stable storage?

15.14 Would it be realistic for a DBMS to dynamically maintain a wait-for-graph rather than create it each time the deadlock detection algorithm runs? Explain your answer.

16 Distributed Database Systems

Chapter Objectives

In this chapter you will learn:

- The need for distributed databases.
- The difference between distributed databases and distributed processing.
- The advantages and disadvantages of distributed databases.
- The problems of heterogeneity in a DDBMS.
- Basic networking concepts.
- The functions that should be provided by a DDBMS.
- An architecture for a DDBMS.
- The problems associated with distributed database design.
- What fragmentation is and how it should be carried out.
- The importance of allocation and replication in distributed databases.
- The levels of transparency that should be provided by a DDBMS.
- How distribution affects concurrency control techniques.
- How to detect deadlock when multiple sites are involved.
- How to recover from database failure in a distributed environment.
- A comparison criterion for DDBMSs.

Database systems have taken us from a paradigm of data processing in which each application defined and maintained its own data, to one in which data is defined and administered centrally. Now, distributed database technology may change the mode of working from centralized to decentralized. Distributed Database Management System (DDBMS) technology is one of the current major developments in the database systems area. In previous chapters, we have concentrated on centralized database systems: that is, systems with a single logical database located at one site under the control of a single DBMS. In this chapter, we discuss the concepts and problems of distributed database management systems, where users can not only access the database at their own site but also access data stored at remote sites. There are claims that in the next 10 years centralized database systems will be an 'antique curiosity' as most organizations move towards distributed database systems.

16.1 Introduction

A major motivation behind the development of database systems is the desire to integrate the operational data of an organization and to provide controlled access to the data. Although integration and controlled access may imply centralization, this is not the intention. In fact, the development of computer networks promotes a decentralized mode of work. This decentralized approach mirrors the organizational structure of many companies, which are logically distributed into divisions, departments, projects, and so on, and physically distributed into offices, plants, factories, where each unit maintains its own operational data (Date, 1995). The development of a distributed database system that reflects this organizational structure, makes the data in all units accessible, and stores data proximate to the location where it is most frequently used, should improve the shareability of the data and the efficiency of data access.

Distributed systems should help resolve the *islands of information* problem. Databases are sometimes regarded as electronic islands that are distinct and generally inaccessible places, like remote islands. This may be a result of geographical separation, incompatible computer architectures, incompatible communication protocols, and so on. Integrating the databases into a logical whole may prevent this way of thinking.

16.1.1 Concepts

To start the discussion of distributed systems, we first give a definition of a distributed database:

Distributed database	A logically interrelated collection of shared data, physically distributed over a computer network.

and following on from this we have:

Distributed	The software system that permits the management of the
DBMS	distributed database and makes the distribution transparent
	to users.

A Distributed Database Management System (DDBMS) consists of a single database that is split into a number of **fragments,** each of which is stored on one or more computers under the control of a separate DBMS; the computers are connected by a communications network. Each site is capable of independently processing user requests that require access to local data (that is, has some degree of local autonomy) and is also capable of processing data stored on other computers in the network.

Users access the distributed database via applications. Applications are classified as those that do not require data from other sites (**local applications**) and those that do require data from other sites (**global applications**). We require a DDBMS to have at least one global application. A DDBMS therefore has the following characteristics:

- A collection of logically related shared data is distributed over a number of different computers.

- The computers are linked by a communications network.

- The data at each site is under the control of a DBMS.

- The DBMS at each site can handle local applications, autonomously.

- Each DBMS participates in at least one global application.

It is not necessary for every site in the system to have its own local database, as illustrated by the topology of the DDBMS shown in Figure 16.1.

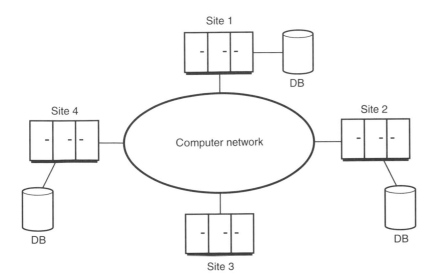

Figure 16.1
Distributed database
management system.

Example 16.1

Using distributed database technology, the *DreamHome* estate agency may implement their database system on a number of separate computer systems rather than a single, centralized mainframe. The computer systems may be located at each local branch office: for example, London, Aberdeen and Glasgow. A network linking the computers will enable the branches to communicate with each other, and a DDBMS will enable them to access data stored at another branch office. Thus, a client living in Glasgow can go to the nearest branch office to find out what properties are available in London, rather than having to telephone or write to London for details.

Alternatively, if each *DreamHome* branch office already has its own (disparate) database, a DDBMS can be used to integrate the separate databases into a single, logical database, again making the local data more widely available.

From the definition of the DDBMS, the system is expected to make the distribution **transparent** to the user. Thus, the fact that a distributed database is split into fragments that can be stored on different computers and perhaps replicated, should be hidden from the user. The objective of transparency is to make the distributed system appear like a centralized system. This is sometimes referred to as the **fundamental principle** of distributed systems (Date, 1987). This additional requirement provides significant functionality for the end user but, unfortunately, creates many additional problems that have to be handled by the DDBMS, as we see in Section 16.5.

Distributed processing

It is worthwhile making a distinction between a distributed DBMS and distributed processing:

Distributed processing	A centralized database that can be accessed over a computer network.

The key point with the definition of a distributed database is that the system consists of data that is physically distributed across the network. If the data is centralized, then even although other users may be accessing the data over the network, we do not consider this to be a distributed DBMS, simply distributed processing. We illustrate the topology of distributed processing in Figure 16.2. Compare this figure, which has a central database at site 2, with Figure 16.1, which shows several sites with their own databases.

16.1.2 Advantages and Disadvantages of DDBMSs

The distribution of data and applications has potential advantages over traditional centralized database systems. Unfortunately, there are also disadvant-

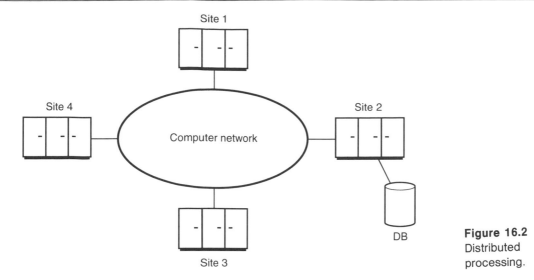

Figure 16.2
Distributed
processing.

ages. In this section, we review the advantages and disadvantages of the
DDBMS.

Advantages

Organizational structure

Many organizations are naturally distributed over several locations. For
example, the *DreamHome* estate agency has many offices in different cities.
It is natural for databases used in such an application to be distributed over
these locations. *DreamHome* may keep a database at each branch office
containing details of such things as the staff that work at that location, the
properties that are for rent and the clients that own or wish to rent out these
properties. The staff at a branch office will make local enquiries of the
database. The company headquarters may wish to make global enquiries
involving the access of data at all or a number of branches.

Shareability and local autonomy

The geographical distribution of an organization can be reflected in the
distribution of the data; users at one site can access data stored at other sites.
Data can be placed at the site close to the users that normally use that data.
In this way, users have local control of the data, and they can consequently
establish and enforce local policies regarding the use of this data. A global
Database Administrator (DBA) is responsible for the entire system. Generally,
part of this responsibility is devolved to the local level, so that the local DBA
can manage the local DBMS (see Chapter 4).

Improved availability

In a centralized DBMS, a computer failure terminates the operations of the DBMS. However, a failure at one site of a DDBMS, or a failure of a communication link making some sites inaccessible, does not make the entire system inoperable. Distributed systems are designed to continue to function despite such failures. If a single node fails, the system may be able to reroute the failed node's requests to another site.

Improved reliability

As data may be replicated so that it exists at more than one site, the failure of a node or a communication link does not necessarily make the data inaccessible.

Improved performance

As the data is located near the site of 'greatest demand', and given the inherent parallelism of distributed systems, it may be possible to improve the speed of database accesses than if we had a remote centralized database. Furthermore, since each site handles only a part of the entire database, there may not be the same contention for CPU and I/O services as characterized by a centralized DBMS.

Economics

In the 1960s, computing power was calculated according to the square of the costs of the equipment – three times the cost would provide nine times the power. This was known as *Grosch's Law*. However, it is now generally accepted that it costs much less to create a system of smaller computers with the equivalent power of a single large computer. This makes it more cost-effective for corporate divisions and departments to obtain separate computers. It is also much more cost-effective to add workstations to a network than to update a mainframe system.

The second potential cost saving occurs where databases are geographically remote and the applications require access to distributed data. In such cases, due to the relative expense of data being transmitted across the network as opposed to the cost of local access, it may be much more economical to partition the application and perform the processing locally at each site.

Modular growth

In a distributed environment, it is much easier to handle expansion. New sites can be added to the network without affecting the operations of other sites. This flexibility allows an organization to expand relatively easily. Increasing database size can usually be handled by adding processing and storage power to the network. In a centralized DBMS, growth may entail changes to both hardware (the procurement of a more powerful system) and software (the procurement of a more powerful or more configurable DBMS).

Disadvantages

Complexity

A distributed system that hides the distributed nature from the user and provides an acceptable level of performance, reliability and availability is inherently more complex than a centralized DBMS. The fact that data can be replicated also adds an extra level of complexity to the distributed system. If the software does not adequately handle data replication, there will be a degradation in availability, reliability and performance compared with the centralized system, and the advantages we cited above will become disadvantages.

Cost

Increased complexity means that we can expect the procurement and maintenance costs for a DDBMS to be higher than those for a centralized DBMS. Furthermore, a distributed system requires additional hardware to establish a network between sites. There are ongoing communication costs incurred with the use of this network. There are also additional manpower costs to manage and maintain the local DBMSs and the underlying network.

Security

In a centralized system, access to the data can be easily controlled. However, in a distributed system, not only does access to replicated data have to be controlled in multiple locations, but the network itself has to be made secure. In the past, networks were regarded as an insecure communication medium. Although this is still partially true, significant developments have been made recently to make networks more secure.

Integrity

Database integrity refers to the validity and consistency of stored data. Integrity is usually expressed in terms of constraints, which are consistency rules that the database is not permitted to violate. Enforcing integrity constraints generally requires access to a large amount of data that defines the constraint, but is not involved in the actual update operation itself. In a distributed DBMS, the communication and processing costs that are required to enforce integrity constraints may be prohibitive.

Lack of standards

Although distributed databases depend on effective communication, we are only now starting to see the appearance of standard communication and data access protocols. This lack of standards has significantly limited the potential of distributed systems. There are also no tools or methodologies to help users convert a centralized DBMS into a distributed DBMS.

Lack of experience

There are currently some prototype and special-purpose distributed systems in use; however, to date, general-purpose distributed systems have not been widely accepted. Consequently, we do not yet have the same level of experience in industry as we have with centralized systems.

Database design more complex
Besides the normal difficulties of designing a centralized database, the design of a distributed database has to take account of fragmentation of data, allocation of fragments to specific sites and data replication. We discuss these problems in Section 16.4.

The advantages and disadvantages of distributed systems are summarized in Table 16.1.

Table 16.1 Summary of advantages/disadvantages of DDBMSs.

Advantages	Disadvantages
Organizational structure	Complexity
Shareability and local autonomy	Cost
Improved availability	Security
Improved reliability	Integrity
Improved performance	Lack of standards
Economics	Lack of experience
Modular growth	Database design more complex

16.1.3   Homogeneous and Heterogeneous DDBMSs

A DDBMS may be classified as homogeneous or heterogeneous. In a **homogeneous** system, all sites use the same DBMS product. In a **heterogeneous** system, sites may run different DBMS products, which need not be based on the same underlying data model and so may be composed of relational, network, hierarchical and object-oriented DBMSs.

Homogeneous systems are much easier to design and manage. This approach provides incremental growth, making the addition of a new site to the distributed system easy, and allows increased performance by exploiting the parallel processing capability of multiple sites.

Heterogeneous systems usually result when individual sites have implemented their own databases and integration is considered at a later stage. In a heterogeneous system, translations are required to allow communication between different DBMSs. To provide DBMS transparency, users must be able to make requests in the language of the DBMS at their local site. The system then has the task of locating the data and performing any necessary translation. Data may be required from another site that may have:

- different hardware,
- different DBMS products, or
- different hardware and different DBMS products.

If the hardware is different but the DBMS products are the same, the translation is straightforward, involving the change of codes and word lengths. If the hardware is the same but the DBMS products are different, the translation is complicated, involving the mapping of data structures in one data model to the equivalent data structures in another data model (for example, relations in the relational data model are mapped to records and sets in the network model). It is also necessary to translate the query language used (for example, SQL SELECT statements are mapped to the network FIND and GET statements). If both the hardware and software are different, then these two types of translations are required. This makes the processing extremely complex.

The typical solution used by some relational systems that are part of a heterogeneous DDBMS is to use **gateways**, which convert the language and model of each different DBMS into the language and model of the relational system. However, the gateway approach has some serious limitations. First, it does not support transaction management, even for a pair of systems. In other words, the gateway between two systems is merely a query translator. For example, a system may not coordinate concurrency control and recovery of transactions that involve updates to both databases. Second, the gateway approach is concerned only with the problem of translating a query expressed in one language into an equivalent expression in another language. As such, it does not address the issues of homogenizing the structural and representational differences between different schemas.

Multidatabase systems

Before we complete this section, it is worth mentioning a particular type of distributed DBMS known as a multidatabase system.

Multidatabase system (MDBS)	A distributed database system in which each site maintains complete autonomy.

In recent years, there has been considerable interest in MDBSs, which attempt to logically integrate distributed database systems, while allowing the local systems to maintain complete control of their operations. One consequence of complete autonomy is that there can be no software modifications to the local DBMSs. Thus, an MDBS requires an additional software layer on top of the local systems to provide the necessary functionality.

An MDBS allows users to access and share data without requiring physical database integration. However, it still allows users to administer their own databases without centralized control, as with true distributed systems. There are **unfederated** (where there are no local users) and **federated** MDBSs. A federated system is a cross between a distributed system and a centralized system; it is a distributed system for global users and a centralized system for local users. The interested reader is referred to Sheth and Larson (1990) for a taxonomy of distributed database systems.

In simple terms, an MDBS is a DBMS that resides transparently on top of existing database and file systems and presents a single database to its users. An MDBS maintains a global schema against which users issue queries and updates; an MDBS maintains only the global schema and the local DBMSs themselves maintain all user data. The global schema is constructed by integrating the schemas of the local databases. The MDBS first translates the global queries and updates into queries and updates on the appropriate local DBMSs. It then merges the local results and generates the final global result for the user. Furthermore, the MDBS coordinates the commit and abort operations for global transactions by the local DBMSs that processed them, to maintain consistency of data within the local databases. An MDBS controls multiple gateways and manages local databases through these gateways.

For example, the multidatabase system UniSQL/M from UniSQL Inc. allows application development using a single global view and a single database language over multiple heterogeneous relational and object-oriented databases (Connolly *et al.*, 1994). We discuss the architecture of an MDBS in Section 16.3.3.

16.2 Overview of Networking

> **Network** An interconnected collection of autonomous computers that are capable of exchanging information.

Computer networking is a complicated and rapidly changing field, but some knowledge of it is useful to understand distributed systems. From the situation a few decades ago when systems were standalone, we now find computer networks commonplace. They range from systems connecting a few personal computers to worldwide networks with thousands of machines and over a million users. For our purposes, the DDBMS is built on top of a network in such a way that the network is hidden from the user.

Communication networks may be classified in several ways. One classification is according to whether the distance separating the computers is short (local area network) or long (wide area network). A **local area network** (LAN) is intended for connecting computers at the same site. A **wide area network** (WAN) is used when computers or LANs need to be connected over long distances. With the large geographical separation, the communication links in a WAN are relatively slow and less reliable than LANs. The transmission rates for a WAN generally range from 2 to 2000 kilobits per second. Transmission rates for LANs are much higher, operating at 10s to 100s of megabits per second, and are highly reliable. Clearly, a DDBMS using a LAN for communication will provide a much faster response time than one using a WAN.

If we examine the method of choosing a path, or **routeing**, we can classify a network as either point-to-point or broadcast. In a **point-to-point** network, if a site wishes to send a message to all sites, it must send several separate messages. In a **broadcast** network, all sites receive all messages, but each message has a prefix that identifies the destination site, so other sites simply ignore it. WANs are generally based on a point-to-point network, whereas LANs generally use broadcasting. A summary of the typical characteristics of WANs and LANs is presented in Table 16.2.

Table 16.2 Summary of WAN and LAN characteristics.

WAN	*LAN*
Distances up to thousands of km	Distances up to a few km
Link autonomous computers	Link computers that cooperate in distributed applications
Network managed by independent organization (using telephone or satellite links)	Network managed by users (using privately owned cables)
Data rate up to 2 Mbits/s	Data rate up to 100 Mbits/s
Complex protocol	Simpler protocol
Use point-to-point routeing	Use broadcast routeing
Use irregular topology	Use bus or ring topology
Error rate about $1:10^5$	Error rate about $1:10^9$

The International Standards Organization (ISO) has defined a set of rules, or **protocol**, governing the way in which systems can communicate (ISO, 1981). The approach taken is to divide the network into a series of layers, each layer providing a particular service to the layer above, while hiding implementation details from it. The protocol, known as the ISO **Open Systems Interconnection (OSI) Model**, consists of seven manufacturer-independent layers. The layers handle transmitting the raw bits across the network, managing the connection and ensuring that the link is free from errors, routeing and congestion control, managing sessions between different machines and resolving differences in format and data representation between machines. A description of this protocol is not necessary to understand the remainder of this chapter and so we refer the interested reader to Halsall (1992) and Tanenbaum (1988).

The International Telegraph and Telephone Consultative Committee (CCITT) has produced a standard known as X.25, which complies with the lower three layers of this architecture. Most DDBMSs have been developed on top of X.25. However, new standards are being produced for the upper layers that may provide useful services for DDBMSs, for example, Remote Database Access (RDA) (ISO 9579) or Distributed Transaction Processing (ISO 10026).

Communication time

The time taken to send a message depends upon the length of the message and the type of network being used. It can be calculated using the formula:

Communication Time = C_0 + (no_of_bits_in_message/transmission_rate)

where C_0 is a fixed cost of initiating a message, known as the **access delay**. For example, using an access delay of 1 second and a transmission rate of 10 000 bits per second, we can calculate the time to send 100 000 records, each consisting of 100 bits as:

$$\text{Communication Time} = 1 + (100\,000*100/10\,000) = 1001 \text{ seconds}$$

If we wish to transfer 100 000 records one at a time, we get:

$$\text{Communication Time} = 100\,000 * [1 + (100/10\,000)]$$
$$= 100\,000 * [1.001] = 100\,100 \text{ seconds.}$$

Clearly, the communication time is significantly longer transferring 100 000 records individually because of the access delay. Consequently, an objective of a DDBMS is to minimize both the amount of data transmitted over the network and the number of network transmissions. We will return to this point again when we consider distributed query optimization in Section 16.5.3.

16.3 Functions and Architecture of a DDBMS

In Chapter 2, we examined the functions, architecture and components of a centralized DBMS. In this section, we consider how distribution affects expected functionality and architecture.

16.3.1 Functions of a DDBMS

We expect a DDBMS to have at least the functionality that we discussed in Chapter 2 for a centralized DBMS. In addition, we expect a DDBMS to have the following functionality:

- extended communication services to provide access to remote sites and allow the transfer of queries and data among the sites using a network;
- extended data dictionary to store data distribution details;
- distributed query processing, including query optimization and remote data access;
- extended concurrency control to maintain consistency of replicated data;
- extended recovery services to take account of failures of individual sites and the failures of communication links.

We discuss these issues further in later sections of this chapter.

16.3.2 Reference Architecture for a DDBMS

The ANSI–SPARC three-level architecture, presented in Section 2.1, has been accepted and implemented by many commercial database systems. Due to the diversity of distributed systems, it is much more difficult to present an equivalent architecture that is generally applicable. However, it may be useful to present a reference architecture that considers data distribution. The reference architecture shown in Figure 16.3 consists of the following schemas:

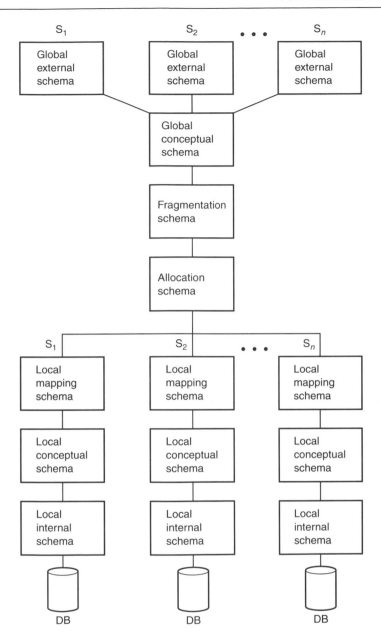

Figure 16.3
Reference architecture
for a DDBMS.

- a set of global external schemas;
- a global conceptual schema;
- a fragmentation schema and allocation schema;
- a set of schemas for each local DBMS conforming to the ANSI–SPARC three-level architecture.

The edges represent mappings between the different schemas. Depending on which levels of transparency are supported, some levels may be missing from the architecture.

Global conceptual schema

The global conceptual schema is a logical description of the whole database, as if it were not distributed. This level corresponds to the conceptual level of the ANSI–SPARC architecture, and contains definitions of entities, relationships, constraints, security and integrity information. It provides physical data independence from the distributed environment. The global external schemas provide logical data independence.

Fragmentation and allocation schemas

The fragmentation schema is a description of how the data is to be logically partitioned. The allocation schema is a description of where the data is to be located. The allocation schema takes account of any replication.

Local schemas

Each local DBMS has its own set of schemas. The local conceptual and local internal schemas correspond to the equivalent levels of the ANSI/SPARC architecture. The local mapping schema maps fragments in the allocation schema into external objects in the local database. It is DBMS independent and is the basis for supporting heterogeneous DBMSs.

16.3.3   Reference Architecture for an MDBS

In Section 16.1.3, we briefly discussed Federated Multidatabase Systems (FMDBS). Federated systems differ from distributed systems in the level of local autonomy. This difference is also reflected in the reference architecture. Figure 16.4 shows a reference architecture for an FMDBS that is **tightly coupled**: that is, it has a Global Conceptual Schema (GCS). In a DDBMS, the GCS is the union of all local conceptual schemas. In an FMDBS, the GCS is a subset of the local conceptual schemas, consisting of the data that each local system agrees to share. The GCS of a tightly coupled system involves the integration of either parts of the local conceptual schemas or the local external schemas.

It has been argued that an FMDBS should not have a GCS (Litwin, 1988), in which case the system is referred to as **loosely coupled**. In this case,

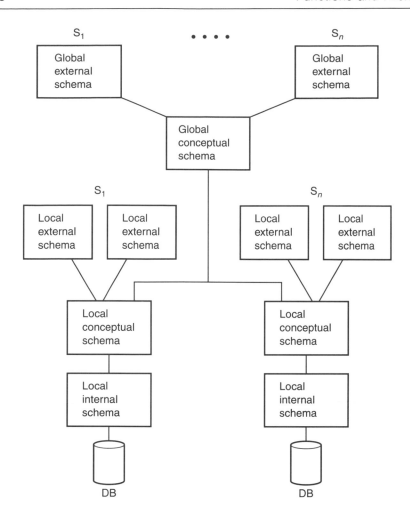

Figure 16.4
Reference architecture
for a tightly coupled
FMDBS.

external schemas consist of one or more local conceptual schemas. For additional information on MDBSs, the interested reader is referred to Litwin (1988) and Sheth and Larson (1990).

16.3.4 Component Architecture for a DDBMS

Independent of the reference architecture, we can identify a component architecture for a DDBMS consisting of four major components:

- Local DBMS (LDBMS) component,
- Data Communications (DC) component,
- Global Data Dictionary (GDD),
- Distributed DBMS (DDBMS) component.

The component architecture for a DDBMS based on Figure 16.1 is illustrated in Figure 16.5. For clarity, we have omitted site 2 from the diagram as it has the same structure as site 1.

Local DBMS (LDBMS) component

The local DBMS component is a standard DBMS, responsible for controlling the local data at each site that has a database. It has its own local data dictionary that stores information about the data held at that site. In a homogeneous system, the local DBMS component is the same product, replicated at each site. In a heterogeneous system, there would be at least two sites with different DBMS products.

Data Communications (DC) component

The Data Communications component is the software that enables all sites to communicate with each other. The DC component contains information about the sites and the links.

Global Data Dictionary (GDD)

The Global Data Dictionary has the same functionality as the data dictionary of a centralized system. The GDD holds information specific to the distributed nature of the system, such as the fragmentation and allocation schemas. It can itself be managed as a distributed database and so it can be fragmented and distributed, fully replicated or centralized, like any other relation, as discussed below.

Distributed DBMS (DDBMS) component

The Distributed DBMS component is the controlling unit of the entire system. We briefly listed the functionality of this component in the previous section and we concentrate on this functionality in the remaining sections of this chapter.

16.4 Distributed Relational Database Design

In Chapters 7 and 8, we presented a methodology for the logical design of a centralized relational database. In this section, we examine the additional factors that have to be considered for distributed relational databases. We look at:

- **Fragmentation** A relation may be divided into a number of sub-relations, called fragments, which are then distributed. There are two main types of fragmentation: **horizontal** and **vertical**. Horizontal fragments are subsets of tuples and vertical fragments are subsets of attributes.

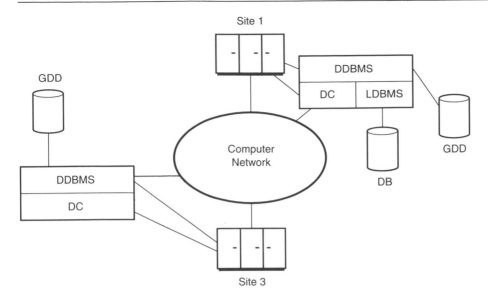

Figure 16.5
Components of a
DDBMS.

- **Allocation** Each fragment is stored at the site with 'optimal' distribution.
- **Replication** The DDBMS may maintain a copy of a fragment at several different sites.

The definition and allocation of fragments are carried out strategically to achieve the following objectives:

- *Locality of reference* Where possible, data should be stored close to where it is used. If a fragment is used at several sites, it may be advantageous to store copies of the fragment at these sites.

- *Improved reliability and availability* Reliability and availability are improved by replication: there is another copy of the fragment available at another site in the event of one site failing.

- *Performance* Bad allocation may result in bottlenecks occurring: that is, a site may become inundated with requests from other sites, perhaps causing a significant degradation in performance. Alternatively, bad allocation may result in under-utilization of resources.

- *Storage capacities and costs* Consideration should be given to the availability and cost of storage at each site, so that cheap mass storage can be used, where possible. This must be balanced against *locality of reference*.

- *Communication costs* Consideration should be given to the cost of remote requests. Retrieval costs are minimized when *locality of reference* is maximized or when each site has its own copy of the data. However, when replicated data is updated, the update has to be performed at all sites holding a duplicate copy, thereby increasing communication costs.

16.4.1 Data Allocation

There are four alternative strategies regarding the placement of data: centralized, partitioned, complete replication and selective replication.

Centralized

This strategy consists of a single database and DBMS stored at one site with users distributed across the network (we referred to this previously as distributed processing). Locality of reference is at its lowest as all sites, except the central site, have to use the network for all data accesses; this also means that communication costs are high. Reliability and availability are low, as a failure of the central site results in the loss of the entire database system.

Partitioned (or fragmented)

This strategy partitions the database into disjoint fragments, with each fragment assigned to one site. If data items are located at the site where they are used most frequently, locality of reference is high. As there is no replication, storage costs are low; similarly, reliability and availability are low, although they are higher than in the centralized case, as the failure of a site results in the loss of only that site's data. Performance should be good and communications costs low if the distribution is designed properly.

Complete replication

This strategy consists of maintaining a complete copy of the database at each site. Therefore, locality of reference, reliability and availability and performance are maximized. However, storage costs and communication costs for updates are the most expensive. To overcome some of these problems, **snapshots** are sometimes used. A snapshot is a copy of the data at a given time. The copies are updated on a periodic basis, for example, hourly or weekly, so they may not be always up to date. Snapshots are also sometimes used to implement views in a distributed database to improve the time it takes to perform a database operation on a view.

Selective replication

This strategy is a combination of partitioning, replication and centralization. Some data items are partitioned to achieve high locality of reference and others, which are used at many sites and are not frequently updated, are replicated; otherwise, the data items are centralized. The objective of this strategy is to have all the advantages of the other approaches but none of the disadvantages. This is the most commonly used strategy because of its flexibility. The alternative strategies are summarized in Table 16.3. For further details on allocation, the interested reader is referred to Ozsu and Valduriez (1991) and Teorey (1994).

Table 16.3 Comparison of strategies for data allocation.

	Locality of reference	Reliability and availability	Performance	Storage costs	Communication costs
Centralized	lowest	lowest	unsatisfactory	lowest	highest
Partitioned	high[†]	low for item; high for system	satisfactory[†]	lowest	low[†]
Complete replication	highest	highest	best for read	highest	high for update; low for read.
Selective replication	high[†]	low for item; high for system	satisfactory[†]	average	low[†]

[†] Indicates subject to good design.

The definition and allocation of fragments must be based on how the database is to be used. This involves analysing applications. Generally, it is not possible to analyse all applications, so we concentrate on the most important ones. The design should be based on both quantitative and qualitative information. Quantitative information is used in allocation; qualitative information is used in fragmentation. The quantitative information may include:

- frequency with which an application is run;
- site from which an application is run;
- performance criteria for transactions and applications.

The qualitative information may include transactions that are executed by the application, including relations, attributes and tuples accessed, the type of access (read or write) and the predicates of read operations.

16.4.2 Fragmentation

Why fragment?

Before we discuss fragmentation in detail, we list four reasons for fragmenting a relation:

- *Usage* In general, applications work with views rather than entire relations. Therefore, for data distribution, it seems reasonable to work with subsets of relations.
- *Efficiency* Data is stored close to where it is most frequently used. In addition, data that is not needed by local applications is not stored.
- *Parallelism* With fragments as the unit of distribution, a transaction can be divided into several subqueries that operate on fragments. This should increase the degree of concurrency or parallelism in the system, thereby allowing transactions that can do so safely to execute in parallel.

- *Security*   Data not required by local applications is not stored, and consequently not available to unauthorized users.

Fragmentation has two primary disadvantages, which we have mentioned previously:

- *Performance*   The performance of applications that require data from several fragments located at different sites may be slower.
- *Integrity*   Integrity control may be more difficult if data and functional dependencies are fragmented and located at different sites.

Correctness of fragmentation

Fragmentation cannot be carried out haphazardly. There are three rules that must be followed during fragmentation:

(1)   *Completeness*   If a relation instance R is decomposed into fragments $R_1, R_2, \ldots R_n$, each data item that can be found in R must appear in at least one fragment. This rule is necessary to ensure that there is no loss of data during fragmentation.

(2)   *Reconstruction*   It must be possible to define a relational operation that will reconstruct the relation R from the fragments. This rule ensures that functional dependencies are preserved.

(3)   *Disjointness*   If a data item d_i appears in fragment R_i, then it should not appear in any other fragment. There is one exception to this, in the case of vertical fragmentation, where primary key attributes must be repeated to allow reconstruction. This rule ensures minimal redundancy.

In the case of horizontal fragmentation, a data item is a tuple; for vertical fragmentation, a data item is an attribute.

Types of fragmentation

There are two main types of fragmentation: **horizontal** and **vertical**. Horizontal fragments are subsets of tuples and vertical fragments are subsets of attributes, as illustrated in Figure 16.6.

There are also two other types of fragmentation: **mixed**, illustrated in Figure 16.7, and **derived**, a type of horizontal fragmentation. We illustrate the types of fragmentation using the instance of the *DreamHome* Database shown in Figure 3.3.

Horizontal fragmentation

Horizontal fragment	A horizontal fragment of a relation consists of a subset of the tuples of a relation.

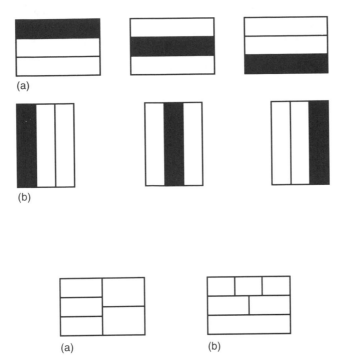

Figure 16.6
(a) Horizontal and
(b) vertical
fragmentation.

Figure 16.7 Mixed
fragmentation:
(a) vertical fragments,
horizontally
fragmented;
(b) horizontal
fragments, vertically
fragmented.

A horizontal fragment is produced by specifying a predicate that performs a restriction on the tuples in the relation. It is defined using the *Selection* operation of relational algebra (see Section 3.4.1). The Selection operation groups together tuples that have some common property; for example, the tuples are all used by the same application or at the same site. Given a relation R, a horizontal fragment is defined as:

$$\sigma_p(R)$$

where p is a predicate based on one or more attributes of the relation.

Example 16.2: Horizontal fragmentation

Assuming that there are only two property types, Flat and House, the horizontal fragmentation of Property_for_Rent by property type can be obtained as follows:

$$P_1 = \sigma_{\text{type}=\text{'House'}}(\text{Property \_for\_Rent})$$
$$P_2 = \sigma_{\text{type}=\text{'Flat'}}(\text{Property\_for\_Rent})$$

This produces two fragments, one consisting of those tuples where the Type value is 'House' and the other consisting of those tuples where the Type value is 'Flat', as shown in Figure 16.8. This particular fragmentation strategy may be advantageous if there are separate applications dealing with flats and houses. The fragmentation schema satisfies the correctness rules:

- *Completeness*   Each tuple in the relation appears in either fragment P_1 or P_2.

- *Reconstruction*   The Property_for_Rent relation can be reconstructed from the fragments using the Union operation, thus:

$$P_1 \cup P_2 = \text{Property\_for\_Rent}$$

- *Disjointness*   The fragments are disjoint; there can be no property type that is both 'House' and 'Flat'.

Fragment P_1

Pno	Street	Area	City	Pcode	Type	Rooms	Rent	Cno	Sno	Bno
PA14	16 Holhead	Dee	Aberdeen	AB7 5SU	House	6	650	CO46	SA9	B7
PG21	18 Dale Rd	Hyndland	Glasgow	G12	House	5	600	CO87	SG37	B3

Fragment P_2

Pno	Street	Area	City	Pcode	Type	Rooms	Rent	Cno	Sno	Bno
PL94	6 Argyll St	Kilburn	London	NW2	Flat	4	400	CO87	SL41	B5
PG4	6 Lawrence St	Partick	Glasgow	G11 9QX	Flat	3	350	CO40	SG14	B3
PG36	2 Manor Rd		Glasgow	G32 4QX	Flat	3	375	CO93	SG37	B3
PG16	5 Novar Dr	Hyndland	Glasgow	G12 9AX	Flat	4	450	CO93	SG14	B3

Figure 16.8
Horizontal fragmentation of Property_for_Rent by property type.

Sometimes, the choice of horizontal fragmentation strategy is obvious. However, in other cases, it is necessary to analyse the applications in detail. The analysis involves examination of the predicates or search conditions used by transactions or queries in the applications. The predicates may be **simple**, involving single attributes, or **complex**, involving multiple attributes. The predicates for each attribute may be single-valued, or multi-valued. In the latter case, the values may be discrete or involve ranges of values.

The fragmentation strategy involves finding a set of **minimal** (that is, *complete* and *relevant*) predicates that can be used as the basis for the fragmentation schema. A set of predicates is **complete** if and only if any two tuples in the same fragment are referenced with the same probability by any application. A predicate is **relevant** if there is at least one application that accesses the resulting fragments differently.

Vertical fragmentation

Vertical fragment	A vertical fragment of a relation consists of a subset of the attributes of a relation.

Vertical fragmentation groups together attributes that are used by some applications. It is defined using the *Projection* operation of relational algebra (see Section 3.4.1). Given a relation R, a vertical fragment is defined as:

$$\Pi_{a_1, \ldots, a_n}(R)$$

where $a_1, \ldots, a_n$ are attributes of the relation.

Example 16.3: Vertical fragmentation

The *DreamHome* payroll application requires the staff number Sno and the Position, Sex, DOB, Salary and NIN attributes of each member of staff; the personnel department requires the Sno, FName, LName, Address, Tel_No and Bno attributes. The vertical fragmentation of Staff for this example can be obtained as follows:

$$S_1 = \Pi_{\text{sno, position, sex, dob, salary, nin}}(\text{Staff})$$
$$S_2 = \Pi_{\text{sno, fname, lname, address, tel\_no, bno}}(\text{Staff})$$

This produces two fragments as shown in Figure 16.9. Note that both fragments contain the primary key, Sno, to enable the original relation to be reconstructed. The advantage of vertical fragmentation is that the fragments can be stored at the sites that need them. In addition, performance is improved, as the fragment is smaller than the original base relation. The fragmentation schema satisfies the correctness rules:

- *Completeness* Each attribute in the Staff relation appears in either fragment S_1 or S_2.

- *Reconstruction* The Staff relation can be reconstructed from the fragments using the Natural Join operation, thus:

$$S_1 \bowtie S_2 = \text{Staff}$$

- *Disjointness* The fragments are disjoint except for the primary key, which is necessary for reconstruction.

Fragment S_1

Sno	Position	Sex	DOB	Salary	NIN
SL21	Manager	M	1–Oct–45	30000	WK442011B
SG37	Snr Asst	F	10–Nov–60	12000	WL432514C
SG14	Deputy	M	24–Mar–58	18000	WL220658D
SA9	Assistant	F	19–Feb–70	9000	WM532187D
SG5	Manager	F	3–Jun–40	24000	WK588932E
SL41	Assistant	F	13–Jun–65	9000	WA290573K

Fragment S_2

Sno	FName	LName	Address	Tel_No	Bno
SL21	John	White	19 Taylor St, Cranford, London	0171–884–5112	B5
SG37	Ann	Beech	81 George St, Glasgow PA1 2JR	0141–848–3345	B3
SG14	David	Ford	63 Ashby St, Patrick, Glasgow G11	0141–339–2177	B3
SA9	Mary	Howe	2 Elm Pl, Aberdeen AB2 3SU		B7
SG5	Susan	Brand	5 Gt Western Rd, Glasgow G12	0141–334–2001	B3
SL41	Julie	Lee	28 Malvern St, Kilburn NW2	0181–554–3541	B5

Figure 16.9 Vertical fragmentation of Staff.

Vertical fragments are determined by establishing the **affinity** of one attribute to another. One way to do this is to create a matrix that shows the number of accesses that refer to each attribute pair. For example, a transaction that accesses attributes a_1, a_2 and a_4 of a relation R with attributes (a_1, a_2, a_3, a_4), can be represented by the following matrix:

$$
\begin{array}{c c c c c}
 & a_1 & a_2 & a_3 & a_4 \\
a_1 & & 1 & 0 & 1 \\
a_2 & & & 0 & 1 \\
a_3 & & & & 0 \\
a_4 & & & &
\end{array}
$$

The matrix is triangular; the diagonal does not need to be filled in and the lower half is a mirror image of the upper half. The 1s represent an access involving the corresponding attribute pair. The 1s are replaced by numbers representing the transaction frequency. A matrix is produced for each transaction and an overall matrix is produced showing the sum of all accesses for each attribute pair. Pairs with high affinity should appear in the same vertical fragment; pairs with low affinity may be separated. Clearly, working with single attributes and all major transactions may be a lengthy calculation.

Therefore, if you know some attributes are related, it may be prudent to work with groups of attributes instead.

This approach is known as **splitting**, and was first proposed by Navathe *et al.* (1984). It produces a set of non-overlapping fragments, which ensures compliance with the disjointness rule defined above. In fact, the non-overlapping characteristic applies only to attributes that are not part of the primary key. Primary key fields appear in every fragment and so can be omitted from the analysis. For additional information on this approach, the reader is referred to Ozsu and Valduriez (1991).

Mixed fragmentation

Sometimes, horizontal or vertical fragmentation of a database schema by itself is insufficient to adequately distribute the data for some applications. Instead, **mixed** or **hybrid** fragmentation may be useful.

Mixed fragment	A mixed fragment of a relation consists of a horizontal fragment that is subsequently vertically fragmented, or a vertical fragment that is then horizontally fragmented.

Mixed fragmentation is defined using the *Selection* and *Projection* operations of relational algebra. Given a relation R, a mixed fragment is defined as:

$$\sigma_p(\Pi_{a_1, \dots, a_n}(R)) \quad \text{or}$$
$$\Pi_{a_1, \dots, a_n}(\sigma_p(R))$$

where p is a predicate based on one or more attributes of R and $a_1, \dots, a_n$ are attributes of R.

Example 16.4: Mixed fragmentation ─────────────────

In Example 16.3, we vertically fragmented Staff for payroll purposes into:

$$S_1 = \Pi_{\text{sno, position, sex, dob, salary, nin}}(\text{Staff})$$
$$S_2 = \Pi_{\text{sno, fname, lname, address, tel\_no, bno}}(\text{Staff})$$

We could now horizontally fragment S_2 according to branch number:

$$S_{21} = \sigma_{\text{bno}='B3'}(S2)$$
$$S_{22} = \sigma_{\text{bno}='B5'}(S2)$$
$$S_{23} = \sigma_{\text{bno}='B7'}(S2)$$

This produces three fragments, one consisting of those tuples where branch number is B3, one consisting of those tuples where branch number is B5, and the other consisting of those tuples where the branch number is B7, as shown in Figure 16.10. The fragmentation schema satisfies the correctness rules:

- *Completeness* Each attribute in the Staff relation appears in either fragment S_1 or S_2; each (part) tuple appears in fragment S_1 and either fragment S_{21}, S_{22} or S_{23};

- *Reconstruction* The Staff relation can be reconstructed from the fragments using the Union and Natural Join operations, thus:

$$S_1 \bowtie (S_{21} \cup S_{22} \cup S_{23}) = \text{Staff}$$

- *Disjointness* The fragments are disjoint; there can be no staff that works in more than one branch and S_1 and S_2 are disjoint except for duplication of primary key.

Fragment S_1

Sno	Position	Sex	DOB	Salary	NIN
SL21	Manager	M	1–Oct–45	30000	WK442011B
SG37	Snr Asst	F	10–Nov–60	12000	WL432514C
SG14	Deputy	M	24–Mar–58	18000	WL220658D
SA9	Assistant	F	19–Feb–70	9000	WM532187D
SG5	Manager	F	3–Jun–40	24000	WK588932E
SL41	Assistant	F	13–Jun–65	9000	WA290573K

Fragment S_{21}

Sno	FName	LName	Address	Tel_No	Bno
SG37	Ann	Beech	81 George St, Glasgow PA1 2JR	0141–848–3345	B3
SG14	David	Ford	63 Ashby St, Partick, Glasgow G11	0141–339–2177	B3
SG5	Susan	Brand	5 Gt Western Rd, Glasgow G12	0141–334–2001	B3

Fragment S_{22}

Sno	FName	LName	Address	Tel_No	Bno
SL21	John	White	19 Taylor St, Cranford, London	0171–884–5112	B5
SL41	Julie	Lee	28 Malvern St, Kilburn NW2	0181–554–3541	B5

Fragment S_{23}

Sno	FName	LName	Address	Tel_No	Bno
SL9	Mary	Howe	2 Elm Pl, Aberdeen AB2 3SU		B7

Figure 16.10 Mixed fragmentation of Staff.

Derived horizontal fragmentation

Some applications may involve a join of two or more relations. If the relations are stored at different locations, there may be a significant overhead in processing the join. In such cases, it may be more appropriate to ensure that the relations, or fragments of relations, are at the same location. We can achieve this using derived horizontal fragmentation.

| **Derived** | A derived fragment of a relation is a horizontal fragment that |
| **fragment** | is based on the horizontal fragmentation of a parent relation. |

We use the term *child* to refer to the relation that contains the foreign key and *parent* to the relation containing the targeted primary key. Derived fragmentation is defined using the *Semi-Join* operation of relational algebra (see Section 3.4.1). Given a child relation R and parent S, the derived fragmentation of R is defined as:

$$R_i = R \triangleright_F S_i, \quad 1 \leqslant i \leqslant w$$

where w is the number of horizontal fragments defined on S and F is the join attribute.

Example 16.5:   Derived horizontal fragmentation _____

We may have an application that joins the Staff and Property_for_Rent relations together. For this example, we assume that Staff is horizontally fragmented according to the branch number, so that data relating to the branch is stored locally:

$$S_3 = \sigma_{bno = \text{'B3'}}(\text{Staff})$$
$$S_4 = \sigma_{bno = \text{'B5'}}(\text{Staff})$$
$$S_5 = \sigma_{bno = \text{'B7'}}(\text{Staff})$$

Thus, it would be useful to store property data using the same fragmentation strategy. This is achieved using derived fragmentation to horizontally fragment the Property_for_Rent relation according to branch number:

$$P_i = \text{Property\_for\_Rent} \triangleright_{bno} S_i, \quad 3 \leqslant i \leqslant 5$$

This produces three fragments, one consisting of those properties managed by staff at branch number B3, one consisting of those properties managed by staff at branch B5 and the other consisting of those properties managed by staff at branch B7, as shown in Figure 16.11. We can easily show that this fragmentation schema satisfies the correctness rules. We leave this as an exercise for the reader.

Fragment P_3

Pno	Street	Area	City	Pcode	Type	Rooms	Rent	Cno	Sno	Bno
PG4	6 Lawrence St	Partick	Glasgow	G11 9QX	Flat	3	350	CO40	SG14	B3
PG36	2 Manor Rd		Glasgow	G32 4QX	Flat	3	375	CO93	SG37	B3
PG21	18 Dale Rd	Hyndland	Glasgow	G12	House	5	600	CO87	SG37	B3
PG16	5 Novar Dr	Hyndland	Glasgow	G12 9AX	Flat	4	450	CO93	SG14	B3

Fragment P_4

Pno	Street	Area	City	Pcode	Type	Rooms	Rent	Cno	Sno	Bno
PL94	6 Argyll St	Kilburn	London	NW2	Flat	4	400	CO87	SL41	B5

Fragment P_5

Pno	Street	Area	City	Pcode	Type	Rooms	Rent	Cno	Sno	Bno
PA14	16 Holhead	Dee	Aberdeen	AB7 5SU	House	6	650	CO46	SA9	B7

Figure 16.11 Derived fragmentation of Property_for_Rent based on Staff.

If a relation contains more than one foreign key, it will be necessary to select one of the referenced relations as the parent. The choice can be based on the fragmentation used most frequently or the fragmentation with better join characteristics; that is, the join involving smaller fragments or the join that can be performed in parallel to a greater degree.

No fragmentation

A final strategy is not to fragment a relation. For example, the Branch relation contains only a small number of tuples, and is not updated very frequently. Rather than trying to horizontally fragment the relation on, for example, branch number, it would be more sensible to leave the relation whole and simply replicate the Branch relation at each site.

16.5 Transparencies in a DDBMS

The definition of a DDBMS given in Section 16.1.1 states that the system should make the distribution **transparent** to the user. Transparency hides implementation details from the user. For example, in a centralized DBMS, data independence is a form of transparency – it hides changes in the definition and organization of the data from the user. A distributed system may provide various levels of transparency. However, they all participate in the same overall objective: to make the use of the distributed database equivalent to that of a centralized database. All of the transparencies we discuss are rarely met by a single system. We can identify four main types of transparency in a distributed system:

- distribution transparency,
- transaction transparency,
- performance transparency,
- DBMS transparency.

16.5.1 Distribution transparency

Distribution transparency allows the user to perceive the database as a single, logical entity. If a DDBMS exhibits distribution transparency, then the user does not need to know the data is fragmented (**fragmentation transparency**), or the location of data items (**location transparency**).

If the user needs to know that the data is fragmented and the location of fragments then we call this **local mapping transparency**. These transparencies are ordered as we now discuss. To illustrate these concepts, we consider the distribution of the Staff relation given in Example 16.4, such that:

$$S_1 = \Pi_{\text{sno, position, sex, dob, salary, nin}}(\text{Staff}) \qquad \text{located at site 5}$$

$$S_2 = \Pi_{\text{sno, fname, lname, address, tel\_no, bno}}(\text{Staff})$$

$$S_{21} = \sigma_{\text{bno} = \text{'B3'}}(S_2) \qquad\qquad\qquad \text{located at site 3}$$

$$S_{22} = \sigma_{\text{bno} = \text{'B5'}}(S_2) \qquad\qquad\qquad \text{located at site 5}$$

$$S_{23} = \sigma_{\text{bno} = \text{'B7'}}(S_2) \qquad\qquad\qquad \text{located at site 7}$$

Fragmentation transparency

Fragmentation is the highest level of distribution transparency. If fragmentation transparency is provided by the DDBMS, then the user does not need to know that the data is fragmented. As a result, database accesses are based on the global schema, so the user does not need to specify fragment names or data locations. For example, to retrieve the names of all Managers, with fragmentation transparency we could write:

```
SELECT fname, lname
FROM STAFF
WHERE position = 'Manager';
```

This is the same SQL statement as we would write in a centralized system.

Location transparency

Location is the middle level of distribution transparency. The user must know how the data has been fragmented but still does not have to know the location of the data. The above query under location transparency now becomes:

> SELECT fname, lname
>
> FROM S_{21}
>
> WHERE sno IN (SELECT sno FROM S_1 WHERE position = 'Manager') UNION
>
> SELECT fname, lname
>
> FROM S_{22}
>
> WHERE sno IN (SELECT sno FROM S_1 WHERE position = 'Manager') UNION
>
> SELECT fname, lname
>
> FROM S_{23}
>
> WHERE sno IN (SELECT sno FROM S_1 WHERE position = 'Manager');

We now have to specify the names of the fragments in the query. We also have to use a join (or subquery) because the attributes Position and FName/LName appear in different vertical fragments. The main advantage of location transparency is that the database may be physically reorganized without impact on the application programs that access them.

Replication transparency

Closely related to location transparency is replication transparency, which means that the user is unaware of the replication of fragments. Replication transparency is implied by location transparency. However, it is possible for a system not to have location transparency but to have replication transparency.

Local mapping transparency

This is the lowest level of distribution transparency. With local mapping transparency, the user needs to specify both fragment names and the location of data items. The example query under local mapping transparency becomes:

SELECT fname, lname

FROM S_{21} *AT SITE* 3

WHERE sno IN (SELECT sno FROM S_1 *AT SITE* 5 WHERE position = 'Manager') UNION

SELECT fname, lname

FROM S_{22} *AT SITE* 5

WHERE sno IN (SELECT sno FROM S_1 *AT SITE* 5 WHERE position = 'Manager') UNION

SELECT fname, lname

FROM S_{23} *AT SITE* 7

WHERE sno IN (SELECT sno FROM S_1 *AT SITE* 5 WHERE position = 'Manager');

For the purposes of illustration, we have extended SQL with the keyword *AT SITE*, to express where a particular fragment is located. Clearly, this is a more complicated and time-consuming query for the user to enter than the first two. It is unlikely that a system that provided only this level of transparency would be acceptable to end users.

Naming transparency

As a corollary to the above distribution transparencies, we have **naming transparency**. As in a centralized database, each item in a distributed database must have a unique name. Therefore, the DDBMS must ensure that no two sites create a database object with the same name. One solution to this problem is to create a central **name server**, which has the responsibility for ensuring uniqueness of all names in the system. However, this approach results in:

- loss of some local autonomy;
- performance problems, if the central site becomes a bottleneck;
- low availability; if the central site fails, the remaining sites cannot create any new database objects.

An alternative solution is to prefix an object with the identifier of the site that created it. For example, the relation Branch created at site S_1 might be named S1.BRANCH. Similarly, we need to be able to identify each fragment and each of its copies. Thus, copy 2 of fragment 3 of the Branch relation created at site S_1 might be referred to as S1.BRANCH.F3.C2. However, this results in loss of distribution transparency.

An approach that resolves the problems with both these solutions uses **aliases** for each database object. Thus, S1.BRANCH.F3.C2 might be known as *local_branch* by the user at site S_1. The DDBMS has the task of mapping aliases to the appropriate database object.

16.5.2   Transaction Transparency

Transaction transparency in a DDBMS environment ensures that all distributed transactions maintain the distributed database's integrity and consistency. A **distributed transaction** accesses data stored at more than one location. Each transaction is divided into a number of **sub-transactions**, one for each site that has to be accessed; a sub-transaction is represented by an **agent**.

Example 16.6:   Distributed transaction _____

Consider a transaction T that prints out the name of all staff, using the fragmentation schema defined above as S_1, S_2, S_{21}, S_{22} and S_{23}. We can define three sub-transactions T_{s_3}, T_{s_5} and T_{s_7} to represent the agents at sites 3, 5 and 7, respectively. Each sub-transaction prints out the names of the staff at that site. The distributed transaction is shown in Figure 16.12. Note the inherent parallelism in the system: the sub-transactions at each site can execute concurrently.

Time	T_{s_3}	T_{s_5}	T_{s_7}
t_1	begin_transaction	begin_transaction	begin_transaction
t_2	read(fname, lname)	read(fname, lname)	read(fname, lname)
t_3	print(fname, lname)	print(fname, lname)	print(fname, lname)
t_4	end_transaction	end_transaction	end_transaction

Figure 16.12
Distributed
transaction.

The indivisibility of the distributed transaction is still fundamental to the transaction concept, but in addition, the DDBMS must also ensure the indivisibility of each sub-transaction (see Section 15.1.1). Therefore, not only must the DDBMS ensure synchronization of sub-transactions with other local transactions that are executing concurrently at a site, but it must also ensure synchronization of sub-transactions with global transactions running simultaneously at the same or different sites. Transaction transparency in a distributed system is complicated by the fragmentation, allocation and replication schemas. We consider two further aspects of transaction transparency: **concurrency transparency** and **failure transparency**.

Concurrency transparency

Concurrency transparency is provided by the DDBMS if the results of all concurrent transactions (distributed and non-distributed) execute *independently* and are logically *consistent* with the results that are obtained if the transactions are executed one at a time, in some arbitrary serial order. These are the same fundamental principles as we discussed for the centralized DBMS in Section 15.2.2. However, there is the added complexity that the DDBMS must ensure that both global and local transactions do not interfere with each other. Similarly, the DDBMS must ensure the consistency of all sub-transactions of the global transaction.

Replication makes the issue of concurrency more complex. If a copy of a replicated data item is updated, the update must eventually be propagated to all copies. An obvious strategy is to propagate the changes as part of the original transaction, making it an atomic operation. However, if one of the sites holding a copy is not reachable when the update is being processed, because either the site or the communication link has failed, then the transaction is delayed until the site is reachable. If there are many copies of the data item, the probability of the transaction succeeding decreases exponentially. An alternative strategy is to limit the update propagation to only those sites that are currently available. The remaining sites must be updated when they become available again. We discuss distributed concurrency control in Section 16.7.

Failure transparency

In Section 15.3.2, we stated that a centralized DBMS must provide a recovery mechanism that ensures that, in the presence of failures, transactions are **atomic** – either all the operations of the transaction are carried out or none at all. Furthermore, once a transaction has committed, the changes are **durable** (or permanent). We also examined the types of failure that could occur in a centralized system, namely system crashes, media failures, software errors, carelessness, natural physical disasters and sabotage. In the distributed environment, the DDBMS must also cater for:

- the loss of a message,
- the failure of a communication link,
- the failure of a site,
- network partitioning.

The DDBMS must ensure the atomicity of the global transaction, which means ensuring that sub-transactions of the global transaction either all commit or all abort. Thus, the DDBMS must synchronize the global transaction to ensure that all sub-transactions have completed successfully before recording a final COMMIT for the global transaction. For example, consider a global transaction that has to update data at two sites, S_1 and S_2, say. The sub-transaction at site S_1 completes successfully and commits, but the sub-transaction at site S_2 is unable to commit and rolls back the changes to ensure local consistency. The distributed database is now in an inconsistent state: we are unable to uncommit the data at site S_1, due to the durability property of the sub-transaction at S_1. We discuss distributed recovery control in Section 16.9.

16.5.3 Performance Transparency

Performance transparency requires a DDBMS to perform as if it were a centralized DBMS. In a distributed environment, the system should not suffer any performance degradation due to the distributed architecture, for example, the presence of the network. Performance transparency also requires the DDBMS to determine the most cost-effective strategy to execute a request.

In a centralized DBMS, the Query Processor (QP) must evaluate every data request and find an optimal execution strategy, consisting of an ordered sequence of operations on the database. In a distributed environment, the Distributed Query Processor (DQP) maps a data request into an ordered sequence of operations on the local databases. It has the added complexity of taking into account the fragmentation, replication and allocation schemas. The DQP has to decide:

- which fragment to access;
- which copy of a fragment to use, if the fragment is replicated;
- which location to use.

The DQP produces an execution strategy that is optimized with respect to some cost function. Typically, the costs associated with a distributed request include:

- the access time (I/O) cost involved in accessing the physical data on disk;
- the CPU time cost incurred when performing operations on data in main memory;
- the communication cost associated with the transmission of data across the network;

The first two factors are the only ones considered in a centralized system. In a distributed environment, the DDBMS must take account of the communication cost, which may be the most dominant factor. This is certainly true for slow communications networks such as WANs with a bandwidth of a few kilobytes per second. In such cases, optimization may ignore I/O and CPU costs. However, some communications networks have a bandwidth comparable with that of disks, such as LANs. In such cases, optimization should not ignore I/O and CPU costs entirely.

One approach to query optimization minimizes the total cost of time that will be incurred in executing the query (Sacco and Yao, 1982). An alternative approach minimizes the response time of the query, in which case the DQP attempts to maximize the parallel execution of operations (Epstein *et al.*, 1978). Sometimes, the response time will be significantly less than the total cost time. The following example, adapted from Rothnie and Goodman (1977), illustrates the wide variation in response times that can arise from different, but plausible, execution strategies.

Example 16.7: Distributed query processing

Consider a simplified *DreamHome* relational schema, consisting of the following three relations:

Property(Pno, City)	10 000 records stored in London
Renter(Rno, Max_Price)	100 000 records stored in Glasgow
Viewing(Pno, Rno)	1 000 000 records stored in London

To list the properties in Aberdeen that have been viewed by clients who have a maximum price limit greater than £200,000, we can use the SQL query:

```
SELECT p.pno
FROM property p, renter r, viewing v
WHERE p.pno = v.pno AND r.rno = v.rno AND
    p.city = 'Aberdeen' AND max_price > 200000;
```

For simplicity, assume that each tuple in each relation is 100 characters long, there are 10 renters with a maximum price greater than £200,000, there are 100 000 viewings for Aberdeen and computation time is negligible compared to communication time. The communication system has a data transmission rate of 10 000 characters per second and a 1 second access delay to send a message from one site to another.

Rothnie identifies six possible strategies for this query and associated response times. We calculate the communication time using the algorithm given in Section 16.2.

Strategy 1: Move the Renter relation to London and process query there:

$$\text{Time} = 1 + (100\,000 * 100/10\,000) \simeq 16.7 \text{ minutes}$$

Strategy 2: Move the Property and Viewing relations to Glasgow and process query there:

$$\text{Time} = 2 + [(1\,000\,000 + 10\,000) * 100/10\,000] \simeq 28 \text{ hours}$$

Strategy 3: Join the Property and Viewing relations at London, select tuples for Aberdeen properties and then for each of these tuples in turn, check at Glasgow to determine if the associated Renter price > £200,000. The check for each tuple involves two messages: a query and a response.

$$\text{Time} = 100\,000 * [1 + 100/10\,000] + 100\,000 * 1 \simeq 2.3 \text{ days}$$

Strategy 4: Select renters with price > £200,000 at Glasgow and for each one found, check at London to see if there is a viewing involving that renter and an Aberdeen property. Again, two messages are needed:

$$\text{Time} = 10 * [1 + 100/10\,000] + 10 * 1 \simeq 20 \text{ seconds}$$

Strategy 5: Join Property and Viewing relations at London, select Aberdeen properties and project result over Pno and Rno, and move this result to Glasgow for matching with price > £200,000. For simplicity, we assume that the projected result is still 100 characters long:

$$\text{Time} = 1 + (100\,000 * 100/10\,000) \simeq 16.7 \text{ minutes}$$

Strategy 6: Select renters with price > £200,000 at Glasgow and move the result to London for matching with Aberdeen properties:

$$\text{Time} = 1 + (10 * 100/10\,000) \simeq 1 \text{ second}$$

The strategies and results are summarized in Table 16.4. The response times vary from 1 second to 2.3 days, yet each strategy is a legitimate way to execute the query! Clearly, if the wrong strategy is chosen, then the effect can be devastating to acceptable system performance. To complete our discussion of query processing, we briefly examine some of the issues that have to be considered when designing a distributed query processor, namely: timing, statistics and distributed joins.

Table 16.4 Comparison of distributed query processing strategies.

	Strategy	Time
(1)	Move Renter relation to London and process query there.	16.7 minutes
(2)	Move Property and Viewing relations to Glasgow and process query there.	28 hours
(3)	Join Property and Viewing relations at London, select tuples for Aberdeen properties and for each of these in turn, check at Glasgow to determine if associated price > £200,000.	2.3 days
(4)	Select renters with price > £200,000 at Glasgow and for each one found, check at London for a viewing involving that renter and an Aberdeen property.	20 seconds
(5)	Join Property and Viewing relations at London, select Aberdeen properties and project result over pno and rno and move this result to Glasgow for matching with price > £200,000.	16.7 minutes
(6)	Select renters with price > £200,000 at Glasgow and move the result to London for matching with Aberdeen properties.	1 second

Distributed joins

The join is the costliest of the relational operations. One approach used in distributed query optimization is to replace joins by combinations of semijoins (see Section 3.4.1). The semi-join operator has the important property of reducing the size of the operand relation. When the main cost component is communication time, the semi-join operator is particularly useful for improving the processing of distributed joins by reducing the amount of data transferred between sites.

For example, suppose we wish to evaluate the join expression $R_1 \bowtie_x R_2$ at site S_2, where R_1 and R_2 are fragments stored at sites S_1 and S_2, respectively. R_1 and R_2 are defined over the attributes $A = (a_1, a_2, \ldots, a_n)$ and $B = (b_1, b_2, \ldots, b_m)$, respectively. We can achieve this using the semi-join operation. First, note that we can rewrite a join as:

$$R_1 \bowtie_x R_2 = (R_1 \ltimes_x R_2) \bowtie R_2$$

We can therefore evaluate the join as follows:

(1) Evaluate $R' = \Pi_x(R_2)$ at S_2 (only need join attributes at S_1).
(2) Transfer R' to site S_1.
(3) Evaluate $R'' = R_1 \ltimes_x R'$ at S_1.

(4)   Transfer R'' to site S_2.

(5)   Evaluate $R'' \bowtie_x R_2$ at S_2.

The use of semi-joins is beneficial if there are only a few tuples of R_1 that participate in the join of R_1 and R_2. The join approach is better if most of tuples of R_1 participate in the join, because the semi-join approach requires an additional transfer of a projection on the join attribute.

16.5.4   DBMS Transparency

DBMS transparency hides the knowledge that the local DBMSs may be different, and is therefore only applicable to heterogeneous distributed systems. It is one of the most difficult transparencies to provide as a generalization. We discussed the problems associated with the provision of heterogeneous systems in Section 16.1.3.

16.6   Distributed Transaction Management

In Section 16.5.2, we noted that the objectives of distributed transaction processing are the same as those of centralized systems, although more complex because the DDBMS must also ensure the indivisibility of the global transaction and each sub-transaction. In Section 15.1.2, we identified four high-level database modules that handle transactions, concurrency and recovery control in a centralized DBMS. The **transaction manager** coordinates transactions on behalf of application programs, communicating with the **scheduler**, the module responsible for implementing a particular strategy for concurrency control. The objective of the scheduler is to maximize concurrency without allowing concurrently executing transactions to interfere with one another and so compromise the integrity or consistency of the database. The **recovery manager** ensures that the database is restored to the state it was in before the start of the transaction, and therefore a consistent state, in the event of a failure occurring during the transaction. There is also the **buffer manager** that transfers data between disk storage and main memory.

    In a distributed system, these modules still exist in each local DBMS. In addition, there is also a **global transaction manager** or **transaction co-ordinator** at each site, to coordinate the execution of both the global and local transactions initiated at that site. Inter-site communication is still through the Data Communications component (transaction managers at different sites do not communicate directly with each other). The procedure to execute a global transaction initiated at site S_1 is as follows:

(1)   The transaction coordinator (TC$_1$) at site S_1 divides the transaction into a number of sub-transactions, using information held in the global data dictionary.

(2)   The data communications component at site S_1 sends the sub-transactions to the appropriate sites, S_2 and S_3, say.

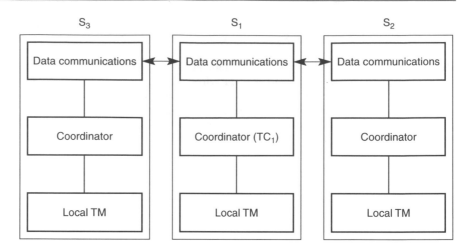

Figure 16.13
Coordination of
distributed
transaction.

(3) The transaction coordinators at S_2 and S_3 coordinate these sub-transactions. The results of sub-transactions are communicated back to TC_1 via the data communications components. The process is depicted in Figure 16.13.

16.7 Distributed Concurrency Control

In this section, we present the protocols that can be used to provide concurrency control in a distributed system. We start by examining the objectives of distributed concurrency control.

16.7.1 Objectives

Given that the system has not failed, all concurrency control mechanisms must ensure that consistency of data items is preserved, and that each atomic action is completed in finite time. In addition, a good concurrency control mechanism for distributed systems should:

- be resilient to site and communication failure;
- permit parallelism to satisfy performance requirements;
- incur modest computational and storage overhead;
- perform satisfactorily in a network environment that has significant communication delay;
- place few constraints on the structure of atomic actions (Kohler, 1981).

In Section 15.2.1, we discussed the types of problems that can arise when multiple users are allowed to access the database concurrently, namely the problems of lost update, uncommitted dependency and inconsistent analysis. These problems also exist in the distributed environment. However, there are additional problems that can arise as a result of data distribution. One such problem is the **multiple-copy consistency problem**. This problem occurs when there is more than one copy of a data item in different locations. Clearly, to maintain consistency of the global database, when a replicated data item is updated at one site all other copies of the data item must also be updated. If a copy is not updated, the database becomes inconsistent.

16.7.2 Distributed Serializability

The concept of serializability, which we discussed in Section 15.2.2, can be extended for the distributed environment to cater for data distribution. If the schedule of transaction execution at each site is serializable, then the **global schedule** (the union of all local schedules) is also serializable provided local serialization orders are identical. This requires that all sub-transactions appear in the same order in the equivalent serial schedule at all sites. Thus, if the sub-transaction of T_i at site S_1 is denoted T_i^1, we must ensure that if:

$T_i^1 < T_j^1$ then
$T_i^x < T_j^x$ for all sites S_x at which T_i and T_j have sub-transactions.

The solutions to concurrency control in a distributed environment are based on the two main approaches of locking and timestamping, which we considered for centralized systems in Section 15.2. Thus, given a set of transactions to be executed concurrently, then:

- Locking guarantees that the concurrent execution is equivalent to *some* (unpredictable) serial execution of those transactions.

- Timestamping guarantees that the concurrent execution is equivalent to a *specific* serial execution of those transactions, corresponding to the order of the timestamps.

If the database is either centralized or partitioned, but not replicated, so that there is only one copy of each data item, and all transactions are either local or can be performed at one remote site, then the protocols discussed in Section 15.2 can be used. However, these protocols have to be extended if data is replicated or transactions involve data at more than one site. In addition, if we adopt a locking-based protocol, we have to ensure that deadlock does not occur. This involves checking for deadlock not only at each local level, but also at the global level, which entails combining deadlock data from more than one site. We consider distributed deadlock in Section 16.8.

16.7.3 Locking Protocols

In this section, we present some two-phase locking (2PL) protocols that can be employed to ensure serializability for distributed systems: centralized 2PL, primary copy 2PL, distributed 2PL and majority locking.

Centralized 2PL

With this protocol, there is a single site that maintains all locking information (Alsberg and Day, 1976; Garcia-Molina, 1979). There is only one scheduler or lock manager for the whole of the distributed DBMS that can grant and release locks. The centralized two-phase locking protocol for a global transaction initiated at site S_1 works as follows:

(1)   The transaction coordinator at site S_1 divides the transaction into a number of sub-transactions, using information held in the global data dictionary. The coordinator has responsibility for ensuring that consistency is maintained. If the transaction involves an update of a data item that is replicated, the coordinator must ensure that all copies of the data item are updated. Thus, the coordinator requests write locks on all copies before updating each copy and releasing the locks. The coordinator can elect to use any copy of the data item for reads, generally the copy at its site, if one exists.

(2)   The local transaction managers involved in the global transaction request and release locks from the centralized lock manager, using the normal rules for two-phase locking.

(3)   The centralized lock manager checks that a request for a lock on a data item is compatible with the locks that currently exist. If it is, the lock manager sends a message back to the originating site acknowledging that the lock has been granted. Otherwise, it puts the request in a queue until the lock can be granted.

A variation of this scheme is for the transaction coordinator to make all locking requests on behalf of the local transaction managers. In this case, the lock manager interacts only with the transaction coordinator and not with the individual local transaction managers.

The advantage of centralized 2PL is that the implementation is relatively straightforward. Deadlock detection is no more difficult than that of a centralized DBMS, because all lock information is maintained by one lock manager. The disadvantages with centralization in a distributed system are bottlenecks and lower reliability. As all lock requests go to one central site, that site may become a bottleneck. The system may be less reliable since the failure of the central site would cause major system failures. Communication costs are relatively low. For example, a global update operation that has agents at n sites may require a minimum of $2n + 3$ messages with a centralized lock manager:

- 1 lock request
- 1 lock grant message
- n update messages
- n acknowledgements
- 1 unlock request.

Primary copy 2PL

This protocol attempts to overcome the disadvantages of centralized 2PL by distributing the lock managers to a number of sites. Each lock manager is then responsible for managing the locks for a set of data items. For each replicated data item, one copy is chosen as the **primary copy**; the other copies are called **slave copies**. The choice of which site to choose as the primary site is flexible, and the site that is chosen to manage the locks for a primary copy need not hold the primary copy of that item (Stonebraker and Neuhold, 1977).

The protocol is a straightforward extension of centralized 2PL. The main difference is that when an item is to be updated, the transaction coordinator must determine where the primary copy is, to send the lock requests to the appropriate lock manager. It is only necessary to write-lock the primary copy of the data item that is to be updated. Once the primary copy has been updated, the change can be propagated to the slave copies. The propagation should be carried out as soon as possible to prevent other transactions reading out-of-date values. However, it is not strictly necessary to carry out the updates as an atomic operation. This protocol guarantees only that the primary copy is current.

This approach can be used when data is selectively replicated, updates are infrequent, and sites do not always need the very latest version of data. The disadvantages of this approach are that deadlock handling is more complex due to multiple lock managers, and that there is still a degree of centralization in the system: lock requests for a specific primary copy can be handled only by one site. This latter disadvantage can be partially overcome by nominating backup sites to hold locking information. This approach has lower communication costs and better performance than centralized 2PL, since there is less locking.

Distributed 2PL

This protocol again attempts to overcome the disadvantages of centralized 2PL, this time by distributing the lock managers to every site. Each lock manager is then responsible for managing the locks for the data at that site. If the data is not replicated, this protocol is equivalent to primary copy 2PL. Otherwise, distributed 2PL implements a Read-One-Write-All (ROWA) replica control protocol. This means that any copy of a replicated item can be used for a read operation, but all copies must be write-locked before an item can be updated. This scheme deals with locks in a decentralized manner, thus avoiding the drawbacks of centralized control. However, the disadvantages of this approach are that deadlock handling is more complex due to multiple lock managers and that communication costs are higher than primary copy 2PL, as all items must be locked before update. A global update operation that has agents at n sites, may require a minimum of $5n$ messages with this protocol:

- n lock request messages
- n lock grant messages

- n update messages
- n acknowledgements
- n unlock requests.

This could be reduced to $4n$ messages if the unlock requests are omitted and handled by the final commit operation. Distributed 2PL is used in System R* (Mohan *et al.*, 1986).

Majority locking

This protocol is an extension of distributed 2PL to overcome having to lock all copies of a replicated item before an update. Again, the system maintains a lock manager at each site to manage the locks for all data at that site. When a transaction wishes to read or write a data item that is replicated at n sites, it must send a lock request to more than half the n sites where the item is stored. The transaction cannot proceed until it obtains locks on a majority of the copies. If the transaction does not receive a majority within a certain timeout period, it cancels its request and informs all sites of the cancellation. If it receives a majority, it informs all sites that it has the lock. Since a read lock is shareable, any number of transactions can simultaneously hold a read lock on a majority of the copies; however, only one transaction can hold a write lock on a majority of the copies (Thomas, 1979).

Again, this scheme avoids the drawbacks of centralized control. The disadvantages are that the protocol is more complicated, deadlock detection is more complex and locking requires at least $[(n + 1)/2]$ messages for lock requests and $[(n + 1)/2]$ messages for unlock requests. The technique works but is overly strong in the case of read locks: correctness only requires that a single copy of a data item be locked, namely the item that is read, but this technique requests locks on a majority of copies.

16.7.4 Timestamp Protocols

We discussed timestamp methods for centralized databases in Section 15.2.5. The objective of timestamping is to order transactions globally in such a way that older transactions, transactions with *smaller* timestamps, get priority in the event of conflict. In a distributed environment, we still need to generate unique timestamps both locally and globally. Clearly, using the system clock or an incremental event counter at each site, as proposed in Section 15.2.5, would be unsuitable. Clocks at different sites would not be synchronized; equally well, if an event counter was used, it would be possible for different sites to generate the same value for the counter.

The general approach in distributed systems is to use the concatenation of the local timestamp with a unique site identifier, ⟨local timestamp, site identifier⟩. The site identifier is placed in the least significant position to ensure that events can be ordered according to their occurrence as opposed to their location. To prevent a busy site generating larger timestamps than slower sites, sites synchronize their timestamps. Each site includes their timestamps in inter-site messages. On receiving a message, a site compares its timestamp with the timestamp in the message and, if its timestamp is smaller, sets it to some value greater than the message timestamp.

16.8   Distributed Deadlock Management

Any locking-based concurrency control algorithm (and some timestamp-based algorithms that require transactions to wait) may result in deadlocks, as discussed in Section 15.2.4. In a distributed environment, deadlock detection may be more complicated if lock management is not centralized, as the following example shows.

Example 16.8: Distributed deadlock _____

Consider three transactions T_1, T_2 and T_3 with:

- T_1 initiated at site S_1 and creating an agent at site S_2,
- T_2 initiated at site S_2 and creating an agent at site S_3,
- T_3 initiated at site S_3 and creating an agent at site S_1.

The transactions set read and write locks as illustrated below, where read_lock(T_i, x_j) denotes a read lock by transaction T_i on data item x_j and write_lock(T_i, x_j) denotes a write lock by transaction T_i on data item x_j.

Time	S_1	S_2	S_3
t_1	read_lock(T_1, x_1)	write_lock(T_2, y_2)	read_lock(T_3, z_3)
t_2	write_lock(T_1, y_1)	write_lock(T_2, z_2)	
t_3	write_lock(T_3, x_1)	write_lock(T_1, y_2)	write_lock(T_2, z_3)

We can construct the wait-for-graphs (WFGs) for each site, as shown in Figure 16.14.

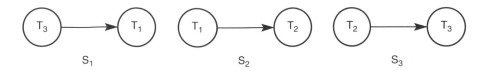

Figure 16.14   Wait-for-graphs for sites S_1, S_2 and S_3.

There are no cycles in the individual WFGs, which might lead us to believe that deadlock does not exist. However, if we combine the WFGs, as illustrated in Figure 16.15, we can see that deadlock does exist: there is a cycle from:

$$T_3 \rightarrow T_1 \rightarrow T_2 \rightarrow T_3.$$

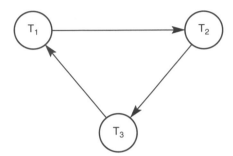

Figure 16.15
Combined wait-for-graphs for sites S_1, S_2 and S_3.

The above example demonstrates that in a distributed system it is not sufficient for each site to build its own local WFG to check for deadlock. It is also necessary to construct a global WFG, which is the union of all local WFGs. There are three common methods for handling deadlock detection in distributed systems: **centralized**, **hierarchical** and **distributed** deadlock detection.

Centralized deadlock detection

With centralized deadlock detection, a single site is appointed as the Deadlock Detection Coordinator (DDC). The DDC has the responsibility of constructing and maintaining the global WFG. Periodically, each lock manager transmits its local WFG to the DDC. The DDC builds the global WFG and checks for cycles in it. If one or more cycles exist, the DDC must break each cycle by selecting the transactions to be rolled back and restarted. The DDC must inform all sites that are involved in the processing of these transactions that they are to be rolled back and restarted.

To minimize the amount of data sent, a lock manager need send only the changes that have occurred in the local WFG since it sent the last one. These changes would represent the addition or removal of edges in the local WFG. The disadvantage with this centralized approach is that the system may be less reliable, since the failure of the central site would cause problems.

Hierarchical deadlock detection

With hierarchical deadlock detection, the sites in the network are organized into a hierarchy. Each site sends its local WFG to the deadlock detection site above it in the hierarchy (Menasce and Muntz, 1979). Figure 16.16 illustrates a hierarchy for eight sites, S_1 to S_8. The level 1 leaves are the sites themselves, where local deadlock detection is performed. The level 2 nodes, DD_{ij}, detect deadlock involving adjacent sites i and j. The level 3 nodes detect deadlock between four adjacent sites. The root of the tree is a global deadlock detector that would detect deadlock between, for example, sites S_1 and S_8.

The hierarchical approach reduces the dependence on a centralized detection site, thereby reducing communication costs. However, it is much more complex to implement, particularly in the presence of site and communication failures.

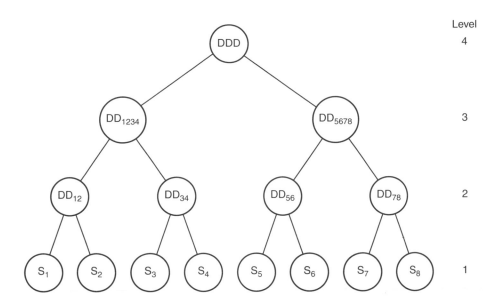

Level
4

3

2

1

Figure 16.16
Hierarchical deadlock detection.

Distributed deadlock detection

There have been various proposals for distributed deadlock detection algorithms, but here we consider one of the most well-known distributed deadlock detection methods that was developed by Obermarck (1982). In this approach, an external node, T_{ext}, is added to a local WFG to indicate an agent at a remote site. When a transaction T_1 at site S_1, say, creates an agent at another site, S_2 say, then an edge is added to the local WFG from T_1 to the T_{ext} node. Similarly, at site S_2, an edge is added to the local WFG from the T_{ext} node to the agent of T_1.

For example, the global WFG shown in Figure 16.15 would be represented by the local WFGs at sites S_1, S_2 and S_3, shown in Figure 16.17. The edges in the local WFG linking agents to T_{ext} are labelled with the site involved. For example, the edge connecting T_1 and T_{ext} at site S_1 is labelled S_2, as this edge represents an agent created by T_1 at site S_2.

If a local WFG contains a cycle that does not involve the T_{ext} node, then the site and the DDBMS are in deadlock. A global deadlock potentially exists if the local WFG contains a cycle involving the T_{ext} node. However, the existence of such a cycle does not necessarily mean that there is global deadlock, since the T_{ext} nodes may represent different agents, but cycles of this form must appear in the WFGs if there is deadlock. To determine whether

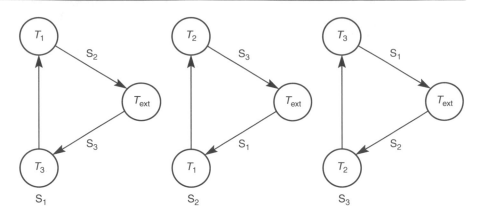

Figure 16.17
Distributed deadlock
detection.

there is a deadlock, the graphs have to be merged. If a site, S_1 say, has a potential deadlock, its local WFG will be of the form:

$$T_{ext} \to T_i \to T_j \to \ldots \to T_k \to T_{ext}.$$

To prevent sites transmitting their WFGs to each other, a simple strategy allocates a timestamp to each transaction and imposes the rule that S_1 only transmits its WFG to the site for which transaction T_k is waiting, S_k say, if $ts(T_i) < ts(T_k)$. If we assume that $ts(T_i) < ts(T_k)$, then to check for deadlock site S_1 would transmit its local WFG to S_k. Site S_k can now add this information to its local WFG and check for cycles not involving T_{ext} in the extended graph. If there is no such cycle, the process continues until either a cycle appears, in which case one transaction is rolled back and restarted together with all its agents, or the entire global WFG is constructed and no cycle has been detected. In this case, there is no deadlock in the system. Obermarck proved that if global deadlock exists, then this procedure will eventually cause a cycle to appear at some site.

The three local WFGs in Figure 16.17 contain cycles:

S_1: $T_{ext} \to T_3 \to T_1 \to T_{ext}$
S_2: $T_{ext} \to T_1 \to T_2 \to T_{ext}$
S_3: $T_{ext} \to T_2 \to T_3 \to T_{ext}.$

In this example, we could transmit the local WFG for site S_1 to the site for which transaction T_1 is waiting: that is, site S_2. The local WFG at S_2 is extended to include this information and becomes:

S_2: $T_{ext} \to T_3 \to T_1 \to T_2 \to T_{ext}.$

This still contains a potential deadlock, so we would transmit this WFG to the site for which transaction T_2 is waiting: that is, site S_3. The local WFG at S_3 is extended to:

S_3: $T_{ext} \to T_3 \to T_1 \to T_2 \to T_3 \to T_{ext}.$

This global WFG contains a cycle that does not involve the T_{ext} node, so we can conclude that deadlock exists and an appropriate recovery protocol must be invoked. Distributed deadlock detection methods are potentially more robust than the hierarchical or centralized methods, but since no one site contains all the information necessary to detect deadlock, a lot of inter-site communication may be required.

16.9 Distributed Recovery Control

In this section, we discuss the protocols that are used to handle failures in a distributed environment.

16.9.1 Failures in a Distributed Environment

In Section 16.5.2, we mentioned four types of failure that are particular to distributed systems:

- the loss of a message,
- the failure of a communication link,
- the failure of a site,
- network partitioning.

The loss of messages, or improperly ordered messages, are the responsibility of the computer network. As such, we assume they are handled transparently by the Data Communications component of the DDBMS, and we concentrate on the remaining types of failures.

A DDBMS is highly dependent on the ability of all sites in the network to be able to communicate reliably with one another. In the past, communications were not always reliable. Although network technology has improved significantly and current networks are much more reliable, communication failures can still occur. In particular, communication failures can result in the network becoming split into two or more **partitions**, where sites within the same partition can communicate with one another, but not with sites in other partitions. Figure 16.18 shows an example of network partitioning where,

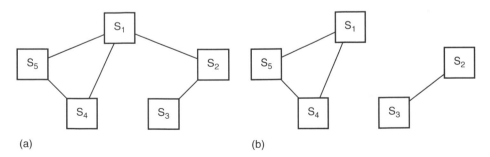

(a)   (b)

Figure 16.18
Partitioning of a network: (a) before failure; (b) after failure.

following the failure of the line connecting sites (S_1, S_2), sites (S_1, S_4, S_5) are partitioned from sites (S_2, S_3).

In some cases, it is difficult to distinguish whether a communication link or a site has failed. For example, suppose that site S_1 cannot communicate with site S_2 within a fixed (timeout) period. It could be that site S_2 has crashed or the network has gone down. It could be that the communication link has failed. It could be that the network is partitioned. It could also be that site S_2 is currently very busy and has not had the time to respond to the message. Choosing the correct value for the timeout, which will allow S_1 to conclude that it cannot communicate with site S_2, is difficult.

16.9.2 How Failures Affect Recovery

As with local recovery control, distributed recovery control aims to maintain the **atomicity** and **durability** of distributed transactions. To ensure the atomicity of the global transaction, the DDBMS must ensure that sub-transactions of the global transaction either all commit or all abort. If the DDBMS detects that a site has failed or become inaccessible, it needs to carry out the following steps:

- Abort any transactions that are affected by the failure.
- Flag the site as failed, to prevent any other site from trying to use it.
- Check periodically to see whether the site has recovered, or alternatively, wait for the failed site to broadcast when it has recovered.
- On restart, the failed site must initiate a recovery procedure to abort any partial transactions that were active at the time of the failure.
- After local recovery, the failed site must update its copy of the database to make it consistent with the rest of the system.

If a network partition occurs as in the above example, the DDBMS must ensure that if agents of the same global transaction are active in different partitions, then it must not be possible for S_1 and other sites in the same partition to decide to commit the global transaction, while S_2 and other sites in its partition decide to abort it. This would violate global transaction atomicity.

Distributed recovery protocols

As mentioned earlier, recovery in a DDBMS is complicated by the fact that atomicity is required for both the local sub-transactions and for the global transactions themselves. The recovery techniques described in Section 15.3 guarantee the atomicity of sub-transactions, but the DDBMS needs to ensure the atomicity of the global transaction. This involves modifying the commit and abort processing so that a global transaction does not commit or abort until all its sub-transactions have successfully committed or aborted. In addition, the modified protocol should cater for both site and communication failures to ensure that the failure of one site will not affect processing at another site. In other words, operational sites should not be left blocked. Protocols that obey this are referred to as **non-blocking** protocols. In this section, we consider two common commit protocols suitable for distributed systems: two-phase commit (2PC); and three-phase commit (3PC), a non-blocking protocol.

We assume that every global transaction has one site that acts as **coordinator** for that transaction. This will generally be the site at which the transaction was initiated. Sites at which the global transaction has agents are called **participants**. We assume that the coordinator knows the identity of all participants, and each participant knows the identity of the coordinator but not necessarily of each other.

16.9.3   Two-Phase Commit (2PC)

As the name implies, 2PC operates in two phases: a **voting phase** and a **decision phase**. The basic idea is that the coordinator asks all participants whether they are prepared to commit the transaction. If one participant votes to abort, or fails to respond within a timeout period, then the coordinator instructs all participants to abort the transaction. If all vote to commit, then the coordinator instructs all participants to commit the transaction. The global decision must be adopted by all participants. If a participant votes to abort, then it is free to abort the transaction immediately; in fact, any site is free to abort a transaction at any time up until it votes to commit. This type of abort is known as a **unilateral abort**. If a participant votes to commit, then it must wait for the coordinator to broadcast either the global-commit or global-abort message. This protocol assumes that each site has its own local log, and can therefore rollback or commit the transaction reliably. 2PC involves processes waiting for messages from other sites. To avoid processes being blocked unnecessarily, a system of timeouts is used. The procedure for the coordinator at commit is as follows:

Phase 1

(1)   Write a *begin_commit* record to the log file and force-write it to stable storage. Send a PREPARE message to all participants. Wait for participants to respond within a timeout period.

Phase 2

(2)   If a participant returns an ABORT vote, write an *abort* record to the log file and force-write it to stable storage. Send a GLOBAL_ABORT message to all participants. Wait for participants to acknowledge within a timeout period.

(3)   If a participant returns a READY_COMMIT vote, update a list of participants who have responded. If all participants have voted commit, write a *commit* record to the log file and force-write it to stable storage. Send a GLOBAL_COMMIT message to all participants. Wait for participants to acknowledge within a timeout period.

(4)   Once all acknowledgements have been received, write an *end_transaction* message to the log file. If a site does not acknowledge, resend the global decision until an acknowledgement is received.

The coordinator must wait until it has received the votes from all participants. If a site fails to vote, then the default vote of abort is assumed by the coordinator and a global abort message is broadcast to all participants. The issue of what happens to the failed participant on restart will be discussed shortly. The procedure for a participant at commit is as follows:

(1)   When the participant receives a PREPARE message, then either:

(a)   write a *ready_commit* record to the log file and force-write all log records for the transaction to stable storage. Send a READY_COMMIT message to the coordinator; or

(b)   write an *abort* record to the log file and force-write it to stable storage. Send an ABORT message to the coordinator. Unilaterally abort the transaction.

Wait for the coordinator to respond within a timeout period.

(2)   If the participant receives a GLOBAL_ABORT message, write an *abort* record to the log file and force-write it to stable storage. Abort the transaction and, on completion, send an acknowledgement to the coordinator.

(3)   If the participant receives a GLOBAL_COMMIT message, write a *commit* record to the log file and force-write it to stable storage. Commit the transaction, releasing all locks, if appropriate, and on completion send an acknowledgement to the coordinator.

If a participant fails to receive a vote instruction from the coordinator, it simply times out and aborts. Therefore, a participant could already have aborted *and* performed local abort processing, before voting. The processing for the case when participants vote commit and abort are shown in Figure 16.19.

The participant has to wait for either the global-abort or global-commit instruction from the coordinator. If the participant fails to receive the instruction from the coordinator, or the coordinator fails to receive a response from a participant, then it assumes that the site has failed and a **termination protocol** must be invoked. The termination protocol is only followed by operational sites; sites that have failed follow the **recovery protocol** on restart.

Termination protocols

A termination protocol is invoked whenever a coordinator or participant fails to receive an expected message and times out. The action to be taken is different, depending upon whether the coordinator or participant has timed out and on when the time out occurred.

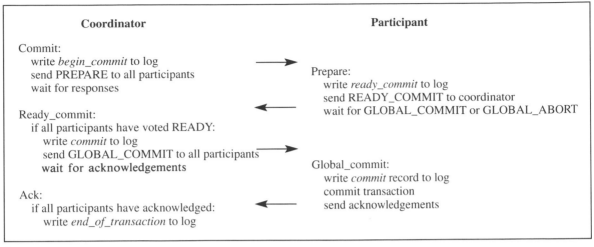

(a)

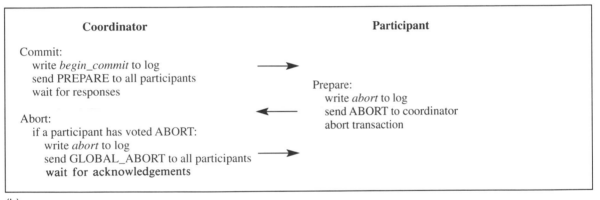

(b)

Figure 16.19
Summary of 2PC:
(a) 2 PC protocol for
participant voting
COMMIT; (b) 2PC
protocol for
participant voting
ABORT.

Coordinator

The coordinator can be in one of four states during the commit process: INITIAL, WAITING, DECIDED and COMPLETED, as shown in the state transition diagram in Figure 16.20a, but can time out only in the middle two states. Actions are as follows:

- *Timeout in the WAITING state* The coordinator is waiting for all participants to acknowledge whether they wish to commit or abort the transaction. In this case, the coordinator cannot commit the transaction because it has not received all votes. However, it can decide to globally abort the transaction.

- *Timeout in the DECIDED state* The coordinator is waiting for all participants to acknowledge whether they have successfully aborted or

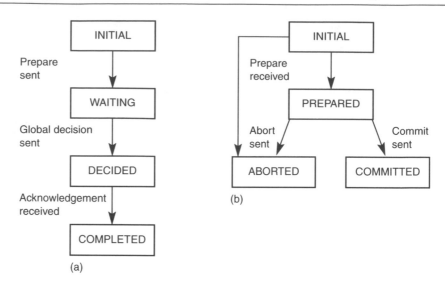

committed the transaction. In this case, the coordinator simply sends the global decision again to sites that have not acknowledged.

Participant

The simplest termination protocol is to leave the participant process blocked until communication with the coordinator is re-established, and the participant can then be informed of the global decision and resume processing accordingly. However, there are other actions that may be taken to improve performance.

A participant can be in one of four states during the commit process: INITIAL, PREPARED, ABORTED and COMMITTED, as shown in Figure 16.20b. However, a participant may time out only in the first two states as follows:

- *Timeout in the INITIAL state* The participant is waiting for a prepare message from the coordinator, which implies that the coordinator must have failed while in the INITIAL state. In this case, the participant can unilaterally abort the transaction. If it subsequently receives a prepare message, it can either ignore it, in which case the coordinator times out and aborts the global transaction, or it can send an abort message to the coordinator.

- *Timeout in the PREPARED state* The participant is waiting for an instruction to abort or commit the transaction. The participant must have voted to commit the transaction, so it cannot change its vote and abort the transaction. Equally well, it cannot go ahead and commit the transaction. Without further information, the participant is blocked. However, the participant could contact each of the other participants attempting to find one that knows the decision. This is known as the

cooperative termination protocol. A straightforward way of telling the participants who the other participants are is for the coordinator to append a participants' list to the vote instruction.

Although the cooperative termination protocol reduces the likelihood of blocking, blocking is still possible and the blocked process will just have to keep on trying to unblock as failures are repaired. If it is only the coordinator that has failed and all participants detect this as a result of executing the termination protocol, then they can elect a new coordinator and so unblock.

Recovery protocols

Having discussed the action to be taken by an operational site in the event of a failure, we now consider the action to be taken by the failed sites on recovery. The action on restart again depends on what stage the coordinator or participant had reached at the time of failure.

Coordinator failure
We consider three different stages for failure of the coordinator:

(1) *Failure in INITIAL state*   The coordinator has not yet started the commit procedure. Recovery in this case starts the commit procedure.

(2) *Failure in WAITING state*   The coordinator has sent the prepare message and although it has not received all responses, it has not received an abort response. In this case, recovery restarts the commit procedure.

(3) *Failure in DECIDED state*   The coordinator has instructed the participants to globally abort or commit the transaction. On restart, if the coordinator has received all acknowledgements, it can complete successfully. Otherwise, it has to initiate the termination protocol discussed above.

Participant failure
The objective of the recovery protocol for a participant is to ensure that a participant process on restart performs the same action as all other participants, and that this restart can be performed independently (that is, without the need to consult either the coordinator or the other participants). We consider three different stages for failure of a participant:

(1) *Failure in INITIAL state*   The participant has not yet voted on the transaction. Therefore, on recovery, it can unilaterally abort the transaction, as it would have been impossible for the coordinator to have reached a global commit decision without this participant's vote.

(2) *Failure in PREPARED state*   The participant has sent its vote to the coordinator. In this case, recovery is via the termination protocol discussed above.

(3) *Failure in ABORTED/COMMITTED states*   Participant has completed the transaction. Therefore, on restart, no further action is necessary.

Election protocols

If the participants detect the failure of the coordinator (by timing out) they can elect a new site to act as coordinator. One election protocol is for the sites to have an agreed linear ordering. We assume that site S_i has order i in the sequence, the lowest being the coordinator, and that each site knows the identification and ordering of the other sites in the system, some of which may also have failed. One election protocol asks each operational participant to send a message to the sites with a greater identification number. Thus, site S_i would send a message to sites S_{i+1}, S_{i+2}, ..., S_n in that order. If a site S_k receives a message from a lower-numbered participant, then S_k knows that it is not to be the new coordinator and stops sending messages.

This protocol is relatively efficient and most participants stop sending messages quite quickly. Eventually, each participant will know whether there is an operational participant with a lower number. If there is not, the site becomes the new coordinator. If the newly elected coordinator also times out during this process, the election protocol is invoked again.

After a failed site recovers, it immediately starts the election protocol. If there are no operational sites with a lower number, the site forces all higher numbered sites to let it become the new coordinator, regardless of whether there is a new coordinator or not.

Communication topologies for 2PC

There are several different ways of exchanging messages, or communication topologies, that can be employed to implement 2PC. The one discussed above is called **centralized 2PC**, since all communication is funnelled through the coordinator, as shown in Figure 16.21a. A number of improvements to the centralized 2PC protocol have been proposed that attempt to improve its overall performance, either by reducing the number of messages that need to be exchanged, or by speeding up the decision making process. These improvements depend upon adopting different ways of exchanging messages.

An alternative is to use **linear 2PC**, where participants can communicate with each other, as shown in Figure 16.21b. In linear 2PC, sites are ordered 1, 2, ..., n, where site 1 is the coordinator and the remaining sites are the participants. The 2PC protocol is implemented by a forward communication from coordinator to participant n for the voting phase and a backward communication from participant n to the coordinator for the decision phase. In the voting phase, the coordinator passes the vote instruction to site 2, which votes and then passes its vote to site 3. Site 3 then combines its vote with that of site 2 and transmits the combined vote to site 4, and so on. When the nth participant adds its vote, the global decision is obtained and this is passed backwards to participants $n - 1$, $n - 2$, ... and eventually back to the coordinator. Although linear 2PC incurs fewer messages than centralized 2PC, the linear sequencing does not allow any parallelism.

Linear 2PC could be improved if the voting process adopts the forward linear sequencing, while the decision process adopts the centralized topology,

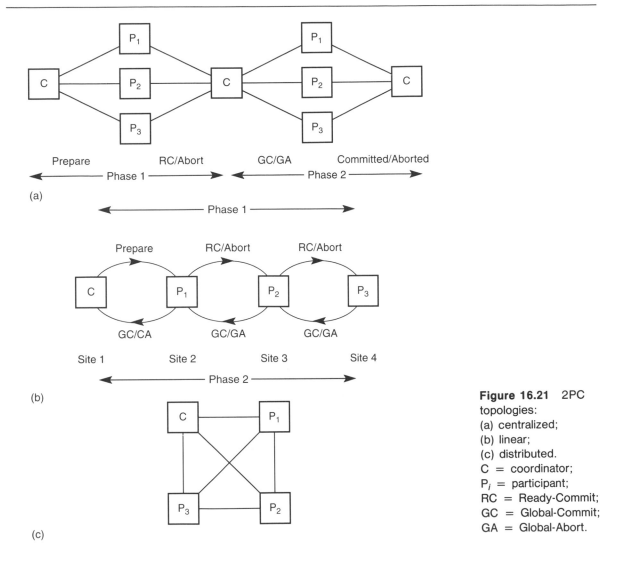

Figure 16.21 2PC topologies:
(a) centralized;
(b) linear;
(c) distributed.
C = coordinator;
P_i = participant;
RC = Ready-Commit;
GC = Global-Commit;
GA = Global-Abort.

so that site n would be able to broadcast the global decision to all participants in parallel (Bernstein *et al.*, 1987).

A third proposal, known as **distributed 2PC**, uses a distributed topology, as shown in Figure 16.21c. The coordinator sends the prepare message to all participants who, in turn, send their decision to all other sites. Each participant waits for messages from the other sites before deciding whether to abort or commit the transaction. This effectively eliminates the need for the decision phase of the 2PC protocol, since the participants can reach a decision consistently, but independently (Skeen, 1981).

16.9.4 Three-Phase Commit (3PC)

We have seen that 2PC is *not* a non-blocking protocol, since it is possible for sites to become blocked in certain circumstances. For example, a process that times out after voting commit, but before receiving the global instruction from the coordinator, is blocked if it can communicate only with sites that are similarly unaware of the global decision. The probability of blocking occurring in practice is sufficiently rare that most existing systems use 2PC. However, an alternative non-blocking protocol, called the **three-phase commit** (3PC) protocol, has been proposed (Skeen, 1981). It is non-blocking for site failures, except in the event of the failure of all sites. Communication failures can, however, result in different sites reaching different decisions, thereby violating the atomicity of global transactions. The protocol requires that:

- No network partition can occur.
- At least one site must always be available.
- At most K sites can fail simultaneously (system is classified as K-resilient).

The basic idea of 3PC is to remove the uncertainty period for participants that have voted commit and are waiting for the global abort or global commit from the coordinator. 3PC introduces a third phase, called **pre-commit**, between voting and global decision. On receiving all votes from the participants, the coordinator sends a global pre-commit message. A participant who receives the global pre-commit knows that all other participants have voted commit and that, in time, the participant itself will definitely commit, unless it fails. Each participant acknowledges receipt of the pre-commit message and, once the coordinator has received all acknowledgements, it issues the global commit. An abort vote from a participant is handled in exactly the same way as in 2PC.

The new state transition diagrams for coordinator and participant are shown in Figure 16.22. Both the coordinator and participant still have periods of waiting, but the important feature is that all *operational* processes have been informed of a global decision to commit by the pre-commit message *prior* to the first process committing, and can therefore act independently in the event of failure.

16.9.5 Network Partitioning

When a network partition occurs, maintaining the consistency of the database may be more difficult, depending on whether data is replicated or not. If data is not replicated, we can allow a transaction to proceed if it does not require any data from a site outside the partition in which it is initiated. Otherwise, the transaction must wait until the sites it needs access to are available again. If data is replicated, the procedure is much more complicated. We consider two examples of anomalies that may arise with replicated data in a partitioned network, based on a simple bank account relation containing a customer balance.

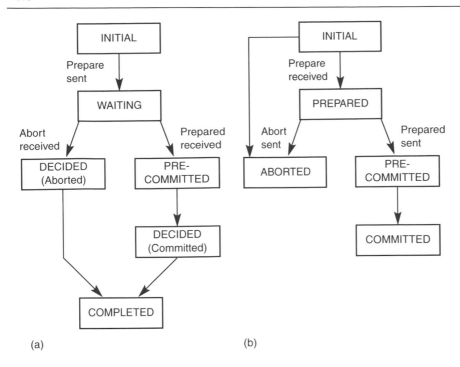

Figure 16.22 State transition diagram for 3PC: (a) coordinator; (b) participant.

Identifying updates

Successfully completed update operations by users in different partitions can be difficult to observe, as illustrated in Figure 16.23. In partition P_1, a transaction has withdrawn £10 from an account (with balance bal_x) and in partition P_2, two transactions have each withdrawn £5 from the same account. Assuming at the start both partitions have £100 in bal_x, then on completion they both have £90 in bal_x. When the partitions recover, it is not sufficient to check the value in bal_x and assume that the fields are consistent if the values are the same. In this case, the value after executing all three transactions should be £80.

Time	P_1	P_2
t_1	begin_transaction	begin_transaction
t_2	$bal_x = bal_x - 10$	$bal_x = bal_x - 5$
t_3	write(bal_x)	write(bal_x)
t_4	commit	commit
t_5		begin_transaction
t_6		$bal_x = bal_x - 5$
t_7		write(bal_x)
t_8		commit

Figure 16.23 Identifying updates.

Maintaining integrity

Successfully completed update operations by users in different partitions can easily violate integrity constraints, as illustrated in Figure 16.24. Assume that a bank places a constraint on a customer account (with balance bal_x) that it cannot go below £0. In partition P_1, a transaction has withdrawn £60 from the account and in partition P_2, a transaction has withdrawn £50 from the same account. Assuming at the start, both partitions have £100 in bal_x, then on completion one has £40 in bal_x and the other has £50. Most important, neither has violated the integrity constraint. However, when the partitions recover and the transactions are both implemented, the balance of the account will be −£10, and the integrity constraint will have been violated.

Processing in a partitioned network involves a trade-off in availability and correctness (Davidson, 1984; Davidson *et al.*, 1985). Absolute correctness is easiest to provide if no processing of replicated data is allowed during partitioning. On the other hand, availability is maximized if no restrictions are placed on the processing of replicated data during partitioning.

Time	P_1	P_2
t_1	begin_transaction	begin_transaction
t_2	$bal_x = bal_x - 60$	$bal_x = bal_x - 50$
t_3	write(bal_x)	write(bal_x)
t_4	commit	commit

Figure 16.24
Maintaining integrity.

In general, it is not possible to design a non-blocking atomic commitment protocol for arbitrarily partitioned networks (Skeen, 1981). Since recovery and concurrency control are so closely related, the recovery techniques that will be used following network partitioning will depend on the particular concurrency control strategy being used. Methods are classified as either pessimistic or optimistic.

Pessimistic protocols

Pessimistic protocols choose consistency of the database over availability, and would therefore not allow transactions to execute in a partition if there is no guarantee that consistency can be maintained. The protocol uses a pessimistic concurrency control algorithm such as primary copy or majority locking, discussed in Section 16.7. Recovery using this approach is much more straightforward, since updates would have been confined to a single, distinguished partition. Recovery or reconnection of the network simply involves propagating all the updates to all other sites.

Optimistic protocols

Optimistic protocols, on the other hand, choose availability of the database at the expense of consistency, and use an optimistic approach to concurrency control, in which updates are allowed to proceed independently in the various partitions. Therefore, when sites recover, inconsistencies are likely.

To determine whether inconsistencies exist, **precedence graphs** can be used to keep track of dependencies among data. Precedence graphs are similar to wait-for-graphs discussed earlier, and show which transactions have read and written which data items. While the network is partitioned, updates proceed without restriction, and precedence graphs are maintained by each partition. When the network has recovered, the precedence graphs for all partitions are combined. Inconsistencies are indicated if there is a cycle in the graph. The resolution of inconsistencies depends upon the semantics of the transactions, and thus it is generally not possible for the recovery manager to re-establish consistency without user intervention.

16.10   Date's 12 Rules for a DDBMS

In this final section, we list Date's 12 rules (or objectives) for DDBMSs (Date, 1987). The basis for these rules is that a distributed system should feel like a non-distributed system to the user. These rules are akin to Codd's 12 rules for relational systems presented in Section 3.6.

(0)   Fundamental principle

> To the user, a distributed system should look exactly like a nondistributed system.

(1)   Local autonomy
The sites in a distributed system should be autonomous. In this context, autonomy means that:

- local data is locally owned and managed;
- local operations remain purely local;
- all operations at a given site are controlled by that site.

(2)   No reliance on a central site
There should be no one site without which the system cannot operate. This implies that there should be no central servers for services such as transaction management, deadlock detection, query optimization and management of the Global Data Dictionary.

(3)   Continuous operation
Ideally, there should never be a need for a planned system shutdown, for operations such as:

- adding or removing a site from the system;
- the dynamic creation and deletion of fragments at one or more sites.

(4) Location independence

Location independence is equivalent to location transparency. The user should be able to access the database from any site. Furthermore, the user should be able to access all data as if it were stored at the user's site, no matter where it is physically stored.

(5) Fragmentation independence

The user should be able to access the data, no matter how it is fragmented.

(6) Replication independence

The user should be unaware that data has been replicated. Thus, the user should not be able to access a particular copy of a data item directly, nor should the user have to specifically update all copies of a data item.

(7) Distributed query processing

The system should be capable of processing queries that reference data at more than one site.

(8) Distributed transaction processing

The system should support the transaction as the unit of recovery. The system should ensure that both the global and local transactions conform to the ACID rules for transactions, namely: atomicity, consistency, independence and durability.

(9) Hardware independence

It should be possible to run the DDBMS on a variety of hardware platforms.

(10) Operating system independence

As a corollary to the previous rule, it should be possible to run the DDBMS on a variety of operating systems.

(11) Network independence

Again, it should be possible to run the DDBMS on a variety of disparate communication networks.

(12) Database independence

It should be possible to run different local DBMSs, perhaps supporting different underlying data models; that is, the system should support heterogeneity.

The last four rules are ideals. As the rules are so general, and due to the lack of standards in computer and network architecture, we can expect only partial compliance from vendors in the foreseeable future.

Chapter Summary

- A **distributed database** is a collection of multiple, logically interrelated databases, distributed over a computer network. The **DDBMS** is the software that transparently manages the distributed database.

- The advantages of a DDBMS are that it reflects the organizational structure, it makes remote data more shareable, it improves reliability, availability and performance, it may be more economical and provides for modular growth. The major disadvantages are cost, complexity, lack of standards and experience.

- Communication takes place over a network, which may be a Local Area Network (LAN) or a Wide Area Network (WAN). LANs are intended for short distances and provide faster communication than WANs.

- A relation may be divided into a number of sub-relations called **fragments**, which may be horizontal, vertical, mixed or derived. Fragments are **allocated** to one or more sites. Fragments may be **replicated** to provide improved availability and performance.

- The DDBMS should appear like a centralized DBMS by providing a series of transparencies. With **distribution transparency**, users should not know that the data has been fragmented/replicated. With **transaction transparency**, the consistency of the global database should be maintained when multiple users are accessing the database concurrently and when failures occur. With **performance transparency**, the system should be able to efficiently handle queries that reference data at more than one site. With **DBMS transparency**, it should be possible to have different DBMSs in the system.

- Two methods that can be used to guarantee distributed serializability are **locking** and **timestamping**. In **two-phase locking (2PL)**, a transaction acquires all its locks before releasing any. 2PL protocols can use centralized, primary copy or distributed lock managers. Majority voting can also be used. With **timestamping**, transactions are ordered in such a way that older transactions get priority in the event of conflict.

- Distributed deadlock involves merging local wait-for-graphs together to check for cycles. If a cycle is detected, transactions must be aborted and restarted until the cycle is broken.

- Causes of failure in a distributed environment are loss of messages, communication link failures, site crashes and network partitioning. To facilitate recovery, each site maintains its own a log file. The log can be used to undo and redo transactions in the event of failure.

- The **two-phase commit (2PC)** protocol comprises a voting and decision phase, where the coordinator asks each participant whether they are ready to commit. If one participant votes to abort, the global transaction and each local transaction must be aborted. Only if all participants vote to commit can the global transaction be committed. The protocol can leave sites blocked in the presence of sites failures.

- A non-blocking protocol is **three-phase commit (3PC)**, which involves the coordinator sending an additional message between the voting and decision phases to all participants asking them to pre-commit the transaction.

REVIEW QUESTIONS

16.1 Explain what is meant by a DDBMS, and discuss the motivation in providing such a system.

16.2 Compare and contrast a DDBMS with distributed processing. Under what circumstances would you choose a DDBMS over distributed processing?

16.3 Discuss the advantages and disadvantages of a DDBMS.

16.4 One problem area with DDBMSs is that of distributed database design. Discuss the issues that have to be addressed with distributed database design. Discuss how these issues apply to the global data dictionary.

16.5 Define and contrast alternative schemes for fragmenting a global relation. State how you would check for correctness to ensure that the database does not undergo semantic change during fragmentation.

16.6 What layers of transparency should be provided with a DDBMS? Give justification for your answer.

16.7 In a distributed environment, locking-based algorithms can be classified as centralized, primary copy or distributed. Compare and contrast these algorithms.

16.8 One of the most well-known methods for distributed deadlock detection was developed by Obermarck. Explain how Obermarck's method works and how deadlock is detected and resolved.

16.9 Outline two alternative two-phase commit topologies to the centralized topology.

16.10 Explain the term 'non-blocking protocol' and explain why two-phase commit protocol is not a non-blocking protocol. Discuss how the three-phase commit protocol overcomes this problem.

16.11 Each item in a distributed database must have a unique name. One solution to this problem is to create a central name server which has the responsibility for ensuring uniqueness of all names in the system. Discuss the problems with this solution and propose an alternative approach.

EXERCISES

A multinational engineering company has decided to distribute its project management information at the regional level in mainland Britain. The current centralized relational schema is as follows:

Employee	(NIN, First_Name, Last_Name, Address, Birth_Date, Sex, Salary, Tax_Code, Dept_No)
Department	(Dept_No, Dept_Name, Manager_NIN, Business_Area_No, Region_No)
Projects	(Proj_No, Proj_Name, Contract_Price, Project_Manager_NIN, Dept_No)
Works_On	(NIN, Proj_No, Hours_Worked)
Business	(Business_Area_No, Business_Area_Name)
Region	(Region_No, Region_Name)

where	Employee	contains employee details and the national insurance number **NIN** is the key.
	Department	contains department details and **Dept_No** is the key. Manager_NIN identifies the employee who is the manager of the department. There is only one manager for each department.
	Projects	contains details of the projects in the company and the key is **Proj_No.**
	Works_on	contains details of the hours worked by employees on each project and **NIN/Proj_No** forms the key.
	Business	contains names of the business areas and the key is **Business_Area_No.**
and	Region	contains names of the regions and the key is **Region_No.**

Departments are grouped regionally as follows:

Region 1: Scotland;   Region 2: Wales;   Region 3: England

Information is required by business area which covers: Software Engineering, Mechanical Engineering and Electrical Engineering. There is no Software Engineering in Wales and all Electrical Engineering departments are in England. Projects are staffed by local department offices.

As well as distributing the data regionally, there is an additional requirement to access the employee data either by personal information (by Personnel) or by work related information (by Payroll).

16.12 Produce a distributed database design for the above system, and include:

(a)   a suitable fragmentation schema for the system;

(b) in the case of primary horizontal fragmentation, a complete and minimal set of predicates;

(c) the reconstruction of global relations from fragments.

State any assumptions necessary to support your design.

16.13 Repeat Exercise 16.12 for the *DreamHome* case study presented in Section 1.7.

16.14 Give full details of the centralized two-phase commit protocol in a distributed environment. Outline the algorithms for both coordinator and participants.

17 Object Databases

Chapter Objectives

In this chapter you will learn:

- The requirements for advanced database applications.
- Why relational DBMSs currently are not well suited to supporting advanced database applications.
- The concepts associated with object-orientation:
  - Abstraction and encapsulation.
  - Objects and attributes.
  - Object identity.
  - Methods and messages.
  - Classes, subclasses, superclasses and inheritance.
  - Overloading.
  - Polymorphism and dynamic binding.
- The evolution of ODBMSs.
- The framework for an object data model.
- Issues underlying object DBMSs.
- Advantages and disadvantages of object DBMSs.
- The distinction between object DBMSs and extended relational DBMSs.
- How the relational model has been extended to support advanced database applications.
- The object-oriented features proposed in the next SQL standard, namely SQL3.
- How to design an object-oriented database.
- The main features of the new Object Database Standard.

Object-orientation is a new approach to software construction that shows considerable promise for solving some of the classic problems of software development. The underlying concept behind object technology is that all software should be constructed out of standard, reusable components wherever possible. Traditionally, software engineering and database management have existed as separate disciplines. Database technology has concentrated on the static aspects of information storage, while software engineering has modelled the dynamic aspects of software. With the arrival of the third generation of database management systems, namely Object Database Management Systems (ODBMSs), the two disciplines have been combined to allow the concurrent modelling of both data and processes acting upon the data. ODBMSs are sometimes called object-oriented DBMSs or object data management systems.

The success of relational systems in the past decade is evident. However, there is currently significant dispute regarding the next generation of DBMSs. The traditionalists believe that it is sufficient to extend the relational model with additional capabilities. On the one hand, the OMG has published the Object-Oriented Database System Manifesto based on the object-oriented paradigm (Atkinson *et al.*, 1989) (see Section 17.3.4). On the other hand, the Committee for Advanced DBMS Function (CADF) have published a Third Generation Database System Manifesto (Stonebraker *et al.*, 1990), which defines a number of principles that a DBMS ought to meet in the near future (see Section 17.4.1). We also discuss the new object model proposed by the ODMG, which in the short term will become a *de facto* standard for ODBMSs (see Section 17.6). The examples in this chapter are once again drawn from the *DreamHome* case study introduced in Section 1.7.

17.1 Introduction

In this section, we discuss the particular database requirements for the new types of advanced applications that are becoming increasingly commonplace. We then examine why current relational DBMSs (RDBMSs) are not well suited for supporting these applications.

17.1.1 Advanced Database Applications

The past decade has seen significant changes in the computer industry. In database systems, we have seen the widespread acceptance of RDBMSs for business applications. However, existing relational systems have proven inadequate for applications whose needs are quite different from those of traditional business database applications. These applications include:

Computer-Aided Design (CAD)

A CAD database stores data relating to mechanical and electrical design covering, for example, buildings, aeroplanes and integrated circuit chips. Designs of this type have some common characteristics:

- Design data is characterized by a large number of types, each with a small number of instances. Conventional databases are just the opposite.

- Designs may be very large, perhaps consisting of millions of parts, often with many interdependent subsystem designs.

- The design is not static but evolves through time. When a design change occurs, its implications must be propagated through all design representations.

- Updates are far-reaching because of topological relationships, functional relationships, tolerances, and so on. One change is likely to affect a large number of design objects.

- Often, many design alternatives are being considered for each component, and the correct version for each part must be maintained. This involves some form of version control and configuration management.

- There may be hundreds of staff involved with the design, and they may work in parallel on multiple versions of a large design. Even so, the end-product must be consistent and coordinated. This is sometimes referred to as **cooperative engineering**.

Computer-Aided Manufacturing (CAM)

A CAM database stores similar data to a CAD system, in addition to data relating to discrete production (such as cars on an assembly line) and continuous production (such as chemical synthesis).

Computer-Aided Software Engineering (CASE)

A CASE database stores data relating to the stages of the software development lifecycle: planning, requirements collection analysis, design, implementation, test, maintenance and documentation. As with CAD, designs may be extremely large and cooperative engineering is the norm.

Office Automation (OA)

An OA database stores data relating to the computer control of information in a business, including electronic mail, documents, invoices, and so on. To provide better support for this area, we need to handle a wider range of data types than names, addresses, dates and money. Modern systems now handle free-form text, photographs, diagrams, audio and video sequences. For example, a multimedia document may handle text, photographs, spreadsheets and voice commentary.

Computer-Aided Publishing (CAP)

A CAP database stores complex documents. As with office automation, CAP applications are being extended to handle multimedia documents consisting of text, audio, image and video data and animation.

Other advanced database applications include scientific applications, expert systems and other applications with complex and interrelated objects and procedural data.

17.1.2 Weaknesses of Relational DBMSs

In Chapter 3, we discussed how the relational model has a strong theoretical foundation, based on first-order predicate logic. This theory supported the development of SQL, a declarative language that has now become the standard language for defining and manipulating relational databases. Other strengths of the relational model are its simplicity, its suitability for Online Transaction Processing (OLTP) and its support for data independence. However, the relational data model, and RDBMSs in particular, are not without their disadvantages. We discuss below some of the disadvantages often cited by the proponents of the object-oriented approach. Readers are left to judge for themselves the applicability of these weaknesses.

Representation of 'real world' entities

The process of normalization generally leads to the creation of relations that do not correspond to entities in the 'real world'. The fragmentation of a 'real world' entity into many relations, with a physical representation that reflects this structure, is inefficient, leading to many joins during query processing.

Semantic overloading

The relational model has only one construct for representing data and data relationships: the relation. For example, to represent an M:N relationship between two entities A and B, we create three relations, one to represent each of the entities A and B and one to represent the relationship. There is no mechanism to distinguish between entities and relationships, or to distinguish between different kinds of relationships that exist between entities. For example, a 1:M relationship might be *Has*, *Owns*, *Manages*, and so on. If such distinctions could be made, then it might be possible to build the semantics into the operations. It is said that the relational model is **semantically overloaded**.

There have been many attempts to overcome this problem using **semantic data models**: that is, models that represent more of the meaning of data. The interested reader is referred to the survey papers by Hull and King (1987) and Peckham and Maryanski (1988). However, the relational model is not completely without semantic features. For example, it has domains and keys (see Section 3.2), and functional, multi-valued and join dependencies (see Chapter 6).

Integrity constraints and enterprise constraints

Integrity refers to the validity and consistency of stored data. Integrity is usually expressed in terms of constraints, which are consistency rules that the database is not permitted to violate. In Section 3.3, we introduced the concepts of entity and referential integrity, and in Section 3.2.1 we introduced domains, which are also types of constraints. Unfortunately, many commercial systems do not support these constraints, and it has been necessary to build them into the applications. This, of course, is dangerous and can lead to duplication of effort and, worse still, inconsistencies. Furthermore, there is no support for enterprise rules in the relational model, which again means they have to be built into the DBMS or the application.

The SQL-92 standard helps resolve this claimed deficiency by allowing constraints to be specified as part of the data definition language (see Chapter 12).

Homogeneous data

The relational model assumes both horizontal and vertical homogeneity. Horizontal homogeneity means that each tuple of a relation must be composed of the same attributes. Vertical homogeneity means that the values in a particular column of a relation must all come from the same domain. Further, the intersection of a row and column must be an atomic value. This fixed structure is too restrictive for many 'real world' objects that have a complex structure and leads to unnatural joins, which, as mentioned above, is inefficient. Among the classic examples is a parts explosion where we wish to represent some object, for example an aeroplane, as composed of parts and composite parts, which in turn are composed of other parts and composite parts, and so on. This weakness has led to research in complex object or non-first normal form (NF^2) database systems, for example Jaeschke and Schek (1982), and Bancilhon and Khoshafian (1989). In defence of the relational data model, it could equally be argued that this symmetric structure is one of the model's strengths.

Many relational systems now allow the storage of **Binary Large Objects (BLOBs)**. A BLOB is a data value that contains binary information representing an image, a digitized video or audio sequence, a procedure, or any large unstructured object. Typically, the database does not manage this information directly, but simply contains a reference to a file. The use of BLOBs is not an elegant solution. Storing this information in external files denies it many of the protections naturally afforded by the DBMS. More importantly, BLOBs cannot contain other BLOBs, so they cannot take the form of composite objects. Also, BLOBs generally ignore the behavioural aspects of objects. For example, pictures can be stored as BLOBs in some relational databases. However, the pictures can only be stored and displayed. It is not possible to manipulate the internal structure of the images, nor is it possible to display or manipulate parts of a picture. An example of the use of BLOBs is given in Figure 10.19.

Limited operations

The relational model only has a fixed set of operations, such as set and tuple-oriented operations. These operations are provided in the SQL-92 specification. However, SQL-92 does not allow new operations to be specified. Again, this is too restrictive to model the behavior of many 'real world' objects. The next SQL standard, SQL3, should help resolve this deficiency by allowing new data types and operations to be specified as part of the data definition language (see Section 17.4.4).

Recursive queries

Atomicity of data means that repeating groups are not allowed. As a result, it is extremely difficult to produce recursive queries: that is, queries about relationships that a relation has with itself (directly or indirectly). Consider the following simplistic Staff relation, which stores staff numbers and the corresponding manager's staff number:

Staff_No	Manager_Staff_No
S5	S4
S4	S3
S3	S2
S2	S1
S1	NULL

How do we find all the managers who directly or indirectly manage staff member S5? To find the first two levels of the hierarchy, we have:

```
SELECT manager_staff_no
FROM staff
WHERE staff_no = 'S5'
UNION
SELECT manager_staff_no
FROM staff
WHERE staff_no =
        (SELECT manager_staff_no
        FROM staff
        WHERE staff_no = 'S5');
```

We can easily extend this approach to find the complete answer to this query. In this particular example, this approach works because we know how many levels in the hierarchy have to be processed. However, if we were to ask a more general query, such as 'For each member of staff, find all the managers who directly or indirectly manage him or her', this approach would be much more difficult to implement using interactive SQL. To overcome this problem, SQL can be embedded in a high-level programming language, which provides constructs to facilitate iteration. Additionally, many relational systems provide a report writer with similar constructs. In either case, it is the application rather than the inherent capabilities of the system that provides the required functionality.

Impedance mismatch

In Section 11.1, we mentioned that SQL lacked *computational completeness*. This is true with most data manipulation languages for relational systems. To overcome this problem, the SQL standard provides embedded SQL to help develop more complex database applications (see Section 12.5). However, this approach produces an **impedance mismatch** because we are mixing different programming paradigms. SQL is a declarative language that handles rows of data, whereas a high-level language such as 'C' is a procedural language that can handle only one row of data at a time. Secondly, SQL and 3GLs use different models to represent data. For example, SQL allows the data types Date and Interval, which are not available in traditional programming languages. Thus, it is necessary for the application program to convert between the two representations, which is inefficient. Furthermore, since we are using two different type systems, it is not possible to automatically type check the application as a whole. It is argued that the solution to these problems is not to replace relational languages by record-level object-oriented languages, but to introduce set-level facilities into programming languages (Date, 1995).

Other problems with RDBMSs

(1)   Transactions in business processing are generally short-lived, and the concurrency control primitives and protocols (such as two-phase locking) are not particularly suited for long-lived transactions, which are more common for complex design objects.

(2)   Schema changes are difficult. Database administrators must intervene to change database structures and, typically, programs that access these structures must be modified to adjust to the new structure. These are slow and cumbersome processes with today's technologies. As a result, most organizations are locked into their existing database structures. Even if they are willing and able to change the way they do business to meet new requirements, they are unable to make these changes because they cannot afford the time and expense required to modify their information systems (Taylor, 1992). To meet the requirement for increased flexibility, we need a system that caters for natural schema evolution.

(3)   Relational systems were designed to use content-based associative access and are poor at navigational access: that is, access based on movement between individual records. This type of access is important for many of the complex applications we discussed in the previous section.

Of these three problems, the first two are applicable to many DBMSs, not just relational systems. In fact, there is no underlying problem with the relational model that would prevent such mechanisms being implemented.

17.2 Object-Oriented Concepts

In this section, we discuss the primary concepts that occur in object-orientation. We start with a brief review of two of the underlying themes: abstraction and encapsulation.

17.2.1 Abstraction and Encapsulation

Abstraction is the process of identifying the essential aspects of an entity and ignoring the unimportant properties. In software engineering, this means that we concentrate on what an object is and what it does, before we decide how it should be implemented. In this way, we delay implementation details for as long as possible, thereby avoiding commitments that we will find restrictive at a later stage.

The concept of **encapsulation**, or information hiding, means that we separate the external aspects of an object from its internal details, which are hidden from the outside world. In this way, the internal details of an object can be changed without affecting the applications that use it, provided the external details remain the same. This prevents a program becoming so inter-dependent that a small change has massive ripple effects. In other words, encapsulation provides **data independence**.

There are two views of encapsulation: the Object-Oriented Programming Language (OOPL) view and the database adaptation of that view. In some OOPLs, encapsulation is achieved through **Abstract Data Types** (ADTs). In this view, an object has an interface part and an implementation part. The interface provides a specification of the operations that can be performed on the object; the implementation part consists of the data structure for the ADT and the functions that realize the interface. Only the interface part is visible to other objects or users. In the database view, proper encapsulation is achieved by ensuring that programmers have access only to the interface part. In this way, encapsulation provides a form of **logical data independence**: we can change the internal implementation of an ADT without changing any of the application programs using that ADT (Atkinson *et al.*, 1989).

17.2.2 Objects and Attributes

Many of the important object-oriented concepts stem from the Simula programming language developed in Norway in the mid 1960s to support simulation of real-world processes (Dahl and Nygaard, 1966). Modules in Simula is not based on procedures, as they are in conventional programming languages, but on the physical objects being modelled in the simulation. This seemed a sensible approach as the objects are the key to the simulation: each object has to maintain some information about its current state, and additionally has actions (**behaviour**) that have to be modelled. From Simula, we have the definition of an object:

Object	A uniquely identifiable entity that contains both the attributes that describe the state of a real-world object and the actions that are associated with a real-world object.

In the *DreamHome* case study, a branch office, a member of staff and a property are all examples of objects that we wish to model. The concept of an object is simple but, at the same time, very powerful: each object can be defined and maintained independently of the others. This definition of an object is very similar to the definition of an entity given in Section 5.2.1. However, an object encapsulates both state and behaviour; an entity only models state.

The current state of an object is described by one or more **attributes**, or **instance variables**. For example, the branch office at 163 Main Street may have the attributes shown in Table 17.1. Attributes can be classified as simple or complex. A **simple attribute** can be a primitive type such as integer, string, real, and so on, which takes on literal values; for example, Bno in Figure 17.1 is a simple attribute with the literal value 'B3'. A **complex attribute** can contain collections and/or references. For example, the attribute Sales_Staff is a **collection** of Staff objects. A **reference attribute** represents a relationship between objects. A reference attribute contains a value, or collection of values, that are themselves objects. For example, Sales_Staff is, more precisely, a collection of references to Staff objects. A reference attribute is conceptually similar to a foreign key in the relational data model or a pointer in a programming language. An object that contains one or more complex attributes is called a **complex object** (see Section 17.2.9).

Table 17.1   Object attributes for branch instance.

BNO	B3
STREET	163 Main St
AREA	Partick
CITY	Glasgow
POST_CODE	G11 9QX
TEL_NO	0141–339–2178
FAX_NO	0141–339–4439
SALES_STAFF	Ann Beech; David Ford
MANAGER	Susan Brand

Attributes are generally referenced using a 'dot' notation. For example, the Street attribute of a Branch object is referenced as:

branch_object.street

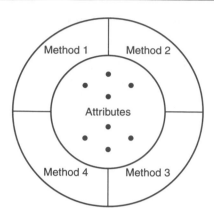

Figure 17.1 Object showing attributes and methods.

17.2.3   Object Identity

A key part of the definition of an object is unique identity. In an object-oriented system, each object has a unique system-wide identifier that is independent of the values of its attributes (that is, its state), and is invisible to the user.

Two objects could have the same state but would have different identities. When an object is created, it is assigned an **Object Identifier (OID)** that is unique and invariant, in the sense that it cannot be altered during its lifetime. The OID distinguishes the object from every other object in the system. Once the object is created, this OID will not be reused for any other object, even after the object has been deleted. Object identity automatically provides entity integrity (see Section 3.3.2).

There are several ways in which object identity can be implemented. In a relational system, the primary key is used to provide uniqueness of each tuple in a relation. Primary keys do not provide the type of object identity that is required in object-oriented systems. First, the primary key is only unique in a relation not across the entire system. Second, the primary key is generally chosen from the attributes of the relation, making it dependent on object state. If the potential key is subject to change, identity has to be simulated by unique identifiers, such as the branch number Bno, but while these are not under system control this does not guarantee protection against violations of identity. Furthermore, simulated keys have little semantic meaning to the user. Other techniques that are frequently used in programming languages to support identity are variable names and memory references or addresses, but these approaches also compromise object identity (Khoshafian and Abnous, 1990).

There are several advantages to using OIDs over keys as the mechanism for object identity:

- *They are efficient.*   OIDs require minimal storage within a complex object. Typically, they are smaller than textual names, foreign keys or other semantic-based references.

- *They are fast.* OIDs point to an actual address or to a location within a table that gives the address of the referenced object. This means that objects can be located quickly whether they are currently stored in local memory or on disk.

- *They are independent of content.* OIDs do not depend upon the data contained in the object in any way.

- *They are invisible to the user.*

(Note the potential for ambiguity that can arise from this last property: two objects can appear to be the same to the user (all attribute values are the same), yet have different OIDs and so be different objects. If the OIDs are invisible, how does the user distinguish between these two objects? From this we may conclude that primary keys are still required to allow users to distinguish objects.)

For each OID defined by the system there must always be an object present in the system that corresponds to the OID: that is, there are no **dangling references**. The OIDs are used in object-oriented systems to provide referential integrity (see Section 17.5.2). With this approach to designating an object, we can distinguish between object identity and object equality. Two objects are **identical** if and only if they are the same object (denoted by '='): that is, their OIDs are the same. Two objects are **equal** if their states are the same (denoted by '= =').

17.2.4 Methods and Messages

An object encapsulates both data and functions into a self-contained package. In object technology, functions are usually called **methods**. Figure 17.1 provides a conceptual representation of an object, with the attributes on the inside protected from the outside by the methods.

Methods define the **behaviour** of the object. They can be used to change the object's state by modifying its attribute values, or to query the value of selected attributes. For example, we may have methods to add a new property for rent at a branch, to update a member of staff's salary or to print out a member of staff's details.

A method consists of a name and a body that performs the behaviour associated with the method name. In an object-oriented language, the body consists of a block of code that carries out the required action. For example, Figure 17.2 represents the method to update a member of staff's salary. The name of the method is *update_salary*, which has an input parameter *increment* that is added to the **instance variable** *salary* to produce a new salary.

```
method void update_salary(float increment)
{
    salary = salary + increment;
}
```

Figure 17.2 Example of a method.

CLASS DEFINITION   CLASS INSTANCES

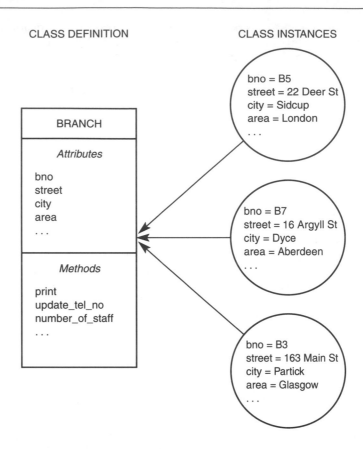

Figure 17.3 Class
instances share
attributes and
methods.

Messages are the means by which objects communicate. A message is
simply a request from one object (the sender) to another object (the receiver)
asking the second object to execute one of its methods. The sender and receiver
may be the same object. Again, the dot notation is generally used to access
a method. For example, to execute the *update_salary* method on a Staff object
and pass the method an increment value of 1000, we write:

    staff_object.update_salary(1000)

In a traditional programming language, a message would be written as a function call:

    update_salary(staff_object, 1000)

17.2.5   Classes

In Simula, classes are blueprints for defining a set of similar objects. Thus,
objects that have the same attributes and respond to the same messages can
be grouped together to form a **class**. The attributes and associated methods
are defined once for the class rather than separately for each object. For example, all branch objects would be described by a single Branch class. The objects

in a class are called **instances** of the class. Each instance has its own value for each attribute, but shares the same attribute names and methods with other instances of the class, as illustrated in Figure 17.3.

In the literature, the terms 'class' and 'type' are often used synonymously. Some authors make a distinction between the two terms. A type corresponds to the notion of an abstract data type (Atkinson and Buneman, 1989). In programming languages, a variable is declared to be of a particular type. The compiler can use this type to check that the operations performed on the variable are compatible with its type, thus helping to ensure the correctness of the software. On the other hand, a class is a blueprint for creating objects that provides methods that can be applied on the objects. Thus, a class is referred to at run-time rather than compile time.

In some object-oriented systems, a class is also an object and has its own attributes and methods, referred to as **class attributes** and **class methods**, respectively. Class attributes describe the general characteristics of the class, such as totals or averages. For example, in the class Branch, we may have a class attribute for the average staff salary. Class methods are used to change or query the state of class attributes. There are also special class methods to create new instances of the class and to destroy unneeded ones. In an object-oriented language, a new instance is normally created by issuing the command *new*. Such methods are usually called **constructors**. Methods for destroying objects and reclaiming the space occupied are typically called **destructors**. Messages sent to a class method are sent to the class rather than an instance of a class. This implies that the class is an instance of a higher-level class called a **metaclass**.

17.2.6   Subclasses, Superclasses and Inheritance

Some objects may have similar but not identical attributes and methods. If there is a large degree of similarity, it would be useful to be able to share the common properties (attributes and methods). **Inheritance** allows one class of objects to be defined as a special case of a more general class. These special cases are known as **subclasses**, and the more general cases are known as **superclasses**. The process of forming a superclass is referred to as **generalization**; forming a subclass is **specialization**. By default, a subclass inherits all of the properties of its superclass and, additionally, defines its own unique properties. However, as we shall see shortly, a subclass can redefine inherited methods. All instances of the subclass are also instances of the superclass.

The concepts of superclass, subclass and inheritance are similar to those discussed for the enhanced entity–relationship model in Section 5.4, except that in the object-oriented paradigm inheritance covers both state and behaviour. The relationship between the subclass and superclass is sometimes referred to as **A KIND OF (AKO)**; for example, a Manager is AKO Staff. The relationship between an instance and its class is sometimes referred to as **IS-A**; for example, Susan Brand IS-A Manager.

There are several forms of inheritance: single inheritance, multiple inheritance, repeated inheritance and selective inheritance. Figure 17.4 shows an example of **single inheritance**, where the subclasses Manager and Sales_Staff inherit the properties of the superclass Staff. The term single inheritance refers

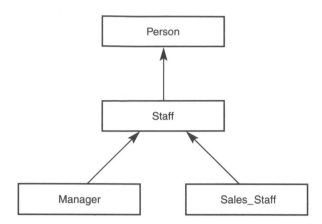

Figure 17.4 Single
inheritance

to the fact that the subclasses inherit from no more than one superclass. The
superclass Staff could itself be a subclass of a superclass, Person, thus forming
a **class hierarchy**.

Figure 17.5 shows an example of **multiple inheritance** where the subclass
Sales_Manager inherits properties from both of the superclasses Manager and
Sales_Staff. The provision of a mechanism for multiple inheritance can be quite
problematic. The mechanism has to provide a way of dealing with conflicts that
arise when the superclasses contain the same attribute or method. Not all
object-oriented languages and database systems support multiple inheritance as
a matter of principle. Some authors claim that multiple inheritance introduces
a level of complexity that is hard to manage safely and consistently. Others
argue that it is required to model reality, as in this example.

Repeated inheritance is a special case of multiple inheritance, in which
the superclasses inherit from a common superclass. Extending the previous
example, the classes Manager and Sales_Staff may both inherit properties from
a common superclass Staff, as illustrated in Figure 17.6. In this case, the
inheritance mechanism must ensure that the Sales_Manager class does not
inherit properties from the Staff class twice.

Selective inheritance allows a subclass to inherit a limited number of properties from the superclass. This feature may provide similar functionality to
the view mechanism discussed in Section 12.1 by restricting access to some
details but not others.

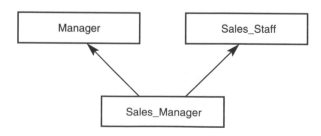

Figure 17.5 Multiple
inheritance.

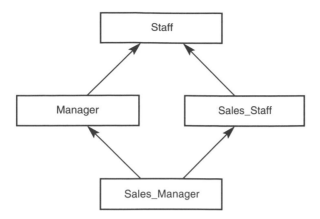

Figure 17.6
Repeated inheritance.

Overriding

As we have just mentioned, properties, namely attributes and methods, are automatically inherited by subclasses from the superclass. However, it is possible to redefine a property in the subclass. In this case, the definition of the property in the subclass is the one used. This process is called **overriding**. For example, we might define a method in the Staff class to increment salary based on a commission:

```
method void give_commission(float branch_profit)
{
    salary = salary + 0.02 * branch_profit;
}
```

However, we may wish to perform a different calculation for commission in the Manager subclass. We can do this by redefining or overriding the method *give_commission* in the Manager subclass:

```
method void give_commission(float branch_profit)
{
    salary = salary + 0.05 * branch_profit;
}
```

The ability to factor out common properties of several classes and form them into a superclass that can be shared with subclasses can greatly reduce redundancy within systems, and is regarded as one of the main advantages of object-orientation. Overriding is an important feature of inheritance as it allows special cases to be handled easily with minimal impact on the rest of the system.

17.2.7   Overloading

Overriding is a special case of the more general concept of **overloading**. Overloading allows the name of a method to be reused within a class definition or across class definitions. This means that a single message can perform different functions depending on which object receives it and, if appropriate, what parameters are passed to the method. For example, many classes will have a print method to print out the relevant details for an object, as shown in Figure 17.7.

```
method void print() {                          method void print() {
    printf("Branch number: %s\n", bno);            printf("Staff number: %s\n", sno);
    printf("Street: %s\n", street);                printf("First name: %s\n", fname);
    printf("Area: %s\n", area);                    printf("Last name: %s\n", lname);
    printf("City: %s\n", city);                    printf("Address: %s\n", address);
    printf("Post code: %s\n", post_code);          printf("Telephone number: %s\n", tel_no);
    printf("Telephone number: %s\n", tel_no);      printf("Position: %s\n", position);
    printf("Fax number: %s\n", fax_no);            printf("Sex: %c\n", sex);
}                                                  printf("Date of birth: %s\n, dob);
                                                   printf("Salary: %f\n", salary);
                                                   printf("NI number: %s\n", nin);
                                               }

(a)                                            (b)
```

Figure 17.7
Overloading print method: (a) for Branch object; (b) for Staff object.

Overloading can greatly simplify applications, since it allows the same name to be used for the same operation irrespective of what class it appears in, thereby allowing context to determine which meaning is appropriate at any given moment. This saves having to provide unique names for methods such as *print_branch_details* or *print_staff_details* for what is essentially the same functional operation.

17.2.8 Polymorphism and Dynamic Binding

Overloading is a special case of the more general concept of **polymorphism**, from the Greek meaning 'having many forms'. There are three types of polymorphism: operation, inclusion and parametric (Cardelli and Wegner, 1985). Overloading, as in the previous example, is a type of **operation** (or **ad hoc**) **polymorphism**. A method defined in a superclass and inherited in its subclasses is an example of **inclusion polymorphism. Parametric polymorphism**, or **genericity** as it is sometimes called, uses types as parameters in generic type, or class, declarations. For example:

```
template ⟨type T⟩
T max(x:T, y:T) {
    if (x > y)
        return x
    else
        return y;
}
```

defines a generic function *max* that takes two parameters of type T and returns the maximum of the two values. This piece of code does not actually establish any methods. Rather, the generic description acts as a template for the later establishment of one or more different methods of different types. Actual methods are instantiated as follows:

> int max(int, int)   or   real max(real, real)

The process of selecting the appropriate method based on an object's type is called **binding**. If the determination of an object's type can be deferred until runtime (rather than compile time), the selection is called **dynamic** or **late binding**. For example, consider the class hierarchy of Staff with subclasses Manager and Sales_Staff shown in Figure 17.4, and assume that each class has its own print method to print out relevant details. Let us further assume that we have a list consisting of an arbitrary number of objects, *n* say, from this hierarchy. In a conventional programming language, we would need a CASE statement or a nested IF statement to print out the corresponding details:

```
FOR i = 1 TO n DO
      SWITCH (list[i].type)
      {
           CASE staff:        print_staff_details(list[i].object); break;
           CASE manager:      print_manager_details(list[i].object); break;
           CASE sales_person: print_sales_person_details(list[i].object); break;
      }
```

If a new type is added to the list, we have to extend the CASE statement to handle the new type, forcing recompilation of this piece of software. If the language supports dynamic binding and overloading, we can overload the print methods with the single name *print* and replace the CASE statement with the line:

> list[i].print()

Furthermore, with this approach we can add any number of new types to the list and, provided we continue to overload the *print* method, no recompilation of this code is required. Thus, the concept of polymorphism is orthogonal to inheritance.

17.2.9 Complex Objects

There are many situations where an object consists of subobjects or components. A complex object is an item that is viewed as a single object in the 'real world', but combines with other objects in a set of complex **a-part-of** relationships (APO). The objects contained may themselves be complex objects, resulting in **a-part-of hierarchy**. In an object-oriented system, a contained object can be handled in one of two ways. First, it can be encapsulated within the complex object and thus form part of the complex object. In this case, the structure of the contained object is part of the structure of the complex object and can be accessed only by the complex object's methods. On the other hand, a contained object can be considered to have an independent existence from the complex object. In this case, the object is not stored directly in the parent object but only its OID. This is known as **referential sharing** (Khoshafian and Valduriez, 1987). The contained object has its own structure and methods, and can be owned by several parent objects.

These types of complex objects are sometimes referred to as **structured complex objects**, since the system knows the composition. The term **unstructured complex object** is used to refer to a complex object whose structure can be interpreted only by the application program. In the database context, unstructured complex objects are sometimes known as Binary Large Objects (BLOBs), which we discussed in Section 17.1.2.

17.3 Object Database Management Systems (ODBMSs)

Now that we have a basic understanding of object-oriented concepts, we examine how these concepts have been adopted by the database community. In this section, we concentrate on the 'revolutionary' approach to the development of third generation DBMSs using pure ODBMSs. In contrast, we address the 'evolutionary' approach (the approach that extends the relational model) in Section 17.4. To put this development in context, we start with a brief history of database management systems leading up to the third generation of databases. We then discuss how, unlike the relational data model, there is no universally agreed object data model. In Section 17.3.3, we examine some issues that arise in a study of ODBMSs. In Section 17.3.4, we briefly review the Object-Oriented Database System Manifesto, which proposes 13 mandatory features for an ODBMS. We conclude this section with a review of the advantages and disadvantages of ODBMSs.

17.3.1 Evolution of the ODBMS

In the late 1960s and early 1970s, there were two mainstream approaches to constructing DBMSs. The first approach was based on the hierarchical data model, typified by IMS (Information Management System) from IBM, in response to the enormous information storage requirements generated by the Apollo moon programme. The second approach was based on the network data model and attempted to resolve some of the difficulties of the hierarchical model. Together, these approaches represented the **first generation** of DBMSs. However, these two models had some fundamental disadvantages:

- Complex programs had to be written to answer even simple queries based on navigational record-oriented access.

- There was minimal data independence.
- There was no widely accepted theoretical foundation.

In 1970, Codd produced his seminal paper on the relational data model. This paper was very timely, and addressed the disadvantages of the former approaches, in particular data dependency. Many experimental relational systems were implemented thereafter, with the first commercial products appearing in the late 1970s and early 1980s. Now there are over 100 RDBMSs for both mainframe and microcomputer environments, though many are stretching the definition of the relational model. Relational systems are referred to as **second-generation** DBMSs.

However, as we discussed in Section 17.1.2, RDBMSs are not without their failings, particularly their limited modelling capabilities. There has been much research since then attempting to address this problem. In 1976, Chen presented the entity–relationship model that is now a widely accepted technique for database design, and the basis for the methodology presented in Chapter 7 of this book. In 1979, Codd himself attempted to address some of the failings in his original work with an extended version of the relational model called RM/T (1979), and more recently RM/V2 (1990). The attempts to provide a data model that represents the real world more closely have been loosely classified as **semantic data modelling**. Some of the more famous are:

- the Semantic Data Model (Hammer and McLeod, 1981);
- the Functional Data Model (Shipman, 1981);
- the Semantic Association Model* (Su, 1983).

In response to the increasing complexity of database applications, two 'new' data models have emerged: the **Object Data Model** (ODM) and the **Extended Relational Data Model** (ERDM). However, unlike previous models, the actual composition of these models is not clear. This evolution represents **third-generation** DBMSs, as illustrated in Figure 17.8.

There is currently considerable debate between the ODBMS proponents and the relational supporters, which resembles the network/relational debate of the 1970s. Both sides agree that relational systems as they exist today are inadequate for certain types of applications. However, the two sides differ on the best solution. The ODBMS proponents claim that relational systems are satisfactory for standard business applications but lack the capability of supporting more complex applications. The relational supporters claim that the relational functionality is a necessary part of any real DBMS, and that complex applications can be handled by extensions to the relational model. At present, it is unclear whether one side will win this debate and become the dominant system, or whether each system will find its own particular niche in the marketplace. Certainly, if ODBMSs are to become dominant they must change their image from being systems solely for complex applications to being systems that can also accommodate standard business applications with the same tools and the same ease as their relational counterparts. In particular, they must support a declarative query language compatible with SQL. We return to this point later in the chapter.

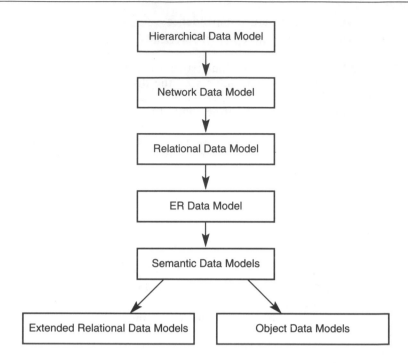

Figure 17.8 History of data models.

17.3.2 Object Data Model (ODM)

Kim (1991) defines an Object Data Model (ODM), Object Database (ODB) and an Object DBMS (ODBMS) as:

> **ODM** A data model that captures the semantics of objects supported in object-oriented programming.

> **ODB** A persistent and sharable collection of objects defined by an ODM.

> **ODBMS** The manager of an ODB.

Unfortunately, there is no one object data model equivalent to the underlying data model of relational systems. Each system provides its own interpretation of base functionality. For example, Zdonik and Maier present a threshold model that an ODBMS must, at, a minimum satisfy:

(1)   It must provide database functionality.
(2)   It must support object identity.
(3)   It must provide encapsulation.
(4)   It must support objects with complex state.

The authors argue that although inheritance may be useful, it is not essential to the definition, and an object-oriented database could exist without it (Zdonik and Maier, 1990). On the other hand, Khoshafian and Abnous (1990) define an object-oriented database as:

> Object-orientation = ADTs + Inheritance + Object identity
>
> Object-oriented database = Object-orientation + Database capabilities

Yet another definition for an ODBMS is given by Parsaye *et al.* (1989):

(1)   high-level query language with query optimization capabilities in the underlying system;

(2)   support for persistence and atomic transactions: concurrency and recovery control;

(3)   support for complex object storage, indexes and access methods for fast and efficient retrieval.

> Object-oriented database = Object-oriented system + (1)–(3)

Studying some of the current commercial ODBMSs, such as GemStone from Servio Logic Corporation, Itasca from Itasca Systems Inc., Objectivity/DB from Objectivity Inc., ObjectStore from Object Design Inc., Ontos from Ontos Inc., O_2 from O_2 Technology and Versant from Versant Object Technology, we can see that the concepts of object databases are drawn from different areas, as shown in Figure 17.9.

17.3.3   Issues in ODBMSs

In this section, we discuss various issues as they relate to ODBMSs

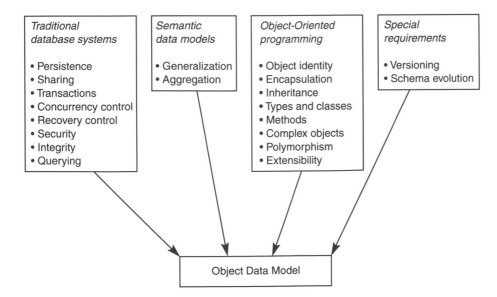

Figure 17.9   Origins of object data model.

Persistence

A DBMS must provide support for the storage of **persistent** objects: that is, objects that survive after the user session or application program that created them has terminated. This is in contrast to **transient** objects that only last for the invocation of the program. Persistent objects are retained until they are no longer required, at which point they are deleted. ODBMSs differ in how an object becomes persistent. The main strategies that are used to create persistent objects are:

- *By class*   A class is declared to be persistent and all instances of the class are made persistent when they are created. Alternatively, a class may be a subclass of a system-supplied persistent class. This is the approach taken by the products Ontos and Objectivity/DB.
- *By call*   An object may be specified as persistent when it is created, or in some cases, dynamically at runtime. This is the approach taken by the product ObjectStore.
- *By reachability*   The system determines persistence of objects by reachability from certain globally persistent database root objects. This is the approach used by the product GemStone. It is analogous to the concept of garbage-collection in programming languages such as Smalltalk: an object that becomes inaccessible from any other object is *garbage* and should be removed from the object space.

Transactions

As discussed in Section 15.1, a transaction is a **logical unit of work**, which should always transform the database from one consistent state to another. The types of transactions found in business applications are typically of short duration. In contrast, transactions involving complex objects, such as those found in engineering and design applications, can continue for several hours, or even several days. Clearly, to support **long duration transactions**, we need to re-examine the protocols that are used in concurrency and recovery control (see Chapter 15).

In an ODBMS, the unit of concurrency and recovery control is logically an object, although for performance reasons a more coarse granularity may be used. Concurrency control prevents database accesses from interfering with one another. Locking-based protocols are the most common type of concurrency control mechanism used by ODBMSs to prevent conflict from occurring. However, it would be totally unacceptable for a user who initiated a long duration transaction to find that the transaction has been aborted due to a lock conflict and the work has been lost. Two solutions have been proposed:

- **conversational transactions**, which allow data to be checked out for a long period (Lorie and Plouffe, 1983);
- **versions**, which we discuss below.

Recovery control ensures that transactions are **atomic** and **durable**. From this point of view, long duration transactions are problematic: significant amounts of work may be lost should the system crash during transaction execution. One approach is to divide the transaction into a number of smaller **nested transactions** (Moss, 1981). In a nested transaction model, there is a top-level transaction that can have a number of child transactions; each child transaction can also have nested transactions. For example, we might have three nested transactions T_1, T_2 and T_3, as shown in Figure 17.10. Transactions have to commit from the bottom upwards. Thus, T_3 must commit before transaction T_2, and T_2 must commit before T_1. However, a transaction abort at one level does not have to affect a transaction in progress at a higher level. The updates of committed transactions at intermediate levels are visible only within the scope of their immediate predecessors. Thus, when T_3 commits, the changes are visible to T_2. However, they are not visible to T_1 or any transaction external to T_1. Long duration transactions are discussed in Korth *et al.* (1988), Skarra and Zdonik (1989) and Khoshafian and Abnous (1990).

Begin_Transaction T_1

. . .

    Begin_Transaction T_2

    . . .

        Begin_Transaction T_3

        . . .

        Commit_Transaction T_3

    . . .

    Commit_Transaction T_2

. . .

Commit_Transaction T_1

Figure 17.10   Nested transactions.

Versions

There are many applications that need access to the previous state of an object. For example, the development of a particular design is often an experimental and incremental process, the scope of which changes with time. It is therefore necessary in databases that store designs to keep track of the evolution of design objects and the changes made to a design by various transactions (see for example, Atwood, 1985; Katz *et al.*, 1986; and Banerjee *et al.*, 1987a).

The process of maintaining the evolution of objects is known as **version management**. An **object version** represents an identifiable state of an object; a **version history** represents the evolution of an object. Versioning should allow changes to the properties of objects to be managed in such a way that object references always point to the correct version of an object. Figure 17.11 illustrates version management for three objects: O_A, O_B and O_C. For example, we can determine that object O_A consists of versions V_1, V_2, V_3; V_{1A} is

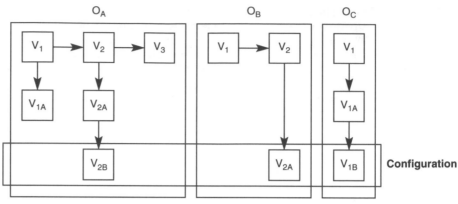

Figure 17.11
Versions and
configurations.

derived from V_1, and V_{2A} and V_{2B} are derived from V_2. This figure also shows an example of a **configuration** of objects, consisting of V_{2B} of O_A, V_{2A} of O_B and V_{1B} of O_C.

Versioning of data can also be used to increase concurrency, since different designers may work concurrently on different versions of the same object instead of having to wait for each others' transaction to complete. In the event that the design appears faulty at any stage, it should be possible to roll back the design to some valid state. Versions have been used as an alternative to conversational and nested transactions for concurrency control (for example, see Beech and Mahbod (1988) and Chou and Kim (1986, 1988)).

The commercial products Ontos, Versant, ObjectStore, Objectivity/DB and Itasca provide some form of version management. Itasca identifies three types of versions (Kim and Lochovsky, 1989):

- *Transient versions* A transient version is considered unstable and can be updated and deleted. It can be created from new by checking out a released version from a public database or by deriving it from a working or transient version in a private database. In the latter case, the base transient version is promoted to a working version. Transient versions are stored in the creator's private workspace.

- *Working versions* A working version is considered stable and cannot be updated, but it can be deleted by its creator. It is stored in the creator's private workspace.

- *Released versions* A released version is considered stable and cannot be updated or deleted. It is stored in a public database by checking in a working version from a private database.

Due to the performance and storage overhead in supporting versions, Itasca requires that the application indicate whether a class is **versionable**. When an instance of a versionable class is created, a **generic object** for that instance is created, along with the first version of that instance. The generic object consists of version management information.

Schema evolution

Engineering design is an incremental process and evolves with time. To support this process, applications require considerable flexibility in dynamically defining and modifying the database schema. For example, it should be possible to modify class definitions, the inheritance structure and specifications of attributes and methods without requiring system shutdown. Schema modification is closely related to the concept of version management discussed above. The issues that arise in schema evolution are complex and not all of them have been investigated in sufficient depth. Typical changes to the schema include (Banerjee *et al.*, 1987b):

(1)   Changes to the class definition:

    (a)   Modifying attributes
    (b)   Modifying methods.

(2)   Changes to the inheritance hierarchy:

    (a)   Making a class S the superclass of a class C.
    (b)   Removing a class S from the list of superclasses of C.
    (c)   Modifying the order of the superclasses of C.

(3)   Changes to the set of classes, such as creating and deleting classes and modifying class names.

The changes proposed to a schema must not leave the schema in an inconsistent state. Itasca and GemStone define rules for schema consistency, called **schema invariants**, which must be complied with as the schema is modified.

Architecture

In this section, we discuss two architectural issues: how best to apply the client–server architecture to the ODBMS environment, and the storage of methods.

Client–server

Many commercial ODBMSs are based on the client–server architecture to provide data to users, applications and tools in a distributed environment (see Section 2.6). However, not all systems use the same client–server model. We can distinguish three basic architectures for a client–server DBMS that vary in the functionality assigned to each component (Loomis, 1992), as depicted in Figure 17.12:

- *Object server*   This approach attempts to distribute the processing between the two components. Typically, the server process is responsible for managing storage, locks, commits to secondary storage, logging and recovery, enforcing security and integrity, query optimization and executing stored procedures. The client is responsible for transaction management and interfacing to the programming language. This is the

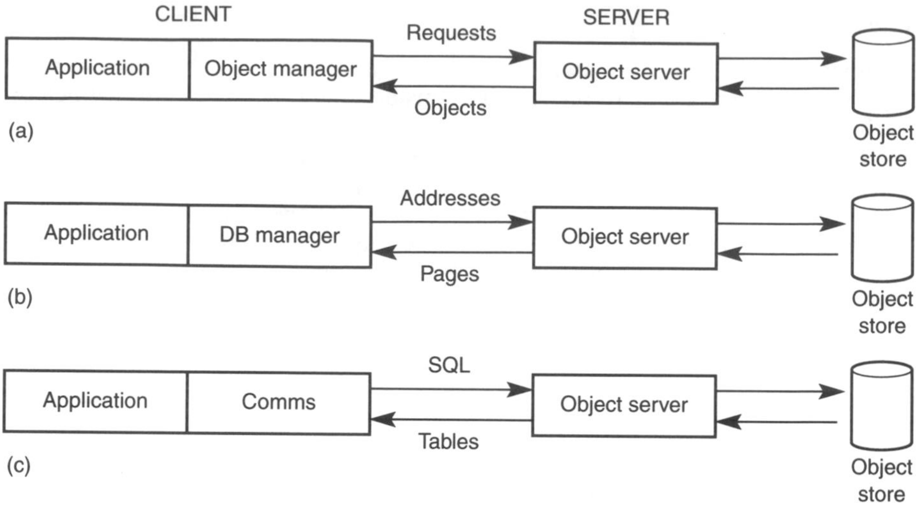

Figure 17.12 Client–server architectures: (a) object server; (b) page server; (c) database server.

best architecture for cooperative, object-to-object processing in an open, distributed environment.

- *Page server* In this approach, most of the database processing is performed by the client. The server is responsible for secondary storage and providing pages at the client's request.

- *Database server* In this approach, most of the database processing is performed by the server. The client simply passes requests to the server, receives results and passes them on to the application. This is the approach taken by many RDBMSs.

In each case, the server resides on the same machine as the physical database. The client, or **object manager** as it is sometimes called, may reside on the same or different machine. If the client needs access to databases distributed across multiple machines, then the client communicates with a server on each machine. There may also be a number of clients communicating with one server: for example, one client for each user or application.

Storing and executing methods
There are two approaches to handling methods: (1) to store the methods in external files, as shown in Figure 17.13(a); and (2) to store the methods in the database, as shown in Figure 17.13(b). The first approach is similar to function libraries found in traditional DBMSs, in which an application program interacts with a DBMS by linking in functions supplied by the DBMS vendor. With the second approach, methods are stored in the database and are dynamically bound to the application at runtime. The second approach offers several benefits:

- It eliminates redundant code. Instead of placing a copy of a method that accesses a data element in every program that deals with that data, the method is stored only once in the database.

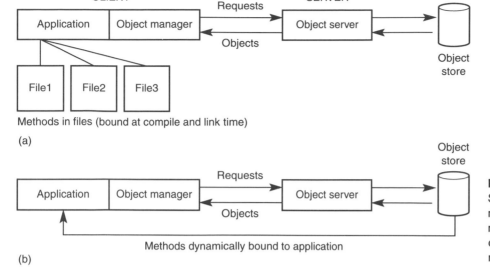

Figure 17.13
Strategies for handling methods: (a) storing methods outside database; (b) storing methods in database.

- It simplifies modifications. Changing a method requires changing it in one place only. All the programs automatically use the updated method. Depending on the nature of the change, rebuilding, testing and redistribution of programs may be eliminated.

- Methods are more secure. Storing the methods in the database gives them all the benefits of security provided automatically by the ODBMS.

- Methods can be shared concurrently. Again, concurrent access is provided automatically by the ODBMS. This also prevents multiple users making different changes to a method simultaneously.

- Improved integrity. Storing the methods in the database means that integrity constraints can be enforced consistently by the ODBMS across all applications.

The products GemStone and Itasca allow methods to be stored and activated from the database.

Alternative strategies for developing an ODBMS

There are several approaches to developing an ODBMS that can be summarized as follows (Khoshafian and Abnous, 1990):

- *Extend an existing object-oriented programming language with database capabilities*   This approach adds traditional database capabilities to an existing object-oriented programming language such as Smalltalk or C++ (see Figure 17.9). This is the approach taken by the product GemStone, which extended Smalltalk.

- *Provide extensible object-oriented DBMS libraries*   This approach also adds traditional database capabilities to an existing object-oriented programming language. However, rather than extending the language, class libraries are provided that support persistence, aggregation, data types, transactions, concurrency, security and so on. This is the approach taken by the products Ontos and ObjectStore.

- *Embed ODB language constructs in a conventional host language*   In Section 12.5, we saw how SQL can be embedded in a conventional host programming language. This strategy uses the same idea of embedding an ODB language in a host programming language. This is the approach taken by the product O_2, which provides embedded extensions for 'C'.

- *Extend an existing database language with object-oriented capabilities*   Due to the widespread acceptance of SQL, vendors are extending it to provide object-oriented constructs. This approach is being pursued by both RDBMS and ODBMS vendors. The next SQL standard, SQL3, will support object-oriented features (see Section 17.4.4). In addition, the new Object Database Standard by the Object Database Management Group (ODMG) specifies a standard for Object SQL (see Section 17.6.5). The products Ontos, Versant and O_2 provide a version of Object SQL and many ODBMS vendors will comply with the ODMG standard.

- *Develop a novel database data model/data language*   This is a radical approach that starts from the beginning again, and develops an entirely new database language and DBMS with object-oriented capabilities. This is the approach taken by SIM (Semantic Information Manager), which is based on the semantic data model and has a novel DML/DDL (Jagannathan *et al.*, 1988).

17.3.4   The Object-Oriented Database System Manifesto

The ODBMS manifesto (Atkinson *et al.*, 1989a) proposes 13 mandatory features for an object-oriented DBMS, based on two criteria: it should be an object-oriented system and it should be a DBMS. The first eight rules apply to the object-oriented characteristic:

(1)   **Complex objects must be supported**
It must be possible to build complex objects by applying constructors to basic objects. The minimal set of constructors are SET, TUPLE and LIST (or ARRAY). The first two are important because they have gained widespread acceptance as object constructors in the relational model. The final one is important because it allows order to be modelled. Furthermore, the manifesto requires that object constructors must be orthogonal: any constructor should apply to any object.

(2)   **Object identity must be supported**
All objects must have a unique identity that is independent of its values.

(3)   **Encapsulation must be supported**
In an ODBMS, proper encapsulation is achieved by ensuring that programmers have access only to the interface specification of methods, and the data

and implementation of these methods are hidden in the objects. However, there may be cases where the enforcement of encapsulation is not required: for example, with ad hoc queries. (We have already noted that encapsulation is seen as one of the great strengths of the object-oriented approach. In which case, why should there be situations where encapsulation can be overriden? The argument given is that it is not an ordinary user who is examining the contents of objects but the DBMS. Second, the DBMS could invoke the 'get' method associated with every attribute of every class, but direct examination is more efficient. We leave these arguments for the reader to reflect on.)

(4) Types or classes must be supported
We mentioned the distinction between types and classes in Section 17.2.5. The manifesto requires support only for one of these concepts. The database schema in an object-oriented system comprises a set of classes or a set of types. However, it is not a requirement that the system automatically maintains the extent of a type, that is, the set of objects of a given type in the database, or if an extent is maintained, to make it accessible to the user.

(5) Types or classes must be able to inherit from their ancestors
A subtype or subclass will inherit attributes and methods from its supertype or superclass.

(6) Dynamic binding must be supported
Methods should apply to objects of different types (overloading). The implementation of a method will depend on the type of the object it is applied to (overriding). To provide this functionality, the system cannot bind method names until run-time (dynamic binding).

(7) The DML must be computationally complete
In other words, the data manipulation language (DML) of the ODBMS should be a general-purpose programming language. This is obviously not the case with SQL (see Section 11.1).

(8) The set of data types must be extensible
The user must be able to build new types from the set of predefined system types. Furthermore, there must be no distinction in usage between system-defined and user-defined types.

The final five mandatory rules of the manifesto apply to the DBMS characteristics of the system:

(9) Data persistence must be provided
As in a conventional DBMS, data must remain (persist) after the application that created it has terminated. The user should not have to explicitly move or copy data to make it persistent.

(10) The DBMS must be capable of managing very large databases
In a conventional DBMS, there are mechanisms to manage secondary storage efficiently: for example, indexes and buffers. An ODBMS should have similar mechanisms that are invisible to the user, thus providing a clear independence between the logical and physical levels of the system.

(11)   **The DBMS must support concurrent users**
An ODBMS should provide concurrency control mechanisms similar to those in conventional systems.

(12)   **The DBMS must be capable of recovery from hardware and software failures**
An ODBMS should provide recovery control mechanisms similar to those in conventional systems.

(13)   **The DBMS must provide a simple way of querying data**
An ODBMS must provide an ad hoc query facility that is high-level (that is, reasonably declarative), efficient (that is, suitable for query optimization) and application independent. It is not necessary for the system to provide a query language, but could instead provide a graphical browser.

The manifesto proposes the following optional features: multiple inheritance, type checking and type inferencing, distribution across a network, design transactions and versions. Interestingly, there is no direct mention of support for security, integrity or views; even a declarative query language is not mandated.

17.3.5   Advantages and Disadvantages of ODBMSs

We conclude this section with a summary of the claimed advantages and obvious disadvantages of object database management systems.

Advantages

Enriched modelling capabilities
The object data model allows the real world to be modelled more closely. The object, which encapsulates both state and behaviour, is a more natural and realistic representation of real-world objects. An object can store all the relationships it has with other objects, including many-to-many relationships, and objects can be formed into complex objects that the traditional data models cannot cope with easily.

Extensibility
ODBMSs allow new abstract data types to be built from existing types. The ability to factor out common properties of several classes and form them into a superclass that can be shared with subclasses can greatly reduce redundancy within systems, and is regarded as one of the main advantages of object-orientation. Overriding is an important feature of inheritance, as it allows special cases to be handled easily, with minimal impact on the rest of the system. The reusability of classes promotes faster development and easier maintenance of the database and its applications.

Removal of impedance mismatch

A single language interface between the Data Manipulation Language (DML) and the programming language overcomes the impedance mismatch. This eliminates many of the inefficiencies that occur in mapping a declarative language such as SQL to an imperative language such as 'C'. We also find that most ODBMSs provide a DML that is computationally complete compared with SQL, the standard language for RDBMSs.

More expressive query language

Navigational access from one object to the next is the most common form of data access in an ODBMS. This is in contrast to the associative access of SQL. Navigational access is more suitable for handling parts explosion, recursive queries, and so on. However, it is argued that most ODBMSs are tied to a particular programming language which, although convenient for programmers, is not generally usable by end users who require a declarative language. In recognition of this, the ODMG standard specifies a declarative query language based on an object-oriented form of SQL (see Section 17.6.5).

Schema evolution

The tight coupling between data and applications in an ODBMS makes schema evolution more feasible. Generalization and inheritance allow the schema to be better structured, to be more intuitive, and to capture more of the semantics of the application.

Support for long duration transactions

Current RDBMSs enforce serializability on concurrent transactions to maintain database consistency (see Section 15.2.2). Some ODBMSs use a different protocol to handle long duration transactions, which are common in many advanced database applications. This is an arguable advantage – as we have already mentioned, there is no structural reason why such transactions cannot be provided by an RDBMS.

Applicability to advanced database applications

As we discussed in Section 17.1.1, there are many areas where traditional DBMSs have not been particularly successful: for example, Computer-Aided Design (CAD), Computer-Aided Manufacturing (CAM), Computer-Aided Software Engineering (CASE), Office Automation (OA), Computer-Aided Publishing (CAP) and other applications with complex and interrelated objects and procedural data. The modelling capabilities of ODBMSs have made them suitable for these applications.

Improved performance

The Object Operations Version 1 (OO1) benchmark is intended as a generic measure of ODBMS performance (Cattell and Skeen, 1992). It was designed to reproduce operations that are common in the advanced applications discussed above. In 1989 and 1990, the OO1 benchmark was run on the ODBMSs GemStone, Ontos, ObjectStore, Objectivity/DB and Versant and the RDBMSs INGRES and Sybase. The results show an average 30-fold performance improvement for the ODBMS over the RDBMS. However, it has been argued that this difference in performance can be attributed to architectural-based differences, as opposed to model-based differences. Dynamic binding and garbage collection in ODBMSs may compromise this performance improvement.

Before we discuss the disadvantages, it is worthwhile pointing out that if domains were properly implemented, relational systems would be able to provide the same functionality as ODBMSs are claimed to have. A domain can be perceived as a data type of arbitrary complexity with scalar values that are encapsulated, and that can be operated on only by predefined functions. Therefore, an attribute defined on a domain in the relational model can contain anything: for example, drawings, documents, images, arrays, and so on (Date, 1995). In this respect, domains and object classes are essentially the same thing.

Disadvantages

Lack of universal data model
As we discussed in Section 17.3.2, there is no universally agreed data model for an object DBMS, and most models lack a theoretical foundation. This disadvantage is seen as a significant drawback, and is equated to pre-relational systems. However, the ODMG has proposed an object model, which we discuss in Section 17.6. The ODMG object model should become a *de facto* standard.

Lack of experience
The use of ODBMSs is still quite limited. This means that we do not yet have the level of experience that we have with traditional systems. Furthermore, the learning curve for the design and management of ODBMSs is steep. This results in resistance to the acceptance of the technology.

Lack of standards
There is a general lack of standards for ODBMSs. We have already mentioned that there is no universally agreed data model. Similarly, there is no standard object-oriented query language. Again, the ODMG has specified an Object Query Language (OQL) that should become a *de facto* standard, at least in the short term (see Section 17.6.5). This lack of standards may be the single most damaging factor for the uptake of ODBMSs.

Query optimization
Query optimization requires an understanding of the underlying implementation to access the database efficiently. However, this compromises the concept of encapsulation. The ODBMS Manifesto, discussed in Section 17.3.4, suggests that this may be acceptable, although as we discussed this seems questionable.

Locking
Many ODBMSs use locking as the basis for a concurrency control protocol. However, if locking is applied at the object level, locking of an inheritance hierarchy may be problematic.

Complexity

The increased functionality provided by an ODBMS, such as long duration and nested transactions, version management and schema evolution, is inherently more complex than that of traditional DBMSs. In general, complexity leads to products that are more expensive and more difficult to use.

Views

Currently, most ODBMSs do not provide a view mechanism, which, as we have seen previously, provides many advantages such as data independence, security, reduced complexity and customization (see Section 12.1.7).

Security

Currently, ODBMSs do not provide adequate security mechanisms. Most mechanisms are based on a coarse granularity, and the user cannot grant access rights on individual objects or classes. If ODBMSs are to expand fully into the business field, this deficiency must be rectified.

17.4 Extended Relational Systems

Many vendors of RDBMS products are conscious of the threat and promise of ODBMSs. They agree that their systems are not currently suited to the advanced applications discussed in Section 17.1.1, and that added functionality is required. However, they reject the claim that extended RDBMSs will not provide sufficient functionality or will be too slow to cope with the new complexity.

The most obvious way to remedy the shortcomings of the relational model is to extend the model. Extended relational data models are based on enhancements of the relational data model to incorporate procedures, objects, versions and other new capabilities. There is no single extended relational model; rather, there are a variety of these models, whose characteristics depend upon the way and the degree to which extensions were made. However, all the models do share the same basic relational tables and query language, all incorporate some concept of 'object', and some have the ability to store procedures as well as data in the database.

In this section, we present a proposal by the Committee for Advanced DBMS Function (CADF) that specifies a number of principles an advanced DBMS ought to satisfy. We also look at Postgres, a research system from the designers of INGRES that attempts to extend the relational model, and at how Postgres has influenced the development of the object management extension to INGRES. To conclude the section, we examine the proposed object-oriented extensions to the SQL2 standard. For additional information on extended relational systems, the interested reader is referred to Cattell (1994b).

17.4.1 The Third-Generation Database Manifesto

The Committee for Advanced DBMS Function (CADF) have published a Third-Generation Database System Manifesto (Stonebraker *et al.*, 1990). The manifesto proposes the following features for a third-generation database system:

(1) A third-generation DBMS must have a rich type system.

(2) Inheritance is a good idea.

(3) Functions, including database procedures and methods and encapsulation, are a good idea.

(4) Unique identifiers for records should be assigned by the DBMS only if a user-defined primary key is not available.

(5) Rules (triggers, constraints) will become a major feature in future systems. They should not be associated with a specific function or collection.

(6) Essentially all programmatic access to a database should be through a non-procedural, high-level access language.

(7) There should be at least two ways to specify collections, one using enumeration of members and one using the query language to specify membership.

(8) Updateable views are essential.

(9) Performance indicators have almost nothing to do with data models and must not appear in them.

(10) Third generation DBMSs must be accessible from multiple high-level languages.

(11) Persistent forms of a high-level language, for a variety of high-level languages are a good idea. They will all be supported on top of a single DBMS by compiler extensions and a complex runtime system.

(12) For better or worse, SQL is 'intergalactic dataspeak'.

(13) Queries and their resulting answers should be the lowest level of communication between a client and a server.

17.4.2 Postgres

Postgres ('Post Ingres') is a research database system designed to be a potential successor to the INGRES RDBMS (Stonebraker and Rowe, 1986). The objective of the project was to extend the relational model to include the following mechanisms:

- abstract data types,
- data of type 'procedure',
- rules.

These mechanisms are used to support a variety of semantic and object-oriented data modelling constructs including aggregation, generalization, complex objects with shared subobjects and attributes that reference tuples in other relations.

Abstract data types

An attribute type in a relation can be atomic or structured. Postgres provides a set of predefined atomic types: **int2, int4, float4, float8, bool, char** and **date**. Users can add new atomic types and structured types. All data types are defined as Abstract Data Types (ADTs). An ADT definition includes a type name, its length in bytes, procedures for converting a value from internal to external representation (and vice versa) and a default value. For example, the type **int4** is internally defined as:

> DEFINE TYPE int4 IS   (InternalLength = 4, InputProc = CharToInt4,
>   OutputProc = Int4ToChar, Default = "0")

The conversion procedures are implemented in some high-level programming language such as 'C' and made known to the system using a **define procedure** command. An operator on ADTs is defined by specifying the number and type of operands, the return type, the precedence and associativity of the operator, and the procedure that implements it. It can also specify procedures to be called to sort the relation containing values of the associated type (Sort) and to negate the operator in a query predicate (Negator). For example:

> DEFINE OPERATOR '+'(int4, int4) RETURNS int4
> IS (Proc = Plus, Precedence = 5, Associativity = 'left')

Again, the procedure Plus that implements the operator + would be programmed in a high-level language. Users can define their own atomic types in a similar way.

      Structured types are defined using type constructors for arrays and procedures. A variable-length or fixed-length array is defined using an **array constructor**. For example, char[25] defines an array of characters of fixed length 25. Omitting the size makes the array variable-length. The **procedure constructor** allows values of type 'procedure' in an attribute, where a procedure is a series of commands written in Postquel, the query language of Postgres. The corresponding type is called the **postquel** data type.

Relations and inheritance

A relation in Postgres is declared using the following command:

> **CREATE** table_name (column_name_1 = type_1, column_name_2 = type_2, . . .)
> [**KEY**(list_of_column_names)]
> [**INHERITS**(list_of_table_names)]

A relation inherits all attributes from its parent(s) unless an attribute is overridden in the definition. If the same attribute can be inherited from more than one parent and the types of the attribute are different, the declaration is disallowed. Key specifications are also inherited. For example, to create an entity Staff that inherits the attributes of Person, we would write:

```
CREATE person   (fname = char[15], lname = char[15], address = char[50],
                 tel_no = char[13], sex = char, date_of_birth = date)
KEY(lname, date_of_birth)
CREATE staff    (sno = char[5], position = char[10], salary = float4,
                 nin = char[9], bno = char[5], manager = postquel)
INHERITS(person)
```

The relation Staff includes the attributes declared explicitly and the attributes declared for Person. The key is the (inherited) key of Person. The Manager attribute is defined as type *postquel* to indicate that it is a Postquel query. A tuple could be added to the Staff relation using the **append** command:

```
APPPEND staff   (sno = "SG37", position = "Snr Asst", salary = 12000,
                 nin = "WL432514C", bno = "B3",
                 manager = "retrieve (S.sno) from S in STAFF
                 where position = "Manager" and bno = "B3")
```

A query that references the Manager attribute returns the string that contains the Postquel command, which, in general, may be a relation as opposed to a single value. Postgres provides two ways to access the Manager attribute. The first uses a nested dot notation to implicitly execute a query:

```
RETRIEVE (S.sno, S.lname, S.manager.sno) from S in STAFF
```

This query lists each member of staff's number, name and associated manager. The result of the query in Manager is implicitly joined with the tuple specified by the rest of the retrieve list. The second way to execute the query is to use the **EXECUTE** command:

```
EXECUTE (S.sno, S.lname, S.manager.sno) from S in STAFF
```

Parameterized procedure types can be used where the query parameters can be taken from other attributes in the tuple. The $ sign is used to refer to the tuple in which the query is stored. For example, we could redefine the above query using a parameterized procedure type:

```
DEFINE TYPE manager is   RETRIEVE (staff_no = S.sno) FROM s in staff
                         WHERE position = "Manager" and bno = $.bno
```

and use this new type in the table creation:

```
CREATE staff    (sno = char[4], position = char[10], salary = float4,
                 nin = char[9], bno = char[4], manager = Manager)
INHERITS(person)
```

The query to retrieve staff details would now become:

```
RETRIEVE (S.sno, S.lname, S.manager.staff_no)
```

The ADT mechanism of Postgres is limited in comparison with ODBMSs. In

Postgres, objects are composed from ADTs, whereas in an ODBMS all objects are treated as ADTs. This does not fully satisfy the concept of encapsulation. Furthermore, there is no inheritance mechanism associated with ADTs.

17.4.3 The INGRES Object Management Extension

The Object Management Extension is an optional INGRES facility that allows ADTs and new SQL functions to be created. A user-defined data type can be used anywhere a system-defined data type can be used. New SQL functions can be used in queries and can manipulate both user-defined and system-defined data types.

An ADT definition consists of a name, an internal data type identifier, and a set of routines required by INGRES to manipulate the data type. The routines given in Table 17.2 must be defined for each new ADT.

Table 17.2 Routines required for a new INGRES ADT.

compare:	compare two elements of the data type
length_check:	check specified length for the data type is valid and return length
keybuild:	build an ISAM, BTREE or HASH key from a specified value
getempty:	construct an empty value for the data type
value_check:	check a value of the data type for valid values
hashprep:	prepare a data value of the data type for becoming a hash key
helem:	create a histogram element for a data value (for query optimization)
hmin:	create a histogram value for the minimum value (for query optimization)
dhmin:	create a default minimum histogram (for query optimization)
hmax:	create a histogram value for the maximum value (for query optimization)
dhmax:	create a default maximum histogram (for query optimization)
hg_dtln:	return the data type and length for a histogram value for the data type (for query optimization)
minmaxdv:	return the minimum/maximum values/lengths for the data type
dbtoev:	determine the external data type to which the data type will be converted
tmlen:	determine the length of the data type as a textual representation
tmcvt:	convert the data type to a displayable format

A function definition provides the names of the functions that are used to invoke operations. It consists of a function name and a function identifier. A function instance definition defines the use of a function or operator in a particular context (for example, the operator '+' may be used differently for different data types). When a new ADT is defined, a function instance must also be defined for each function or operator that the new ADT requires. A function instance definition includes:

- a function instance identifier;

- a function instance complement identifier (if the function is a comparison function; for example, '<');
- a function identifier for which this is an instance;
- an operator type;
- the number and types of any arguments;
- the data type of the result;
- the length of the result;
- the address of the routine that implements the instance.

Functions must be written in a language that conforms to the calling and operational conventions of C. The functions are compiled and linked into the INGRES executable image, thus forming part of the underlying system. This implies that a fault in a user-defined function may result in some indeterminate error, which may affect the integrity of the database.

17.4.4   SQL3

In Chapters 11 and 12, we provided an extensive tutorial on the features of the 1992 ISO (International Standards Organization) SQL standard, commonly referred to as SQL2 or SQL-92. In this section, we briefly examine the proposed object-oriented features of the next release of the SQL standard, SQL3. We will see that many of the concepts that we discussed in Section 17.2 are in the proposal. It is expected that SQL3 will be issued as an official standard around 1996–97. At the time of writing, SQL3 is not yet at the draft standard stage: therefore, some of the details in this section may change.

Abstract Data Types (ADTs)

SQL3 allows the definition of an abstract data type that specifies the behaviour of similar objects, called instances of the ADT. The ADT definition consists of **attribute specifications** and **function specifications**. Encapsulation is enforced, so that only the definition of attributes and functions are visible outside the type definition, not their implementation. Attributes and functions can be further protected using the tags *public*, *private* or *protected*, as in C++. If no tag is specified, the last specified tag is assumed. The default for the first tag is public. Figure 17.14 shows an example of an ADT definition for a **person**.

This example illustrates the use of **stored** and **virtual attributes**. A **stored attribute** is the default type with an attribute name and data type. The data type can be any known data type, including other ADTs. In contrast, **virtual attributes** do not correspond to stored data, but to derived data. The Age attribute is declared to be virtual and is derived using the *get_age* function and assigned using the *set_age* function. The value of an attribute can be accessed using the standard dot notation. Attributes can be specified as UPDATABLE (the default), READONLY or CONSTANT. Read only attributes cannot be updated; constant attributes can be assigned values only at the time of creation.

```
CREATE TYPE person(
    PRIVATE
        date_of_birth DATE CHECK (date_of_birth < DATE '1995-01-01'),
    PUBLIC
        fname VARCHAR NOT NULL,
        lname VARCHAR NOT NULL,
        address VARCHAR NOT NULL,
        tel_no VARCHAR NOT NULL,
        sex CONSTANT CHAR,
        age UPDATABLE VIRTUAL GET WITH get_age SET WITH set_age,
        next_of_kin REF (person),
        EQUALS DEFAULT,
        LESS THAN NONE,
        CONSTRUCTOR FUNCTION person (P person, FN VARCHAR, LN VARCHAR,
            ADD VARCHAR, TEL VARCHAR, S CHAR, DOB DATE)
          RETURNS person
        BEGIN
            SET P.fname = FN;
            SET P.lname = LN;
            SET P.address = ADD;
            SET P.tel_no = TEL;
            SET P.sex = S;
            SET P.date_of_birth = DOB;
            RETURN P;
        END,
        DESTRUCTOR PROCEDURE remove_person(P person);
        BEGIN
            /* Any necessary cleanup actions go here */
            DESTROY P;
        END,
        ACTOR FUNCTION get_age (P person) RETURNS INTEGER;
            RETURN /* code to calculate age from date_of_birth */
        END,
        ACTOR FUNCTION set_age (P person, DOB: DATE);
            RETURN /* set date_of_birth */
        END
        );
```

Figure 17.14
Example ADT type
definition in SQL3.

SQL3 defines three types of functions that can be used in an ADT: constructors, destructors and actors. **Constructors** are used to initialize new instances of an ADT, and **destructors** are used to release instance resources. In the present SQL3 specification, constructors and destructors do not actually create and destroy instances of an ADT, as we might expect. **Actor functions** perform all other operations on instances of an ADT. In Figure 17.14, the functions *person* and *remove_person* are the constructor and destructor functions, and *get_age* and *set_age* are actor functions. It is also possible to specify equality and less-than comparison functions through EQUAL and LESS THAN clauses. In Figure 17.14, we specify the default equality function, which compares the equality of the values in two instances, and we specify LESS THAN as undefined.

Object identity

A unique Object Identifier (OID) is associated with each ADT instance. The OID is assumed to be an implicit stored attribute of the ADT, although it cannot be assigned or updated by users. An OID has a type of REF, similar to the notion of a pointer type in C++, and is used to model shared objects. In our example, the value of the Next-of-Kin attribute is an OID corresponding to a Person instance. The same Next-of-Kin can then be shared by multiple Person instances. Using the keyword WITHOUT OID, it is also possible to specify that an ADT should not have an associated OID.

Subtypes and supertypes

SQL3 allows ADTs to participate in a subtype/supertype hierarchy using the UNDER clause. For example, to create a subtype Staff of Person we could write:

```
CREATE TYPE staff UNDER person(
        sno VARCHAR NOT NULL,
        position VARCHAR NOT NULL,
        salary DECIMAL(6,2),
        nin VARCHAR NOT NULL,
        . . . .)
```

A subtype can define attributes and functions like any other ADT. Names of functions can be overloaded. SQL3 supports the concept of **substitutability**: that is, whenever an instance of a supertype is expected an instance of the subtype can be used in its place.

Creating tables

To maintain upwards compatibility with the SQL2 standard, it is still necessary to use the CREATE TABLE statement to create a relation, even if the relation consists of a single ADT. For example, to create a table using the Person ADT we write:

```
CREATE TABLE persons(
        info PERSON);
```

We can also use an ADT within a table. For example:

```
CREATE TABLE renter(
        info PERSON,
        pref_type VARCHAR,
        max_rent DECIMAL(6,2));
```

We can also create a table that inherits all the attributes of an existing table using the UNDER clause. For example:

```
CREATE TABLE owner UNDER person;
```

Querying data

SQL3 provides the same syntax as in SQL2 for querying and updating tables. For example, to find the names of Managers, we could write:

```
SELECT s.lname
FROM staff s
WHERE position = 'Manager';
```

To find the telephone number of the next of kin for a person named Brand, we use the subobject Next-of-Kin directly in the SELECT clause as follows:

```
SELECT tel_no (next_of_kin)
FROM person
WHERE lname = 'Brand';
```

In SQL2, this query would have required a nested subquery. It is also possible to use actor functions within a query. For example, if we have an actor function *get_city* that extracts the city component from an address, we could write:

```
SELECT lname, get_city(address)
FROM staff
WHERE position = 'Manager';
```

SQL3 enforces the encapsulation level, so that we are not allowed to access private or protected attributes, such as *date_of_birth*.

17.5   Object-Oriented Database Design

In this section, we discuss how to adapt the methodology presented in Chapter 7 for an ODBMS. We start the discussion with a comparison of the basis for our methodology, the Enhanced Entity–Relationship Model and the primary object-oriented concepts. In Section 17.5.2, we examine the relationships that can exist between objects and how referential integrity can be handled. We conclude this section with some guidelines for identifying methods.

17.5.1   Comparison between Object Data Modelling and Logical Data Modelling

The methodology for logical database design presented in Chapter 7, based on the Enhanced Entity–Relationship (EER) model, has similarities with Object Data Modelling (ODM), as shown in Table 17.3. The main difference is the encapsulation of both state and behaviour in an object, whereas the EER model only accounts for state and has no knowledge of behaviour. Thus,

Table 17.3   Comparison of ODM and LDM.

ODM	LDM	Difference
Object	Entity	Object includes behaviour
Attribute	Attribute	None
Relationship	Relationship	Associations are the same but inheritance in ODM includes both state and behaviour
Messages		No corresponding concept in LDM
Class	Entity Type	None
Instance	Entity	None
Encapsulation		No corresponding concept in LDM

Logical Data Modelling (LDM) has no concept of messages and consequently no provision for encapsulation.

The similarity between the two approaches makes the logical data modelling methodology presented in Chapter 7 a reasonable basis for a methodology for object-oriented database design. Although this methodology is aimed primarily at relational database design, the model can be mapped with relative simplicity to the network and hierarchical models. The data model produced had many-to-many relationships and recursive relationships removed (Step 1.2.1). These are unnecessary changes for object-oriented modelling and can be omitted. These changes were introduced because of the limited modelling power of the traditional data models. The use of normalization in the methodology is still important, and should not be omitted for object-oriented database design. Normalization is used to improve the model so that it satisfies various constraints that avoid unnecessary duplication of data. The fact that we are dealing with objects does not mean that redundancy is acceptable. In object-oriented terms, second and third normal form should be interpreted as:

'Every attribute in an object is dependent on the object identity.'

Object-oriented database design requires the database schema to include both a description of the object data structure and constraints, and the object behaviour. We discuss behaviour modelling in Section 17.5.3.

17.5.2   Relationships and Referential Integrity

Relationships are represented in an object data model using **reference attributes** (see Section 17.2.2), typically implemented using OIDs. In the methodology presented in Chapter 7, we decomposed all non-binary relationships (for example, ternary relationships) into binary relationships. In this section, we discuss how to represent binary relationships according the their cardinality: one-to-one (1:1), one-to-many (1:M) and many-to-many (M:N).

1:1 relationships

A 1:1 relationship between objects A and B is represented by adding a refer-ence attribute to object A and, to maintain referential integrity, a reference attribute to object B. For example, there is a 1:1 relationship between the entities Manager and Branch, as represented in Figure 17.15.

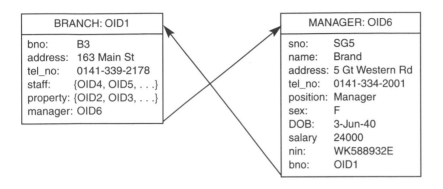

Figure 17.15 A 1:1 relationship between Manager and Branch.

1:M relationships

A 1:M relationship between objects A and B is represented by adding a reference attribute to object B and an attribute containing a set of references to A. For example, there are 1:M relationships represented in Figure 17.16, one between Branch and Sales_Staff, and the other between Sales_Staff and Property_for_Rent.

M:N relationships

An M:N relationship between objects A and B is represented by adding an attribute containing a set of references to each object. For example, there is a M:N relationship between the entities Renter and Property_for_Rent, as represented in Figure 17.17. For relational database design, we would decom-pose the M:N relationship into two 1:M relationships linked by an inter-mediate entity. It is also possible to represent this model in an ODBMS, as shown in Figure 17.18.

Referential integrity

In Section 3.3.3, we discussed referential integrity in terms of primary and foreign keys. Referential integrity requires that any referenced object must exist. For example, consider the 1:1 relationship between Manager and Branch in Figure 17.15. The Branch instance, OID1, references a Manager instance, OID6. If the user deletes this Manager instance without updating the Branch instance accordingly, referential integrity is lost. There are several techniques that can be used to handle referential integrity:

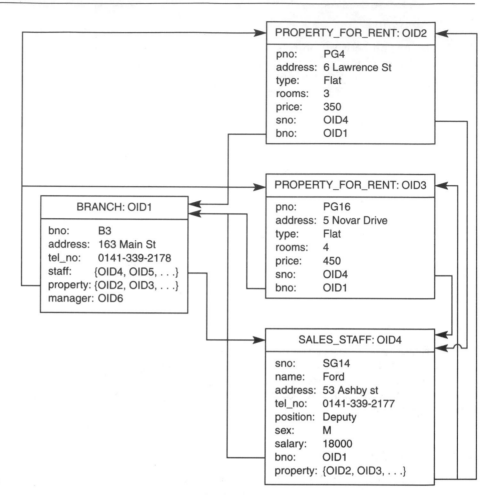

Figure 17.16 1:M relationships between Branch, Sales_Staff and Property_for_Rent.

- Do not allow the user to explicitly delete objects. In this case, the system is responsible for 'garbage collection'; in other words, the system automatically deletes objects when they are no longer accessible by the user, the approach taken by GemStone.

- Allow the user to delete objects when they are no longer required. In this case, the system may detect invalid references automatically and set the reference to NULL (the null pointer) or disallow the deletion. The Versant ODBMS uses this approach to referential integrity.

- Allow the user to modify and delete objects and relationships when they are no longer required. In this case, the system automatically maintains the integrity of objects. Inverse attributes can be used to maintain referential integrity. For example, in Figure 17.15, we have a relationship from Branch to Manager and an inverse relationship from Manager to Branch. When a Manager object is deleted, it is easy for the system to

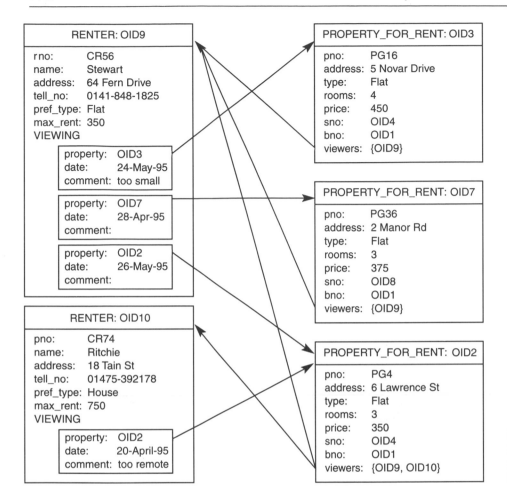

Figure 17.17 An M:N relationship between Renter and Property_for_Rent.

use this inverse relationship to adjust the reference in the Branch object accordingly. The Ontos, Objectivity/DB and ObjectStore ODBMSs provide this form of integrity.

17.5.3   Identifying Methods

The EER approach by itself is insufficient to complete the design of an object-oriented database. The EER approach must be supported with a technique that identifies and documents the behaviour of each class of object. This involves a detailed analysis of the processing requirements of the enterprise. In a conventional data flow approach using Data Flow Diagrams (DFDs), for example, the processing requirements of the system are analysed separately from the data model. In object-oriented analysis, the processing requirements are mapped onto a set of methods that are unique for each class. The methods

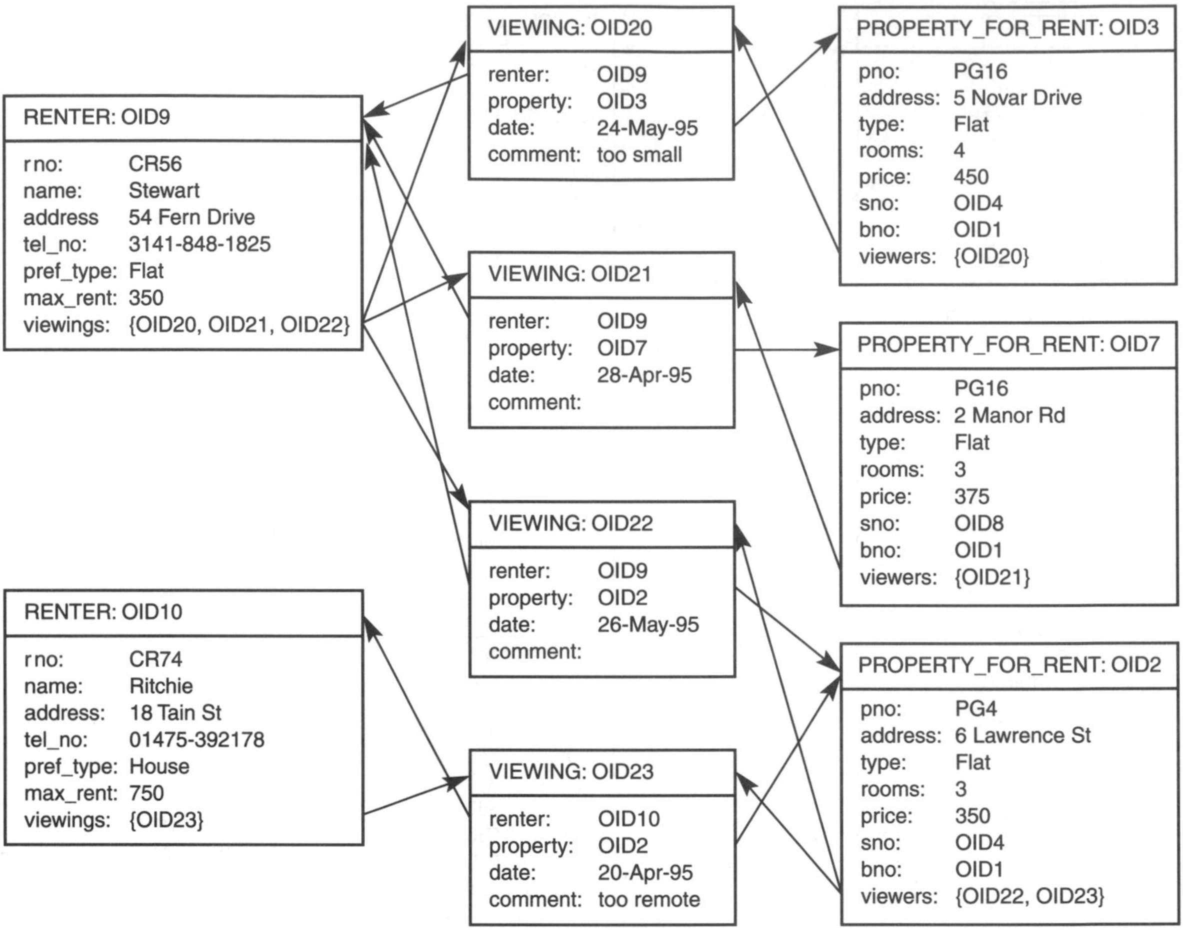

Figure 17.18
Alternative design of M:N with intermediate class.

that are visible to the user or to other objects (**public methods**) must be distinguished from methods that are purely internal to a class (**private methods**). We can identify three types of public and private methods:

- constructors and destructors,
- access,
- transform.

Constructors and destructors

Constructor methods generate new instances of a class. Each new instance is given a unique OID. Destructor methods delete class instances that are no longer required. In some systems, destruction is an automatic process:

whenever an object becomes inaccessible from any other object it is automatically deleted. We referred to this previously as garbage collection.

Access

Access methods return the value of an attribute or set of attributes of a class instance. It may return a single attribute value, multiple attribute values or a collection of values. For example, we may have a method *get_salary* for a class Sales_Staff, which returns a member of staff's salary, or we may have a method *get_contact_number* for a class Person, which returns a person's telephone and fax number. An access method may also return data relating to the class. For example, we may have a method *get_average_salary* for a class Sales_Staff, which calculates the average salary of all sales staff. An access method may also derive data from an attribute. For example, we may have a method *get-age* for Person, which calculates a person's age from their date of birth.

Transform

Transform methods change (transform) the state of a class instance. For example, we may have a method *increment_salary* for the Sales_Staff class, which increases a member of staff's salary by a fixed annual inflation rate.

A more complete description of identifying methods is outside the scope of this book. There are several methodologies for object-oriented analysis and design, and the interested reader is referred to Rumbaugh *et al.* (1991), Coad and Yourdon (1991) and Graham (1993).

17.6   Object Database Standard (1993)

In this section, we review the new standard for the Object Data Model (ODM) proposed by the Object Database Management Group (ODMG). It consists of an object model (Section 17.6.3), an object definition language (Section 17.6.4), equivalent to the Data Definition Language (DDL) of a conventional DBMS, and an object query language with an SQL-like syntax (Section 17.6.5). We start with a brief presentation of the function of the OMG.

17.6.1   The Object Management Group

The Object Management Group (OMG) is an international nonprofit-making industry consortium founded in 1989 to address the issues of object standards. The group currently has more than 430 member organizations including virtually all platform vendors and major software vendors such as IBM, Microsoft, Apple, AT&T/NCR. All of these companies have agreed to work together to create a set of standards acceptable to all. The primary aims of the OMG are promotion of the object-oriented approach to software engineering, and the development of standards in which the location, environment, language and other characteristics of objects are completely transparent to other objects.

The OMG is not a recognized standards group, unlike the International Standards Organization (ISO) or national bodies such as the American National Standards Institute (ANSI) or the Institute of Electrical and Electronics Engineers (IEEE). The aim of the OMG is to develop *de facto* standards that will eventually be acceptable to ISO/ANSI. The OMG does not actually develop or distribute products, but they will certify compliance with the OMG standards.

The OMG seeks to define standard object-based facilities for supporting a number of advanced features:

- **concurrent execution**, allowing many objects to execute their methods simultaneously, on either the same or different computers;

- **distributed transactions**, allowing interactions between groups of objects to be atomic;

- **versioning**, allowing changes to the properties of objects to be managed in such a way that object references always point to the correct version of an object;

- **event notification**, allowing objects to be automatically activated whenever certain events occur;

- **internationalization**, allowing country-specific variations to be handled transparently.

In 1990, the OMG published its Object Management Architecture (OMA) Guide document (Soley, 1992). This guide specified a single terminology for object-oriented languages, systems, databases and application frameworks; an abstract framework for object-oriented systems; a set of technical and architectural goals; and a reference model for distributed applications using object-oriented techniques. Four areas of standardization were identified for the reference model: the Object Model (OM), the Object Request Broker (ORB), the object services and the common facilities, as illustrated in Figure 17.19. Already some vendors, including DEC, Hewlett-Packard, IBM, Object Design Inc and Objectivity, have announced products that comply with the Common Object Request Broker Architecture (CORBA), and many more will soon follow.

The Object Model (OM)

The OM is a design-portable abstract model for communicating with OMG-compliant object-oriented systems (see Figure 17.20). A requester sends a request for object services to the ORB, which keeps track of all the objects in the system and the types of services they can provide. The ORB then forwards the message to a provider who acts on the message and passes a response back to the requester via the ORB.

The Object Request Broker (ORB)

The ORB handles distribution of messages between application objects in a highly interoperable manner. In effect, the ORB is a distributed 'software bus' that enables objects (requesters) to make and receive requests and responses from a provider. On receipt of a response from the provider, the ORB translates the response into a form that the original requester can understand. The ORB is analogous to the X500 electronic mail communications standard, wherein a requester can issue a request to another application or node without having detailed knowledge of its directory services structure. In this way, the ORB removes much of the need for complex Remote Procedure Calls (RPCs) by providing the mechanisms by which objects make and receive requests and responses transparently. The objective is to provide interoperability between applications in a heterogeneous distributed environment and to connect multiple object systems transparently.

The object services

The object services provide the main functions for realizing basic object functionality. Many of these services are database-oriented.

The common facilities

The common facilities comprise a set of tasks that many applications must perform but are traditionally duplicated within each one. In the OMG

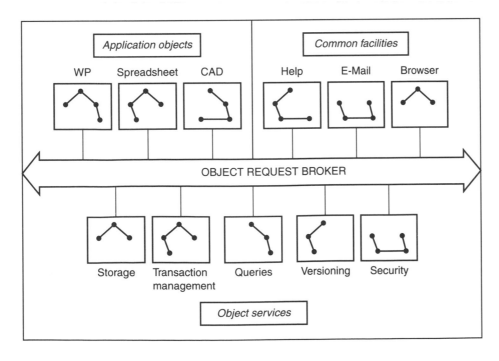

Figure 17.19
Object reference model.

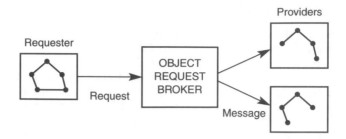

Figure 17.20 Object model.

Reference Model they are made available through OMA-compliant class interfaces.

17.6.2 The ODMG Object Model

Several important vendors have formed an Object Database Management Group (ODMG) to define standards for ODBMSs. These vendors include Object Design, Ontos, O_2 Technology, Versant Object Technology and Objectivity. The ODMG has produced an object model that specifies a standard model for the semantics of database objects. The model is important because it determines the built-in semantics that the ODBMS understands and can enforce. The design of class libraries and applications that use these semantics should be portable across the various ODBMSs that support the object model (Connolly, 1994).

The major components of the ODMG architecture for an ODBMS are:

- Object Model (OM),
- Object Definition Language (ODL),
- Object Query Language (OQL),
- C++ language binding,
- Smalltalk language binding.

We discuss the first three components in the remainder of this section. For information on the latter two components, the interested reader is referred to Cattell (1994a, 1994b).

17.6.3 The Object Model (OM)

The ODMG object model specifies the following basic modelling primitives:

- The basic modelling primitive is the **object**.
- Objects can be categorized into **types**. All objects of a given type exhibit common behaviour and state. A type is itself an object.

- Behaviour is defined by a set of **operations** that can be performed on an object.

- State is defined by the values objects carry for a set of **properties.** A property may be either an **attribute** of the object or a **relationship** between the object and one or more other objects.

Objects

Object types are decomposed orthogonally as (1) mutable or immutable and (2) atomic or structured. The values of an immutable object's properties may not change. Immutable objects are generally referred to as **literals** and mutable objects simply as **objects**. The term **denotable object** is used to refer to both types of objects using a single term. The type structure has been flattened into a hierarchy by using mutability as the primary decomposition, as illustrated in Figure 17.21. In this figure, the types shown in bold are abstract types; the types shown in normal typeface are directly instantiable. In other words, we can specify only types that are instantiable.

Denotable objects also have characteristics that consist of properties and operations. Properties model the **state** of an object, which includes its attributes and relationships to other objects. Operations model the **behaviour** of an object.

Each object has a unique identity that does not change and is not reused when the object is deleted. The identity of a literal is its value. For an object, a unique identifier is created, called the OID. An object may also be given one or more names that are meaningful to the user in addition to the OID, provided each name identifies a single object within the scope of the definition of the name. The model specifies built-in operations that allow objects to be created and deleted.

The standard specifies that the lifetime of an object is orthogonal to its type. This means that persistence is independent of type. The lifetime is specified when the object is created and may be:

- **Coterminus_with_procedure**: The object's storage is allocated from the programming language's runtime stack when the procedure is invoked and is released when the procedure returns.

- **Coterminus_with_process**: The object's storage is allocated dynamically by the programming language runtime from either static storage or the heap.

- **Coterminus_with_database**: The object's storage is managed by the ODBMS.

Types and classes
A type has one **interface** and one or more **implementations**. The (external) interface defines the properties and operations that can be invoked on instances of the type. An implementation defines data structures and methods that operate on the data structures to support the required state and behaviour. The combination of the type interface and one implementation

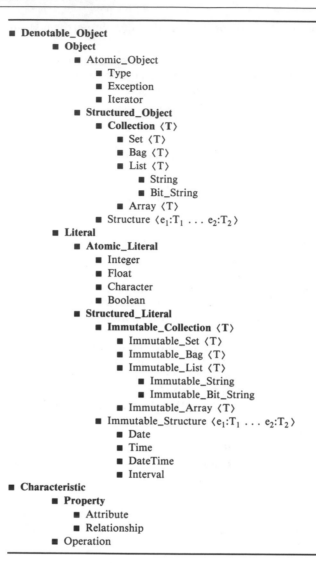

■ **Denotable_Object**
  ■ **Object**
    ■ **Atomic_Object**
      ■ Type
      ■ Exception
      ■ Iterator
    ■ **Structured_Object**
      ■ **Collection** $\langle T \rangle$
        ■ Set $\langle T \rangle$
        ■ Bag $\langle T \rangle$
        ■ List $\langle T \rangle$
          ■ String
          ■ Bit_String
        ■ Array $\langle T \rangle$
      ■ Structure $\langle e_1:T_1 \ldots e_2:T_2 \rangle$
  ■ **Literal**
    ■ **Atomic_Literal**
      ■ Integer
      ■ Float
      ■ Character
      ■ Boolean
    ■ **Structured_Literal**
      ■ **Immutable_Collection** $\langle T \rangle$
        ■ Immutable_Set $\langle T \rangle$
        ■ Immutable_Bag $\langle T \rangle$
        ■ Immutable_List $\langle T \rangle$
          ■ Immutable_String
          ■ Immutable_Bit_String
        ■ Immutable_Array $\langle T \rangle$
      ■ Immutable_Structure $\langle e_1:T_1 \ldots e_2:T_2 \rangle$
        ■ Date
        ■ Time
        ■ DateTime
        ■ Interval
■ **Characteristic**
  ■ **Property**
    ■ Attribute
    ■ Relationship
  ■ Operation

Figure 17.21 The full built-in type structure of the ODMG object model.

is a **class**. Thus, type is an abstract concept and class is an implementational concept. The interface definition of a type specifies its **supertype(s)**, its **extent** and its **keys**:

- *Supertypes*   Object types are related in a supertype/subtype lattice. All of the attributes, relationships and operations defined on a supertype are inherited by the subtype. The subtype may define additional properties and operations and may redefine inherited properties and operations.

- *Extents*   The set of all instances of a given type is its extent. The programmer may request that the ODBMS maintain an index to the members of this set. Deleting an object will remove the object from the extent of a type of which it is an instance.

- *Keys* A key uniquely identifies the instances of a type (similar to the concept of a candidate key defined in Section 3.2.5).

Attributes

An attribute is defined on a single object type. It does not have an OID but takes as its value a literal or set of literals. The following built-in operations are defined on attributes (which may be overridden):

- set_value(new_value: Literal)   Sets attribute to a new literal value.
- get_value() : Literal   Returns current value of an attribute.

Relationships

Any (mutable) object may participate in relationships with other (mutable) objects. However, the current model supports only binary relationships with cardinality 1:1, 1:M and M:N. A relationship does not have a name; instead, **traversal paths** are defined in the interface for each direction of traversal. For example, a Branch *Has* a set of Staff and a member of Staff *WorksAt* a Branch, would be represented as:

```
interface Branch
{
        Has: Set ⟨Staff⟩ inverse Staff :: WorksAt
}
interface Staff
{
        WorksAt: Branch inverse Branch :: Has
}
```

Referential integrity of relationships is maintained automatically by the ODBMS and an exception (that is, an error) is generated if an attempt is made to traverse a relationship in which one of the participating objects has been deleted. The model specifies built-in operations to create, add, delete and traverse relationships.

Operations

The instances of an object type have behaviour that is specified as a set of operations. The object type definition includes an **operation signature** for each operation that specifies the names and types of each argument, the names of any exceptions that can be raised and the types of the values returned, if any. An operation can be defined only in the context of a single object type. Overloading operation names is supported. The model assumes sequential execution of operations, and does not require support for concurrent or parallel or remote operations, although it does not preclude such support.

Structured objects

Besides atomic objects, the ODMG model also supports structured objects. The type **Structured_Object** has two subtypes: *Collection* and *Structure* (see Figure 17.21). A **structure** contains a fixed number of named heterogeneous elements. Each element is a ⟨name, value⟩ pair, where *value* may be any subtype of *Denotable_Object*. For example, we could define a structure Date, consisting of elements Year, Month and Day. In this respect, a structure is similar to the **struct** or **record** type in programming languages. Since structures are literals, they may occur as the value of an attribute in an object definition. The ODMG model also supports structured literals. Structured literals are created by applications, but once created cannot be modified. As with atomic literals, they do not have OIDs.

On the other hand, a **collection** contains an arbitrary number of unnamed homogeneous elements. For example, we could define the set of all branch offices as a collection. A collection has an OID, and may be defined over any instantiable subtype of *Denotable_Object*. Iteration of a collection is achieved by defining an iterator that maintains a current position within the given collection. There are ordered and unordered collections. Ordered collections must be traversed first to last, or vice versa; unordered collections have no fixed order of iteration. The type Collection has operations to create a collection, create an iterator, insert, remove, retrieve and select elements from a collection. The model specifies four built-in collection subtypes:

- Set: unordered collections that do not allow duplicates;
- Bag: unordered collections that do allow duplicates;
- List: ordered collections that allow duplicates;
- Array: one-dimensional array of dynamically varying length.

Each subtype has operations to create an instance of the type and insert an element into the collection. Sets and Bags have the usual set operations: union, intersection and difference.

Transactions

The ODMG object model supports the concept of transactions, which are logical units of work that take the database from one consistent state to another (see Section 15.1). The model supports nested transactions, using standard read/write locks in a pessimistic concurrency control protocol. All access, creation, modification and deletion of persistent objects must be performed within a transaction. The model specifies built-in operations to begin, commit and abort transactions, as well as a checkpoint operation. A checkpoint commits all modified objects in the database without releasing any locks before continuing the transaction.

Databases

The ODMG object model supports the concept of databases as storage areas for persistent objects of a given set of types. A database has a schema that is a set of type definitions. Each database is an instance of type **Database** with the built-in operations open() and close() and contains_object?() to check whether a database contains a specified object.

Metadata

As we discussed in Section 2.7, metadata is 'the data about data': that is, data that describes objects in the system, such as classes, attributes and methods. Many existing ODBMSs do not treat metadata as objects in their own right, and so a user cannot query the metadata as he or she can query other objects. The ODMG model defines all of the types shown in Figure 17.21 to be instances of type *Type*, which is itself a subtype and an instance of type *Atomic_Object*. The type *Type* has attributes and operations that can be queried, providing a user-accessible catalogue.

17.6.4   The Object Definition Language (ODL)

The Object Definition Language (ODL) is a specification language for defining the interfaces to object types for ODMG-compliant systems. Its main objective is to facilitate portability of schemas between compliant systems while helping to provide interoperability between ODBMS vendors. ODL is equivalent to the Data Definition Language (DDL) of traditional DBMSs. It defines the attributes and relationships of types and specifies the signature of the operations. It does not address the implementation of signatures. The syntax of ODL extends the Interface Definition Language (IDL) of the Common Object Request Broker Architecture (CORBA) (OMG and X/Open, 1992). The ODMG hope that the ODL will be the basis for integrating schemas from multiple sources and applications.

A complete specification of the syntax of ODL is beyond the scope of this book. However, the following example illustrates some of the elements of the language. The interested reader is referred to Cattell (1994a) for a complete definition.

Example 17.1:   The Object Definition Language _____

Consider the simplified Property for Rent schema for the *DreamHome* agency, as shown in Figure 17.22. An example ODL definition for part of this schema is shown in Figure 17.23.

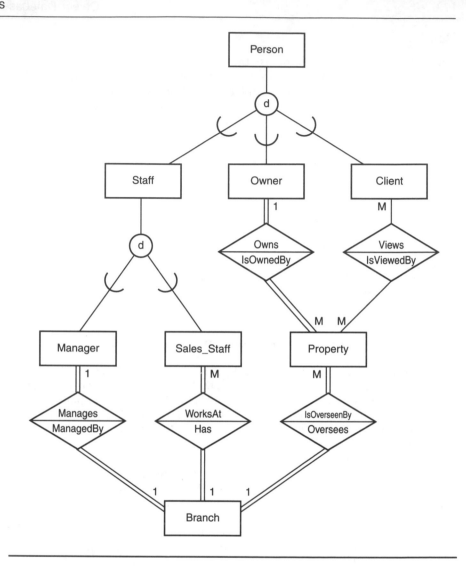

Figure 17.22
Example *DreamHome*
property for Rent
schema.

Figure 17.23 ODL
definition for part of
the *DreamHome*
Property for Rent
schema

```
interface Branch {
        extent branch_offices;
        key bno;
/* Define attributes */
        attribute string bno;
        attribute ⟨struct⟨string street, string area, string city, string post_code⟩⟩;
        attribute string tel_no;
        attribute string fax_no;

/* Define relationships */
        relationship Manager ManagedBy inverse Manager :: Manages;
        relationship Set⟨Sales_Staff⟩ Has inverse Sales_Staff :: WorksAt;
        relationship Set⟨Property_for_Rent⟩ Oversees
```

```
                          inverse Property_for_Rent :: IsOverseenBy;
/* Define operations */
                  take_on_property_for_rent(in Property_for_Rent)
                      raises(property_already_for_rent);
        }


        interface Person {
/* Define attributes */
                  attribute ⟨struct⟨string fname, string lname⟩⟩;
                  attribute string address;
                  attribute string tel_no;
                  attribute string sex;
                  attribute date date_of_birth;
/* Define operations */
                  age();
        }


        interface Staff:Person {          /* Inherits from Person */
                  extent staff;
                  keys sno, nin;
/* Define attributes */
                  enum {Manager, Deputy, Snr_Asst, Assistant} position_type; /*
                  Enumerated type for position */
                  attribute string sno;
                  attribute position_type position;
                  attribute float salary;
                  attribute string nin;
/* Define operations */
                  delete_staff() raises(no_such_staff_member);
                  increase_salary(in float);
        }


        interface Manager:Staff {        /* Inherits from Staff */
                  extent managers;
/* Define relationships */
                  relationship Branch Manages inverse Branch :: ManagedBy;
        }


        interface Sales_Staff:Staff {    /* Inherits from Staff */
                  extent sales_staff;
/* Define relationships */
                  relationship Branch WorksAt inverse Branch :: Has;
/* Define operations */
                  transfer_staff(in from:Branch, in to:Branch)
                  raises(does_not_work_in_branch);
        }
```

Figure 17.23
Continued.

17.6.5   The Object Query Language (OQL)

The Object Query Language (OQL) provides declarative access to the object database using an SQL-like syntax. It does not provide explicit update operators, but leaves this to the operations defined on object types. As with SQL, OQL can be used as a standalone language and as a language embedded in another language. An OQL query is a function that delivers an object whose type may be inferred from the operator contributing to the query expression. Before we define an OQL query, we first have to understand the composition of expressions.

Expressions

- **Query definition expression**   A query definition expression is of the form: **DEFINE Q AS e**. This defines a query with name Q, given a query expression e.

- **Elementary expressions**   An expression can be a variable, an atom, a named object or a query definition expression (Q above).

- **Construction expressions**

  - If T is a type name with properties $p_1, \ldots p_n$, and $e_1, \ldots e_n$ are expressions, then $T(p_1{:}e_1, \ldots p_n{:}e_n)$ is an expression. An example of an expression is:

    Branch(bno:"B3", manager: "Susan Brand")

  - Similarly, we can construct expressions using struct, set, list, bag and array. For example:

    struct(bno:"B3", street:"163 Main St")

  is an expression, which dynamically creates an instance of this type.

- **Arithmetic expressions**   Expressions can be formed using the standard unary and binary operations on expressions.

- **Collections expressions**   Expressions can be formed using universal quantification (**for all**), existential quantification (**exists**), membership testing (**in**), select clause (**select from where**), sort-by operator (**sort**), unary set operators (**min, max, count, sum, avg**) and the group-by operator (**group**). The format of the SELECT clause is:

SELECT [DISTINCT] ⟨expression⟩
FROM ⟨from_list⟩
WHERE ⟨expression⟩

---

where:

   ⟨from_list⟩   ::=   ⟨variable_name⟩ **IN** ⟨expression⟩ |
                    ⟨variable_name⟩ **IN** ⟨expression⟩, ⟨from_list⟩

The result of the query is a set for SELECT DISTINCT and a bag for SELECT

- **Indexed collections expressions**　If e_1, e_2 are lists or arrays and e_3, e_4 are integers, then $e_1[e_3]$, $e_1[e_3:e_4]$, first(e_1), last(e_1) and $(e_1 + e_2)$ are expressions.

- **Binary set expressions**　If e_1, e_2 are sets or bags, then the set operators union, except and intersect of e_1 and e_2 are expressions.

- **Structure expressions**　If e is an expression and p is a property name, then $e.p$ and $e \rightarrow p$ are expressions, which extract the property p of an object e.

- **Conversion expressions**

  - If e is an expression, then element(e) is an expression that checks e is a singleton, raising an exception if it is not.

  - If e is a list expression, then listtoset(e) is an expression that converts the list into a set.

  - If e is a collection-valued expression, then flatten(e) is an expression that converts a collection of collections into a collection, that is, it flattens the structure.

  - If e is an expression and c is a type name, then $c(e)$ is an expression that asserts e is an object of type c, raising an exception if it is not.

- **Object expressions**　If e is an expression and f is an operation, then $e.f$ and $e \rightarrow f$ are expressions that apply an operation to an object. The operation can optionally take a number of expressions as parameters.

Queries

A query consists of a (possibly empty) set of query definition expressions followed by an expression. The result of a query is an object with or without identity.

Example 17.2:　The Object Query Language _____

(1)　To get a set of all staff (with identity), the query would be simply:

> staff

(2)　To get a set of all branch managers (with identity), the query would be:

> branch_offices.ManagedBy

(3)　To get a set of all staff who live in London (without identity), the query would be:

> define Londoners as
> 　　　select x
> 　　　from x in staff
> 　　　where x.address.city = "London"
> select x.name.lname from x in Londoners

This returns a literal of type set⟨string⟩.

(4)   To get a structured set (without identity) containing name, sex and age for all staff who live in London, the query would be:

```
select struct (lname:x.name.lname, sex:x.sex, age:x.age)
from x in staff
where x.address.city = "London"
```

This returns a literal of type set⟨struct⟩.

(5)   To get a structured set (with identity) containing name, sex and age for all deputy managers over 60, the query would be:

```
type deputies {attribute lname : string; age : integer;}
deputies (select struct (lname:x.name.lname, sex:x.sex, age:x.age)
        from x in (select y from staff where position = "Deputy")
        where x.age > 60)
```

This returns a mutable object of type *deputies*.

(6)   To get a structured set (without identity) containing branch number and the set of all Assistants at the branches in London, the query would be:

```
select struct (bno:x.bno, assistants: (select y from y in x.WorksAt where
y.position = "Assistant"))
from x in (select z from branch_offices where z.address.city = "London")
```

This returns a literal of type set⟨struct⟩.

Creating objects

A type name constructor is used to create an object with identity. For example, to create a Person, we would write:

```
Person(fname:"John", lname:"White", address:"19 Taylor St, Cranford,
London", tel_no:"0171-884-5112", sex:"M", date_of_birth:"1-Oct-45")
```

Any properties that are not initialized are given a default value. It is also possible to build objects from a query. For example, if we have a type **retirer**, say, then we could create an object of this type using:

```
retirer(select struct (lname:x.name.lname, sex:x.sex, age:x.age)
from x in staff
where x.age > 60)
```

Objects without identity are created using **struct**, as illustrated in Example 17.2(4).

Chapter Summary

- Advanced database applications include Computer-Aided Design (CAD), Computer-Aided Manufacturing (CAM), Computer-Aided Software Engineering (CASE), Office Automation (OA) and Computer-Aided Publishing (CAP), as well as applications with complex and interrelated objects and procedural data. The limited modelling capabilities of relational systems have made them unsuitable for advanced database applications.

- An **object** is a uniquely identifiable entity that contains both the attributes that describe the state of a real-world object and the actions that are associated with a real-world object. Objects can contain other objects. A key part of the definition of an object is unique identity. In an object-oriented system, each object has a unique system-wide identifier that is independent of the values of its attributes and invisible to the user.

- **Methods** define the behaviour of the object. They can be used to change the object's state by modifying its attribute values or to query the value of selected attributes. **Messages** are the means by which objects communicate. A message is simply a request from one object (the sender) to another object (the receiver) asking the second object to execute one of its methods. The sender and receiver may be the same object.

- Objects that have the same attributes and respond to the same messages can be grouped together to form a **class**. The attributes and associated methods can then be defined once for the class rather than separately for each object. A class is also an object and has its own attributes and methods, referred to as **class attributes** and **class methods**, respectively. Class attributes describe the general characteristics of the class, such as totals or averages.

- **Inheritance** allows one class of objects to be defined as a special case of a more general class. These special cases are known as **subclasses** and the more general cases are known as **superclasses**. The process of forming a superclass is referred to as **generalization**; forming a subclass is **specialization**. A subclass inherits all of the properties of its superclass and additionally defines its own unique properties. All instances of the subclass are also instances of the superclass.

- **Polymorphism** allows the name of a method to be reused. Dynamic binding allows the determination of an object's type and methods to be deferred until runtime.

- An **ODBMS** is a manager of an ODB. An ODB is a persistent and sharable repository of objects defined in an ODM. An ODM is a data model that captures the semantics of objects supported in object-oriented programming. There is no universally agreed ODM.

- **Extended relational data models** are based on enhancements of the relational data model to incorporate procedures, objects, versions and other new capabilities. There is no single extended relational model.

- Several important vendors have formed an **Object Database Management Group (ODMG)** to define standards for ODBMSs. The ODMG has produced an object model that specifies a standard model for the semantics of database objects. The model is important because it determines the built-in semantics that the ODBMS understands and can enforce. The design of class libraries and applications that use these semantics should be portable across the various ODBMSs that support the object model. The major components of the ODMG architecture for an ODBMS are: an Object Model (OM), an Object Definition Language (ODL), an Object Query Language (OQL) and C++ and Smalltalk language bindings.

REVIEW QUESTIONS

17.1 Discuss why the weaknesses of relational DBMSs may make them unsuitable for advanced database applications.

17.2 Discuss each of the following concepts in the context of an object data model:

(a)   objects and attributes;

(b)   object identity;

(c)   methods and messages;

(d)   classes, subclasses, superclasses and inheritance;

(e)   overloading;

(f)   polymorphism and dynamic binding.

Give examples using the *DreamHome* sample data shown in Figure 3.3.

17.3 Compare and contrast the three generations of database management systems.

17.4 Discuss the main strategies that can be used to create persistent objects.

17.5 Discuss the types of transaction protocols that can be useful in design applications.

17.6 Discuss why version management may be a useful facility for some applications.

17.7 Discuss why schema control may be a useful facility for some applications.

EXERCISES

17.8 For the relational schema in the exercises at the end of Chapter 3, suggest a number of methods that would be applicable to the system. Produce an object-oriented schema for the system.

17.9 Using the schema produced above, show how the following queries would be written in OQL:

    (a)   List all hotels.

    (b)   List all single rooms with a price below £20.00 per night.

    (c)   List the names and addresses of all guests.

    (d)   List the price and type of all rooms at the Grosvenor Hotel.

    (e)   List all guests currently staying at the Grosvenor Hotel.

    (f)   List the details of all rooms at the Grosvenor Hotel, including the name of the guest staying in the room, if the room is occupied.

    (g)   List the guest details (guest_no, name and address) of all guests staying at the Grosvenor Hotel.

17.10 Produce an object-oriented database design for the *DreamHome* case study presented in Section 1.7. State any assumptions necessary to support your design.

17.11 Produce an object-oriented database design for the *Wellmeadows* Hospital student project presented in Section 1.8. State any assumptions necessary to support your design.

17.12 Show how you would implement the designs of 17.10 and 17.11 using the proposed SQL3 standard.

17.13 Analyse the relational DBMSs that you are currently using. Discuss the object-oriented facilities provided by the system. What additional functionality do these facilities provide?

Appendices

A File Organization and Storage Structures

Objectives

In this appendix you will learn:

- The distinction between primary and secondary storage.
- The meanings of file organization and access method.
- How heap files are organized.
- How ordered files are organized.
- How hash files are organized.
- What an index is and how it can be used to speed up database retrievals.
- The distinction between a primary and secondary index.
- How indexed sequential files are organized.
- How multilevel indexes are organized.
- How B^+-Trees are organized.

A.1 Introduction

In this appendix, we introduce the main concepts regarding the physical storage of the database on **secondary storage** devices such as magnetic disks and optical disks. The computer's **primary storage**, that is main memory, is inappropriate for storing the database. Although the access times for primary storage are much faster than secondary storage, it is not large or reliable enough to store the quantity of data that a typical database might require. As the data stored in primary storage disappears when power is lost, we refer to primary storage as **volatile** storage. In contrast, the data on secondary storage persists through power loss, and is consequently referred to as **non-volatile** storage. Further, the cost of storage per unit of data is an order of magnitude greater for primary storage than for disk.

In the remainder of this section, we introduce the basic concepts of physical storage. In the following three sections, we discuss the main types of file organization, namely heap, sorted and hash files. In Section A.5, we discuss how indexes can be used to improve the performance of database retrievals. In particular, we look at indexed sequential files, multilevel indexes and B^{+}-Trees. In Chapters 9 and 10, we presented a methodology for physical database design for relational systems, which provided guidelines for choosing appropriate file organizations for a given logical data model.

A.1.1 Basic Concepts

The database on secondary storage is organized into one or more **files**, where each file consists of one or more **records** and each record consists of one or more **fields**. Typically, a record corresponds to an entity and a field to an attribute. Consider the reduced Staff relation from the *DreamHome* case study shown in Figure A.1.

Sno	Lname	Position	NIN	Bno
SL21	White	Manager	WK442011B	B5
SG37	Beech	Snr Asst	WL432514C	B3
SG14	Ford	Deputy	WL220658D	B3
SA9	Howe	Assistant	WM532187D	B7
SG5	Brand	Manager	WK588932E	B3
SL41	Lee	Assistant	WA290573K	B5

Figure A.1 Reduced Staff relation from *DreamHome* case study.

We may expect each tuple to map on to a record in the operating system file that holds the Staff relation. Each field in a record would store one attribute from the Staff relation. When a user requests a tuple from the DBMS, for example Staff tuple SG37, the DBMS maps this **logical record** into a **physical record** and retrieves the physical record into the DBMS **buffers** in primary storage using the operating system file access routines.

The physical record is the unit of transfer between disk and primary storage, and vice versa. Generally, a physical record consists of more than one logical record, although sometimes, depending on size, a logical record can correspond to one physical record. It is even possible for a large logical record to span more than one physical record. The terms **block** and **page** are sometimes used in place of physical record. In the remainder of this appendix we use the term page. For example, the Staff tuples in Figure A.1 may be stored on two pages, as shown in Figure A.2.

Sno	Lname	Position	NIN	Bno		Page
SL21	White	Manager	WK442011B	B5		
SG37	Beech	Snr Asst	WL432514C	B3		1
SG14	Ford	Deputy	WL220658D	B3		
SA9	Howe	Assistant	WM532187D	B7		
SG5	Brand	Manager	WK588932E	B3		2
SL41	Lee	Assistant	WA290573K	B5		

Figure A.2 Storage of Staff relation in pages.

The order in which records are stored and accessed in the file is dependent on the file organization.

File organization	The physical arrangement of data in a file into records and pages on secondary storage.

The main types of file organization are as follows:

- **Heap** or unordered; records are placed on disk in no particular order.
- **Sorted** records are ordered by the value of a specified field.
- **Hash** records are placed on disk according to a hash function.

Along with a file organization, there is a set of access methods:

Access method	The steps involved in storing and retrieving records from a file.

Some access methods can be applied only to certain file organizations. For example, we cannot apply an indexed access method to a file without an index. In the remainder of this appendix, we discuss the main types of file organization and access techniques. Chapter 9 presented a methodology for physical database design. The chapter provides guidelines for selecting suitable storage structures for relational systems.

A.2 Heap Files

A **heap file**, sometimes called a **pile** or **sequential file**, is the simplest type of file organization. Records are placed in the file in the same order as they are inserted. A new record is inserted in the last page of the file; if there is insufficient space in the last page, a new page is added to the file. This makes insertion very efficient. However, as a heap file has no particular ordering with respect to field values, a linear search must be performed to access a record. A linear search involves reading pages from the file until the required record is found. This makes retrievals from heap files that have more than a few pages relatively slow, unless the retrieval involves a large proportion of the records in the file.

To delete a record, the required page first has to be retrieved, the record marked as deleted and the page written back to disk. The space with deleted records is not reused. Consequently, performance progressively deteriorates as deletions occur. This means that heap files have to be periodically reorganized by the Database Administrator (DBA) to reclaim the unused space of deleted records.

Heap files are one of the best organizations for bulk loading data into a table, as records are inserted at the end of the heap; there is no overhead of calculating what page the record should go on.

A.3 Ordered Files

The records in a file can be sorted on the values of one or more of the fields, forming a key-sequenced data set. The field(s) that the file is sorted on is called the **ordering field(s)**. For example, consider the following SQL query:

```
SELECT *
FROM staff
ORDER BY sno;
```

If the tuples of the Staff relation are already ordered according to the ordering attribute Sno, it should be possible to reduce the execution time for the query, as no sorting is necessary. (Although in Section 3.2 we stated that tuples are unordered, this applies as an external (logical) property not as an implementational (physical) property. There will always be a first record, second record and nth record.) If the tuples are ordered on Sno, under certain conditions we can use a binary search to execute queries that involve a search condition based on Sno. For example, consider the following SQL query:

```
SELECT *
FROM staff
WHERE sno = 'SG37';
```

If we use the sample tuples shown in Figure A.1 and for simplicity assume there is one record per page, we would get the ordered file shown in Figure A.3. The binary search proceeds as follows:

(1)   Retrieve the mid-page of the file. Check whether the required record is between the first and last record of this page. If so, no more pages need to be retrieved; the required record lies in this page.

(2)   If the value of the key field in the first record on the page is greater than the required value, the required value, if it exists, occurs on an earlier page. Therefore, we repeat the above steps using the lower half of the file as the new search area. If the value of the key field in the last record on the page is less than the required value, the required value occurs on a later page, and so we repeat the above steps using the top half of the file as the new search area. In this way, half of the search space is eliminated from the search with each page retrieved.

In our case, the middle page is page 3, and the record on the retrieved page (SG14) does not equal the one we want (SG37). The value of the key field in page 3 is less than the one we want, so we can discard the first half of the file from the search. We now retrieve the mid-page of the top half of the file, that is, page 5. This time the value of the key field (SL21) is greater than SG37, which enables us to discard the top half of this search space. We now retrieve the mid-page of the remaining search space, that is, page 4, which is the record we want.

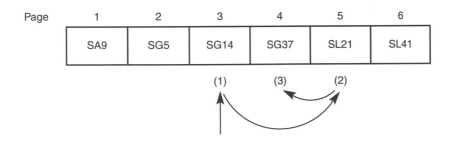

Figure A.3   Binary search on ordered file.

In general, the binary search is more efficient than a linear search. However, binary search is applied more frequently to data in primary storage than secondary storage.

Inserting and deleting records in a sorted file is problematic because the order of records has to be maintained. To insert a new record, we must find the correct position in the ordering for the record and then find space to insert it. If there is sufficient space in the required page for the new record, then the single page can be reordered and written back to disk. If this is not the case, then it would be necessary to move one or more records onto the next page. Again, the next page may have no free space and the records on this page must be moved, and so on. Inserting a record near the start of a large file could be very time-consuming. One solution is to create a temporary unsorted file, called an **overflow** or **transaction file**. Insertions are added to the overflow file and, periodically, the overflow file is merged with the main sorted file. This makes insertions very efficient, but has a detrimental effect on retrievals. If the record is not found during the binary search, the overflow file has to be searched linearly. Inversely, to delete a record we must reorganize the records to remove the now free slot.

Ordered files are rarely used for database storage unless a primary index is added to the file (see Section A.5.1).

A.4 Hash Files

In a hash file, records do not have to be written sequentially to the file. Instead, a **hash function** calculates the address of the page in which the record is to be stored based on one or more of the fields in the record. The base field is called the **hash field**, or if the field is also a key field of the file, it is called the **hash key**. Records in a hash file will appear to be randomly distributed across the available file space. For this reason, hash files are sometimes called **random** files or **direct** files.

The hash function is chosen so that records are as evenly distributed as possible throughout the file. One technique, called **folding**, applies an arithmetic function such as addition to different parts of the hash field. Character strings are converted into integers before the function is applied using some type of code – for example, alphabetic position or ASCII values. For example, we could take the first two characters of the staff number, Sno, convert them to an integer value, then add this value to the remaining digits of the field. The resulting sum is used as the address of the disk page in which the record is stored. An alternative, more popular technique, is the **division-remainder** hashing. This technique uses the MOD function, which takes the field value, divides it by some predetermined integer value and uses the remainder of this division as the disk address.

The problem with most hashing functions is that they do not guarantee a unique address because the number of possible values a hash field can take is typically much larger than the number of available addresses for records. Each address generated by a hashing function corresponds to a page, or **bucket**, with **slots** for multiple records. Within a bucket, records are placed in order of arrival. When the same address is generated for two or more records, a **collision** is said to have occurred. The records are called **synonyms**. In this situation, we must insert the new record in another position, since its hash address is occupied. Collision management complicates hash file management and degrades overall performance.

There are several techniques that can be used to manage collisions:

Open addressing

If a collision occurs, the system performs a linear search to find the first available slot to insert the new record. When the last bucket has been searched, the system starts back at the first bucket. Searching for a record employs the

Before	Bucket
Staff SA9 record Staff SL21 record	0
Staff SG37 record	1
Staff SG5 record Staff SG14 record	2

After	Bucket
Staff SA9 record Staff SL21 record	0
Staff SG37 record Staff SL41 record	1
Staff SG5 record Staff SG14 record	2

Figure A.4 Collision resolution using open addressing.

same technique used to store a record, except that the record is considered not to exist when an unused slot is encountered before the record has been located. For example, assume we have a trivial hash function which takes the digits of the staff number MOD 3, as shown in Figure A.4. Each bucket has two slots and staff records SG5 and SG14 hash to bucket 2. When record SL41 is inserted, the hash function generates an address corresponding to bucket 2. As there are no free slots in bucket 2, it searches for the first free slot, which it finds in bucket 1, after looping back and searching bucket 0.

Unchained overflow

Instead of searching for a free slot, an overflow area is maintained for collisions that cannot be placed at the hash address. Figure A.5 shows how the collision illustrated in Figure A.4 would be handled using an overflow area. In this case, instead of searching for a free slot for record SL41, the record is placed in the overflow area. At first sight, this may not appear to offer much performance improvement. However, using open addressing, collisions are located in the first free slot, potentially causing additional collisions in the future with records that hash to the address of the free slot. Thus, the number of collisions that occur is increased and performance is degraded. On the other hand, if we can minimize the number of collisions, it will be faster to perform a linear search on a smaller overflow area.

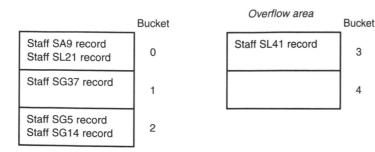

	Bucket
Staff SA9 record Staff SL21 record	0
Staff SG37 record	1
Staff SG5 record Staff SG14 record	2

Overflow area	Bucket
Staff SL41 record	3
	4

Figure A.5 Collision resolution using overflow.

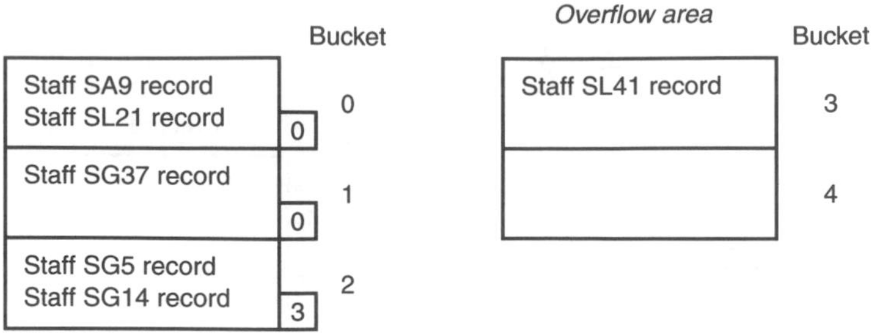

Figure A.6 Collision resolution using chained overflow.

Chained overflow

As with the previous technique, an overflow area is maintained for collisions that cannot be placed at the hash address. However, with this technique, each bucket has an additional field, sometimes called a **synonym pointer**, that indicates whether a collision has occurred and, if so, points to the overflow page used. If the pointer is zero no collision has occurred. In Figure A.6, bucket 2 points to an overflow bucket 3; buckets 0 and 1 have a 0 pointer to indicate that there have been no collisions with these buckets yet.

A variation of this technique provides faster access to the overflow record by using a synonym pointer that points to a slot address within the overflow area rather than a bucket address. Records in the overflow area also have a synonym pointer that gives the address in the overflow area of the next synonym for the same target address, so that all synonyms for a particular address can be retrieved by following a chain of pointers.

Multiple hashing

A second hashing function is applied if the first results in a collision. The intention is to produce a new hash address that will avoid a collision. The second hashing function is generally used to place records in an overflow area.

With hashing, a record can be located efficiently by first applying the hash function and, if a collision has occurred, using one of these approaches to locate its new address. To update a hashed record the record first has to be located. If the field to be updated is not the hash key, the update can take place and the record written back to the same slot. However, if the hash field is being updated, the hash function has to be applied to the new value. If a new hash address is generated, the record has to be deleted from its current slot and stored at its new address.

A.4.1 Dynamic Hashing

The above hashing techniques are *static* in that the hash address space is fixed when the file is created. When the space becomes too full it is said to be saturated, and the DBA must reorganize the hash structure. This may involve creating a new file with more space, choosing a new hashing function and mapping the old file to the new file. An alternative approach is **dynamic hashing**, which allows the file size to change dynamically to accommodate growth and shrinkage of the database.

There have been many different dynamic hashing techniques proposed (see, for example, Larson, 1978; Fagin *et al.*, 1979; Litwin, 1980). The basic principle of dynamic hashing is to manipulate the number generated by the hash function as a bit sequence, and to allocate records to buckets based on the progressive digitization of this sequence. A dynamic hash function generates values over a large range, namely b-bit binary integers, where b is typically 32. We briefly describe one type of dynamic hashing called **extendible hashing**.

Buckets are created as required. Initially, records are added to the first bucket until the bucket becomes full, at which time we split the bucket up depending on i bits of the hash value, where $0 \leqslant i < b$. These i bits are used as an offset into a **Bucket Address Table (BAT)** or directory. The value of i changes as the size of the database changes. The directory has a header that stores the current value of i, called the depth, together with 2^i pointers. Similarly, for each bucket there is a local depth indicator that specifies the value of i used to determine this bucket address. Figure A.7 shows an example of extendible hashing. We assume that each bucket has space for two records and the hash function uses the numeric part of the staff number, Sno:

SL21	010101
SG37	100101
SG14	001110
SA9	001001

Figure A.7(a) shows the directory and bucket 0 after staff records SL21 and SG37 have been inserted. When we come to insert record SG14, bucket 0 is full so we have to split bucket 0 based on the most significant bit of the hash value, as shown in Figure A.7(b). The directory contains 2^1 pointers for the bit values 0 and 1 ($i = 1$). The depth of the directory and the local depth of each bucket becomes 1. Again, when we come to insert the next record SA9, bucket 0 is again full so we have to split the bucket based on the two most significant bits of the hash value. The directory contains 2^2 pointers for the bit values 00, 01, 10 and 11 ($i = 2$). The depth of the directory and the local depth of buckets 0 and 2 becomes 2. Note that this does not affect bucket 1, so the directory for bits 10 and 11 both point to this bucket, and the local depth pointer for bucket 1 remains at 1.

When a bucket becomes empty after a deletion, it can be deleted together with its entry in the directory. In some schemes, it is possible to merge small buckets together and cut the size of the directory by half.

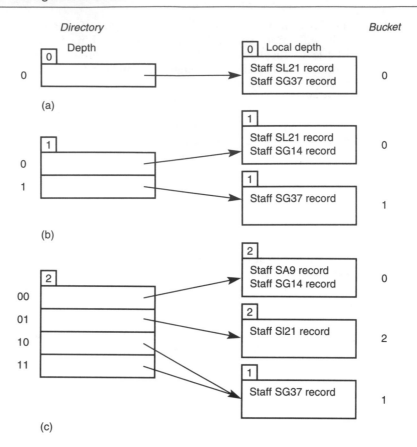

Figure A.7 Example of extendible hashing: (a) after insert of SL21 and SG37; (b) after insert of SG14; (c) after insert of SA9.

A.4.2 Limitations of Hashing

The use of hashing for retrievals depends upon the complete hash field. In general, hashing is inappropriate for retrievals based on pattern matching or ranges of values. For example, to search for values of the hash field in a specified range, we require a hash function that preserves order: that is, if r_{min} and r_{max} are minimum and maximum range values, then we require a hash function h, such that $h(r_{min}) < h(r_{max})$. Further, hashing is inappropriate for retrievals based on a field other than the hash field. For example, if the Staff table is hashed on Sno, then hashing could not be used to search for a record based on the Lname field. In this case, it would be necessary to perform a linear search to find the record, or add Lname as a secondary index (see Section A.5.2).

A.5 Indexes

In this section, we discuss techniques for making the retrieval of data more efficient using **indexes**.

> **Index**   An index is a data structure that allows the DBMS to locate par-
> ticular records in a file more quickly, and thereby speed response
> to user queries.

An index in a database is similar to an index in a book. It is a structure
associated with a file that can be referred to when searching for an item of
information, just like searching the index of a book. An index obviates the
need to scan serially or sequentially through the file each time. In the case of
database indexes, the required item will be one or more records in a file. As
in the book index, each index entry contains the item required and one or more
locations (record identifiers) where the item can be found.

An index structure is associated with a particular search key, and contains records consisting of the key value and the address of the logical record
in the file containing the key value. The file containing the logical records is
called the **data file** and the file containing the index records is called the **index
file**. The values in the index file are ordered according to the **indexing field**.
If the data file is sequentially ordered, and the indexing field is a key field
of the file, that is, it is guaranteed to have a unique value in each record, the
index is called a **primary index**. If the indexing field is not a key field of the
file, so that there can be more than one record corresponding to a value of
the indexing field, the index is called a **clustering index**. An index that is
defined on a non-ordering field of the data file is called a **secondary index**.
A file can have *at most* one primary index or one clustering index, and in addition can have several secondary indexes. An index can be **sparse** or **dense**: a
sparse index has an index record for only some of the search key values in
the file; a dense index has an index record for every search key value in the file.

A.5.1   Indexed Sequential Files

A sorted data file with a primary index is called an **indexed sequential file**.
This structure is a compromise between a purely sequential file and a purely
random file, in that records can be processed sequentially or individually
accessed using a search key value that accesses the record via the index. An
indexed sequential file is a more versatile structure. An indexed sequential file
normally has:

- a primary storage area,
- a separate index or indexes,
- an overflow area.

IBM's Indexed Sequential Access Method (ISAM) uses this structure, which
is closely related to the underlying hardware characteristics. Periodically, these
types of file need reorganizing to maintain efficiency. The later development,
Virtual Sequential Access Method (VSAM), is an improvement on ISAM in
that it is hardware independent. There is no separate designated overflow area,
but there is space allocated in the data area to allow for expansion. As the
file grows and shrinks, the process is handled dynamically without the need
for periodic reorganization. Figure A.8 shows an example of a dense index

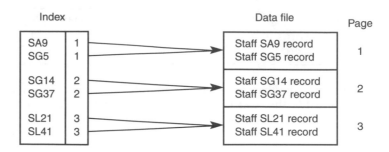

Figure A.8 Example of dense index.

on a sorted file of Staff records. However, as the records in the data file are sorted, we can reduce the index to a sparse index as shown in Figure A.9.

Typically, a large part of a primary index can be stored in main memory and processed faster. Access methods, such as the binary search method discussed in Section A.3, can be used to further speed up the access. The main disadvantage of using a primary index, as with any sorted file, is maintaining the order as we insert and delete records. These problems are compounded as we have to maintain the sorted order in the data file and in the index file. One method that can be used is the maintenance of an overflow area and chained pointers, similar to the technique described in Section A.4 for collision management with hash files.

A.5.2 Secondary Indexes

A secondary index is also an ordered file similar to a primary index. However, whereas the data file associated with a primary index is sorted on the index key, the data file associated with a secondary index may not be sorted on the indexing key. Further, the secondary index key need not contain unique values, unlike a primary key index. For example, we may wish to create a secondary index on the branch number field Bno of the Staff table. From Figure A.1, we can see that the values in the Bno column are not unique. There are several techniques for handling non-unique secondary indexes:

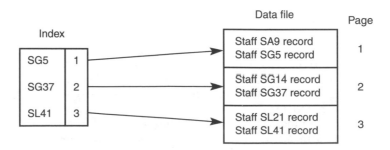

Figure A.9 Example of sparse index.

- Produce a dense secondary index that maps onto all records in the data file, thereby allowing duplicate key values to appear in the index.

- Allow the secondary index to have an index entry for each distinct key value, but allow the block pointers to be multi-valued, with an entry corresponding to each duplicate key value in the data file.

- Allow the secondary index to have an index entry for each distinct key value. However, the block pointer would not point to the data file but to a bucket that contains pointers to the corresponding records in the data file.

Secondary indexes improve the performance of queries that use attributes other than the primary key. However, the improvement to queries has to be balanced against the overhead involved in maintaining the indexes while the database is being updated. This is part of physical database design, and was discussed in Chapter 9.

A.5.3 Multilevel Indexes

When an index file becomes large and extends over many pages, the search time for the required index increases. For example, a binary search requires approximately $\log_2 p$ page accesses for an index with p pages. A **multilevel index** attempts to overcome this problem by reducing the search range. It does this by treating the index like any other file, splits the index into a number of smaller indexes and maintains an index to the indexes. Figure A.10 shows an example of a two-level partial index for the Staff table of Figure A.1. Each page in the data file can store two records. For illustration, there are also two index records per page, although in practice there would be many index records per page. Each index record stores an access key value and a page address. The stored access key value is the highest in the addressed page.

    To locate a record with a specified Sno value, SG14 say, we start from the second-level index and search the page for the last access key value that is less than or equal to SG14, in this case SG37. This record contains an address to the first-level index page to continue the search. Repeating the above process leads us to page 1 in the data file, where the record is stored. If a range of Sno values had been specified, we could use the same process to locate the first record in the data file corresponding to the lower range

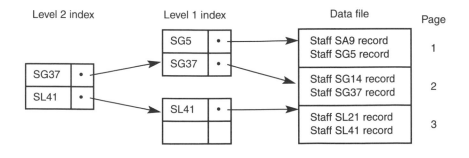

Figure A.10
Example of multilevel index.

value, and as the records in the data file are sorted on Sno, we can find the remaining records in the range by reading serially through the data file.

IBM's ISAM is based on a two-level index structure. Insertion is handled by overflow pages, as discussed in Section A.4. In general, an n-level index can be built, although three levels are common in practice; a file would have to be very large to require more than three levels. In the next section, we discuss a particular type of multilevel full index called a **B-Tree**.

A.5.4   B$^+$-Trees

Many DBMSs use a data structure called a **tree** to hold data or indexes. A tree consists of a hierarchy of **nodes**. Each node in the tree, except the **root** node, has one **parent** node and zero or more **child** nodes. A root node has no parent. A node that does not have any children is called a **leaf** node.

The **depth** of a tree is the maximum number of levels between the root node and a leaf node in the tree. Depth may vary across different paths from root to leaf, or depth may be the same from the root node to each leaf node, producing a tree called a **balanced tree**, or **B-Tree** (Bayer and McCreight, 1972; Comer, 1979). The **degree** or **order** of a tree is the maximum number of children allowed per parent. Large degrees, in general, create broader, shallower trees. Since access time in a tree structure depends more often upon depth than on breadth, it is usually advantageous to have 'bushy', shallow trees. A binary tree is one of order 2 in which each node has no more than two children.

The rules for a B$^+$-Tree are as follows:

- If the root is not a leaf node, it must have at least two children.
- For a tree of order n, each node (except the root and leaf nodes) must have between $n/2$ and n pointers and children. If $n/2$ is not an integer, round the result up.
- For a tree of order n, the number of key values in a leaf node must be between $(n - 1)/2$ and $(n - 1)$ pointers and children. If $(n - 1)/2$ is not an integer, round the result up.
- The number of key values contained in a nonleaf node is 1 less than the number of pointers.
- The tree must always be balanced: that is, every path from the root node to a leaf must have the same length.
- Leaf nodes are linked in order of key values.

Figure A.11 represents an index on the Sno field of the Staff table in Figure A.1 as a B$^+$-Tree of order 1. Each node is of the form:

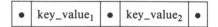

where ● can be blank or represents a pointer to another record. If the search key value is less than or equal to key_value$_i$, the pointer to the left of

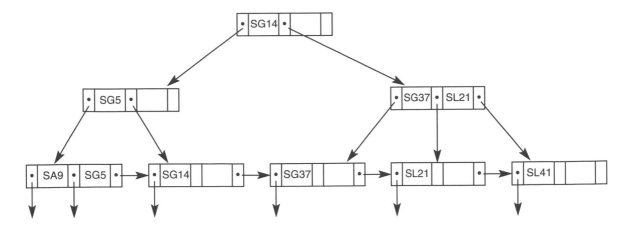

Figure A.11
Example of a B$^+$-Tree index.

key_value$_i$ is used to find the next node to be searched; otherwise, the pointer at the end of the node is used. For example, to locate SL21, we start from the root node. SL21 is greater than SG14, so we follow the pointer to the right, which leads to the second level node containing the key values SG37 and SL21. We follow the pointer to the left of SL21, which leads to the leaf node containing the address of record SL21.

In practice, each node in the tree is actually a page, so we can store more than three pointers and two key values. If we assume that a page has 4096 bytes, each pointer is 4 bytes long and the Sno field requires 4 bytes of storage, and each page has a 4 byte pointer to the next node on the same level, we could store $(4096 - 4)/(4 + 4) = 511$ index records per page. The B$^+$-Tree would be order 512. The root can store 511 records and can have 512 children. Each child can also store 511 records, giving a total of 261 632 records. Each child can also have 512 children, giving a total of 262 144 children on level 2 of the tree. Each of these children can have 511 records giving a total of 133 955 584. This gives a theoretical maximum number of index records as:

root:	511
Level 1:	261 632
Level 2:	133 955 584
TOTAL	134 217 727

Thus, we could randomly access one record in the Staff file containing 134 217 727 records within four disk accesses (in fact, the root would normally be stored in main memory, so there would be one less disk access). In practice, however, the number of records held in each page would be smaller as not all pages would be full (see Figure A.11).

A B$^+$-Tree always takes approximately the same time to access any data record by ensuring that the same number of nodes is searched: in other

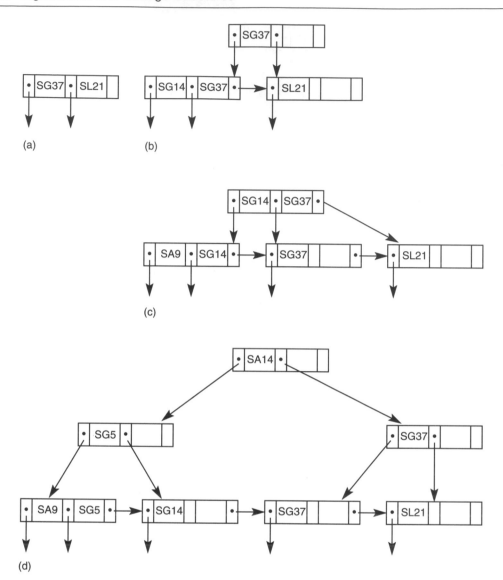

Figure A.12

Insertions into a B$^+$-Tree index: (a) after insertion of SL21, SG37; (b) after insertion of SG14; (c) after insertion of SA9; (d) after insertion of SG5.

words, by ensuring that the tree has a constant depth. Being a full index, every record is addressed by the index so there is no requirement for the data file to be sorted; for example, it could be stored as a heap file. However, balancing can be costly to maintain as the tree contents are updated. Figure A.12 provides a worked example of how a B$^+$-Tree would be maintained as records are inserted using the order of the records in Figure A.1.

Figure A.12(a) shows the construction of the tree after the insertion of the first two records SL21 and SG37. The next record to be inserted is SG14. The node is full, so we must split the node by moving SL21 to a new node.

In addition, we create a parent node consisting of the rightmost key value of the left node, as shown in Figure A.12(b). The next record to be inserted is SA9. SA9 should be located to the left of SG14, but again the node is full. We split the node by moving SG37 to a new node. In addition, we move SG14 to the parent node as shown in Figure A.12(c). The next record to be inserted is SG5. SG5 should be located to the right of SA9 but again the node is full. We split the node by moving SG14 to a new node and add SG5 to the parent node. However, the parent node is also full and has to be split. In addition, a new parent node has to be created, as shown in Figure A.12(d). Finally, record SL41 is added as a new node to the right of SL21, and SL21 is added to the parent node, as shown in Figure A.11.

B Network Data Model

Objectives

In this appendix you will learn:

- The basic architecture of a CODASYL (network) DBMS.
- The basic structures available in CODASYL.
- How database structures (schema diagrams) can be developed.
- The manner in which a CODASYL DBMS is typically implemented.
- How a schema is defined in CODASYL.
- How the Data Manipulation Language (DML) commands can be used to manipulate data.

In Chapter 3, we discussed the relational model, which represents the second generation of DBMSs. Relational systems are primarily used in business applications, but there is an earlier generation of DBMS that continues to exist in many business areas. This earlier generation is mainly composed of two data models, the **network data model** and the **hierarchical data model**. The systems based on these data models are sometimes referred to as **navigational systems**, for reasons which will become obvious as you read the following sections. These systems may also be referred to as **legacy systems**. However, this term is also used to describe any existing inherited system, and not just network and hierarchical-based systems.

In this appendix we discuss the network data model, typified by the CODASYL approach. CODASYL systems have been important in the area of commercial applications, and continue to be important. Indeed, as Gillenson (1991) found in his survey, a majority of the companies surveyed had invested heavily in a navigational DBMS and made substantial use of them. The navigational DBMS in the survey was either a network (CODASYL) system, or a hierarchical system. Sometimes it was both.

In the area of CODASYL DBMS development, there has been a conscious effort to determine standards that should be applied to the DBMSs, some of which have been subsequently implemented by different commercial developers. For many applications these systems proved efficient, despite the inherent complexities of 'navigating' around the database.

All examples in this appendix use the *DreamHome* case study described in Section 1.7.

B.1 Network Data Model

Network Data Model	A model comprising records, data items and one-to-many (1:M) associations between records.

The term 'network' might imply this model has its origins in graph structures. However, there is in fact no formal network data model to which reference can be made, although the theory underlying network structures could be used as a basis for a network data model. A CODASYL implementation is more restrictive than a network implementation might be. CODASYL arose from the Database Task Group (DBTG) specifications. It is likely that the term network was used simply to indicate that components of the model were, or could be, interconnected. We examine the network data model as developed and specified by the CODASYL work, which is the network data model most commonly used. For reasons given above, the treatment is inevitably practical, and although we do not follow a specific implementation, we present the CODASYL 'model' in general terms.

B.2 Terminology

There are some subtle differences in the terminology used with respect to CODASYL systems compared with that currently used for relational systems and, more generally, in database design. In Table B.1 we present the CODASYL terms to facilitate further discussion and hopefully to avoid confusion from misinterpretation.

Table B.1 CODASYL terminology.

CODASYL term	*Explanation*
Data (elementary) item	Named field (or sub-field).
Group item	Named collection of sub-fields.
Record type	Named collection of fields and sub-fields.
Set type	Named 1:M relationship between two record types.
Schema	Definition of the global database structure.
Subschema	Definition of an external/logical view of a portion of the database.
Storage/internal schema	Definition of the physical database.
User work/working area (UWA)	Area of memory controlled by an executing program in which all relevant variables, and so on are stored and allocated space. Data is transferred between the database and the UWA.
Run-unit	An instance of an executing program. A run-unit is created each time an application program is invoked.
Schema Data Description Language (Schema DDL)	A declarative language used to define the database structure.
Sub-schema Data Description Language (Sub-schema DDL)	A declarative extension to a programming language that can define a user's view of the database.

B.3 Architecture

The CODASYL DBTG committee proposed a particular structure for a DBMS, which is shown in Figure B.1.

We can see from this figure that end users are expected to access the database using an application program written in a host language, which in

Users

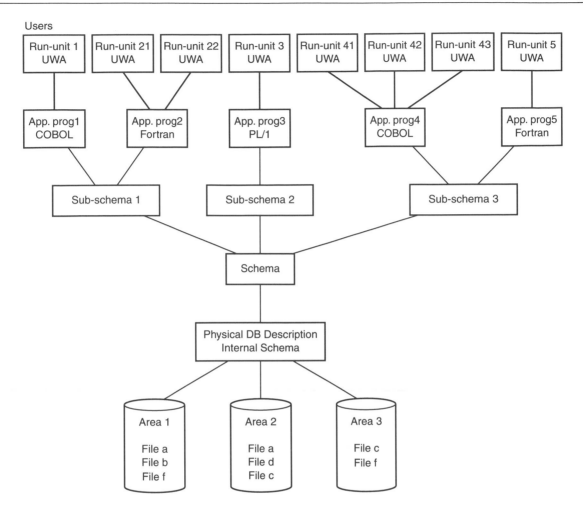

Figure B.1
Architecture of a
CODASYL DBMS.

practice is usually COBOL. Each application program must use a sub-schema, which is essentially a restricted view of the overall database, before it can gain access to the data in the database. It is possible for more than one program to use the same sub-schema concurrently, but each program is only permitted to use one sub-schema. Moreover, a sub-schema is defined over one schema only, but may overlap another sub-schema. A CODASYL DBMS may support several different databases, each of which is defined by its own schema.

The schema and sub-schemas are defined using their own distinct DDL. As mentioned previously, the Sub-schema DDL is considered as an extension to a programming language. After the schema has been defined using the Schema DDL, it must be translated from this source form into an object form before it can be used by the DBMS software. In a similar process, each sub-schema source definition has to be translated into object form before it can be used by a compiled program, and the schema object definition must first exist before this can be done. The sub-schema definitions are kept separate from the application programs and may be developed by programmers, but it is assumed that this is a responsibility of the Database Administrator (DBA).

Normally, within an application program, there has to be temporary storage declared either to hold data that is extracted from secondary storage, or to place data prior to storing it. In a COBOL program, this is accomplished by specifying appropriate record types in the **working storage section** of the **data division**. This working storage is still required even when the programmer is dealing with a DBMS, because data is still exchanged between the application program and the database. The use of a sub-schema by an application program implicitly declares the sub-schema items in working storage. This space reserved for the sub-schema items was termed User Working Area or User Work Area (UWA) by the DBTG, and is set up by the DBMS. The Database Language Task Group (DBLTG) proposals dropped the term, although it is still used. We continue to use the term UWA in this appendix.

The most recent CODASYL proposals define a data storage description language or internal schema DDL, which describes all aspects of physical storage details. These include specifying the initial size of the storage area, how and where records are to be stored, defining internal data item formats, defining indexes and specifying the storage characteristics of sets. Some statements of the schema DDL that do, in fact, define physical storage (and thus reduce physical data independence) have been moved to this internal schema DDL. Corresponding changes have also been proposed to the schema DDL. We limit our discussion to the schema and sub-schema DDLs.

The physical database comprises records which are stored in one or more **areas**. These areas in turn, are mapped into physical files. It is possible for areas to span several files or for a physical file to contain more than one area, but this is very implementation dependent.

B.4   Basic Structures

The fundamental structures used in a CODASYL DBMS are taken from COBOL and the early Integrated Data Store (IDS) system (a prototype network DBMS), with influences from PL/1. We briefly explain these basic structures and show how database structures can be built using these constructions.

B.4.1   Record Type

Record type	A named structure that comprises one or more named distinct data items, each with a specified format. Some data items may comprise two or more named data items, each with a specified format.

The term **data item** (or elementary item) represents a field or sub-field in CODASYL terminology. Record types have names and generally comprise several data items. These data items can comprise other data items, in which case the term **group item** is used. Each data item has a name and format: that is, a data type. An example of a record type is shown in Figure B.2.

01 STAFF.	– record name
02 SNO; PICTURE IS XX999.	
02 FNAME; PICTURE IS X(15).	data items
02 LNAME; PICTURE IS A (15).	
02 ADDRESS.	group item
03 ALINE1; PICTURE IS A(15).	
03 ALINE2; PICTURE IS A(15).	data items
02 TEL-NO; PICTURE IS A(13).	

Figure B.2   COBOL record structure for Staff record type.

Diagrammatically, each record type is illustrated by a name in a rectangle, as for example in Figure B.3, which shows two record types: Staff and Property_for_Rent. A record type defines a specific structure that usually relates to a particular entity type. Where values are shown for a record type, these are called occurrences or instances.

Staff		Property_for_Rent

Figure B.3   Record type diagram.

Intra-record structures

An intra-record structure is a structure permitted within a record type. Apart from the group item structure *Address* shown above, COBOL also permits repeating groups or tables, to be defined. (In PL/1, the term aggregate is used for a repeating group, and is used where PL/1 is the application program language.) These repeating groups may be 1, 2 or 3 dimensioned, and are accessed using subscripts. The proposed 1971 schema DDL was oriented towards PL/1 as a result of IBM's protests that it was too COBOL oriented. PL/1 has more powerful intra-record structuring facilities. However, since then, there has been greater emphasis on database design and having normalized relations, and so the use of this feature is discouraged. In fact, it is not fully supported by all implementations.

B.4.2   Set Type

Set type	A named one-to-many (1:M) relationship between an owner record type and one or more member record types.

A set type is a construction that supports inter-record structures, that is, structures between record types, and hence can be used to store relationships between different record types. A set type supports a 1:M relationship, with the record type at the one end termed the **owner** record type, and the record type at the many end termed the **member** record type. By using record types and set types, a database designer can construct the data structure diagram, or schema diagram, to illustrate the structure of a CODASYL database. A simple example of a set type is illustrated in Figure B.4.

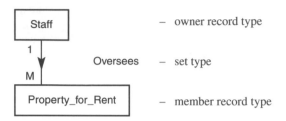

Figure B.4 Set type diagram with cardinality shown.

This type of diagram is also known as a Bachmann diagram. When creating set types, the following points are applicable:

- All set types *must* be named.
- There may be several **occurrences** of a set type (there is one exception to this, which is described later).
- A set may be empty: that is, there is only an owner record present.

B.5 Developing Database Structures

Record types and set types are used to develop database structures and, subsequently, a schema diagram. However, there are some rules that must be observed:

- Only one record type can be an owner in any one set type, although a record type can be an owner in more than one set type.
- One or more record types can be members in the same set type (a multi-member set type).
- A record type can be a member in more than one set type.
- A record type can be an owner in one set type and a member in other set types.
- Any number of set types can be defined between any two record types.
- Set types can be defined that result in cyclic structures.
- A record may not be a member of two **occurrences** of the same set type.
- A record type need not be a member of a set type (a standalone record type).

Figures B.5–B.8 illustrate some possible types of structure that can be created. Figure B.11 also illustrates a cyclic structure, and Figure B.13 shows two set types defined between two record types.

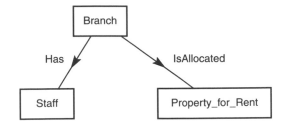

Figure B.5 Branch is the owner of the Has and Is_Allocated set types.

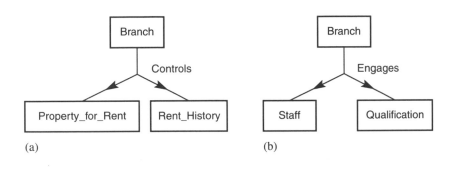

(a)   (b)

Figure B.6 Two multi-member set types. (a) The Branch record type owns the Controls set type containing both Property_for_Rent and Rent_History record types. (b) The Branch record type owns the Engages set type containing both the Staff and Qualification record types.

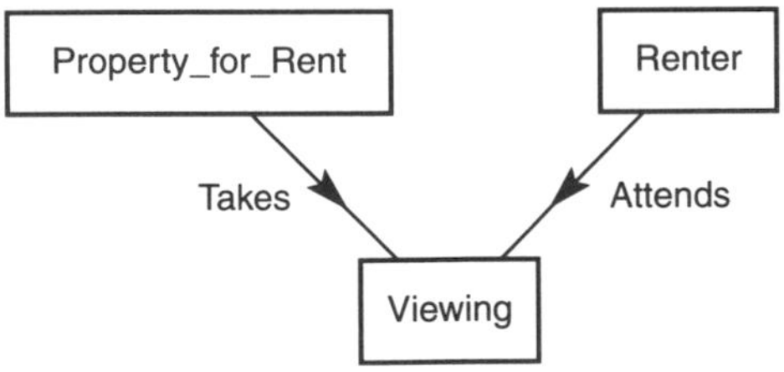

Figure B.7 The Viewing record type is a member of both the Takes and Attends set types.

B.5.1   Resolving Many-to-Many (M:N) Relationships

Since sets are the only method of representing relationships between records, and as a set can only have one owner, there is no direct way to represent a many-to-many relationship in this model. Consequently, a link or intersection record type has to be inserted between the two records, thus forming two 1:M relationships that can easily be handled by set types. For example, a prospective renter views many properties for rent, and a property for rent is viewed by many prospective renters. Consequently, there is an M:N relationship that occurs between Renter and Property_for_Rent, which is expressed by a Viewing relationship that is represented by a link record, as shown in Figure B.7.

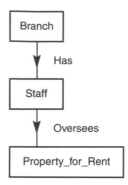

Figure B.8 A hierarchical structure in which the Branch record type owns many Staff record types, each of which own many Property_ for_Rent record types.

If there is only a requirement to know which people had viewed which properties, the link record would have no need to hold any information; it would simply act as the link between the two principal record ypes. However, if data about the viewings themselves are required, the Viewing record type would still link the other two record types, but would also hold data items itself. This process of handling M:N relationships mirrors the decomposition of M:N relationships as discussed in Chapter 7.

B.5.2 Handling Recursive Relationships

A recursive relationship exists where an occurrence of a record type can participate in a relationship with another occurrence of the *same* record type. Recursive relationships can be 1:1, 1:M or M:N. For example, amongst the staff employed at any Branch, there is one person who manages all the other staff. The staff management relationship can be illustrated using the Bachmann diagram shown in Figure B.9.

The problem with this structure is that many CODASYL DBMSs do not permit the definition of a recursive set in which the same record type is both an owner and member in the same set type. To overcome this, a link record is created, and two set types are defined between the two record types, as shown in Figure B.10.

Figure B.9 A one-to-many recursive relationship.

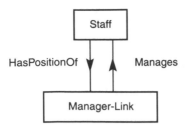

Figure B.10 Data structure for a one-to-many recursive relationship.

Note that the set type *HasPositionOf* represents a 1:1 relationship between Staff and Manager-link, whereas *Manages* represents a 1:M relationship in the other direction. There are also no data items in the link record. This is not the only way of handling a 1:M recursive relationship. An alternative method of handling this recursive relationship is to create a Manager record type with *one* set *Manages* between the Manager record type and the Staff record type. This removes the recursive relationship, but may cause difficulties if both record types participate in common relationships with other record types. Similar comments apply to a 1:1 recursive relationship, although instances of these are rare.

An M:N recursive relationship is handled in a similar manner to the resolution of ordinary M:N relationships. The difference is that only *one* record type is involved. To illustrate an example of this, we extend our *DreamHome* case study to include a staff development programme containing details of specific training or educational courses that staff members can attend. Whether they qualify to attend a particular course depends upon their level of qualification and/or previous courses they have successfully completed. All course details include not only the qualification obtained on successful completion, but also the equivalent qualifications from other external programmes. Consequently, for any given course, we must be able to determine what prerequisite courses are needed, and conversely, we must also be able to determine what courses any particular course is a prerequisite for. Course, therefore has an M:N recursive relationship with itself, as shown in Figure B.11.

As before, a link record is created and two sets defined between the two record types, as shown in Figure B.12. Note that in comparison with the 1:M example, both resulting sets have the same direction as each other: that is, the owner record type and member record type are the same for both set types.

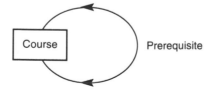

Figure B.11 A many-to-many recursive relationship.

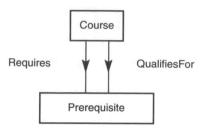

Figure B.12 Data structure for many-to-many recursive relationship.

B.5.3   System Sets

System set type	A named relationship between the notional owner record type, which is System, and (usually) a single member record type.

System sets are also referred to as **singular sets,** and are a means of connecting all occurrences of a record type that only occur as an owner record type in other set types. As the name suggests, the owner of these set types is System, which exists only in name. There is no definition of the System record type, and consequently, it cannot be accessed. There is also only *one* occurrence of any System set type. System sets are useful if the requirements include sequentially processing a given record type that otherwise cannot be ordered because it only occurs as an owner record type. An example of a System set is shown in Figure B.13, where a system set *Branch-set* is owned by the System and contains Branch as the member record type.

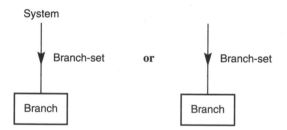

Figure B.13   System set type.

B.6   Implementation of Sets

An appreciation of how set types can be implemented in a CODASYL DBMS is important, although we are now discussing storage level details. Awareness of the methods clarifies the portrayal of set occurrences, and enables many of the specific DDL statements and DML operations to be properly understood. The interested reader is referred to Stubbs and Webre (1993) and Standish (1994).

B.6.1 Pointer Chains

The most common method used to implement sets is to use pointers between records, such that they are effectively chained or linked together. These links can be followed from one record through all the other records, back to the original record at the start, so that a ring structure is present. These ring structures can either be singly or doubly linked, the latter allowing movement in both directions. To illustrate both cases, we use an example of an owner with property for rent using the following simplified data:

Owner	Owns	Property_for_Rent
CO46		PA14
CO87		PL94 and PG21

If the set type was implemented singly-linked (linked to Next), the two set occurrences would be represented as shown in Figure B.14.

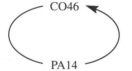
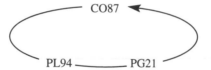

Figure B.14
Singly linked set
implementation
(next pointers).

However, if the set type was doubly linked (linked to Next and Prior), the set occurrences would have two sets of pointers, as shown in Figure B.15.

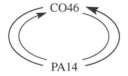
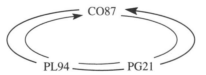

Figure B.15
Doubly linked set
implementation (next
and prior pointers).

A further pointer can be implemented, which is really a feature of a member record type, and that is a pointer to the owner of the set. This is illustrated, in conjunction with the singly linked set implementation, in Figure B.16.

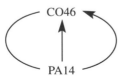
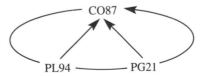

Figure B.16
Singly linked set
implementation with
member-to-owner
pointers.

It is obvious that in this simple example implementation of a direct link between member records and owner records is excessive, and would have the disadvantage of additional overheads in storing and maintaining the structures. However, in cases where sets are large and access would frequently be required from a member record to an owner record, then it would be beneficial to implement such a pointer. It is also possible, in multi-member sets (see Section B.5), for one member record type to have these member-to-owner pointers implemented, but not the others. For example, to facilitate processing the multi-member *Engages* set illustrated in Figure B.6, it may be desirable to have the Staff member records linked to owner. If the set is singly linked, the representation for Branch B3 using sample data is as shown in Figure B.17.

Figure B.17
Multi-member set occurrence with member-to-owner links for one record type.

B.6.2 Pointer Arrays

A second method of implementing sets is to use pointer arrays. These effectively allow access from an owner record to each member record, and dispense with the idea of Next and Prior pointers. The representation without owner pointers for the example presented in Figure B.16 is shown in Figure B.18.

Figure B.18
Pointer array set implementation.

In this implementation, owner pointers can still be defined from member records to owner records. The pointer array may be stored as part of the owner record, as the diagram implies, or it may be stored elsewhere in the database. If stored elsewhere, the owner record contains a pointer to the array.

Originally, the specification for how a set should be implemented was entered in the schema DDL, but this was removed in the most recent proposals because implementation details were rightly considered not appropriate at this level. Such details now belong to the internal schema DDL. For further information regarding the CODASYL proposals, the interested reader is referred to Frank (1988).

B.6.3 Occurrence Diagram

We have already used occurrence diagrams to illustrate aspects of set implementation. However, they are useful in another way. Generally, the usual method of connecting up the record values in an occurrence diagram is as a singly linked ring structure, although this is not intended to imply any particular implementation. The benefit of occurrence diagrams is in better understanding how the actual data is arranged in the structures, which should lead to a better appreciation of how the Data Manipulation Language (DML) statements process the data contained in the structures.

As a typical example, Figure B.14 illustrates two occurrences of the set type Owns. This is a simple hierarchy with one owner record occurrence (Owner) associated with one or more member record occurrences (Property_for_Rent). Note that this construction can be used to remove repeating groups. More complex examples of occurrence diagrams are shown for the structures illustrated in Figures B.5 and B.7 using simplified data. Figures B.19 and B.20 show the data for each structure and the resulting occurrence diagrams.

Branch	Has	**Staff**
B3		SG5, SG14 and SG37
B5		SL21 and SL41

Branch	IsAllocated	**Property_for_Rent**
B3		PG4, PG16, PG21 and PG36

Figure B.19 Sample data and occurrence diagram for Figure B.5.

B.7 Schema Data Description Language (DDL)

There are two DDLs, one for the schema and another for sub-schemas (views). In the previous section, we described the fundamental structures of CODASYL DBMSs, and it is these structures that have to be specified in the schema and sub-schema descriptions. Although there are two DDLs, we describe only the Schema DDL.

Property_for _Rent	IsViewedBy	Renter
PG4		CR56 and CR76
PG16		CR76
		CR74
PG21		

(Note – a blank indicates no value)

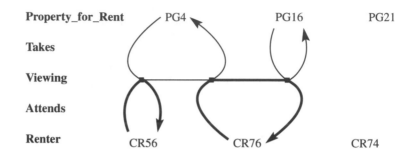

Figure B.20 Sample data and occurrence diagram for Figure B.7.

B.7.1 Schema DDL

Figure B.21 shows part of a schema definition for the *DreamHome* Estate Agency, consisting of the record types for Staff and Property_for_Rent and the set type Supervises between these two record types.

The Schema DDL defines the conceptual or global structure of the database (see Figure B.1), in which *all* record types and set types are defined. There may be several schema definitions handled by a CODASYL DBMS. Any schema definition will comprise the following sections:

(1) **Schema description** This is the initial section that specifies the name of the schema.

(2) **Area description** This section identifies physical storage areas and may give other physical storage information.

(3) **Record description** This section gives a complete description of each record structure with all its data items, and may also include details of record locations and how they are stored.

(4) **Set description** This section identifies all the sets specifying the owner and member record types for each, and gives other set details such as orderings.

B.8 Data Manipulation Language (DML)

Historically, CODASYL DML was considered as an extension to a programming language that operated on a sub-schema, defined using its own Sub-

SCHEMA NAME IS Estate-agent

AREA NAME IS Estate-Area

RECORD NAME IS Property_for_Rent
LOCATION MODE IS VIA Manages
WITHIN Estate-Area;
  02 Pno;   PICTURE IS XX999.
  02 Street;   PICTURE IS A(15).
  02 Area;   PICTURE IS X(10).
  02 City;   PICTURE IS X(10).
  02 Postcode; PICTURE IS A(8).
  02 Type;   PICTURE IS X(8).
  02 Rooms; PICTURE IS 99.
  02 Rent;   PICTURE IS 9999.99.
  02 Ono;   PICTURE IS XX999.

RECORD NAME IS Staff
LOCATION MODE IS CALC USING Sno
DUPLICATES ARE NOT ALLOWED;
WITHIN Estate-Area;
  02 Sno;   PICTURE IS XX999.
  02 FName; PICTURE IS X(15).
  02 Lname; PICTURE IS A(10).
  02 Address; PICTURE IS A(30).
  02 Tel-no; PICTURE IS X(13).
  02 Position; PICTURE IS A(9).
  02 Sex;   PICTURE IS X.
  02 Salary; PICTURE IS 999999.99.
  02 NI-No; PICTURE IS XX9(6)X.

SET NAME IS Supervises;
 OWNER IS Staff;
 ORDER IS SORTED BY DEFINED KEYS
 DUPLICATES ARE NOT ALLOWED
 MEMBER IS Property_for _Rent
 KEY IS ASCENDING Pno
 NULL IS NOT ALLOWED
 INSERTION IS AUTOMATIC RETENTION IS MANDATORY
 SET SELECTION IS THRU Supervises OWNER IDENTIFIED BY CALC-KEY

Figure B.21 Partial schema description for *DreamHome* property rentals.

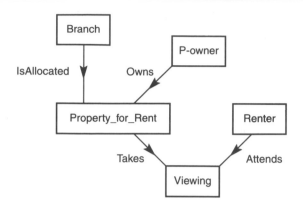

Figure B.22 Schema diagram for sample queries.

schema DDL. In this way, the programming language is a host language. Ideally, any application program written in a host language and containing DML statements should be compiled by a modified language compiler, but in practice a language pre-processor translates the source code into a form that can be compiled by the language compiler (see Section 2.2). The sub-schema, which is defined and stored separately from an application program, is included in a COBOL application program by an appropriate statement in the Data Division. This automatically sets up working space in memory for the sub-schema.

The DML commands operate on a single record at a time, and not on a set of records. Consequently, there is a need for ordinary programming constructions such as conditionals and loops in order to manipulate many records.

B.8.1 DML Examples

We demonstrate the use of the DML in the following three examples, which are based on the schema diagram shown in Figure B.22. The aim of the examples is to show the method of navigating around the sets without the distraction of other aspects of the programming, such as error trapping, that would be necessary in a real situation. Two of the examples use a special DBMS variable (termed a register) called DB-STATUS. A program can inspect this variable for returned values to determine whether an error has occurred.

(1)   **Add a new Branch to the database**

```
MOVE 'B2' TO Bno
MOVE '56 Clover Dr' TO Street
MOVE 'EastEnd' TO Area
        and so on
STORE Branch
⟨error routine⟩
```

(2)   **List the details of all properties for rent handled by Branch B7**

    MOVE 'B7' TO Bno
    FIND ANY Branch USING Bno
    ⟨error routine⟩
    GET
    ⟨print details⟩
    FIND FIRST Property_for_Rent WITHIN IsAllocated
    WHILE DB-STATUS = 0
        GET
        ⟨print details⟩
        FIND NEXT Property_for_Rent WITHIN IsAllocated
    ENDLOOP

(3)   **List the details of properties with who viewed them and when for property owner CO87**

    MOVE 'CO87' TO Ono
    FIND ANY P-owner USING Ono
    ⟨error routine⟩
    GET
    ⟨print details⟩
    FIND FIRST Property_for_Rent WITHIN Owns
    WHILE DB-STATUS = 0
        GET
        ⟨print details⟩
        FIND FIRST Viewing WITHIN Takes
        WHILE DB-STATUS = 0
            GET
            FIND OWNER WITHIN Attends
            GET
            ⟨print details⟩
            FIND NEXT Viewing WITHIN Takes
        ENDLOOP
        FIND NEXT Property_for_Rent WITHIN Owns
    ENDLOOP

C Hierarchical Data Model

Objectives

In this appendix you will learn:

- The characteristics of a hierarchical structure.
- The terminology and architecture for IMS, an example hierarchical DBMS.
- The basic database structures available in IMS.
- How the basic structures have been extended to enable a limited networking capability.
- How the structures are implemented and stored in IMS.
- How data definition is carried out in IMS.
- How data can be manipulated in IMS.

In this appendix, we discuss the hierarchical data model. The best-known system based on the hierarchical data model is the Information Management System (IMS) developed by IBM. Hierarchical DBMSs, and IMS in particular, are still used, and consequently merit discussion. There have been many commercial applications developed using IMS, and these, in conjunction with other applications developed on different types of DBMS, form part of an organization's existing applications portfolio. Hierarchical systems are still used because of the level of investment in existing systems, the costs of changing, and the fact that they continue to perform satisfactorily against the organization's requirements, often supporting crucial system functions. The structuring and implementation of hierarchical DBMSs has led to them also being referred to as 'navigational' systems, like CODASYL DBMSs.

The continuing use of these earlier systems is a reason for describing them. Another reason is the anticipation that many of these older application systems may require transferring onto newer types of DBMS when they require upgrading. Consequently, an appreciation of how information is handled by these earlier types of DBMS is helpful, particularly if the original design details are obscure, out of date, or non-existent, as may be the case. This knowledge is useful when adjustments are needed where, as occasionally occurs, performance needs to be improved in data retrieval. Major adjustments are not normally made (or desirable) on these older systems. It should be noted that for some implementations, automatic conversions to a relational data model have been commercially developed.

All examples in this appendix use the *DreamHome* case study described in Section 1.7.

C.1 Hierarchical Data Model

Hierarchical data model	A model comprising **records** stored in a general tree structure. There is one root record type which has zero or more dependent record types. Each dependent record type can itself have zero or more dependent record types.

As the name implies, data is structured hierarchically. Although defined types of hierarchical structures exist in the field of computing, there was no formal hierarchical data model defined initially. Hierarchical DBMSs were developed first, and a data model subsequently inferred from them. This is a similarity shared with the network data model. However, unlike the network model, there was never any formal body established to determine standards for the architecture or language syntax.

In the following sections we initially describe the concepts behind a hierarchical structure and discuss its capabilities, as well as recognizing the deficiencies that are inherent in a hierarchical structure. Then we proceed to focus on IMS specifically as an example and to discuss the structuring and definition of this typical hierarchical DBMS, and to broadly describe the manner in which data can be manipulated. IMS has extensions to the basic concepts of a hierarchical structure. Originally, IMS only supported hierarchically structured data, but subsequent enhancements have enabled a limited networking capability, amongst other features.

C.2   Hierarchical Structure

The fundamental computing structure that supports a hierarchy is a tree. Where a tree structure is applied to modelling information, it is a **general** tree, as shown in Figure C.1.

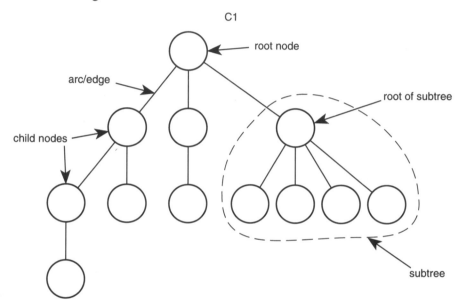

Figure C.1   General tree structure.

This figure illustrates an abstract representation in which the structure comprises **nodes** connected by **links** termed arcs or edges. The topmost node is termed the **root node**, which can have zero or more **child nodes**, each of which can also have zero or more child nodes. Consequently, the structure can be defined recursively. All nodes in a tree, apart from the root node, must have a parent node. Any portion of the tree rooted at one node, apart from the root, is termed a **subtree**. In practical terms, each node can be represented by a **record type**, and each link either by a **pointer** (or **address**) embedded in each record type, or by the physical arrangement of the records.

The nodes represent objects of interest, and the relationships between them are represented by the arrangement of the nodes and the edges that connect them in the structure. The objects can be of the same type. For example, at a *DreamHome* branch office, the individual staff details can be arranged hierarchically as shown in the type diagram of Figure C.2(a). In this diagram, the Staff-Manager type is directly senior to the Staff-Senior type, which in turn is directly senior to the Staff-Clerical type. Figure C.2(b) illustrates an occurrence of this structure for Branch B3. The Branch Manager is in root position at the top, followed by the Deputy and Senior Assistants on the level below, then the Assistants on the next level below, subordinate to the Senior Assistants.

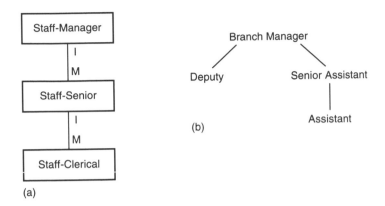

(a)

(b)

Figure C.2 Hierarchy of same record type: (a) type diagram with cardinality; (b) occurrence diagram.

Alternatively, the objects of interest can be distinct entities, as shown in the type diagram of Figure C.3(a). Here, Branch forms the root node for this tree, with Staff and Property_for_Rent as child nodes, and Viewing as the child node of Property_for_Rent. Figure C.3(b) illustrates *one* occurrence of the structure depicted in Figure C.3(a). In this example, the occurrence is of branch B3 with its associated data for Staff, Property_for_Rent and Viewing. Note that the occurrences of Viewing are shown by the number assigned to the particular renter who viewed the property. This diagram shows that a hierarchical structure naturally supports both one-to-many (1:M) and one-to-one (1:1) relationships.

The diagram might imply that only one link is possible between nodes, and that within the structure the links have a particular arrangement. However, in practice several links could be implemented: for example, from parent to child node, and vice versa. The arrangement of the pointers may be such that all occurrences of the same type are connected together. The main effect caused by the type of links implemented is on the algorithms that maintain the structure. Methods of implementation pertinent to IMS are discussed in Section C.6.

When a general tree is used to hold information, it is also usually **ordered**, in the sense that apart from the root, the position of record types in the tree is significant. This ordering conventionally is from left to right. The record **occurrences** are also likely to be ordered. In Figure C.3(a), because the Staff record type is to the left of the Property_for_Rent record type, Staff records will occur first, so that any processing carried out on the structure will always process the Staff records before the Property_for_Rent records. Ordering the record types in this way can facilitate efficient retrieval.

In a general tree structure, there are two possible methods of accessing all the nodes or record types within the tree. One method is to access the root first, and then proceed down the tree accessing the subtrees in order from left

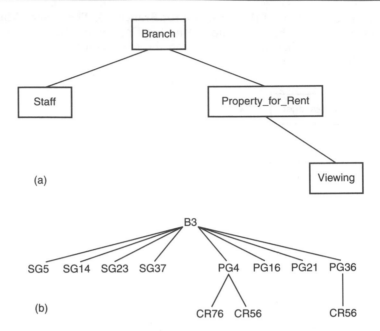

Figure C.3 Hierarchy of different record types: (a) type diagram showing different record types; (b) occurrence diagram for branch B3.

to right (termed **pre-order traversal,** or top down). The other method is to start at the bottom and proceed upwards accessing the subtrees in order from left to right, and finishing with the root (termed **post-order traversal,** or bottom up). Figure C.4 shows the order in which the records are retrieved in pre-order and post-order traversals for the occurrence of the tree presented in Figure C.3(b).

Figure C.4 General tree traversals: (a) pre-order traversal sequence; (b) post-order traversal sequence.

B3 SG5 SG14 SG23 SG37 PG4 CR76 CR56 PG16 PG21 PG36 CR56
(a)
SG5 SG14 SG23 SG37 CR76 CR56 PG4 PG16 PG21 CR56 PG36 B3
(b)

For information structures, the usual access required is top down. This is because the most significant data that is frequently accessed is placed in the highest levels of the tree. Data stored at the lower levels is usually logically dependent on data at the higher levels, and therefore, if required, would normally be retrieved in conjunction with this higher level data. For example, accessing only the Viewing records of Figure C.3(b) may indicate how many viewings have occurred, but will not indicate which properties have been viewed. Consequently, a pre-order traversal facilitates retrieval of data at the higher levels, and its subsequent dependent data, if present. Selective access can be accomplished as a variation on the general access strategy: that is, a general pre-order traversal can be modified to access only data of interest, rather than all the data.

The collection of record occurrences for one root occurrence is termed **one occurrence of the tree**. In specific implementations, one occurrence of a tree equates to a database record.

C.2.1   Advantages and Disadvantages of Hierarchical Structures

An important feature of a hierarchical structure is that child occurrences cannot occur without a parent occurrence. There is therefore a dependency built into the structure, such that if a root occurrence is deleted, the whole tree (or sub-tree) occurrence is deleted. This dependency has both advantages and disadvantages. One advantage is that referential integrity (see Chapter 3) is enforced where record occurrences are wholly dependent on other record occurrences. For example, in Figure C.3(b), deletion of a Property_for_Rent record occurrence also deletes the associated Viewing record occurrences. Alternatively, a Viewing record could not be inserted unless the appropriate Property_for_Rent record already existed. The structure therefore enforces automatic referential integrity (see Section 3.3).

The disadvantages, however, include the inability to store occurrences of record types that do not currently have a parent occurrence. For example, in Figure C.3(b), deletion of a Branch record occurrence results in deletion of all its dependent record occurrences. It is not easy to retain either Staff records or Property_for_Rent records in the structure if they do not belong to an existing Branch record. There are, of course, ways around this problem – a dummy Branch record could be inserted, for instance. However, the fundamental problem is that the structure does not readily model the pattern of the real world data occurrences.

Another major disadvantage of the hierarchical data model is the difficulty of modelling many-to-many (M:N) relationships or other complex, non-hierarchical relationships, in which a record type has distinct relationships with several other record types. For example, there is a relationship between Staff and Property_for_Rent, in addition to the relationship each has with Branch. There is also a relationship between Renter and Viewing in addition to the relationship between Property_for_Rent and Viewing. Extra hierarchical structures are required in order to store these relationships, in addition to those shown in Figure C.3(a). This results in data replication and increased overheads of data maintenance. Figure C.5 shows these additional structures.

We now proceed to discuss briefly aspects of the IMS system as an example of a hierarchical DBMS. The discussion is simplified out of necessity, because space precludes a more detailed treatment. However, IMS is a large and very complex system requiring considerable skill and knowledge to use it effectively, which is one reason why it may be a difficult decision to replace it.

C.3   IMS Terminology

We have introduced the basic concepts behind hierarchical structures and now consider the IMS DBMS specifically. IMS does not use the same terminology

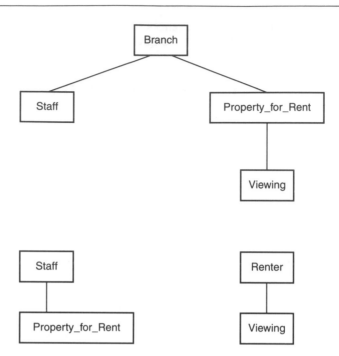

Figure C.5 Additional hierarchical structures required for complex relationships.

as used for tree structures, and also has some specific terms of its own. These are explained in Table C.1.

In the table, the term **logical database** has been included. Some of the earlier texts that described IMS employed this term, and originally it caused some confusion. The confusion arose because **physical databases** can include logical relationships, and it was unclear what was being referred to: that is, was it the physical database with logical relationships, or the logical database structure that resulted from the logical relationships? However, we use the term logical database to refer to the logical view, and logical database structure to refer to the virtual structure created by the use of logical relationships.

C.4 IMS Architecture

The general architecture for an IMS DBMS is shown in Figure C.6.

Like the CODASYL proposals, IMS was developed as a DBMS accessed by host languages such as COBOL and PL/1. Each user sees, or interacts with, a logical database, which is defined in the PSB. Within a PSB, the PCBs provide the definitions of the structures that can be accessed by the program. These structures are all hierarchical. Each PCB maps onto either a physical DBD or a logical DBD. Usually, each PCB defines a subset of the DBD, but

Table C.1 IMS terminology.

IMS term	Explanation
Field	Fields are contained in **segments**. There are three types of field, one of which is data. Data fields hold a user's data.
Segment type	This is equivalent to a node, or more generally a record type. It need not contain fields.
Segment occurrence	An instance of a segment type. Segment occurrences constitute a physical database record.
Physical database	This comprises several database records. A physical database maps into one specific storage structure. There may be several physical databases that correspond to a conceptual schema.
Logical relationship	A logical relationship can be used to resolve the problem posed when determining an appropriate data structure in which a segment type needs to be shared by two or more other segment types. This type of problem commonly occurs when modelling M:N relationships. The shared segment is physically stored in the structure along the path where it is most frequently accessed. For the less frequent access paths, the other segments that need access to it have a logical relationship implemented by storing a pointer to the shared segment. Consequently, a logical relationship allows segments from different hierarchies to be associated with each other, effectively creating a logical hierarchical structure that does not exist in storage, but which can be processed.
Physical Database Description (DBD)	This defines the structure and characteristics of a physical database to IMS, and is written in the language DL/I. A specific database can only contain one type of database record. Where logical relationships occur between different databases, the necessary pointers must be included in the DBD. The physical DBD specifies the rules for all pointers.
Logical Database Description (DBD)	This defines a logical data structure to IMS. The facility permits the definition of a distinct logical database description based on several physical database descriptions. This logical DBD can utilize logical pointers in the physical DBDs to form a more complex structure, which in appearance is still hierarchical, although its effect on access is that of a network.

Table C.1   *(cont'd)*

Logical database	This is a term that may refer to an external/logical/ user view of a database, and may be exactly the same as a physical database, or it may be a subset of one or more physical databases. It is still hierarchical in structure.
	Another interpretation of logical database refers to the logical database structure that results from the use of logical relationships in physical databases, and is therefore defined in a Logical DBD. In a sense, it may still equate to a user view, but strictly, the actual view must be defined on top of it.
Program Communication Block (PCB)	This defines a program's view and use of a database and can only be defined over one physical or logical DBD. However, there may be several PCBs defined over the same DBD. A program can have different views and uses of the same database, and can also access several different databases. Consequently, it may have several PCBs. A logical view can only be hierarchical, therefore it may be necessary to have more than one PCB for more complex structures.
Program Specification Block (PSB)	This contains one or more PCBs and is required by an application program.

it is possible for a PCB to define the entire DBD. If the view that a program needs to use is complex, it requires several PCBs to define it.

Each physical database is defined by a physical DBD, which may be a strictly hierarchical arrangement of segments, or it may also include logical relationships. Where logical relationships are defined in a Physical DBD, the resulting logical structure must be defined to IMS before it can be used. This is done using a logical DBD, which effectively defines a virtual structure on the underlying physical DBDs that are involved. A program can then use this virtual structure by having a PCB that references the logical DBD, not a physical DBD. Each physical database comprises segments arranged hierarchically and stored in a physical file. The physical files each have a particular storage structure specified, which is determined by the processing requirements. The main storage structures fall into the following two groups, although there are other types:

- sequential access storage structures,
- direct access storage structures.

Within these two groups, the most commonly known are:

- Hierarchical Sequential Access Method (HSAM),
- Hierarchical Indexed Sequential Access Method (HISAM),

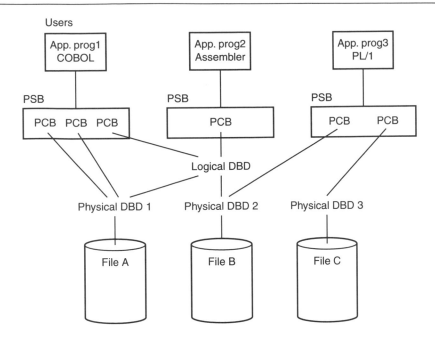

Figure C.6
Architecture of an
IMS DBMS.

- Hierarchical Direct Access Method (HDAM),
- Hierarchical Indexed Direct Access Method (HIDAM).

In the sequential access method structures, segments are physically adjacent to each other in hierarchical order. However, in the direct access method structures, segments contain pointers to other segments. Further information on these storage structures can be found in Appendix A.

C.5 Database Structures

A **physical database** is expressed by a database storage structure which represents a hierarchy of segment types, some of which may contain logical pointers that reference segment types in other database structures (physical databases). Each segment type is defined within the physical Database Description (DBD) that defines the database structure. The complexity of the DBD reflects the complexity of the data modelled; see Section C.7.

C.5.1 Segment Type

Segment type	A named specification of a node in a hierarchical database, which includes the segment on which it is dependent, if it is not a root segment. It may comprise zero or more fields, including key fields, and details of any pointers to other database structures.

Each segment type is defined by a description contained in the physical DBD. The description includes a definition of each data field in the segment and the name of the parent segment type on which it is dependent. This is set to zero if it is a root segment type. Figure C.7 shows the description of a root (parent) and dependent (child) segment types. For each segment description, the segment's name, size in bytes, and parent segment's name are specified first, followed by each field's description. Each field has a name, a size, a start position within the segment and a type specified, such as 'C' meaning character. If the field name is followed by SEQ, this indicates that the field is designated as a unique key field.

SEGM NAME = Branch, BYTES = 23, PARENT = 0

segment name, size and parent

FIELD NAME = (Bno, SEQ), BYTES = 3, START = 1, TYPE = C

field name, key field indicator, size and datatype

FIELD NAME = Street, BYTES = 20, START = 4, TYPE = C

field name, size and datatype

SEGM NAME = Staff, BYTES = 35, PARENT = Branch
FIELD NAME = (Sno, SEQ), BYTES = 5, START = 1, TYPE = C
FIELD NAME = Fname, BYTES = 15, START = 6, TYPE = C
FIELD NAME = Lname, BYTES = 15, START = 21, TYPE = C

Figure C.7 Parent and child segment descriptions.

C.5.2 Hierarchical Structures

A physical database is, of course, a hierarchical structure, that can handle 1:M and 1:1 relationships. A simple hierarchy is shown in Figure C.8(a). A general hierarchy, allowing more than one record type to be dependent on another is depicted in Figure C.8(b).

C.5.3 Handling Many-to-Many (M:N) Relationships

As previously mentioned, hierarchical structures do not easily handle M:N relationships. In IMS, one way in which they can be handled is by storing data in two places: that is, by having redundant data in the database. Another

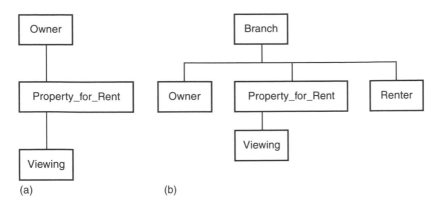

Figure C.8 Basic IMS hierarchical structures: (a) simple hierarchy; (b) general hierarchy.

method is to define a logical relationship between the segment types, which usually, but not necessarily, are in different physical databases. The addition of logical relationships extends the capability of a strictly hierarchical structure to that of a limited network. This can be done in several ways, only one of which we describe below. Essentially, the differences between the methods affect how the data can be accessed and maintained.

To illustrate this method, we use the portion of the *DreamHome* Rentals system shown in Figure C.9 as our example.

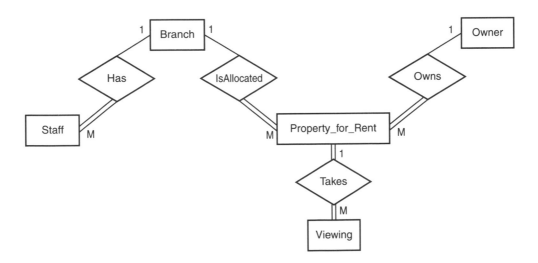

In the diagram, Property_for_Rent needs to be accessed from both Branch and Owner. The entity types are represented by segment types, and two database structures are used to handle the data. One of the structures has Branch as the root segment, and the other has Owner as the root segment. As Property_for_Rent and Viewing are most frequently accessed from Branch, they are put into the same physical database as the Branch segment. The resulting database structures are illustrated in Figure C.10.

Figure C.9 ER diagram for part of the *DreamHome* rentals database.

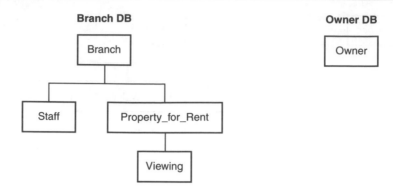

Figure C.10 IMS database structures.

To create a link between the Property_for_Rent and Owner segment types requires a logical relationship to be defined in one or both Physical DBDs. Focusing on Branch, Property_for_Rent and Owner, one method of doing this is as follows.

Unidirectional logical relationship

As the name implies, the link set up is in *one direction only*. If we determine that Owner data is accessed only through Branch and Property_for_Rent or on its own, and no access path is needed from Owner to Property_for_Rent, then a unidirectional arrangement is adequate. The link is created by making Property_for_Rent a logical child of Owner. This arrangement is illustrated in Figure C.11 in terms of both the pointer arrangement and the resulting logical database structure.

This arrangement only permits access through the **physical parent** segment, which in this example is Branch. A logical parent is defined using a

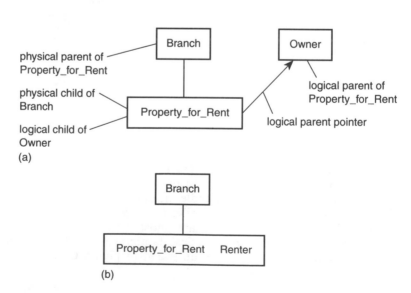

Figure C.11
Unidirectional logical relationship: (a) pointer arrangement; (b) logical database structure sharing concacenated segment.

pointer embedded in the segment description of the logical child. Note that it is not necessary for all segment types to be in the same physical database. We discuss the Database Descriptions (DBDs) for this example in Section C.7.

C.5.4   Handling Recursive Relationships

In the previous section, we showed how M:N and other complex relationships are handled by the use of logical relationships between segment types. Our example illustrated the associated segment types that are in different database structures. However, logical relationships can be established between segment types in the *same* database structure, and this facility permits a recursive structure to be defined. For example, a 1:M recursive relationship exists where one member of staff manages several other members of staff. The ER diagram is shown in Figure C.12(a), and the corresponding database structure in Figure C.12(b).

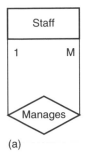 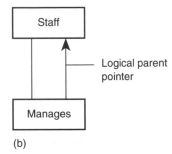

Figure C.12
Handling a recursive relationship: (a) ER diagram; (b) database structure.

C.6   Implementation

A general awareness of the method of implementation and the underlying storage structures enables a better understanding and appreciation of IMS. We indicated previously that there are two main ways of representing and implementing a hierarchical structure. One method is to place all segment occurrences in a hierarchical sequence so that they are stored physically adjacent to one another. The sequence in which they are stored corresponds to a pre-order traversal, and this is the method used in the sequential access storage structure. Let us assume the following simplified data is held in the BranchDB database structure of Figure C.10.

Branch B3	Has	**Staff** SG5, SG14 and SG37
Branch B3	Is_Allocated	**Property_for_Rent** PG4, PG16, PG21 and PG36
Property_for_Rent PG4 PG36	Takes	**Viewing** CR76 and CR56 CR56

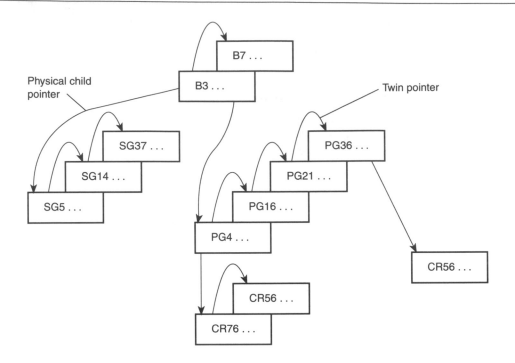

Figure C.13 **Figure C.13** Example of pointer arrangement in an IMS hierarchical structure.

Storing the segments physically adjacent to each other in a pre-order traversal sequence results in the order of values, as shown in Figure C.4(a).

The other method of implementing a hierarchical structure is to use pointers, which can be arranged in different ways. However, a common method of implementation is to have pointers between parent and child segments and between segment occurrences of the same type (twin pointers). This method is shown in Figure C.13, and although only one set of pointers is shown (forward links), in practice it is possible to specify a reverse set of pointers (backward links). The predominant logical order of the segments remains that of a pre-order traversal. However, the inclusion of additional pointers facilitates movement in ways other than strictly pre-order.

Other implementations use combinations of these methods. For example, pointers can be used to connect a parent segment to the first occurrence of a child segment, with the other child segment occurrences being stored physically adjacent to the first child segment occurrence. The method used has implications for the flexibility of a structure and consequently the performance of an application, and is determined by the storage structure selected for the physical database. We discuss storage structures in Appendix A.

C.7   Database Description (DBD)

There are two types of DBD. One, a physical DBD, defines the physical database structure, and the other, a logical DBD, defines a virtual database structure, which is based on underlying physical database structures. Figure C.6 illustrates the relationship between logical and physical DBDs. Both types of DBD define hierarchical structures.

C.7.1 Physical DBD

An IMS physical DBD names a physical database, its underlying file organization, and also describes the database structure. The structure comprises a root segment type together with all its dependent segment types. Each segment type is defined in the order in which it is stored in the structure. For example, if we consider the database structure in Figure C.8(b), the segment types would be defined in the order Branch, Staff, Property_for_Rent and Viewing. A segment type description includes the name of its parent segment, if it is not a root segment, its length and field details. Usually segment types contain data fields, each of which has specified a start byte position within the segment, and a length in bytes. It is also possible to have one field defined as a key field, which may or may not be unique. Key fields allow segments to be identified. In particular, if a key field is defined in a root segment (not in HSAM databases) an application program can get access easily to a specific database record. A key field is defined in IMS as a **sequence** (SEQ) field, which defaults to unique if no indication is given. Normally a 'U' is used to signify unique values and an 'M' is used to signify there may be multiple occurrences. The root segment of HISAM, HDAM and HIDAM databases must have a unique sequence field. Figure C.14 shows the physical DBDs for the database structures shown in Figure C.10. Each DBD has a unique name specified initially, followed by the storage structure. For example, BranchDB is stored as a HIDAM structure. The segment types are then specified in hierarchical sequence followed by the terminating statements to generate the DBD and finish. Figure C.14 also includes a definition of a logical relationship between Property_for_Rent and Owner, which is illustrated in Figure C.11(a).

   All pointers are specified in the physical DBD. These include not only the types of pointers allowed by the stated file organization (excluding HSAM), but also any **logical pointers** used to define a logical database structure across different physical database structures. As previously stated, Figure C.14 defines such a logical relationship between Property_for_Rent and Owner. Accordingly, the segment description for Property_for_Rent defines not only its **physical** parent (Branch), but also its **logical** parent (Owner), together with the name of the physical database in which the logical parent is located (OwnerDB). In addition to specifying the logical parent, the type of pointer used is also specified. This is given by the 'V' and 'POINTER =' clause. The 'V', signifying virtual pointer, together with the 'POINTER =' clause indicates that the pointer stores the physical address of the logical parent, which gives fast access. To correspond with the Property_for_Rent description, the segment description for Owner must include a statement (LCHILD) indicating that Owner has a logical child, and stating its name and the name of the physical database in which this logical child is stored.

   Although at first it may appear that a logical relationship can be used to resolve all complex relationship problems easily, there are a number of constraints on their use. This, of course, may lead to compromises in defining database structures. Some of the constraints are listed as follows:

DBD   NAME = BranchDB,   ACCESS = HIDAM

SEGM   NAME = Branch, BYTES = 23, PARENT = 0
FIELD   NAME = (Bno, SEQ), BYTES = 3, START = 1, TYPE = C
FIELD   NAME = Street, BYTES = 20, START = 4, TYPE = C

SEGM   NAME = Staff, BYTES = 35, PARENT = Branch
FIELD   NAME = (Sno, SEQ), BYTES = 5, START = 1, TYPE = C
FIELD   NAME = Fname, BYTES = 15, START = 6, TYPE = C
FIELD   NAME = Lname, BYTES = 15, START = 21, TYPE = C

SEGM   NAME = Property _for_Rent, BYTES = 79, PARENT = ((Branch),
(Owner, V, OwnerDB)), POINTER = LPARNT
segment name, size, physical parent, logical parent with pointer type and location

FIELD   NAME = (Pno, SEQ), BYTES = 5, START = 1, TYPE = C
FIELD   NAME = Street, BYTES = 20, START = 6, TYPE = C

SEGM   NAME = Viewing, BYTES = 13, PARENT = Property_for_Rent,
FIELD   NAME = (Rno, SEQ, M), BYTES = 5, START = 1, TYPE = C
FIELD   NAME = Date, BYTES = 8, START = 6, TYPE = C

DBDGEN
FINISH
END

DBD   NAME = OwnerDB,   ACCESS = HIDAM

SEGM   NAME = Owner, BYTES = 103, PARENT = 0
FIELD   NAME = (Ono, SEQ, U), BYTES = 5, START = 1, TYPE = C
FIELD   NAME = Fname, BYTES = 15, START = 6, TYPE = C

⋮

FIELD   NAME = Tel-no, ...
LCHILD NAME = (Property_for_Rent, BranchDB)
logical child name and location

Figure C.14 Physical DBDs for part of the *DreamHome* rentals database illustrating a unidirectional logical relationship.

DBDGEN
FINISH
END

- A root segment cannot be a logical child: that is, a logical child must always be a dependent segment.
- A logical child must have only one physical and logical parent segment.
- A logical child cannot have a physical child which is also defined as a logical child.
- A segment cannot be defined as both a logical child and a logical parent.
- A logical parent can have one or more logical children.

DBD NAME = PropLog,   ACCESS = LOGICAL
DATASET LOGICAL

SEGM NAME = Branch, PARENT = 0, SOURCE = ((Branch, data, BranchDB))
segment name, root indicator, source segment name with indicator that both data and key
values are required and source segment location

SEGM NAME = PropOwn, PARENT = Branch, SOURCE = ((Property_for _Rent,
data, BranchDB), (Owner, data, OwnerDB))
concatenated segment comprising Property_for_Rent and Owner

DBDGEN
FINISH
END

Figure C.15 Logical DBD for logical database structure of Figure C.11(b).

C.7.2 Logical DBD

As stated previously, a logical DBD defines a virtual database structure. Within physical DBDs, logical pointers may be embedded, which associates segments from one physical structure with those of another. Before a program can access segments associated in such a way, a logical DBD must first be defined. This essentially defines a logical database structure, and includes all segments that are part of this logical structure and where they are located. For example, if we consider the view of Figure C.11(b), which shows the Branch segment type having a dependent segment type which is a concatentation of Property_for_Rent and Owner segment types. In the logical DBD, this concatenated segment type must be named distinctly and include where the source of the data is located. Figure C.15 shows the logical DBD for this view in which the concatenated segment type is named PropOwn.

The logical DBD has a unique name specified, but in place of a storage structure the term LOGICAL is used to indicate it is a logical DBD. Accordingly, it also has a logical dataset. Each segment type within the logical DBD is named, similar to segment types in a physical DBD, except that there is also a SOURCE clause that states which segment type(s) supply the values required and where they are located. No fields need to be specified. The concatenated segment PropOwn has two segments to supply its values: Property_for_Rent in BranchDB and Owner in OwnerDB. The term *data* indicates all values including key values are required. There are certain rules governing how a logical database structure can be defined. In particular:

- The root segment in a logical DBD must be a root segment in one of the physical databases.
- The dependent segments in a logical DBD must be in the same relative order with respect to their parent as in the physical database.

PCB   DBDNAME = BranchDB, KEYLEN = 13

SENSEG   NAME = Branch, PROCOPT = K

SENSEG   NAME = Property_for Rent, PROCOPT = G
SENFLD   NAME = Pno, START = 6
SENFLD   NAME = Street, START = 11

SENSEG   NAME = Viewing, PROCOPT = G,I

Figure C.16 A logical view defined on the Physical DBD for BranchDB.

C.7.3   Views

IMS does not use the term view; instead the term **logical database** may be used, or PSB. As previously indicated, a logical database may be based on a physical or a logical DBD. It comprises one or more PCBs defined within a PSB, through which an application program can access the database.

An important rule in defining a logical database is that if a segment is omitted, then so are all its dependent segments. Consequently, the root segment must always be included. However, in a PCB it is possible to restrict access to only the key field (SEQ field) if none of the other fields of the root segment are required. This also applies to other segments. If all fields of a segment type are required, it is not necessary to specify them because by default they are all included. Figure C.16 illustrates a logical view for both checking and inserting the viewings of a property for rent, but which omits branch details.

In the PCB the programmer or database administrator must state the name of the physical or logical database structure to be used, and the maximum length of the concatenated key for this hierarchy (KEYLEN =). This concatenated key is the sum of all the bytes used for sequence fields in each segment. If the length is not specified, IMS reserves a maximum default amount. In our example, the physical database is BranchDB and the maximum key length is 13 bytes, that is, the sum of the key field lengths for Branch, Property_for_Rent and Owner.

All segments and fields required by the view are termed **sensitive**, and if only a segment is named then it is assumed all fields are required. In addition to specifying the segments and fields using SENSEG and SENFLD, the type of processing to be carried out must also be specified. This is the PROCOPT (Processing Option) clause, and can take one of the values shown in Table C.2.

C.8   Data Manipulation Language (DML)

The DML comprises DL/I (Data Language with Indexes) commands that are embedded within host language programs. The host language may be COBOL,

Table C.2   Valid processing options (PROCOPT) for segments in a PCB.

G – Get (Retrieve)

I – Insert

R – Replace (Modify)

D – Delete   or

A – All (GIRD)   or

K – Key sensitive, which prevents access to the segment fields because they are
        not required. However, access is needed to the key field in order to access its
        dependent segments.

PL/1 or Assembler. Data is manipulated in the database by the host language
making external calls to the appropriate DL/I command. The DML commands operate on one segment at a time, not groups of segments. In this
respect they are similar to the CODASYL DML commands, in that ordinary
programming constructions are needed with the CALL statements. We give
brief examples of the use of DL/I in performing certain queries based on the
database structure of Figure C.10. The examples do not show full CALL
statements, only the essential parts of them. The DL/I commands are stated
in full, with the abbreviation following in parentheses.

(1)   **Add a new Branch to the database**

⟨construct record in the I/O area, for example,
MOVE 'B2' TO Bno
MOVE '56 Clover Dr' TO Street
MOVE 'EastEnd' TO Area
        and so on ⟩
INSERT (ISRT) Branch

(2)   **List the details of all properties for rent handled by branch B7**

GET UNIQUE (GU) Branch Bno = 'B7'
WHILE NOT FINISHED
        GET NEXT WITHIN PARENT (GNP) Property_for_Rent
        ⟨print details⟩
ENDLOOP

(3)   **Update comments for a viewing on property PG4 handled by branch B3**

GET UNIQUE (GU) Branch Bno = 'B3'
GET HOLD UNIQUE (GHU) Property_for_Rent Pno = 'PG4',
                      Viewing Rno = 'CR56'
                this puts a lock on the segment prior to update
MOVE 'Riddled with rot' TO comments
REPLACE (REPL)

D Comparison of Network, Hierarchical and Relational Database Systems

Objectives

In this appendix you will learn:

- How the different systems can be compared.

In this appendix, we compare each type of model by focusing on the particular characteristics of each one. Finally, we present a summary of comparisons between the different systems.

D.1   Network Data Model

- Directly supports 1:1 and 1:M binary and higher degree relationships.
- Supports M:N binary and higher-degree relationships by decomposition.
- Supports recursive relationships by decomposition.
- Record types are directly related to each other through the set type construction.
- Referential integrity is supported through the set type construction.
- Limited flexibility to changing data and access requirements.
- Access to record types is accomplished by 'navigating' through the structure. There are specific statements to be used, depending upon where the target record type is in relation to the starting point in the structure.

D.2   Hierarchical Data Model

- Directly supports 1:1 and 1:M binary relationships.
- M:N binary and higher-degree relationships are supported only by decomposition and duplicating data in different hierarchies.
- Recursive relationships are supported only by decomposition and duplicating data, or decomposition and duplicating data in different hierarchies.
- Record types are directly related to each other through the hierarchical structure.
- Referential integrity is supported where a dependent child record type has total participation in the relationship with its parent record type.
- Inflexible structure to changing data and access requirements.
- Access to record types is usually achieved by 'navigating' from the root record type to record types lower down in the hierarchy in a pre-order traversal.

D.3   Relational Data Model

- Directly supports 1:1 and 1:M binary and higher-degree relationships and also 1:1 and 1:M recursive relationships.
- Supports M:N binary and higher-degree relationships by decomposition.
- Supports M:N recursive relationships by decomposition.
- Record types are related to each other symbolically by using the primary key/foreign key construction.
- Referential integrity is supported in the relational model.
- Flexible structure to changing data and access requirements.
- Access to record types is achieved by using relational algebra or relational calculus statements. These can be nested to produce complex queries.

D.4   Summary of Database Systems Comparison

See Table D.1.

Table D.1   Summary of database systems comparison.

Criterion	CODASYL	IMS (hierarchical)	Relational
Development work carried out	1960s–1970s	1960s–1970s	1970s–present
Continuing development	In separating physical and logical aspects.	In providing communications with other systems and types of DBMSs.	In improving performance, ensuring compliance with SQL2 and adding object-oriented features.
Implementation	Records and pointers.	Usually records and pointers, but can be simply physically contiguous records.	Records which contain values that are used as logical pointers.
Underlying physical data structure	A network in which records are linked together in a set using an arrangement of pointers. Records may have pointers embedded within them.	A general tree structure in which one record type forms the root of the tree and all others form dependencies.	A two-dimensional table.
Common file organizations	Direct access methods and Indexed Sequential Access methods (includes VSAM).	HIDAM, HDAM, HISAM and HSAM. Variants on direct access methods and Indexed Sequential Access methods (includes VSAM).	Varies from serial files with indexes through direct access methods to complex search tree structures.

Table D.1 *(contd).*

Criterion	CODASYL	IMS (hierarchical)	Relational
Logical data structure	A set in which one owner record type can be linked to many member record types. More complex network structures can be constructed from the set types.	A general tree structure.	A collection of two-dimensional tables.
Relationships handled	1:1, 1:M. M:N and recursive handled by decomposition. Easier to handle than in a hierarchical system.	1:1, 1:M. M:N commonly handled by using logical pointers that link different physical data structures together. Recursive handled by decomposition and duplication.	1:1, 1:M. M:N and M:N recursive handled by decomposition.
Basic referential integrity of parent–child relationship	Enforced by the DBMS using the set structure insertion and retention rules. If member records are fixed to an owner, deletion of an owner has a cascading effect. If member records need not be part of a set, the effect of deleting an owner is equivalent to setting the relationship to null. Other actions must be programmed. Normally foreign keys are not needed in record types.	Enforced by the DBMS using the dependencies in the tree structure. That is, if a root of a tree or subtree is deleted, then so are all of its dependents. This is equivalent to the cascade action. Normally foreign keys are not needed in record types. Complications may arise where M:N relationships are represented by logical pointers.	Enforcement varies from development of procedures and rules or triggers for use by the DBMS, to routines developed in the application programs. Support for SQL92 will build this into the DBMS.
Logical data independence	The conceptual schema can be extended without altering the external schemas (sub-schemas). Where record, field and set types are removed from the conceptual schema or restructured, only those external schema that accessed them require to be amended.	This is supported in a similar manner to CODASYL.	This is supported as for CODASYL.
Physical data independence	Where aspects of physical storage are contained in the conceptual schema, the conceptual schema must be altered to change the storage structure. This may cause changes to be made to application programs. Therefore, the implementation of a database design can become very complicated.	To change from one storage structure to another requires changes to the conceptual schema (DBD) and may require changes to be made to application processing logic. Utilities exist to facilitate changing storage structures.	Where a choice of structures exists, some DBMSs permit different file organizations and secondary indexes to be defined as required.

Table D.1 *(contd).*

Criterion	CODASYL	IMS (hierarchical)	Relational
Flexibility to changing applications	New or altered applications may not have such good performance because the database is structured for the original applications. It may not be possible to support all applications efficiently.	New or altered applications may be inefficient because the underlying structures suit the original applications. It may not be easy or possible to alter the underlying structures to accommodate all applications. Additional structures may have to be created.	New or altered applications should be more easily accommodated. For DBMSs with a choice of file organization, the appropriate ones are selected for the tables.
Ease of design	Guidance should be available especially when determining the structures needed and developing the associated application programs.	This should be left to an expert.	Most users (including end-users) find the logical structure easy to understand, and consequently to design and map to physical structures. Unfortunately, lack of knowledge or awareness of database design techniques can result in poor, inefficient and inflexible designs.
Accessing the database	The standard method of access is through an Application Programming Interface (API), in which an application program contains embedded subroutine calls to the DBMS. The statements operate on one record at a time, although they could potentially affect other records. Additional programming constructions are needed to enable a user to 'navigate' through the database and process sets of records.	Access is again via an API in which subroutine calls are embedded within a host language. The statements operate on one record (segment) at a time, but could affect dependent records. Use of particular 'navigational' statements enables a user to move to various places within the hierarchical structure. Programming constructions may be needed to process sets of records.	Access can vary from the use of an API to an interactive query language. Query languages allow end-users to interrogate a database in an ad hoc manner. There are many types of such query languages available which operate on sets of data. A commonly provided command language interface is SQL, for which standards are defined. It is possible to embed SQL statements within an application program.
Standards	A set of standard concepts exists for the CODASYL data model, although there are variations between implementations.	There is no precise set of standard concepts for a hierarchical data model, nor do implementations of the model conform to a specific standard.	A set of standard concepts exists for the relational data model, although there are variations between implementations.

E Summary of the Database Design Methodology for Relational Databases

Objectives

In this appendix you will learn:

- That database design is composed of two main phases: logical and physical database design.
- The steps involved in the main phases of the database design methodology.

In this book, we present a database design methodology for relational databases. This methodology is made up of two main phases: logical and physical database design, which are described in detail in Chapters 7 and 9, respectively. In this appendix, we summarize the steps involved in these phases for those readers who are already familiar with database design.

Step 1 Build Local Conceptual Data Model from User View

Build a local conceptual data model of an enterprise for a specific user view.

Step 1.1 Identify entity types

Identify the main entity types in the user's view of the enterprise. Document entity types.

Step 1.2 Identify relationship types

Identify the important relationships that exist between the entity types that we have identified. Determine the cardinality and participation constraints of relationship types. Document relationship types. Use Entity–Relationship (ER) modelling when necessary.

Step 1.3 Associate attributes with entity or relationship types

Associate attributes with the appropriate entity or relationship types. Identify simple/composite attributes, single-valued/multi-valued attributes and derived attributes. Document attributes.

Step 1.4 Determine attribute domains

Determine domains for the attributes in the local conceptual model. Document attribute domains.

Step 1.5 Determine candidate and primary key attributes

Identify the candidate key(s) for each entity and, if there is more than one candidate key, choose one to be the primary key. Document primary and alternate keys for each strong entity.

Step 1.6 Specialize/generalize entity types (optional step)

Identify superclass and subclass entity types, where appropriate.

Step 1.7 *Draw Entity–Relationship diagram*

Draw an Entity–Relationship (ER) diagram that is a conceptual representation of a user's view of the enterprise.

Step 1.8 *Review local conceptual data model with user*

Review the local conceptual data model with the user to ensure that the model is a 'true' representation of the user's view of the enterprise.

Step 2   Build and Validate Local Logical Data Model

Build a logical data model based on the conceptual data model of the user's view of the enterprise, and then validate this model using the technique of normalization and against the required transactions.

Step 2.1 *Map local conceptual data model to local logical data model*

Refine the local conceptual data model to remove undesirable features and to map this model to a local logical data model. Remove M:N relationships, complex relationships, recursive relationships, relationships with attributes and redundant relationships. Re-examine 1:1 relationships.

Step 2.2 *Derive relations from local logical data model*

Derive relations from the local logical data model to represent the entity and relationships described in the user's view of the enterprise. Document relations and foreign key attributes. Also, document any new primary or candidate keys that have been formed as a result of the process of deriving relations from the logical data model.

Step 2.3 *Validate model using normalization*

Validate a local logical data model using the technique of normalization. The objective of this step is to ensure that each relation derived from the logical data model is in at least Boyce–Codd Normal Form (BCNF).

Step 2.4 *Validate model against user transactions*

Ensure that the logical data model supports the transactions that are required by the user view.

Step 2.5 *Draw Entity–Relationship diagram*

Draw an Entity–Relationship (ER) diagram that is a logical representation of the data given in the user's view of the enterprise.

Step 2.6 Define integrity constraints

Identify the integrity constraints given in the user's view of the enterprise. These include specifying the required data, attribute domain constraints, entity integrity, referential integrity and enterprise constraints. Document all integrity constraints.

Step 2.7 Review local logical data model with user

Ensure that the local logical data model is a true representation of the user view.

Step 3 Build and Validate Global Logical Data Model

Combine the individual local logical data models into a single global logical data model that can be used to represent the part of the enterprise that we are interested in modelling.

Step 3.1 Merge local logical data models into global model

Merge the individual local logical data models into a single global logical data model of the enterprise. Some typical tasks in this approach are as follows:

- Review names of entities and their primary keys.
- Review the names of relationships.
- Merge entities from the local views.
- Include (without merging) entities unique to each local view.
- Merge relationships from the local views.
- Include (without merging) relationships unique to each local view.
- Check for missing entities and relationships.
- Check foreign keys.
- Draw the global logical data model.
- Update the documentation.

Step 3.2 Validate global logical data model

Validate the global logical data model using normalization and against the required transactions, if necessary. This step is equivalent to Steps 2.3 and 2.4, where we validated each local logical data model.

Step 3.3 Check for future growth

Determine whether there are any significant changes likely in the foreseeable future, and assess whether the global logical data model can accommodate these changes.

Step 3.4 Draw final Entity–Relationship diagram

Draw the final entity–relationship diagram that represents the global logical data model of the enterprise.

Step 3.5 Review global logical data model with users

Ensure that the global logical data model is a true representation of the enterprise.

Step 4 Translate Global Logical Data Model for Target DBMS

Produce a basic working relational database schema from the global logical data model.

Step 4.1 Design base relations for target DBMS

Decide how to represent the base relations we have identified in the global logical data model in the target DBMS. Document design of relations.

Step 4.2 Design enterprise constraints for target DBMS

Design the enterprise constraint rules for the target DBMS. Document design of enterprise constraints.

Step 5 Design and Implement Physical Representation

Determine the file organizations and access methods that will be used to store the base relations: that is, the way in which relations and tuples will be held on secondary storage.

Step 5.1 Analyse transactions

Understand the functionality of the transactions that will run on the database and analyse the important transactions.

Step 5.2 Choose file organizations

Determine an efficient file organization for each base relation.

Step 5.3 Choose secondary indexes

Determine whether adding secondary indexes will improve the performance of the system.

Step 5.4   Consider the introduction of controlled redundancy

Determine whether introducing redundancy in a controlled manner by relaxing the normalization rules will improve the performance of the system. Consider introducing derived data and duplicating attributes or joining relations together.

Step 5.5   Estimate disk space

Estimate the amount of disk space that will be required by the database.

Step 6   Design and Implement Security Mechanisms

Design the security measures for the database implementation as specified by the users.

Step 6.1   Design and implement user views

Design the user views that were identified in Step 1 of the logical database design methodology.

Step 6.2   Design and implement access rules

Design the access rules to the base relations and user views. Document the design of the security measures and user views.

Step 7   Monitor and Tune the Operational System

Monitor the operational system and improve the performance of the system to correct inappropriate design decisions or reflect changing requirements.

References

Alsberg P. A. and Day J. D. (1976). A principle for resilient sharing of distributed resources. In *Proc. 2nd Int. Conf. Software Engineering*, San Francisco, CA, pp. 562–570

American National Standards Institute (1975). ANSI/X3/SPARC Study Group on Data Base Management Systems. Interim Report, FDT. *ACM SIGMOD Bulletin*, **7**(2)

Astrahan M. M., Blasgen M. W., Chamberlin D. D., Eswaran K. P., Gray J. N., Griffith P. P, King W. F., Lorie R. A., McJones P. R., Mehl J. W., Putzolu G. R., Traiger I. L., Wade B. W. and Watson V. (1976). System R: Relational approach to database management. *ACM Trans. Database Systems*, **1**(2), 97–137

Atkinson M. and Buneman P. (1989). Type and persistence in database programming languages. *ACM Computing Surv.*, **19**(2)

Atkinson M., Bancilhon F., DeWitt D., Dittrich K., Maier D. and Zdonik S. (1989). Object-Oriented Database System Manifesto. In *Proc. 1st Int. Conf. Deductive and Object-Oriented Databases*, Kyoto, Japan, pp. 40–57.

Atwood T. M. (1985). An object-oriented DBMS for design support applications. In *Proc. IEEE 1st Int. Conf. Computer-Aided Technologies*, Montreal, Canada, pp. 299–307

Bailey R. W. (1989). *Human Performance Engineering: Using Human Factors/Ergonomics to Archive Computer Usability* 2nd edn. Englewood Cliffs, NJ: Prentice-Hall

Bancilhon F. and Khoshafian S. (1989). A calculus for complex objects. *J. Computer and System Sciences*, **38**(2), 326–340

Banerjee J., Chou H., Garza J. F., Kim W., Woelk D., Ballou N. and Kim H. (1987a). Data model issues for object-oriented applications. *ACM Trans. Office Information Systems*, **5**(1), 3–26

Banerjee J., Kim W., Kim H. J. and Korth H. F. (1987b). Semantics and implementation of schema evolution in object-oriented databases. In *Proc. ACM SIGMOD Conf.*, San Francisco, CA, pp. 311–322

Batini C., Ceri S. and Navathe S. (1992). *Conceptual Database Design: An Entity–Relationship Approach* Redwood City, CA: Benjamin/Cummings

Bayer R. and McCreight E. (1972). Organization and maintenance of large ordered indexes. *Acta Informatica*, **1**(3), 173–189

Beech D. and Mahbod B. (1988). Generalized version control in an object-oriented database. In *IEEE 4th Int. Conf. Data Engineering*, February 1988

Bernstein P. A., Hadzilacos V. and Goodman N. (1987). *Concurrency Control and Recovery in Database Systems*. Reading, MA: Addison-Wesley

Boyce R., Chamberlin D., King W. and Hammer M. (1975). Specifying queries as relational expressions: SQUARE. *Comm. ACM*, **18**(11), 621–628

Brathwaite K. S. (1985). *Data Administration: Selected Topics of Data Control* New York: John Wiley

Cannan S. and Otten G. (1993). *SQL – The Standard Handbook* Maidenhead: McGraw-Hill International

Cardelli L. and Wegner P. (1985). On understanding types, data abstraction and polymorphism. *ACM Computing Surv.*, **17**(4), 471–522

Cattell R. G. G. and Skeen J. (1992). Object operations benchmark. *ACM Trans. Database Systems*, **17**, 1–31

Cattell R. G. G. ed. (1994a). *The Object Database Standard: ODMG – 93*. San Mateo, CA: Morgan Kaufmann

Cattell R. G. G. (1994b). *Object Data Management: Object-Oriented and Extended Relational Database Systems* revised edn. Reading, MA: Addison-Wesley

Catterell T. E. (1990). Why security? In *Computer Security: Policy planning and Practice* (Roberts D. W., ed.), pp. 1–9. London: Blenheim Online

Chamberlin D. and Boyce R. (1974). SEQUEL: A Structured English Query Language. In *Proc. ACM SIGMOD Workshop on Data Description, Access and Control*

Chamberlin D. *et al.* (1976). SEQUEL2: A unified approach to data definition, manipulation and control. *IBM J. Research and Development*, **20**(6), 560–575

Chen P. P. (1976). The Entity–Relationship model – Toward a unified view of data. *ACM Trans. Database Systems*, **1**(1), 9–36.

Childs D. L. (1968). Feasibility of a set-theoretical data structure. In *Proc. Fall Joint Computer Conference*, pp. 557–564

Chou H. T. and Kim W. (1986). A unifying framework for versions in a CAD environment. In *Proc. Int. Conf. Very Large Data Bases*, Kyoto, Japan, August 1986, pp. 336–344

Chou H. T. and Kim W. (1988). Versions and change notification in an object-oriented database system. In *Proc. Design Automation Conference*, June 1988, pp. 275–281

Clarke R. A. (1988). Information technology and dataveillance. *Comm. ACM*, **31**(5) 498–512

Coad P. and Yourdon E. (1991). *Object-Oriented Analysis* 2nd edn. Englewood Cliffs, NJ: Yourdon Press/Prentice-Hall

CODASYL Database Task Group Report. (1971). ACM, New York, April 1971

Codd E. F. (1970). A relational model of data for large shared data banks. *Comm. ACM*, **13**(6), 377–387

Codd E. F. (1971). A data base sublanguage founded on the relational calculus. In *Proc. ACM SIGFIDET Conf. on Data Description, Access and Control*, San Diego, CA, pp. 35–68

Codd E. F. (1972a). Relational completeness of data base sublanguages. In *Data Base Systems, Courant Comput. Sci. Symp 6th* (R. Rustin, ed.), pp. 65–98. Prentice-Hall

Codd E. F. (1972b). Further normalization of the data base relational model. In *Data Base Systems* (Rustin R., ed.), Prentice-Hall

Codd E. F. (1974). Recent investigations in relational data base systems. In *Proc. IFIP Congress*

Codd E. F. (1979). Extending the data base relational model to capture more meaning. *ACM Trans. Database Systems*, **4**(4), 397–434

Codd E. F. (1982). The 1981 ACM Turing Award Lecture: Relational database: A practical foundation for productivity. *Comm. ACM*, **25**(2), 109–117

Codd E. F. (1985a). Is your DBMS really relational? *Computerworld*, 14 October 1985, 1–9

Codd E. F. (1985b). Does your DBMS run by the rules? *Computerworld*, 21 October 1985, 49–64

Codd E. F. (1986). Missing information (applicable and inapplicable) in relational databases. *ACM SIGMOD Record*, **15**(4)

Codd E. F. (1987). More commentary on missing information in relational databases. *ACM SIGMOD Record*, **16**(1)

Codd E. F. (1988). Domains, keys and referential integrity in relational databases. *InfoDB*, **3**(1)

Codd E. F. (1990). *The Relational Model for Database Management Version 2* Reading, MA: Addison-Wesley

Comer D. (1979). The ubiquitous B-tree. *ACM Computing Surv.*, **11**(2), 121–138

Connolly T. M. (1994). The 1993 object database standard. *Technical Report 1(3)*, Computing and Information Systems, University of Paisley, Paisley, Scotland

Connolly T. M., Begg C. E. and Sweeney J. (1994). Distributed database management systems: have they arrived? *Technical Report 1(3)*, Computing and Information Systems, University of Paisley, Paisley, Scotland.

Dahl O. J. and Nygaard K. (1966). Simula – an ALGOL-based simulation language. *Comm. ACM*, **9**, 671–678

Database Architecture Framework Task Group. (1986). Reference Model for DBMS Standardization. *SIGMOD Record*, **15**(1)

Date C. J. (1986). *Relational Database: Selected Writings* Reading, MA: Addison-Wesley

Date C. J. (1987). Where SQL falls short. *Datamation*, May 1987, 83–86.

Date C. J. (1987). Twelve rules for a distributed database. *ComputerWorld*, 8 June, **21**(23), 75–81

Date C. J. (1990). Referential integrity and foreign keys. Part I: basic concepts; Part II: further considerations. In *Relational Database Writing 1985–1989* (Date C. J.). Reading, MA: Addison-Wesley

Date C. J. (1992). *Relational Database Writings 1989–1991*. Reading, MA: Addison-Wesley

Date C. J. (1995). *An Introduction to Database Systems* 6th edn. Reading, MA: Addison-Wesley

Davidson S. B. (1984). Optimism and consistency in partitioned distributed database systems. *ACM Trans. Database Systems*, **9**(3), 456–481

Davidson S. B., Garcia-Molina H. and Skeen D. (1985). Consistency in partitioned networks. *ACM Computing Surv.*, **17**(3), 341–370

Denning D. E. and Denning P. J. (1979). Data security. *ACM Computing Surv.*, **11**(3), 227-249

Dunnachie S. (1984). Choosing a DBMS. In *Database Management Systems Practical Aspects of Their Use* (Frost R. A., ed.), pp. 93–105. London: Granada Publishing

Earl M. J. (1989). *Management Strategies for Information Technology* London: Prentice-Hall

Elbra R. A. (1992). *Computer Security Handbook* Oxford: NCC Blackwell

Elmasri R. and Navathe S. (1994). *Fundamentals of Database Systems* 2nd edn. New York: Benjamin/Cummings

Epstein R., Stonebraker M. and Wong E. (1978). Query processing in a distributed relational database system. In *Proc. ACM SIGMOD Int. Conf. Management of Data*, Austin, TX, May 1978, pp. 169–180

Eswaran K. P., Gray J. N., Lorie R. A. and Traiger I. L. (1976). The notion of consistency and predicate locks in a database system. *Comm. ACM*, **19**(11), 624–633

Fagin R. (1977). Multivalued dependencies and a new normal form for relational databases. *ACM Trans. Database Systems*, **2**(3)

Fagin R. (1979). Normal forms and relational database operators. In *Proc. ACM SIGMOD Int. Conf. on Management of Data,* pp. 153–160

Fagin R., Nievergelt J., Pippenger N. and Strong H. (1979). Extendible hashing – A fast access method for dynamic files. *ACM Trans. Database Systems*, **4**(3), 315–344

Fernandez E. B., Summers R. C. and Wood C. (1981). *Database Security and Integrity*. Reading, MA: Addison-Wesley

Fisher A. S. (1988). *CASE – Using Software Development Tools*. Chichester: John Wiley

Fleming C. and Von Halle B. (1989). *Handbook of Relational Database Design*. Reading, MA: Addison-Wesley

Frank L. (1988). *Database Theory and Practice*. Reading, MA: Addison-Wesley

Frost R. A. (1984). Concluding comments. In *Database Management Systems Practical Aspects of Their Use* (Frost R. A., ed.), pp. 251–260. London: Granada Publishing

Gane C. (1990). *Computer-Aided Software Engineering: The Methodologies, the Products, and the Future*. Englewood Cliffs, NJ: Prentice-Hall

Gardarin G. and Valduriez P. (1989). *Relational Databases and Knowledge Bases*. Reading, MA: Addison-Wesley

Garcia-Molina H. (1979). A concurrency control mechanism for distributed data bases which use centralised locking controllers. In *Proc. 4th Berkeley Workshop Distributed Databases and Computer Networks*, August 1979

Gillenson M. L. (1991). Database administration at the crossroads: The era of end-user-oriented, decentralized data processing. *J. Database Administration*, **2**(4), 1–11

Graham I. (1993). *Object Oriented Methods* 2nd edn. Wokingham: Addison-Wesley

Gray J. N., Lorie R. A. and Putzolu G. R. (1975). Granularity of locks in a shared data base. In *Proc. Int. Conf. Very Large Data Bases*, pp. 428–451

Greenblatt D. and Waxman J. (1978). A study of three database query languages. In *Database: Improving Usability and Responsiveness* (Shneiderman B., ed.), pp. 77–98. New York: Academic Press

Guidc/Sharc. (1970). *Database Management System*

Requirements. Report of the Guide/Share Database Task Force. Guide/Share

GUIDE (1978). *Data Administration Methodology.* GUIDE Publications GPP-30

Haerder T. and Reuter A. (1983). Principles of transaction-oriented database recovery. *ACM Computing Surv.*, **15**(4), 287–318

Halsall F. (1992). *Data Communications, Computer Networks and Open Systems* 3rd edn. Wokingham: Addison-Wesley

Hammer R. and McLeod R. (1981). Database description with SDM: A semantic database model. *ACM Trans. Database Systems*, **6**(3), 351–386

Hearnden K. ed. (1990). *A Handbook of Computer Security* revised edn. London: Kogan Page

Herbert A. P. (1990). Security policy. In *Computer Security: Policy, planning and practice* (Roberts D. W., ed.), pp. 11–28. London: Blenheim Online

Holt R. C. (1972). Some deadlock properties of computer systems. *ACM Computing Surv.*, **4**(3), 179–196

Howe D. (1989). *Data Analysis for Data Base Design* 2nd edn. London: Edward Arnold

Hull R. and King R. (1987). Semantic database modeling: Survey, applications and research issues. *ACM Computing Surv.*, **19**(3), 201–260

IDE (1994). *Software Through Pictures, Integrated Structured Environment – Using the StP Editors.* Interactive Development Environments

ISO (1981). *ISO Open Systems Interconnection, Basic Reference Model* (ISO 7498). International Standards Organization

ISO (1987). *Database Language SQL* (ISO 9075:1987(E)). International Standards Organization

ISO (1989). *Database Language SQL* (ISO 9075:1989(E)). International Standards Organization

ISO (1990). *Information Technology – Information Resource Dictionary System (IRDS) Framework* (ISO 10027). International Standards Organization

ISO (1992). *Database Language SQL* (ISO 9075:1992(E)). International Standards Organization

ISO (1993). *Information Technology – Information Resource Dictionary System (IRDS) Services Interface* (ISO 10728). International Standards Organization

Jaeschke G. and Schek H. (1982). Remarks on the algebra of non-first normal form relations. In *Proc. ACM Int. Symposium on Principles of Database Systems*, Los Angeles, March 1982, pp. 124–138

Jagannathan D., Guck R. L., Fritchman B. L., Thompson J. P. and Tolbert D. M. (1988). SIM: A database system based on the semantic data model. In *Proc. ACM SIGMOD*

Katz R. H., Chang E. and Bhateja R. (1986). Version modeling concepts for computer-aided design databases. In *Proc. ACM SIGMOD Int. Conf. Management of Data*, Washington, DC, May 1986, pp. 379–386

Kim W. (1991). Object-oriented database systems: strengths and weaknesses. *J. Object-Oriented Programming*, **4**(4), 21–29

Kim W. and Lochovsky F. H., eds. (1989). *Object-Oriented Concepts, Databases and Applications.* Reading MA: Addison-Wesley

Khoshafian S. and Abnous R. (1990). *Object Orientation: Concepts, Languages, Databases and Users.* New York: John Wiley

Khoshafian S. and Valduriez P. (1987). Persistence, sharing and object orientation: A database perspective. In *Proc. Workshop on Database Programming Languages*, Roscoff, France, 1987

Kohler W. H. (1981). A survey of techniques for synchronization and recovery in decentralised computer systems. *ACM Computing Surv.*, **13**(2), 149–183

Korth H. F., Kim W. and Bancilhon F. (1988). On long-duration CAD transactions. *Information Science*, October 1988

Kung H. T. and Robinson J. T. (1981). On optimistic methods for concurrency control. *ACM Trans. Database Systems*, **6**(2), 213–226

Lacroix M. and Pirotte A. (1977). Domain-oriented relational languages. In *Proc. 3rd Int. Conf. Very Large Data Bases*, 370–378

Larson P. (1978). Dynamic hashing. *BIT*, 18

Leiss E. L. (1982). *Principles of Data Security.* New York: Plenum Press

Litwin W. (1980). Linear hashing: A new tool for file and table addressing. In *Proc. Conference on Very Large Data Bases*, 212–223

Litwin W. (1988). From database systems to multidatabase systems: why and how. In *Proc.*

British National Conf. Databases (BNCOD 6), (Gray W. A. ed.), Cambridge: Cambridge University Press, pp. 161–188

Loomis M. E. S. (1992). Client-server architecture. *J. Object Oriented Programming*, **4**(9), 40–44

Lorie R. (1977). Physical integrity in a large segmented database. *ACM Trans. Database Systems*, **2**(1), 91–104

Lorie R. and Plouffe W. (1983). Complex objects and their use in design transactions. In *Proc. ACM SIGMOD Conf. Database Week*, May 1983, pp. 115–121

Maier D. (1983). *The Theory of Relational Databases*. New York: Computer Science Press

McClure C. (1989). *CASE Is Software Automation*. Englewood Cliffs, NJ: Prentice-Hall

Menasce D. A. and Muntz R. R. (1979). Locking and deadlock detection in distributed databases. *IEEE Trans. Software Engineering*, **5**(3), 195–202

Mohan C., Lindsay B. and Obermarck R. (1986). Transaction management in the R* distributed database management system. *ACM Trans. Database Systems*, **11**(4), 378–396

Moss E. (1981). Nested transactions: An approach to reliable distributed computing. *PhD dissertation*, MIT, Cambridge, MA

Moulton R. T. (1986). *Computer Security Handbook: Strategies and Techniques for Preventing Data Loss or Theft*. Englewood Cliffs, NJ: Prentice-Hall

Navathe S. B., Ceri S., Weiderhold G. and Dou J. (1984). Vertical partitioning algorithms for database design. *ACM Trans. Database Systems*, **9**(4), 680–710

Obermarck R. (1982). Distributed deadlock detection algorithm. *ACM Trans. Database Systems*, **7**(2), 187–208

OMG and X/Open. (1992). CORBA Architecture and Specification

Ozsu M. and Valduriez P. (1991). *Principles of Distributed Database Systems*. Englewood Cliffs, NJ: Prentice-Hall

Papadimitriou C. H. (1979). The serializability of concurrent database updates. *J. ACM*, **26**(4), 150–157

Parsaye K., Chignell M., Khoshafian S. and Wong H. (1989). *Intelligent Databases*. New York: John Wiley

Peckham J. and Maryanski F. (1988). Semantic data models. *ACM Computing Surv.*, **20**(3), 143–189

QED. (1989). *CASE: The Potential and the Pitfalls*. QED Information Sciences

Revella A. S. (1993). Software escrow. *I/S Analyzer*, **31**(7), 12–14

Rogers U. (1989). Denormalization: Why, what and how? *Database Programming and Design*, **2**(12), 46–53

Rosenkrantz D. J., Stearns R. E. and Lewis II P. M. (1978). System level concurrency control for distributed data base systems. *ACM Trans. Database Systems*, **3**(2), 178–198

Rothnie J. B. and Goodman N. (1977). A survey of research and development in distributed database management. In *Proc. 3rd Int. Conf. on Very Large Data Bases*, Tokyo, Japan, pp. 48–62

Rumbaugh J., Blaha M., Premerlani W., Eddy F. and Lorensen W. (1991). *Object-Oriented Modeling and Design*. Englewood Cliffs, NJ: Prentice-Hall

Sacco M. S. and Yao S. B. (1982). Query optimization in distributed data base systems. In *Advances in Computers*, **21** (Yovits M.C., ed.), New York: Academic Press, pp. 225–273

Schmidt J. and Swenson J. (1975). On the semantics of the relational model. In *Proc. ACM SIGMOD Int. Conf. on Management of Data* (King F., ed.), San Jose, CA, pp. 9–36

Senn J. A. (1989). *Analysis and Design of Information Systems*. New York: McGraw-Hill

Sheth A. and Larson J. L. (1990). Federated databases: architectures and integration. *ACM Computing Surv., Special Issue on Heterogeneous Databases*, **22**(3), 183–236

Shipman D. (1981). The functional model and the data language DAPLEX. *ACM Trans. Database Systems*, **6**(1), 140–173

Shneiderman D. (1992). *Design the User Interface: Strategies for Effective Human–Interaction* 2nd edn. Addison-Wesley

Sieber U. (1986). *The International Handbook on Computer Crime*. Chichester: John Wiley

Silberschatz A., Stonebraker M. and Ullman J., eds. (1991). Database systems: Achievements and opportunities. *Comm. ACM*, **34**(10)

Skarra A. H. and Zdonik S. (1989). Concurrency control and object-oriented databases. In *Object-Oriented Concepts, Databases and Applications*

(Kim W. and Lochovsky, F. H., eds.), pp. 395–422. Reading, MA: Addison-Wesley

Skeen D. (1981). Non-blocking commit protocols. In *Proc. ACM SIGMOD Int. Conf. Management of Data*, pp. 133–142

Soley R. M., ed. (1992). Object Management Architecture Guide Rev 2, 2nd edn. *OMG TC Document 92.11.1*, Object Management Group

Sommerville I. (1992). *Software Engineering* 4th edn. Reading, MA: Addison-Wesley

Standish T. A. (1994). *Data Structures, Algorithms, and Software Principles*. Reading, MA: Addison-Wesley

Strachan A. D. (1994). Taking care of the corporate data resource: So you think you have a database administrator? *Computing and Information Systems*, **1**(1), 11–22

Stonebraker M. and Neuhold E. (1977). A distributed database version of INGRES. In *Proc. 2nd Berkeley Workshop on Distributed Data Management and Computer Networks*, Berkeley, CA, May 1977, pp. 9–36

Stonebraker M. and Rowe L. (1986). The design of POSTGRES. In *ACM SIGMOD Int. Conf. on Management of Data*, pp. 340–355

Stonebraker M., Rowe L., Lindsay B., Gray P., Carie Brodie M. L., Bernstein P. and Beech D. (1990). The third generation database system manifesto. In *Proc. ACM SIGMOD Conf.*

Stubbs D. F. and Webre N. W. (1993). *Data Structures with Abstract Data Types and Ada*. Belmont, CA: Brooks/Cole Publishing Co.

Su S. Y. W. (1983). SAM*: A Semantic Association Model for corporate and scientific-statistical databases. *Information Science*, **29**, 151–199

Tanenbaum A. S. (1988). *Computer Networks* 2nd edn. Englewood Cliffs, NJ: Prentice-Hall

Taylor D. (1992). *Object Orientation Information Systems: Planning and Implementation*. New York: John Wiley

Teorey T. J. (1994). *Database Modeling & Design: The Fundamental Principles* 2nd edn. San Mateo, CA: Morgan Kaufmann

Teorey T. J. and Fry J. P. (1982). *Design of Database Structures*. Englewood Cliffs, NJ: Prentice-Hall

Thomas R. H. (1979). A majority consensus approach to concurrency control for multiple copy databases. *ACM Trans. Database Systems*, **4**(2), 180–209

Todd S. (1976). The Peterlee relational test vehicle – a system overview. *IBM Systems J.*, **15**(4), 285–308

Ullman J. D. (1988). *Principles of Database and Knowledge-base Systems* Volumes I and II, Rockville, MD: Computer Science Press

Wiederhold G. (1983). *Database Design* 2nd edn. New York: McGraw-Hill

Zdonik S. and Maier D., eds. (1990). Fundamentals of object-oriented databases in readings. In *Object-Oriented Database Systems*, San Mateo, CA: Morgan Kaufmann, pp. 1–31

Zloof M. M. (1977). Query-By-Example: A database language. *IBM Systems J.*, **16**(4), 324–343

Further Reading

Chapter 2

Batini C., Ceri S. and Navathe S. (1992). *Conceptual Database Design: An Entity–Relationship approach.* Redwood City, CA: Benjamin/Cummings

Brodie M., Mylopoulos J. and Schmidt J., eds. (1984). *Conceptual Modeling.* New York: Springer-Verlag

Gardarin G. and Valduriez P. (1989). *Relational Databases and Knowledge Bases.* Reading, MA: Addison-Wesley

Tsichritzis D. and Lochovsky F. (1982). *Data Models.* Englewood Cliffs, NJ: Prentice-Hall

Ullman J. (1988). *Principles of Database and Knowledge-Base Systems* Vol 1. Rockville, MD: Computer-Science Press

Chapter 3

Aho A. V., Beeri C. and Ullman J. D. (1979). The theory of joins in relational databases. *ACM Trans. Database Systems*, **4**(3), 297–314

Chamberlin D. (1976a). Relational data-base management systems. *ACM Computing Surv.*, **8**(1), 43–66

Codd E.F. (1982). The 1981 ACM Turing Award Lecture: Relational database: A practical foundation for productivity. *Comm. ACM*, **25**(2), 109–117

Dayal U. and Bernstein P. (1978). The updatability of relational views. In *Proc. 4th Int. Conf. on Very Large Data Bases*, pp. 368–377

Ozsoyoglu G., Ozsoyoglu Z. and Matos V. (1987). Extending relational algebra and relational calculus with set valued attributes and aggregate functions. *ACM Trans. on Database Systems*, **12**(4), 566–592

Reisner P. (1977). Use of psychological experimentation as an aid to development of a query language. *IEEE Trans. Software Engineering*, **SE3**(3), 218–229

Reisner P. (1981). Human factors studies of database query languages: A survey and assessment. *ACM Computing Surv.*, **13**(1)

Rissanen J. (1979). Theory of joins for relational databases – a tutorial survey. In *Proc. Symposium on Mathematical Foundations of Computer Science*, pp. 537–551. Berlin: Springer-Verlag

Schmidt J. and Swenson J. (1975). On the semantics of the relational model. In *Proc. ACM SIGMOD Int. Conf. on Management of Data*, pp. 9–36.

Chapter 4

Brancheau J. C. and Schuster L. (1989). Building and implementing an information architecture. *Data Base*, Summer, 9–17

Fox R. W. and Unger E. A. (1984). A DBMS selection model for managers. In *Advances in Data Base Management, Vol. 2* (Unger E. A., Fisher P. S. and Slonim J., eds.), pp. 147–170. Wiley Heyden

Grimson J. B. (1986). Guidelines for data administration. In *Proc. IFIP 10th World Computer Congress* (Kugler H. J., ed.), pp. 15–22. Amsterdam: Elsevier Science

Loring P. and De Garis C. (1992). The changing face of data administration. In *Managing Information Technology's Organisational Impact, II, IFIP Transactions A [Computer Science and*

Technology] vol A3 (Clarke R. and Cameron J., eds.), pp. 135–144. Amsterdam: Elsevier Science

Nolan R. L. (1982). *Managing The Data Resource Function* 2nd edn. New York: West Publishing Co.

Peat L. R. (1982). *Practical Guide to DBMS Selection.* Berlin: Walter de Gryter & Co.

Ravindra P. S. (1991a). Using the data administration function for effective data resource management. *Data Resource Management*, **2**(1), 58–63

Ravindra P. S. (1991b). The interfaces and benefits of the data administration function. *Data Resource Management*, **2**(2), 54–58

Robson W. (1994). *Strategic Management and Information Systems*: *An Integrated Approach.* London: Pitman

Teng J. T. C. and Grover V. (1992). An empirical study on the determinants of effective database management. *J. Database Administration*, **3**(1), 22–33

Weldon J.-L. (1981). *Data Base Administration.* New York: Plenum Press

Chapter 5

Benyon D. (1990). *Information and Data Modelling.* Oxford: Blackwell Scientific

Elmasri R. and Navathe S. (1994). *Fundamentals of Database Systems* 2nd edn. New York: Benjamin/Cummings

Gogolla M. and Hohenstein U. (1991). Towards a semantic view of the Entity–Relationship model. *ACM Trans. Database Systems*, **16**(3)

Hawryszkiewycz I. T. (1991). *Database Analysis and Design* 2nd edn. Basingstoke: MacMillian

Howe D. (1989). *Data Analysis for Data Base Design* 2nd edn. London: Edward Arnold

Chapter 6

Date C. J. (1995). *An Introduction to Database Systems* 6th edn. Reading, MA: Addison-Wesley

Elmasri R. and Navathe S. (1994). *Fundamentals of Database Systems* 2nd edn. New York: Benjamin/Cummings

Ullman J. D. (1988). *Principles of Database and Knowledge-base Systems* Volumes I and II, Rockville, MD: Computer Science Press

Chapter 7

Avison D. E. and Fitzgerald G. (1988). *Information Systems Development*: *Methodologies, Techniques and Tools.* Oxford: Blackwell

Elmasri R. and Navathe S. (1994). *Fundamentals of Database Systems* 2nd edn. New York: Benjamin/Cummings

Howe D. (1989). *Data Analysis for Data Base Design* 2nd edn. London: Edward Arnold

Chapter 9

Howe D. (1989). *Data Analysis for Data Base Design* 2nd edn. London: Edward Arnold

Senn J. A. (1989). *Analysis and Design of Information Systems* 2nd edn. New York: McGraw-Hill

Tillmann G. (1993). *A Practical Guide to Logical Data Modelling.* New York: McGraw-Hill

Wertz C. J. (1993). *Relational Database Design*: *A Practitioner's Guide.* New York: CRC Press

Willits J. (1992). *Database Design and Construction*: *Open Learning Course for Students and Information Managers.* Library Association Publishing

Chapters 11 and 12

ANSI (1986). *Database Language – SQL* (X3.135). American National Standards Institute, Technical Committee X3H2

ANSI (1989a). *Database Language – SQL with Integrity Enhancement* (X3.135-1989). American National Standards Institute, Technical Committee X3H2

ANSI (1989b). *Database Language – Embedded SQL* (X3.168-1989). American National Standards Institute, Technical Committee X3H2

Date C. J. and Darwen H. (1993). *A Guide to the SQL Standard* 3rd edn. Reading, MA: Addison-Wesley

Date C. J. (1995). *An Introduction to Database Systems* 6th edn. Reading, MA: Addison-Wesley

Chapter 13

Borland (1994). *Borland Paradox for Windows User's Guide.* Borland International Inc.

Borland (1994). *Borland Paradox for Windows Guide to ObjectPAL*. Borland International Inc.

Smith L. (1994). *Understanding and using Paradox 5.0 for Windows*. West Publishing Co.

Townsend J. J. and Lindsay J. (1994). *Using Paradox for Windows*. Que Corp.

Chapter 14

Ackmann D. (1993). Software Asset Management: Motorola Inc. *I/S Analyzer*, **31**(7), 5–9

Bawden D. and Blakeman K. (1990). *IT Strategies for Information Management*. London: Butterworth Scientific

Berner P. (1993). Software auditing: Effectively combating the five deadly sins. *Information Management & Computer Security*, **1**(2), 11–12

Bhashar K. (1993). *Computer Security: Threats and Countermeasures*. Oxford: NCC Blackwell

Brathwaite K. S. (1985). *Data Administration: Selected Topics of Data Control*. New York: John Wiley

Collier P. A., Dixon R. and Marston C. L. (1991). Computer Research Findings from the UK. *Internal Auditor*, August, 49–52

Hsiao D. K., Kerr D. S. and Madnick S. E. (1978). Privacy and security of data communications and data bases. In *Issues in Data Base Management, Proc. 4th Int. Conf. Very Large Data Bases*. North-Holland

Kamay V. and Adams T. (1993). The 1992 profile of computer abuse in Australia: Part 2. *Information Management & Computer Security*, **1**(2), 21–28

Martin J. (1976). *Principles of Data-Base Management*. Englewood Cliffs, NJ: Prentice Hall

Perry W. E. (1983). *Ensuring Data Base Integrity*. New York: John Wiley

S. W. R. H. A. (February 1993). *Report on the Inquiry into the London Ambulance Service*. Communications Directorate, South West Thames Regional Health Authority

Chapter 15

Bayer H., Heller H. and Reiser A. (1980). Parallelism and recovery in database systems. *ACM Trans. Database Systems*, **5**(4), 139–156

Bernstein P. A., Shipman D. W. and Wong W. S. (1979). Formal aspects of serializability in database concurrency control. *IEEE Trans.*

Software Engineering, **5**(3), 203–215

Bernstein P. A. and Goodman N. (1983). Multiversion concurrency control – theory and algorithms. *ACM Trans. Database Systems*, **8**(4), 465–483

Bernstein P. A., Hadzilacos V. and Goodman N. (1988). *Concurrency Control and Recovery in Database Systems*. Reading, MA: Addison-Wesley

Chandy K. M., Browne J. C., Dissly C. W. and Uhrig W. R. (1975). Analytic models for rollback and recovery strategies in data base systems. *IEEE Trans. Software Engineering*, **1**(1), 100–110

Davies Jr. J. C. (1973). Recovery semantics for a DB/DC system. In *Proc. ACM Annual Conf.*, pp. 136–141

Elmasri R. and Navathe S. (1994). *Fundamentals of Database Systems* 2nd edn. Redwood City, CA: Benjamin/Cummings

Gray J. N. (1978). Notes on data base operating systems. In *Operating Systems: An Advanced Course, Lecture Notes in Computer Science* (Bayer R., Graham M. and Seemuller G., eds.), pp. 393–481. Berlin: Springer-Verlag

Gray J. N. (1981). The transaction concept: virtues and limitations. In *Proc. Int. Conf. on Very Large Data Bases*, pp. 144–154

Gray J. N., McJones P. R., Blasgen M., Lindsay B., Lorie R., Price T., Putzolu F. and Traiger I. (1981). The Recovery Manager of the System R database manager. *ACM Computing Surv.*, **13**(2), 223–242

Gray J. N. (1993). *Transaction Processing: Concepts and Techniques* San Mateo CA: Morgan-Kaufmann

Kadem Z. and Silberschatz A. (1980). Non-two phase locking protocols with shared and exclusive locks. In *Proc. 6th Int. Conf. on Very Large Data Bases*, Montreal, pp. 309–320

Kohler K. H. (1981). A survey of techniques for synchronization and recovery in decentralized computer systems. *ACM Computing Surv.*, **13**(2), 148–183

Korth H. F. (1983). Locking primitives in a database system. *J. ACM*, **30**(1), 55–79

Kung H. T. and Robinson J. T. (1981). On optimistic methods for concurrency control. *ACM Trans. Database Systems*, **6**(2), 213–226

Lorie R. (1977). Physical integrity in a large segmented database. *ACM Trans. Database Systems*, **2**(1), 91–104

Moss J., Eliot J., and Eliot B. (1985). *Nested*

●
Transactions: An Approach to Reliable Distributed Computing. Cambridge, MA: MIT Press

Papadimitriou C. (1986). *The Theory of Database Concurrency Control*, Rockville, MD: Computer Science Press

Thomas R. H. (1979). A majority concensus approach to concurrency control. *ACM Trans. Database Systems*, 4(2), 180–209

Chapter 16

Bell D. and Grimson J. (1992). *Distributed Database Systems.* Wokingham: Addison-Wesley

Bhargava B., ed. (1987). *Concurrency and Reliability in Distributed Systems.* New York: Van Nostrand Reinhold

Bray O. H. (1982). *Distributed Database Management Systems.* Lexington Books

Ceri S. and Pelagatti G. (1984). *Distributed Databases: Principles and Systems.* New York: McGraw-Hill

Chang S. K. and Cheng W. H. (1980). A methodology for structured database decomposition. *IEEE Trans. Software Engineering*, 6(2), 205–218

Knapp E. (1987). Deadlock detection in distributed databases. *ACM Computing Surv.*, 19(4), 303–328

Rozenkrantz D. J., Stearns R. E. and Lewis P. M. (1978). System level concurrency control for distributed data base systems. *ACM Trans. Database Systems*, 3(2), 178–198

Stonebraker M. (1979). Concurrency control and consistency of multiple copies of data in distributed INGRES. *IEEE Trans. Software Engineering*, 5(3), 180–194

Traiger I. L., Gray J., Galtieri C. A. and Lindsay B. G. (1982). Transactions and consistency in distributed database systems. *ACM Trans. Database Systems*, 7(3), 323–342

Chapter 17

Bertino E. and Martino L. (1993). *Object-Oriented Database Systems: Concepts and Architectures.* Wokingham: Addison-Wesley

Kim W., ed. (1995). *Modern Database Systems: The Object Model, Interoperability and Beyond.* Reading MA: Addison-Wesley

Loomis M. E. S. (1995). *Object Databases.* Reading MA: Addison-Wesley

Appendix A

Austing R. H. and Cassel L. N. (1988). *File Organization and Access: From Data to Information.* Lexington MA: D.C. Heath and Co.

Baeza-Yates R. and Larson P. (1989). Performance of B^+-trees with partial expansion. *IEEE Trans. Knowledge and Data Engineering*, 1(2)

Folk M. J. and Zoellick B. (1987). *File Structures: A Conceptual Toolkit.* Reading, MA: Addision-Wesley

Frank L. (1988). *Database Theory and Practice.* Reading, MA: Addison-Wesley

Gardarin G. and Valduriez P. (1989). *Relational Databases and Knowledge Bases.* Reading, MA: Addison-Wesley

Johnson T. and Shasha D. (1993). The peformance of current B-Tree algorithms. *ACM Trans. Database Systems*, 18(1)

Knuth, D. (1973). *The Art of Computer Programming Volume 3: Sorting and Searching.* Reading, MA: Addison-Wesley

Larson P. (1981). Analysis of index-sequential files with overflow chaining. *ACM Trans. Database Systems*, 6(4)

Livadas P. (1989). *File Structures: Theory and Practice.* Englewood Cliffs, NJ: Prentice-Hall

Mohan C. and Narang I. (1992). Algorithms for creating indexes for very large tables without quiescing updates. In *Proc. ACM SIGMOD Int. Conf. on Management of Data*, San Diego, CA

Salzberg B. (1988). *File Structures: An Analytic Approach.* Englewood Cliffs, NJ: Prentice-Hall

Smith P. and Barnes G. (1987). *Files & Databases: An Introduction.* Reading, MA: Addison-Wesley

Appendix B

Bachmann C. W. (1989). The programmer as navigator. In *Readings in Artificial Intelligence and Databases* (Mylopolous J. and Brodie M., eds.), pp. 52–59. San Mateo, CA: Morgan Kaufmann

Boulanger D. and March S. T. (1989). An approach to analyzing the information content of existing databases. *DataBase*, 20(2), 1–8

Fadok G. T. (1985). *Effective Design of CODASYL Data Base.* New York: Macmillan

Hawryszkiewycz I. T. (1991). *Database Analysis and Design* 2nd edn. New York: Macmillan

Olle T. W. (1978). *The Codasyl Approach to Data Base Management.* Chichester: John Wiley

Ozkarahan E. (1990). *Database Management: Concepts, Design, and Practice.* Englewood Cliffs, NJ: Prentice-Hall

Peat L. R. (1982). *Practical Guide to DBMS Selection.* Berlin: Walter de Gruyter

Appendix C

IBM Corp. (October 1990). *IMS/ESA Version 3 Database Administration Guide Release 1* 2nd edn. (SC26-4281-1)

IBM Corp. (February 1993). *IMS/ESA Version 3 Utilities Reference Release 1* 2nd edn. (SC26-4284-01)

Peat L. R. (1982). *Practical Guide to DBMS Selection.* Berlin: Walter de Gruyter

Index